Echoes in the Wind

Also by Anthony Joseph Sacco, Sr.—

Fact Based Fiction:

THE CHINA CONNECTION
(Available in Hardcover and Trade Paperback)

Creative Non-Fiction:

LITTLE SISTER LOST
(Available in Trade Paperback Only)

Biography:

ECHOES IN THE WIND: A Biography of Guy Vitale, East Boston High
School Sports Great

Echoes in the Wind

A Biography of Guy Vitale, East Boston High School Sports Great

Anthony Joseph Sacco, Sr.

iUniverse, Inc.
New York Lincoln Shanghai

Echoes in the Wind
A Biography of Guy Vitale, East Boston High School Sports Great

iUniverse books may be ordered through booksellers or by contacting:

iUniverse
2021 Pine Lake Road, Suite 100
Lincoln, NE 68512
www.iuniverse.com
1-800-Authors (1-800-288-4677)

Because of the dynamic nature of the Internet, any Web addresses or links contained in this book may have changed since publication and may no longer be valid.

The views expressed in this work are solely those of the author and do not necessarily reflect the views of the publisher, and the publisher hereby disclaims any responsibility for them.

ISBN: 978-0-595-45522-5 (pbk)
ISBN: 978-0-595-89831-2 (ebk)

Printed in the United States of America

This book is a work of creative non-fiction, based upon records of actual events in the life of Guy Vitale, interviews with many who knew him, and the memories of those who did not know him personally but knew of him.

Occasionally, places and incidents have been created and inserted into events that actually happened. In those cases, dialogue is the result of fictional interpretation by the author of certain events—*what might have been said or done*—thus giving each event a plausible explanation or meaning. Where this occurs, this interpretation is the product of the author's imagination and has been used fictitiously.

Tell all the Truth but tell it Slant—
Success in Circuit lies
Too bright for our infirm Delight
The Truth's superb surprise
As lightening to the Children eased
With explanation kind
The Truth must dazzle gradually
Or every man be blind.

—Emily Dickinson[1]

---

1   Nancy Ekholm Burkert and Jane Langton, *Acts of Light, Emily Dickinson,* New York Graphic Society, Little, Brown and Company, Boston, MA 1980.

This book is dedicated to two outstanding people:

The first is Margaret Spencer Vitale, who passed away on Saturday, August 6, 2005 at her home in Sanford, Florida. Having met Guy Vitale later in life, my Aunt Margaret helped him achieve the happiness, intimacy and stability he so richly deserved.

Born Margaret Esther Spencer in Sanford on July 13, 1923, she was a daughter of Morris Houston Spencer and Ruth Roberts Spencer, one of Sanford's pioneer families. Both parents predeceased her. She grew up in Sanford.

When she and Guy met, Margaret was working for the United States Department of State as a Secretary/Administrative Assistant, in Athens, Greece. Whether or not she was a CIA operative, I can only speculate. She did, however, work out of the U.S. Embassy.

When Guy retired, she had a bit less than two years of service remaining before she could receive her pension, so Guy leased an apartment in Munich, Germany, to be closer to her. They were married in Sanford, on April 7, 1969, in a civil ceremony at the Maitland, Florida home of Margaret's sister, Katherine Spencer Dean.

The second is Joe "Rock" Rocciolo, who, although several years younger, knew Guy and played baseball with him at East Boston High School. No slouch as a baseball player, in 1937 Joe was named to the *Boston Post's* All-Scholastic Baseball team as a left fielder.

Joe Rocciolo devoted a lifetime to the youth of East Boston, serving as president of the Little League and the Pony League, and either coaching or managing teams for seventeen years. He also spent twenty-five years with St. Lazarus' football team as its backfield coach, equipment manager and recruiter. At the 43rd Banquet of Champions, sponsored by the East Boston Athletic Board, Joe received the "Flashback" of the year award.

An able historian and chronicler of East Boston athletes, Joe provided many clippings, documents and valuable information, all of which were used in the writing of this book. And during my research trip to Boston in 2002, he generously spent much time arranging for Guy's former friends and acquaintances to meet with me at our East Boston "office," the Burger King on Bennington Street, prior to my heading downtown to the Public Library. There isn't a better man in East Boston!

May God look with favor upon them both!

CONTENTS

AUTHOR'S NOTE

For the author, *Echoes in the Wind* is a departure from the Matt Dawson series.[2] A biography, it's my attempt to chronicle the life of my uncle, a very interesting man, and, at the same time, lay to rest a mystery that has puzzled his family, friends, and all who knew him, through the medium of fact-based fiction or creative nonfiction.

The task of a creative nonfiction writer is to tell the truth, of course, but in addition to laying out the bare facts, to relate a story utilizing the tools available to all writers; style, meaning and effect, and by doing so, to bond with and *move* the reader to understand the subject matter.[3]

In this case, the subject matter is my uncle's life and how he lived it. Though this work contains some elements invented by the author, it is solidly rooted and grounded in fact and in the real world. There is much truth to it!

2   Anthony J. Sacco, *The China Connection*, Lincoln, NE., Writers Club Press, an imprint of iUniverse, Inc., 2003, and Anthony J. Sacco, *Little Sister Lost,* Lincoln NE., Writers Club Press, an imprint of iUniverse, Inc., 2004.

3   William Noble, *Writing Dramatic Non-Fiction*, Paul S. Erikson, Publisher. Forestdale, VT. 2000.

ACKNOWLEDGEMENTS AND ATTRIBUTIONS

Without the help of the following individuals and organizations, this book would not have been possible. I'll try not to leave anyone out:

Christopher Lundquist and his staff at the Sturgis Library, Barnstable, Massachusetts, where I was underfoot for several days in August 2002, researching copies of old newspapers and records dealing with Guy Vitale's accomplishments while playing baseball in the Cape Cod League in 1936, 1937, and 1938.

Henry F. Scannell, Director of Research, Boston Public Library, and his able staff, for their help. I spent a full week there, from August 10 through August 16, 2002, accompanied by a severe case of the flu, searching the sports sections of old newspapers such as the *Boston Globe*, the old *Boston Record-American*— formerly a Hearst newspaper before its sale and name-change to *The Boston Herald*—the *Boston Post*, *The Boston Traveler*, and others, while harassing one and all for assistance. When even that length of time proved inadequate, Henry helped by e-mail, locating records of East Boston High School's Thanksgiving Classic games and the Boston Metropolitan area's All-Scholastic selections from 1933 through 1937.

The Barnstable Patriot, the *Hyannis Patriot,* and the *Cape Cod Standard Times.* The latter entered the scene in October 1936, too late to chronicle Guy's exploits that year, but handily did so for the next two seasons. From these newspapers I was able to glean articles about the Cape Cod League and the Barnstable and Falmouth teams on which Guy Vitale starred.

And special thanks to author, director, writer, and composer, Jack Sacco of Los Angeles, CA, for permission to use an excerpt from his book, *Where the Birds Never Sing,* which appears in Chapter 43.

THANKS

First, I'd like to thank my wife, Carol. Being married to an author isn't easy. Oh, sure, there are the good times, like state-wide book tours which bring us into contact with lots of wonderful people. But there's also the other part—the "Oh my God! I'm married to a madman" part—which often occurs when I go to sleep wrestling with a scene that isn't quite right, until, at 2:30 a.m., I toss off the covers and dash for my office to write it the way my subconscious has worked it out. After three books, she finally understands how I operate. And we're still together. Carol also helped as a back up proof reader, and did an excellent job of picking up grammatical errors. The sainted Carol.

In writing this book, I commandeered the valuable time of many people, bothering them unmercifully, depending upon their indulgence, their knowledge, advice, and, of course, their good memories of times long past and the people who shared those times. I'd like to mention and thank each of them:

To the Kents Hill School Crowd:

Matthew R. Crane, Director of Admissions and Financial Aid, who put me in touch with Howard Doyle.

Howard Doyle, Academy Program Student, Class of 1936, who steered me to Chester Parasco, Academy Program student, Class of 1938.

Chester Parasco, a classmate of Guy's at Kents Hill and a retired Insurance lawyer, now living in Walpole, Massachusetts who good-naturedly shared his recollections of Guy and Kents Hill's 1937 football team with me.

Cheryl W. Freye, Office of Development and Alumni Affairs, for her invaluable help in searching for records.

Lillian MacDonald Washburn, nee Lillian Beatrice MacDonald, Junior College Program, Class of 1938, President, Class of 1938, now of Jaffrey, NH., who shared her memories and sent me a fine photo of Guy at Kents Hill, and several other records.

Janet Spalding Pratt, nee Janet Elisabeth Spalding, for information she provided.

Terry Greco Paquette, nee Marie Theresa Greco, originally from Arlington, MA, now of Centerville, MA, who shared her memories of Guy at Kents Hill.

To my Cape Cod League Information Helpers:

Alfred G. Irish, of Falmouth, MA, a member of the Cape Cod League's Hall of Fame Advisory Committee, for his gifts of time and effort in locating hard-to-find records.

Dudley Jensen, of Cataumet, MA, also a Cape Cod League Hall of Fame Advisory Committee member, for his willingness to help, and the records he provided.

Another word about these two men: after finishing the chapters on Guy Vitale's Cape Cod League exploits, I sent copies to each of them with the suggestion that, if they thought him worthy, they might nominate Guy to the Cape Cod League Hall of Fame. At the meeting in late 2006, Al and Dudley submitted Guy's name. This nomination will remain active until he is eventually elected and takes his rightful place among the all-time best of those who starred in that League.

Christopher Price, author of *Baseball by the Beach*, Parnassus Imprints, Hyannis, MA, 1998, for his description of the thrilling ending to the Cranberry Circuit's 1937 season, contained in his aforementioned book.

To the Librarians and Helpers in Northern New Hampshire and Vermont:

Barbara Mellor, Littleton Public Library, Littleton, NH, for being the first to find for me evidence that Guy Vitale had played baseball in the Twin States League in 1939.

Barbara Robarts, Weeks Memorial Library, Lancaster, NH, for corroborating that Guy played in the Twin States League in '39, and for sending me copies of a few articles describing games in which he played, and a copy of the final listing of players, graded by batting averages.

Lisa von Kahn, Director, and Alice Carpenter, volunteer research assistant, at the St. Johnsbury Athenaeum, St. Johnsbury, VT, for voluminous information gleaned from the pages of the *Caledonian Record* regarding the Twin States League, the St. Johnsbury Senators, and Guy Vitale's performance in the League during the summer of 1939.

To the Brave Men of the 78th Lightning Division, 311th Infantry Regiment, United States Army, and especially to the men of its Service Company:

Joseph F. Lemon, Lewisburg, WV, for many hours of conversations, his recollections and willingness to help;

The 78th Division has an active veteran's association and an excellent publication, *The Flash,* dedicated to the friendships established by its fighting men of two world wars. To its editor, Bill Parsons, of Wappingers Falls, NY, and its membership secretary, Herman (Red) Gonzalez, of Pittsburgh, PA, a great big thanks for all their help.

Louis J. Spano, Service Company, 311th Infantry Regiment, now of Aiken, SC, and Laverne J. Lander, St. Paul, MN, for their letters outlining some of Guy's activities while the 78th Lightning Division and the 311th Infantry Regiment were at Camp Butner, NC;

Joseph Lewandoski, for his willingness to talk about Guy and "the game," and sharing his memories.

Elizabeth M. Purnell of South Deerfield, MA, wife of deceased Captain Frederick Purnell, for information and photos she provided from her late husband's records.

And all the men of Service Company, 311th Infantry Regiment, who, although they didn't do much shooting, were indispensable to the fighting mission of their regiment and the 78th Infantry Division.

To Guy's Friends and Acquaintances in East Boston:

Joe "Rock" Rocciolo, an acquaintance of Guy's, a fellow student at East Boston High School, member of the 1937 baseball team, Honorable Mention All-Scholastic baseball team in '37, and one of two people to whom this book is dedicated;

Anthony Marmo, East Boston High School Class of '35, currently of Winthrop, MA, a great athlete in his own right, and the force behind the annual Old Timer's Breakfast in East Boston.

Lennie Merullo, East Boston High School's Class of '33, currently of Reading, MA, a baseball teammate of Guy's for one year when he was a senior and Guy was a freshman, St. John's Preparatory School, Villanova and Boston College, Class of '40, who later played professional baseball for seven years with the Chicago Cubs from 1941 through 1947, for talking to me and sharing his memories of Guy and himself.

Professor Ernest A. Siciliano, currently of Newton, MA, retired from the Romance Languages Department at Boston College, for sharing one of Guy's first "moments in the sun," on Saturday, August 8, 1931, when, as young boys, they appeared in a photograph with "Babe" Herman and "Lefty" O'Doul, then outfielders for the Brookline Dodgers.

<u>To a Relative Who Cared Enough to Help:</u>
   Some years ago I sent packets containing copies of voluminous newspaper clippings to Guy's brother (my Uncle Frank Vitale), and to Guy's wife, Margaret Spencer Vitale, of Sanford FL. One of these packets made its way to a cousin, Teri Vitale Gallant, of Dracut, MA. Guy Vitale was, of course, her uncle as well as mine. Teri was farsighted enough to save this material. Eventually, upon learning I was writing this book, she sent it to me. Thanks, Teri.

<u>To My Very Able Proof-reader, Joleen Marquardt:</u>
   Now and then the planets align, the stars shine brighter, and the result is someone like Joleen. Intelligent, bright, and interested in my books from the beginning, she has been one of the biggest fans of the Matt Dawson series, so it was only natural when looking for a proof-reader in southeastern Wyoming, that I'd turn to her. Thank you for a super job, Joleen.

PROLOGUE

Pine Bluffs, WY
Thursday, September 2, 2004
703 Beech Street
11:00 p.m.

It's late. My wife is already asleep, but I sit in my office staring at a blank computer screen, engrossed in my own uneasy thoughts. Fall has come already, here on the High Plains, our chosen new home. The wind we were forewarned about back during the balmy summer days when it was no threat and therefore not understood by new arrivals, is whistling across the dark prairie tonight, bending before it unharvested corn and pinto beans growing in the limitless fields outside of town.

The powerful gusts whisper his name and mine; the two of us are inextricably bound by empathy, a bond so strong that for years I've felt compelled to write his story.

Much of the research is done. It involved investigative work, telephone interviews and delving into musty archives at several newspapers; begun in early 2000 and continued through the middle of 2004 while we still lived in Towson, Maryland. A ten-day trip to Boston and Cape Cod in August 2002 was also part of it. And it's not finished. I still must piece together a part of Guy Vitale's life. Our long-distance telephone bill will, by the time I'm through, rival the national debt.

It's been hard and expensive. It's also been interesting beyond anything I could have imagined, bringing me into contact with numerous wonderful people; individuals eager to help, some of whom knew Guy, others who knew of him, and many who didn't fit either category, but who just helped because they were asked and because it was something they wanted to do.

Now, it's time to write. Tonight, even if it turns into an all-nighter, I'll make a start ...

1

*　　*　　*　　*

Boston, MA
Friday, June 1, 2000
Santarpio's Pizza and Bar
Porter & Chelsea Streets
12:30 a.m.

"Whatever became a Guy Vitale?" Around Boston, when the old-timers and their better halves get together for an evening, it's not long before his name comes up and someone asks that question.

After a hearty dinner of a huge antipasto followed by lasagna with thick layers of Mozzarella cheese and ground beef and black bread, and after they've had a drink or two and mellowed out—age having taken its toll, none of them are heavy drinkers any more—they dredge up stories about the past, the people, the events, and pretty soon *his* name is on someone's lips.

It's the same in the bars around East Boston, from Piers Park and Harborside Drive to Suffolk Downs, from Logan International to Chelsea. As it gets on toward closing time and the late-stayers in the watering holes over in Orient Heights and in the saloons along Bennington, Boardman, Porter, Chelsea, and Saratoga Streets have had their fill, the stories begin to flow, replacing the booze.

Santarpio's, a popular gathering spot for locals, is no exception. On this warm early June evening, the upstairs pizza place is dark, its patrons having long-since departed, but the regulars in the dimly-lit basement bar remain, reminiscing. Amid thick cigarette smoke, the clicking of glasses and bottles, good-natured insults and creative profanity, stories of local former sports greats bubble to the surface. Guy's name is one of the first to be spoken.

"Were you at the Eastie-Brighton game that day in '35? Vitale was a senior then. That was the best kickin' I ever seen at a high school football game."

"Hell, I was there an' that was the best kickin' I ever saw, *period*. High school, college, or pro."

"The first kick he made, Eastie had the ball right after the game started. They couldn't move it and had ta punt. Guy took the snap on his thirty-yard line and kicked it inta Brighton's end zone. I seen it with my own eyes!"

"He was a good baseball player, too. His senior year at East Boston High, didn't he hit .621 for the season?"

"Yeah." The man whipped out a pen, pulled a paper napkin toward him and began scribbling furiously. "Thirty-six hits in fifty-eight trips ta the plate," he said. "That's 0.6206896. Nobody ever done that before. Or *after*, either."

And so it goes. All around Boston, at christenings, wedding receptions, funerals, and wherever the older people gather. After they've worked up a sweat dancing with their wives to very loud but only so-so music and their feet begin to swell and start to hurt in shoes that are too tight, the men pull their chairs up, and over beer and chips, or maybe just a wee bit of the hard stuff, everybody has a story to tell about Guy Vitale's exploits.

"In 1936, he played a few weeks for Saint Lazarus afta Eastie's season finished and before he went down the Cape that first time. Hit .444."

"Best natural hitter I ever saw. Musta had great eyesight."

"He once told me he never went ta the movies. Wanted ta protect his vision."

"First year he played down the Cape, he came close ta winnin' the battin' championship."

"Vitale made All-Scholastic in football *and* baseball two years in a row. How many athletes from around here ever done *that*? Now *you* tell *me*."

"*The Herald-Traveler* named him Athlete of the Year for baseball in '36. So how come he never made it to the big leagues?"

"I dunno. He tore up the Cape Cod League the three summers he played ball down there. And that was a damn good league back then. Let me tell ya somethin'. Vitale could a made it."

"It's *still* a good league. Thurman Munson was battin' champion in '67. Terry Steinbach won the title in '82, Chuck Knoblauch did it in '88, and Jason Veritek won it in '93.

That's the way it is. The kid was a good football player and a great baseball player. He even ran track one or two years. Broke a couple of records, too.

From humble beginnings, Guy was the son of hard-working immigrant parents, Nicola Vitale and Rosaria Moscaritolo, both from the Naples area in Italy. At first, his family was so poor he had to quit high school for two weeks during his freshman year to help out at the grocery store his mother ran from the apartment building over on Breed Street. That was in January 1933. It's right there in his transcript.

The youngest of a bunch of kids, he matured fast, as the youngest often does in a large family. That the great athletic ability was there should not have surprised anyone who knew the Vitale clan. His older brother, Frank, broke ground and smoothed the way a few years before.

As an athlete, especially a baseball player, Guy was the "can't miss" kid." But he did. Miss, I mean. Although he *did* sign a professional contract and played a year of professional ball on Maryland's Eastern Shore in 1941, he never made it to the Big Leagues like everyone thought he would, even though several major league clubs had been interested in him. Why not? People still wonder.

Well, with help from some old timers who knew Guy personally—especially Joe Rocciolo—some who didn't know Guy but heard or read about his exploits, his widow—my Aunt Margaret Spencer Vitale—a bit of family lore here and there, newspaper accounts, and much that I pieced together myself, I think the mystery, a family mystery of sorts, has been unraveled, and I'm going to tell you what happened to him.

Anybody who knows me knows about my first two books, *The China Connection,* published in January 2003, and *Little Sister Lost,* released in November, 2004. They also know I'm a private investigator as well as a writer and author. This book, a biography, is a departure for me from the usual fact-based fiction I've been writing.

William Noble, in his *Writing Dramatic Nonfiction,*[4] quotes biographer Patricia Bosworth, who penned biographies of actor Marlon Brando and photographer Diane Arbus, as saying, "… the biographer … should display talents of an historian, psychiatrist and novelist when going about their tale, and yet even that will provide only a measure of completeness. 'If one is lucky,' she says, 'one comes away with the essence of the character, a version of a life. But there is always more than one version.'" That sounds correct to me. In writing about my uncle, I quickly became aware that in addition to my investigator's talents, I'd need to use all the skills Bosworth mentioned.

My uncle was, to me as I grew up, a distant figure; elusive and inaccessible. I was not a part of his life. In 1937, the year I was born, he was a twenty year old phenom, already well known among baseball people in the Boston area and on Cape Cod. In the summer of '41, he played his first and only year of professional baseball on Maryland's Eastern Shore. Of course my mother must have known about it, but I cannot remember her ever passing that information along to me. Yet, I knew, from an early age that she felt a strong bond of love for her younger brothers; both Frank[5] and Guy. To me, however, he meant little. He was just my mother's youngest brother.

But when I reached my early teens and started to play sports myself, and it became apparent that my own skill level was higher than most, I began to wonder about him. The stories of his awesome exploits fascinated me, and a bond of some sort developed, spawned at a distance and always one way only; he was, by then, living in Washington, D.C. and working for the CIA.

---

4   Ibid.

5   Francis J. Vitale was born January 25, 1915 in East Boston, MA.

Later still, I began to experience a strange though subtle compulsion to know what happened to him. Was he really as excellent a football player as they said he was? Could he really punt sixty-five and seventy yards? And baseball. Was he as good as the stories I'd heard? Why, then, did it take so long for him to play in 'organized' ball? And the sixty-four thousand dollar question? Why didn't he make it to the Big Leagues?

Feeling compelled to answer these questions and to write his story, I researched a whole lot, studied and pondered, wrote a draft and tore it up, backtracked, re-interviewed, expanded on some notes, discarded other material—and wrote again.

My goal was to write an accurate version of Guy's life, making it as complete as possible. Along the way, I confirmed what I'd come to believe; that Guy Vitale, although aloof from his family and friends, was so mostly because of the secrecy requirements of his chosen calling. A basically good person, he was tough but vulnerable, a complicated human being who lived a life made up of a mix of many things, some good and some bad.

After reading this biography, his friends might say that perhaps a few things I discovered about my uncle should have been left unreported. But had I done that, the young man he was, the man he became, and the motivations for many of his actions might have remained cloudy.

As mentioned above, there's always more than one version of the life of a person like Guy; more than one way to interpret his life events, actions and experiences. Newspapers and records clearly show his accomplishments. So in addition to recounting those, I tried to move beyond them, to an understanding of what he was like as a person; his strengths and weaknesses, his inner vulnerabilities and how they came to be. I tried to capture the essence of the man who was my uncle. When you finish reading, you will have *my* version, hopefully an accurate and complete one, of Guy Vitale's life.

PART ONE

THE EARLY YEARS

Part One

The Early Years

CHAPTER I

East Boston, MA
Tuesday, October 16, 1917
2 Emmet Place
1:15 a.m.

Emmet Place is a short, insignificant strip of macadam situated a few blocks north of the murky waters at the entrance to Boston's Inner Harbor. Less than half a mile away is busy Logan International Airport. Named after General Edward L. Logan[6], those concrete runways are all that separates *that* part of East Boston from the black expanse of Boston Harbor to the east.

The residential street runs west to east for only a few blocks, dead-ending at the marsh where Joe Porzio Park now stands but didn't back then. Some nights, thick, heavy fog rolls in off the water and settles over the entire area, muffling somewhat the low, brutal sounds of the oceangoing behemoths; cargo ships in the Harbor.... OOOOOOOWaa. Pause. OOOOOOOWaa. Pause.

Another thing the fog blocks out sometimes is the whining engine noises of the big planes making use of the concrete runways across the water at Logan. Back then, incoming flights made people's teeth chatter, with noise levels of sixty-five decibels or higher. And as bad as it was in East Boston, Winthrop, under the glide path of those planes, was worse, with sound levels above seventy-five decibels. What's it like now? Well, thirty listening stations around

---

6   A first generation Irish-American, military leader, Commander of the 101st Infantry Regiment of the 26th Yankee Division. Logan was a state representative and senator from South Boston, and a Justice in the South Boston Municipal Court. He also was active in charitable programs such as the Home for Destitute Catholic Children. In 1929, Pope Pius made him a Knight of the Order of Malta in recognition of his charitable endeavors. During a $4.75 million expansion in 1943, the East Boston Airport was officially named in his honor.

Boston gather data that's used to minimize the impact of Logan's noise on nearby communities. Apparently, the problem has improved some.

That evening was not particularly noteworthy. Nothing spectacular had happened anywhere in the Greater Boston Metropolitan area that day, and the weather was just what was expected for an evening in the middle of October.

All the homes on the street were dark, their inhabitants, for the most part laborers who used their brawn and muscle power to eke out a living, have retired early, shutting themselves in as tightly as possible to block out the noise of those planes taking off and landing only a few hundred yards away. All day and all night. It was never quiet. Sometimes, as the planes roared overhead, dishes and cups rattled in the cupboards or on the tables, and the locals could not even hear themselves think, much less sleep well. Eventually, it would get to them and they'd move somewhere else. If they could.

But this night *was* different. In the wee hours of the blustery October morning, a solitary light burned in one of the small, second floor bedrooms in the home of Nicola[7] and Rosaria[8] Vitale and their four children. The bare light bulb dangling at the end of a black wire suspended from the ceiling cast shadows across the room's only wall decoration, a cheap print of Michelangelo's Pieta in a pressed metal frame.

Rosaria Vitale, all the color drained from her comely face, her lips contorted in pain, sat on the edge of the double bed, her bare toes touching the cold linoleum floor. Thirty-one years old, she spoke in the Italian dialect common around Avellino, approximately fifty miles east of Naples, where she and her husband—their marriage arranged by both sets of parents—had been born and had spent their early childhood years.

"Nicola!"

"Hmm?" Exhausted from a long, hard day as a ship fitter's helper at the nearby Bethlehem Steel Ship Building Company, Nicola's shoulders twitched. He'd been sleeping on his side, his back to his wife.

"Get up. It's time," she said curtly, beads of sweat standing out on her line-creased forehead. In addition to the fact that she was in pain, her tone conveyed her lack of affection for the man in the double bed beside her.

---

7   Nicola (sometimes spelled Nicolo) Vitale was born in 1871 in Naples, Italy, entered the U.S. through New York City in 1880 at the age of 9, and acquired U.S. citizenship in 1895, in Boston, MA.

8   Rosaria Moscaritolo (sometimes spelled Moscaritola and Moscaritello) Vitale was born in 1884 in Naples, Italy, entered the U.S. through New York City in 1892 at the age of 8, and acquired U.S. citizenship (date unknown) in Boston, MA.

Blinking away sleep, Nicola obeyed quickly. He pushed back the blanket and sheet and swung his short legs over the side of the bed until his feet contacted the floor. His movement was not violent, but done gently so as not to cause his wife any more pain. For several years after he first came to America, he had worked as a barber. But unable to make a living at it, he'd given it up and gone to work at the shipyard. That had been hard for awhile, but he had eventually adapted to it. Now, his wiry body displayed muscles still firm at the age of forty-four. "Are you sure, Rosaria?" he asked. "Maybe ..."

"Damn it! Yes, I'm sure!" She snapped. "The contractions ..."

"Madonna Mia! It's always at night. Late at night," he announced rhetorically as he reached for his trousers. "Why can't she do this during the day? Then I'd have an excuse to take a few hours off from work."

Ignoring him, Rosaria wrapped both arms tightly around her ample body but continued to sit on the edge of the bed while her husband speedily dressed. Minutes later she looked up to see the heads of their children, Maria, Anna, Albert and Frankie, crowding the doorway; the two girls first, then a boy, and then another boy. All were wearing pajamas and slippers. All looked sleepy but concerned.

"What's happening, Ma?" Maria Antonetta asked.[9] As is often the case with the eldest, somewhere along the line she had become the spokesperson for the other kids. Rosaria had noted *that* more than once. This time, fighting the pain of another contraction, she cannot respond, which allowed her husband, for one of the infrequent occasions in their lives together, to answer *for* her.

"It's time for the baby, Maria," Nicola, now clad in his pants and socks, said. "Get dressed and run for Doctor Bloom!"

"But Pa—" It was cold and dark outside. And foggy. Maria, twelve years old and afraid of what the wet, gray vapor might conceal, did not relish the idea of venturing forth at this hour, even though the doctor's home was only in the next block.

"Maria! Quickly!" Rosaria, knowing how stubborn her eldest could be at times, used her stern tone, hoping to cut off any further discussion. Tossing a sullen glance at her mother, the girl disappeared. But the other kids stayed, watching through wide, sleepy brown eyes.

Rosaria reached for her maternity frock, a shapeless, sack-type dress, gasped and placed both fists against her sides. "My God in Heaven!" she cried as another contraction engulfed her. "No more bambinos," she murmured through clenched teeth. "None! Not ever."

---

9   Maria Antonetta Vitale was born on January 25, 1905, at 2 Emmett Place, East Boston, MA.

Nicola, a short, pleasant-looking man with a full head of dark brown hair and a neatly-trimmed mustache resembling the wings of a bird, was not at a loss for what to do. Crossing the small room in three strides, he spoke to the kids. "Anna Marie? Albert! Go down to the kitchen. We need a big fire in the stove. Fill the large kettle with water. Put it on the stove. Lots of coal. Bring the water to a boil."

"Yes, Pa," Anna Marie Vitale said. Three years younger than her sister, Maria, she was second in command and a favorite with *both* parents. She knew it and relished the position. Turning to carry out their fathers' instructions, she shoved five-year old Albert ahead of her. Frankie, a year younger than Albert, trailed after them.

Rosaria's eyes were fastened on her husband as he returned to her side. She watched him suppress what in her present mood appeared to her as a lecherous grin.

"You say that *every* time, caro mia," he chided. "But you still come to our bed regularly. Whenever the urge arises." He picked up the threadbare quilt. "Come on, now," he said gently. "Lay back and stretch out. The doctor will be here soon."

*   *   *   *

East Boston, MA
Tuesday, October 16, 1917
2 Emmet Place
4:05 a.m.

Speaking Italian, Nicola Vitale led Doctor D. N. Bloom to the Vitale living room, where they both collapsed into chairs. Like all the houses on this street, this one lacked central heating; not like the homes on the next street over, which had furnaces in their basements, fueled by chunks of black coal delivered on coal company trucks and emptied into the lower reaches by use of a metal chute thrust through a small basement window. Lacking this modern development, the Vitales seldom used the living room, preferring instead to sit around the kitchen table, enjoying the heat from the nearby cooking stove.

The room was frigid, sparsely furnished, and smelled the way a seldom heated room does. A tattered couch with a washed out floral pattern was the focal point. Two overstuffed chairs with worn spots in their arms despite the presence of circular white antimacassars to protect them, flanked it. A floor lamp with tassels hanging from its pale pink shade stood beside one, its low wattage bulb losing a battle with the darkness. On a wall hung an obscure artist's imitation of Joseph Mallord William Turner's watercolor, *Sunset on Grand Canal*, it's isolation of brilliant colors—reds, golds and blues—already fading with age.

"Ahh! That was not so bad this time, was it Nicola?" Doctor Bloom, a tall, heavy man with a round, jovial face, began.

Nicola, tired and wanting only to return to his bed, surveyed the doctor in the meager light. *He speaks Italian well for a Jew,* he thought. *So many Italians moved in here this last ten years, for him, it was either learn the language or move and start over somewhere else*

"Not too bad," he heard himself agreeing. "She did okay during *this* pregnancy. No miscarriage, like …"

"How many miscarriages?"

"Too many. I've lost count."

"Yes. The melody of birth and death," Doctor Bloom responded judgmentally. "We've been instilled with the idea that large families are a good thing. So, most parents want lots of kids."

Troubled by the thought that he was a father again and had another mouth to feed, Nicola was not in the mood to listen to anyone pontificating on this subject. For a fleeting second, images of his own father, Francesco, a former Mayor of Naples in the mid-1890s, and his mother, Anna Sirignano, floated into his mind. He willed them away. Elderly, distant and unattainable, they were part of his past. He didn't want them intruding. "She says she'll have no more."

The doctor sighed. "I don't blame her. Besides the miscarriages, she's lost several during birth." He looked up brightly. "This one, however, is sturdy and strong. He has made it safely out of the starting gate." Doctor Bloom, a horse racing fan, frequented nearby Suffolk Downs whenever he could get away, and often peppered his speech with racing metaphors. Sitting back, he folded his huge hands over an ample belly and waited for the appreciative laugh he felt his words deserved.

It didn't come. Instead, Nicola yawned and stood. "It's been rough for her," he said. "She works hard and saves our money. But when we lost Tony …"

Doctor Bloom, looking unappreciated, examined his fingernails. "Pneumonia, wasn't it?"

Despite his best efforts, Nicola's eyes filled with tears. "Yes. He was only eleven."

Bloom pretended not to notice. Adjusting his gold, wire-rimmed glasses, he pulled a Department of Health form from his jacket pocket and unfolded it. "She'll sleep for awhile. But right now, I need to get some information for the Registry Division," he announced. "What will you name this one?"

"Salvatore Crescenzio Gaetano Vitale."

The doctor, his pen poised above the form, squinted at his patient's husband in the dim light, but Nicola's face was lost in shadow. "All of that?"

"Yes!" the new father said sharply, failing to conceal his impatience. Then, conscious that this man, too, had risen from a warm bed to come and care for his Rosaria, he elaborated a bit. "Besides Tony, he had a sister named Bedelia and a brother named Salvatore; both only lived a few days." He looked away, for a moment lost in the memory of the daughter and two sons who did not live to grow into adulthood. Then, "But we'll probably call *this* one Gaetano."

Finished filling out the form, the doctor signed his name—D. N. Bloom— with a flourish, rose and reached for his topcoat. "What will you bet the boy doesn't shorten it further? I'd say he'll be calling himself 'Guy' before too long."

*   *   *   *

Pine Bluffs, WY
Friday, September 3, 2004
703 Beech Street
11:30 p.m.

And that's exactly what happened. To his family and friends the kid *was* known as 'Guy.' He was my mother's youngest brother. My uncle. I'm proud of that.

Guy's parents were my maternal grandparents. When Nick wrote his name, which wasn't often, he wrote it 'Nicola' and at first, that's how most people addressed him. Later, assimilated into his new American culture and somewhat upwardly mobile, he used 'Nick.' When *she* wrote in Italian she spelled hers 'Rosalia.' I found a letter from her addressed to him that proves it. But when she was doing business someone usually wrote her name out for her as 'Rosaria' and she'd place her 'X' next to it.

As mentioned, Guy had a sister named Bedelia and several older brothers, Tony, Salvatore, Albert[10] and Frank. Tony was felled by pneumonia when he was eleven years old, and Bedelia and Salvatore died a few days after birth. Anna

---

10   Albert Ronald Vitale was born July 26, 1912 in East Boston, MA. According to church records, he was not baptized until October 21, 1914, at the Church of Our Lady of Mount Carmel, East Boston, MA. Peculiar? Yes, because back then priests all said that a kid was supposed to be baptized within a few short weeks after his birth, to cleanse his soul from original sin; otherwise, if he died he might go to Limbo, instead of Heaven.

Marie, at the age of nine a few years before, had had a serious brush with rheumatic fever, an illness which left her little heart severely damaged.

With the memory of those painful incidents etched forever in their minds, Rosaria and Nicola, perhaps overly protective, watched Guy like a hawk as he grew. And this, when he was six, proved to be a prudent thing.

*   *   *   *

East Boston, MA
Monday, June 2, 1924
2 Emmet Place
6:15 p.m.

"Ma! Guy spilled his milk. And now he's got his face in it." Nineteen year old Maria Vitale looked up from the novel she'd been reading, in time to observe her youngest brother perform the action she had just described. The Vitale family had finished its evening meal. Anna Marie, Albert and Frankie had vacated the dining room table, leaving Maria, a pretty, five foot two inch dynamo, so helpful to Rosaria as to be almost a surrogate mother, to watch Gaetano play listlessly with the last of his food. Rosaria and Nicola had retired to the kitchen to wash dishes, scrub pans and bicker over Nicola's announcement that he would apply for his barber's license again, and leave the hard life of a ship fitter behind. Bored, Maria had been reading instead of cajoling her brother to eat the remnants of his supper.

Her mother stuck her head into the dining room. "What?" she said in rapid Italian. "Maria, I told you to see that he finished eating." Entering the room, she advanced toward the table, wiping her hands on an apron.

"I was, Ma," Maria said, laying aside the novel. "But he just now knocked the glass over with his arm."

"Guy? Get up off the table," Rosaria commanded as she came to a stop next to her son. "Ah! What's this?" Leaning over, she touched the boy's forehead with the back of her hand, and quickly drew it back.

"What is it?" Nicola, sensing something amiss, had followed his wife from the kitchen. "Gaetano! Lift your head up off the table. What a mess you've made."

The boy sat up sluggishly, his eyes glassy, his face a rosy red flush. "Sorry, Pa," he mumbled.

Ignoring her father, Maria turned to her mother. "Ma! I think …"

"What?" Rosaria demanded.

"Is it like … Tony?" Maria asked.

"Yes," Nicola interjected. "Quickly. To the hospital."

*   *   *   *

Boston, MA
Friday, July 11, 1924
The Children's Hospital[11]
300 Longwood Avenue
11:00 a.m.

"This young man was a very sick puppy when you brought him in five weeks ago, Mrs. Vitale," the Superintendent, Doctor J. C. Smith said, as he ran his hand across the top of Guy's head. Rosaria Vitale and her daughter, Maria, were standing next to Guy's bed in Ward One on the second floor of busy Children's Hospital, listening to the doctor. "His fever got up to a hundred and six before we brought it down."

"I didn't like the ice baths very much," Guy said, swinging his legs out from under the sheet and placing his bare feet on one of the huge black and white squares of the ward's linoleum floor.

Chuckling, the elderly doctor took a baseball glove from the top of the bundle of clothing in Rosaria's arms and handed it to Guy. "You can get dressed now, son," he said. "You're being discharged today."

Although she could understand English somewhat, Rosaria, a bit heavier now at thirty-eight, was still unable to speak it. *Listen—think in the new language—talk. Listen—think in the new language—talk. The listening part is okay, but somewhere between that and the talking, I always seem to get lost. Ahh! After Tony died … I don't care. It's all too damn much.*

Unwilling to invest the time to learn, and not wanting to rely upon her husband, who was far ahead of her in understanding their second language, although he, too, still had trouble speaking it, she had come to depend on her daughter, Maria, to convey her wishes to others. She turned to her eldest daughter now. "Maria, tell the doctor we thank him for all he did," she said, and listened while her words were translated.

"Don't mention it," Doctor Smith said. "That's what we're here for." He turned to leave. "We'll follow your boy as an outpatient for a few weeks to make sure the fever doesn't return. Come by the office after he's dressed and take care of your bill before you leave."

Rosaria watched the doctor's back as he left them. When he was far enough away, the cordial smile receded from her face. Snatching the baseball glove from

---

11   A highly regarded medical center in Boston during the early part of the 20th Century, specializing in children's illnesses.

her son, she handed him a pair of pants. "Get dressed quickly," she commanded coldly. "I had to close the store to come for you. No one's there to tend the customers. If I'm not back soon, they'll go over to Fiorillo's on Boardman Street and I'll lose them."

CHAPTER 2

Pine Bluffs, WY
Friday, September 10, 2004
703 Beech Street
11:a.m.

In America, the period between the first and second World Wars was remarkable in many ways. During the 1920s, this country was, generally speaking, a laissez-fair country with a self-regulating economy. For the most part, businessmen were free to make their own arrangements and workers free to bargain for the best wages at the market rate.

But there were several significant factors out there on the American scene. The first? Industry was protected from foreign competition by high tariffs. Neither Harding, Coolidge, nor Hoover pursued Wilson's attempts to reduce tariffs and move to free trade. This produced consequences, both at home and abroad.

The second was that America's presidents and Congressional leadership failed to stand up to the National Federation of Manufacturers (NFM), and the American Federation of Labor (AFL), other lobbying groups formed by particular industries, and local pressure from within industrial states, to pursue the policies of economic freedom they claimed to favor. Among the rank and file, the new fashion of social engineering preached by "progressive" eminent sociologists (read Socialists) like Thorsten Vehblen—the notion that action from above could determine the shape of society and that humans could be manipulated like commodities—had taken hold. Although Prohibition was in force, jobs were plentiful, earnings were up, Ford and GM were turning out affordable cars at a fast pace, and life for most was good.

The ordinary man and woman on the street were unaware of the sinister forces already at work on the business scene and in the markets. There had been a mini-depression in 1920–21, but it did not last, and the general public took little notice.[12]

The Presidential election of 1928 featured Herbert Hoover, who had served as Secretary of Commerce for eight years during the 1920s, as the Republican candidate, and Alfred E. Smith, the popular and successful governor of New York, as the Democrat. Smith, a Roman Catholic, openly campaigned *against* Prohibition, while Hoover *defended* it. But significant anti-catholic prejudice still existed in America at the time and despite his tendency toward social engineering, Hoover seemed to exemplify old fashioned moral values. His promise of "a chicken in every pot and a car in every garage" resonated with the common man, winning him the popular vote by slightly more than five million. Sweeping the Electoral College 444–87, he took office in March 1929—just seven months prior to the Wall Street Market collapse and the Great Depression which followed.

*   *   *   *

East Boston MA
Thursday, November 28, 1929
21 Ford Street
6:45 a.m.

Marie Antonetta Vitale lay in her bed, wide awake, her hands behind her head, staring at the ceiling. This was her wedding day! *My wedding day,*[13] she thought. *Myweddingdaymyweddingdaymyweddingday,* she said to herself. Liking the way she thought that would sound, she said the words again, out loud, letting them run together like some sort of tongue twister.

"Myweddingdayyyy, myweddingdayyyy, myweddingdaaaaayyyyy!" she said. Rolling over, she kicked the blanket and sheet off herself. Since she disliked pajamas, she wore only a slip to bed each night. *Now Devina*[14] *and the others will have ta shut up about me bein' an old maid.* She sniffed. *Twenty-four isn't all that old.*

---

12 Paul Johnson, *A History of the American People,* New York, N.Y 10022. HarperCollins Publishers, Inc. 1997.

13 On Thanksgiving Day, Thursday, November 28, 1929, Maria Antoinetta Vitale and Edward George Sacco were joined in holy matrimony.

14 Devina Vitale, a cousin, born December 8, 1896. Daughter of Gaetano Vitale and Marianna Falcucci, she was 9 years older than Maria, divorced, but re-married to Constantine Cogliani at the time.

Even though it was Thanksgiving Day, it was too early to get up. Nobody expected her to be up and about. There was nothing for her to do, except get ready for the ceremony, which was not scheduled until late in the afternoon.

What a delicious feeling! To have nothing to do and plenty of time to do it.

"Nothin'tadooooonothin'tadoooooooonothin'ta doooooo," she repeated, dragging the words out as long as she could, until she ran out of breath.

Things were different back in January 1905 when Marie was born. The average life expectancy was a mere 47 years. Only 8 percent of homes had a telephone and television had not yet been invented. There were just 8,000 cars and 144 miles of paved roads in all of America. The average hourly wage was 22 cents an hour and the average annual wage was between $200 and $400 per year. At the time, the Vitale family had been living in the house on Emmett Place. Marie's earliest memories involved the planes roaring overhead as they landed at Logan, and the foghorns of ships in the nearby harbor.

By the middle of this decade, she would have been two years out of high school. Would have been, that is, had she not quit school at the end of the sixth grade to help her mother in the family grocery store.

Grabbing a pillow, she placed it behind her head and lay back, thinking. *Had that been the right decision?* She certainly had thought so at the time. But now? What did she think now? It was hard to think. She was needed, Rosaria had argued, because the family was struggling, the business was growing, and besides, everybody knew that schooling was not necessary for girls, since they were just going to grow up, marry and have babies. *I didn't like school very much anyway,* she recalled. Her mother and father had disagreed over this, as they had disagreed over so many things during that period of time. So, although her father had tried to convince her to finish school, she had sided with her mother and gone to work.

What about Eddie? she asked herself now. *What does he think? I mean really think about me not going to high school.*

The man who would be Marie's future husband, Edward George Sacco,[15] was younger than she. Born on November 18, 1909, he was one of five children of Antonio Sacco and Anna Cicco; his brothers and sisters were Joseph, Louise, Henry and Helen. The family lived at 88 Leyden Street until moving to Everett a couple of years ago. *Probably because of that trouble between Henry and his mother,* she thought.

---

15   Edward George Sacco grew up at 82 Leydon Street, East Boston, MA. Interestingly, at birth his middle name was listed as Albert, but it was apparently changed later, to George. He was the fourth child and youngest son of Antonio Sacco and Emmanuela Annie Cicco.

Maria rolled over onto her stomach. *He's soooo smart,* she thought proudly. *Maybe he's smart enough for both of us.*

As a kid, Edward (Eddie to family and friends) was a bright, strong-willed child. *When it was time to pick a high school, he stood right up and said he wanted to be an engineer and would go to Mechanic Arts.* She rolled over and looked out the window. *That took real guts,* she decided. *But how the hell did he know? Just exactly how did he know he wanted to be an engineer and go to the school where all boys with that ambition went? He did, too, graduating with the Class of '28.*

Rising from the bed, she went to her dresser, picked up his class directory, the graduation issue of *The Artisan,* which she kept right out on top where everyone could see it, and read his brief Bio:

> *1927, honor roll, dramatic club,*
> *1928, service committee (escort)*

Woooooeeee! Smart, alright. Ambitious and a hard worker, too. For three summers while he was in high school, 1925, 1926 and 1927, he had gone to the Massachusetts Institute of Technology (MIT), where he took courses in Architectural and Engineering Design.

It was during the summer of 1925 that she had attended nursing school in New York, at the academy run by Vittoria Simone. She sniffed. *I'm smart, too. I still remember the address—398 Marcy Avenue, Brooklyn.*

She'd kept all his letters. He had written almost every day, and when he didn't, she wrote *him* and indignantly wanted to know why. *Anybody with half a brain could see he was a real go-getter who'd make a good provider,* she thought. *I was afraid some other girl would snatch him up while I was away.*

Their letters show a developed and serious relationship. Clearly, Maria felt it was necessary to show him that she cared about him. And it worked. Caught up in that, being as young as he was, Eddie certainly seemed to enjoy the attention he was getting from this "older woman."

She opened her dresser drawer, extracted a small box crammed full of his letters to her, and pulled out the one on top; one she'd written to him. She'd asked him if she could have it because it was the last one she had written to him.

July 23, 1925

Dear Eddie
    Aren't you glad about my last two letters? I can't make them long for I have no more writing paper and I have to go out to 18th Street

with Vittoria and we are going to be away all day so I have to hurry. No, Oh no, my wrist isn't sore. I've had to wear a wrist band of Emil's all this week. And I don't mean maybe! It's all right. You see I'm trying to meet most of your demands BUT where do you get the idea I should write only to you and a few times a week at that, to Anne? Boy, what a monkey you turned out to be! ... Say, don't you dare have any other girl while I'm gone, and tell that girl you HAVE got a girl and can't be bothered with her. IF YOU DON'T, I'll get after her myself. That's why I want to put you in a glass case, so I'll be the only one can have you! See? Forever and ever! I hope you'll like the souvenirs too, Eddie. I'll feel rotten if you don't. Oh, I've got loads to tell you when I get home so I'll not write so much in this letter. You won't have to answer this letter for I'd not be here to get it. I'm coming home! Home Eddie! Gee! But it's grand! I'm so excited I can hardly write and it's still Thursday. How will I be tomorrow? The train leaves Grand Central at 7:35 and I'm expecting to get there 2:35 Standard time or earlier. That will mean 3:35 daylight saving time. But if I get there before you, I'll wait, shall I? When you get to South Station ask the man what time the express from N.Y. will get there and on what track so that you'll be the first one I'll see when I get off ...

Tucking the letter in its box with the others, she carefully placed the box back in the drawer. He had been so young; only fifteen, while she'd been twenty. *And here we are* four years later, she thought. *Thanksgiving Day, November 28, 1929. Just ten days after his twentieth birthday, and one month after the stock market crash, we're about to be married. And Pa? He says it's not a good time to start out.* She sniffed again. *What does he know? I've never listened to him, anyway. Ma doesn't listen to him either. Why should I?*

Returning to the bed, she sat on the edge and wrapped her arms around herself. *Is this the right thing? Is Eddie really the right man for me? Will we have a good life together? Holy Mother, Mary, help me. I need ta know!* She waited for a moment as if expecting an immediate answer from The Virgin. Nothing happened. Scared and feeling very alone, she tossed herself face down on the bed and began to sob uncontrollably.

*   *   *   *

East Boston, MA
Thursday, November 28, 1929
St. Lazarus Roman Catholic Church
8:30 a.m.

Father Francisco Berti, pastor of Saint Lazarus Church, had risen early that morning, washed his face, brushed his teeth and dressed in his older black suit. He grimaced as he wrestled to secure the frayed, white collar of a Roman Catholic priest around his thin neck.

What with the Sacco-Vitale wedding that afternoon at four, he thought it best to carry communion to his shut-ins and return as quickly as possible. The Parish could not afford to pay a Sacristan to maintain the church and since this was a week day, the Sodality members were all working their regular jobs, even though it was Thanksgiving Day. He'd need to turn the heat on, light the candles and go over the pews with a dust cloth before the ceremony. After that, if there was time, he'd take a few minutes to bathe, shave and change into his best black suit and the stiff, white collar he saved for special occasions, so he'd look presentable.

Weddings were one of the things about being a priest that he enjoyed, and *this* one, Rosaria Vitale's oldest daughter, Marie Antonette, promised to be a real social event. He understood that almost a hundred people would be there; family and friends of the bride and groom. *That* would fill the little wooden church to overflowing. And the reception to follow, at the Vitale home on Ford Street, promised to be memorable, what with all those great cooks in that Italian family.

He knew both the bride and the groom well. When he'd first been assigned to this parish, the girl was away, in Brooklyn, New York, attending nursing school at a place run by a friend of her mother. She'd returned a few months later, near the end of July 1925, but, unable to get work as a nurse, she'd been forced to take a job at W.F. Schrafft & Sons Corporation, a chocolate factory nearby. It was around then that she'd begun fiddling with her name some. Although at home, her parents still called her by the name they gave her when she'd been born—Maria Antonetta, the rest of the family referred to her as Marie Antoinette, or simply as Marie, and at work and among her friends she was known by the more Americanized first name—Mary. Her parents had apparently capitulated to her desires, because, on her wedding invitation, her name was printed as Marie Antonette.

The groom? He'd been born and raised right here in East Boston, but his family had moved to Everett a year or two ago. Father Berti frowned. *Some trouble there, between Annie, the mother and one of her sons, Henry, who was two years older than Eddie,* he thought.

The bride was twenty-four years old—she'd be twenty-five in January. The boy was young; he'd just turned twenty ten days ago, on November 18th. This was the first marriage for both.

An industrious sort, Eddie Sacco had attended Mechanic Arts School, where boys who had half a brain and wanted to be engineers went to school. While still in high school he'd taken summer courses at MIT. He'd been taking night courses at the Boston Architectural Club for the past three years, in Manufacturing, Industrial, and Public Building Design, while working during the day.

Checking to see that he had everything he needed, Father Berti left the Rectory, locking the door carefully behind him. *But what a time to get married!* He thought. *What with the market taking a dive like that and people being laid off left and right, jobs were becoming scarce. True, this past July the boy had been hired by the John G. McGann Architectural firm as an Associate Architect and Engineer, a pretty good position for a kid his age.* He shrugged. After their wedding, the couple was slated to move into a small apartment at 21 Ford Street, the building owned by her parents. *They'll do alright,* he thought. *Wouldn't they?*

*   *   *   *

Pine Bluffs, WY
Monday, September 13, 2004
703 Beech Street
9:30 a.m.

So Guy, who had just turned twelve the month before, saw his first sibling, his eldest sister, marry and leave the nest, although she didn't go far—yet; only to an apartment on one of the floors above his own.

The wedding went off without a hitch. The bride, my mom, looked beautiful in a long, white gown with a flowing train. Wearing a veil and headpiece, and carrying a bouquet of flowers, she appeared tired, like maybe she had not slept well the night before. My Dad, handsome and looking *very* serious, wore a black tux, the standard white shirt, and a black bow tie.

Their well-framed wedding portrait, re-conditioned by my wife and hanging in our home, was done by the Falk Studio, 14 Scollay Square, Boston. It's a nice photo. My wife says the Vitales must have had some money by then, because a wedding photo like *that* was not cheap.

For years, I've studied that picture, puzzling over the looks on each of their faces, trying to read something there that might give me insight into what they were feeling that day. I'm not very good at that.

My Aunt Madeline Vitale told me that after the wedding, Nicola and Rosaria gave the bride and groom three hundred dollars as a wedding present to help them get started. That was a lot of money in those days. Were my mothers' parents generous with their money? Yes and no. I'll explain later.

Aunt Madeline also told me that her mother-in-law and father-in-law did the same for Frank and her when they married in 1936. She was a Riley, the daughter of a fireman, who had grown up in Chelsea. They probably did it for Anne and her husband Alexander Tosi when those two tied the knot in June 1933, about four years after my mother and father. The son of Aldo Tosi and Josephine Drudy, Alec was an older guy from Hyde Park.

I don't know if the Sacco newlyweds went off on a honeymoon or not. I don't recall ever hearing any stories about it so I think they didn't, what with the market crash being so recent and things so uncertain. Perhaps, had they gone off by themselves for a few days, their marriage might have turned out better.

Anyway, after tying the knot, my parents moved into a third floor apartment in that same building in Orient Heights, at 21 Ford Street. That was the plan. It says as much on their wedding invitation. I have a copy of that, too.

That's where I was born, on Friday, August 20, 1937. My brother, Edward George, Junior, and my sister, Edwina Rosalie, were also born there.[16]

I remember my Mom telling me that in those days few women went to a hospital to deliver their babies. The doctor, or in some cases, the midwife, came to the house and did the job there. I was delivered on the kitchen table. One of my earliest memories is of that table; a metal job with black legs and a white, Formica top. On one corner, the Formica had been damaged; a round piece about the size of a half-dollar was chipped off, as if someone had hit it with a hammer or something.

Saint Lazarus' Church was across Breed Street and down the block at 125 Leydon Street. That was their parish for a while. I was baptized there.[17] The

---

16 My brother, Edward George Sacco, Jr., was born on April 16, 1931, at 21 Ford Street, East Boston, MA. He died on June 19, 1987, in Towson, MD. My sister's date of birth was January 9, 1933. She was also born in East Boston, MA. and she died on August 16, 1988, in Randallstown, MD.

17 On September 19, 1937.

old wooden church is gone now, but the brick rectory building still stands, although in private hands. The neighborhood changed. Lots of people moved to the newer suburbs. My mother and father did that, too, moving to West Roxbury when I was three. Not enough parishioners stayed on to support two Roman Catholic churches in that area, so the Diocese merged that parish with Saint Joseph's at 59 Ashley Street a couple of blocks away. It's a nice brick building. They now call the parish Saint Joseph/Saint Lazarus. Progress!

CHAPTER 3

Boston, MA
Saturday, August 8, 1931
Braves Field
12:45 a.m.

The boy was five feet four inches tall and sturdily built. His skin was olive, his hair thick and dark brown, almost black. He was Italian but could have passed for Greek. Or Cuban. He was with another, smaller boy and a stern, pale, mustachiod Boston Parks and Recreation official who looked like he might benefit from a day at the beach. They had walked through the rows of seats behind the first base dugout, opened the gate next to the photographer's box, let themselves down onto the field, and were standing on the grass near the on-deck circle on the Brooklyn Dodgers side of Braves field, waiting about as patiently as kids their age do, which isn't very patient at all.

Both kids were decked out in the uniforms of the local baseball teams for which they played. They didn't know each other well, having only just met the day before, but they stood together, not saying a word, and nervously fingered their new bats, shifting from one foot to the other the way kids sometimes do, and peering into the visitor's dugout where they could see two Dodger players moving around.

When he glimpsed Floyd Caves Herman, right fielder for the Brooklyn Dodgers, and saw him gesturing toward them as he moved to the front of the dugout for a better look, Guy Vitale grinned a satisfied grin. An avid reader of the Sports section of a local daily newspaper, he knew who "Babe" Herman was;[18] and the other

---

18 Floyd Caves "Babe" Herman, born June 26, 1903, in Buffalo, N.Y., played in the Major Leagues for thirteen consecutive years, from 1926 through 1937, mostly as a right fielder for the National League's Dodgers. His lifetime batting average was a hefty .326.

one, O'Doul, too.[19] He knew their latest batting averages, that both threw the ball with their left hands, that one batted from the left side of the plate and the other from the right, and how fast each could get to first base from home plate.

He was glad it was Herman they were going to meet because he was an outfielder, and that's where Guy saw himself playing in his fantasies. He was never in the infield or on the pitcher's mound; always in the outfield, mostly in center, because he was a faster runner than all the kids his age in East Boston. He imagined himself out there, taking off at the crack of the bat, tearing back, back, back as fast as he could run, reaching out to stab the ball out of the air at the last second before sprawling headlong on the lush outfield grass. But he always held onto the white pill. And the crowd always went wild.

Another thing; his collection of baseball cards, put together over the last two years with money he earned on Coke bottle returns, was the envy of all the neighborhood boys. Guy liked that. It made him feel important when the other kids drooled over his Babe Ruth or Lou Gehrig, Bill Terry, or Cy Young, and he'd savor the moment, thumbing slowly through his stack while the others looked on. He had cards for all the Dodger players, as well as the ones for the Braves. "Babe" Herman and "Lefty" O'Doul, among his favorites before, were about to be elevated to *the* favored spots.

Frank "Lefty" O'Doul was Herman's closest friend and the team's left fielder that year. Finished wrapping tape around his right ankle, he joined his teammate and squinted at the youngsters. "Those must be the two kids gonna get their picture took wit' us," he said. "Won the Boston Parks Department's fungo hittin' and outfield throwin' contests yesterday. The prize was a free ticket ta this afternoon's game, a medal, a new Loueyville Slugger 'n a picture wit' a couple a Dodger ball players. You 'n me."

Herman was a six foot four inch, well-muscled young man, with washboard abs and rope-like arms. He had come up to the Dodgers in the spring of 1926, after spending a few summers in the minors working to fulfill his goal of making it to the "big show." Honing his skills, you might say.

Twenty-three when he got the call, Herman was now five years older and a seasoned veteran with a good bat and a cannon for an arm. He had reached, even surpassed the great potential he had displayed in high school, and along the way he became a hard-boiled, fence-challenging outfielder who could wise crack with the best around and spit tobacco juice as far as anyone in that Brooklyn dugout.

---

19 Francis Joseph "Lefty" O'Doul, born March 4, 1897 in San Francisco, CA, played eleven seasons, for five teams in both Leagues. He retired after the 1934 season, with a lifetime batting average of .349.

Last season had been his best yet. Playing in a hundred fifty-three games, all but three in right field, he had hit thirty-five home runs, and batted .393. Although his bat was his best weapon, he was no slouch in the field, either. He handled almost three hundred chances in the outfield, made two hundred sixty put outs and committed only six errors the *whole* season.

But his left arm was his most valuable asset, strong enough to easily make that long throw from right field to third base. In the '30 season, he cut down ten runners trying to move from first to third on line drive singles to right. In '31, the year this little story I'm telling you about happened, the number was seventeen and counting.

Resting his right foot on the unpadded dugout bench, he re-tied a frayed shoelace. He was weary. The season was taking its toll, and at his age, going on twenty-nine, his body was beginning to show the wear and tear all professional ball players start to feel somewhere along the line.

Herman's knick-name was "Babe," a moniker stuck on him by a long forgotten teammate on some minor league club, years before. He was standing in the dugout on the third base side, the one traditionally reserved for visiting teams. Today, the Dodgers, in town for a three-game series with the Braves—the Bees, as they were affectionately called by their fans back then—were filling that role. The umpire would sing out, "Play ball!" in less than an hour and a half.

The smell of freshly cut grass filled his nostrils. Turning toward the playing field where most of his teammates were already sweating under the scorching August sun as they danced their way through the drills their coaches called 'pre-game practice,' he climbed the three concrete steps to the grass, nodded at the Parks official and pointed at the closest boy. "What's yer name, kid?"

"Gaetano Vitale," was the prompt response. The boys were young; Guy was thirteen, going on fourteen.

"Yeah? You a wop?" Herman asked.

Guy's dark eyes narrowed and he dropped his gaze. Back then, calling an Italian a 'wop' was like calling a black man a 'nigger' today. But Herman was a pretty big ballplayer and Guy was just a boy. So Guy was not going to start anything. Like he might have had it been another kid down at the playground doing the name calling.

"I guess so," he answered in a real low voice, looking like he wanted to be anyplace else but there. Then, raising his eyes to meet Herman's, he changed the subject. "I won the gold medal for fungo hitting yesterday," he announced importantly. "My friend here won a silver medal in the outfield-throwing contest. His name's Ernie Siciliano. He ain't Italian, though."

"Am so!" The other boy wailed.

"Are not. You're Sicilian."

"Haw, Haw," Herman bellowed. "There's a diffrunce?"

"Cut the crap, Babe," O'Doul said, coming out of the dugout behind Herman.

"Sorry," he grinned. "Lost my head there for a sec."

"Come on, people," the Parks Department official said. He had a little Brownie box camera in one hand, and he smiled agreeably. "I'll take a couple a shots of all four a you guys."

Minutes later, the picture-taking session was over. Herman, thinking he'd gone too far with that "wop" thing and eager to make amends, turned to the two local kids.

"You like playin' baseball, boys?"

"*I* do," young Vitale said. "I play for my school team."

"Yeah? What school you go to?"

"Blackinton Elementary. I got a certificate for playin' ball, two years in a row." He paused and started to wipe his nose on the back of his hand, but he remembered that his oldest sister, Maria, was always telling him not to do that, so he wiped it on his sleeve instead. "I'm gonna play again next year, too."

"So, ya gonna be a ballplayer like me when ya grow up, Guy?"

"I sure hope so, Mr. Herman," Guy answered, his large, intense eyes blazing.

"Not me," Ernie said, shaking his head. He was a bit older than Guy, but several inches shorter. "I wanna be a teacher."

The Parks man turned to Herman. "Too bad you didn't get batting champ last year, Babe. Who'd ever thought Bill Terry would go and hit .401?" He grinned nervously.

"Yeah," Herman said, a tinge of disappointment in his voice. He ran a hand through his straw-colored hair and turned away so the others wouldn't see his face.

"But that's baseball for ya."

With a nondescript waive of his hand at Herman and O'Doul, the Parks official gathered his two fledgling ballplayers and led them off toward the stands, where they found their seats and joined a few fervid fans, early arrivals, who were already seated and watching the pre-game practice, their thermos bottles full of ice cold lemonade. Many carried sandwiches of tuna salad or ham and Swiss cheese on rye, packed in brown paper bags, to be eaten later during the seventh inning stretch. You could bring lots of that stuff to the ballpark back then. Guy didn't have a thermos or any sandwiches. His mother had been working in the vegetable garden across the street when he left for the field. Not having it, he didn't seem to miss it, but settled back comfortably in his seat, enjoying the spectacle, absorbing everything going on around him.

Back on the field, Wilbert "Will" Robinson, Brooklyn's manager, was standing on the outfield grass down the third base line, holding a long, narrow fungo bat in his hand. "Babe! Lefty! *If* you're finished. Outfield drill. Let's go."

O'Doul and Herman stood together briefly, near home plate. Herman gazing thoughtfully at the two boys in the stands until O'Doul slapped him on the rump.

"What?" he wanted to know. "Those kids get to ya?"

"Naw." Herman said. The two men fell into step and began jogging across the infield. "Ya know what? Most kids wanna be ball players when they grow up. They forget about it later. But that Vitale kid? Somethin' about his eyes. I think he's really serious."

"Hell, who cares?" O'Doul said. "Better git yer mind back on baseball real quick. A few more a those bonehead base runnin' mistakes you been makin' lately 'n you'll be on the bench just like that." He snapped the thumb and forefinger of his throwing hand and grinned at Herman.

The two men separated behind the pitcher's mound, Herman heading for right field and O'Doul to left. Just then, the sun broke out from behind a few clouds that had briefly hidden it. Another hot, humid August day in Boston. The "dog days of summer" were hard on fans and players alike.

Ignoring the dull ache in his lower back, Herman glanced skyward. He had not told anyone about the back pain yet, afraid that if he showed up in the training room for treatment, the trainer would tattle to the manager and Robinson might bench him. With his stats, he knew he was a valuable commodity, prime for sale. Trade rumors were in the wind. He liked the idea of a solid pay raise if that happened, so he did not want to miss a single game. And he didn't need any *stories* floating around that he might be damaged goods.

The sun was now high in the midday sky. Herman's spikes penetrated the soft outfield turf at every stride. He reached his position, turned, pulled a pair of sunglasses from his shirt pocket and slipped them on. Under his wool shirt, rivulets of sweat began running down his chest. He heard the familiar sound of baseballs meeting catchers' mitts as the pitchers loosened up in the bullpen behind him. He listened as nearby players traded good natured jibes and mild obscenities, and he was about as happy with his life as anybody could be.

Punching a huge fist into his well-oiled glove, he assumed the outfielder's crouch as Robinson pointed at him with the fungo bat, then glided effortlessly to his left to get under the lazy fly ball arced his way off the long barrel of the metal bat in the hands of his manager. Squeezing the ball as it settled into his glove, with an almost effortless, fluid motion, he fired it into second base on one hop.

That season, 1931, Babe Herman hit .313. Pretty respectable considering the nagging back problem. But those "bonehead base running mistakes" that O'Doul had mentioned got Herman traded to Cincinnati at the end of the season. And the bonehead plays must've continued—or maybe it was back trouble—because scuttlebutt began circulating about a massive trade in which he was to be involved. The alleged deal had Gabby Hartnet, Pat Malone and Ki-Ki Cuyler of the Chicago Cubs going to the New York Giants for Freddie Lindstrom and Frank Hogan, and then Cuyler was to move on to Cincinnati in exchange for Herman. This canard produced denials all the way around, including from the Cubs owner. But the buzz persisted, as rumors often do. On October 18th, 1932, the *Boston Post*, the most popular newspaper in New England for over a hundred years before it folded in 1956, ran this small article:

NO DEAL FOR HERMAN
Reds Boss has not been approached in Trade. Cincinnati, O., Oct. 17 (AP)—Sidney Wells, president of the Cincinnati Reds baseball club denied tonight there is any deal being consummated involving Babe Herman, his heavy-slugging outfielder.

"I have not been approached by any club on any trade since returning from the World's Series," Wells said. "From the Cincinnati angle, there is nothing to it. I am undecided as to whether I will trade Herman.

Which meant he was thinking about it, though. And a couple of months later, Wells *did* trade "Babe" to the Cubs. From 1933 to 1937 Herman played with several teams; Chicago, Pittsburgh, and Cincinnati again, then Detroit. The back problem finally got to him in '37 and he quit baseball. Ten years later, he made a try at a comeback with Brooklyn, but didn't get to play much. It was a young man's game even back then. So that's it. He was history.

On Tuesday, September 8th, 1931, young Guy Vitale entered the eighth grade at Blackinton Elementary School.[20] He'd turn fourteen a month later. I didn't find a baseball certificate for either the seventh or eighth grade in with my mother's stuff after she passed on, like the one I found for the sixth grade, but I'm just going to assume he played baseball *both* those years. Why not? He loved baseball and he was good at it. Unless his mother put him to work in the store

---

20   This was the closest elementary school to Guy's home at that time.

afternoons and weekends, or he got run over by a milk truck or something, what was going to stop him? He was already a standout.

Then, in September of '32, he was off to East Boston High School for his freshman year and all the wonderful, unimaginably exciting experiences that lay ahead in the life of a young, wide-eyed high school kid.

And that's when things really began to get interesting!

PART TWO

HIGH SCHOOL DAZE

CHAPTER 4

Boston, MA
Wednesday, September 7, 1932
East Boston High School
3:00 p.m.

Aside from the fact that the Japs had invaded Manchuria and the Boston newspapers were reporting that the League of Nations' Lytton Commission had condemned their action, it was an otherwise glorious September afternoon, even if some media pundits *were* beginning to speculate that Japan might weaken the League by withdrawing from it.

Built in 1924, East Boston High School's facilities were first-rate. On this, the second day of school, the eight year old gray walled locker room was crawling with boys of different sizes and shapes. Seventy-five boisterous kids were suiting up, trying out for the football team. Within minutes they'd all be out on the field going through their paces under the watchful eyes of Fred L. O'Brien, Eastie's head coach since 1916, and a guy named Merrill, the athletic director who also doubled that season as O'Brien's assistant.

The football budget allowed for only forty players that year. Cuts would take place at the end of the week. About half of these young hopefuls wouldn't be there the following Monday when the first serious practice was scheduled. The opening game, traditionally against Brighton, was just three weeks away.

With a loud crash, the heavy locker room doors swung open. Coach Merrill, tall, thin, and wearing his serious face, appeared in the doorway. He stood there for a few seconds, hands on hips. "Famulari! Vitale! Coach wants both of you." He gestured with a thumb toward the hallway. "Right now!"

Charlie Famulari, short, heavily-muscled, black hair parted in the middle, tossed his helmet into his locker, closed it and headed for the door. He was the first string center, and a solid football player. Over in the next aisle, quarterback Frank Vitale finished lacing up his cleats. He glanced down the row of green lockers toward his kid brother, Guy, who had heard and was watching him. With a cavalier wave, Frank heaved his thick young body off the bench, slammed his locker shut, and followed Famulari into the hall.

*   *   *   *

Boston, MA
Wednesday, September 7, 1932
East Boston High School
3:10 p.m.

Fred O'Brien sat in his office just down the hall with the door shut, waiting. A Probation Officer in East Boston's Municipal Court system, he'd been coaching part-time here for sixteen years, and he'd always had good teams, some better than others. *A lot of great athletes have come through this place over the years,* he thought. *The boys around here seem to absorb football with their mothers' milk.*

O'Brien's feet were up on his scarred metal desk and he was studying a list containing names of all the boys who signed up to try out for the team that year. No great passer or team leader had miraculously appeared on the list since he'd last glanced at it, nor had any huge lineman unexpectedly transferred from Hyde Park or Chelsea. No six foot two end with glue on his fingers, either. He shook his head. *Good, but not great,* he thought. *It's gonna be an interesting season.*

Famulari and Vitale entered the coach's office. Jostling each other good-naturedly like boys do, they pulled up in front of O'Brien's desk, wiped the grins off their faces and waited respectfully. Their coach was a legend and they knew it. A kid was expected to show respect around a legend.

Pretending to be busy for maybe half a minute, O'Brien let the boys cool their heels. Then he looked up. His voice took on a kindly quality. "Have a seat, boys," he said, peering over his glasses. He had already decided on his team captain for that season.

"Famulari? You're a senior, right?" O'Brien asked. He already knew the answer.

"Yes, sir."

"You played well at center last year and if the boys look up to anybody on this squad, it's you. I think you deserve to be team captain this year. That okay by you, young man?"

"Yes, sir! That's great." Famulari exclaimed, his face beaming.

"Frank, you did well last year, too. You're my starting quarterback this season. You'll have your hands full learning all the plays and running the team on the field, without the stuff that goes along with bein' team captain, too."

Frank Vitale exhaled. "Okay," he said. Dropping his gaze to the floor, he half turned away.

"Now, I want you guys ta come ta practice every day and work hard," Coach O'Brien said. "The others will be lookin' ta *both* a you for direction."

Vitale brightened a bit. "Yes, sir."

O'Brien picked up the list of hopefuls from his desk. "There's another Vitale on this list. He a relative of yours, Frank?"

"Yeah. My kid brother. He's a good punter."

"Really?" O'Brien looked interested. "We'll see about that." He turned back to his star center. "Charlie? Your father still brew that great muscatel wine down in the basement?"

"Yes, sir. He just finished makin' a batch."

"Muscatel's my favorite. You think maybe you could bring me a bottle?"

*   *   *   *

Boston, MA
Wednesday, September 7, 1932
East Boston High School
3:20 p.m.

All the boys except one had gone out onto the practice field when Frank Vitale re-entered the quiet locker room. He found his younger brother alone, sitting on the bench in front of his closed locker.

"I was waitin' for ya," Guy said.

Frank sat heavily on the scarred wooden bench next to him. "Coach made Charlie captain this year," he said glumly. "I was hopin' he'd pick me."

Guy looked at his brother. His dark eyes expressed sympathy but he didn't say anything. Something else was on his mind.

"Frankie? Did you tell Mr. O'Brien I wanna try out for quarterback?"

"Naw. You're only a freshman. I told him you were a good kicker."

"Frankie!" Guy's eyes flashed anger.

"Look, Guy," Frank said, showing a degree of patience with his young brother that he really didn't feel. "You wanna make this team? Try out for punter. There's nobody tryin' out this year who can kick as well as you. Make the team *first*. Then you can work *up* ta quarterback in a year or two."

Guy thought that over for a minute. He was not at all sure of the logic behind the advice, nor the wisdom of the move. But he looked up to his big brother. Like younger brothers do.

"Okay," he finally said doubtfully. The two boys rose and moved toward the rear door leading out to the athletic field, their cleats beating a kind of tattoo on the concrete floor. They passed under a well worn poster which read, "Socrates once said 'To develop the mind and neglect the body is to create a cripple.' The converse of his statement is also true." A few more steps and they were outside.

"Remember now," Frank said. "When they ask who's tryin' out for punter, raise your hand. Then go out there and kick the best you know how." He put an arm affectionately around his younger brother's shoulders. "You'll make it. Okay, Guy?"

"Okay, Frankie."

So, that's how I think it went. Frank's advice turned out to be good. Guy made the '32 East Boston High football team. That was his freshman year. I have a humongous newspaper photo of that year's team. As the starting quarterback, Frank is in the front row next to O'Brien. Team captain, Charlie Famulari is on O'Brien's left. Guy? He's up in the back row with the other freshmen. But the important thing was, he got his chance. What he did with it was really something to see.

*   *   *   *   *

Boston, MA
Thursday, October 6, 1932
Fenway Park
6:15 p.m.

Back when the Vitale boys were in high school, Boston's high school football teams played most of their games at Fenway Park under an arrangement with the Boston Red Sox Baseball Club that allowed them to use the park a couple of days each week. The schools played two grid double-headers every week during the winter, at Fenway. I'm going to tell you about the 1932 season, when Frank Vitale was East Boston's quarterback and Guy, a freshman, played for the first time.

The afternoon of Thursday, October 6th was a brisk fall day. The trees showed the vivid gold, bright orange and flaming red that would only last for another week before giving way to winter's dull hues.

Jamaica Plain beat South Boston in the first game of the twin bill, 6–0, in a defensive struggle played between the two thirty-yard lines until the third quarter, when right guard John Murphy blocked a South Boston punt on Southie's thirty-two, which set up the only score a few downs later.

East Boston, coming off a win over Brighton in its first game the week before, was set to battle Trade School in the second game that day. A large number of enthusiastic fans—maybe a thousand people—had taken the subway over to Fenway so they could watch. Two Saccos—Jerome at right end, and George, at right halfback—were in the lineup for Eastie, and Frank Vitale was at quarterback as the game got under way. Guy, only a freshman, was on the bench.

Eastie received the opening kickoff and put the ball in play around its twenty-five. Frank called Leo Corsetti's number right away, and the strong fullback plowed for three yards off right tackle. On the next play, Frank took the snap and tossed a bullet to Bobby Rawson, who then passed it back to tall, thin, right end Jerome Sacco, who ran for twenty-two yards and a first down near midfield. Then, halfback George Sacco lugged it for eleven more. It looked like Eastie was really moving. But two plays later, an offside penalty caused that drive to sputter.

In the second period, Trade threatened to score. Baylor, their quarterback, recovered a fumble on Eastie's twenty-yard line. Two plays later on third down, Baylor passed to Kelley at Eastie's nine. Then Novak ran over center for three yards on the next play and East Boston drew an offside penalty, which set them back to their own one yard line. Things were looking grim, and Eastie's fans were temporarily out of the game. But Trade's fans were not.

In the defensive huddle, Frank Vitale was fired up. "We gotta hold 'em," he yelled above the noise of the Trade crowd.

"Yeah," Famulari yelled back. "If we stop 'em here, it's gonna knock the wind right outta these guys."

And that's what Eastie did. With Charlie Famulari and big Frank Ciampa leading, they mounted a goal line stand that held for three plays. Eastie got the ball back on downs at its own one, but when Famulari got up off the cold turf after assisting with the tackle, he was holding his shoulder and his face was twisted in pain. He had to leave the game at that point.

Frankie took a deep breath and called Corsetti again, but Trade, instead of wilting, was now angered and nailed him after only a yard. Second and nine. He called a pass play, but Tommy Hegner, his left end, dropped the ball in the flat. It was third and nine on the one. Frank signaled time and went to the sidelines to talk things over with his Coach.

"I can't move it," he said, his breath coming in short gasps.

O'Brien turned to his bench. His regular kicker, George Sacco, has not been punting well at all that day, and Eastie needed a good punt here to get them out of this jam. He gestured toward Guy, who was sitting on the bench next to left tackle Roland Indrisano, following the game action intently.

Guy was off the bench like a shot. "Get in there, young man," O'Brien said. "Kick it out of bounds as far up field as you can."

As the two Vitale boys trotted back to the huddle, Frank glanced at his kid brother, who appeared serene. He couldn't tell if Guy had nerves of steel or if he simply didn't realize how desperate the situation was. He shook his head. "Jest get the kick away, Guy, that's all I want," he said, and slapped his brother on the rear.

The shrill sound of the referee's whistle split the air and the clock started to run. In Eastie's huddle, Corsetti wiped his nose on his sleeve and spoke up. "Shit, Frankie. What's *he* doin' in here?"

"Shut up, Leo," Frank said hotly. "Coach sent him in 'cause he's been kickin' good in practice." He glared around the huddle at the others. "There ain't much room back there, so you guys up front gotta hold until he gets the kick away. Okay?"

They broke from the huddle and moved to the line of scrimmage. Guy was standing very deep in his own end zone, one step in front of the out of bounds stripe, but he was less than ten yards behind his line. It was his first time off the bench in a game. He glanced left, then right, and saw Trade's big ends digging in. *They'll be comin' like freight trains, tryin' ta block this kick,* he thought. He wished Famulari was still at center. *With him out, the middle's not solid, either.* His stomach contracted like a fist. He remembered that Mr. O'Brien wanted him to kick it out of bounds as far up field as he could. *I'm gonna have ta hurry,* he thought. He licked his dry lips, extremely aware that this was his first big chance. If he muffed it, he'd be on the bench for a long, long time.

There was no more time. As if from a great distance, Guy heard the clamoring crowd getting into the game, and the pulsating, reassuring staccato of his brother's voice shouting the signals. Suddenly the ball was spiraling back, a perfect snap from the substitute center. There was the sound of contact by the brawny linemen in front of him; pads against pads, helmets against helmets, and gasps of violent effort as one set strained to break through while the other set strained to keep them out. Guy's arms felt like lead as he plucked the ball out of the air. The leather felt cold in his hands. In a split second he had the laces positioned just right. He took his stride, let the ball drop and swung his right leg up as hard as he could, shoe pointing straight out, toe down, just like he'd been doing in practice. He felt his foot make contact with the pigskin— solid contact. Expelling a breath loudly, he followed through. The ball exploded off his foot, evaded several pairs of desperate hands reaching for it, and soared skyward. The punt was away!

A thousand other pairs of eyes were fastened on that ball as it rose; a perfect spiral, arcing high in the chill air. It had good height, which allowed Guy's front line to get up-field to cover it. The ball descended like some prehistoric bird without wings and hit the ground at Trade's forty-nine-yard line before bouncing, end over end, out of bounds at the forty-three. It had traveled sixty yards in the air! The crowd roared its approval.

His eyes shining with pride and pleasure, Frank Vitale wiped his dirt-streaked face on his sleeve and slapped his brother on the back as they jogged up field to the new line of scrimmage. Leo Corsetti, who had thrown a desperation block on one of Trade's huge guards coming through the middle and sustained a hip-pointer for his trouble, limped over to Guy. "Nice punt, kid," he grunted.

Over on the sidelines, Fred O'Brien's ears and nose were red from the October cold, but he was grinning from ear to ear as he sent in a sub for his freshman punter.

"What d'ya know about that!" he said out loud.

A couple of plays later the half ended. Thanks to Guy's kick, the game was still scoreless. As the teams surrendered the field to the marching bands at half time, O'Brien was next to Guy. "Nice kick, Vitale," he said.

"Thanks, Coach!" Guy replied earnestly, his face flushed with excitement. "I wasn't sure I was gonna get that kick away."

O'Brien let out a loud belly laugh. "Kid, there wasn't a soul in this *ballpark* who thought you'd get that kick away." As if to put an exclamation point to O'Brien's words, Eastie's marching band, now in sole possession of the same end zone from which Guy had made his kick, struck up the first notes of John Phillip Souza's piece; "Ta-Da, Ta-Di-Da, Ta-Di-Da, pause. Ta-Di-Da, Ta-Di-Da, Ta-Di-Da-Daaa …"[21]

The second half began with Guy back on the bench. Trade received the kick-off to start the third quarter, but its drive went nowhere. Baylor, Trade's punter, got off a short kick to his own forty, where Eastie took over.

On the first play, Frank Vitale handed off to his left halfback, Bob Gambino, who gained eleven yards around left end. Then, after hauling in a short pass,

---

21 One of the most popular Marches of all time, John Philip Sousa's *Stars and Stripes Forever* was often played by marching bands at high school and college football games, and when Army and Marine Corps troops were reviewed on parade grounds. Sousa's band was the most popular band in the U.S. for over thirty years. Yes, even more popular than Benny Goodman, Tommy and Jimmy Dorsey, Guy Lombardo and his Royal Canadians, and Glenn Miller.

Jerome Sacco broke loose and ran down to Trade's two-yard line. But a fumble by Frank on the next play turned the ball over to Trade. After a couple of first downs *their* drive stalled. Baylor kicked it away and Eastie took over at midfield. Things went back and forth like that for a while.

As the fourth quarter began, George Sacco ran for seven on a reverse from right end, and Gambino then went off tackle for a first down at Trade's twenty-five. But two downs lost five yards as Trade's defense stiffened. Frank then tossed a pass to Jerome Sacco, who couldn't hang onto it, but a Trade defender was called for interference and Eastie had a first down at Trade's three-yard line!

First and goal. Eastie's loyal fans were now back in the ballgame, making lots of noise as Gambino tried the center of the line and moved the ball to the one foot line. On the next play, Frank handed off to Larry Currie who went over on an off tackle slant. Because they didn't yet have a reliable place kicker, and because they might need two points to win this game if Trade scored a late touchdown and kicked the extra point, Eastie tried a rush play for the point after. It failed and the second game of the day came to an end by the same score as the first; East Boston six, Trade nothing.

✳   ✳   ✳   ✳

East Boston, MA
Thursday, October 13, 1932
East Boston High School
5:15 p.m.

In the rapidly fading light of a cold, dreary Thursday afternoon, Fred O'Brien's football players were nearing the end of their practice session, a light drill without pads, in preparation for their game the next day. At one end of the field, two squads, one directed by Frank Vitale on offense, the other by second string quarterback, Frank Ford on defense, were running their plays; the same ones they'd use against Commerce High at Fenway Park the next afternoon.

In those days, offenses were relatively unsophisticated, the running game dominant, passing still only an afterthought, although gaining in popularity. Guy was at the other end of the field, taking snaps from a center, and kicking the football to a lone receiver standing out around the fifty yard line. In between punts, he was scrutinizing the drills, watching his brother and Ford with fierce concentration as they ran the team using the old single wing formation. In a sawdust pit nearby, the tackling dummy hung from a rope, temporarily neglected.

"Vitale?" Assistant Coach Merrill was calling him.

"Yes, sir?" With difficulty, Guy forced himself to look away from the action.

"Coach O'Brien wants you to start practicing place-kicking."

"Place-kickin'?" Guy's eyebrows shot up in surprise.

"Yeah. It's a new thing. Red Grange or Andy Kerr, or some big-time coach thinks it's gonna replace drop-kicking, rushing, and passing for the point after."

"But, I don't …"

Merrill raised a hand to stop him. "Don't *worry*, Guy. Coach O'Brien'll show you what you need to know. Starting Monday afternoon, okay?"

CHAPTER 5

The twin bill featuring Jamaica Plain against Charlestown and East Boston versus Commerce was played on a glorious day; the kind that filled people with energy and made them glad to be alive. Lots of spectators turned out to see their favorite teams play football that afternoon. Bostonians cared little about the stirrings of dictators in a crazy Europe that seemed so far away on that fall afternoon in 1932.

In the first game, an interference call on a pass play, a blocked punt and an intercepted pass helped Jamaica beat Charlestown, 20–0. The game featured a 57-yard run by Jamaica's left end, Herb Kelleher, about whom we'll hear more later, which almost produced a touchdown but fell short when he was hit and knocked out of bounds just three yards shy of the goal line.

The contest between Eastie and Commerce later that day turned out to be a defensive battle that saw hard hitting, several fumbles at key times, and many penalties. Frank Vitale, now a strapping eighteen year older, and left end, Tommy Hegner, *did* team up for two spectacular pass plays, but neither led to a score as both drives were stymied, one by a penalty, the other by a fumble. The game ended in a scoreless tie. Guy, despite his good showing in the game against Trade, did not see action in this one, as Coach O'Brien, who had not been substituting freely, used only three subs the entire game.

*   *   *   *

Boston, MA
Tuesday, November 1, 1932
Fenway Park
6:15 p.m.

The day was frigid and overcast, with the smell of snow hanging heavy in the air as East Boston and Charlestown took the field after Hyde Park had soundly thrashed South Boston, 27–0.

J.W. Mooney, a sportswriter who covered high school sports back then for the *Boston Post*, one of the largest newspapers in the country, with a circulation in the 1930's of well over a million readers, had this to say about the Eastie-Charlestown game:

> *East Boston had its own fun in its own way with the competition right within the fold. Coach Fred O'Brien has an Irish backfield and an Italian backfield and the two had it out all afternoon seeing which could gain the most ground and score more often. Well, the Italian boys knocked off the first score in the first period and the Irish boys lugged it right down to within a couple of feet of the goal line in their period before a fumble stopped the march. So it was a racial affair when the touchdown was made in the last quarter as there were two of each in the backfield, although (George) Sacco crashed over for the touchdown.*

This contest saw some strong and accurate passing by Frank Vitale, and exceptional running by George Sacco, who also did the punting again that day.

Early in the game, Frank threw a fifteen-yard pass to Ben Morse, which was complete to Charlestown's twenty-eight-yard line. Gambino then picked up five yards, but two running plays netted only a yard. An incomplete pass on fourth down and Charlestown had stopped Eastie's drive at its own twenty-two.

On the next series of downs, the Ferry Boat Riders mounted another drive. Frank heaved a pass to Bobby Rawson at Charlestown's twenty-two-yard line. Next, Frank pitched out to George Sacco who raced around left end and went in for the touchdown, but it was called back because of an offside penalty. Undeterred, Frank called Gambino's number again, and he hit the right side for what looked like no gain, but kept digging, broke a couple of tackles and dented the goal line for the first score. As the half was ending, Frank had his team back in enemy territory, but his final pass, though complete, was out of bounds at the back of the end zone.

The second half began with Ford at quarterback for the Noddle Islanders. J. W. Mooney described the action:

> *In the third period, the Irish ball carriers got going. Coulty was away for 35 yards on a punt (return) to the Charlestown 45-yard line. Doherty was hemmed in for what was a set-up for a loss but he reversed his field and got away for forty yards to the 10-yard line. But, the ball was fumbled a few rushes later.*

As was his custom, Mooney did not say who fumbled. Didn't want to embarrass the kids. In any event, the Irish boys, despite some dazzling running plays, did not score during the third period, and the Italian backfield took over in the fourth quarter.

Early in the final stanza, unnoticed by Mooney, O'Brien inserted Guy, not Ford, as a sub at quarterback, so his brother could rest. From the skimpy coverage I can't tell how long he was in the game. It was probably not more than two or three series of downs. Because Mooney did not comment, we can assume Guy's brief playing time was uneventful. Apparently it was *also* mistake-free. And that was a harbinger of things to come for East Boston High.

When Frank came back in, he dialed Corsetti, and the low-slung fullback punched through the right side for twenty yards. George Sacco followed by making the first down inside Charlestown's fifteen-yard stripe. But Charlestown's defense tightened up and they took the ball back on downs inside their own seven. Unable to move the ball in three tries, they kicked it away. Here was an example of why a good kicker is so valuable to a team. That punt was not a long one. Eastie took over again at Charlestown's forty.

This time things were different. A steady march saw them grind out a first down inside the five-yard line. Four hard tries later, George Sacco went over for the final touchdown and Eastie won it 13–0.

So the Ferry Boat Riders came out of that game still undefeated and unscored upon, although with a scoreless tie against Commerce on its record. They were now one of only a handful of teams in the entire State with no losses. Their remaining games included one against Jamaica Plain, also unbeaten to this point, a first-time game with Memorial, a team from Roxbury having a hot year, one against Hyde Park, who they had not beaten since 1926, and the annual Turkey Day classic against South Boston.

The Jamaica and Hyde Park games ended in ties and Eastie defeated Memorial. Guy, in those remaining games, played some, but for only one or two series of downs. Mostly, he spent the rest of that season, including that year's Thanksgiving Classic, on the bench, watching and learning, and working hard in practice to perfect his ball-handling and kicking skills. Since Frank Ford was a junior and a quarterback, Guy expected to play behind him in the fall of '33, or maybe start at another position, because Fred O'Brien liked to bring his boys along that way, giving each a chance in his own time.

But with baseball, as we'll see later, O'Brien handled his teams differently.

*   *   *   *

Boston, MA
Tuesday, November 22, 1932
Fenway Park
3:30 p.m.

In 1932, the Thanksgiving Classic rivalries were *not* played on Thanksgiving Day, but whenever during that time frame the Fenway Park card would permit.

Tuesday, November 22, dawned clear and cold, with a wind that promised to be a factor in the game between rivals East Boston, a team which had had a successful season, and South Boston, which had sputtered and misfired all year. The game, though a mismatch on paper, was played before a huge crowd of emotionally charged locals, who, anticipating a win for their side, rooted hard for their team.

"Okay, listen up." Coach O'Brien, his lineup ready, addressed the team prior to he game. "Rawson, right end; Indrisano, right tackle, Famulari, center, DeLeo, left tackle, Morse, left end, Vitale, quarterback, Sacco, right half, Gambino, left half, and Corsetti, fullback." He paused and waited for his boys to settle down. Moments passed. A locker door was slammed in the back of the room. A pair of cleats was dropped off to one side. Then, the desired silence.

"This will be the last game at Eastie fa you seniors," he said. "For some a you guys, it'll be your last football game ever as a player. I know you wanna do well today." Glancing around, he met the eyes of each of his seniors. "We've been together for four seasons. I've seen each a you grow, put on inches and pounds, learn the game, persevere, and play through the pain of injuries, school troubles, and even family troubles. I feel like each a you is my own son, and I'm proud a you guys. It's been a pleasure knowin' ya."

Again, O'Brien paused, letting his words sink in. "The papers say we're gonna beat Southie today. Well, I don't know. Southie has *always* gotten up fa *this* game, no matter what. It ain't gonna be any different today. But if you seniors play the way I know ya can, and if the *rest* a you guys concentrate and play hard, we *will* win, and the game will be what you want it ta be." He pointed to the door. "The crowd's waitin'. Let's go show 'em how East Boston High plays football!"

East Boston won the toss and elected to receive. It looked like O'Brien's pre-game pep talk had worked wonders, as his boys reeled off three quick first downs, moving the ball from their own eighteen to Southie's thirty-six. But like O'Brien said, Southie always got up for this rivalry. Their defense stiffened at that point, and Eastie had to punt.

Eastie didn't allow much yardage on South Boston's first series of downs, as its quarterback and captain, Eddie Hankard, a star two years before but hampered all season by injuries, got warmed up.

On Eastie's next series, O'Brien, who always called the plays from the sidelines, made a tactical error. Although operating with a wind advantage for the first quarter, he elected to have his team run the football instead of passing. Still the kids made some headway, but it was tough going. Mastrullo, South Boston's star center, a senior who had been out with an injury, returned for this, his last game, and was proving a formidable opponent for Charlie Famulari in the center of the line.

"That son-of-a-bitch is strong! I'm havin' a hard time keepin' him out," Charlie said, his breath coming in quick, short gasps.

"Well keep workin' on him," Frank said. "I gotta have some time back here." He called one of the few pass plays of the quarter and they moved to the line of scrimmage. But at the snap, Mastrullo and several others broke through and Frank had to scramble for his life. It looked like a thirty yard loss, but he kept his cool and looked for an eligible receiver in front of him. Spotting his right end Rawson downfield, he flung the ball in his direction. The pass was incomplete, but at least they would run the next play from the line of scrimmage, not thirty yards behind it.

This is how J.W. Mooney described the game:

> A South Boston eleven, which had sputtered and misfired all season, suddenly got rolling on all 16 cylinders yesterday at Fenway Park, and accomplished the surprising stunt of holding a strong East Boston favorite and rival to a scoreless tie.
>
> The Noddle Islanders didn't get many of the breaks and never could gather momentum. Invariably something happened, like a fumble,

pass interception or penalty, to clog up the works for the Ferry Boat Riders.

But it all turned out to be a wonderful battle between two scrappy young school elevens, and the way the game swung for the most part, a scoreless tie, was the best result that could be offered. There were individual battles of prowess all along the fronts. Mastrullo, the Southie center, was back in form, giving Captain Famulari one of his bitterest fights of the year. The biggest shot on the field was Captain Eddie Hankard, a 1931 star, who never got going this fall until yesterday. He had been saving it up for East Boston with the result that he was all over the field, once lugging out from his own goal for twenty-five yards on a kick formation. On the defense he played a great game as well.

The long and short of it was that neither team dented the end zone that day. Eastie, in a game it had been favored to win big, did not get many breaks and Frank Vitale could not fire his team up. Each time the Noddle Islanders gathered momentum, something happened—a fumble or an intercepted pass—that would bring their offense to a screeching halt. The contest ended in a 0–0 tie, and there were a lot of disappointed football players in the locker room that afternoon, not the least of whom was Frank Vitale.

Although the game against South Boston ended in a tie, the season had been a good one for the Sacco boys, and also for Frank Vitale, who, in his senior year at quarterback, did a fine job for his high school, displaying sound field leadership, a strong, mostly accurate passing arm, and ball-handling skills that kept the fumbles to a minimum.

*   *   *   *

Boston, MA
Monday, November 28, 1932
Noyes Playground, East Boston
9:30 p.m.

The moon was a large silver sliver in the sky over East Boston on that cold November night, as young Guy Vitale approached the temporary seats erected for spectators along the third-base line of the baseball diamond at Noyes Field, the neighborhood ball park a couple of blocks from the Vitale home.

"Frankie? Is that you?" he asked, peering into the gloom.

"Yeah, it's me. What d'ya want?" Dressed in a heavy plaid jacket with the collar turned up and a Boston Red Sox baseball cap, Frank was sprawled on one of the scarred wooden benches, ankles crossed, hands thrust deep in his jacket pockets, but otherwise oblivious to the cold. Next to his head on the bench was a copy of the *Boston Post,* open to the sports pages. He did not sit up.

"We were worried when ya didn't come home for dinner," Guy responded. He had on an old navy pea coat, a crew-neck woolen sweater, and jeans. "Ma told me ta call around and see if I could find ya. I couldn't, so I came lookin' for ya." He picked up the open newspaper, saw the headline where J.W. Mooney named the *Post's* All-Scholastic Football Team that day, and he knew what was wrong with his brother.

"Look, Frankie. You played really well this year. Nobody can take that away from ya."

Frank sat up and shook his head slowly from side to side. "I thought I'd make all-scholastic for sure. At least second or third team, anyway."

Guy examined the newspaper article quickly in the scant silvery moonlight. "Mr. Mooney didn't pick *anyone* from East Boston High," he said indignantly. "Either first, second or third team."

"No," Frank's voice was constricted. "And this was real important ta me, since I ain't gonna go ta college."

"But you'll still have the *memories,* Frankie. You know that." Guy said. He punched his brother on the arm and broke into a wide grin. "Another good thing. We didn't lose to Southie in your senior year, either."

Frank laughed cynically. "I guess a nothin' ta nothin' tie *is* better than a loss," he said. "But we shoulda beat the livin' crap outta them."

"Every one a Eastie's games is written up in the newspapers," Guy said. "We can collect all the clippings and put them in a scrapbook."

Frank shrugged. "You're right," he said, but his eyes still had a wounded look.

He rose slowly to his feet and studied his younger brother for a minute before giving him a playful push. "Thanks for comin' ta look for me," he said.

CHAPTER 6

East Boston, MA
Tuesday, September 14, 2004
Pine Bluffs, WY
3:15 p.m.

During 1931 and 1932, the collapse of thousands of banks nationwide brought the banking system almost to a standstill, and unemployment continued its steady rise from a low of 3.2 percent in early '29 to over 20 percent.

FDR's inauguration took place to the strains of *Happy Days Are Here Again,* and Roosevelt's famous calming words resonated across the troubled nation: "Let me assert my firm belief that the only thing we have to fear is fear itself." Despite his upbeat language, on March 6th, 1933, the President felt it necessary to declare a three day "bank holiday," making it impossible for many people to access their money and causing mortgages, other loan payments, and utility bills to be made late. In many cases, even essentials such as grocery shopping, for those who lived paycheck to paycheck, ground to a halt.

Internationally, Japan, instead of withdrawing its troops from Manchuria as the League of Nations insisted, gave notice that it would withdraw from the League. And the League did nothing.[22] Also in 1933, Adolph Hitler became Chancellor in Germany and there was a bonfire of books at Berlin University, as the Fuhrer quickly began dictating how the people of the Third Reich should think. But other than some in the U.S. government, Americans, preoccupied with more pressing personal matters, seemed not to notice these happenings across the big pond.

---

22   Sound familiar? Faced with Japanese aggression, the League of Nations, predecessor to the United Nations, did little more than hold meetings when faced with this serious world situation. Apparently its member nations felt that they could talk their enemies to death, just as the United Nations and its European member-nations believe today.

Budding trees and shrubs were beginning to turn green throughout the area, as adolescent Guy Vitale turned out for the baseball tryouts that spring.

In the past, Fred O'Brien had spent an occasional free evening watching kids play at nearby schools like Blackinton Elementary, and local Recreation and Parks League teams like Saint Lazarus, which performed at Noyes Field. He'd seen Guy play once or twice, knew a little about what he could do, and was happy to see him come out.

Tall, thin, Lennie Merullo was a senior at East Boston High in the '32–'33 school year. A bright student, Lennie had been given a double promotion earlier, which moved him from fifth to seventh grade. As a result, he was younger than everybody in his senior class. But he was a slick baseball player, so Coach O'Brien appointed him team captain despite his tender age. Not bad for a fifteen year-old kid.

"I grew up over on Byron Street," Lennie told me. "Met my future wife, Mary Eugenia (Jean) Geggis over there. Guy was from East Boston. The Heights. He was in Saint Lazarus Parish and I was in Saint Mary's, so we didn't grow up together. First time I ever met Guy was the spring of '33 when he came out for the baseball team. I played shortstop that year and a kid named Ritchie McDonald played second base. Guy was an outfielder. I don't recall anything specific about him, but I *do* remember he was a real good athlete. He did everything well. And, he *played*."[23]

*   *   *   *

East Boston, MA
Monday, May 8, 1933
North Brighton
3:45 p.m.

And play he *did*. I don't know what his competition was during tryouts that spring, but in early May, when Fred O'Brien's baseball team took the field for its first game, Guy, though only a freshman, was firmly ensconced as its starting left fielder.

Lennie Merullo may not recall anything specific about Guy's play, but beginning with the third game against Mechanics, the box scores show Lennie playing shortstop and batting second, and Guy Vitale, playing left field and hitting

23 Telephone interviews with Lennie Merullo, on 9/25/01, 10/30/01, and 11/5/01. Merullo and his wife were then living at 159 Summer Avenue, Reading, MA. 01867.

in the third slot right behind him. That lineup remained in place for the entire '33 season. Oh, and George Sacco was the catcher that year.

The game against Mechanic Arts High School, otherwise known as Mechanics, was played on a beautiful spring day at Smith Field in North Brighton. As mentioned earlier, Mechanics was the high school where boys who wanted to become Engineers went. My dad went there, but except for a short, undistinguished stint on the football team, he did not play sports.

Eastie's players, apparently sensing how good they could be that year, came ready to play. They pounded out seventeen hits in a three-hour contest, defeating Mechanics 16–9. In this game, Merullo collected three hits in five plate appearances, walked once and figured in two double plays. One of his hits was a double. Guy? He went two for six, stole a base and made two put-outs in left field. In the ninth, Larry Seggese smashed the only homer of the day, for Eastie.

A week later, on May 16th, the Noddle Islander's faced Roxbury Memorial at Memorial and racked up another win. Lennie did very well with the stick, going two for four—a double and a home run—and he figured in two double plays in the field while making one error. Guy collected one hit in four at-bats, made one put-out in left, was hit by a pitch once, and committed one miscue in the outfield. The final score was Eastie 10, Memorial 1.

The following week, May 23rd, saw East Boston playing Hyde Park. Patsy Rago, on the mound for Eastie, fanned ten Hyde Park batters while giving up just four hits and walking six. Neither Lennie nor Guy got a hit that day, but Guy, who had begun the habit of going to Mass on game-day mornings, handled two chances in left flawlessly. Both boys stole a base after getting on with walks from Howland, Hyde Park's pitcher, who gave up eight free passes. Howland was lifted for a pinch hitter in the ninth; a guy named Tominey batted for him, but didn't collect a hit. Tominey would re-appear in Guy's life later, when they both played for Barnstable in '37. Anyway, when the smoke cleared, it was East Boston 8, Hyde Park 3.

So, did East Boston lose a game that season? Yes. One. To Jamaica. Here's how it happened.

When Jamaica took the field that day, Reveliotis was playing second base and leading off. The pitcher, Hopkins was batting second. Norton was playing first base and hitting third. The clean-up hitter was their center fielder, Francis Goode. Kelliher was at third, hitting fifth. Both of these guys would be named by the *Boston Post* to its 1933 All-Scholastic teams. Another guy named Keleher,—spelled with one l—was behind the plate, batting sixth. Sholes was at short, Connolly was playing left and Mahoney was in right, batting ninth.

For Eastie, it was Bill Doherty leading off and playing third base, Lennie Merullo at shortstop hitting second, Guy was in left again, batting third, Hegner was in center batting fourth, H. McDonald was batting fifth and playing first. George Sacco was the catcher, batting sixth. Ritchie McDonald was at second, swinging the bat in the seventh slot. Larry Seggese was patrolling right field and batting eighth, and Larry Hesenius did the pitching.

The first inning was uneventful; lots of chatter from the benches of both clubs. Doherty led off for Eastie with a hard grounder to Reveliotis at second, who threw him out. Merullo lined out to Goode in center, and Vitale hit a one-hopper to Herb Kelliher at third, who knocked it down, picked it up and threw Guy out. In their half of the first, Jamaica sent up Reveliotis, who drew a walk and moved to second on Hopkins's slow grounder to Merullo, who slung it over to first just in time. But Norton flied out to Guy in left, and Goode struck out to end the inning.

In the second, both pitchers settled down. Hopkins notched three of his eleven strikeouts, by getting Hegner, H. McDonald and Sacco to fan. Hesenius responded by striking out Kelliher, getting the other Keleher on a foul fly to Seggese in right and Sholes on a grounder to short.

The third was also uneventful. Rich McDonald lined a single to left field just over the outstretched glove of Sholes. But Seggese and Hesenius struck out, and Doherty popped out to Reveliotis to end the inning. In Jamaica's half of the third, Connolly flied out to Seggese in right, Mahoney struck out, and Reveliotis ground to Doherty at third. Still no score, and the few fans who had shown up to watch, were restless for some offense.

"Merullo, Vitale and Hegner! Let's go boys. Start things off." It was the top of the fourth inning. Fred O'Brien was standing in front of the bench, holding a piece of lined paper with the batting order scribbled on it. Hopkins, Jamaica's pitcher had finished his warm-up tosses. Lennie Merullo grabbed a bat and stood in the batter's box, while Guy walked to the on-deck circle and began swinging three bats to loosen up.

In the on-deck circle, Guy watched Lennie take the first pitch from Hopkins, a curve that broke low and outside. Then Lennie took a fastball for a strike, watched the third pitch sail high, and swung at a fastball but fouled it off. With the count 2–2, he guessed right on a fastball again, but got under it and popped it up to third, bringing Vitale to the plate.

Guy liked to stand deep in the batter's box because it gave him an extra split second to follow the ball as it came in. He checked the third base coach for any signs, got none, and stepped into the batter's box. *His first pitch to Lennie was a curveball,* he thought, as he waited. Sure enough, Hopkins started him off with a curve, low and inside, then came back with a fastball for a strike. Instinctively, Guy knew Hopkins would try to get ahead of him here by throwing another pitch over the plate. *It's gonna be the fastball again,* he guessed. Hopkins wound and delivered. Guy swung and lined a shot into the alley between left and center. There were maybe a hundred fans in the wooden grandstand along the third base line, and they began to make noise. Thinking double all the way, Guy rounded first, but saw that left fielder Connolly had raced over to cut the ball off. *Whoa!* he thought, as he slammed on the brakes and hustled back to first, looking serious.

"Where d'ya think you're goin' kid?" Norton, Jamaica's tall, skinny first baseman needled. Guy ignored him because he was watching Mr. Merrill, the third base coach, and saw the steal sign. Hegner was the batter. *Gotta get my lead,* Guy thought. He took three steps off first, but Hopkins lobbed a throw over there to keep him close.

"Head's up, Guy!" With a runner on base, O'Brien had come over to the first base coaching box. Guy got his lead again, and when Hopkins moved toward the plate, he took off. The pitch was high and outside, the throw from Keleher was slightly higher than it should have been and Guy, with a good hook slide, notched a stolen base. Hegner was still the batter, and he worked the count to 2–2. On the next pitch, he smashed a single to center. Guy, who would later break a track and field record for East Boston High in the 50-yard dash, scored easily from second. Hopkins, however, bore down and struck out H. McDonald and Sacco to get out of trouble. But Eastie had a 1–0 lead.

In their half of the fourth, Jamaica roared back. Hopkins, a good hitter as well as an excellent pitcher, singled to left. He moved to second on a passed ball by Sacco behind the plate. Goode hit the ball hard but right to Lennie at short, but Kelliher followed with his first hit of the day, and Keleher did likewise, a line drive down the right field line that scored both Hopkins and Kelliher. Jamaica was not done yet, as Sholes slapped a single to left, moving Keleher to third. Connolly then struck out on a high hard one, but Mahoney poked a pitch over Merullo's head into left center, to plate another run for Jamaica, before Hesenius could get the final out of the inning.

Jamaica went on to beat Eastie 6–4 in a game that took an hour and fifty minutes to play. Lennie went one for five. Guy had a big game, going three for four, one of his hits a double, walked once, stole a base and scored a run. Hesenius struck out seven that afternoon, but Hopkins did better, striking out eleven and walking only one.

Here's an example of a kid—I'm talking about Guy, now—serving notice that he was going to be a great one. Against a good team whose pitcher threw nothing but strikes, he got on base four out of five times—three hits and a walk—and drove in one of his teams four runs that afternoon.

For a high school freshman to make a varsity baseball team is pretty good. For a freshman to actually *play* every day is quite an achievement. Lennie Merullo again: "Guy Vitale was a *good* athlete. Football, baseball and track. Coach O'Brien, who was a probation officer out of Station Seven in East Boston, had been an ex-big leaguer. At least that's what he always *told* us. He was impressed with Guy." True. But apparently Guy's parents, a different breed entirely, were not.

*   *   *   *

East Boston, MA
Monday, May 8, 1933
20 Breed Street
6:15 p.m.

In 1933, with Adolph Hitler already in power, the leftist British Labor Party, at its annual convention, voted overwhelmingly to totally eliminate the Royal Air Force. Fortunately for the people of England, the liberal Labor Party, political home to the pacifist crowd in England, was not the Party in power at the time, but only the Party in opposition.

On that steamy spring evening in May—the evening of Eastie's loss to Jamaica—Guy Vitale, his face flushed with excitement, took all three front steps at once and entered the first-floor apartment where his family lived. Knowing he'd performed well that day, he was eager to share the news. "Ma? Pa? Ya home?" Guy yelled, slamming the screen door behind him.

"Don't bang the door, Guy!" His father, still wiry but quieter now and more resigned to the things life had sent his way, was hunched in an overstuffed chair, laboring through a copy of the *Boston Globe,* a newspaper written in a language he could now read, but which told of people he did not understand and a country he could still barely comprehend. He didn't look up as Guy entered. The delicious aroma of spaghetti sauce with chunks of fat Italian sausage wafted from the kitchen, where his mother was adding the finishing touches to their dinner.

"Pa! Listen. I did real well in the game today. Got a double and two singles."

He tossed his schoolbooks on the worn sofa and threw himself down beside them so hard that his young body bounced once before coming to a stop. He was speaking Italian with the dialect of the Avellino area, which his parents used.

"That's nice, Guy. Wash up for dinner right away."

Rosaria, hearing Guy come in, walked into the dining room, wiping her hands on her apron. She stopped next to the sideboard on which was a cheap metal triptych that displayed a copy of Pietro Lorenzetti's Fourteenth Century work, *The Birth of the Virgin*. A yellow votive candle burned in front of it, a bright reminder of whatever special intention for which Rosaria was praying that day.

"Hey, Ma! I got three hits in the game today, an' one a them was a double. I—"

"Oh, Guy," Rosaria said in Italian. "I'm glad your home. We'll eat in about five minutes. Go down the cellar and bring up one of those big blocks of Parmesan cheese, will you?" She disappeared back into the kitchen.

Guy stared at the empty kitchen door for a few seconds and then turned back to his father. But Nicola had resumed reading his newspaper.

"Okay, Ma," he said. "Okay." But his dark brown eyes displayed a look that should never be seen in the eyes of any kid; wounded, puzzled, hurt, all there together.

*   *   *   *

East Boston, MA
Monday, May 8, 1933
150 Orient Avenue
8:05 p.m.

"Ma's not too happy about me playin' sports," Guy said out loud. It was a pleasant spring night at the Shrine of the Madonna, Queen of the Universe, on Orient Avenue, high atop the hill north of East Boston.

The month of May was quickly drawing to a close. Except for a young couple at the other end of the terrace holding hands and looking out over the iron railing at the shimmering lights of East Boston, he was alone. But he didn't *feel* alone. The statue of the Madonna on its marble pedestal towered above him, glistening green and black in the night air. Across the street, visitors to the Don Orione Home for the Sick Elderly were leaving, a few at a time. "Pa's not, either. I guess they'd rather see me workin' in the store or somethin'." His voice held resentment, resignation and a touch of understanding.

He was quiet for a minute. "But I sure wish they'd come out ta watch one a my games, now that I'm doin' so well."

A gentle breeze from off the water next to Logan Airport caressed his face. "I know. Ma doesn't speak any English, and Pa only speaks a little. They prob'ly feel outta place around my school. They never saw Frankie play, either."

The young couple left the Shrine and walked arm-in-arm to a black Packard sedan parked at the curb on Orient Avenue. The man, dressed in a polo shirt and Bermuda shorts, unlocked the woman's door. Laughing, she climbed in. Guy heard her door slam and watched absently as the young man ran around to the driver's side, slid behind the wheel, and they drove away.

A bright, silver moon glowed overhead. He rose from his concrete bench and moved to a spot at the black wrought iron railing. From there, he could look down on all of East Boston. His eyes roved over the familiar scene, picking out his own house below but several blocks away, old Saint Lazarus Church around the corner on Ashley Street, and newer Saint Joseph's Church a couple of blocks further. A muted whine of airplane engines reached him from the nearby airport, while to the south, the lights of Boston's tall buildings sparkled against the dark sky.

Reaching into his pants pocket, Guy pulled out a well-used rosary. "Still," he said, "if it's okay with you, I'm gonna say a rosary for the intention that maybe God will get them ta come out and watch. Or at least that they'll listen ta me when I try ta tell them about a game."

He moved to the base of the Madonna and glanced around self-consciously. No one was there. Kneeling quickly, he began to recite the rosary, under the outstretched arms of Mary, Queen of the Universe, his friend and comforter.

*   *   *   *

East Boston, MA
Tuesday, June 6, 1933
East Boston High School
5:30 p.m.

Fred O'Brien was sitting in his office, a room about the size of a prison cell you might find in Nicaragua or Bolivia, just down the hall from the boy's lockers, when a tall, thin man with sandy hair, wearing a navy blue sport coat, gray slacks, and a straw boater walked through the open door and into the sweltering cubicle. O'Brien removed his feet from the cluttered desk, loosened his tie and smiled at Dan Quigley, an employee of the National League's Boston Braves Baseball Club, who spent his time looking at local baseball talent. Quigley was carrying a brown paper bag in one hand.

"Quig! How ya doin'?"

"Okay, Fred. Just passin' by."

"Saw ya watchin' practice earlier. I was hopin' you'd stop in. You people made any decision on Merullo, yet?"

"Merullo? Naw. Nuthin' yet." The ancient electric fan perched on O'Brien's metal file cabinet in the corner was losing its battle with the heat in the windowless office. Removing his sport coat, Quigley carefully hung it over the back of the only chair in front of O'Brien's desk. In the oppressive humidity, his white dress shirt clung limply to his back.

"They're takin' their sweet time about it." O'Brien said, as he put on his glasses.

"Kid's awful young, Fred. Only fifteen now, right?"

"Nope. Turned sixteen last month."

The Bees scout frowned and started pacing up and down the small room. "Fred, be realistic, will ya? No major league club's gonna sign a kid that young. Besides, at five foot eleven and a hunnerd fifty pounds, they're worried he might not make it physically. Too light."

O'Brien's face fell. "He's a hundred fifty-five pounds and he'll sure as *hell* fill out a lot over the next two or three years," he responded indignantly." He stood up behind the desk. "What about tyin' him up fer a coupla years? Give him some help with college tuition or somethin', and sign him later on?"

"I don't think so, Fred," Quigley responded. "But we appreciate the fact that you thought of us first." He reached into the paper bag and brought out a fifth of Johnny Walker Red Label. "Ya *did* think of us first, didn't ya, Fred?"

"Yeah, Dan. I always try ta take care a the local teams first."

"Good. I brought ya a little somethin' to show our appreciation. Keep us in mind the next time you have a hot prospect, okay?" He handed the bottle to O'Brien and stood to leave.

O'Brien, who had progressed from wine to the hard stuff, took it, waved at Quigley's back as the man walked out, stashed the bottle in the lower left-hand drawer of his desk and dropped back heavily into his chair. What he had *not* told Dan Quigley was that the Braves, although the first, weren't the *only* team he had contacted about his slick fielding kid shortstop. *Maybe the Yankees or the Cubs'll have more of an interest in a top talent like Merullo,* he mused.

*   *   *   *

East Boston, MA
Monday, June 12, 1933
20 Breed Street
5:00 p.m.

On Monday, June 12th, 1933, J. W. Mooney announced the *Boston Post's* 1933 All-Scholastic Baseball Team. These, remember, were the athletes the *Post* thought were the best baseball players in the Greater Boston area that year. Francis "Cowboy" Crawley, a Senior from Cambridge Latin, who would later play with Guy for Barnstable in the Cape Cod League, was named to the *Post's* Second Team, and Mooney selected Lennie Merullo as a shortstop on the Third Team, claiming that the talent at that position was so deep that at least five local shortstops, including Lennie, deserved to be on the First Team.

In a lesser category called the "Honor Roll," George Sacco was named by Mooney as one of eight catchers. Both Sacco and Merullo were seniors. Freshman Guy Vitale was selected as one of twenty-five outfielders in the "Honor Roll" category that year.

One other thing. East Boston High was in the Boston District League. Although back then it was not as strong as the Boston Suburban League, according to Lennie Merullo, "... it was a pretty strong league. Not like it is today." That 1933 baseball team, with Lennie and Guy on it, won the District League Championship.

*   *   *   *

East Boston, MA
Thursday, June 15, 1933
East Boston High School
8:30 p.m.

Lennie Merullo graduated from high school in June 1933, and because he was a hot baseball prospect, a couple of teams were interested in him. But he had just turned sixteen on May fifth, way too young to sign. So he decided to go to prep school, get some extra credits and see if he could go on to college before signing with a big league club.

"I took the Commercial Course at East Boston High," Lennie told me. "That would prepare you to work in an office if you didn't want to work in the local shoe factory or in the Bethlehem Steel shipyard over on Webster Street. You could be a bookkeeper or something like that. But I realized I might be able to go to college because of my athletic ability, so I spent the next two years at Saint John's Prep in Danvers, Massachusetts, getting the credits I needed. Played baseball there, too. I was the shortstop and captain of the team both years."

How did he manage the cost? "I was able to get some financial help. Saint John's cost three hundred a year for tuition and books back then. My parents couldn't even afford the extras, so me, Jerome Sacco, and another fella, would drive down there [and back] every day instead of boarding. We'd stay overnight in a room over a local store on the nights when we couldn't get a ride back home."

What about Guy and *his* academics? What kind of student was he? I was able to get a copy of his transcript from East Boston High. As a freshman, he took English (five credits), Math (five credits), General Science (three credits), Drawing (3 credits), Manual Arts (four credits), Hygiene (1 credit), Military Drill (1 credit), and Phys Ed (1/2 credit).

The record shows he was a B and C student during his first high school year, as he rationed his time between the books, his sports, and work at the grocery store his mother ran in one room on the first floor of the apartment house. He finished the year successfully, earning the required twenty-two and one-half credits.

At that time, East Boston High School, like many other high schools across the country, had a Reserve Officer Training Corps (ROTC) unit. All the boys were required to participate. It seems that back then, educators understood that an early introduction to some light military training was an excellent way to instill in male students the discipline that's so necessary in later life.

George "Red" Baccigolupo, whose family lived at 29 and 60 Leydon Street until they moved from East Boston in 1952, agrees. "Guy was a Lieutenant Colonel in the ROTC during his senior year," he said. "He was a good officer, too."

Joe Rocciolo: "Military Drill seemed real popular until 1948 or 1950, when a few misguided mothers began to complain that too many of their sons were going into the armed forces after high school. So the school stopped offering the course."

Later, Military Drill was eliminated from school curricula around the nation, for the most part, a victim of ideological resentment of the military by certain elements of society who unfortunately had taken control of most of America's public schools.

But what was Guy actually like personally at this point in his young life?

Madeline Vitale, Frank's wife, put it this way: "Guy and his brother Frank were very different. Frank had more of an ego; he had opinions about everything and wouldn't hesitate to let you know what they were. More so than Guy, who was a very quiet, modest person."

This was not at all what I thought she'd tell me. Guy was the youngest in his family, and as you might expect, probably a bit spoiled by his older sisters and brothers. He was a kid who, up to this point in his life, was successful at everything he had tried. Someone like that is seldom "a very quiet, modest person." He's more likely to be an extrovert; self-assured, outgoing, somewhat loud, and possibly even boisterous at times.

Puzzling? Yes. On the gridiron and the diamond Guy seemed more true to the type of young person I thought he would have been. Is the explanation there, in his sister-in-law's words? Did Guy Vitale lack a strong ego as a child? Had he not picked up that healthy sense of self-worth or self-esteem that a person needs if he is to develop an integrated personality as he grows older? There were indications that this was so, and that this lack would cause him serious harm until later events helped him to partially overcome it.

*   *   *   *

East Boston, MA
Sunday, June 25, 1933
Saint Lazarus Roman Catholic Church
1:30 p.m.

On a sunny Sunday morning in June 1933, Guy's second sister Anna, surely his favorite, married Alessandro Henry Tosi in a wedding ceremony that took place at Saint Lazarus Church in Orient Heights. One of Alessandro's brothers was probably the Best Man—I have their Certificate of Marriage from the parish, but I can't make out his name—and a young lady named Norma Nickerson, probably Anna's closest friend at the time, was the Maid of Honor.

Father Berti having been reassigned to another parish the year before, the ceremony was performed by Father Leo Toma, who had taken his place. An extremely well-liked parish priest, Father Toma later baptized my brother, sister and me. Guy was fifteen years old at the time of Anna's wedding; he'd be sixteen that October.

Anna Marie Vitale, born in 1908, was twenty-five years old when she married Alessandro. These Vitale girls married late by comparison to the custom of their day. Anna did not seem to mind that most of the girls her age married earlier than she did; that people gossiped and speculated about her, as she toiled in the Vitale grocery store year after year without seeming to be interested enough in marriage to set her cap for a man. But one look at Al, who like most Italians of that day, "Americanized" his name to Alexander, and then to Al, was all it took. Anna was smitten.

So was Al. Shy and retiring, he'd not had much experience with women before he and Anna Vitale met. The son of Italian immigrants Aldo Tosi and Josephine Drudy, who, at the time of their son's wedding, lived at 27 Magnolia Avenue, Cambridge, not too far from that citadel of learning, Harvard College, he'd been born on January 17, 1904, and raised in Hyde Park. Aldo was a cook in a well-known Boston restaurant, who made a comfortable income; his mother was a stay-at-home mom.

A draftsman, Al was employed in the same engineering firm in which my dad, Edward George Sacco, Anna's brother-in-law worked. Sensing that Al Tosi was a good man, it was he who introduced them. My dad's judgment was sound in this. When Al died on July 8th, 1974, in Randallstown, Maryland, forty-one years later, he and Anne—she had also "Americanized" her name by then— were still together.

Incidentally, my dad died on July 15th of that year, just a week after Al passed away. When I called that to my Aunt Anne's attention a few weeks after their respective funerals, she dabbed at her eyes with a damp handkerchief and said: "Yeah, it would be just like Al to want some company."

After their wedding, Al Tosi and his wife bought a home on Lowden Avenue in Somerville, across the Charles River from Boston. Tiring of engineering during the early years of World War II, he answered a nationwide ad for engravers at the U.S. Treasury Department in Washington, D.C., was hired, and he and his wife relocated to the Nation's capitol, where they lived at 714 31st Street, N.W. until he retired. Shortly thereafter, they moved out of Washington to Maryland. An influx of blacks had resulted in deterioration of homes and businesses in their area, and shrinking property values. When gangs of young, undisciplined kids began making living conditions intolerable for whites, they abandoned any thought of recouping their investment or making a profit on their home, and left the area. They were happy to get out when they did, salvaging what they could. Besides, Anne wanted them to be near her older sister, Mary, in Randallstown, during their retirement years.

However, it was while Anne and Al resided in the District of Columbia, that they were able to provide Guy Vitale with a home after the war ended, and the emotional support he so sorely needed, until his recruitment by the newly formed Central Intelligence Agency (CIA) gave his life a sense of purpose, direction and meaning. But I'm getting ahead of myself again.

CHAPTER 7

East Boston, MA
Monday, October 2, 1933.
East Boston High School
3:00 p.m.

Across the stormy Atlantic in Europe, Chancellor Adolph Hitler pulled Germany from the General Disarmament Conference at Geneva and nobody paid much attention until he followed up a few days later by withdrawing his country from the League of Nations. *That* produced mild anxiety, which spreads through the U. S. diplomatic community, and Americans around the country began taking notice.

As school kids throughout the Boston area took to the fields for the first week of the '33 football season, the unemployment rate topped out at 24.9 percent. That meant that almost one in four of their fathers was out of work, and for the seniors among them, the prospects of finding a job after graduation were slim and none.

But for Guy and the younger kids, it was business as usual, and the business was football.

In his *Post* column on Monday October 3rd, J. W. Mooney wrote:

> *The Boston High School grid season starts this afternoon at Fenway Park, where the first of a series of double-headers will get under way. For the opening bargain bill English meets East Boston as leadoff and Commerce then takes on Charlestown.*
> ## 50 GAMES CARDED
> *The spacious ballpark, with its perfect turf, makes a real layout for the Hub teams and the drawing power under these ideal conditions is expected to prove itself today. Football is the hottest sport on the Hub athletic card and, with a schedule of 50 games to play at the ball*

park, there will be something doing there nearly every afternoon until Thanksgiving.

Since he expected them to have a strong team, Mooney gave the nod to English High, but went on to say:

> But *the Noddle Islanders are just in the mood to spring a surprise and uphold their fine record of not having been defeated since 1931, when they lost only one game by the trypoint. There are nine of the eleven players of last year back for East Boston, so Coach Fred O'Brien and Captain (Randolph) Indrisano aren't worried a whole lot about what the old Blue and Blue has.*

Maybe Mooney was right and Eastie was not concerned about English High going *into* the game, but it quickly became clear that if they weren't worried they *should* have been.

As expected, the Junior, Frank Ford, was at quarterback. Bobby Rawson started at right end, McGee was at right tackle, Silva at right guard, Carabott at center, Siraco at left guard, Indrisano at left tackle and Morse at left end. The starting backfield included Festa at right half, Currie at left half, and Corsetti at fullback.

English won the toss and elected to receive. After they moved to midfield on two first downs, East Boston stopped their drive, English punted, and Eastie took over. But on the second play, Eastie fumbled. Mooney this year changed his long-standing policy and began reporting who the culprit was. In this case it was Ford, standing on his own ten-yard line. But he recovered it himself on the four.

Eastie could not move the ball, however, and Ford had to punt. That's right. Ford. But it was a very poor kick, traveling only out to the twenty-seven, where English's left halfback, Little, gathered it in and ran it back for a touchdown, just like that.

In the second period, another poor punt got Eastie in trouble again. They moved the ball out to around their thirty-three yard stripe before they were forced to kick it away. But Ford hit it off the side of his foot and the punt only went ten yards. English got the ball on Eastie's forty-four. From there, English's quarterback Roger Battles tossed a pass to Little at the twenty-nine. A new backfield then made another first down at Eastie's seventeen-yard line. But English was called for holding, and a few plays later the Ferryboat Riders took the ball back on their own eighteen.

Midway into the third quarter, McGrath blocked a punt for English and Paul Agrillo recovered on the Eastie forty-one. Battles then carried it down to the twenty-seven, where East Boston's defense tightened and they took the ball back on downs at their own twenty-two. But it wasn't Eastie's day. Another fumble—at that point Mooney became inconsistent and did not say who, but it may have been Ford again—and English had the ball once more. Battles ran it for ten yards, and then hauled in a pass from Little and dented the end zone for the second score. They missed the extra point and that's how the third period ended.

The teams lined up for English's kick-off and Guy was inserted into the game for the first time. He'd be sixteen years old in a few days. His face flushed and his shoulder pads pushing up around his ears, he looked smaller than he was at five foot six and a hundred forty-five pounds. A high school band began playing somewhere in the stands, and the PA system began announcing how to get tickets for next week's games, while on opposite sidelines, two sets of cheerleaders performed their routines.

Lining up with the others to receive the kick, Guy, who had again attended morning Mass at Saint Lazarus,[24] felt a curious exhilaration at being in the game. *Big crowd a people out here today,* he thought, feeling it rather than seeing it. He heard the referee's whistle, saw the football in the air, and watched the defense commit itself to a full-out rush downfield, yelling like a bunch of wild Indians as they came.

Guy experienced a mix of relief and disappointment as the ball angled to the other side of the field where Festa took it on the eighteen and carried it only six yards before he was hit hard and knocked flat.

The referees, in their black and white vertical striped shirts, spotted the football at the twenty-four and one of them was waiting there astride it, a silver whistle dangling from a black cord around his neck.

For Guy, everything compressed into a tiny area around himself. He moved back to the ten-yard line, his teammates following. They leaned in to hear the play. They waited and Guy waited, too. Maybe five seconds went by before Guy realized that *he's* the quarterback and *he's* supposed to call the play. His face turning crimson, he tried to act like he had just been thinking of exactly the right one. He called the only play that came to mind.

---

24   Guy apparently sensed at an early age, that the holy sacrifice of the Mass is the best way of offering our lives to the Lord, because he attended Mass daily throughout his high school years. He understood that in the Mass we have the sacrifice of Jesus' death on the cross made present, and we have the chance to offer all our virtues and talents to the Father, along with Jesus.

"Two left five-six squeeze, on hut-two," he yelled and wondered if his voice had been loud enough for his teammates to hear above the noisy crowd.

This was a running play where the quarterback takes a direct snap from the center, drops straight back two steps, and hands it off to his fullback who is moving laterally from right to left. The fullback then cuts into the hole between left guard and left tackle. If there's a hole.

Eastie broke from the huddle and lined up. "Down. Set." Guy's voice sounded thin and small against the crowd noise. "Hut. Hut-one, hut-two!" Carabott's snap was perfect. Guy took it, but he felt like his shoes were weighted with lead. As if in slow motion, he faked a pitch-out right, then whirled and slapped the ball into Corsetti's middle as the low-slung fullback came across behind him. Siraco and Indrisano had cleared a small hole between tackle and guard and Corsetti slammed into it, almost losing his footing, recovered and made it into the secondary where he was brought down at the thirty-six yard line. A gain of twelve yards and a first down. *"This isn't so hard,"* Guy thought, grinning.

In the huddle, Guy paused for a second and then called the play. "Three, left-right, ten. On hut-one." He had called for his left halfback to go ten yards downfield and cut across the middle from left to right, turn and take a pass from him.

At the line of scrimmage, Guy started the play. "Down. Set. Hut. Hut-one." The ball was snapped and he faked a pitch-out again, moved left and saw that Currie had a step on his defender eight or ten yards away. He fired a perfect spiral, but Currie slipped on some loose turf and sprawled full-length. The ball sailed harmlessly over his head for an incomplete pass. Guy shrugged as his teammates formed the huddle again.

Well, that was how it went. Guy played the rest of the way, but although he moved the team well between the twenties and did not fumble, he could not dent the goal line or do anything miraculous to pull the game out. English won it 12–0.

A review of that game showed a couple things. First, Frank Ford, apparently nervous as the starting quarterback, hurt Eastie by fumbling several times. Second, Leo Corsetti, ordinarily unstoppable at fullback, had an off-day and didn't figure in this game, although he *did* substitute at right guard for Silva, as O'Brien tried to plug a hole in the front line to protect his neophyte quarterback. Also, Ford, who did the punting that day, didn't do well at all. His bad punts figured in both English touchdowns. And Guy? While he was in there he must have played reasonably well, because he was given his first start the following week. If he had played poorly in the English game, O'Brien would not have assigned him a start a week later.

As for East Boston's kicking game to this point in the season, we can glean a bit from a comment Mooney made in his report of the English-East Boston, Commerce-Charlestown twin-bill on Wednesday, October 5:

> *Rossana, the Charlestown kicker, got away the best kick of the double bill when he stood near his end line and kicked one out to Paul Healy on the Charlestown 45-yard line.*

*   *   *   *

Boston, MA
Tuesday, October 10, 1933
Fenway Park
3:30 p.m.

The day dawned cold, windy and raining, but by game time at Fenway, the wind had died down and the rain had stopped, so weather was not a factor in either contest.

East Boston took the field for its game against Commerce with the same lineup it displayed in its game against English a week earlier, except that Silva and Siraco traded places at the guards and Doherty got the nod over Festa at right halfback, while Currie sat down and Guy started the game at left halfback. Yes, left halfback. To this point, Coach O'Brien was still sticking with Ford as his starting quarterback, and young Guy, a week shy of his sixteenth birthday, was not questioning the coach's decision.

As the contest got under way, it quickly became obvious that O'Brien, who'd been coaching football since 1908 when he began at Roxbury and Brighton, knew what he was doing with those line and backfield adjustments.

Mooney, ever the astute observer, said this:

> *There was lots of improvement in the East Boston team and the fast jump of the forwards kept them all over the Commerce linemen. The fast, light backfield the Noddle Islanders offered made plenty of yardage ...*

Guy and Doherty were deep to receive the kick-off for East Boston, and a thousand or more fans had turned out to watch. Standing on his own twenty yard line, Guy felt the same exhilaration again as he waited for the whistle that started the game. This time, the ball, high, end over end, came to him. But several Commerce players were ripping downfield under full heads of steam, anxious to nail the ball carrier. Conscious of that, it seemed to Guy that the ball hung in the air forever.

"Come ahn, come ahn!" he muttered under his breath as the ball descended. He caught it cleanly and cradled it before tucking it under his right arm at his own twenty-five. Getting a block, he sprinted to the sideline and immediately served notice that he was on the field by returning it fifteen yards on the soggy turf, to his own forty.

But Eastie could not move the ball and had to kick. Ford was doing the punting again, and his first boot traveled only to the Commerce thirty. However, Commerce could not get anything going, so they kicked it away. That's the way the game went for a while until Morse, Eastie's left end, began to assert himself by nailing Commerce quarterback Heggerty in his tracks at the Commerce thirty-six.

East Boston's defense was waiting as Commerce broke from its huddle and lined up over the ball for the next play, in a kicking formation. But as Heggerty began calling signals, Morse diagnosed the play. "It's a run! A run," he yelled. He was right. It was a fake kick and run, but Morse, reading it perfectly, penetrated and stopped the ball carrier for a ten-yard loss.

So Commerce punted for real this time, and Ford ran it back to Commerce's forty-six yard line. On the next play, Ford dialed Corsetti, who made six yards on an off-tackle slant. Ford then called his own number for another six and a first down at the Commerce thirty-four. Next, he passed to Festa, complete to the twenty. Corsetti then tried the center of the line and gained seven yards. It was first and ten at the ten-yard stripe and the teams changed direction at the end of the quarter.

As the second quarter began, Guy found a small hole between left tackle and left end and carried for three yards. DeLeo then went around the same end and moved to the one-yard line before he was hit and brought down. But on the next play somebody fumbled. Mooney, reverting to his former practice, did not tell us who, but Commerce recovered the ball in their end zone for a touchback, and took over on their own twenty.

Later, with the help of some good running and a penalty, Commerce had moved to Eastie's forty-five yard line when Indrisano intercepted a pass to end that drive.

Eastie took the pigskin back, but another costly fumble, this one on their twenty-five, turned the ball over, and on the sidelines, Fred O'Brien threw his hat on the ground. Commerce then ran two plays, but on the second one Ford intercepted a pass on his own sixteen and that was the way the first half ended.

The second half began with Eastie mounting a strong attack. Ford, maybe sensing a threat from Guy and not wanting to give Guy an opportunity to look good, didn't call his number much. Corsetti and DeLeo did most of the hard work, and they were moving for a score when Byrne, Commerce's left end, made his presence felt with several hard tackles in a row to stop the drive. On the next exchange, Eastie got the ball back but yet another fumble coughed up the football to Commerce on Eastie's twenty-one. That was the way this game went; every time Eastie began to move, somebody fumbled the ball away. Final score? A 0–0 tie.

Next morning, Mooney's report of the games started this way:

> ... *the double-header at Fenway Park, where East Boston fumbled its way out of a win over Commerce when it bobbled on the Commerce one-yard line and the ball was recovered by Captain (Walter) Hazell of Commerce for a touchback that kept the game a scoreless tie throughout.*

CHAPTER 8

Boston, MA
Tuesday, October 17, 1933
Fenway Park
2:30 p.m.

It was another beautiful fall day for football as the East Boston squad suited up in the locker room at Fenway Park for its game against Brighton.

J. W. Mooney again, in Tuesday morning's *Boston Post:*

> *One of the classics among the District League gridsters will be put on as part of a double-header at Fenway Park this afternoon at 2:45 o'clock. This scrap will bring together East Boston and Brighton, while the other end of the bargain bill will be the Charlestown-Memorial game.*
>
> *UNBEATEN TO DATE*
>
> *Both East Boston and Brighton are well set up this year and both are undefeated by district rivals, although English took the Noddle Islanders, who showed so much improvement in a week that they held Commerce to a scoreless tie …*
>
> *The Ferry Boat Riders have a good, sturdy line, which is capable of leaving its impression on the terrors in the Brighton backfield, Mallard and McCarthy. Both of these boys are triple threats as they pass and kick with the best of the schoolboys. It may be that the passing and kicking game that Brighton might lean back on will bring home the bacon for Coach Tom Scanlon. East Boston's ends can't be run to any advantage and its line now has a fast, heavy charge that is poison.*

*   *   *   *

Boston, MA
Tuesday, October 17, 1933
Fenway Park
2:45 p.m.

"Listen up!" Fred O'Brien called when the boys were dressed. "Here's the lineup for today. Morse, left end. Indrisano, left tackle. Siraco, left guard. Carabott, center. Silva, right guard. McGee, right tackle. Rawson, right end. Ford, quarterback. Festa, left halfback. Vitale, right halfback. Corsetti, fullback." He pocketed the lineup paper and gestured toward the door with a thumb. "Let's go get em!"

I'm not going to dwell on this game, except to tell you that it was a very sloppy, poorly played game and East Boston lost.

J. W. Mooney described it this way:

> *For ruggedness and competition the Brighton-Eastie game, which featured the double-header at Fenway Park yesterday, was a whiz. Brighton came through 12 to 6 ...*
>
> *Instead of a rush and kick game, it became as open as the great outdoors. Neither team showed particular brilliancy in team generalship, but it was the mistakes that make it so interesting to the fans. Brighton got the best of the breaks on fumbles and by taking advantage of their rival's weak kicking.*
>
> *While McCarthy, the Brighton quarter wasn't any Carideo, he proved to be the most valuable player on the field. Even though he seemed all for tossing the game to the Noddle Islanders at times, it was his work in the pinches that assured victory and his ball lugging and tackling stamped him as a back of ability even though not a quarterback.*
>
> *East Boston had much the same trouble in its backfield with poor selection of plays, although fullback Corsetti made up for a lot of the mistakes ...*

Mooney, while trying to be kind to both teams, put his finger on two glaring problems that both East Boston and Brighton had; weak quarterbacks and a poor kicking game. Here are just a couple of examples.

The game began with Brighton kicking off to East Boston. The boot went to the twenty-six, where Eastie put it in play. Ford called Corsetti's number and he looked like he'd be trapped for no gain, but spun away from a tackler and broke loose for twenty-two yards, out to midfield. If it hadn't been for a great open-field tackle by Brighton's Maguire, Corsetti would have gone all the way. But that tackle prevented a touchdown, and Brighton's defense bucked up, forcing Eastie to punt. As they huddled, Guy, playing right halfback, was hoping Ford would call on him to kick it away, but Ford didn't. So Guy and Corsetti were the blockers for Ford.

The signal call was long. Carabott's snap was good. The linemen had been drilled and drilled not to leave to cover a punt until they heard the sound of the football being kicked. But anxious to get downfield, several left too quickly and Brighton's right guard and tackle broke through. Guy was the shallow blocker. *Oh, shit!* he thought.

He immediately threw his block, knocking the guard down. But Ryan, Brighton's right tackle, blocked the punt and then recovered it on Eastie's forty-yard line.

One Brighton play later, Maguire fumbled on the Ferry Boat Rider's forty, and Carabott recovered it. Corsetti then went off-tackle for fifteen yards. But Brighton's defense stiffened at that point and after three more plays Eastie had to kick, and it was Ford again.

Next morning, Mooney described the play:

> *... and when Ford tried to kick, the punt bent back over his head, Maguire caught it on the gallop and went to the Eastie 30, Ford stopping a touchdown run. There, Maguire partly fumbled but recovered and ran his left end for 20 yards to the five-yard line, Indrisano making quite a tackle. On a fake reverse play, McCarthy looped it around his right flank for a touchdown without being tagged. The trypoint was missed.*

The error-prone ballgame continued after the kickoff. Maguire flopped on an East Boston fumble on Eastie's eighteen. Two running plays gained zilch, but then Maguire heaved Reddam a pass for a touchdown, just five plays after Brighton's first score.

In the third quarter, Eastie started a strong running attack. Doherty, subbing at halfback, went for seven yards, and Corsetti carried for sixteen to Brighton's forty-six.

They walked back to the huddle and Guy, disgusted that he had not had much work in the game, was surprised to hear Ford call his number. "Four right sweep. One-two down. On hut-three. Let's go!"

Ford had called for Guy to line up a few steps farther to his right than usual, take a pitch-out and go around his right end behind his end and right tackle, who would pull out of the line to be his blockers.

They broke from the huddle and lined up. The referee's whistle sounded. *Don't telegraph the play,* Guy thought. He made sure his feet were straight and he was not leaning in the direction the play would go. The ball was snapped back to Ford, who, without any fake, immediately pitched out to Guy. Nobody on the Brighton team was fooled. Guy took two steps and saw that both Rawson and McGee had been mowed down. He had no blockers in front of him and Brighton's left end and linebacker were clogging up what should have been a hole.

"Damn it!" he yelled. He cut left and moved laterally. Indrisano got off the turf and threw a block. Guy, much to his surprise, was now across the line of scrimmage and still on his feet. For just a split second, no one was in front of him and he sprinted for nine yards before the safety moved up and slammed him hard.

On the way back to the huddle, Guy, a big grin on his face, adjusted his shoulder pads and looked for Indrisano. "Great block," he said, slapping his left tackle on the rump.

"Thanks, Guy. I seen you was in trouble back there," Indrisano said.

"Nice run, kid." Corsetti said as they leaned in to hear the play. Ford called a pass play to Morse at left end, but this wasn't Eastie's game. McCarthy intercepted and *that* march was stopped, too. That's the way the game went, right to its bitter end.

CHAPTER 9

Boston, MA
Tuesday, October 31, 1933
Fenway Park
3:30 p.m.

East Boston's next game was against Jamaica, and it was played on a bitter cold and dreary day, with snow threatening. But the game was anything but dreary for the Noddle Islanders. As was now his habit, Guy started his day off well, with morning Mass and the Eucharist. However, his game didn't start off well at all.

"Quiet down, boys," Coach Fred O'Brien yelled over the usual locker room din. "Here's the starting team for today." When the babble had died and all the players were grouped around and he had their attention, O'Brien read off the names from his list. "Rawson, left end. Indrisano, left tackle. Siraco, left guard. Carabott, center. Silva, right guard. McGee, right tackle. Morse, right end. Corsetti, quarterback. Ford, left halfback. Harris, right halfback, and Doherty, fullback." No one but Guy, who thought he played well against Brighton the week before, noticed that he was not a starter. But no one failed to notice the other changes; Corsetti at quarterback, Ford moved to left half and Doherty playing fullback. Several boys exchanged I-told-you-so glances.

The Coach wasn't done. He ran his hand across his chin, where a stubble of beard indicated he had not applied a razor to his face that morning. "Things haven't been goin' so good for us up to now," he said. Several players nodded their agreement. "But today's the day we're gonna turn this season around."

"Right!" Captain Indrisano yelled.

"You bet!" Morse said, slamming his fist into his locker.

"I wanna see good, heads-up ball out there today," O'Brien continued. "No *fumbles*. Hold onta da football. Fumbles have been *killin'* us all season. Hard blockin' and solid tacklin'. If we buckle down out there, we can *win* this game. And we *will!*"

Their coach's pep-talk over, the boys jumped to their feet and moved into the tunnel connecting the locker room area to the field. O'Brien waited until the last of them had left. Walking quickly to the small office in the back reserved for coaches, he closed the door tightly behind him, opened a gray metal locker and took out a brown paper bag. A bottle of Kentucky Gentleman bourbon was inside, where he'd stashed it earlier. He raised the bottle to his lips, tilted his head back and drank deeply. The golden liquid burned his throat on the way down. Satisfied, he shook his head to clear it, replaced the bottle in the dented locker and followed his team onto the field.

Well, East Boston lost the toss and Jamaica elected to receive. Indrisano kicked off for Eastie. He did all the kicking that day. With both school bands blasting away, and a nice crowd in the stands, he booted it down to the Jamaica twenty-five where Jamaica's quarterback, Ring, took it and ran it back almost to midfield. But Rawson nailed him there and he fumbled. Morse, Eastie's other end, fell on the loose ball. Rawson jumped up quickly.

"Yeah! Yeah!" he yelled, pumping a fist in the air.

"Way ta go!" Siraco shouted, delivering two quick open-hand slaps to Morse's helmet.

Corsetti was calling the signals. Eastie began its first drive. Ford and Doherty alternated in a series of off-tackle slants, first the left side, then the right. But Jamaica's line quickly came to grips with things, and it was fourth and eight at Jamaica's thirty-five yard line. Instead of punting, Corsetti called an old criss-cross play with Doherty to carry the pigskin. Carabott snapped it directly to his fullback and he started around the left side, cut back to the right and went all the way in for the score.

East Boston kicked off and Jamaica couldn't move the ball. It was three and out for them and Eastie got the ball back on a short punt that traveled only to Jamaica's thirty-six yard line. Then Corsetti called Ford's number on a fake reverse and Ford made it down to the twenty before being run out of bounds. Doherty then tried the criss-cross again and made nine more. But Corsetti fumbled on the next play, and Herb Kelliher, who later that year would be named as a Third Team All-Scholastic pick by the *Boston Post*, recovered for Jamaica to end Eastie's drive.

O'Brien, over on the sideline, punched his left fist into his right hand. "Goddam fumbles gotta stop," he yelled. Only a few of his players heard, as he sat heavily on the end of the bench, his anger festering. A few plays later, he jumped up.

"Currie! Get in there for Corsetti," he yelled.

But Currie didn't make a difference, and the game seesawed back and forth for the rest of the period.

In the second stanza, Guy was substituted at right halfback for Harris, and DeLeo was put in at right guard. After an exchange of punts, Eastie got the ball on Jamaica's thirty-nine.

In the huddle, the boys leaned in to hear Currie call the play. "Pitch Three-four-ten-right," he said. He had called for him to pitch-out to the number three back, Doherty, who would fake a run but toss it to the number four back, ten yards downfield on the right side. That was Guy. "On hut-three," Currie said. He looked pretty confident for a kid who had never played quarterback before.

The teams lined up and waited for the referee's whistle. Guy, butterflies in full force, listened to the cadence as Currie called the signals. On the snap, he moved quickly right, faked as if to block, slipped into the hole between Silva and McGee, and raced ten steps downfield. As he turned, the ball was there, a perfect spiral from Doherty, and Guy, in full stride, gathered it in.

"Yeah!" he yelled. Under a full head of steam, he could not be caught. Nobody laid a hand on him until he neared the goal line, where Jamaica's free safety closed the angle and nailed him with a jarring tackle, dropping him just over the goal line in the end zone. The play had covered forty yards. Guy had scored his first touchdown! Indrisano kicked the point after.

Well, the rest of the game passed quickly. Eastie scored another touchdown, with Corsetti taking it in, but the score was called back on a pushing penalty at the goal line. Jamaica filled the air with passes as they tried desperately to catch-up, but each time they got moving a pass was intercepted to stop them.

Eastie's players were a boisterous group in the locker room after the game, and a jubilant Guy Vitale showered, dressed and headed for home that evening hoping to tell his mother and father how well he did.

Next morning, J. W. Mooney described the action in the *Post:*

> *With a more capable set of backs, who functioned behind a willing front line, East Boston High outplayed Jamaica Plain yesterday at Fenway Park and won, with a 13–0 score, another touchdown having been taken away from the Noddle Islanders on a pushing penalty close to the goal line.*

*   *   *   *

Boston, MA
Tuesday, November 7, 1933
Fenway Park
6:15 p.m.

The next game was against Roxbury Memorial. Corsetti started at quarterback again and Ford, more comfortable at left halfback did well there. Guy played some, going in at right halfback, but he didn't figure in anything. The two teams battled to a scoreless tie.

Mooney again:

> Although Memorial outrushed East Boston at Fenway Park yesterday, they wound up in a scoreless tie. They were two strapping strong teams and the advantage the Roxbury club had in its running attack was lost on fumbles and intercepted passes ...
>
> Before the half ended East Boston was down on Memorial's 30-yard line when Captain Indrisano flopped on Kenney's fumbled punt and DeLeo and Corsetti moved on to the 20-yard line. This was the only real shot the Ferryboat riders had and it was ruined when Captain Geraghty intercepted a pass.

*   *   *   *

Boston, MA
Wednesday, November 15, 1933
Fenway Park
3:25 p.m.

With the temperature far below freezing and the playing surface like concrete, East Boston and Hyde Park took the field at Fenway Park in front of a scant group of chilled spectators, for their annual game. O'Brien shuffled his lineup again. He put Ford back at quarterback, gave Struzzerio his first start at right halfback, installed Festa at fullback, and started Guy at left halfback.

Mooney, in his column the next day:

> Hyde Park and East Boston elevens did much more than go through the motions in their ... game ... yesterday and rather made it one of

the greatest scraps of the year in a battle that Hyde Park won 13 to 6 to break the two tie games of the two previous years.

Yes, East Boston lost. And it'd be nice if I could tell you that Guy played his entire sophomore year without fumbling the ball, missing a key block, or tossing an interception. But that wouldn't be true. After all, he was only a sophomore and he was still learning the game.

About midway in the first quarter, Eastie got the ball out around its own twenty and started a march. Ford was calling a series of off-tackle slants, alternating Struzzerio, Festa, and Vitale, and the line, behind the guards and tackles, was opening some nice holes. It was first and ten at the forty and Ford called Guy's number. "Four left sweep. Six-seven down. On hut-three. Let's go!" They broke from the huddle.

Guy was having a good day. His confidence was high. Maybe too high. You might say he was a bit cocky as he ambled to his position to the left and several steps behind Ford. On the other side of the line, Hyde Park's big linemen were waiting, helmets glistening in the feeble afternoon sun, and close behind them were the linebackers, poised, hands extended, tense.

"Down!" Ford bellowed. "Set! Hut. Hut-one, hut-two, hut-three." The play began. Ford had the ball, faked right, turned and pitched out to Guy, who was already moving left behind his number six and seven blockers. Taking short, quick steps until clear of the line, he thought he was loose and began to extend his stride. He didn't know where Hyde Park's right linebacker came from until he felt a shoulder blasting into his right arm and side, the arm where he'd tucked the football! Horrified, he watched the ball pop loose, sail away and bounce crazily on the frozen turf.

"Loose ball!" he heard Indrisano scream.

"Aw, shit!" Carabott yelled.

To Guy, it seemed like his feet each weighed a ton as he stumbled after the ball, but Walter Bracken, Hyde Park's senior left halfback, who would be a *Post's* First Team All-Scholastic pick that year, got to it first and fell on it at the forty-six yard line.

A disappointed East Boston team lined up on defense. Guy, his face crimson, was with them as, across the line of scrimmage, Losardo called the signals for Hyde Park. But Eastie's right tackle, McGee was overanxious and jumped offside. The referee's whistle stopped the play before it could be run, and Eastie was penalized ten yards, back to their own thirty-six. On the next play, MacInnes, Hyde Park's fullback carried, but the Noddle Islander's front line was fired up and the play lost four yards. Just when Guy was beginning to think his fumble wouldn't be a costly one, MacInnes took a direct snap, faked a plunge into the line, pulled up and heaved a pass to Bracken over center. Bracken grabbed it on the dead run at the twenty-yard line and went all the way for the touchdown. Bracken then missed the extra point. Hyde Park six, East Boston zip.

A few minutes later, with Eastie in possession of the football on its own twenty-nine, another break went Hyde Park's way as Ford fumbled and Olson, its left end recovered. But Carabott, Siraco and Indrisano clogged up the middle for three plays, and East Boston took the ball back on downs at its twenty-three. It was three and out for them, too, and they had to punt at their own nine, but the kick only traveled to the thirty. MacInnes got a first down in two tries and the ball was spotted at East Boston's fifteen-yard line.

On the next play Losardo pitched out to Bracken, who started around his right end. Guy, playing linebacker on the left side, moved up quickly and was engaged by a blocker who slowed him down just long enough for him to see Bracken, who was hit hard by Morse, fumble. "Loose ball!" he yelled. This time, he reacted more quickly, and flopped on the ball at Eastie's five-yard stripe.

So Eastie got the ball back and Guy had partially redeemed himself, although he didn't see it that way. He was still feeling terribly bad about his own earlier fumble.

But this time Eastie couldn't get anything going and they were forced to kick it away. The game seesawed back and forth for a while, until the Noddle Islander's had the ball out around mid-field. On first and ten, Ford called a pass play in the flat to Struzzerio, but Bracken read the play perfectly and raced over to break it up. Cutting in front of Struzzerio, he reached low, lifted the ball up with one hand, pulled it in with the other and ran it all the way back for Hyde Park's second score of the day.

The third period was all East Boston. Mooney described it this way:

> ... started from its own twenty, with a load of deceptive plays, spin-ners and delayed passes. With Corsetti featured in the lugging, it swept the rivals off their feet with first downs to the 35, the 45, then to Hyde Park's 45, its 31, and to the 20, getting another break, its second in a row, on a five-yard penalty for extra time out to the 15 from where Corsetti lugged to the seven, then to the five and to the three with Doherty taking a turn to the two-yard line as the period ended, giving Corsetti the honor of cracking the left of center for the touchdown on the opening play of the final period. The rush on the trypoint failed.

Guy, although still on the field, was absent from this sequence of plays.

In the final stanza, Eastie mounted another sustained drive, but an offside penalty and a five-yard loss on a broken running play forced them to kick, saving Hyde Park from further trouble. Final score: Hyde Park 13, East Boston 6.

CHAPTER 10

East Boston, MA
Wednesday, November 15, 1933
Orient Avenue
8:15 p.m.

"Ma tole me you come up here a lot," Frank Vitale said as he parked himself on the cold concrete bench next to his younger brother. He'd heard about the Hyde Park loss by late afternoon, from Ritchie Cutillo, one of Guy's friends, who also told him about Guy's fumble. Unusually quiet at supper and wanting to be alone, Guy had disappeared quickly afterward. Concerned a couple of hours later when he didn't come home, Frank decided to go looking for him.

"She doesn't pay much attention ta me," Guy shot back. "How would *she* know?" There was just a touch of bitterness in his young voice.

The air was frigid, and clumps of clouds skimmed silently across the cold, black sky above the two boys. Frank had on the same plaid Mackinaw with the big collar that he'd been wearing the last couple of years. Unable to find work after he finished school, he'd been helping out in the family grocery store. His mother didn't pay him much but he was grateful he'd been able to get even that.

"You upset about that fumble in the game today?"

Guy shrugged but didn't answer. Moving down the bench a few inches, he continued to stare out at the lights of the City in the distance.

Frank looked over at his brother, sucked in his breath and exhaled loudly. "Come ahn, Guy! Everybody fumbles once in a while. Hell! I fumbled once or twice myself." He grinned ruefully. "In every *game*."

Chuckling in spite of himself, Guy said, "Did any a *your* fumbles ever lead to a touchdown by the other team?"

"Naw. Only about every other one."

This time Guy laughed out loud. "I was real embarrassed," he confessed.

"Well, how d'ya think Frankie Ford feels? Shit! He fumbles half a dozen times a game."

"I guess that's why Coach wouldn't let him play quarterback any more."

"O'Brien!" Frank struck a theatrical pose, both arms extended, head tilted down, mimicking O'Brien's way of looking out over his bifocals. "'Hang onta da bahl, fellas. Teams dat fumble alla time don't win no games.'" Both boys guffawed loudly.

"Listen, kid," Frank said. "That was yer first fumble a the season. It won't be yer last. It's natural ta feel embarrassed. But ya gotta jest forget about it and keep playin'. Like it never happened. Okay, Guy?"

"Okay, Frankie," Guy said. He looked at his brother. "You didn't come ta the game today. How d'ja hear about my fumble anyway?"

"Ritchie Cutillo stopped by the store jest before supper."

"Ritchie never *could* keep his mouth shut," Guy said hotly.

Frank grinned at his brother. "What are friends for?" He rubbed his cold hands together. "Hey, let's go over ta the garage and tease Albert about that plane he's buildin'. The wings are so long, I don't think he's gonna be able ta get it outta there."

"Okay! Ya know what? Ma called Albert 'the grease monkey' yesterday, 'cause when he goes in there he's all cleaned up but when he comes out, he's covered with grease and oil."

∗   ∗   ∗   ∗

East Boston, MA
Wednesday, November 15, 1933
Ford Street, East Boston
10:00 p.m.

The two Vitale boys approached the old garage that fronted on Ford Street in high spirits. But their clowning around stopped abruptly as they noticed a luxurious, black and red Plymouth seven-seater sedan parked out front.

Frank let out a long low whistle. "Wow! Would ya just look at that?" he breathed. Jumping onto the running board, he peered eagerly inside the vehicle. "It's a Model PB," he said. "Brand new, too. It's gut a hunderd and twelve inch wheel base. I read about this car in the *Post*."

"Ritzy lookin'," Guy said, brushing a tentative hand along the sleek hood. "I wonder where Al's friends get the money ta buy cars like this?" He would have said more but he was interrupted by the sound of loud, angry voices coming from inside the old garage.

The boys exchanged concerned looks, but before either could move, the small side door burst open and two men, elegantly dressed in dark, pinstriped suits, long, dark overcoats and black fedoras, emerged. The last one out stopped and looked back inside through the open door. "Don't push too hard, Al," he said, his face red and swollen from yelling. "Ya might live ta regret it." Slamming the door behind him, he and the other man headed for their car. That's when they saw Guy and Frank.

"Hey, you kids! Get away frum that car," the first man yelled. Approaching the boys, he pulled up and glared at each of them. "What the hell's the idea?" he said to Frank, who was so surprised by the unfolding events that he was still standing on the running board. Grabbing him by the front of his plaid woolen coat, he yanked Frank off his perch and slammed him hard against the side of the vehicle.

"It's only Al's kid brothers, Mario," The other man said. "Go easy."

"I don' care who it is," the man called Mario responded in tones that sounded like they emanated from his nose. "I don' wan nobody messin' with my car." Releasing Frank, he moved around to the driver's side, unlocked the vehicle and slipped into the driver's seat.

The other man paused, staring at Guy. "Hey, kid. You live here?" he asked, jerking a thumb toward the nearby apartment house.

"Yeah," Guy shot back. "What of it?" He recognized the man as an unsavory character who lived around the corner on Whitby Street.

Inside the vehicle, Mario leaned over and rolled down the passenger side window. "C'mon, Vito! Let's get outta here."

"Keep yer shirt on. I'm comin'," Vito replied. With a thoughtful last look in Guy's direction, he opened the passenger door and climbed in. The big car's engine sprang to life. Backing quickly out of the driveway, Mario pulled away, squealing rubber as he went, leaving Guy and Frank watching as the auto turned right on Breed Street and accelerated up the hill.

What, exactly was going on here? Who were these two men who apparently had some problems with young Albert Vitale?

Jeanne Vitale Winter, Al's daughter and one of my cousins, was born on September 9th, 1935. She had just turned five years old when her father was killed on October 28th, 1940. What little she recalls was gleaned from her memories of what her mother's relatives had told her as she was growing up. Since these two families did not get along, the accuracy of much of what she'd heard as a child is questionable.

"My father got mixed up with the gangs—Mafia—running numbers. He stepped on some toes and they came after him."

"What did he do to them?" I wanted to know.

"I really don't know," she replied at first.

"Was he skimming?"

"Yes, I think so," was her response.

Was this true? What little I was able to find and confirm, and it wasn't much, will be revealed as we go along.

*   *   *   *

East Boston, MA
Monday, November 27, 1933
Fenway Park
3:20 p.m.

As grudge rivals East Boston and South Boston took the field for their annual match-up in front of a sell-out crowd of excited fans, a couple hundred miles north, in South Bristol, Maine, George Herman "Babe" Ruth, relaxing by taking random shots at rabbits, geese, ducks and other small game, ended speculation about whether he'd retire or play ball one more year. "I'm in the pink," he told reporters. "I got at least one more year left in me—and a good one, too."

The football game got off to a fast start—for Southie. Taking a short kick-off on its own forty yard line, halfbacks Bushman and Purvitsky and quarterback Repetti carried the ball down to Eastie's ten yard line, reeling off four straight first downs in the process.

Southie smelled blood as it emerged from the huddle and came to the line of scrimmage. But perhaps overanxious, a snap from center Venetsky went wild and Leo Corsetti, Eastie's quarterback, fell on it on the twenty-four. That ended Southie's drive and took some wind out of the sails of the Southie kids.

Corsetti started this game at quarterback. Guy started at right halfback. Frankie Ford was at left halfback and doing the kicking. As you know, back then there were no specialty teams. Players played both ways; offense *and* defense.

With Corsetti and Ford doing the work, Eastie moved to a first down at its thirty-four, but a few plays later, Ford's partially blocked punt was recovered by Hannigan at Eastie's twenty-nine. But Southie could not capitalize on this break, and East Boston, fired up now, took the ball back on downs. Corsetti, on a quarterback keeper, ran for twenty yards, and he and Doherty moved the ball another ten, to Southie's forty-four. Then Guy and Ford earned another first down and Corsetti went nearly ten more to Southie's twenty-three. But the first quarter ended at that point, and after the teams changed ends of the field, Eastie could not get moving and lost the ball on downs.

In the second quarter, both teams moved the ball to midfield, but could not do more. Eastie got a break when Randolph Indrisano recovered a fumble on his forty-three, but they could only move to Southie's forty before giving up the football. And that's how the half ended. Each team had reeled off five first downs in the half.

The second half was a duel of defenses. Neither team could mount any offense, there were lots of punts from both sides of the line and the game ended in a scoreless tie.

The following day, J.W. Mooney's column headline said this:

> ### EAST BOSTON AND SOUTHIE IN TIE
> *Evenly Balanced Rivals Go Scoreless—Corsetti, Noddle Island Back, the Star of Game*
> *These two grudge rivals, East Boston and South Boston High elevens, fought it out tooth and nail yesterday afternoon at Fenway Park, and after a brilliant exhibition wound up in a scoreless tie, the most satisfactory result that could be offered with the pair so evenly balanced.*

Now here's a curious thing. On the day of the game, Monday, November 27th, 1933, the *Boston Post* named its All-Scholastic Football Team for 1933. Only Randolph Indrisano was named from East Boston High. He made Third Team at tackle.

Then, the following day, in writing up the Thanksgiving Classic, J.W. Mooney said this about Leo Corsetti:

> *Some boys stood out prominently in their final game of the year and the king pin of them all was Leo Corsetti of East Boston, practically a whole football team in himself. Always a steady plugger this fall, Corsetti reached new heights against the Southie foes and besides doing most of the lugging for the Noddle Islanders, he gave a demonstration of defensive play that was nothing less than startling, and it all made us wonder if perhaps he didn't deserve a better break on the All Scholastic team.*

So here we have Mooney, who *made* the All Scholastic team selections just the day before, second guessing *himself* one day later in not picking Corsetti. In the article announcing his picks, Mooney talked about the awards:

The selection is the result of study through 12 weeks on the school gridirons. It embraces only the Greater Boston teams as every team in the State cannot be seen, nor can they all be properly 'scouted.' It is even impossible to see every one of the 40 teams in Greater Boston. About 25 different teams were seen by the writer, some only once ...

If Mooney figured he'd get complaints about his picks that year, he needn't have worried. A few days later, in December 1933, the Twenty-first Amendment was ratified, officially ending prohibition in America, and people all over the country went wild. It was as if they had not had alcohol to drink all that time and no bootleggers had ever been operating. Parties were thrown everywhere, featuring kegs of beer and lots of the hard stuff. After being dry for so long, Americans couldn't seem to get enough of the booze. And for months afterwards that's all anybody talked about.

*   *   *   *

Boston, MA
Friday, December 4, 1933
Ford Street, East Boston
5:40 p.m.

The sedan was back. The big, shiny Plymouth Model PB was parked in front of the garage when Guy came out of the Vitale's front door, a football in his hands, and headed for Noyes Field, where, under the lights, he expected to find a few local kids with whom he could practice his passing.

His eyes went to the garage doors. No lights were on in there. His older brother, Al, who had become more serious since meeting and beginning to date an Irish gal named Emma Hughes, recently opened a solo welding business in there. But Guy knew Al was not inside. *They're not here lookin' for Al,* he thought.

There was no way he could walk in that direction without passing the vehicle. He had cut the distance in half before he was able to make out the two men in the front seat; the same two who'd left the garage last week after a shouting match with his twenty-one year old brother. Mario, the owner of the car, was in the driver's seat. As Guy approached, the passenger door opened and Vito stepped out.

"Hey, Guy," Vito used his most engaging tone. "C'mere. I wanna talk to ya."

Frowning, Guy debated crossing the street, but decided not to do it. *There really isn't any harm in talking ta these guys,* he thought. A few safe strides from Vito, he stopped, folded his arms across his chest and waited.

"What d'ya want?"

"I got a proposition for ya," Vito responded. "We … I need yer help."

Guy glanced up and down the dark street to see if anyone else was around. The street was empty. "My help? Doin' what?"

Vito grinned and jerked his thumb toward the apartment building. "Nothin' very hard," he said. "All ya have ta do is, once a week, on Friday afternoon, knock on the doors of everybody who lives in that building there, and tell 'em Vito sent ya."

"That's it?"

"Well, then they'll give ya an envelope fer me, see. You collect all the envelopes and run 'em over ta my place around the corner. I'll be waitin' for ya and I'll take the envelopes."

Guy hesitated. Something wasn't right, but he did not know what it was. He had only just turned sixteen and he was neither a worldly teenager, nor a street-wise kid. Between his sports and his studies, he'd had no time to waste standing on the street corner with the other kids.

"I don't know …" he said.

Seeing Guy hesitate, Vito decided maybe he had him. He played his ace. "One other thing, Guy. I wouldn't ask ya ta do this fer nothin'." He glanced back at the car, where his friend, Mario sat behind the wheel, smoking a cigarette and waiting. "I'll give ya a five spot every week, afta ya turn over the envelopes ta me."

Guy's eyes widened. "Five dollars?"

"Yep. What d'ya say, kid. You can collect a lotta baseball cards with that kind a dough."

"If I say yes, when do I start?" Guy wants to know.

"Right now's as good a time as any," Vito said. "Jes' collect the envelopes and bring 'em down. We'll make it easy this first time, and wait right here for ya."

"Okay," Guy said. He did not see any harm in what Vito was asking him to do. It did not occur to him to ask what was in the envelopes because, raised to be polite, he didn't think *that* was any of his business. "I'll be right back." Turning on his heel, he headed for the side door and a flight of stairs which led to the upper levels of the building.

CHAPTER 11

East Boston, MA
Monday, April 8, 1934
20 Breed Street
8:30 p.m.

"Frankie, look at this, will ya?" Twenty year old Albert Vitale, two months shy of his twenty-first birthday, tall and thin, his thick, wavy black hair neatly combed because, even though he'd marry Emma Francis Hughes a few months later, he was headed for Scolley Square that evening and the strip clubs located there, entered the kitchen and approached his younger brother, his face dark, like a thundercloud, wishing the thoughts swirling through his mind were not swirling through his mind.

Frank, sitting at the white, Formica-topped table reading *South Moon Under*,[25] a just-released novel by Marjorie Kinnan Rawlings, did not look up. The realization that he would not be able to go to college had hit home. I mean *really* hit home; with a force that, when it happened, just before Christmas 1932, had knocked the wind from him like a punch in the stomach. Although not an intellectual, he was bright and more practical than introspective. Soon, he'd figured out that there were other ways of acquiring an education. Reading was one. So since that significant holiday, he'd been spending most of his spare time doing exactly that; devouring every book he could lay his hands on.

"What, Al?" Frank responded impatiently. He did not look up from his book.

"This." Albert placed two cigar boxes containing Guy's baseball card collection on the table under Frank's nose, forcing him to stop reading.

---

25 Marjorie Kinnan Rawlings, *South Moon Under,* Charles Scribner's Sons, New York, N.Y. 1933. Rawlings also later wrote *The Yearling*.

It worked. Setting the novel aside, Frank glanced at the cards and looked up at his older brother with a quizzical expression. "That there is Guy's baseball card collection," he said. His tone was that of someone lecturing a child. "He's been collectin' since he was in the sixth grade. So what?"

"If ya look close, peach fuzz," Albert said, referring to the fact that Frank only shaved twice a week, "you'll see that some a these cards are *really* valuable." Sitting down next to Frank, he opened one of the boxes. "Fer instance, this one." He handed Frank a shiny Mickey Cochrane card in mint condition, much-in-demand because Cochrane had grown up in Bridgewater, Massachusetts and had made it to The Bigs, where he had played for the Philadelphia Athletics and the Detroit Tigers. Everyone who knew anything about baseball cards knew that *that* card was extremely valuable and very hard to come by.

Frank took the card, scanned the front, turned it over in his hands and noted its pristine condition. "Whewwww!" he whistled, long and low.

"And *this* one," Al said, handing his brother an equally fine specimen of Honus Wagner. Nicknamed the "Flying Dutchman," this two hundred pound shortstop for the Pittsburgh Pirates was on his way to the Hall of Fame. Baseball card collectors everywhere coveted Wagner's card.

Examining the thin, colorful slip of cardboard, Frank's eyes narrowed. He handed it back to his brother.

"So," Al demanded, "where's our little brother gettin' the money ta buy cards like them?"

"I don't know. You ask Ma or Pa about this?"

"Not yet. Ma's over closin' up the store. Pa's in the shop chit-chattin' with a couple a his cronies."

"Where's Guy now?" Frank asked.

"Ma said he went up ta the statue. He'll be back soon."

"You thinkin' what I think you're thinkin'?"

Al nodded. "Let's have a little talk with him when he gets back."

*   *   *   *

East Boston, MA
Monday, April 8, 1934
20 Breed Street
9:15 p.m.

"Where ya been, Guy?" Albert Vitale asked, as Guy entered the kitchen a few minutes later, after collecting his schoolbooks from his room upon returning.

Albert's hands were on his hips, his feet spread apart, his tone accusatory. Guy noticed.

"No place, jest out," he replied, a bit defensively, as he dropped his books onto the table. "What's it ta *you*, anyway?" Throwing himself into the only vacant chair, he opened a Math book to the lesson he'd been assigned as homework. Seeing the cigar boxes on the corner of the table, he glanced from Albert to Frank. "Okay, what's up?"

"Nice card collection ya got there, Guy," Frank began.

"Especially these two cards here," Albert chimed in, placing the Cochrane and Wagner cards face up in front of him. "We were jest curious. Where ya getting' the money ta buy baseball cards like those?"

Guy was relieved. "Oh, is *that* all? I earn the money from my part-time job collectin' for Vito."

His face flushed, Al came closer and leaned over his youngest brother. "Vito? Vito Scarpello?"

"Yeah," Guy said.

Frank's eyebrows shot up. "You're collectin' for Vito Scarpello and Mario Ragazzi?"

"Yeah. What's wrong with that?"

Albert spun around, walked to the stove and quickly returned. "Guy, don't ya know what those guys do?"

"No! I …"

"They're drop men for the Mob."

"Drop men? What's that?"

"They're inta the numbahs racket. These guys collect the receipts from numbahs and bookmakin' operations here in the Heights."

"Numbahs runnin' is illegal, Guy." Frank explained. "You could get inta trouble."

"How long you been doin' this collectin'?" Albert demanded.

"Since December," Guy answered. "Vito pays me five bucks every time."

"So that's how you were able ta buy the nice Christmas presents for everybody in the family," Frank said.

"Where do ya collect'?" Albert wanted to know.

"Well … right here in *this* building," Guy said. "And on our street, too."

Albert threw up his hands. "Damn it!" he exclaimed angrily.

Placing a restraining hand on Albert's shoulder, Frank said: "He didn't know, Al. All he does is go ta Mass every mornin' on his way ta school. And he spends all his free time with Ritchie Cutillo, one a the altah boys at St. Lazarus. He doesn't know shit from shinola about what's goin' on around here."

"Ritchie's goin' away soon ta study for the priesthood," Guy explained brightly. "I wanna spend as much time as I can with him before he goes."

Albert's eyes met Frank's. Collapsing into a ladder-back chair, he burst out laughing. "Oh my God! The kid's soooo naïve."

Frank grinned and turned to Guy. "Look, Guy, you could get arrested and wind up in the Pokey fer doin' what yer doin'. Don't do it any more, ya hear? No more."

"But what'll I tell Vito?" Guy asked, concerned.

Albert's eyebrows shot up. Hot tempered and sometimes impetuous, he glanced at Frank, an unspoken question in his eyes. Frank nodded agreement. "We'll take care a that *for* ya," he said.

*   *   *   *

East Boston, MA
Wednesday, April 10, 1934
Noyes Field
5:30 p.m.

"You boys see the newspaper this morning?" Nicola Vitale asked his sons, Albert and Frank. Sixty-two years old now, his full head of hair was completely gray and he did not move quite as fast as he once did, but his body still had not gone to fat, and his mind was still sharp as a tack.

He had seen the morning paper, had recalled that Albert and Frank had come home late last night; that Frank's hair was mussed and his left cheek was swollen, and Albert had a bruised chin and bloodied knuckles. With that sixth sense that sometimes blesses fathers, this morning Nicola had connected the events and knew, instinctively, that his sons had been involved. So he had closed his shop a few minutes early that afternoon to hunt up his two boys. His powers of observation being acute, he had a pretty good idea where they'd be this time of day, if they weren't at home.

The boys were lounging in the otherwise empty grandstand along the third base line watching a few kids play a pickup baseball game. They were talking quietly, a copy of that morning's *Herald* open on the bench next to them. Startled, they turned and saw their father standing there.

"Pa!" Albert said, obviously flustered. "I didn't see ya come up."

"I didn't intend for you to, Alberto," Nicola said dryly. He gestured to the open newspaper. "Terrible, what happened to Vito Scarpello last night, isn't it? And just over there." He jerked a thumb in the direction of the small parking area next to the field. "Right across from his home," he observed. "You know where he lives don't you?"

Frank's eyes narrowed. He ignored his father's question. "Got beat up pretty bad, the paper sez."

"Yeah," Albert chimed in. "Some guy walkin' his dog found him unconscious late last night. Called the cops. They took him ta the hospital." His tone of voice did nothing to conceal a certain satisfaction.

Nicola searched his topcoat pockets and brought out a pipe and a small leather tobacco pouch. Slowly, he built himself a smoke, tamping the tobacco down firmly in the bowl, his eyes never leaving his sons. Finished, he spoke again.

"In Italy, when someone did a family member dirt, they seldom called in the police. Instead, the father and the sons would pay the guy a little visit. Mess up his face a bit, or break an arm or even a kneecap."

Albert wheeled around until he could look at his father. "You told us that story before, Pa. Don't ya remember."

"I *do*," Nicola responded. Striking a match, he lit his pipe, puffed twice, and watched the smoke drift quickly away on the evening breeze. "And I plead guilty to having said those things. For that, I'm sorry, because I may have ... given a wrong impression. But you know what?"

"What, Pa?" His eyes locking with his fathers, Albert tried brazenly to stare the old man down. But Nicola's steely brown eyes held his gaze.

"This is *not* Italy," he said quietly. "Things are *not* done that way here."

Albert dropped his gaze. Beside him on the bench, Frank squirmed.

Turning to leave, Nicola stopped as if he'd just had another thought, and turned back. "I'd sure hate to be whoever did this to Vito," he said. "You know why?" Without waiting for their answer he continued. "Two reasons. One, even though Vito was into the numbers game, assault and battery are crimes. The police will investigate. They'll probably find the culprits. Two, if the police don't find them, Mario Ragazzi and his ... associates will *certainly* find them. The Mob takes care of its own." Puffing on his pipe again, he made a nondescript hand gesture. "See you at home, boys," he said. "Don't be late for dinner."

CHAPTER 12

Pine Bluffs, WY
Wednesday, September 15, 2004
703 Beech Street
10:00 p.m.

In the spring of 1934, Guy was a sophomore. Material was hard to come by for his tenth grade exploits on the baseball diamond, so I'm going to assume that he continued to improve and develop as a baseball player during his sophomore year.

We don't need to speculate about his school work, however. As I previously mentioned, his transcript was made available to me. It shows that in Tenth Grade he took English, Geography—Biology, Clerical Practice—Bookkeeping, Commercial Geography, Manual Arts, Physical Education, Military Drill and Choral Practice. His grades? Two As and three Bs in the courses required for graduation. In addition, he received the necessary credits in Physical Education, Military Drill and Choral Practice, which gave him the twenty-two credits required that year.[26]

*   *   *   *

East Boston, MA
Wednesday, May 10, 1934
Noyes Field
6:00 p.m.

As spring turned into summer, Vito Scarpello recovered from his injuries, Mario Ragazzi welcomed his associate back into the numbers racket, and the police, more important things to do, conducted only a cursory investigation.

---

26 I'm grateful to Mr. Karl De Ninno, Registrar at East Boston High School, who, in November 2000, provided me with a copy of Guy's transcript.

Let me just say here that the names Scarpello and Ragazzi are not the real names of the two men who had something against Albert Vitale. But the only person I could find who recalled the events dealing with them did not remember their names and was hazy about details, so I've assigned fictitious names to each of them.

The cops had a pretty good idea who had bloodied and bruised the man I call Scarpello, alright; but they had no proof. Reluctant to commit manpower to further investigate a crime perpetrated on someone they thought of as "scum," the local cops placed Scarpello's file on inactive status, justifying the move with a notation that the victim would not cooperate. Soon it was gathering dust at the back of a file drawer in the office of the Precinct Captain.

Scarpello? He obviously knew who had worked him over, but he would not assist the police. He had his own reasons for that—one of them revenge. And he had the means to obtain it.

The Mob didn't forget …

*   *   *   *

East Boston, MA
Saturday, May 13, 1934
Noyes Field
5:30 p.m.

The spring afternoon was a pleasant one as Guy Vitale and a few of the local boys came off the baseball field and removed their spikes on one of the benches. Guy, feeling the need to practice throwing from the outfield to each of the bases and to home plate, had convinced three of them to help. Each had stationed himself at a base; second, third and home plate, and fielded Guy's throws for fifteen minutes, until, his arm warm and tingly, he felt he'd had enough.

Guy relaxed on the third base bench as each of the boys replaced spikes with sneakers and, one by one, left for home and dinner with their families.

The field was now deserted; the sun low in the western sky beyond the left field fence. Guy stood and scraped the bottoms of his spikes against the chain link fence that comprises the backstop, knocking the accumulated dirt from them. Looking up, he frowned as he saw Mario Ragazzi's big Packard pull to the curb and Ragazzi, Scarpello and two other toughs emerge from it.

Of course, Guy knew about Scarpello's beating a month before; all of Orient Heights had been abuzz with it. But not having been involved himself, and having accepted his brother's explanation that it must have been done by some dissatisfied or competing 'mob members,' he had no reason to fear as the men approached him. Until he saw the looks on their faces.

Too late, his alarm bell went off. He tried to run but large, powerful arms reached out, intercepted him, and threw him against the backstop so hard that the back of his head hit the crossbar, bringing tears to his eyes.

"Hey! Cut the shit," he yelled.

The man was big, perhaps six feet tall and two hundred twenty pounds. A weight room type, his beefy face was pock-marked, like he'd had a bad case of acne as a kid. He spun Guy around and pinned him against the fence, a huge forearm against the back of his neck.

"What the hell's goin' on?" Guy breathed through clenched teeth.

"What's yer hurry, Guy?" Ragazzi asked innocently. "Headin' home fer dinnah?"

Scarpello joined the others behind Guy. Mafia street justice? Not just yet. "Relax, kid," he said. "We ain't gonna hurt ya. We jest want ya ta deliver a message ta them two brothers a yours."

"What kinda message?" Guy tried to sound like he wasn't afraid, but he was, and he was not a good enough actor to conceal his fear, which was written all over his face.

"You tell yer brother, Frank, that if he knows what's good fer him, he'll get outta East Boston," Scarpello said.

"Yeah," Ragazzi affirmed. "And Albert? We gut sumethin' better in store fer him." He shook the chain link fence next to Guy's head. "You tell 'im his days is numbered. We're gonna git 'im no matter what." With that, he placed a hand against the back of Guy's head, pushed his face against the fence as if for emphasis, turned and with the others following, strode back to his car.

Guy, breathing hard, stayed where he was for a few moments after the big Packard pulled away from the curb. His shirt had come un-tucked. Adjusting it, he noticed that two buttons had popped loose. "Uh, Oh," he said aloud. "I don't understand what just happened, but I think we got trouble."

Feeling his nose carefully with his fingers to make sure it wasn't broken, he picked up his spikes from the ground and tossed them over his shoulder. "Punks," he said a bit louder, but there was no one around to hear. His courage returning, he shook his fist in the direction of Vito Scarpello's house across the street and a few doors down the block, and walked unsteadily away.

* * * *

Boston, MA
Thursday, October 4, 1934
Fenway Park
3:00 p.m.

At this point, we'll fast-forward to October 1934, the beginning of Guy's junior year, and take a look at his football season.

In this, East Boston's second game of a still young season, these players took the field for the game against Memorial: Pease—left end, Turchinetz—left tackle, Pearson—left guard, Carabott—center, DeFrancisco—right guard, Silva—right tackle, Bianco—right end, Ryan—left halfback, Guy—right halfback and Harris—fullback. Frank Ford having graduated, Fred O'Brien tapped Alex Struzzerio, a senior, as his starting quarterback.

Eastie won the toss, and of course, elected to receive. The wind picked up immediately after the opening kickoff, blowing directly into their faces, destroying any hope of mounting a passing attack.

From their own twenty, with Harris, Struzzerio and Guy alternating on criss-crosses and fake spinners, they moved all the way down to Memorial's seventeen yard line before a fumble ruined their drive.

With the wind at their backs, Memorial then began a drive of its own with some success. A series of passes from Brennan, its left halfback to Rogers, the right halfback, seemed to confuse the Eastie players. In the defensive huddle, with the ball resting on their own thirty-two, Struzzerio shouted at his defensive backs. "C'mon you guys! They ain't invisible. Let's knock down a pass or two, huh?"

"Rogers is big," Guy said, breathing hard, "and it's like he has glue on his fingers."

"Yeah," tall, gangly Bill Ryan chimed in. "He ain't dropped nuthin' yet."

"Well, goddam it." Struzzerio shot back. "Ya gotta get in the way a one a those passes. Let's go!"

But continuing to mix up his plays, quarterback Panton handed off to his fullback, Connolly, who gained eight. Then a quick down and in pass to Rogers, who caught the ball over Guy's outstretched hands, gave Memorial a first down on Eastie's nineteen. The Ferry Boat riders seemed unable to stop their opponents, who had it all going their way up to this point.

"They're matchin' up Rogers against Guy," Ryan said in the huddle, wiping sweat from his eyes. "Gives 'em a huge height advantage."

"Six inches at least," Guy added, licking his lips nervously. "I can keep up with him but I can't out jump him."

Struzzerio, who knew the game well, glanced from Ryan to Guy. "Okay. Let's try somethin'" he said. "We line up the same way, but after the ball's snapped, you two switch the coverage. See if that doesn't help."

It did, but not before Memorial penetrated to the ten yard line. There, Eastie took over on downs but could not move beyond their twenty-five, where they had to kick it away.

Memorial came roaring back with passes, Brennan to Rogers again, and they went to Eastie's eleven before the Noddle Islander's front line stiffened and caused a fumble, which was recovered by Guy on the fifteen. Fired up, Guy carried twice during the next series of downs and almost broke loose for a touchdown, but was tackled from behind at Memorial's thirty-seven. Unable to move the ball any farther, they had to punt.

The game went like that for awhile. In the final stanza, Struzzerio fired a long pass to Guy, who was in full stride and would have scored, but the pass was slightly overthrown and hit off his fingertips at the twenty-four. Later in the game, Eastie mounted another promising drive, but a pass to Ryan also failed at the twenty, and this game went into the books as a scoreless tie.

*   *   *   *

Boston, MA
Thursday, October 18, 1934
Fenway Park
6:15 p m.

The following week in the game against Brighton, Coach O'Brien juggled his lineup, hoping to field a team with some scoring punch. His changes involved sitting Harris and moving Pearson—who had played left guard the week before—to fullback. O'Brien started Siraco at left guard and also switched Guy to left half and Ryan to right half.

The results were dramatic. East Boston reeled off nineteen points in this contest, and would have had more except that Guy dropped a pass on Brighton's seven yard line, which would have been a certain touchdown had he held onto it. The game featured an interception of a Brighton pass by Pearson, who tucked it under his arm and ran from his own forty, sixty yards for the score. Also, in this battle we saw that Guy had mastered placekicking. He kicked one point after touchdown. Pepicelli, a year ahead of Guy, was asked to kick the others.

He hit the goalpost with one attempt and missed clean with the other. Final score? East Boston 19, Brighton 6.

*   *   *   *

Boston, MA
Thursday, October 25, 1934
Fenway Park
6:10 p.m.

Narragansett Park Race Course listed the weather as clear and the track slow on its fifteenth day of racing, as Eastie squared off against Charlestown that chilly Thursday evening.

J.W. Mooney described the game at Fenway Park this way:

> *Those Charlestown lads, as small as they were, made it mighty hot for East Boston, and held the Noddle Islanders to a scoreless tie in the first half. Charlestown was in the wrong at the start when Casey's short kick went out (of bounds) on his own 45. Vitale ran the next Charlestown kick (back) 34 yards to the Charlestown 22 but Potter intercepted a pass to break up the march.*
>
> *After O'Neil picked up 11 yards Casey booted out of danger. Vitale again carried back for 18 yards to the Charlestown 40 and starting the second quarter Charlestown held for downs on its 34 yard line. After the kick, Ryan and Vitale clicked for a first down on the Charlestown 44 and Pearson was going for another first down when O'Neil tumbled on his fumble. After the kick out, Ryan tossed Vitale a 20 yard pass to the Charlestown 40 yard line where the half ended.*

Notice that Guy was not only playing, but he was figuring in lots of plays and handling the ball frequently. He was running back punts, catching passes and—guess what? Struzzerio apparently having been injured, Guy was now handling the team at quarterback.

Mooney again:

> *In the third period, East Boston started a concerted march of 70 yards that scored the touchdown. The backs were banging away for three or four yards and making headway on kick exchanges until it landed on the Charlestown 40 from where Vitale heaved Ryan a 10 yard pass and Ryan lugged 10 to the 20. The Noddle Islander backs*

alternated on more severe thrusts at the tackles until Pearson went over and Vitale kicked the trypoint.

Guy also scored one of Eastie's two touchdowns that day, taking it over on a quarterback sneak from the three after a drive of some sixty yards which featured his passing to Ryan, Pease and Harris, while fullback Carozza did some of the brute work. Final score of this one was Eastie 13, Charlestown zip, as Guy played most of this game at quarterback.

*   *   *   *

Boston, MA
Tuesday, October 30, 1934
Fenway Park
3:15 p.m.

On a cold, dreary October afternoon, Jamaica Plain and East Boston, both undefeated, were set to clash at Fenway Park. One team would emerge from this game unbeaten. It had rained earlier, and the playing surface was sloppy and the ball slippery. A large crowd, bundled up against the cold, had turned out to root for their favorite team.

In the locker room before the game, Bill McCarthy, an English teacher and volunteer assistant coach, substituting for O'Brien, who was "under the weather" that day, addressed the team.

"Listen up, boys," he said. "Coach O'Brien's not here today, but he left me his starting lineup for the game." He waited until the team settled down and then read from a sheet of paper in his hand: "Pease—left end, Turchinetz—left tackle, Siraco—left guard, Carabott—center, Sartini—right guard, Silva—right tackle, Sacco—right end, Vitale—quarterback, Ryan—left half, Pearson—right half, Carozza—fullback."

Apparently Struzzerio was still out with an injury, so once again Guy was called upon to run the team. From the opening whistle, the game went badly for Eastie.

The kickoff, a good one from Jamaica Plains' point of view, was killed at the Noddle Islander's one yard line. Three running plays found them only at their five, in a kicking situation. Guy was the punter.

Lining up deep in his end zone, his brain replayed the time—as a Freshman—when he was called upon in a situation much like this, to punt from almost at the end zone out-of-bounds stripe. *God? Please make Carabott's snap a good one*, he prayed silently. It wasn't.

The muddy ball came back high, and Guy had to leap for it. He dropped it and for an agonizing moment, he sensed the charging Plainers linemen, heard the familiar sounds of pads on pads and saw the ball bouncing crazily at his feet.

Everything moved in slow motion. Snatching at the ball, he got his muddy hands on it, lined the laces and dropped it to his foot. The pigskin and his foot united as one. The ball sailed over the outstretched hands of the oncoming linemen and—the kick was away. But Guy, unable to sidestep Jamaica's beefy guard and tackle because of the sloppy field, was hit hard and slammed to the ground. In those days, there was no penalty for roughing the kicker.

In his column the next day, here's what Mooney had to say about Guy's kick:

> *… Humphrey Sullivan's kick was killed on the Eastie one yard line and [when Eastie could not move the ball] Vitale had to kick from his end zone. He fumbled but recovered and got away a pip out to the 38 yard line. Buccigross fumbled and Eastie recovered …*

To be sure, there were many fumbles by players on *both* teams in that game. Also, several pass interceptions. Guy fumbled twice and had one of his passes picked off. The match went that way until the middle of the fourth quarter, when Eastie started a drive from its own twenty.

They moved it out to their forty-seven yard line, and Guy called a criss-cross play with sub left halfback McCormick carrying around his own left end. It was a good call, and the play gained ten yards to the forty-three. Buoyed by that success, Guy called a criss-cross reverse play, with Bill Ryan carrying the football.

As the teams lined up, Eastie's formation looked to the kids of Jamaica Plain like the same one used on the previous criss-cross.

"Down." Guy yelled above the din of the excited throng. "Hut one, Hut two, Hut!" As the Plainers swung to meet the play, Guy hid the ball on his hip for several seconds before handing off cleanly to Ryan.

"Other side! Other side!" cried Buccigross, Jamaica's quarterback who was calling defensive signals. Attempting to pursue, he slipped and went down in the mud. Both Burke and Sullivan tried to stop Ryan, but he evaded their tackles and carried it around right end, galloping forty-three yards for the score.

Mooney waxed eloquent in his report the next morning:

Grabbing the wheel of the undefeated band wagon from the reckless hands of Jamaica Plain, Bill Ryan swerved around the corner of Defeat and Victory street, sending Jamaica skidding completely off the seat while he tore along a now none too crowded Victory highway at a terrific clip until he wound up with the lone touchdown and six points that kept old East Boston in the class of the very elite.

The *Post's* sportswriter said nothing about the extra point. If it was attempted by Guy, he must have shanked it.

Maybe the fans didn't notice something else, but Mooney did. He ended his column with two lines that would soon be oft repeated:

As Fred O'Brien, Eastie coach was sick, Bill McCarthy ran the team.

CHAPTER 13

Boston, MA
Friday, November 16, 1934
Fenway Park
3:30 p.m.

"Okay, fellas. Listen up! Here's the lineup for today." Fred O'Brien stood in the middle of the visitor's locker room at Fenway Park, his raucous, exuberant boys clustered around him. They were happy, excited and ready to face off against Hyde Park. Their team, undefeated so far, was perched on top of the District League. "Sacco—right end; Silva—right tackle; Sartini—right guard; Carabott—center; Siraco—left guard; Turchinetz—left tackle; Pease—left guard; Struzzerio—quarterback; Vitale—right half back; Ryan—left half back; Pearson—fullback."

Standing next to his locker, Guy looked up. Expecting to play quarterback again that day, he was surprised to hear his name called as the right halfback. And *disappointed*, too. His face looked briefly like a storm cloud. But, understanding that he'd turned in a bad game the week before and respectful of his coach, he left the locker room with his teammates without saying a word. *I'll just have ta play real well today,"* he thought. *No fumbles. Then maybe next week, Coach will put me back at quarterback.*

This game was not an offensive contest, but rather, a defensive struggle. It featured bone crushing tackling by Alex Struzzerio and some good punting by Guy, who twice had to kick his team out of trouble from inside his own end zone.

Toward the end of the first quarter, after a series of kick exchanges, East Boston began a drive at midfield and reeled off three straight first downs to Hyde Park's fourteen yard line, where the quarter ended. Moving to the opposite end of the field, Hyde Park's big line dug in and stopped Eastie for three downs at the eleven.

In the huddle on fourth down, there was no thought of kicking a field goal. Eastie wanted a score. Guy was pleased to hear Struzzerio call a pass play; a down and in pattern from Ryan to him. He'd score the touchdown and make his coach and teammates proud.

They lined up. Guy, on the right side, listened to Struzzerio's cadence. The memory of his brother's strong young voice calling signals two years before, came back to him like a voice floating in the ether. At the snap, he faked a block, slipped into Hyde Park's backfield under a full head of steam, turned at the four yard line and—the ball was there, but it was higher than it should have been. With everything he had, Guy leaped for the pigskin. No one was around him. If he pulled it in, he'd score by simply falling across the goal line without a hand being laid on him.

It was not to be. The ball skipped off his fingertips and skittered harmlessly away. Guy, sprawled full-length in the dirt, his body half in and half out of the end zone, furiously pounded a fist into the turf. Hyde Park had escaped damage and would get the ball back on downs.

But it wasn't until the final minutes of play that either team scored. Hyde Park drew the first and only blood when Fagerberg, subbing for quarterback Narcisso, heaved a pass to Dray, who collected it at Eastie's goal line and scored the only touchdown of the game. Hyde Park's kicker missed the extra point, and that's how the game ended. Hyde Park six, Eastie nothing.

The next morning, Mooney wrote:

> *In a grid game packed with bone crushing tackles, featured espe-*
> *cially by the defensive work of Alex Struzzerio East Boston quarter-*
> *back, Hyde Park High knocked the Tunnel Tourists from the peak of*
> *the District League standing with a close 6 to 0 victory at Fenway Park*
> *yesterday afternoon.*

*   *   *   *

East Boston, MA
Friday, November 16, 1934
East Boston High School
7:30 p.m.

Fred O'Brien, his sport coat off and tie untied, stood in front of the gray file cabinet in his office. His blood pressure was high now from several years of heavy drinking, which gave his face a florid look. Several tiny, red veins stood out on his nose.

His mood was somber; his thoughts dark—as dark as the halls of the school beyond the locker rooms. The boys, subdued and quiet, had returned to school, showered, dressed and gone home. He was alone, except for a custodian who was checking that all the doors were locked before leaving.

Shit! We can't hold onta da football. Vitale droppin' that pass maybe cost us da game. He catches that ball, we're six points up and da game ends in a tie or maybe we win and we're still on top a the league. How the hell can a coach win games without a decent quarterback? He groused. *Haven't had one since Guy's older brother Frank, back in '32, It just ain't fair.*

Trying to develop a reliable quarterback, he'd experimented with several boys; Alex Struzzerio, the senior, of course; Guy Vitale, a junior, and the new kid, Tony Geraci, who had transferred in just this year.

Struzzerio was capable and had done an adequate job. He'd graduate that year. Geraci, a good athlete, was still developing. *I can play him at fullback or halfback for a year,* he thought. *Vitale seems ta be the best of the lot; a born leader, a savvy play caller, a reasonably good passer and a great kicker. Hell, the other kids already look up ta him even though he's only a junior. No doubt about it. He'll be the starting quarterback next season. But he's gotta learn ta hold onta da ball!*

Sliding the file cabinet drawer open, O'Brien glanced at the bottle of Jim Beam inside and then closed it again. *Maybe I'll go over to Santarpio's. The fellas from Probation'll all be there bendin' their elbows and rehashin' the game.* But he didn't *want* to rehash the game. He didn't want to think about it at all. And he *definitely* did not feel like putting up with the ribbing he'd get from them, good natured as it would be.

He pulled the drawer open again, and closed it again. His mouth was dry, his lips parched. He craved the warm feeling of good whiskey flowing down his gullet into his stomach. He wanted that feeling repeated over and over, until his overactive brain ceased thinking about the team, the game, his coaching job, everything. The hell with how he'll feel tomorrow morning. He could always sleep in, phone his secretary and tell her he'd be late. He'd been doing that a lot lately. *Hell, I been at the Department so long, they wouldn't dare hand me the old pink slip.*

Licking his lips, he slid the file drawer open once more. Removing the bottle and a shot glass from inside, he shut the drawer firmly, returned to his desk and poured himself a full shot. Then he sat, elevated the glass in an imaginary toast to no one, raised it to his lips, drained it and poured another.

*   *   *   *   *

Boston, MA
Monday, November 26, 1934
Fenway Park
3:30 p.m.

Perhaps because of his fumbling in several games, or maybe just because there were so many good Seniors playing quarterback that year, J.W. Mooney did *not* name Guy for the *Post's* All-Scholastic honors at that position for 1934. Instead, Roger Battles of English High was named First Team Quarterback and Alex Struzzerio was selected as Second Team quarterback.[27]

However, too good to be overlooked, Guy received Mooney's nod as one of the halfbacks in the Honorable Mention category.

A final note: Buddy McLaughlin of Boston Latin was selected as one of the *Post's* First Team's halfbacks on Monday, November 26, 1934. Later in the column, Mooney wrote about him:

> ... *McLaughlin of Latin features in running and was account-*
> *able for 37 punts in the last two games. His stepping and cutting is*
> *something to watch. It may be that he will never be a college [foot-*
> *ball] player as he is too valuable as a [base] ball player, being the best*
> *infielder in the last 20 years in the local school ranks.*

Just two thoughts about that: Mooney, of course, had seen Guy's punting during this, his junior year. He'd also seen Lennie Merullo play shortstop for East Boston two years before. Did he rate Buddy McLaughlin as better in these categories than Vitale and Merullo? If so, McLaughlin must have been *something else*. But he didn't make it to the Bigs. I checked.

Joe Rocciolo thinks McLaughlin did his college at Dartmouth, where he played football and baseball in the Ivy League. Perhaps he marched to a different drummer, with no interest in playing pro baseball, or suffered an injury that stopped him from going any further. Or maybe he went to work or got

---

27 I asked Joe Rocciolo if he knew what became of Alex Struzzerio (whose name, by the way, I've seen spelled several different ways; Struzzierio, Struzzieri, Struzziero, and the way I elected to spell it in this book—Struzzerio). "After he graduated from East Boston High School," Joe told me, "he went on to become a Hall of Fame athlete at Northeastern University, where he played football and captained the baseball team. Later, he started his own machine shop in Lynn, MA, and became wealthy supplying airplane parts for General Electric."

married right after college and put his sports aside. If I ever get time, I'll do more research on him. There goes an entire afternoon.

*   *   *   *

Boston, MA
Tuesday, November 27, 1934
Fenway Park
3:30 p.m.

The annual Thanksgiving battle between rivals East Boston and South Boston was played before a large, boisterous crowd at Fenway Park on the afternoon of November 27th. O'Brien's team, if it won today, might still be able to claim the Division title. Here's how J.W. Mooney, writing in the *Boston Post*, saw it:

EAST BOSTON TIPS OVER SOUTHIE

VITALE GOES OVER FOR SCORE OF NODDLE ISLANDERS
Two close grid games kept the fans at Fenway Park howling yes-terday. After Mechanic Arts and Trade made a scoreless tie of their annual scrap, East Boston stepped in to take the rival Southie team 6 to 0, the first time that a Steve White team has been beaten by the Noddle Islanders. This, the feature game, gave the Tunnel Tourists an opportunity to argue it out with Hyde Park as to which team deserves the District title. Hyde Park played one less game, won four and lost to Jamaica. Eastie beat Jamaica but lost to Hyde Park and tied Memorial but beat Charlestown, a team Hyde Park could whip any day.

The game featured some good play calling by Alex Struzzerio, fully recov-ered, who was back at quarterback, and great defensive tackling by Carabott, Eastie's underrated but steady center. It also saw Guy do some of his best punt-ing yet, constantly pinning Southie back against its own goal line by kicking the coffin corner, and doing it going in either direction, into and against the wind.

Eastie's scoring drive came in the second half, after Pearson, playing fullback that day, intercepted a Southie pass at midfield. On the first play after that, Struzzerio, back to pass, could not find any open receivers. Keeping the ball himself, he ran it to Southie's thirty-eight. Then Guy, playing left half back that day, ran around his left end and carried down to the twenty-nine. Struzzerio then carried three times, to the sixteen, the ten and seven. Guy lugged it to the five and Pearson churned out two more to the three. Two off-tackle plays by

Struzzerio only made it to the one, and it looked like Southie would stymie East Boston's touchdown drive.

Dragging himself off the frozen turf, Alex adjusted his shoulder pads and trotted back to the huddle, his mind racing. This was important! They needed this touchdown. But he was drawing a blank. He didn't know what play to call!

Suddenly, Vitale was at his elbow. "Gimme the ball, Alex," he said through dried lips. "I can do it! I know I can."

Struzzerio glanced from one of his backs to the other; Ryan, at right half, Pearson playing fullback. Both were working hard and were having good games. *But Guy's right,* he thought. *He's been the standout today. He deserves it.* Looking straight at Guy, he called Guy's number. "On hut two," he said with a grin.

"Thanks, pal," Guy breathed, wiping his sweaty face on a dirty sleeve.

They broke from the huddle and Guy took his position a few feet to Struzzerio's left, his face expressionless, being careful to position his feet pointing straight ahead and not to lean one way or the other so he didn't telegraph the play.

As if from a great distance, he heard his quarterback calling signals. At the snap, Guy began to move, but he had to hesitate, timing his forward motion to take Struzzerio's hand-off. When it came, it was clean and crisp, right into his midsection, and his feet churned the ground in short, quick steps as he searched for the hole that must be created by the straining Turchinetz and DeAngelis; a space big enough and just at the right time.

His small frame hit the line behind Turchinetz. But there was no hole! Thinking to help, he extended his hand to the big left tackle's shoulder, just in time to feel him slip and go down to his knees in the mud.

Instinctively, with the agility and grace of a good runner, Guy moved to his right, feeling for DeAngelis. *DeAngelis of the angels, the angel!* he thought.

Guy could hear the big linemen from both teams cursing and straining in front of him, and for a moment, his confidence flagged. Then, DeAngelis, with a Herculean effort, moved Donahue, Southie's huge right guard and there it was—a small hole just large enough for Guy.

His legs churning in short steps, he slipped through and into the end zone. He was immediately hit hard by Mason, the defensive back on that side, with a bone-jarring tackle. But it was too late. Guy had scored.

The extra point attempt by a very elated Guy Vitale was blocked, but that did nothing to dampen his jubilation. The game ended with East Boston winning it, six to nothing. Guy had scored the only touchdown.

*   *   *   *   *

Boston, MA
Wednesday, November 28, 1934
Fenway Park
3:30 p.m.

Well, Lady Luck was certainly smiling on Fred O'Brien and his entire East Boston football team that season. Here's why I say that. East Boston's only defeat was a 6–0 loss to Hyde Park. Hyde Park's record included a 6–0 loss to Jamaica. *That* caused Eastie and Hyde Park to finish their seasons tied for first and the Division championship.

However, the *Boston Traveler*, on a tip, had been investigating one of Hyde Park's players, Art Dray. Discovering that he'd been ineligible, the newspaper broke the story. A complaint was lodged with League authorities by Albert West, President of the East Boston High School Alumni Association. Hyde Park's headmaster investigated, found that Dray had, in fact, been ineligible, and forfeited all his team's games. The game between Eastie and Hyde Park was forfeited to East Boston. Here's the article from the *Boston Traveler*, clipped from that newspaper in '34 by my grandfather and kept all these years. Because the handwriting on the article is illegible, it may have been dated either December 11th or December 17th:

> *EAST BOSTON WINNER ON HYDE PARK FORFEITURES*
> *East Boston High followers are doing the rooting now over their District championship team, which won the title when Hyde Park, which tied for the lead was forced to forfeit its games. It had beaten East Boston 6 to 0 and then lost to Jamaica by the same score.*
> *The East Boston alumni, headed by President Albert West, protested the eligibility of Art Dray, a star halfback, and Headmaster Haley of Hyde Park, after an investigation, forfeited the games. Dray had played a year of hockey under the direction of a player teacher-coach, and it had been assumed that it did not count as a year of athletics. Superintendent Patrick Campbell, to whom the protest was referred, wrote President West as follows:*
> *It is a pleasure to know that the Alumni of East Boston High School continue their interest in the welfare of the school and its organizations. I am informed that Mr. Haley has written letters to every school with whom its football team has played, forfeiting the games on the ground that one of his boys actually was ineligible.*

Thus, East Boston High ended its season still undefeated and perched atop the District League, alone as Division champ. That's a big story. But I think the bigger one is the action of Hyde Park's Headmaster, whose respect for the rules and his teaching of sportsmanship to his "boys" was such that he forfeited all of Hyde Park's games, knowing that his football team had come so close to tying for the District championship. Hey, can you see that happening today, when in sports, both high school and college, winning is everything?

CHAPTER 14

Pine Bluffs, WY
Wednesday, September 15, 2004
703 Beech Street
11:30 p.m.

In August 2002, I spent seven days in Boston, searching microfilm at the Boston Public Library. Not wanting to deal with heavy crowds and long security lines at Logan International, I flew to Providence, Rhode Island, rented a car and drove north to Boston on roads extremely good and well-marked. You've heard Massachusetts referred to as "Taxachusetts?" Well, at least the people seem to be getting something for their tax dollars—good highways.

Henry Scannell and his research staff got to know me well that week, as I opened the place at ten o'clock each morning and closed it at night. Burdened by a very bad case of the flu, I was unable to collect all the articles and box scores for every baseball game East Boston High played in the spring of 1935. But the ones I found are referred to here.

Before we get to that, a personal note: I like to eat. No, I'm not a food aficionado or a gourmet, but I appreciate good food. So it was a bright spot in an otherwise bad week for me, when, looking for some hot soup to soothe my aching throat, I dropped into a Thai restaurant not far from the Library for lunch on the third day. The Bangkok Blue, at 6512 Boylston Street, was something else. If you like Asian cooking, I heartily recommend this place for atmosphere, cuisine, and service the next time you're in Boston.

*   *   *   *

East Boston, MA
Thursday, May 9, 1935
World War Park
3:15 p.m.

That spring, Guy's junior year, East Boston High School's baseball team sported a new look. Many of the old names had disappeared and new players had taken their places. Gone were the McDonald brothers, Hesenius, Sacco, and of course, Lenny Merullo.

Eastie's lineup in their May 9, 1935 game against Brighton read this way: Beaton leading off and playing second base, Barrasso at third, hitting second, Matera playing first and batting third. Guy Vitale patrolling center field and hitting in the cleanup slot, Alex Struzzerio at shortstop, playing his final season of varsity sports for East Boston High and batting fifth, Sam Fiorini batting sixth and playing right field, Buontempo in left batting seventh, and Blanchard, the catcher, batting eighth. Callahan was the starting pitcher in this game, but he was later relieved by Lavoie.

The *Boston Post's* unaccredited article described the game this way:

EAST BOSTON WINNER, 11–10

Tunnel Tourists Shade Brighton Team
In a nip and tuck battle that found the starting twirlers being chased to the showers, East Boston High edged out Brighton 11 to 10 yesterday at World War Park, East Boston.

It looked like Brighton's game by a mile when it had a nine to four lead going into the fifth, after stacking up six runs in the third and chasing Captain Callahan off the mound. But the Noddle Islanders came back strong in the fifth with five runs and Pallas was yanked off the mound.

Lavoie, who relieved Callahan, had a shaky start but settled down to twirl a fine game, fanning six to help win his first varsity game. Struzzerio, in the third, and Callahan, in the second, banged out homers. Lavoie also came through with a four ply wallop as did Pessa of Brighton.

Playing the entire game in center field, Guy collected one hit in five trips, apparently a single. He made three putouts in the outfield and committed no errors, a solid though unexciting performance in what was either the first or second game of the 1935 season.

*   *   *   *

East Boston, MA
Tuesday, May 14, 1935
World War Park
3:25 p.m.

Sooner or later every baseball team will notch a game the players would just as soon forget. For Eastie, the contest against Jamaica Plain was one of those. They were pounded thirteen to two. However, Guy batted cleanup again, went one for four—a double—and made four flawless plays in center field.

Also, in an effort to create some scoring punch, Coach O'Brien played several new boys in this game. Rodriguez relieved Barrasso at third, Matero and Alves each played some at first base, and Tony Geraci, about whom we'll hear more later, patrolled left field for a few innings. Danner and Siraco took turns at catcher, and Callahan, Lavoie and Kelly did the pitching, walking two, three, and one respectively.

Another unaccredited article in the *Boston Post* the following day said this:

> *NODDLE ISLANDERS BURIED BY JAMAICA*
> *Jamaica Plain High won its third in a row yesterday at World War Park when it buried East Boston 13 to 2. Hyde Park and Latin were recent foes the Jamaica team crushed but they were not expected to give the Noddle Islanders such a trimming.*
>
> *Callahan, who started on the mound for the Tunnel Tourists, lasted only a couple of innings. Jamaica got six runs off him in the second, mostly on timely hitting. Seery, the Jamaica twirler, allowed eight hits but kept them scattered and never seemed to be in danger.*

*   *   *   *

East Boston, MA
Friday, May 17, 1935
World War Park
3:10 p.m.

Spring was in full swing as the boys took the field for the game against Charlestown. In this one, things were different for the East Boston nine. Again playing at home, the kids pounded out eighteen hits and as many runs in crushing a hapless Charlestown team 18–2.

Guy, apparently off to a slow start that year, did better, collecting three hits in six trips to the plate, one of them a triple, and playing errorless ball in center field again. Buontempo roamed left and smacked a home run for Eastie. Callahan went the distance and struck out eleven batters. Charlestown may have been a sub-par team, but if they were, Eastie made the most of it. The entire team looked improved this time around.

Here's the description in the *Post*, next morning:

> ### EAST BOSTON WHIPS CHARLESTOWN NINE
> *Playing errorless ball and whaling the old apple for 18 blows, the East Boston High Club walloped Charlestown 18 to 2, yesterday at World War Park, East Boston.*
>
> *Captain Callahan twirled good ball for the Norfolk Downs crowd, fanned 11 Bunker Hillers and tightened up in the pinches. Struzzerio, his shortstop, came up with the star play of the game, when he robbed Salerno of a hit in the sixth …*

*   *   *   *

East Boston, MA
Tuesday, May 21, 1935
World War Park
3:10 p.m.

The weather was bright and sunny for this contest as East Boston defeated Roxbury Memorial eight to two. Their lineup featured Alves playing first, Buontempo in left, Guy in center, Struzzerio at short, Callahan, pitching, Fiorini in right, Beaton at second, Danner doing the catching and Barrasso at third.

Here, we saw Guy going one for four and making two put outs in center field, while being hit by a pitch once. We also saw that he'd been moved up in the batting order to third, with Alex Struzzerio now hitting in the cleanup spot. However, maybe a bit nervous about batting there, Alex went hitless in four trips, although he *did* pull off an unassisted double play in the game. Callahan allowed only six hits and fanned nine in winning his second game in a row, while his opposite, a "colored boy"[28] named Singleton, walked fifteen batters, according to the *Post's* May 22nd account of the game.

---

28   That's the way he was described in the *Post's* article the next day.

*   *   *   *

East Boston, MA
Friday, June 7, 1935
World War Park
3:15 p.m.

This one must have been the last game of the 1935 season and Guy's junior year. Guy again roamed center field for Eastie, as his club defeated Trade, six to four.

O'Brien, juggling his lineup so that more kids got a chance to play, used Hansford at catcher and Lavoie did the pitching that day, allowing seven base hits and four runs to a strong Trade team, which had beaten Eastie two years in a row. He struck out six and walked four.

Collecting two hits in four trips, one of them a home run and the other a double, and scoring both times he was on base, Guy accounted for half of his team's run production that day. Hansford, responding to the opportunity to catch, smacked a home run in the first inning. Guy hit his in the fourth. That was the scoring for East Boston.

At game's end, Sammy Fiorini was named captain for the following year. I thought that Guy, with his record of accomplishments to this point, had earned that honor. But quiet and modest, he either did not push for it or told his team-mates he did not want the job, perhaps believing that the responsibility would be too much for him.

CHAPTER 15

Pine Bluffs, Wyoming
Monday, September 27, 2004
703 Beech Street
3:10 p.m.

Annually, after the high school baseball season had ended, it was traditional for the Hub League, the Greater Boston League, the All-Catholic League and the All-Middlesex County League to play a series of games to determine which league was the strongest.

The Hub League included all the high schools in Boston proper; South Boston, Commerce, English, Brighton, Dorchester, Boston Latin, Jamaica Plain, Mechanic Arts, Memorial, and of course, East Boston. The Greater Boston League was comprised of schools in Somerville, Medford, Everett, Revere and Malden. Their series of games began on Monday, June 17th, 1935.

In addition, there was to be a game the following evening between the All-Mystic Valley stars and the All-Middlesex County stars. Then on that Wednesday, the All-Catholic League team was to play the All-Suburban League team. The winners of these games would square off the following week.

Who was the star sent to represent East Boston High School? Guy Vitale.

*　　*　　*　　*

East Boston, MA
Monday, June 10, 1935
East Boston High School
3:30 p. m.

The boy's locker room was quiet. Baseball season over, the players had cleaned out their lockers the previous Friday, turning in their uniforms and padlocks, and removing their worn spikes, dirty socks and hot pin-up pictures of Hollywood starlets. Only the last few stragglers were on hand to perform that chore this afternoon, and they were buzzing about the *Post's* All-Team selections announced that morning. East Boston had not been treated kindly by J. W. Mooney, in this, Guy's junior year. Guy was the only player selected, and he was picked on the second team.

Guy had stopped by that afternoon to clean out his locker. Finished, he was about to leave when Sammy Fiorini approached him.

"Guy? Coach O'Brien wants ta see ya in his office."

"Yeah?"

"Yeah," Fiorini said with a lecherous grin. "He's got a girl in there for ya." It was common knowledge around school that Guy had not yet had a date. Aware of that, Sammy and his other teammates had been ribbing Guy mercilessly about it the entire season.

"Sure, sure," Guy responded, having heard this kind of stuff before. But his neck showed splotches of red above his clean, white tee shirt.

"I'm *serious*," Fiorini said. "She said she'd go out with ya, and Coach wanted ta make sure she didn't change her mind, so he tied her up and stashed her in his office."

"Har, har, har! Yer really funny, Sammy," Guy said. Turning, he headed for the door leading to the athletic fields. He didn't get there. O'Brien, under a full head of steam, barged through the double doors of the locker room leading to the hallway.

"Guy. I wanted ta see ya," O'Brien said. "Mooney from the *Post* called. Wanted me ta remind ya that the *Post's* All team players need ta play for the All-Hub team next week. I told him you'd be there."

Among those who made first team All-Scholastic that year were Andy Wright, ace pitcher from South Boston, Joe Zagami, first baseman from Somerville, Walter Berry, second baseman also from Somerville, and Buddy McLaughlin, shortstop from Boston Latin.

Along with Guy as second team selections were Everett pitcher, Bellafatto, Brighton catcher, Gincauskas and Southie's first baseman, Cruickshank.

This was a big year for Guy. He was also named as an all-star on the All-Boston League team as its left fielder, along with such standouts as Wright and Connolly, South Boston pitchers, Byrne, Commerce and Gincauskas, Brighton, both catchers, Blasser, Dorchester second baseman, Buddy McLaughlin, Latin's slick shortstop, Cohen, Memorial's centerfielder and Munichello, English's right fielder. Pessa from Brighton and Munroe from Dorchester were named utility outfielders.

*   *   *   *

Boston, MA
Monday, June 17, 1935
The Boston Post
7:00 a.m.

On Monday, June 17th, 1935, J.W. Mooney wrote a terrific column about the All-Star series, no doubt seeking to stir up interest among baseball fans in Boston and vicinity, because proceeds from the games supported the *Post's* Santa Claus Fund. In order to play in the series, one had to have been an All-Scholastic pick that year.

HUB SCHOOLBOYS PLAY SUBURBANS
ALL—STAR TEAMS FROM HIGH SCHOOLS IN FIRST OF
SERIES TONIGHT AT TOWN FIELD AT DORCHESTER.

What high school leagues have the best ballplayers? This is a much discussed question. But it is to be settled again this year starting this evening at 6 o'clock at the Dorchester Town Field, where the stars from the Boston schools clash with the stars from the Greater Boston League schools ... This is a continuation of an annual series. Boston started against the Suburban league and invariably came out on top. The Catholic League has cut in, and the Mystic Valley loop has also held a title.

FOR POST SANTA FUND

This, the opening game of the Post Santa Claus Fund Series, should be a success this evening. Every boy on each team has been contacted either personally or through his coach and as each league dotes on taking the 1935 All League honors, a true representation of their strength will be offered. Every boy is expected to be on hand at 5:30 o'clock with his uniform, glove and bat. They must bring bats.

The strong Somerville team, champion in the State High School title series recently concluded at Fenway Park, will be strongly represented on the Greater Boston league team with such stars as Walter Berry, second sacker, known as Somerville's second Horace Ford, Lefty Joe Zagami, the copy of Babe Ruth, at first, Russ McNamara and Munzo Iannacaone, two of the finest gardeners in the business, and the battery of Flynn, catcher, and either White or Fitch on the mound.

Bellafatto, twirler from Everett and his catcher, Trafton will also get a whack at battery work.

Other stars on the club are Gordee, Revere shortstop, Lewis, Medford third sacker, Wakeham, Medford outfielder, Cervini, Medford infielder, and Lyons, Malden's heavy hitting outfielder.

"BABE" ZAGAMI TO PLAY

Zagami, who lifted a home run over 400 feet into the center field stands at Fenway Park, is one of the Greater Boston heavy stickers who will give such star twirlers as Andy Wright, Southie strikeout king, and Jim Connolly of Commerce plenty of worry. Wright, who recently made a record by fanning 22 batters, has a load of stuff. He will have a fine catcher holding him as Frank Byrne of Commerce is one of the best and was considered clever enough to be chosen to go South with the Braves this spring. Lack of funds on the part of the Braves denied him the trip. Connolly, who gave English only four hits, and Ginkauskas, Brighton catcher, will aid in the battery work.

Cruickshank, Southie first sacker, is a steady lad and a good sticker. He is the best in Boston. Blasser, heavy sticker from Dorchester, will play second, with the noted Buddy McLaughlin of Boston Latin at short for his third year as an All Scholastic player....

HAVE FINE OUTFIELDERS

In the garden, Al Munichello of English, and Guy Vitale of East Boston, Cohen of Memorial, Pessa of Brighton, and Munroe of Dorchester, considered the cream of the Boston crop, will give their twirlers plenty of encouragement under flies and at the bat.

*   *   *   *

Dorchester, MA
Monday, June 17, 1935
Dorchester Town Field
6:00 p.m.

The game was everything Mooney had predicted it would be. Nearly six thousand avid baseball fans turned out to watch, as Andy Wright threw a one-hitter at the all-stars from the Greater Boston League, thereby settling the issue, at least for that season, of which was the stronger circuit.

Wright was opposed on the mound by Somerville's ace, White, who had recorded one hundred fifty-nine strikeouts in ninety innings that season, and

Nick Bellafatto of Everett High, who allowed only five hits and fanned six while walking three during his stint on the hill.

Hitting third in the batting order, Guy walked in the first inning on four pitches, as White, who opened the game for the Greater Boston League, got off to a rocky start by walking four straight batters, allowing the Hub team to score several times.

Guy came to the plate again in the second inning with Cohen on second and Pessa on first base. Hyped by this huge crowd and eager to make a good impression, he was looking for a pitch he could drive.

As he stepped into the batter's box, Guy thought about the pitcher on the mound. *He's got some heat. He's faster than most pitchers in our league.*

Taking the first pitch from Bellafatto for a ball, he fouled off a fast ball on the next pitch, and then watched a lazy curve break outside for ball two.

It's gonna be the fast ball again, Guy reasoned. He was right. Bellafatto, who could bring it, liked throwing his fast ball and did so frequently when he was behind in the count.

Not having seen this kind of speed very often before, Guy swung a bit late and smashed a screaming line drive toward right field, which was down the line and would have meant extra bases. But at the last second, big Joe Zagami at first base, playing a bit closer to the bag than usual to keep the runner from taking a long lead, leaped high and pulled it down, robbing Guy of the extra-base hit. With two men on, that hit would have meant at least one and probably two runs batted in.

Next day, J.W. Mooney described it this way:

> *Some fine playing was produced by both clubs. Zagami, the Babe Ruth of the school game who poled a homer into the Fenway center field stands Saturday, yanked down a scorching drive in the second inning that robbed Vitale of a hit with two on. Vitale evened it up in the third by robbing Lyons of Malden with a sweet running catch in center field.*

Mooney did not mention the score, but the All-Hub stars won this battle and went on to play at least one more game the following week before being eliminated.

CHAPTER 16

East Boston, MA
Tuesday, October 8, 1935
East Boston High School
5:45 p.m.

Fred L. O'Brien pulled his tie loose at his neck and settled into his office chair. The strain of nineteen years as a coach had been getting to him mentally for some time. Now it was beginning to catch up with him physically. Alone, he was on the telephone, answering questions from a Boston *Post* reporter for an article the latter was writing for the newspaper the next day. O'Brien did not want a long conversation with a reporter. What he wanted was a stiff drink.

"Well, yeah," he said thoughtfully, his glance straying to the file cabinet in which he kept his liquor stash. "This late start in Boston schools hurts *me* as well as the rest."

"What about your first team?" the unnamed reporter asked. "How good?"

O'Brien tried to conceal his impatience. "I can put a good *starting* team on the field next week," he said, "but with about a hundred boys on the squad, the time for preparation is too short to allow picking out serviceable material for the spares. But, I think my first team will give them all a battle."

"But after that?"

O'Brien rolled his eyes, made a nondescript hand gesture and let his arm fall heavily to the desk. "After that, it's only a guess or a hope," he responded.

"What about East Boston-Hyde Park? Ya think it'll be a grudge game this year?"

O'Brien frowned. "I don't worry about stuff like that," he said. "Sure, they beat us last year all right, but their win was wiped out on a forfeit. Before that we hadn't lost a game since the '33 season. And this year, we have a lighter backfield, but we have a heavier line in front a them. I think we'll do okay." He answered a few more questions before hanging up and running a hand across the stubble on his chin. *Goddam reporters! Always diggin' fer controversial stuff,* he thought. *Wonder if I shoulda been so specific about the changes I've made. Well, too late now.*

The following morning, the *Post's* unattributed article read like this:

O'BRIEN TO FIELD GOOD E. B. TEAM

NODDLE ISLANDERS MAY HAVE
ANOTHER FINE CAMPAIGN

Not having been beaten legally all last fall, East Boston High eleven will field a fairly strong club, according to Coach O'Brien ...

The Noddle Islanders haven't lost a game since Hyde Park won in 1933. Hyde Park slipped over a 6–0 win last year also, but that was washed out on a forfeit. The club this year will offer a lighter backfield with a heavier line in front.

In Guy Vitale, the triple threat, the tunnel tourists have one of the best backs in the Boston ranks. The lad does everything well and is a slippery boy lugging the ball. Larry Ryan is also a left over in the backfield, while Pease, an end, is likely to be shifted to center to give the line the proper balance. He was such a fine end that the coach isn't hot for making the change, but believes it will be for the team's good. DeFrancisco, scrub guard last year, has shown enough stuff in practice to land him a steady berth. Silva, a veteran guard, will be moved over to a tackle berth.

The shift of Pease from end to center gives O'Brien a chance to use some capable wing candidates who include Sullivan, who received some experience last year; Spinney, and Mike Scopa, who made a name for himself in track last winter.

And there's a wealth of backfield material also, for besides Vitale and Ryan, there is Tuck, who won his letter; Carrozza, who made a fine impression starting out last year, but caught fumbleitis; Geraci, a light but shifty boy, who was on the squad a year ago and is now about set; and the third of the Carrozza brothers, Ralph, brother to Rocco, who once captained the team. Ralph is expected to develop into a pip and outclass his brothers."

Eight days later, in Eastie's first game of the season, O'Brien would get a chance to see just how successful his changes would be for the 1935 season.

By the way, in its sports section the *Post* printed daily entries from racetracks around the country. That day's entries—October 9, 1935—for Laurel Raceway in Baltimore, Maryland, showed that Alfred G. Vanderbilt's Sagamore Farm had a two-year old, *Speed to Spare*, running in the fifth—a six furlong, one thousand dollar allowance race. An elderly Alfred Vanderbilt and his Sagamore Farm would later become one of my steady clients during the years I practiced law in Maryland.

✳   ✳   ✳   ✳

Boston, MA
Thursday, October 17, 1935
Fenway Park
6:00 p.m.

The schoolboy twin bill featured Boston Latin and Roxbury Memorial squaring off in the top half, and East Boston playing it's usual opener against Brighton in the nightcap.

Nicola Vitale could not help hearing the buzz about East Boston's football team and the part his son was playing on it. That was all his customers at the barber shop wanted to talk about. For the past week, they'd been exuberantly proclaiming that Eastie would have a great season, and that Guy would, also. Nicola did not understand the game at this point in his life, had little use for sports of any kind, and had only watched his son play once before. But to quiet the good-natured ribbing he was taking at the shop when his patrons learned he'd not been following his son's heroics in either football or baseball, he decided to close the shop early and take the subway to Fenway Park that evening. On the train, he'd grudgingly admitted to himself that he *was* somewhat curious about what his youngest son was doing.

Brighton won the toss and elected to receive, but was forced to punt from its forty after only three plays. The kick went to Eastie's ten, and Guy, playing quarterback, drove the Tunnel Tourists out to his forty-two with a series of well-selected plays, where it was fourth and six from there; a punting situation.

"Okay, I'll kick it away," Guy said in the huddle. "Gonna try ta get it up high so you can get under it. Let's go!"

Nice ta have big guys like Scopa, Silva, Pease, DeFrancisco and Calla on the line in front of me, he thought as he confidently awaited the snap at his own thirty.

True to his word, O'Brien had switched Pease to center, and his transition was smooth. That young man, taking his new position seriously, snapped the ball perfectly, and Guy was able to get off a high, precise spiral that sailed downfield

… landing five yards deep in Brighton's end zone. At first the crowd was quiet, unwilling to believe what it had just seen. Then, as Guy trotted off the field for a breather, the Eastie crowd showed its approval by applauding politely. Under his helmet, Guy's face reddened, but otherwise, he made no sign that he knew the applause was for him

Eastie's next possession was slightly better than its first. This time they moved the ball across midfield, to Brighton's forty-five before being forced to punt. Guy, in sole possession of the punter's job now, again did the kicking, this time standing at his own forty yard stripe. Again the snap was good and Guy put his whole body into it; a high, spiraling kick that traveled into Brighton's end zone, for a touchback. This time, a deafening roar went up—from both sides of the field. It was only the first stanza and Guy had punted twice, the first for seventy yards, the second for sixty.

In the stands on Eastie's side of the field, a puzzled Nicola Vitale's eyes darted from one fan to another around him, wondering what his son had done that merited such wild approval.

The second quarter went by without either team denting the other's goal line. Guy's kicking continued to set Brighton back on its heals. In the third period, after running a punt back twenty yards to the Brighton forty, he was unable to mount a drive and Brighton took over on a fumble. Mooney didn't tell us who the culprit was. Immediately, McNamara, Brighton's fullback, tossed a pass to Shea, good for twenty-five yards, but coughed up the football two downs later. This time Eastie capitalized on the opportunity.

From his own thirty-nine, Guy ran for six yards and then called on Geraci, who was at fullback that day. The slender back, previewing how good he'd later be, simply shot through a hole made for him by Silva and Scopa, left end and left tackle, respectively, and carried for fifteen, to Brighton's forty-yard line. Vitale and Tuck reeled off another first down to the thirty. Then they did it again, down to the thirteen yard line, and Eastie's fans were whooping it up, sensing blood.

On the next play, drawing the Brighton team to his right by faking a pitchout to Carrozza at right halfback, Guy tucked the ball on his hip and went off left tackle for the score, standing up. His placekick for the extra point was good and Eastie led by seven.

For the rest of the game, Guy's deceptive play calling had Brighton on the run. He had his team down on Brighton's five yard line as time ran out. East Boston seven, Brighton zip.

This is how Mooney described the game in his *Post* article on October 18th:

LATIN SMOTHERS MEMORIAL, 19–0; TAKES ADVANTAGE OF BREAKS TO WIN.

EAST BOSTON COPS OTHER HALF OF TWIN BILL

... in the nightcap, of the doubleheader, East Boston made some kind of history by beating Brighton 7–0. It was the first time since 1924 that one team or another in this long series had been able to cop two games in a row.

GREAT KICKING

Those who took in the clashes got a peek at some of the best kicking they ever saw in any ranks, school, college or pro. This lad Vitale, veteran quarterback of East Boston, gave the demonstration. On the very first kick with the [line of] scrimmage around his 42-yard line, he was back on his own 30-yard line and spiraled a pip that sailed all the way into the end zone. On the next kick he stood on his own 40-yard line and kicked for a touchback, the first one going 70 yards in the air and the second 60 yards.

And Ernest Dalton, of the *Boston Globe*, described it this way on October 18th:

EAST BOSTON TAKES BRIGHTON BY 7–0 SCORE

The Eastie-Brighton game [featured great] kicking. Guy Vitale, Eastie leader, cut loose with a boot that traveled 60 yards from scrimmage, and followed that up with several for fifty yards from scrimmage, and for the latter, he was 'pulling his punches' to avoid kicking for touchback.

*   *   *   *

Boston, MA
Friday, November 1, 1935
Fenway Park
6:00 p.m.

On a gray November evening, East Boston, unbeaten and unscored upon, took the field at Fenway Park, squaring off against Jamaica Plain. Playing conditions were poor; the field a sea of mud after an entire day of rain.

The starting lineup for that game featured Spinney at left end, Silva at left tackle, Covino at left guard, Pease at center, Capucci at right guard, Colla at right tackle, Scopa at right end, Tuck at left half, Carozza at right half and Geraci at fullback. Guy was the quarterback.

Tony Geraci, a senior, rapidly developing as a football player, was now showing too much talent for O'Brien to keep him out of the lineup. His favored position was quarterback, but Guy was firmly ensconced at that position and was too good to be dislodged by anyone. In this game, it didn't take long for Guy to show why.

Eastie had received the opening kickoff, but after reeling off two first downs, its drive stalled. Guy, quarterbacking, punted the ball out of bounds at the Jamaica Plain thirty. Broderick, Jamaica's quarterback fumbled on the next play and Eastie recovered at the twenty-seven. Here's Ed Earle, for *The Boston Herald,* the following day:

> *The long range booting of Vitale began counting soon after the start of the East Boston-Jamaica Plain game. The Eastie quarterback got off a 55-yarder which went outside at the Jamaica 30 and the Noddle Islanders recovered a Jamaica Plain fumble on the next play …*

On their first play from scrimmage after recovering that fumble, Guy called Harvey Tuck's number and Tuck, playing left halfback today, used a straight-arm to break a tackle and run to the twenty-two. Tuck again, got seven, to the fifteen. Geraci, in the fullback slot, tried an off-tackle slant between Scopa and DeLeo but no hole opened up and he barely made it back to the line of scrimmage.

In the huddle, Guy wiped his muddy face with a sleeve, thinking. He realized that in this slop, long passes would be impossible, and razzle-dazzle running plays would be difficult. But he decided to gamble here. It was first and ten at Jamaica's fifteen. If the play failed, he'd have three more downs to get the touchdown.

"Okay, one, right reverse 2, 5. On hut, hut."

Tuck and Ed Spinney, Eastie's left end, smiled. Guy had just called for himself to take the snap, start out to the right, and hand off to Tuck, who would move left and toss a pass to Spinney as close to the goal line as possible.

They lined up. On a quick snap, Guy started right, almost slipped in the mud, but managed a smooth exchange with Harvey Tuck, who was churning left. The line held. Tuck managed to slog his way several yards into the left flat, Spinney was open in the end zone fifteen yards away, and Eastie had its first touchdown of the day.

Mooney's article about this game started off as follows:

> *… while Jamaica fumbled its clash with the rival East Boston team which, behind the cleverness of Charlie Vitale, ran up a 13–0 score over the Jamaica kids, who showed enough improvement in the second half to keep that end scoreless.*

This was the first of only two times that Mooney would print Guy's name wrong. Here's the rest of his article describing the game:

> *A 55-yard kick by Vitale had Jamaica back on its 27-yard line early in the Eastie game. Jamaica fumbled the first rush and Eastie recovered on the 30. Vitale belted the right tackle to the 18 and Tuck passed a spiral to Spinney in the end zone for a quick touch—down, Vitale kicking the placement.*
>
> ### EAST BOSTON RECOVERS
>
> *After receiving the next kick, Jamaica had a bad pass back which Eastie recovered on the Jamaica 26-yard line. Vitale was off on a right sweep to the 5-yard line where Jamaica got stubborn and held for three plays on its own one-yard line. Vitale finally lunged through the left side of his line for the second touchdown. Before the half ended Jamaica had Eastie on the run, Keough, who was to feature the game as rival to Vitale, doing the bulk of the work in a pair of first downs to the Eastie 30-yard line where East Boston held. On an odd play, Vitale started to hit his left guard broke off to the left and raced to mid-field to relieve the pressure.*
>
> *Pasquale, who went in at quarter for Jamaica, knocked off 15 yards on the Eastie third quarter kickoff and Keough banged away to his 38-yard line. [Bernie] Pasquale threw Murphy a pass to the Eastie 47, but another weird center pass lost 15 and Eastie recovered it. After a kick exchange, Tuck, apparently stopped, squirmed loose and made up 25 yards before the third period ended.*
>
> *In the fourth quarter, Jamaica tried all it had in the air but lost the ball on downs on its 30-yard line. Tuck picked up eight yards and Eastie went into the air, Jamaica holding on downs as one Eastie lad muffed a throw just over the goal line.*

One more comment: among family records are two original newspaper articles with photos taken in this game. The paper is yellowed with age but the type is still clear after seventy years. The first, captioned *EAST BOSTON STAR IN*

ACTION, shows Guy, a huge grin on his face, breaking a tackle and running the ball. Under the photo is this:

> Gaetano 'Guy' Vitale, schoolboy punting king and leading leather lugger of unbeaten East Boston High, shown cutting through Jamaica Plain High for a gain on the road to the first touchdown as the Noddle Islanders blanked the purple and gold, 13–0 yesterday at Fenway Park.

The second original photo is captioned, *EAST BOSTON MARCHING THROUGH JAMAICA,* and shows Eastie's Harvey Tuck (*Globe* writer, Ernest Dalton refers to him as Mel 'Friar' Tuck[29] in his article about the Charlestown game) carrying the ball on third down, advancing to the Jamaica Plain one. Its defense having stiffened, they'd held Eastie for three downs in a courageous goal line stand. But on fourth and one, Guy carried on a quarterback keeper and scored. Under the photo is this:

> Harvey Tuck of East Boston plowing through the Jamaica Plain frontier to the one-yard line in the play preceding East Boston's second touchdown in the mud at Fenway Park.

*   *   *   *

Boston, MA
Wednesday, November 6, 1935
Fenway Park
6:00 p.m.

Guy's early performance on the gridiron as a senior was … well, spectacular. And it did not go unnoticed. Here's what was said about him a few days after the Jamaica Plain game by sportswriter Vic Stout of the *Boston Traveler* in a portion of his column given over to information about upcoming local high school games. That part of his article was called *Spotlighting the Schools*. It appeared on November 6th, 1935:

SPOTLIGHTING THE SCHOOLS
East Boston v. Commerce and Latin v. B.C. High tomorrow after-
noon at Fenway, in what looms as a grand take-in … The Noddle

---

29 The reference is to a beloved character in Howard Pyle's *The Merry Adventures of Robin Hood,* Grosset & Dunlap, Publishers. 1952.

Islanders, paced by Guy Vitale, are undefeated, as is Charley Fitzgerald's Latin eleven ..." Incidentally, have you noticed the resemblance of Brode Bjorklund to Buddy McLaughlin? ... Brode is not far behind Buddy in football ability either ...

We've already learned who Buddy McLaughlin was, and we know how well thought of he was in local football and baseball circles. But just who is this Brode Bjorkland? We'll find out a bit later.

Unfortunately, I was unable to locate any articles describing the Eastie-Commerce game, but we can assume that East Boston won, because it was undefeated and unscored upon going into its game against Mechanic Arts on Thursday, November 14th. In the Mechanic Arts game, Guy rose to new heights.

CHAPTER 17

Boston, MA
Thursday, November 7, 1935
East Boston High School
6:00 p.m.

On days when Fred O'Brien came in early, several of the junior and senior members of the football squad liked to squeeze into his sardine-can office during the lunch break to talk football and rag each other, either about their performances in the previous game or about a topic which, at their age, was always on their minds; girls. Today, O'Brien sat behind his scarred metal desk, listening as they unburdened themselves. The topic was *not* the opposite sex.

"He's gonna make a terrific quarterback, coach. Ya know he is," Leo Carrozza said. "And he's been workin' hard in practices." He was referring to a fellow teammate, Tony Geraci.

"Too bad he graduates this year," Pease tossed in.

"But if he stayed back a year ..." Spinney aired the thought that was on their minds; especially the juniors. Smelling an undefeated season behind the quarterbacking of senior Guy Vitale, they wanted *another* next year, when *they* would be seniors, and they thought they had hit upon a way to bring it about.

"I admit the thought *has* crossed my mind," O'Brien responded genially. "If a kid failed English in his senior year, he'd *have* ta stay back a year. English is a required subject for graduation." He swiveled his chair a bit so he could see all the boys better.

"Ha! But would he do it?" Silva asked rhetorically. "Stay back I mean."

O'Brien glanced from one boy to another and waited. It would be unseemly for him to be the one to suggest it—especially in front of witnesses. But he'd been doing more than just thinking about it. In fact, he'd been toying with the notion of approaching Geraci privately and feeling him out about it. A transfer student who had entered East Boston High in the fall of '34, the boy was developing quickly. Disciplined and hard-working, he was the number two back this year. If Geraci could take over next season, it would be fantastic; like finding the proverbial pot of gold at the end of the rainbow.

Four undefeated seasons in a row would be a feather in my cap, O'Brien thought. *Steve White at Southie and "Dutch" Holland at Mechanics would be envious as hell.*

"I think he would," Pease said, interrupting O'Brien's reverie. "He's been talkin' about goin' ta college. But ta do that he's gotta git himself a football scholarship."

"A football scholarship?" Leo Carrozza interjected. "Playin' behind Guy all this year, he ain't gonna cut it. He has ta be a lot more visible ta get noticed by a good college."

From out in the hall, a bell sounded, ending the lunch break. The boys rose, noisily collected the remains of their lunches and grabbed their book bags.

"Somebody needs ta talk to 'im," Pease said, glancing back at his coach as the boys filed through O'Brien's door and dispersed to their next classes.

*   *   *   *

Pine Bluffs, Wyoming
Friday, October 1, 2004
703 Beech Street
8:25 a.m.

So, did Fred O'Brien actually ask Tony Gerasi to stay back a year? The evidence is circumstantial. Gerasi *did*, in fact, fail English in his senior year. He *did* repeat that year, and he *did* take over from Guy Vitale as quarterback during the 1936 football season. While researching during 2001, I'd picked up a whiff of this, and realized that, if it were true, O'Brien was … sailing close to the wind ethically, as the saying goes. I needed to learn more.

*   *   *   *

Pine Bluffs, Wyoming
Saturday, October 2, 2004
703 Beech Street
8:30 a.m.

On December 1, 2001, my purpose in attempting to track down Tony Geraci was to find out what his recollection was of his years at East Boston High

School, what he thought of Guy Vitale, and how it felt to play behind him. Of course, if I could gain his confidence and he chose to confirm what I'd been hearing, it would lend credence to my theory that Fred O'Brien, an alcoholic under the stress of a long coaching career, was deteriorating; that his usually good judgment was impaired, and he was now doing things that he might not otherwise have done.

Only three people with the name 'Anthony Geraci' were listed in the Boston area telephone directory. The first was an elderly gentleman who said he had not attended East Boston High School, was not the Geraci I was looking for, and that he thought he'd seen an obituary for another Anthony Geraci in a local newspaper recently.

My second call that day turned up the son of the Geraci for whom I was looking. "Yes," he said, "my father went to East Boston High School and he played football there. He used to talk about your uncle all the time."

"Did he? Terrific!" I responded. "How can I reach him?"

"That's impossible," young Tony said. "He passed away a few months ago. But he shared lots of stories about Guy Vitale with me and my brother, Jim, and later, with my kids." He laughed. "So your uncle is known by two generations of the Geraci family."

I didn't need to prompt Tony Geraci's son. Eager to talk about a father whom he had obviously loved and revered, Anthony A. (Tony) Geraci started by explaining that he was not Anthony Geraci, Junior, because his father did not have a middle name. Then he quickly branched out. "My dad said Guy Vitale was the best athlete to ever come out of East Boston High School," he said emphatically. Hearing that, I felt like one of those Gold Rush miners back in 1849 who had just struck the mother load.

"Did he say anything specific about Guy?" I asked.

"Yes," Tony fired back. "On Sunday afternoons during the NFL seasons, we'd watch New York Giants football games together and he'd tell us that Guy could kick better than the punter for the Giants. It didn't matter who was doin' the kickin' that game. Guy was better. 'Vitale could kick the coffin corner regularly, and he could kick inta the wind or against the wind,' he'd say."

"What formations were high school teams using back then, Tony?"

"They used the direct snap from center, with either a hand off to other backs or a pass. Sometimes, they'd snap it directly to another back in the 'shotgun' position."

"What position did your father play?"

"My dad didn't play much the first year he was on the team. He was a quarterback. The second year, your uncle was the number one back and played quarterback, so dad played behind Guy—halfback and even fullback, during that year."

"Was your father a year behind Guy in school?" I asked.

There was a pause. "Actually, that's an interesting thing," he responded. "I'd always thought my father graduated in 1936. When I was teaching at East Boston High School, I went and looked up his records. He graduated in '37."

"What else did you find?"

"I learned that he'd entered East Boston High in the fall of 1934 as a Junior, and that he'd begun playing football that year. He played in 1935, too. And in '36, after your uncle graduated, he took over the team as quarterback. He actually graduated on June 16, 1937. That was differed from what he'd always said, so I went and asked him about it."

"Well, did he repeat a year or something?"

"Yes. He repeated his senior year."

"Why?"

Tony hesitated for a few seconds. Then he said, "My father wanted to go to college. But his folks—my grandparents—had no money to send him, so he knew he'd need to get a football scholarship. For *that* he needed to showcase himself. But playin' behind someone like Guy Vitale, he was not gonna be able to do it."

"Is that why he decided to stay back a year?"

"Yeah. He got that idea from some of the guys on the team. They told him if he failed English, he couldn't graduate. *They* got the idea from Fred O'Brien and passed it along to him." He paused again. "Later, he may have actually had a meeting with O'Brien about it, too, because he told *me* that O'Brien had *asked* him to stay back one year so he could quarterback the team in the fall of '36."

"How did he deliberately set about failing a year?" I asked, puzzled.

"He started missing a lot of school. Especially English classes. His records show he was absent forty-one times that year."

"Well," I said, "it apparently worked. In the '36 season, with him as quarterback they had a great year again, right?"

"Yep. They were undefeated. But the Southie game wasn't played. It got canceled because of snow that year."

"I'm not following. Was that important?"

"That meant something to dad. In Guy's senior year, Eastie lost to Southie thirteen to seven. I think dad had wanted to beat Southie to show that Eastie's team was better in '36, and he was a better quarterback than Guy. But he never got the chance."

"Where did your father go to college, Tony?" I asked, prepared to wrap up the telephone interview.

"He didn't."

"Why not? He had a terrific senior year, didn't he?"

"Yeah. And North Carolina State was interested in him. But he'd hurt his left knee somewhere along the line, bad enough to need surgery on it. That ended it for him."

Listening to Geraci, I heard the note of melancholy in his voice. "That's a shame," I said, sharing his sadness for a moment.

"Dad thought so. Apparently he really took it hard."

I thanked Tony Geraci's son for talking to me and sharing these stories about his father. I did not want to ask him more; for instance, would a top Atlantic Coast Conference (ACC) college like North Carolina State really offer a scholarship to a kid who'd repeated a year of high school?

As I was about to hang up, he said, "You know, my brother's a member of the East Boston Athletic Board. There are a couple of old-timers on that Board; guys like Sonny Buttiglieri, for instance, who may know something more about Guy."

He gave me a telephone number and started to hang up. "One more thing," he said. "Every year they have an Old Timer's Breakfast. It's held at Finelli's Restaurant."

"I didn't know that."

"Tony Marmo is the prime mover behind it. He was a good athlete in the East Boston area in his younger days, too. But the story goes he ran afoul of the law—a minor juvenile problem—and Fred O'Brien told him never to come out for any team at East Boston High because he'd be cut."

"Really? That seems like a pretty harsh way to treat a kid."

"Yep. You might wanna talk ta Marmo."

*   *   *   *

Pine Bluffs, Wyoming
Saturday, October 2, 2004
703 Beech Street
8:50 a.m.

The conversation with young Tony Geraci had been interesting and thought-provoking. That a high school coach would encourage one of his players to flunk a course and stay back a year is ... well, not the height of ethical behavior. That, if true, said a lot more about Fred O'Brien than I had already known.

And why had Geraci suggested that I talk with Tony Marmo? Was there something more he thought I should know? I decided not to just leave things there, but to follow up with Marmo. So I found his phone number and called him. This was shortly before Christmas, in 2001.

"Yeah, I knew Guy Vitale. Everybody did," Marmo said after I introduced myself and told him why I was calling. "He was one of only two or three athletes ever to be named All-Scholastic and All-State, from East Boston."

"What was your connection with Guy?" I asked.

"I was a year ahead of him at East Boston High. Graduated in June 1935. Guy was a super athlete. He played football and baseball. He's a legend in baseball around here."

"Did you know any of Guy's friends? Jimmy Rosetti, Ritchie Cutillo or Lenny Merullo?"

"Oh, sure. Ritchie Cutillo was a good friend. He was a religious kid. Studied for the priesthood but came out after a year or two. Jimmy Rosetti [30]became secretary to Jack Kennedy when Kennedy was in Congress.[31] I grew up with Lenny Merullo. He was from a family of ten. Lenny played baseball, too. For at least one year, he was one a Guy's teammates."

"I understand you have something to do with the Old Timer's Club. Tell me about that."

"The Old Timer's Club isn't really a club. It's an annual breakfast, held each year ta honor local athletes in their eighties and nineties. I run it. Every year I alert over a hundred people, and thirty to forty turn out for it. Three years ago, we honored Lenny Merullo."

I brought the conversation around to the subject most important to me. "What do you know about Fred O'Brien?" I asked.

There was a pause before Marmo answered. "O'Brien? A great coach at Eastie for a long time. The East Boston Athletic Board has a scholarship in his name. I think it's a thousand dollars. They have a Banquet every year ta raise money, and they distribute it to a local kid."

"How long have they been doing that?"

---

30 Joseph E. "Jimmy" Rosetti (1921–1992) initially worked as a campaign worker in John F. Kennedy's successful 1946 Congressional campaign. After that he hired on as a staff member in the Boston office of Representative Kennedy from 1947–1951. Later he became an investigator; was Chief, Department of Security from 1961–1962, and Chief, Domestic Operations, Department of State from 1961–1966.

31 Recall that John F. Kennedy served in the U.S. House of Representatives from 1947–1952 and in the Senate from 1953–1960 before being elected President.

"For at least thirty years. Funny thing. Twenty-five years ago, the Fund had fifty grand in it, but the money disappeared in six years. So now they have ta hold that annual banquet I mentioned."

"So you think O'Brien was a great coach?"

"No doubt about that," Marmo responds. "But as a person ..." He let the sentence hang in the air.

"As a person? What?"

"As a person, he was no good."

"What do you mean, Tony?"

"Well, O'Brien was a drunk. He'd ask the athletes, 'Does your father make wine?' and if they said yes he'd tell the kid 'ask your father ta send me a gallon.' The kid would go home and tell his father ta make a gallon for his coach."

I thought back. "Seems like I've heard that before."

"Another thing," Marmo continued. "I was a pretty decent athlete, too. I was from the Ghetto and had ta work selling bread. Then I had a minor juvenile offense that came ta O'Brien's attention. He told me never ta come out for a team at East Boston High. So I had ta play sports elsewhere."

"That must have been rough," I commented.

"For a kid like me? Yeah, it was. I could have made the teams." He paused and took a breath. "Here's something else. O'Brien would take a bunch a Irish kids who were only mediocre athletes and put them on the Eastie teams with a few super stars like Guy and Lenny, who would carry them."

We talked for a few more minutes, about the Sacco families in East Boston, about his wife, Dede, whom he obviously adored, and about the Old Timer's Breakfast, which he invited me to attend if I could. Then I hung up.

*   *   *   *

Pine Bluffs, WY
Saturday, October 2, 2004
703 Beech Street
9:30 a.m.

Sonny Buttiglieri was next. Tony Geraci had told me he was a member of the East Boston Athletic Board.

"I'm not just a member," he said with a laugh when I called him, "I'm the *oldest* member."

"Did you know Guy Vitale?"

"I didn't know him personally, but I know Guy was one of the greatest football players to ever come out of East Boston."

"Did you go to high school there?" I asked.

"Yes, I went there in 1940 and would have been in the graduating class of '43 if I'd stayed. But I left school in September of '41 and joined the Navy. When I first entered in '40, Coach O'Brien told me I was too small ta play football. So I became the equipment manager."

"Can you tell me anything else about my uncle?"

"I can tell ya that my friends always argue about who was the greatest football player ever at East Boston High. Joe Zito, Johnny Poto and Guy Vitale are the three names that everyone says were the best."

CHAPTER 18

East Boston, MA
Thursday, November 14, 1935
Fenway Park
6:00 p.m.

The double header at Fenway Park had Boston Latin and Dorchester in the early game, while East Boston played Mechanic Arts in the nightcap. Both were exciting contests as Latin trimmed Dorchester by one point, seven to six, the margin of victory being a missed extra point, and East Boston reeled off three touchdowns to defeat Mechanic Arts nineteen to six.

East Boston's lineup that day featured Spinney at left end, Silva at left tackle, DeFrancisco at left guard, Pease again at center, Capricio at right guard, Colla at right tackle, Scopa at right end, Leo Carrozza at left half, Tony Geraci at right halfback and Harvey Tuck at the fullback spot. Guy again was the field general.

Several thousand fans had braved the bone-chilling cold to witness these games. Many had come especially to watch an undefeated East Boston team and to see young Guy Vitale play. Among the fans again that evening was white-haired Nicola Vitale. Wearing a new topcoat, scarf and gloves, his cheeks rosy from the cold, "Nick" was now frequently seen in the stands on the Eastie side of the field. He had, belatedly, become his son's biggest fan.

Eastie won the toss and elected to receive. As the bands dueled in the stands, the opening kick went to Guy on his thirty-six yard line, and he tucked the football under his left arm, took two steps left and then, seeing he had blocking in the middle, cut behind it and carried for ten yards to the forty-six.

Calling on Tuck, Geraci and Carrozza, Guy moved his team steadily down field to Mechanic's sixteen yard line. It was his turn to handle the ball. He called a quarterback keeper off-tackle slant. "On hut, two!" he yelled above the deafening crowd noise.

The teams lined up. Guy took a direct snap from Pease and found a hole between Silva, playing left tackle, and Spinney, at left end. His short legs churning like pistons, he evaded a tackler in the secondary, cut to the left sideline and raced sixteen yards for Eastie's first score of the day. He then kicked the extra point. East Boston led seven to nothing, and Nick Vitale began telling everyone within earshot, in a thickly accented but unflawed English, that Guy was his son.

Mechanic Arts played well in the second quarter. Using a series of fake spinners, quarterback Calabrese guided his team down to Eastie's thirty-eight yard line. He then tossed a bullet to his right halfback, Nevin, at the eighteen. On the next play, a pass interference penalty was called against East Boston, which placed the ball at the two, where Calabrese called his own number and scored. But he missed the extra point and that's the way the half ended.

Early in the third period, Scopa fell on an Artisan fumble on their twenty-one yard stripe. Three plays netted nine yards. Guy then dialed Carrozza's number and the speedy left halfback carried to the one-foot line where he stepped out of bounds. But Guy, knowing Leo deserved the chance to score, called his number again and Carrozza did not disappoint. The extra point was blocked. East Boston thirteen, Mechanic Arts 6.

Here's how J.W. Mooney described Eastie's final touchdown in his column the next morning:

> *Near the end of the game, the little champion Vitale chased his interference to the right, cut just in time to break into the clearing and faded to the right as he tore down the field for 49 yards and the final score.*

Rhetoric like "the little champion" aside, Guy *did* have an outstanding game that day. And in the wooden stands on Eastie's side of the field, Nick Vitale, who had, at first, only started coming to the games at the urging of his patrons at the shop and a few of his barber friends that he should "see for himself" what his son was doing, swelled with pride as he heard the fans cheering for his boy.

*   *   *   *

Pine Bluffs, WY
Saturday, October 2, 2004
703 Beech Street
10:00 a.m.

Back at that time, the city schools held a competition for individual scoring honors. On Tuesday, November 19th, 1935, sports columnist Vic Stout of the *Boston Traveler* wrote:

> *East Boston's Guy Vitale and Boston Latin's Brode Bjorkland are bracketed in a two-way tie for the individual scoring honors in the city school competition. Vitale and Bjorkland, both captains of their respective teams, boast a total of 28 points.*
>
> *The Noddle Islander has been the outstanding back in Boston School football this year. His grand ball-carrying has been instrumental in East Boston's undefeated record, while his punting is probably better than that of any schoolboy in the state. Practically all his scores have resulted from long runs, either from scrimmage or on the end of a pass.*

Stout, in this column, went on to say:

> *John 'Red' Flaherty of Boston College High is ensconced in third place with a total of 27 points. The well-set up halfback was not too impressive in the Eaglet's early season games, but his play in his last few starts has been exceedingly brilliant.*
>
> *Although he is not included on the scoring lists, English High's place-kicker, Mantos, has scored eight points on touchdown conversions and has yet to fail in this important point after touchdown assignment. The only boy in the state who can compare with Mantos as a place-kicker is Marblehead's Eddie Phelan who has converted 13 out of his last 14 attempts.*

A few days later, on November 22nd, 1935, Stout's column contained the *Spotlighting the Schools* section once again:

> *The South Boston-East Boston game next Tuesday should be a standout … Both elevens are exceptionally strong this season … it will be your last chance to see Guy Vitale, the best back in the Boston schools this year, in action …*

And a few paragraphs further on, this:

> *A correction is in order: 'Red' Tully is captain of [Boston] Latin and not Bjorkland, as we stated earlier this week.*

Even great sportswriters like Vic Stout sometimes make mistakes.

And while I'm on the subject of sportswriters, it seems clear that Guy Vitale had captured the hearts and minds of the Boston writers with his gutsy play, and they were not shy in writing about him.

Here's another interesting note about Guy as a student at East Boston High School. According to Joe Rocciolo, in his senior year, Guy ran for class President. "He got almost all the boys votes because of his sports, but lost to John Ligiotti, who got a few of the boy's votes and all the girls' votes."

"Why was that?" I asked.

"Well, Guy didn't date at all. He was only interested in sports. So the girls thought somethin' was wrong with him; that maybe he didn't like them or somethin'. So they voted for the other fella."

*   *   *   *

Pine Bluffs, WY
Monday, October 4, 2004
703 Beech Street
8:00 a.m.

As I mentioned, the annual Turkey Day Classic football game was not played on Thanksgiving Day, although perhaps at one time it had been. In 1935, the contest between East Boston and archrival South Boston received more hype leading up to it than usual. Why? Certainly because both teams were stronger than usual; but probably also because of East Boston's "little champion," Guy Vitale.

Before we get to the game, it's important to note that on Monday, November 25th, the Boston *Post's* football All-Scholastic picks were announced for 1935. Guy was named All-Scholastic again, but not at the position he played all season long; quarterback. Two first team All-Scholastic picks were made at that position; Walter Carew of Medford and Charles O'Rourke of Malden. Guy, the only player from East Boston to be selected, was named as a back. In view of *his* performance as a field general, these two other kids must have been super stars.

The *Post's* second team All-Scholastic picks list an end named King from South Boston, who we'll hear from again soon. On the *Post's* third team, we find Johnny Maloney of Rindge Tech, selected as a quarterback—he'll later play baseball with Guy on the Cape—and Brode Bjorkland of Boston Latin, selected as a back.

Also on Monday, November 25th, 1935, Vic Stout of the *Boston Traveler* again wrote about the Eastie-Southie game.

RUGGED CLASH AT FENWAY TOMORROW
AS EAST BOSTON MEETS SOUTHIE RIVAL

East Boston, one of the few undefeated elevens in the State, will seek to write a glorious finis to one of its best seasons in recent years tomorrow afternoon at Fenway Park where the Noddle Islanders will match blocks and tackles with a South Boston team which, although defeated, takes rank with the most powerful machines which Steve White has fashioned in many years

GAME ANNUALLY ONE OF MAJOR ATTRACTIONS

The East Boston-Southie game is annually one of the major attractions on the Hub football card. It has always been characteristic of East Boston and South Boston boys that they love to hit, with the result that this spirited rivalry produces more hard tackling and decisive blocking than any other game of the season.

Tomorrow afternoon will mark the final appearance of one of the most talented backs which has represented a Boston school eleven in recent years, Gaetano Vitale of East Boston.

Without question Vitale is the most accomplished back in Hub school competition this season. As far as punting is concerned, there's not a player in the state outdistancing the Noddle Island captain. He is a fast, elusive ball-carrier, and powerful runner for his weight. He passes well, receives excellently, throws a beautiful block and plays grand defensive football.

Stout went on to laud several other Eastie players:

Although Vitale has been instrumental in East Boston's bid for an undefeated season, there are other stars in the Noddle Island line-up. Harvey Tuck, for instance, is an outstanding fullback. He is a powerful plunger, an excellent blocker and an outstanding defensive back.

Then Leo Carozza and Ralph Carozza, those two half-pint halfbacks, have been outstanding all season. The East Boston line, while not big, is about as aggressive a forward wall as you'd find on any schoolboy team and no team has been able to launch a sustained running attack against it ...

Ending his article, Stout printed the starting line-ups for the big game the next day: for East Boston, he listed Spinney at left end, Silva at left tackle,

Cavano at left guard, Pease at center, DePaula at right guard, Calla at right tackle, Johnson at right end, Vitale at quarterback, Ralph Carozza at left halfback, Leo Carozza at right halfback and Harvey Tuck at fullback. Conspicuously absent from this starting line-up? Tony Gerasi.

So who played for South Boston that day? Doherty at right end, Lantry at right tackle, Flaherty at right guard, Rogers at center, Smith at left guard, Caddigan at left tackle, Mat King at left end, Hurney was the quarterback, Frank Gottlich was at right half, McNiff was at left half, and Pieculewicz was their fullback.

And on Tuesday, November 26th, 1935, the day of the big game, the Boston *Post* carried this short, un-attributed article:

SOUTH, EAST BOSTON VIE
KEEN RIVALS BATTLE ON FENWAY GRID TODAY

The undefeated and unscored upon East Boston High team steps out on Fenway Park this afternoon at 2 o'clock to do three things, to beat the old rivals from Southie, to keep unscored upon, and to cop the so-called District Championship of the Boston Schools. And it isn't going to be any cinch to do any one of those things for Southie isn't a pushover by any means. Southie was trimmed but by a fast, on—going B.C. High team which caught Southie out of stride and plagued with injuries.

There will be two of the slickest ball carriers around. Guy Vitale, All-Scholastic back from Eastie and Joe Hurney, Southie's star, are the lads who have made names for themselves this year. They are a couple of pips, do everything well, and have been great aids with their sensational running this fall. Paul McNiff is another fancy stepping and speedy back from Southie while the Tunnel Tourist sport one of the best quartets of any school in Greater Boston with the Carrozza brothers and Tuck aiding Vitale.

This series is 21 years old and Southie has the edge in wins, 9–7, four games having wound up in ties. Eastie was running behind until last year when it won 6–0, for it hadn't beaten Southie in eight starts, although the two games previous to last years were scoreless ties.

*   *   *   *

Boston, MA
Tuesday, November 26, 1935
Fenway Park
3:00 p.m.

A light dusting of snow had turned the gridiron white as East Boston and South Boston elevens took the field for their annual clash. Guy, in the middle of a bout with the flu, knew this would be a tough game because he'd participated in three of them before this one. He was right.

Southie drew first blood. Hurney was its quarterback. He called on Peck, his fullback, and McNiff, his right halfback, who did most of the grunt work that day, and they ground their way from their own thirty-seven yard line to Eastie's thirty where they were forced to punt. But the Southie punter was not skilled at kicking the corners. His punt traveled into the end zone.

Eastie then took over at its own twenty but could not move the ball and had to kick it away. In the exchange, Southie wound up on East Boston's thirty-nine. Hurney then handed off to McNiff, who ran for sixteen yards. At this point, King made his presence felt by catching a pass from Hurney at Eastie's three yard line. Hurney crashed the left side through Silva and Spinney for the touchdown. But Eastie stopped the rushing attempt for the extra point. Southie six, Eastie nothing.

Late in the quarter, Southie mounted a drive which brought it to Eastie's forty yard line. But, there it coughed up the football at the thirty-seven. Guy began alternately calling on the two Carozza brothers and Harvey Tuck, and carrying the pigskin himself. After grinding out several first downs, Eastie had to kick, but held Southie to three and out. This exchange put Eastie on its own twenty-nine.

Guy dialed his own number and made ten yards. Then he called on Ralph Carozza, who ran for eight more. Guy immediately went back to Ralph on a reverse play, which moved them to Southie's forty-eight yard line. On the play, Guy thought he'd seen a weakness at Southie's left end.

"I'm gonna lug it around right end," he said, calling his own number. "But, Covino and Di Paula gotta pull out and nail King good. On hut, two. Let's go!"

At the snap, Covino, playing the guard position on the right side, and Di Paula playing left guard, faked blocks and moved on King, Southie's big left end. That opened two gaping holes in Eastie's forward wall, but Guy was already on the move. With King smothered, he raced around the end and made the long touchdown jaunt.

Eastie's fans went wild. As the teams lined up for the extra point attempt, Guy glanced first at Di Paula and then at Covino, giving each a big grin and the thumbs up sign. He then kicked the extra point. Eastie seven, Southie six.

However, South Boston's captain, Mat King, was not victimized again in this game. In fact, possibly embarrassed and even a bit angry that he'd been effectively taken out of the play on which Eastie had scored, he became a one man wrecking crew for the rest of the contest. Here's Mooney's description of the game, in his Wednesday, November 27th, 1935 column:

FIRST DEFEAT FOR EAST BOSTON HIGH
SOUTHIE TEAM SMASHES ITS PERFECT RECORD BY 13 TO 7
DECISION AS CAPT. KING STARS

East Boston's unbeaten and untied team went down to defeat before its bitterest foes from South Boston at the Fenway Park gridiron, which came from behind, 6 to 7, in the last period to win 13–7. It was a whale of a game between these traditional rivals who have been banging away at each other for over 20 years.

Both clubs played hard, smart football. Captain King of Southie covered himself with glory and as usual, played himself right into the ground. It was his two sensational catches on forward passes that gave Southie their opportunity to knock the Tunnel Tourists off the undefeated bandwagon. The little fellow played a remarkable game and while they swung his end once, two Eastie boys [had to] hit him with everything but the water bucket to get him out of the play.

As usual, Guy Vitale was the Eastie star. He was watched like a hawk and with the Southie backs moving up fast to fill the gaps in the line, Guy didn't get the chance he usually does of running all over the lot. But he did come through with one 47-yard touchdown run.

· · ·

After Carozza was called back to the 40-yard line on the next kick-off, Vitale threw Ralph a pass to the Southie 47, and the pair combined for a pass to the Southie 32, where Hurney intercepted the next pass to kill off the last desperate effort of Eastie to go through its season undefeated.

As I mentioned earlier, Tony Gerasi did not start this game. Nor did he appear as one of Eastie's subs. Perhaps that knee injury his son told me about kept him from playing in this game. I don't know. There's no way to tell. But one thing seems clear. Had he participated, the outcome might have been different.

Here's how Ed Earle of *The Boston Herald,* saw the game:

SENSATIONAL PASS CLUTCHES BY KING
SET STAGE FOR SOUTH BOSTON TO CRACK
EAST BOSTON'S UNBEATEN RECORD, 13–7
By ED EARLE

A pair of hair-raising, acrobatic clutches out of the blue by Capt. Mat King on long-range, looping bombs from Joe Hurney put the ball in plunging distance for two touchdowns as South Boston High spoiled East Boston High's unbeaten record, 13 to 7, yesterday at Fenway Park in one of the greatest football games played by the two ancient rivals.

80-YARD MARCH IN FINALE WINS

Southie roared out from the underdog role and un-leashed a powerful attack in taking the lead, then trailed at the half, but came back to chew off the game in a last quarter, 80-yard march via terra firma and ether.

The chunky Hurney, Southie triple-threater, accounted for both Peninsula touchdowns, with Capt. King turning in a sensational performance at end as he played himself literally into the ground. The never surrender spirit of Southie was typified by the path-clearing and tackling of Frank Gottlich, the blocking back who kept plugging through disguised in a blood-streaked mask of mud.

Capt. Gaetano "Guy" Vitale, the East Boston ace, was the flashing spearhead of the Noddle Island attack, and his 48-yard touchdown gallop, followed by his accurate toe work, gave the Tunnel Towers a 7–6 edge in the second period.

The Southie secondary crashed in fast to hurry kicks and smear plays before they were fully developed and gambled successfully in stopping the Eastie air attack."

A few days later, on Friday, November 30th, 1935, the *Boston Traveler* surfaced with its All-Scholastic Roster. As with the *Post,* it did not name Guy as the first team quarterback, going instead with Wells from Marblehead. Arlington High's Madden was named to the second team and Carew of Medford was selected to the third team quarterback slot.

Guy? The *Traveler* picked him as a fullback, despite the fact that his weight was listed as one hundred sixty pounds and his height as five feet eight inches. Here's what the *Traveler* said about him:

FULLBACK—VITALE, EAST BOSTON—Although Guy Vitale is a quarterback we had to find a spot for him on this 1935 eleven. He is the best back which Fred O'Brien has ever developed at East Boston High. As a punter he has no peers. He runs, passes, blocks and does everything in the approved fashion. He unquestionably will go far in college football.

And *The Boston Globe,* in naming Guy to their All-Boston High School Eleven, picked him as a left halfback. Ernest Dalton wrote the article for the *Globe*:

POWERS [at] QUARTERBACK
Now for the backfield, always a puzzler, this corner is sure it has assembled the best. Quarterback is Tom Powers of English. Halfbacks are Joe Hurney of South Boston and Guy Vitale of East Boston. And at fullback is Al Keough of Jamaica Plain.
Tom Powers, besides being a fine ball toter, is a heady quarterback. And as for the halfbacks, Vitale and Hurney, both are streaks with the pigskin, both can turn on a dime and are experts at cutting back and sprinting through and beyond the secondary. Running back punts is their specialty. Vitale is 50-yard average punter and Hurney is right behind him. And both these lads can pass accurately.

Was not being selected as an All-Scholastic performer at his quarterback slot a concern to Guy? Fast-forward to early fall, 1952. At the time, Guy was living in Washington, D.C. with his sister, Anne, and brother-in-law, Al Tosi. My family was there on one of its annual visits.

Everyone was in the kitchen except Guy and me. We had excused ourselves to watch a Washington Redskins exhibition game on television that afternoon, featuring Eddie LeBaron, a former college standout at the University of the Pacific, quarterbacking for the Redskins. After LeBaron, five feet seven inches tall and one hundred sixty-five pounds soaking wet, had completed a pass for a touchdown, Guy, obviously pleased, jabbed my side with a finger and said, "He's my favorite player."

"LeBaron?"

"Yeah," he said, those intense brown eyes sparkling. "Reminds me of me."

CHAPTER 19

East Boston, MA
Monday, April 20, 1936
East Boston High School
4:30 p.m.

Excited and happy about receiving so many accolades at the end of the '35 football season, Guy turned out for baseball, determined to have a good season, convinced that if he did so, he'd be signed quickly by a major league club. Every sports fan in the Boston Metropolitan area thought so, too.

In addition to Guy, Fred O'Brien's team that season featured Tony Geraci playing second base and another Merullo at shortstop—Lenny's younger brother, Manny.

Because schoolboy sports in the Boston area got off to a late start to begin the 1935–1936 school year, the baseball season began later than usual. That meant fewer games for all the schools, including East Boston High.

I didn't find all the articles on East Boston's team. As I mentioned before, I have an excuse; the flu bug had bitten me early in my research trip to Boston during August 2002, and it simply got worse as the week wore on, progressing to the point where I was carrying a fever, coughing my head off and had lost my voice. It was so bad that it interfered with two visits to close relatives, part of the reason I'd scheduled the trip when I did. One was Guy's brother, my uncle Frank Vitale, who was in a nursing home in Rochester, New Hampshire at the time. He and my Aunt Madeline had been living in a retirement village in that city until Frank became infirm and had to be moved to the nursing home. Because of his age, his immune system was weakened, and when I visited my Aunt and cousin, Linda, it was decided that I should not go to see my uncle, to avoid giving him my bug.

At the same time, my cousin, Jeanne Sacco Waruszyla, was having a bad time with her husband, Ben, who was dying with cancer. Jeanne was the youngest daughter of my father's oldest brother, Joseph. Knowing that Ben was close to death, I'd wanted to see him, too. But for the same reason it was decided that I should not. Ben died three days later.

However, the trip *was* productive. In various newspapers, I found enough games to give you a picture of what kind of club Eastie had during Guy's final high school baseball season.

*   *   *   *

East Boston, MA
Tuesday, May 12, 1936
East Boston High School
3:30 p.m.

The first game I'm going to write about was probably not the first game of their season. I say this because the first article I found said:

> *Guy Vitale again was the batting star with two doubles and three singles in a lost cause.*

But it was, well … a throwaway game, the first of the two games against Brighton. And the first loss. Eastie out-hit those guys twenty-two to fifteen, but errors and walks did our boys in. Eight runs in the fourth inning decided things in Brighton's favor.

*   *   *   *

East Boston, MA
Thursday, May 14, 1936
East Boston High School
3:30 p.m.

I'm guessing about the date of this one, too. But it was against Jamaica Plain, and according to an unattributed article in the *Globe*, their fifth win of the year. Here's what was said about it:

> *The [East Boston's] greatest win of the season was the victory against Jamaica Plain, when Ed Kelly pitched a five-hit shutout as East Boston pounded out 17 hits for a 20–0 win. Twelve runs in the*

first two innings clinched this game. Little 'Manny' Merullo was the hitting star with a homer, a double, and two singles.

*   *   *   *

East Boston, MA
Tuesday, May 19, 1936
East Boston High School
3:30 p.m.

On this date, East Boston played Charlestown and came away with their sixth win., 15–3. Sam Fiorini and Guy each contributed four hits.

*   *   *   *

East Boston, MA
Thursday, May 21, 1936
East Boston High School
3:30 p.m.

The contest between Eastie and Roxbury Memorial was played quickly, but it resulted in Eastie's second loss of the season. That would be it for this team.

Only thirty-seven batters went to the plate for Roxbury and only thirty-four for East Boston, as Spinney pitched great ball for the Noddle Islanders until the ninth inning. Guy, firmly ensconced as East Boston's center fielder, had one hit in four trips and made one put-out in the field. In the ninth inning, Roxbury, behind by two, plated three runs in their half of the ninth, paced by the Cohen brothers, to come from behind to win it, six to five. An error, a walk and a hit batter contributed to Roxbury's three runs.

*   *   *   *

East Boston, MA
Tuesday, May 26, 1936
East Boston High School
3:35 p.m.

The second Brighton game was next on Eastie's schedule. It was played at Brighton's field. In this game, the Tunnel Tourists sent forty-two batters to the plate and scored two runs in the fourth inning, three in the seventh, one in the eighth, and five in the ninth.

Tony Geraci played second base again and got one hit in five plate appearances. Manny Merullo did the catching that day. He went three for four, as Kelley twirled a four hitter and struck out ten Brighton hitters.

Guy turned in a good performance, going three for five at the plate with two put-outs in center field. He scored two of his team's runs, and Eastie thumped Brighton, eleven to three.

*   *   *   *

East Boston, MA
Tuesday, May 31, 1936
East Boston High School
3:20 p.m.

In the game against Trade, Guy collected three hits in six trips to the plate, made two put-outs and no errors in center field. One of his hits was a double. However, he was somewhat overshadowed by Geraci, who walloped two home runs in the game. The *Boston Post*, in a tiny article the next morning, described the game:

> TRADE TEAM BURIED BY EAST BOSTON, 16 TO 7
> *Out of a cluster of 27 hits, 17 of them by East Boston High, the Tunnel Tourists walloped Trade 16 to 7 yesterday at the Fens Stadium. At the start it looked as though the teams would run the score up into the hundreds, Eastie leading off with three runs and Trade getting four in return. Then the twirlers settled down to business, Spinney of Eastie having a slight edge over Mulkern, who later got badly scraped sliding and lost his effectiveness. Geraci had hit him for a homer in the fifth.*
>
> *Dwyer took the Trade mound in the seventh but was relieved in the eighth, Barker taking his place for awhile until Sweetman was moved from third to wind it up. Geraci connected with another homer in the eighth with two on to aid the cluster of six runs. The fine foul catching of both backstops helped feature the game.*

*   *   *   *

East Boston, MA
Thursday, June 11, 1936
East Boston High School
3:20 p.m.

This contest against Jamaica Plain, the last game of the season for both teams, was played under a blazing sun. And since it was the final game for both teams, many fans had turned out to watch.

Guy, apparently not bothered by either the heat or the humidity, turned in a great game. I can't say it was his *best* of the spring, however, because, not having seen any other articles but these, I simply don't know. I'm going to say it was *not*, and I'll explain why later.

Anyway, here's the way it was described the following day in the *Post*:

> *EAST BOSTON BEATS JAMAICA PLAIN 17–11*
> *East Boston High and Jamaica wound up their baseball season yesterday at the Murphy diamond Jamaica, where the Tunnel Tourists ran up a 17 to 11 score. Guy Vitale, clever Noddle Island outfielder, helped in the victory getting four for five including a homer and a double. Eldridge of Jamaica was up six times and got six hits, all singles.*

In addition to a home run and a double, Guy's other two hits in this game were singles. Manny Merullo? He was up six times, too, as Eastie sent forty-six batters to the dish, and he produced two hits on the day.

When the bats were finally stilled for the 1936 baseball season, East Boston's nine was the District champion. Their record was ten wins and two losses. Guy led his team with a batting average of either .671, .621 or .585; again, depending upon which newspaper was the most accurate about that.

On Monday, June 15th, the *Post* came out with its All-Scholastic baseball selections for 1936. J.W. Mooney wrote the article:

> *POST ALL TEAMS FOR 1936 NAMED*
> *Whether it was the late start this spring in schoolboy baseball or just one of those years that pop up now and again, the fact is that it has been much more difficult to find a representative Boston Post All-Scholastic nine this year than it has been for years. But the club the Post presents this morning is the very cream of the lot and in another*

Anthony Joseph Sacco, Sr.   155

*week or two, to make up for the late start, undoubtedly these lads
would be right up with the wonder stars of other years.*

...

CLEVER OUTFIELDERS

*The 1936 outfielders are a clever lot. Guy Vitale of East Boston,
Charlie O'Rourke of Malden and Dick Conley of Everett made the All
football team along with Al Baniewicz, bashing outfielder from Rindge
Tech. For hitting, Vitale perhaps is in a class of his own, around the
.500 mark, although in some instances he has not faced the pitching of
the rest. Baniewicz has got his two or more in practically every game,
O'Rourke was a find this year at Malden and came rapidly, while
Conley's sticking and fast traveling made him a natural for a job.*

However, all was not sunshine and roses for our young hero. Guy, who played
center field the entire spring at East Boston, was *not* picked at that position, but
rather as the left fielder. Al Baniewicz of Rindge Tech got the nod as the *Post's*
All-Scholastic center fielder.

This is a pattern that repeated itself in Guy's case for two years, and in *both*
football and baseball. I suppose that it was indicative of how many good athletes competed in the Boston area during those years, and I found no evidence
anywhere that it bothered Guy. A modest, unassuming kid, he seemed to simply enjoy all the accolades sent his way by the press and others. But deep down
inside? I think it did. If you were a star quarterback and center fielder, but the
local press habitually named other kids to your positions two years running,
wouldn't it bother you?

Anyway, here's the *Post's* list of All-Scholastic baseball players for 1936:

Ray Chamberlain,	*Watertown*	*pitcher*
John Maloney,	*Rindge Tech*	*pitcher*
Connie O'Leary,	*Milton*	*pitcher*
Pat O'Brien,	*Arlington*	*catcher*
Howard Truesdale,	*Stoneham*	*catcher*
John Flaherty,	*B.C. High*	*first base*
Edward Pelligrini,	*Roxbury Memorial*	*second base*
Joe Walsh,	*Brookline*	*shortstop*
Frank Davis,	*Somerville*	*third base*
Guy Vitale,	*East Boston*	*left field*
Al Baniewicz,	*Rindge Tech*	*center field*
Charlie O'Rourke,	*Malden*	*right field*

Dick Conley,	*Everett*	*outfield*
Fred Wakeham,	*Medford*	*infield*
Dave White,	*Somerville*	*honorary pitcher*

The *Post* also named the All-Scholastic Suburban League players and the All Boston High School players. Guy *was* selected as the center fielder on those teams. Here's *that* group:

Singleton,	*Roxbury Memorial*	*pitcher*
Murray,	*English*	*pitcher*
Kelley,	*East Boston*	*pitcher*
Ahearn	*English*	*catcher*
O'Donnell,	*Roxbury Memorial*	*catcher*
Williams,	*English*	*first base*
Geraci	*East Boston*	*second base*
Pelligrini,	*Roxbury Memorial*	*shortstop*
Green,	*Brighton*	*third base*
Histon,	*Latin*	*left field*
Vitale,	*East Boston*	*center field*
McPhale,	*English*	*right field*
Handley,	*English*	*utility infielder*
E. Cohen,	*Roxbury Memorial*	*utility infielder*

As weeks go, this *"was the week that was"* for young Guy Vitale. The *Boston Herald* also named its All-Scholastic team, and Guy was on it, but as its right fielder; Al Baniewicz having been selected as its center fielder. The *Herald's* selections were only slightly different from those of the *Post*:

Ray Chamberlain,	*Watertown*	*pitcher*
Pat O'Brien,	*Arlington*	*catcher*
Frank Moran,	*Somerville*	*first base*
Fred Wakeham,	*Medford*	*second base*
Joe Walsh,	*Brookline*	*shortstop*
Frank Davis,	*Somerville*	*third base*
Charles O'Rourke,	*Malden*	*left field*
Al Baniewicz,	*Rindge Tech*	*center field*
Guy Vitale,	*East Boston*	*right field*

And here's what Will Cloney of the *Herald* had to say about Guy:

> *VITALE ALSO HAS ARM AND COMPETITIVE SPIRIT*
> *Vitale deserves more than passing mention, for he has the distinc-*
> *tion of being the only Boston representative on the team. His East*
> *Boston team played fewer games than most of the outside clubs, but*
> *his .621 batting average stands scrutiny just the same. He has a great*
> *arm and a competitive spirit hard to match.*

Did *The Boston Traveler* also pick Guy to their All-Scholastic team in 1936? Yes, and this is what Vic Stout had to say about him:

> *GUY VITALE—EAST BOSTON—Outfield Some of the boys may*
> *overlook this fellow this year but that will be only because they have*
> *not seen him. The Noddle Islander pounded out 36 hits in 58 trips to*
> *the plate this year for almost an unbelievable average of .621. He is*
> *fast as greased lightning, possesses a great arm, is intelligent and a real*
> *major league prospect.*

Another good note: "Red" Baccigalupo, again. "In 1936, I was in the eighth grade at Blackinton Elementary School. Because of the hubbub about Guy, the Principal, Bertram Richardson, decided he wanted ta have an Assembly, to present Guy with his old uniform in front of the entire student body."

"Did that ever happen?" I asked.

"Yeah. Guy was embarrassed but he was thrilled, too. He was our hero. Especially to the eighth grade boys."

Just one more thing. When the *Herald* named its All-Scholastic Team for Guy's senior season, a cartoon or caricature—a series of nine sketches of each of the first team ballplayers—was included. In a corner of each sketch, a notation of the place where the boy would be going to college or prep school the following year, if known, was inked in. Guy's sketch is second from the left in the top row. In the lower right hand corner, two words appear: "*Kents Hill*". This is a reference to an exclusive preparatory school in Readville, Maine, where kids who needed certain courses in order to enter college might get them.

How could that be? Had he made plans to enter there in September 1936? That he had such a plan seems indicated by those two words penned onto his caricature in June 1936. After all, the artist didn't just pull that bit of information from thin air.

Why did he want to go there at all? And why the year's delay? When I first saw that sketch, I didn't have the foggiest idea. Guy actually *did* attend Kents Hill, but not until the fall of 1937, a whole year later. Eventually, I came up with a plausible explanation.

In November 2005, while trying to find information about the Twin States League, I was put in touch with Dana Sprague, a writer for the Brattleboro Reformer. He provided the answer to at least part of this little mystery.

"I don't know much about the Twin States League, Tony. The Northern League is my focus."

"The Northern League? Lenny Merullo played in that league, didn't he?"

"Yeah. For Burlington, in '37 and '38. The League had a rule that all its players had to be college kids. If your uncle was not in college, he would *not* have been allowed to play in that league."

So, here's the way I see it. We know that Guy had taken the general course at East Boston High, not the academic or college prep course. In order to play in the Northern League, where the top quality ballplayers were showcasing themselves, or were invited to play by an interested major league club, he needed to get into college. But in order to get into college, he needed some academic courses. As a senior in the 1935–36 school year, he must have known this or been made aware of it by someone. So he planned on going to Kents Hill to pick up those courses. In fact, he might have even gone so far as to contact the Registrar and make preliminary plans to attend in the fall of '36.

But two other parts of that riddle remained; first, if Guy had planned on going to Kents Hill in the fall of 1936, why didn't he follow through? And second, how did he expect to come up with tuition, room and board at a prestigious place like Kents Hill? More about these later.

There you have it. What an amazing finish to a brilliant high school athletic career; being named All-scholastic by every single Boston newspaper was quite an honor. It had never happened before, and as far as I can tell, it has never been accomplished since.

What happens next to this wholesome kid with the nice smile and serious brown eyes? Hang in there and you'll find out.

CHAPTER 20

"Glad you could stop by, Apple." Fred O'Brien stood, came around his desk and extended a hand to a tall, skinny fellow dressed in a plaid sport coat with frayed sleeves, navy blue slacks, and a white shirt that was damp and badly wrinkled from the heat and humidity of a June day in Boston. O'Brien, fresh from a hard day on his job at the Probation Office, had arrived only a few minutes before. Pale and harried, he had immediately sought solace in a bottle of Jack Daniels Black Label, which he now kept handy in his file cabinet drawer.

Jimmy "Apple" Fallon had played college baseball at Stanford, in the sunny State of California, before moving East and signing with the Boston Red Sox as a hard-throwing left-hander with a curveball that fell off the table, a slider that confused hitters because it looked so much like a fast ball, and reasonably good control. Elbow trouble caused him to hang up his spikes four seasons later, but not before Red Sox owner, Tom Yawkey had taken a liking to him. Back in those days, club owners were on a first-name basis with all the people who worked for them. It isn't too much different even today. A job as a scout was found for Jimmy in the organization. He'd been doing that ever since, with some success.

"Apple" Fallon shook the outstretched paw, noted the odor of alcohol on O'Brien's breath, and moved toward the single chair in front of O'Brien's battered metal desk. He sat, but not before observing the empty shot glass on O'Brien's blotter.

Fallon had acquired the nickname because of a huge Adam's apple that bobbed up and down when he became excited or annoyed. It was his most striking feature.

"What you said on the phone the other day about young Vitale? Inneresting. You actin' as his agent?"

"Yep. Know the boy and his family well. He's like a son to me."

A frown creased Fallon's forehead. "You see the *Traveler's* All-Scholastic picks the other day? They confirmed everything you said about the young fella."

O'Brien returned behind his desk and sat heavily. He tried to adopt his most earnest expression. "I kid you not, Apple. This one's the real McCoy. We keep good records here. He went thirty-six for fifty-eight this season. Broke a track record in the fifty yard dash, too. He's fast and has a great arm."

A tentative smile spread across Fallon's face. He'd heard it all before—the high school coach acting as a kid's representative, making a strong pitch. *Kid's the second comin' of Babe Ruth, to hear this guy,* he thought.

But there *were* questions. Did Vitale face as strong pitching playing in the Hub League as some of the players out in the counties like Kimball in Lowell, or Davis over in Somerville? At five foot seven and only a hundred and sixty or sixty-five pounds, was he strong enough physically to withstand the grind of playing professional baseball every day? But it was early in the process yet. These were concerns that he could bring up later, when the *serious* negotiations started.

"What's it gonna take ta sign 'im, Fred?"

"Ten grand up front. Maybe a car tossed in for the boy. Nothin' flashy. A Packard sedan will do. You start 'im off in the Northern League, keep him there for a year before movin' him up. Voila! Ya got a major league outfielder."

Fallon heard the dollar figure and his Adam's apple began to bob up and down crazily. "Did you say ten grand?"

"Yep. And he's worth every penny of it, too. Kid's got such good eye sight he can see the laces on the ball as it come to the plate. Watches the ball spinnin' and knows whether it's a curve or a fast ball comin' in."

Brushing that aside, Fallon shrugged. He'd met Fred O'Brien several years before during the Merullo negotiations, which had never gotten very far, didn't like the man and marveled that anyone else *did*. "Sox'll never go for it. Why so much up front?"

"Five's for the boy. The other five's fer me for developin' him," O'Brien responded. "The boy's family is needy. They want 'im ta go ta work in the ship-yard ta bring in some cash. The money will sweeten the pot for them. Make it easier fer Guy ta leave home."

Fallon studied O'Brien's face for a moment. *Fella's got beady eyes. Shifty, too. Wonder if he can be trusted?* He rose to leave. "I'll pass the word along," he said with a scowl. "We know the kid's got ability. Nobody hits over .600 who doesn't.

But that's a lotta money for a signin' bonus." He shot O'Brien once with a finger. "I'll get back to ya on this."

*   *   *   *

Pine Bluffs, WY
Saturday, October 9, 2004
703 Beech Street
6:45 a.m.

What Fallon and O'Brien were talking about that afternoon was the Boston Traveler's selections for their 1936 All-Scholastic Baseball Team on Saturday, June 13th, just two days prior to their meeting, and what the *Boston Post* and *The Boston Herald* wrote that very morning, when each announced its All-Scholastic Baseball Team for that year. I've described those articles in detail in a previous chapter.

The things said about Guy in these newspapers provided ammunition for Fred O'Brien. But a closer reading revealed doubts in some minds about the efficacy of Guy's All-Scholastic selection.

In an article attributed to Vic Stout, the *Traveler* started off with this:

> Several days ago an enthusiastic follower of schoolboy baseball remarked that the caliber of the high school ball players this season was decidedly below par. "In contrast to other seasons," he said, "there are very few outstanding ball players around this year."
>
> The writer, however, does not share that opinion. After observing more than 50 schoolboy teams this season and more than 500 players, it is his opinion that there are just as many around this season as there ever have been. In fact, the 1936 Traveler all-scholastic team, to our way of thinking, is the strongest Traveler team in several years. Below is a brief discussion of the individuals."

Stout went on to describe each of the players, including Buddy Kimball, a first-baseman from Lowell, John Maloney, a pitcher from Rindge Tech, about whom we'll hear more later, Frank Davis, a third-baseman from Somerville, and Guy, who was selected as one of three outfielders:

> GUY VITALE, EAST BOSTON—OUTFIELD—Some of the boys may overlook this fellow this year, but that will be only because they haven't seen him. The Noddle Islander pounded out 36 hits in 58 trips

to the plate this year for [an] almost unbelievable average of .621. He is fast as greased lightning, possesses a great arm, is intelligent and a real major league prospect.

If O'Brien was happy with this write-up in the *Traveler* the previous Saturday, he must have been ecstatic after reading the Sports Sections of the *Boston Post* and *The Boston Herald* that day. Both newspapers named their All-Scholastic players for 1936 on Monday, June 15th. Both selected Guy as one of their outfielders.

The *Boston Post*, J.W. Mooney writing, offered this:

POST ALL TEAMS FOR 1936 NAMED

CHAMBERLAIN, MALONEY, O'LEARY, WIN ALL—SCHOLASTIC MOUND BERTHS—WALSH CLASS AT SHORT.

Whether it was the late start this spring in schoolboy baseball or just one of those years that pop up now and again, the fact is that it has been much more difficult to find a representative Boston Post All-Scholastic nine this year than it has been for years. But the club the Post presents this morning is the very cream of the lot and in another week or two, to make up for the late start, undoubtedly these chosen lads would be right up with the wonder stars of other years.

CLEVER OUTFIELDERS

The 1936 outfielders are a clever lot. Guy Vitale of East Boston, Charlie O'Rourke of Malden and Dick Conley of Everett made the All football Team and they are there again on the All baseball team, along with Al Baniewicz, bashing outfielder from Rindge Tech. For hitting, Vitale, perhaps, is in a class by himself, around the .500 mark, although in some instances he has not faced the pitching of some of the rest. Baniewicz has got his two or more in every game, O'Rourke was a find this year at Malden and came rapidly, while Conley's sticking and fast traveling make him a natural for the job.

And Will Cloney of *The Boston Herald* said this:

> *"SOMERVILLE HIGH PLACES TWO ON THE HERALD'S*
> *ALL-SCHOLASTIC TEAM*
> *CHAMBERLAIN, WATERTOWN PITCHER*
> *NAMED HERALD'S ALL TEAM CAPTAIN;*
> *VITALE, EAST BOSTON, HITS FOR .621*
> *Outstanding hurler in a season of star moundsmen, Ray Chamberlain of Watertown is honored with the captaincy of The Herald's 1936 all-scholastic baseball team published this morning. With Somerville high usurping two places, eight schools are the glory of this nine-man team.*
> *VITALE ALSO HAS ARM AND COMPETITIVE SPIRIT*
> *Vitale deserves more than passing mention, for he has the distinction of being the only Boston representative on the team. His East Boston team played fewer games than most of the outside clubs, but his .621 batting average stands scrutiny just the same. He has a great arm and a competitive spirit hard to match."*

What about *The Boston Globe,* the one with the widest circulation and certainly the most influential, although most liberal newspaper in the Boston metropolitan area? They published their All-Scholastic Baseball Team a week later, on Monday, June 22nd, 1936. Here's what Ernest Dalton, *The Globe's* Sports Editor had to say:

> *Now that the 1936 state baseball championship has been settled, it is time for the Globe to present its annual all-scholastic diamond outfit. Two teams, a first and second, and a choice list of honorable mentions drawn up.*
> *There are twelve boys named to the first team, representing 11 schools. Somerville High, Eastern Division winners, and finalists in the state final, with two boys, was the only school to place more than one player.*
> *All during the year just finished, the 'experts' moaned about the lack of high-class pitching, which is hardly understandable when two boys hurled no-hit, no-run ball on the same afternoon, tow all-scholastics of last year were still doing business, and there were plenty of four and five hit games turned in every week.*
> *CHAMBERLAIN LEADS PITCHERS*
> *This corner took the early stand that the pitching was just as good, if not better than in other years. On our first team today are*

four pitchers that could hardly be matched in the past. They are Ray Chamberlain, Watertown, Dave White, Somerville, Conny O'Leary, Milton and Johnny Maloney, Rindge Tech.

Of this group, Chamberlain is probably destined to go the farthest. He won seven and lost three this year.

Johnny Maloney, stocky, powerful and courageous, Carried Rindge to a tie in the Suburban League with an Ordinary team behind him and should have beaten Lowell in the Eastern Tourney, while both O'Leary and White were unbeaten until the tourney, O'Leary having 12 wins to his credit and White, perhaps the most publicized of them all, 10. White lost in the state title final last Saturday.

FINE INFIELD AND OUTFIELD

Now for the infield, which is a beaut—John Flaherty, B.C. High, first, Ed Pellagrini, Memorial, second, Joe Walsh, Brookline, short, and Frank Davis, Somerville, third.

This infield can hit, and how it can hit. Afield it is immense. Flaherty is big and experienced, while shortstop Joe Walsh is making the Globe team for the third straight year, the other two years being as a pitcher and third sacker. Davis at third was a wow all year, and rose to great heights in the tourney, while Pellagrini, though he played short this year, could not be left out.

The outfield is not only fast and a heavy trio but a clever bunch. Guy Vitale clouted the ball for better than .600 this year, and roamed his garden in grand fashion. Dick Conley slaughtered the ball all year ...

I quoted extensively from Dalton's article because it sheds light on an issue that caused some raised eyebrows about the quality of 1936 schoolboy baseball in the Boston area; the pitching. It seems the *Globe* did not share the concern of some, but felt that the pitching was, perhaps, better than in prior years. This was the pitching against which young Guy Vitale compiled a .671, .621 or .585 average. Yet later, this concern, whether legitimate or not, may have come back to haunt Guy with at least one professional team. More about that later, too.

In another article, this one unattributed, describing the *Globe's* All-Scholastic picks that year, it says this about Guy. Remember earlier, when I said Guy hit .671, .621, or .585, depending upon which newspaper was the most accurate on that? Well, here's where that *lowest* figure came from, and I don't know what evidence the writer had for it, because no source is quoted and no stats are offered as proof:

GUY VITALE ON ALL-TEAM

Guy Vitale, East Boston's pride in the sporting world received his reward for supremacy on Monday by being elected on every all-scholastic team selected by the Boston papers and in one instance was the only Boston player to be so chosen. Guy led all the fielders with a batting mark of .585. This was the second successive year that he received that honor and he will again be in those championship games tonight, Thursday, and possibly, next week. Tony Geraci, second baseman, and Ed Kelly, pitcher, received honorable mention."

Anyway, with these kinds of honors bestowed upon him, Guy was the "can't miss kid." But he did. So what happened? We'll find out.

*   *   *   *

East Boston, MA
Friday, June 19, 1936
East Boston High School
7:30 p.m.

It was a beautiful evening at the beginning of summer. Rain had fallen earlier in the day, but a gentle breeze had sprung up, sweeping the clouds before it to the northeast, out over the Atlantic. The full moon, now revealed in all its splendor, bathed the earth with a soft white light, and the heavens as far as one could see were filled with stars that twinkled brightly, as if pleased with what was about to happen. It was a wonderful night for new beginnings; a graduation ceremony—and the signing of an agent.

Frank Vitale, wearing the only sport coat he owned—navy blue with gold brass buttons and frayed cuffs—tried the door of the corridor leading to the boy's locker rooms and Fred O'Brien's small office.

"It's open," he advised his brother, Guy, who was following closely. "We don't wanna be late." The day before had been the last day of school, and the students had all dispersed, gleefully anticipating a summer away from their books, the demands of teachers, deadlines and homework. He and his brother had entered through the wide front doors, open this evening to receive members of the Senior class, who would be rehearsing at 8:00 p.m., for their graduation ceremony two days hence.

Freshly showered, his hair slicked back and clad in a white shirt open at the collar and tan slacks, Guy was flushed with excitement. "Nope. Wouldn't wanna be late," he echoed. It felt strange to him, being in the building when it was devoid of kids. The empty hallways seemed twice as large, and the sounds of their voices seemed twice as loud.

Their shoes making clicking noises on the corridor floor, the boys reached O'Brien's office. For a moment they stood still outside his door, listening to sounds of the great one moving about inside. Then Frank rapped.

"Come in!" A voice thundered from inside. Frank opened the door and they stepped inside as O'Brien rose to his feet, glanced at his wristwatch and mustered a smile. But his eyes were watery and his legs a bit unsteady. "Evenin' boys," he said, and gestured at two chairs in front of his desk. "What did ya wanna see me about?"

The brothers sat. Not having seen his old coach since graduation in 1933, Frank did not even *know* of O'Brien's drinking problem, much less how *serious* it had become. He was a bit intimidated, because, not to take anything away from him, Fred O'Brien was well-thought of by most, an excellent coach—of football, baseball and track—one of the best of his day in the Boston Metropolitan area. As a former player of his remarked: "It was like bein' coached by a human encyclopedia of football and baseball knowledge."

"We came ta ask if you'd represent Guy with the Major League ball clubs, Mr. O'Brien," Frank began, self-consciously.

O'Brien raised his long legs and placed his feet up on his desk. "Where are your parents, boys? Why aren't they here with you tonight?"

"Our parents don't speak much English," Frank responded. "It's … kinda hard for them, ya know?"

O'Brien's gaze moved from one boy to the other. "It's a bit irregular, fellas," he said. "Usually, I have one or both of the players' parents sign an authorization."

"They can't write much English, either," Frank said. "My dad might be able ta sign his name, but about all my mom can do is make an x-mark on a paper."

"Is that what *you* want me ta do, Guy? Deal with the Major League clubs on your behalf?"

Guy didn't answer right away. Many things were happening in his young life just then. Graduation was a couple of days away. Final rehearsal was to take place that evening in the school's auditorium. Uncertain as to his immediate future, he'd been interviewing locally, and expected to land a job at the nearby shipyard in a few weeks. He glanced apprehensively at his older brother. Reassured, he nodded. "Yes, sir. We … I'd like that."

"You know I'll do my best for ya, don't ya, son?"

"Yes, sir." Guy said again.

"Okay, then." O'Brien's feet came off his desk and he stood. "Let's shake on it."

That done, Frank Vitale asked the burning question. "D'ya think any teams are interested in Guy?"

O'Brien dropped his gaze. He did not tell them about his meeting with Red Sox scout, Apple Fallon a few days before. "Well I don't exactly know. Guy bein' named All-Scholastic by so many newspapers will certainly help," he said. "I can make a few calls and maybe drum up some interest. Come back ta see me again in two weeks. I may have some news for ya by then."

*   *   *   *

Boston, MA
Tuesday, June 30, 1936
Administrative Offices, Boston Red Sox Baseball Club
9:45 a.m.

"So, without battin' an eye, he says 'ten grand,'" Apple Fallon said. He was in the office of his boss, Walter Steele,[32] head of Player Development for the Sox, discussing his recent meeting with Fred O'Brien regarding Guy Vitale.

Steele's eyebrows shot up. "Ten grand? Good lord! Why so much?"

"O'Brien said five was fer the family and five was fer him fer developin' the kid."

Steele shook his head. "We ain't ever paid *anybody* ten grand as a signing bonus," he commented. "This kid? He's got talent, alright, but ..."

"Well, if we go fer 'im, the move might pay fer itself. Him bein' a local boy, I mean. He might sell a lotta tickets at Fenway once he gets to the big club."

"Possibly. *If* he ever makes it. His size is a problem, ya know. And there are those questions some a the sportswriters raised."

Steele rose and walked to the only window in his office. "Who signed for O'Brien to represent the kid?"

"As far as I could find out," Apple said, "nobody signed. His older brother and him were the only ones at the meetin' with O'Brien."

"Hmm! I don't like the smell a that. Makes me wonder if O'Brien's agency is valid. The boy's not twenty-one yet. And what about his parents?"

---

32 The names Jimmy "Apple" Fallon and Walter Steele are fictitious. This and the previous scene in which Fallon appears are products of the author's imagination. Yet, since the Red Sox, who were very interested in Guy early on, did not pursue him, I believe these scenes, or something like them, must have taken place.

"I did some checkin'. The Vitales don't speak or write much English. Father's more advanced than the mother. She runs a small grocery store outta one room in their apartment. The father used to be a laborer. Gave that up and went ta barber's school. Now he's a barber. Has a shop in a room on the *other* end. They also have some rental property. Nothin' spectacular."

Returning to his desk, Steele sat heavily. "You see the sportswriter's comments about Vitale a week or so ago?"

"Yep."

"It's true the city league isn't as strong as some a the suburban leagues. Pitching may not have been as good."

"Vitale was picked for the All-Boston Team. But in the All-Hub game against the Greater Boston lads, he went oh for two. Game was called on account a rain after six."

"Does that tell us anything?"

"I'm not sure. The kid had a great day in the outfield. Played all three positions and all six innings. Got robbed of an extra base hit with two men on in the second inning."

Turning from the window, Steele nodded and spoke again. "Go back and talk ta O'Brien. See if ya can get him ta forget the five grand for *him*. Develop him? Hell. All *he* did for Vitale was what *every* high school coach does for his players."

"What if he won't budge?"

"Then we just back off. Suggest that we're worried about the kid's size and durability. Say we got questions about his hittin' and wanna see the boy spend a season playin' ball in a *good* league. Since he ain't goin' ta college, we can't suggest the Northern League. The Cape Cod League might be the perfect place for him this summer. Then, we'll see what happens."

*   *   *   *

East Boston, MA
Friday, June 25, 1936
Department of Parole & Probation
10:30 a.m.

"Come right on in, boys," Fred O'Brien said expansively from behind the desk in his office on the second floor of the old District Court Building which housed the Department of Parole & Probation for East Boston. He stood and greeted Guy Vitale and his brother, Frank. It was only mid-morning, but he'd already been drinking. His eyes were watery and his face puffy with a florid cast.

"Any word, yet?" Frank Vitale asked as he and Guy took chairs in front of O'Brien's desk.

O'Brien examined his finger nails. "I've had two meetings with Jimmy Fallon, a scout for the Red Sox. Very preliminary, you understand."

Guy brightened. "What did he say?"

"The Sox are interested, alright. But the sportswriters raised some questions with those articles a couple of weeks ago. The Sox Player Development office read them. They wanna see Guy playin' for a really good team on a daily basis before they commit."

Frank and Guy exchanged glances. "So," Frank said, "they didn't make any offer?"

"Oh, no," O'Brien responded. He spread his hands in a theatrical gesture. "Boys, you gotta understand. These things don't just happen overnight. They take time."

Guy's face was stormy. Concern lines etched his forehead. "Are they worried about my ability?" he asked.

"Not exactly, Guy," O'Brien evaded. "But … the Boston schoolboy league isn't as strong as some leagues in the area. The pitchin' ain't quite as good. *That* raised questions about yer hittin' in some minds."

"About my hitting?"

"Yeah," O'Brien said.

"So I gotta show 'em I can hit for real? Well, where can I play this summer?"

"I'd like ta see ya in the Northern League, but they have strict rules. Ya gotta actually be in college ta play there." O'Brien reached for a pencil, scribbled a name and phone number on a piece of paper and handed it to Guy. "Call this man right away. He's Commissioner of the Cape Cod League. Tell him I want ya ta play down the Cape this summer. He can arrange it for ya."

PART THREE

BASEBALL AT THE BEACH, GUY'S COLGATE DANCE, AND THE KENTS HILL AND NEW YORK CITY CAPERS

CHAPTER 21

Pine Bluffs, WY
Thursday, October 14, 2004
703 Beech Street
11:15 a.m.

In June 1936, after he and his brother had their meeting with Fred O'Brien, there was no question whether or not Guy would play baseball that summer; only where it would be.

Having been led to believe that all he had to do was prove he was capable of playing in fast company, Guy came out of high school like a rocket off a launching pad. Fresh from his final season of high school baseball, accolades ringing in his young ears, he probably felt he could compete in the Northern League. But a few telephone calls would have been all it took to confirm what O'Brien had said: there was a rule permitting only college kids to compete in that league. Other than losing that election for Senior class president, this was, perhaps, the first major setback of his young life.

However, displaying the resiliency of youth, he no doubt assessed his situation along these lines. *I can't play in the Northern League unless I'm in college. But I can't get inta college without takin' some college-level courses first. I need ta figure out how ta get them, but in the meantime, the next best thing is ta play in the Cape Cod League this summer, like Mr. O'Brien says.*

Why not? The old Cape Cod League turned out some fine ball players. One, Danny MacFayden, pitched in the Cape Cod League in the early '20s before going on to a seventeen year career in the majors.[33]

---

33   Daniel Knowles (Deacon Danny) MacFayden, born June 10, 1905 in North Truro, MA, played in the Majors from 1926 through 1943, for several teams; the Boston Red Sox, New York Yankees, Boston Braves, Pittsburgh Pirates, and Washington Senators. His record: 132 wins, 159 losses, with an ERA of 3.96. Today, pitchers would kill for a career ERA like that.

In September 2001, I spoke by telephone to Judy Scarafel, Cape Cod League President, to see if the League had any records on Guy. "No, we don't have any records prior to 1965, when the 'modern era' began and the League became NCAA sanctioned. At that time Major League baseball began sending us grant money. Since then we've been able to keep excellent records."

In response to my questions, Scarafel told me that one in every six major league ball players started out in the Cape Cod League. "In the so-called 'modern era,'" she said, "players like Thurman Munson, Terry Steinbach, Mike Bordick, Chuck Knoblauch, John Valentin, Scott Erickson, Jason Varitek and many others got their first taste of top-quality baseball playing on the Cape."

With help from Ralph Wheeler, the man whose name O'Brien had given him, and maybe because he had made inquiries of the Athletic Director at Kents Hill about the availability of an athletic scholarship if he went there in the '36–'37 school year, Guy was able to secure a berth on the Barnstable club. In the thirties, Wheeler was the Boy's Sports Editor at the *Boston Herald*. He also managed the Malden City Club, a local team in the Suburban Twi-League, and ran the Cape Cod League, as its Commissioner.

Guy's decision to play for Barnstable led to his actually meeting and getting to know Edward "Pete" Herman. During the school year, Herman, in his early thirties at the time, was the Athletic Director, football, baseball and ice hockey coach at Kents Hill. Pete had played his high school baseball at Hyde Park, a Boston suburb, and his college ball at Boston College, where, as a six foot two, two hundred and twenty pound right-handed hitter, he was highly regarded.

Whether Herman was not a genuine major league talent, simply lacked the desire to try for the Bigs, or just liked working with kids, I don't know. But one thing is certain; he enjoyed baseball. For several years he had spent his summers as the player-manager for the Barnstable team. That worked for him in two ways; one was he got to rub elbows with some pretty fair young ball players and possibly recruit one or two as students for Kents Hill's Post-Graduate program. The other was he could bring a kid from Kents Hill down to the Cape with him to play summer baseball in fast company. In '36 he brought a new student, a kid who'd just signed up to attend the school that fall, a pitcher named John Maloney. Yes, it's the same kid who played for Rindge Tech.

The *Boston Post*, on July 2, 1936, in a two-inch, un-attributed article, said this about young Maloney:

JOHNNY MALONEY SURE TO MAKE KENTS HILL TEAM
Kents Hill will get a star athlete in the fall when Johnny Maloney
of Rindge Tech enters to polish up in his studies before going to college.

Maloney made the Post All-Scholastic baseball team this spring and is considered one of the best twirlers in the local school ranks. Last fall he was also one of the best halfbacks in the Suburban league and was named on one of the Post teams. In hockey, he played goaltender, so in all [he] should be a valuable addition to the Kents Hill athletic programme.

Why didn't Guy do what Maloney did that year? I don't know for sure. Had he done so, he'd have avoided at least one serious problem: he could have prepared himself to enter college a year later.

*   *   *   *

Pine Bluffs, WY
Thursday, October 14, 2004
703 Beech Street
3:15 p.m.

During the middle 1930s, there was more than cranberries growing on the Cape. It was also a hotbed of amateur baseball. Several leagues operated all up and down its seventy-five mile length. This gave tourists something else to do besides baking their backsides on the sandy beaches. There was also an Upper Cape League, a Lower Cape League, and the Industrial League, all for local kids with some talent but who were not big-league material.

However, those who knew about these things as they were in the middle thirties felt that the Cape Cod League, which annually fielded four or five teams, attracted the best ball players from among the top talent in the New England area who were not yet "connected" to or "tied up" by a major league team.

"But," Joe Rocciolo, who played ball with Guy at East Boston High School and later became a local historian of note in the Boston area says, "a kid needed a connection to get anywhere back in those days."

What about the kids who *were* connected or tied up? Where did they play during their summers? On October 30th, 2001, I talked to Lenny Merullo, who was then living in Reading, Massachusetts, with his wife, Jean—the former Mary Eugenia Geggis—about this.

"They'd play in the Northern League, which had at least four teams at that time; a couple from around Saranac Lake in New York state, and one each from Vermont and New Hampshire."

"Why did they go all the way out there, when the Cape Cod League was closer?" I asked.

"Well, the Cape Cod League had been the best at one time, but it had regressed slightly," he said. "During the middle and late '30s the Northern League was the strongest amateur league in the country. There was little or no minor league baseball at the time, but the teams in that league were 'connected' to major league teams. If a major league club was interested in a player, they'd recommend that he play for a certain team in the Northern League. I played in that League for the Burlington, Vermont club in '37 and '38. They were the Burlington Cardinals at the time. That team had players recommended by the Yankees organization. The Saranac Lake team was [made up of] players recommended by the Red Sox."

"Were there any other leagues around for the unconnected but better ball players?" I asked this question because I had some indication that in 1939, and perhaps in 1940, Guy may have played in a league known as the Twin States League.

"Yeah," Lenny said. "There was an amateur league called the Twin States League. It was an inferior league that ran at the same time as the Northern League, and it had some good ballplayers. It operated in New Hampshire and Vermont, with six or eight teams in it. I think Keene and Brattleboro each had a team in that league."

I then asked Lenny about Ralph Wheeler.

"Ralph? He was my 'Godfather,'" Merullo told me. "He was very well-thought of by athletes in the area at the time. If you had some talent and wanted to play for a club team, you'd call Ralph. He'd check around, find a team in the League that was interested, and send you down to talk with them. He helped me that way during the '35 season when I played down the Cape, for Barnstable. He probably was the one who steered Guy to Barnstable in '36."

Another good thing for some of these kids was that several Cape Cod teams were able to pay their players. Lenny Merullo again. "They'd pay ten dollars a week plus room and board. And because you could eat with any number of families, you could save nine of it."

Rocciolo had heard the same thing. "Barnstable, for at least one of those years Guy played, was able to pay its ballplayers," he said.

Dudley Jensen, of Bourne, Massachusetts, was a teacher of Kinesiology—the study of human motion—and a coach of the swimming team at William & Mary College in Virginia for fifty years. He played for Bourne's entry in the Cape Cod League for the entire '46 season, and part of the seasons in '47 and '50. I spoke to him by telephone in 2002, and learned that he is a member of the Cape Cod League's Hall of Fame Advisory Committee. He recalled it this way:

"The players came in for the summer and they'd stay at a host's home. Back before World War II, the clubs paid twenty dollars a week and provided the men with free room and board. Some Bourne players stayed at Mrs. Alden Eldridge's rooming house, although there was also a place over on Buzzard's Bay where the whole team could stay [if they had wanted to]. After the war, the teams did not pay their players, so when I played, I wasn't paid."

When Jensen learned that I was writing this book, he was very interested. "I'll send you copies of some articles I have," he volunteered. "And next week, I'll go over to the Falmouth library and copy articles from '36, '37 and '38 and send 'em to ya."

At the time Jensen and I talked, I was still living in Towson, Maryland. When I gave him my mailing address, I was surprised that he knew where it was.

"Towson? I used to bring my swimming team there, to compete against Towson State College."

"It's surely a small world," I said. "That school's only a few blocks from where I live."

Anyway, as the Cape Cod League's Commissioner, Ralph Wheeler carried a great deal of weight. His recommendation to a club manager meant a kid was a cinch to get a berth on that team. There was no direct evidence that Wheeler was the man who suggested Guy play at Barnstable. But Joe Rocciolo also believes that's the way it happened.

So, full of confidence after a spring that saw him do so well at Eastie, Guy tossed a few belongings into a brown leather bag and headed for the Cape, anxious to show what he could do and to see for himself how he stacked up in a league where *everybody* had talent. He thought all he had to do was play well, add some weight and muscle to his frame over the summer months, and Fred O'Brien would take care of the rest. After all, O'Brien had his best interests at heart, right?

Not exactly. But Guy *was* destined to add to his reputation as a damn good baseball player.

*   *   *   *

Hyannis, MA
Monday, June 29, 1936
Hallett's Field
2:20 p.m.

"Who's the leetle fella?" George Colbert, behind the plate catching batting practice for his Barnstable teammates, spit a huge mouthful of tobacco juice onto the grass behind home plate, stood and gestured toward the makeshift parking area along the field's third base line where a new arrival had just debarked from an old Ford automobile. Since Colbert was a huge, beefy giant who had played both football and baseball at Boston College many years before, to him everyone else was "leetle."

Thirty-two year old Edward 'Pete' Herman, on the mound throwing batting practice to loosen up his aging arm, glanced in the direction Colbert was indicating. "No idea," he said. "Looks like we're gonna find out, though."

He watched the new arrival, carrying a leather bag in one hand, wave good bye to an elderly man who had dropped him off, turn, and approach the field tentatively. *He walks like he's tired,* Pete thought. *Must've made the long car ride from Boston.* In those days, the Cape was difficult to reach by car, and it remained so until after World War II.

As if a bit uncertain of his welcome, the young man trudged slowly along the third base foul line until he came to the bag. There, he stopped.

"I'm lookin' for Mr. Herman," he announced.

Herman gestured to Normie Merrill, another hurler who hailed from Augusta, Maine, to take over on the mound and approached the new arrival. "*I'm* Pete Herman," he said, and stuck out a hand. "Who might you be?"

"Guy Vitale," was the cryptic response. "Mr. Wheeler said he spoke ta you about me."

"Yeah, I had a call from Ralph Wheeler," Herman responded with a smile that he hoped was welcoming. "Pretty high on ya, too." He gestured to a dilapidated wooden building down the right field line. "Uniforms are hangin' in there. Find one that fits an' change into it quick. We're just startin' battin' practice."

As Guy, bag in hand, hurried off, Colbert glowered and replaced his catcher's mask. "Don't look like he could hit his way outta a paper bag," he said to no one in particular. But the remark was loud enough for Guy to hear.

"Yeah?" Herman said to his former college chum and friend, whom he had sought out to catch for Barnstable that season. "Well that 'leetle' fella hit over .600 for his high school team this past spring. Played a pretty fair outfield for them, too."

The next batting practice batter, a right handed hitter, stepped into the box. Colbert squatted behind the plate. Unimpressed with Herman's response, the burly catcher raised his mitt and made a target for Merrill. A player and coach in the League for a number of years, Colbert was a fan favorite because of his banter and antics on the field and in the dugout. He spat another huge wad of tobacco juice in the direction of Guy's back and hollered after Herman, who had grabbed his glove and was heading for first base. "Does he shave yet?" he asked innocently.

*   *   *   *

Hyannis, MA
Monday, June 29, 1936
Hallett's Field
3:00 p.m.

Dressed in a scratchy, woolen uniform, the kind baseball players wore from the days of Abner Doubleday until well into the '50s when I played the sport, Guy left his bag in the sweltering, un-heated, un-cooled equipment shed which did double duty as a locker room of sorts, trotted back onto the field and joined several of his new teammates shagging flies in the outfield as, one after another, the hitters took their ten cuts in the batter's box. His piercing brown eyes were focused on the big catcher behind the plate, whose name he didn't yet know, but whose cutting remarks he'd clearly heard. In the past, he'd undergone his share of hazing, so he decided that, if there was to be a hazing period, he'd try to put up with it in a good natured way. *But I hope it won't last too long,* he thought. He raced to his left to catch a fly ball and rifled it into second base. *Why the hell do I feel like I'm about to audition for my high school play?*

Finally, when all had taken their turn, he saw his new manager gesturing for him to come in and hit. Trotting into the infield, Guy flipped his glove aside, grabbed two bats and began swinging them to limber his arms and shoulders.

"Don't know why yer doin' that, kid. Ain't gonna do ya no good," Colbert said as he waited for Guy to step into the box.

"Jest an old habit I picked up," Guy responded as he tossed one of the bats aside.

"Old habit, huh?" Colbert pointed to home plate. "Well, git up there an' let's see what ya can do with that toothpick."

Guy, his eyes smoky, stepped to the plate as Bob Cash, another of Barnstable's pitchers, took over on the mound. Each hurler needed to get a certain amount of throwing done between games, and tossing batting practice was the way it was accomplished. Guy didn't see the brief exchange of nods between Cash and Colbert as he addressed the plate and waited, but he had an idea what was coming, and when the big curveball came in, aimed to break inside far enough to hit him, he was not surprised.

Playing along, he dutifully bailed out of the batter's box, landing on his backside. Lots of loud laughter and a few catcalls greeted him as he regained his feet and dusted himself off, a broad grin on his face.

"What's a mattah, kid? Ain't seen a good curveball like that before?" Colbert said from behind his mask.

No answer from Guy. He stepped back in but moved up a foot to catch the next pitch, which he knew would be another curveball, before it could break very much, and waited.

"Sorry, kid. It slipped," Cash hollered from the mound. "Hit this one." He lifted his long leg into the air, reared back with lots of motion, as if he were going to carefully deliver his best heat right over the plate and threw—another big curveball.

Guy was ready. A right handed hitter, he lined it at the fellow stationed at third base, almost knocking him into left field with a rope that, in a game, would have been down the left field line for extra bases.

"Oh! I didn't mean to hit it so hard," Guy exclaimed, feigning concern. "You okay out there?" This was addressed to Bobby Maier, Barnstable's second baseman who was taking ground balls at third in case he might need to play there at some point during the season.

George Colbert had played both baseball and football in college. As a sophomore, he had led the nation's college ballplayers in hitting, a feat that earned him offers from several big league clubs wanting to tie him up. But he had turned them all down because, in exchange for their financial help, they insisted that he quit football. Because he loved the game of football, he didn't want to do that. By his senior year, he'd acquired a reputation as somewhat difficult to deal with. The offers dried up.

Could he have made it to the Bigs? He didn't know, but by now he'd convinced himself that he didn't care; that he was enjoying his life playing baseball in the summers and coaching at Franklin High during the school year. Still, deep down inside he nurtured a nagging feeling of inferiority because a baseball career hadn't materialized. *That* had led to an aggressive, somewhat hostile disposition, which he had worked to conceal with boisterous behavior during his ten previous seasons playing in the Cranberry Circuit.[34]

Big George came up out of his catcher's crouch and wiped the sweat from his brow with a huge forearm. "A wise leetle shit, ain't cha?" he bellowed, and lunged toward Guy, grabbing hold of his arm with his free hand.

---

34   Colbert had begun playing at Chatham in 1926; then managed and played for the Harwich Club in the 1930s.

Guy, taken aback, pulled away and retreated a few steps, brandishing his bat as if he might use it as a club if the situation demanded it, and thinking that he'd like to be somewhere, anywhere else just then.

Listening from the nearby bench where he was going over some papers, Pete Herman jumped up. "Okay, fellas! That's enough," he cried as he stepped between Guy and his burly catcher. "The season's only a few days away. Save your energy for that."

CHAPTER 22

Hyannis, MA
Wednesday, July 1, 1936
Hallett's Field
3:00 p.m.

Back in those days, the Cape Cod League played a bifurcated season. Each half had a champion. If different teams won the championship for each half, a play-off series was held over the Labor Day weekend, for the amusement of the fans who traveled up and down Route 6 to watch the games.

Courtesy of Alfred G. Irish, of Falmouth, Massachusetts, another member of the Old Timers Advisory Committee for the Cape Cod League's Hall of Fame, who was the assistant manager of Northeastern University's baseball team in 1939 and 1940 and its manager in 1941, this is the roster of players for Barnstable in 1936, together with their positions:

Guy Vitale,	*Left Field*
George Colbert,	*Catcher*
John Spirada,	*Right Field*
Norman Merrill,	*Pitcher, Outfielder*
"Muggsey" Kelley,	*Pitcher, Outfielder*
Bob Cash,	*Pitcher*
Wally "Red" Sullivan,	*Pitcher, Utility Infielder*
Myron "Jack" Kelley,	*Pitcher*
Harry Lane,	*Pitcher*
Norman Pilote,	*Shortstop*
Bobby Maier,	*Second Base, Third Base*
Tim Ready,	*Second Base, Utility Catcher*
Dick Conley,	*Center Field*

And of course, Edward "Pete" Herman was the manager. He played first base and also twirled a bit on the mound. On Thursday, July 9, 1936, the column *Batteries For Barnstable* said this about Herman:

> This is 'Pete' Herman's tenth season on the Cape. [Myron] Ruckstull
> of Falmouth and 'Pete' are rivals for the honor of being in the league
> for the longest period.

Playing mostly at second and a bit at third base for Barnstable in 1936 was a wise-cracking, gum-chewing kid named Robert Phillip Maier, from Dunellen, New Jersey. Did he and Guy get to be friends that summer? Probably. Two years older than Guy, Bobby Maier would make another appearance in Guy Vitale's life several years later on Maryland's Eastern Shore where, in 1941, Guy would play his first year of professional ball for the Salisbury Indians.

Maier? He went on from the Eastern Shore League, eventually spending the 1945 season as a third baseman with the Detroit Tigers. The smooth-fielding infielder would play in one hundred thirty-two games for the Tigers in 1945, including an appearance in the World Series, where he would bat a *perfect* 1,000, going one for one in his only plate appearance. But there I go getting ahead of myself again.

*   *   *   *

Barnstable, MA
Thursday, July 9, 1936
Hallett's Field
1:35 p.m.

The first half of the 1936 baseball season opened officially on Friday, July 3rd, with Barnstable opposing Falmouth. Bob Cash was Pete Herman's choice as his opening day hurler, but the long layoff since the close of the college baseball season found his control lacking. A guy named Drisko pitched for Falmouth. It must have been an intimidating experience having this guy with a hook nose and a skinny neck firing fast balls at their knees and breaking off curveballs over the plate, because Drisko had the situation well in hand for several innings.

Normie Merrill, the kid from Augusta, Maine, who could pitch, play some outfield, and hit, slugged a grand slam for Barnstable in the bottom of the ninth, but Jack Walsh's Falmouth club had piled up a big lead by then, which Barnstable, off to a slow start, could not overcome. The final score was Falmouth 11, Barnstable 5.

To cap things off, Colbert, sliding into second, wrenched a knee and was lost to Barnstable for several games, something that only exacerbated his foul mood.

On the Fourth of July, Barnstable played two games against Harwich; one in the morning and another in the afternoon, changing parks in the process. Harwich won the morning game, six to four, a base running boo-boo snuffing out a Barnstable rally in the ninth inning.

But the boisterous Fourth of July fans were treated to a fine game at Hallett's Field in the afternoon, as Barnstable edged Harwich three to one in a pitching duel between 'Muggsey' Kelley of Barnstable and Ken Wiedaw of Harwich.

It wasn't until Sunday, July 5th, that Barnstable's hitters made themselves heard when they went on a hitting spree against Bourne in a lengthy game that didn't end until almost 6:00 p.m. Barnstable pounded out fourteen hits including a home run by Bobby Maier. Final score? Barnstable 12, Bourne 4. After four games, all four clubs were tied with two wins and two losses.

*   *   *   *

Pine Bluffs, WY
Thursday, October 14, 2004
703 Beech Street
1:05 p.m.

Actually, much to Colbert's chagrin, Guy, motivated by the thought that major league clubs were interested in him, got off to a pretty good start that summer. A couple of weeks after the bifurcated season began, Vic Stout, sports writer for *The Boston Traveler,* who, twenty years later, in 1956, would trade his job at the newspaper for the post of Athletic Director at Boston University, wrote this in his column:

> *Congrats to Guy Vitale, one of the finest all-around athletes to graduate from E. B. High this year, who is now playing ball with the Barnstable Club of the Cape Cod League. In his first week facing experienced flingers, Vitale made 13 hits out of 19 trips to the plate … and six of 'em were two-base clouts.*

A week or two later, Stout mentioned Guy again:

> *Peter Herman at Barnstable has a star in Guy Vitale, East Boston boy who is making them all step for outfield honors. Vitale broke into*

*the fast Cape company with a bang and still is banging away. Herman
is enthusiastic in his praise of Vitale.*

Why did Stout write that? Because in Guy's first week of regular play at
Barnstable, hitting against quality pitchers who were probably a lot better than
those he had faced in the Boston District League, his thirteen hits in nineteen
plate appearances included six doubles; a slugging average of almost .500. This
from a kid who was only eighteen years old and would not turn nineteen until
October of that year.

Later that season, Stout wrote about Guy yet again:

> *Guy Vitale, the youngest player in the league, continues to mace the
> ball for Pete Herman's Barnstable team. The recent East Boston High
> School athlete is in the runner-up position with an average of .389 and
> a goodly number of his base hits have been for extra bases.*

At the time, Guy's .389 batting average put him in second place in the
league, behind Joe Cusick, a catcher from Holy Cross, who was backstopping
that summer for Falmouth. Cusick, who had played for Falmouth in 1935 and
had caught all five playoff games against Barnstable that year, emerging as the
hitting star of that series, was batting .405 to that point. Guy's average placed
him ahead of both stringy John Spirada and big George Colbert, two teammates who were hitting .384 and .333 respectively.

He also was doing better than another older man named Tony Plansky, who
was playing baseball for Bourne that summer. I went back to Dudley Jensen
and asked who this fellow was:

"Tony Plansky? He was named one of the top one hundred athletes of the
Twentieth Century by the *Boston Globe*, recently. Number sixty-two, I think"

"It seems a bit presumptuous of a newspaper to do that," I responded. "Is he
really that good?"

"Well, he played four years of college football at Georgetown as a halfback.
Also, ran track and played baseball. While he was there, he participated in a
decathlon and set a relay record. Then he broke his own record the next year."

"What's a decathlon?"

"That's an athletic contest with about ten different events in it. The contes-
tant with the highest total score wins."

"Oh."

"Yep. Then he played professional football for the old New York Football
Giants in 1928 and 1929. After that, he disappeared for a year and then surfaced

in the Braves farm system. He'd been drafted by the Philadelphia Phillies and traded to them."

"Did he ever play in the Majors?" I asked.

"No. Never made it to the Majors. But he played baseball on the Cape in 1934 and then from 1936 through 1939. Made the Cape All-Star team each year."

"Is that all?" I joked.

"Actually, it's not," Jensen deadpanned. "He was a star left halfback in 1932 for the Pere Marquettes football team, which I think was a six-man semi-professional team in the Boston area."

"What did this fella do for a living?"

"He became the track coach at Williams College in Williamstown, Massachusetts. That stuck in my head because the name of the college was so close to the name of the school I coached at. He stayed there for twenty years, and then retired."

Would the kid from East Boston hang onto that second spot all season, or fade as the hot, sultry July and August weather sapped the strength from his young body? I asked Bruce Hack, the Cape Cod Baseball League's Historian, to check this out for me, and he e-mailed me the results of his research:

> I found a reference on July 30 that said Tony Plansky led the league in hitting and was the 'best batter in the league and the fastest'.

*   *   *   *

Barnstable, MA
Thursday, August 20, 1936
Hallett's Field
10:30 a.m.

The season had been long, hot and anything but boring. Bourne won the first half championship, as Barnstable, although leading the League in team batting, could not seem to get that timely hit to drive needed runs across. However, the second half was different.

On Thursday, August 20th, 1936, exactly one year before I was born, the *Batteries For Barnstable* column reported this:

> Speaking of the Cape League, the [Barnstable] team will be in a close contest for the championship of the second half over this weekend
> ... The standings on Thursday had Harwich leading with 7 wins and

6 losses, Falmouth with 6 and 4, Bourne with 6 and 6, and Barnstable with 5 wins and 6 losses. It's anybody's race. As this is the case, there ought to be record crowds on hand for the weekend games.

Barnstable would be matched against Falmouth on Friday and Bourne on Saturday, playing both games away from home. Then, on Sunday and Monday, they'd play Bourne and Falmouth at home. On both Saturday and Sunday, the ninth inning proved fatal to Herman's Hitters.

That Saturday, Bourne, behind nine to seven, staged one of the biggest rallies of the season at Hallett's Field, scored eight runs, including three homers, and defeated Barnstable fifteen to nine. History repeated itself on Sunday, as Falmouth came from behind to tie the score at nine all in the ninth, and then pushed across the winning run in the tenth.

But despite the misfortunes of his club, Guy was doing very well. He missed going to daily Mass at Saint Lazarus, but to compensate for that, he'd set up a little prayer table in a corner of his room. A crucifix sticking out of a global map of the world was on it. Every morning, he knelt before it and said the *Acts of Faith, Hope and Charity, the Morning Offering,* and a few other prayers before heading off to the field for practice or a game. Still, with no Roman Catholic church in the area, he missed the Eucharist; his communion, if you will, with God and Jesus.

Here's what *Batteries For Barnstable* had to say about him, also on Thursday, August 20th, 1936:

> *Guy Vitale, the Greater Boston football and baseball All-Scholastic star, is measuring up to expectations. He has been right on top of the Cape Cod League in the matter of hitting and to date is the leading hitter on the [Barnstable] club. Colbert is right on his heels with a pretty respectable batting average.*

But the team's spotty play continued. On Sunday, August 23rd, Bob Cash lost a game against Bourne when his defense fell apart behind him in the first two innings, making two errors that left him behind four to zip by the top of the third. Bourne added two more in the ninth to win it six to nothing, but Guy and Bobby Maier were the only Barnstable players to get hits off the Bourne pitcher.

Batteries For Barnstable, on August 27th, lamented:

> *The Barnstable team has appeared helpless at bat the whole week.*
> *The sudden slump in hitting accounts largely for the recent losses.*
>
> *The whole Barnstable team has been hitting the ball hard but right*
> *into sombody's hands and altogether too often for double plays. It has*
> *been tragic to see Barnstable get the first man on base and often the*
> *second and third and have him (sic) die there. The club must have set*
> *some kind of record for the number of men left on bases and for the*
> *number of [double] plays which it has hit into.*
>
> *The 1934 and 1935 Barnstable teams that were champions of the*
> *league and of the half [respectively], were noted for their ability to*
> *stage last inning rallies and to pull games out of the fire … It has been*
> *a different story with the 1936 outfit. It has been victimized by late*
> *inning uprisings by its opponents and has lost several games in the*
> *final frames.*
>
> *The team is made up of a fine lot of fellows and Manager Pete*
> *Herman has handled them conscientiously and has taught them a lot*
> *of ball. The team just hasn't been able to come through in the pinches*
> *or to have the punch to keep in there until the final gun. It has given*
> *the fans some good ball games and turned in some good plays and the*
> *fans have been pleased with the conduct of the boys.*
>
> *There will be games over the Labor Day weekend whether champi-*
> *ons or not. An announcement of the schedule for the final games will*
> *appear in this column next week.*

And games there were. But Barnstable did not fare well, dropping decisions on Sunday, Monday and Tuesday, each by one run. On Monday evening, Pete Herman left for Kents Hill to resume his duties there, and George Colbert, who had managed in the League before at Harwich during the early '30s, took over the struggling ball club.

On September 3, 1936, *Batteries For Barnstable* reported this:

> *Guy Vitale has been the leading hitter of the team and league dur-*
> *ing this half. He has turned in a performance that shows he was wor-*
> *thy of the All-Scholastic honors that he gained.*

On the evening of Thursday, September 3rd, at the League meeting of Directors, Bourne protested its game played against Falmouth that afternoon. After considering the matter, the Directors awarded the game to Bourne, thus making that Club champion of the second half. Since it had also won the first half championship, it was automatically named League Champion for 1936. Barnstable finished second to Bourne, with a record of 20 wins and 24 losses.

The League had originally planned to hold a playoff series over the Labor Day weekend. However, Bourne's Directors reported that, although it had financed itself successfully to that point, it was out of money and could not play any more games. Falmouth, looking at the number of players it would lose to colleges, decided it could not participate, either. So, simply for the enjoyment of tourists and local fans, Barnstable and Falmouth played several exhibition games over the holiday weekend.

And Barnstable won the Saturday game, behind the pitching of Harry Lane. Guy started in right field that day, and produced the games' only triple to begin the scoring for Barnstable. His team went on to win, six to two.

They lost on Sunday and again on Monday morning, but closed out their season with a win on Monday afternoon, seven to two.

Several days after the season finale, on Thursday, September 10th, 1936, the *Batteries For Barnstable* column, referenced Guy once more:

> *Guy Vitale led the Barnstable club [in the second half] in hitting with an average of .371. He finished second in the League standing, with Tony Plansky in first place with an average of .374.*

So there's your answer. Guy *did* have a great second half of the bifurcated season. He *did* hold on to second place and finished the season in that spot.

For a kid still a month shy of his nineteenth birthday to finish only three percentage points behind a man who'd been picked as one of the Nation's one hundred top athletes, was not too shabby.

And now we see another interesting thing; a new wrinkle that appeared in Guy Vitale's life, which at one and the same time, threatened to both solve a problem and complicate matters for him. Here's what I'm talking about.

In that same column mentioned above, a reference to Guy Vitale and Colgate University appeared:

> *The fans will follow the boys with interest during the coming year and especially with the opening of college baseball in the spring. It will be rather easy to keep tabs on Bob Cash, Myron Kelley, Harry Lane and Norman Pilote, since they will all be at B.C. It will be a bit harder to get information on Bob Maier from New Jersey ... and Wally 'Red' Sullivan will be in Quincy and Guy Vitale enters Colgate. John Spirada will be at St. Andrews. Tim Ready was not certain as to*

his plans when he left Labor Day night. He graduated from college this year and plans to embark upon a career. The other two members of the Barnstable squad are Pete Herman and George Colbert. The supporting public follows them to see how their respective teams are turning out at Kents Hill and Franklin High.

How did this reporter know that Guy would "enter Colgate" in the fall? Apparently that tidbit of information was gleaned from Guy himself. How it came about, we'll get to in a minute.

So anyway, the 1936 summer season came to an end, the players dispersed to their homes and went about their business; college, work or whatever. A few months later, toward the end of 1936, *The Boston Traveler* published its Schoolboy Hall of Fame for that year. As it explained:

> *Continuing a custom established two years ago, the Traveler today prints its 1936 Schoolboy Hall of Fame. Membership in this elite group is attained as a result of individual excellence in the various major sports, while a special niche in this gallery of scholastic brilliants is reserved for the most versatile athlete of the year.*

The winner in the Baseball category? Guy Vitale.

> *BASEBALL—GUY VITALE. East Boston—Peculiar thing about this Noddle Islander. He was not a unanimous all-scholastic baseball choice last spring. But this was only because some of the boys picking the teams failed to see him play. His batting average in schoolboy competition was almost unbelievable. He wound up the year with an average in excess of .650. He was also a great base runner, a fair fielder, and the possessor of a great 'gun'.*
>
> *That he was no flash in the pan was indicated when he went down to the Cape League last summer and led the league in batting. Guy attended Colgate for several days this past fall, but was forced to quit college owing to financial reasons. But his future in organized baseball is a most promising one.*

The reference to "led the league in batting" is an erroneous reference to Guy's performance in the second half of the summer season. We know he finished second to Tony Plansky. *The Traveler's* overall assessment of Guy, however, was accurate. Joe Rocciolo again:

"My memory of Guy was he could have signed with the Boston Red Sox, New York Yankees, or the Cleveland Indians at the end of 1936 when he was number one or number two hitter in the Cape Cod League, with a .360+ batting average. He was (just) eighteen years old, youngest in the league that year, as most were either in or already out of college."

CHAPTER 23

Pine Bluffs, WY
Saturday, October 16, 2004
703 Beech Street
7:25 a.m.

In January 1936, Adolph Hitler nullified the arms limitations imposed on Germany after Word War I by the Treaty of Versailles. The world took a look at that, bowed to the Kraut lovers, sympathizers and appeasers of Europe and America, and let him get away with it. If the League of Nations had taken a united stand and forceful action against Germany at that time, World War II might not have happened.

At the beginning of this book, I said one of Guy's dreams was to play professional baseball and the other was to get a college degree. At this point in his young life, Guy Vitale, the boy, had no way of knowing that a European Hitler and an Asian Hirohito would eventually drive the final stakes into the dreams of Guy Vitale, the man. But we'll get to that later. We've been talking about his baseball dream. Now, I'm going to tell you about his other dream.

Back when he was growing up most kids wanted to go to college. A lot of their parents were immigrants without much education, so they were anxious for their kids to get more schooling and do better than they did. That's why they did whatever it took, sometimes working day and night to pay for it, and they drilled it into the kids. "Learn! Get an education. Finish high school. Go to college."

Did Guy's parents, Nicola and Rosaria, share that view? I don't think so. Not totally. Other than the vague idea that people ought to improve themselves, busy making a living in a new country, they just didn't have the time to think about it much, if at all. So they really didn't see the value of a college education for their kids.

It was difficult for them. Nick worked from seven in the morning until six at night, as a barber in his little shop in what had been a bedroom on one end of their apartment. Rosaria ran the grocery store out of a space on the other end. She got up at five every day to till, weed, and water the fruit and vegetables she grew on their little sliver of land across the street. Then she'd pick the ripe stuff, carry it into the house in her apron, wash and clean it all, and arrange it in the store's display trays for sale later that day.

They worked hard. But I think their inability to understand the culture and the language caused anxieties and fears way out of proportion to what was real. So even though they struggled and eventually made some money, they were always reluctant to part with any of it. The only thing they spent money on, besides ordinary living expenses was their investments in real estate. *That* was so they could make *more* money. They weren't exactly stingy people. But in a strange new country, living among people who were … different, they just never understood how much money was going to be *enough.* College tuition? They couldn't visualize the benefit to them, down the road.

For girls back then it was worse. Parents didn't consider an education all that important for daughters, so they didn't even insist that they finish high school. My mother was the oldest. The story she always told was that she quit school after the sixth grade. If that were true, she would have been twelve or thirteen, and since she could not have gone out to work in a factory anywhere until she turned sixteen, I think she probably was put to work in Rosaria's grocery store for a few years. Later, after that stint down in Brooklyn at the nursing school, finding that she was unable to break into the nursing ranks, she hired on at W. F. Schrafft & Company, a chocolate factory in Boston.

So, she worked in the chocolate factory for a few years. She would have turned twenty-one on January 25th, 1926. The following June she was still there, making $26.50 a week. I *know* that's true because I found an old pay envelope for the week of June 30th, 1926 in with her personal stuff after she died. She'd kept it all those years.

When my Uncle Frank finished high school in 1933, jobs were *really* scarce. He couldn't find anything, so he, too, helped out in the grocery store until he could get something else. Eventually, he found a job at Roslynoid's, the eyeglass factory nearby. The following year he met the girl he'd marry, Madeline Riley. The Italians and the Irish didn't get along back then, and Maddy's father didn't approve of Italian boys. So they eventually eloped to Manchester, New Hampshire, where Frank found work in the printing business. But that job didn't last long. Later, after returning to Boston he drove a cab for awhile until he hired on at *The Boston Globe.*

Joe Rocciolo again: "To fill up time, Frank Vitale played baseball for Saint Lazarus's team for two or three years. Then he came to the attention of Julio Santo, a local guy who was head of the Typesetter's Union. Santo recruited locals from Saint Lazarus to play for the Typos, the Union's baseball team. He would get them jobs at the *Globe* as line-o-type operators. They'd work nights and play baseball during the day. So, Frank played ball for the Typos for years after that, while working at the *Globe*."

*   *   *   *

Pine Bluffs, WY
Sunday, October 17, 2004
703 Beech Street
5:00 p.m.

At *this* point, Guy didn't know that, wary of Fred O'Brien's demand for a ten grand signing bonus, a very large sum of money at that time, the professional clubs interested in him had backed off. Both the Boston Red Sox and the Detroit Tigers had been approached by O'Brien. But when they heard what O'Brien said his prospect wanted in order to sign, they told him that, despite Guy's terrific showing on the Cape that summer, they considered him too small for them to make that kind of investment at the time, but that maybe after he attended college for a couple of years and filled out more, they'd reconsider and tie him up; perhaps give him some cash for tuition or do something for him in return for his agreement to sign.

O'Brien, concealing what was by that time, in my opinion, a huge alcohol problem, was having trouble juggling his job at the Probation Department, his coaching of football, baseball and track at Eastie, and the agent's thing for Guy and a few other top athletes. I'd already been told of O'Brien's problem by two people; Joe Rocciolo and Tony Marmo, and had some additional corroboration by J.W. Mooney, at the end of an article previously described. But, I felt that I needed more before writing about it. So on October 1st, 2001, I went back to Joe Rocciolo and told him I wanted some additional information.

"Another person you wanna talk to is Joe Sarro. He's the head Historian for the Boston Public Library. Been there for twenty-nine years. He grew up in East Boston. Knew the Vitale family *and* the Sacco family, too." He gave me a number and hung up.

The next morning, I called the Library. My long-distance telephone bill was now approaching the value of all the gold deposited in Fort Knox. After a brief wait, Sarro came on the line. I told him who I was and who referred me to him.

"Yes, Joe Rocciolo's a great guy. Him, me and Carmen Merullo get together on Saturday mornings at the Burger King for breakfast."

"Did you know my uncle?" I asked.

"Yeah, I knew Guy Vitale, too. He was on East Boston's track team with my brother during their junior and senior years. Ran in relays. Won some awards in track while he was there. But a few years back, there was a break-in at East Boston High and your uncle's trophies and awards were stolen outta the trophy case in the lobby, along with lots of others."

"What about Fred O'Brien? What can you tell me about him?"

"The coach? He was a Probation Officer in the Boston Municipal Court System. Had an office in the East Boston District Court Building for years. He was a drunk!"

I sucked in my breath. Was this the independent corroboration I was looking for? And from a man who had no axe to grind?

"Why do you say that?" I asked.

"It was common knowledge around East Boston in the mid 1930s" he said. I waited for more. Then, "Too bad old McCarthy isn't still alive."

"Who?"

"McCarthy. He was a teacher at Eastie who helped out with the teams for years. O'Brien's assistant. Had ta handle the teams many, many time because O'Brien was too drunk ta do it. He took over for O'Brien later, when he retired in '46 or '47. Coach O'Brien was seventy years old by then. You know "Red" Baccigalupo?"

"No."

"Well, get a hold of him. He's retired now. Grew up in East Boston and later moved ta Winthrop and became Fire Chief over there. He knows some stuff about O'Brien."

*   *   *   *

East Boston, MA
Sunday, August 23, 1936
20 Breed Street
4:30 p.m.

With the kind of judgment that gets clouded by the sauce when you've been drinking heavily over a long period of time, O'Brien apparently kept stringing Guy along, telling him that no less than three clubs were interested, and that signing was a sure thing. But to cover his tail, he also told Guy that maybe he should think about college first.

Since college was one of Guy's dreams, I believe he'd already made overtures to Kents Hill in his senior year of high school, and had perhaps even made tentative plans to attend that school in the fall of 1936. That would certainly explain the notation on his sketch when the *Herald* named its All-Scholastic Baseball team that year. But it would *not* explain where he thought he'd get the money for tuition. For that, he'd either need to approach his parents or ... push for an athletic scholarship.

By August 1936, young and inexperienced in matters of the world, but nearing the end of a great summer season of baseball, which made the Kents Hill thing seem doable, I think he bought O'Brien's story and began to firm up his plan to go to Kents Hill; tuition, room and board would be needed but might be covered by an athletic scholarship.

But first, like any good kid would, he went to his parents to see if they could provide the financial help he needed. And their weekly Sunday afternoon dinner was the place he chose to do it.

"You want to do what, son?" Nick Vitale occupying his regular place at the head of the old oak dining room table with lion's claw feet, looked up from his dinner of pork chops, mashed potatoes and home-grown beets. A decanter of Port wine stood in the center of the table. Next to his plate was a bill for a new roof to replace the leaky one on the property at 18 Everett Street, East Boston, which they had recently bought to rent out. So you can see that Guy's timing was not the best. Nick, now fairly fluent in English, spoke in the language of his adopted country.

"College, Pa. I wanna go ta college." Guy had just returned from a swim in nearby Chelsea Creek with some of the neighbor kids. His dark hair was still damp, but since he often came home with wet or damp hair due to showering at school after practices or games, his parents didn't take any notice.

Nick glanced across the table at his wife, and caught the set of her chin and the almost imperceptible shaking of her head to indicate a negative.

"Guy, you know we can't afford college tuition," he said.

"Well, it's not college tuition I need. It's for prep school."

Nick's eyebrows shot up. "Prep school?"

"Yeah, Pa. I need ta get some courses that Eastie didn't have, so I can get inta a good college later on."

"It doesn't matter," Nick said. "We can't afford that, either." Picking up his knife and fork, he began attacking a pork chop.

"Why not? The store's doin' good now. And so's the barber shop."

"Your ma and I didn't do that for Albert or Frank. They went to work after high school. They're making their own way. Maria and Anna, too."

Guy slumped in his chair. As the youngest, he was accustomed to getting his way. Not always, but most of the time. "But it's *only* a few hundred dollars, Pa. And I could pay ya back later, after I finished school and got a job …" Remembering the professional baseball thing, he added, "… or somethin'."

Rosaria cleared her throat, her dark eyes now a steely gray. "No, Guy! And that's final. Let's not hear another word about it."

Guy slammed his fork down next to his plate. "You don't understand," he said. "This is important ta me." His eyes searched the faces of one parent, then the other, but getting no further response from either, he felt the bitter sting of defeat.

"Okay!" he said. "But I'm goin'. If you won't help, I'll find a way ta do it myself." Pushing his chair back, he jumped up from the table and stomped out of the room.

*　　*　　*　　*

Pine Bluffs, WY
Monday, October 18, 2004
703 Beech Street
7:35 a.m.

It's not uncommon for boys Guy's age to disagree with their parents. They're growing up, developing their own ideas and opinions about things; life, the world, politics, religion. They're becoming their own persons. Lots of people say disagreements are necessary if a kid is going to develop his own identity and become independent of his parents. That's true, and inevitable. But I'm not talking about huge blow-ups; big traumatic things that cause hatred and anger. I don't think those things are necessary at all in order for a kid to mature.

Now Guy, being the youngest, was more grown up than most kids his age. He'd already developed an independent streak; the extent of which was probably not known by either Rosaria or Nicola, as preoccupied with making a living as they were. But it was there.

A good example was the swimming thing in Chelsea Creek. The neighborhood boys all went there for a cool swim during those sizzling summer days. It was against the law to swim there. And dangerous, too, because of tidal currants. But that didn't stop them. They swam buck naked, with one eye out for girls and the other for cops. Their parents had told them not to do it. But they did it anyway. It wasn't done from hatred, or malice, nor to deliberately disobey.

You remember how that was? Usually, we didn't mean to defy our parents or lie to them, either. It was just something we did, like walking on a railroad track or experimenting with cigarettes out behind the garage, even though we'd been told time and time again not to, and we knew it was not smart to do those things. We'd do them and we never told our parents. It was a right of passage. We had to grow up, and taking a few risks now and then was part of it.

So being kind of independent, when Guy said he was going to find a way to get to prep school and college, he meant it. And I think this was just one of several issues that caused serious resentments to develop between him and his mother and father; wounds that would fester until their deaths years later.

*   *   *   *

Pine Bluffs, WY
Wednesday, October 20, 2004
703 Beech Street
7:05 a.m.

I don't know exactly how, when, or why Guy decided on Colgate. It might have been the other way around. Maybe Colgate decided on *him*. And it had to have happened late in the summer of '36, after he'd begun talking to people at Kents Hill about an athletic scholarship, and possibly making plans to attend that school. I say this because, even way back then, some advance planning was necessary, and some advance discussions had to take place before a kid would be admitted to a place like Kents Hill.

What happened to make him change direction from prep school to college? Colgate happened. That's what. But prep school or college, Guy still had the same problems; money for tuition, room and board and the need to acquire the necessary courses or if he could get in, the need to show that he could cut it in college.

Now, Guy wasn't a big kid, only about five foot seven and maybe a hundred sixty-five pounds. Not many top college teams were interested in either a quarterback or a halfback that small, and Colgate's Red Raiders, unscored upon and unbeaten in the 1932 season, were still, in 1936, fielding one of the best college football teams in America.

But Guy was the exception to that rule. In high school, he'd been a triple threat; he could run, pass and kick the pigskin. On the field, he displayed a *presence* not often found in kids his age. And his kicking was outstanding. I figure *that* had to be it; the talent that tipped the scales of Colgate's interest toward him. You don't have to be big to punt, kick off or place-kick extra points—just good. Without money for tuition, if Guy was going to be the first Vitale to go to college, it would have to be on the basis of his athletics.

Joe Rocciolo has another explanation of how Guy became interested in Colgate or how Colgate became interested in him.

"Guy could run, pass and punt," he said. "Skip Sherlock, who was coaching at Hyde Park, had graduated from Colgate. I heard he went to O'Brien and asked him if Guy would be interested in goin' ta Colgate ta play football and baseball. But Skip told O'Brien they wanted Guy ta play football full-time rather than ta just do the punting."

I could not find evidence to back this up, but it *is* plausible. While looking into it, however, I *did* find out that Pete Herman had gone to Hyde Park High and probably played sports for Skip Sherlock; another possible tie between Sherlock and Guy.

That Guy had *some* involvement with Colgate back at that time was known. As I said before, Guy was named *The Boston Traveler's* Schoolboy Hall of Fame's baseball player of the year for '36. That article was written in November 1936, and there was a mention of Colgate in it in relation to Guy:

> *... Guy attended Colgate for several days this past fall, but was forced to quit college owing to financial reasons ...*

Another mention of Guy and Colgate appeared a year later in *The Barnstable Patriot*, on Thursday, July 1, 1937. In that one they were talking about the opening of the 1937 baseball season on the Cape, describing the teams and their players.

> *... Edward 'Pete' Herman, coach at Kents Hill prep in Maine will again be skipper for the Barnstable team. His roster of players includes John 'Muggsy' Kelly of Boston College, Norman Merrill of John Carroll, and Maloney of Kents Hill as pitchers, with Pete himself taking an occasional turn. Stanley Bergeron of Bates at first, Francis 'Cowboy' Crawley of Villanova at second, Paul Sharkey of B.C. at shortstop, and Roy Williams of English High, Boston at third. For outfield, Herman will have John Spirada of St. Augustine, Guy Vitale of Colgate, and Tim Ready of B.C ...*

Where were these reporters getting information that Guy may have attended Colgate? Probably from Guy himself. That was understandable as to late '36, but a bit troubling as late as '37, when Guy obviously knew that Colgate was out of the picture.

What's my problem with this Colgate thing? Well, from my own knowledge of family events I knew Guy didn't graduate from Colgate, and I also knew that if he ever went there at all it had to have been for *only* a very short time. Furthermore, I know for a fact that, in the late '40s, while living in Washington, D.C., he attended night school at George Washington University, still chasing that elusive college degree.

And what happened to the Kents Hill thing? When he was released from the Army in 1945, his discharge papers didn't say anything about attendance at any college. But they *did* mention Kents Hill, a prep school in Maine, as the last school he ever attended before entering the Army on February 7, 1942.

Guy's brother, Frank, had moved to a retirement community in Rochester, New Hampshire with my Aunt Madeline and a daughter, Linda.[35] I talked to him several times about Guy and Colgate, the first time as early as 1995. He remembered it like this:

"Yes, Guy went to Colgate. Was up there for a while. But they wanted him to play football full-time and he didn't want to. So he came home."

Knowing that memories tend to blur with the passage of time, I still wasn't satisfied. I thought it would be great to know when he went there and how long he stayed. So I decided to work on it some to find out what actually happened.

My first step was to contact Robin Summers, who was the Associate Director of Alumni Affairs at Colgate, and describe my problem to her.

"Well Carl Peterson, the current Archivist at the University, may be able to help with this," she told me. "I'll give you his number and tell him you're going to call him."

Which I did, later that afternoon, and when I got hold of him I asked him if it was possible for a kid back then to get into Colgate on his athletic ability alone; a scholarship, maybe. Peterson was really cooperative.

"He (Guy) would not have had a scholarship as such, but it's my understanding that students at that date sometimes were admitted largely because of their football skills." I took that to mean it could have happened.

I went back to Robin Summers for more help. "Now that I know it was possible for him to get in," I said, "I need to find some record that he actually went there."

"I understand," she said. "Vicky Stone, my assistant in the Alumni Office might be able to find something. Let me get her on the line."

---

35 Frank J. Vitale died December 24, 2004 in Rochester, NH. Madeline Riley Vitale died one week before, on December 16, 2004.

When Vicki came on, Robin explained the situation. "Well," Vicki said, "I can crank up the main computer. It has the names and addresses of every student who ever went here. We should be able to pull your uncle's name up."

"How long will that take," I asked skeptically.

"Only a few minutes. If you can hold the line, I'll do it now while you wait."

She put me on hold and I waited, listening to Colgate's canned music and drumming my fingers on the table. It took more than a few minutes, but I didn't mind waiting. When she came back, the news was not good.

"I went all the way back to 1930, Tony. His name's not in there."

"Well thanks for your help," I said and was about to hang up.

"Wait. There's one more thing we might try," Vicki said. "Robin and I can examine the old yearbooks from 1938 through 1940 to see if there's any mention of him. I'll get back to you later today."

I thanked her and hung up, thinking I'd probably never hear from her again. I was wrong. A couple hours later, Vicki was back on the line.

"We looked in the old yearbooks, but we couldn't find any sign of him," she said.

"No?"

"Nope. We also looked in the class lists, class pictures, and the sections on football, baseball and track. Nothing. So then Robin asked Carl Peterson to check old yearbooks for 1936 and 1937 down there in the Archives. When he reported back, his note said, 'I can find no record that Guy Vitale attended Colgate. I checked football pictures in the '36 and '37 yearbooks and could not locate him there, either.'"

"I guess we're kind of at a dead end, huh?"

"Well, no," she said. "There's something *else* we can do. You should talk to Carol Swam in the Records Department because they have hard files on every student who was ever here, whether they graduated or not."

"Even if they were only there for a day or two?"

"Yes."

"Great. I'll call her tomorrow morning."

Next day, when I called there Carol was out, so I spoke to Jeanette Lollman, her assistant. If you ever need to research something at Colgate, Jeannette is the kind of person you want to talk to; helpful and quick, too. She searched old Alumni Directories from 1923 through 1964, which listed students who were there for a semester or more. No luck. Then she searched other records for "people who stayed only a short time." Drew a blank there, too. So I hung up, puzzled. The mystery was still unsolved.

CHAPTER 24

Pine Bluffs, WY
Thursday, October 21, 2004
703 Beech Street
7:05 a.m.

Well, did Guy ever actually go to Colgate? The answer is "yes and no," and don't get smart with me, that's the best I can do.

That he *was* at Colgate for at least a short time is fairly certain. We have his brother's recollection and several independent references in newspaper articles to go by.

So why wasn't there a record of him at the University? Maybe he wasn't there very long. Maybe it was a *very* short time, like a week or less.

*   *   *   *

Hamilton, NY
Tuesday, September 8, 1936
Colgate University
9:30 a.m.

Hamilton is in upstate New York, where they have some really frigid winters. It warms up in the spring, but not until later. So schools up that way don't emphasize baseball. The season's not long enough. Football and basketball are the biggies. That, in and of itself, tended to raise a question in my mind as to why, if Guy wanted to play professional baseball, he would have tried to get into a school that didn't have a very good baseball program. The answer? At this point, which college he attended was not important to him. What mattered was that he play baseball in the Northern League, and for that he simply had to be in college—any college. And, because of a lack of funds, he probably didn't have any choice as to which school he'd attend. His ability as a football player

202

was going to be his ticket into college, and Colgate, being interested, was the "bird in the hand," so to speak.

Back then Colgate, under Coach Andy Kerr,[36] had a great football program, possibly the fourth or fifth best in the nation. For example, just look at this. In 1932, the Red Raiders reeled off seven successive wins and by November 7th they were unbeaten and unscored upon. Colgate's president at the time, George B. Cotton, announced that the team had received a Rose Bowl bid, and if it finished with a perfect record, the team would travel to Pasadena to play on New Year's Day. Well, the team finished strong that year, crushing Brown 21–0 on Turkey Day, but unfortunately Colgate did not get the expected Rose Bowl invitation. It went to Pitt instead.

Anyway, Coach Kerr, with teams like Notre Dame, Army, and Michigan on the schedule, recruited hot and heavy, going after some of the best high school talent in the country. By '36 he had been coaching there for five years, and was well-liked at the school and well-respected in coaching circles. But also by '36, there was a rumor floating around that he'd been bringing in ringers; kids who didn't have a snowball's chance in hell of graduating from any college. But they'd play at Colgate for a year two and then leave.

Well, Guy wasn't a ringer. Matter of fact, he was a pretty bright kid. We're going to see just how bright when he spent the 1937–38 school year at Kents Hill.

After reviewing all the information I developed, this is the way I think it went down.

*   *   *   *

Hamilton, NY
Tuesday, September 8, 1936
Colgate University
10:00 a.m.

On a secondary gridiron near the main practice field, Guy Vitale and two other punters were working under the watchful eyes of an assistant coach, a new guy

---

36   Andrew Kerr, IV was born in Cheyenne, WY on October 7, 1878. A graduate of Dickinson College in 1900, where he played 3 years of varsity baseball, he became head football coach at Colgate in 1931, and served there for 18 seasons. His teams were outstanding, using the double wing with precise lateral "razzle-dazzle" offensive inventions. His 1932 team was unbeaten, untied, and unscored upon, with a record of 9–0 and a point total of 264. In 1946, he left Colgate due to their mandatory retirement age rule, but continued coaching at Lebanon Valley College until 1950. He died on February 17, 1969, at the age of 90.

named Bob Gillson. No one else was there except a center to snap the ball to them. They'd been at it for about a half hour, not talking to each other by then, settled into their routines, just taking the snap, kicking, taking another snap and kicking again.

Guy had the application papers for Colgate in his dorm room but he had not applied for admission yet. Sweat was pouring off his muscular frame and he was feeling loose. He was kicking them fifty-five and sixty yards with no effort. He was so loose that when he followed through, his strong right leg was almost vertical to his body and his foot was well above his head, toe pointed forward. Every now and then he would really get into one and it would sail seventy yards. Just like back in high school. The other two kickers? Nothing to worry about there.

But Guy wasn't happy. From the spot where the kickers were practicing, he could look down on the main practice field where the rest of the boys who would be his teammates if he made the squad were working out.

Big, he thought to himself. *Nobody here weighs less than one ninety except me And they're all six feet tall or more.*

He wasn't scared exactly. With four years of high school football behind him, he had taken plenty of hits and just kept getting back up. That's the way it was. If you ever played any football or ice hockey, you know what I mean. But he *was* concerned.

He had been excited when the letter from Coach Kerr had arrived in the mail asking him to come up for a tryout. It meant he might actually be able to go to college. Not having anyone to advise him, the Colgate thing seemed definite enough for him to cancel his plans to attend Kents Hill that fall, and shift his attention to the idea of going directly into college at Colgate, instead.

Perhaps *that* was a mistake in judgment. He still needed those extra courses that had not been available to him at East Boston. How he thought he'd handle that if he got into Colgate on a football scholarship, I don't know, unless he felt that if he could just get in and hold on long enough, he could prove he had the ability to do college work by actually doing it.

Just now, however, his practice uniform jersey soaked in sweat, he was not thinking about it, because yesterday, Coach Kerr had hinted that if he made the team, a hundred and fifty to three hundred dollars in tuition money might be found by tapping into a couple of wealthy boosters. But after two days on the practice field, Guy was having second thoughts.

As we've seen, he'd had a great summer on the Cape. Pete Herman, encouraging Guy to come to Kents Hill that fall, had said he had quite a future in baseball ahead of him. The Boston newspaper reporters were all writing the same thing. And Mr. O'Brien had let him know that no less than three big league teams were now interested, though no contract had been received yet.

Guy wanted to play pro baseball so bad he could taste it. And he didn't want to do anything that might hurt his chances. *Playin' football every day with those guys over there could be a problem,* he thought.

Assistant Coach Gillson's whistle cut off his thoughts. "Okay, men. That's enough for today. Go take your showers. Don't forget the team meeting in Coach Kerr's office in an hour."

*   *   *   *

Hamilton, NY
Tuesday, September 8, 1936
Colgate University
7:30 p.m.

That night, our boy was in the dorm to which he'd been assigned; one of the rooms temporarily reserved for players trying out for the football team. It was the usual dorm room, small, with just enough space for two of everything; two beds, two dressers with mirrors, two tables and two chairs. Only one window though, and no computers. Back then, computers were still way in the future. Kids somehow did without them and still managed to learn a thing or two.

The door was open. His roommate, another football hopeful, had gone off with a couple other guys to get dinner in nearby Hamilton. Guy could not afford that, so he had made an excuse and eaten some stuff from the vending machine in the entrance hall. When you're that age, you can get away with things like that.

There was this soft knock on the door, and Coach Kerr poked his head in. A short, stocky Welshman, maybe fifty-five years old, he was in the prime of his coaching career.

"Guy? Can I come in?"

Guy was off the bed like a shot. He was embarrassed that his coach was there, not only because it was unusual, but because he had not gone to Kerr's office earlier that afternoon like Coach Gillson told him to at the end of practice.

Kerr came right to the point. "Coach Gillson tells me you were kicking pretty good out there yesterday and today," he said. "And I was watching you running the Frosh offense yesterday. You handled yourself pretty well. So naturally I was wondering why you didn't come to the team meeting this afternoon."

Guy settled into a chair over by the window. Like most boys that age, he was self-conscious around grown-ups. "I uh … had a lotta thinkin' ta do," he mumbled.

"A lot of thinking?" A light went on above Kerr's head. *The kid's worried about not making the team,* he thought. "Well, what I have to say might help a bit there," he announced with a grin. "We want you to be our kicker this season. And you'll also run one of the offenses during practice sessions, so you can be available in a game if you're needed." He smiled again. "In between, I might even give you some playing time at halfback this year."

"Oh!" Guy said, but the noise he made wasn't a happy sound. Kerr noticed. "What's the matter, son?"

"Coach Kerr, I don't wanna play football full-time this year," Guy blurted out. "I wanna play pro baseball. There's a good chance I might be offered something soon. If I play football every day and get hurt …"

Kerr raised his eyebrows. "But I thought you wanted to go to college, Guy."

"I *do.* And I really appreciate gettin' this chance. It's just that I wanna play pro baseball. One of the major league teams may tie me up any time now."

Kerr stiffened. "I see," he said. He plopped himself down in the other chair. "But you *do* understand that if you don't play football there'll be no tuition money available for you here at Colgate?"

"What about if I just do the kickin' and promise ta play baseball in the spring?"

Kerr shook his head. "No. We can't waste a slot on someone who just kicks the football. And besides, baseball isn't very important around here. It used to be. From the 1890s until around 1920. But it's been de-emphasized since then. Football is *the* big program here, Guy. It's the only one the boosters will help out with."

"Oh," Guy said. "I see. But yesterday and today I thought about it a lot. My mind's just about made up."

Kerr was worried, now. He had spent some time personally scouting this kid and knew how good a kicker Guy was, and how well, as a quarterback, he could run an offense. And after two days of tryouts, his assistant coach had confirmed that Guy was the real goods. Kerr was salivating over those sixty and seventy yard punts that can set an opposing team back on its heals, and a freshman quarterback just about as good as his second string field general, who was a junior.

Kerr waited for Guy to say something more, but Guy didn't know what else to say. He was just a kid. He didn't have the answers yet. As a matter of fact, he still didn't even know all the questions.

The coach stood and moved to the door. "Think it over carefully, Guy," he said real icy-like, "and let me know what you decide by tomorrow. Okay?"

*   *   *   *

Pine Bluffs, WY
Thursday, October 21, 2004
703 Beech Street
7:05 a.m.

That's how I see it. Guy wanted to go to college so he could play baseball in the Northern League, and Colgate was interested in him as a punter and as a quarterback down the line. Why wouldn't they be? He could run, pass and kick, and had demonstrated leadership ability. Any kid just out of high school who could kick the pigskin seventy yards would add something to your team right away, and a talented kid, with regular work, would soon be ready to take over the first string offense.

So Guy settled on Colgate as the place to go. But, he'd just finished the '36 baseball season on the Cape where everyone who saw him play made noises about what a great baseball future he had ahead of him. He believed it and thought maybe a major league team would tie him up soon. If that happened, he could get his college tuition paid for four years, either here or somewhere else closer to home with a better baseball program. It apparently happened a lot back then, according to Lenny Merullo:

"Guy had a good body. He could run, throw, and hit. He was what all the scouts were looking for. If a major league team got interested in you, they'd tie you up; do something for you or give you some money. As long as you agreed to sign with that club after you graduated."

I believe that's the way Guy saw it. He still thought O'Brien was working for him with several big league clubs and he was only a hair away from signing with one of them. So when he was invited up to Colgate for a football tryout, he went. But one look at the size of his future teammates was enough to convince him that this may have been a bad decision because he could get hurt real easy out there on the old gridiron if he was playing every day. If he came up with a serious injury? Poof! End of his baseball prospects. So he told the coach he didn't want to be an everyday player, but he was willing to be the team's kicker and, also, to play baseball in exchange for tuition.

But Andy Kerr didn't care about some kid's dream. He was only concerned with building a football program and winning football games. He wanted Guy on that team, but he wanted the boy on *his* terms. If a kid wasn't willing to do it *his* way, then Kerr had no further interest in him. You know how that goes with some people. So he told Guy, in effect, "It's my way or the highway, son," and left Guy's dorm room. And when he went, Guy's chance for a college education based on his athletic ability went with him. At least for a while. And his chance to play in the Northern League dimmed, like a flashlight whose battery was running down.

A couple of days later, Guy left Hamilton, New York and returned home without ever even filling out any application forms. That, I think, is why nobody at Colgate can find any record of him ever being there.

As for Coach Kerr, he continued to have good football teams at Colgate for a few more years. But somewhere in there, he was forced to stop bringing in those ringers. He was never fired for it, but as a result, his program dropped a notch or two. Colgate was just too hard, academically, for jocks without smarts. After WWII, Colgate changed its schedule and wasn't playing big name teams like it did before.

Andy Kerr retired from coaching at Colgate in '46. He was so well-thought of there that in 1964, Colgate conferred an honorary doctorate of law degree upon him, and in September 1966, they named their new football stadium after him. Yeah! Things like that *do* happen.

*   *   *   *

Pine Bluffs, WY
Friday, October 22, 2004
703 Beech Street
8:00 a.m.

Remember that a fella named Gillson was a new assistant football coach back in '36, when Guy was first invited to Colgate University? Well, in the summer of 1940, he turned up briefly in Guy's life once more.

I don't know for certain whether Guy had again been invited to try out for the team, or whether he simply decided, once more, to try to get into college, and Colgate was a known quantity, dangling a possible means of getting that college education in return for simply playing football. But in the summer of 1940, a letter was delivered to Guy's home from the Colgate University Athletic Council, signed by Robert W. Gillson, who apparently was the Freshman football coach:

Dear Guy:

There is a lot of football in the air these summer days. The Sunday papers are full of pre-season football dope. The coaches have their plans worked out and are eager to get to work. Players all over the country are feeling the call of America's greatest game, and it time for the players to do some real thinking about what they are going to do this fall.

As a member of the Colgate Freshman Football Squad of 1940, you have a tradition to build up and give to Colgate. How well you carry on depends a great deal upon your seriousness of effort the remainder of the summer. Be loyal yourself, your new team mates and to Colgate, by conditioning your body and preparing yourself for the coming season.

A CHALLENGE TO THE FRESHMAN FOOTBALL MEN OF 1940

Cornell Freshmen, Penn State Frosh, Syracuse Frosh, Blair Academy, and Canisius Frosh. That is our schedule—To come out of each game with a victory, our desire.

Of equal value and importance this first year of football at Colgate, is to develop your ability in the fundamentals of the game and to thoroughly prepare your self for your years on the Varsity. The Varsity team is your ultimate and greatest desire in football. Set yourself for a good, solid season of preparation, so that your desires may be realized.

The information in the article enclosed with this letter is meant to be elementary fundamentals and is somewhat general in character. Make a careful study of the article. The more technical football you know, the better player you will be.

I would like to hear from you before college opens. If you have any questions I shall be glad to answer them. Have you made all arrangements for your room?

You will receive from the Dean of Admissions a letter announcing the date college will open.

I hope you are enjoying a very pleasant summer.

Sincerely,
Robert W. Gillson

The way that letter was worded, it sounded like Guy had already applied and been accepted for the 1940–1941 school year at Colgate. And at the beginning of the summer of 1939, there's a reference to him and Colgate in a newspaper in the St. Johnsbury, VT area. So certainly he must have continued his interest in Colgate and football—the pigskin as a means of obtaining that elusive sheepskin. So what happened? We know he didn't go there in 1936. Did he finally do it in the fall of 1940?

And, the answer is ... No. Why not? Perhaps once again he could not get the tuition and expense money together. If that's what happened, it might be partially because of something that occurred during the summer of '40, about which we'll talk more later. Or, perhaps, with war looming, he decided not to begin college, since he might have had to interrupt his studies to answer Uncle Sam's call. I don't know what happened. In any event, by the time Gillson's letter arrived in Guy's mailbox in August, Guy may have already decided his future regarding Colgate and the 1940–41 school year. Why do I say that? At the bottom of that letter, this handwritten note appears:

> *I would appreciate hearing from you at once in regard to your entering Colgate this fall. Lack of information from you leads us to believe you may not be with us.*
> *Let me hear from you, Guy.*
>
> > *Sincerely,*
> > *Bob.*

And with this, Guy's dream to obtain a college education seemed to have been put on hold once again, for awhile. But I'm getting ahead of myself again.

CHAPTER 25

In the summer of 1937, with the pleasant smell of freshly mowed grass heavy in the June air, Guy, *still* unsigned by any professional club, and *still* not a college boy, again headed for the Cape to patrol left field for Barnstable in the Cape Cod League. To him, this seemed like his only choice.

Pete Herman motored back down from Maine, to again manage the team, play a little first base and even take a turn on the mound now and then, and Joe Rocciollo finished his senior year at East Boston High School by starring in center field and being named second team All-Scholastic. I asked him about O'Brien's drinking problem in the spring of '37.

"O'Brien couldn't handle the team very well that year," he said. "When he came to practices and to games, he was always late. He'd tell people he'd been held up at the courthouse, but you could see he'd been drinking."

"Well, how did the team function?" I wanted to know.

"O'Brien would call the team captain and ask him to run the team that day," Joe responded. "Sometimes, he'd get Bill McCarthy to handle things for him. That year and the following year, O'Brien was a very heavy drinker."

Joe's story about O'Brien's heavy drinking was further corroborated by George "Red" Baccigalupo, a retired Fire Chief from Winthrop, whose name had been mentioned to me by Joe Sarro. I wanted to speak to him but had done nothing about it until, on that trip to Boston I mentioned, the opportunity came. Joe Rocciolo, working like a Trojan, arranged for me to meet some of Guy's old friends and people who had been acquainted with him or had known of him. We were using the Burger King in East Boston as a sort of headquarters.

Each morning, before I went off to the Boston Public Library, these old timers would come in and talk to me. On August 11, 2002, Baccigalupo showed up.

"Sure, I knew Guy," he said. "I lived on Leydon Street. Knew the Vitale family and both Sacco families, too. Louise, Rose, Helen and Henry were children of Antonio Sacco. Jerome Sacco's family was at 35 Leydon."

"What can you tell me about Mr. O'Brien?" I asked.

"I played football for him," Baccigalupo said. "He used to drink a lot. Especially on Wednesdays over at Santarpio's Bar on Chelsea Street. Then he'd come over to coach. He'd be in a very happy mood."

"Anything else?"

"Fred O'Brien coached most of the sports at East Boston High. He started ice hockey and coached football, baseball and basketball. I think 'Okie' O'Connell was the assistant back then, but he died. O'Brien finally stopped coaching in the mid to late forties. By then, they were trying ta get rid a him because he was the only coach who wasn't a teacher. But they couldn't do it because he was politically connected. He was seventy-four or seventy-five when he finally quit."

*   *   *   *

Cape Cod, MA
Thursday, July 1, 1937
Barnstable, MA
8:00 a.m.

On Thursday, July 1st, 1937, two days before opening day, the *Hyannis Patriot,* which later became the *Barnstable Patriot,* ran an article about the teams in the Cape Cod League:

> *Cape Cod Baseball league teams will open the 1937 season next Saturday afternoon at 3:30 p.m. in Hyannis and Orleans. Falmouth will cross bats at Barnstable High field with the Barnstable team, and Harwich invades Orleans for the lower Cape opener …*
>
> *Edward 'Pete' Herman, coach at Kents Hill prep in Maine will again skipper for the Barnstable team. His roster of players includes John 'Muggsy' Kelly of Boston College, Norman Merrill of John Carroll, and John Maloney of Kents Hill as pitchers, with Pete himself taking an occasional turn. Stanley Bergeron of Bates at first; Francis 'Cowboy" Crawley of Villanova at second; Paul Sharkey of B.C. at shortstop; and Roy Williams of English High at third; for outfield Herman will have John Spirada of St. Anselms, Guy Vitale of Colgate, and Tim Ready of B.C.; as utility George*

Colbert of B.C. will catch. Robert 'Bob' Cash of Hyannis will pitch if he doesn't respond to the Nova Scotian League lure.

Probably unaware of the facts and not having the time to check, this reporter appeared to be simply repeating what was already written about Guy and Colgate.

Five teams competed in the Cape Cod League that summer; Barnstable, Bourne, Falmouth, Harwich, and Orleans. Three of the four, Barnstable, Bourne, and Harwich, put on a hot, season-ending pennant race. If you read Christopher Price's book, *Baseball by the Beach*,[37] you know he called it "a pennant race for the ages." The winner was decided in the last game of the season, on Labor Day, Monday, September 6th, when Barnstable—28 wins, 17 losses—played Bourne—26 wins, 18 losses—for the championship. Jeez! What more could baseball fans anywhere want?

On June 29th, an article in the *Cape Cod Standard Times* said this:

> *Judging from the list of players submitted by each club baseball fans along the Cape may see some real fast ball played here this summer. The clubs will be limited to 12 players when the league gets under way and the lineup of each club can include two professionals.*
>
> *Most of the players listed by the managers are college men, a large number coming from Boston College and Holy Cross ...*
>
> *Barnstable: Manager 'Pete' Herman, J. Kelly, J. Maloney, Walter Barson, Roy Williams, John Spirada, Guy Vitale, Norman Merrill, Bob Cash, Tim Ready, and George Colbert, catcher, who has been released by Falmouth and is now ready to play for Barnstable.*

Of the players named in these two lists, only Stanley Bergeron and Walter Barson failed to materialize. Colbert? Apparently he'd signed with Falmouth, but decided not to play for them since his old friend and college chum, Pete Herman, was returning to coach Barnstable. So he switched clubs. That, of course, put him back on the same team as Guy, with whom he'd not gotten along the previous season, although by the end of the summer, the relationship between the two had changed from a hot burn to a warm simmer.

---

37 Christopher Price, *Baseball by the Beach: A History of America's National Pastime on Cape Cod*, Cape Cod Publications. 1998. Another well-written and informative book about baseball on Cape Cod is Dan Crowley, *Baseball on Cape Cod*, Arcadia Publishing. 2006.

The season got under way on Saturday, July 3rd, 1937. The day was designated as Governor's Day, and the Bay State's Governor, Charles F. Hurley, was on hand in Orleans by special invitation, to throw out the first ball at the game between Hyannis and Orleans.

On July 10th, the *Cape Cod Standard Times* published a nice photograph of the Barnstable club, which shows them in two rows, one kneeling and one standing. From left to right, kneeling are Frank "Cowboy" Crawley, George Colbert, John Maloney, Guy Vitale, William Conway and Roy Williams. Standing, left to right are Manager Pete Herman, Norman Merrill, John Spirada, Mike Maleski, Frank Zammarchi and John "Muggsey" Kelly.

Barnstable got off to a fast start. So did Guy. On Tuesday, July 6th, after defeating Bourne 14–10 in eleven innings and Orleans 17–3, the Barnstable club found itself in first place, and Guy, having gone two for seven against Bourne and three for five against Orleans, including a home run and a double, was a happy camper.

George Colbert collected two hits in five trips for Barnstable against Bourne. Oh, yeah. A fellow named Tony Plansky was back, playing left field for Bourne. Batting in the fourth hole that day, he went five for six, including two doubles and a triple.

The following afternoon, however, Barnstable tasted defeat for the first time at the hands of Falmouth, 5–4. Guy played center field, but was blanked at the plate in three appearances, while Colbert was behind the plate and went one for five.

The story appearing in the *Cape Cod Standard Times* the next morning:

> At the outset it looked as if Barnstable was going to keep that undefeated record, getting two runs in the first inning to Falmouth's none. Neither team scored in the second, and then Falmouth tied the score with two runs in the third, Barnstable getting nothing. In the fourth, Barnstable pulled in one and led the game 3–2 until the exciting seventh inning, when again the score was tied after Falmouth brought in two runs and Barnstable one. It looked like anybody's game at the scoreboard at this point and neither team did any more scoring until the ninth inning when Falmouth achieved the winning run.

On July 9th, Barnstable defeated Orleans 7–4, with Guy collecting one hit in four shots, while Colbert went two for four.

The next day, Barnstable lost to Bourne, 12–11, as Guy smashed two hits in five plate appearances. Plansky had an even bigger day for Bourne, going four for six, with seven put outs in left field. Colbert? Bad day; no hits in five attempts.

Well, something must have happened because by July 12th, Barnstable's win over first place Harwich, 9–5, only solidified third place for them. Two days later, Barnstable moved back into first by trouncing Bourne, 7–2, even though Plansky solved Barnstable's pitchers and went three for three. Guy also did well with the bat, going two for five.

Three days later, the *Cape Cod Standard Times* reported this way:

> *Orleans, July 15—Barnstable put itself within short striking distance of first place in the Cape Cod League here yesterday, by pouring hail, rain and sleet on Orleans for a flattening score of 20–3.*

On July 16th, Guy had a big day in a twelve-inning loss to the Falmouth nine, 13–12, as he collected five hits in seven plate appearances, two of them home runs, and scored three of his teams twelve runs. After ten games the league standings looked like this:

TEAM	WON	LOST
Harwich	6	3
Barnstable	6	4
Falmouth	5	4
Bourne	4	5
Orleans	2	7

That several Cape teams were fairly evenly matched as far as player ability was shown by an article in *the Cape Cod Standard Times* two days later, on July 18[th:]

THREE-FIFTHS OF CAPE LEAGUE THROWN INTO TIE FOR FIRST PLACE

> *Harwich, Barnstable and Falmouth have won six games and lost four each in the Cape Cod League and are tied for first place after yesterday's games which Falmouth won over Harwich at Harwich 2–1, and which Bourne won from Orleans 13–7.*

The next day, Barnstable's 4–2 win over Bourne was written up, and the *Cape Cod Standard Times* also listed the batting averages in the Cape Cod League after its first two weeks of play. It showed Tony Plansky of Bourne with the highest average among regular players at .468, with twenty-one hits in forty-seven trips to the plate. Bill Barrett of Harwich was second among the regulars at .467, with twenty-one hits in forty-five plate appearances. In eleventh place, batting .396 is—Guy Vitale.

Worthy of reporting at this stage of the season by the *Times*:

> *Vitale of Barnstable heads the home run list with three circuit clouts …*

A week later, on July 26th, the *Cape Cod Standard Times* again listed the leading hitters in the League. Guy must have had a torrid week at the plate because he is now in seventh place, and two of the players in front of him are not regulars. Eliminate them and Guy is in the fifth spot, hitting .421. George Colbert, after a lukewarm week at the plate, is far down the list at .269. Here's the article:

> *Stavies of Orleans, a pitcher who came to bat only 18 times and connected for ten hits, continues to lead the Cape Cod League batters with an average of .556 percent while Ruckstull, Falmouth batting ace, leads the regulars with .442 percent, or 19 hits out of 43 trips to the plate.*
>
> *The top batter, Stavies, only played in one game last week and is followed by Brown of Harwich, who played in only three games thus far. Brown has an average of .553, while Ruckstull stands third in the lineup of hitters. Barrett of Harwich and Gallagher of Bourne, are pressing the leaders closely for high stick honors.*

Examine this list carefully and three things leap out at you: first, Guy had increased his average twenty-five points in one week. Second, only twenty-one points separated him from the League's leading batter. Third, there was no mention of Tony Plansky, who led the League just the week before.

Barnstable closed out the month of July in first place, after a 7–1 win over hapless Orleans, behind the seven-hit pitching of Normie Merrill, who also got three hits in four plate appearances. Mike Maleski, another Barnstable pitcher, was also throwing quite well. Maleski, who was not listed on the roster at the start of the season, apparently joined the team later.

During the first week of August, the Barnstable club apparently cooled off some. However, it was still in first place on August 8th, winning over Falmouth, 6–4. Guy went one for two, a double, and walked several times, while handling three chances in the outfield flawlessly.

The *Times* reported the game this way:

> *League standings today shows Barnstable still easily the leader. In spite of last week's many reverses, with 17 won and 10 lost. Second is Bourne, 15 wins, 13 lost, and then comes Falmouth, 14 won, 11 lost, followed by Harwich, won 14, lost 15, trailed by Orleans, won 8, lost 19.*

Another interesting thing about that season; many extra inning games were played around the League that summer. This one, a ten inning scrap between Barnstable and Falmouth is typical. A slugfest for eight innings, it entered the tenth tied 7–7.

Mike Maleski had started the game but gave way to two other pitchers before Giovannangeli came on in relief. "Gio" was still in the game in the bottom of the tenth.

"Tominey, Sharkey, 'Gio,' Crawley," Pete Herman hollered, as his team came off the field for its turn at bat. "Let's win this thing now so we can go out ta dinner tonight."

Walter Morris, Falmouth pitcher, who had played for Harwich the previous summer, started Tominey off with fast balls. On a two-one count, Barnstable's speedy center fielder hit a towering fly ball to left, which was caught by Gendron after a long run.

That brought Barnstable's shortstop, Sharkey to the plate. This time Morris went to his curveball. Same result—a deep fly ball to center field for out number two.

Giovannangeli was next. The Barnstable dugout was into the game. "Come on, 'Gio,'" Guy yelled, as Spirada set up a rhythmic clapping. "Gio" took a curve right at the knees for a strike. The next pitch, another curve, hit him on the arm.

"Take yer base!" the umpire bellowed.

A grinning Francis "Cowboy" Crawley stepped into the batter's box amid a loud hue and cry from the Barnstable bench, and crowd noise from Barnstable's fans, who sensed a rally in the making. Hyped, Crawley lined a two-two fastball into center field for a single. Runners were now at the corners with two down.

Next batter was Normie Merrill, a good stick as well as a great pitcher. Falmouth's manager, knowing that Merrill was in the midst of a hot streak with the bat, decided to walk Merrill to get at Guy.

Guy, who had grabbed a couple of bats and was standing in the on-deck circle, saw what was happening. *No respect for me, huh?* he thought. *Well, that's a mistake. Yer gonna pay fer that.*

Barnstable's fans set up a howl but Falmouth's fans were deadly still as Guy walked to the plate and tossed away one of the bats. He loved this kind of situation; bases loaded, two outs, the game on the line. And, he'd been hitting Morris well all season.

Will it be the big ole curve or the heat? he wondered. It was the curveball. A hanging curveball. He could see the laces spinning, spinning as the pill came to the plate, but the break was not there. Swinging a bit early, he drilled the ball over third baseman Baker's head and down the third base line, dropped his bat and sprinted for first base.

"Fair Ball!" the home plate umpire yelled. As Guy crossed first base and headed for second, "Gio" touched the plate with the winning run. Barnstable 8, Falmouth 7.

All smiles, Guy came off the field. He glanced over at Falmouth's bench, saw Falmouth's manager glaring at him, and shot him a look that said *I bet ya won't do that again any time soon.*

Guy's jubilant teammates met him at home plate, thrilled that he'd been able to win another game for them. Finished grabbing the extended hands, he turned and ran head-on into George Colbert, who'd also had a good day at the dish, going two for three. Startled, Guy threw up his hands defensively, but quickly realized that big George's hand was not closed in a fist but extended, like his teammates, to be shaken.

"Nice, clout, kid," the burly catcher said, grabbing Guy's hand and pumping it.

The following day saw yet another extra-inning game; this one an eleven-inning contest between Barnstable and Orleans, which Barnstable won by the identical score of 8–7. In the bottom of the eleventh, Normie Merrill singled to right, Guy was hit on the thigh by a pitch from Orleans's chucker, Fred Cavanaugh, and Colbert singled to center, scoring Merrill from second with the winning run.

On August 16th, Normie Merrill, who'd been pitching exceptionally well, won his tenth game of the season against Orleans, scattering eight base hits and just three runs as his teammates tallied fourteen times to win it 14–3. At this level of baseball, most of the players were not into the booze habit. But that night, with Pete Herman's blessing—in fact he was with them—the entire team, including Guy, who'd gone two for five at the dish, helped Merrill celebrate. Until two a.m. the following morning, at a local bar and grill in Sandwich. Guy partied with his teammates by doing some heavy drinking, something with which he'd had no experience at all up to this point in his young life.

No wonder, then, that in their next game, played after very little sleep, they barely squeaked by Orleans. Two days later, apparently still recuperating, they lost to Harwich, 13–1. Not used to this sort of thing, Guy had had more than his share to drink. It was not surprising that he went hitless in these two games.

*   *   *   *

Barnstable, MA
Wednesday, August 18, 1937
Sandy Neck Beach
8:40 p.m.

Sandy Neck is a barrier beach not too far from Barnstable. A stretch of fine white sand about six miles long, it had been built up by eroding sand traveling along the coast. To reach it, you took a left off of Route 6A and drove along Sandy Neck Road, which was not too far from the boarding house where Guy had a room that summer. At the end of Sandy Neck Road was a small parking area.

Guy, alone, had walked from his boarding house after the loss to Harwich. He was beginning to feel better. The soles of his sneakers scuffed against the macadam of the small parking area. At the edge of the beach he stopped to remove them before taking to the sandy trail on the outer side of the beach nearest the water. He was deep in thought.

Although pleased with himself because of the good showing he was again making with Barnstable, his furrowed brow proclaimed that he was not totally happy.

The sticky stuff with O'Brien had eliminated his chance to sign with a major league club immediately after graduation from high school. But unaware of the real reason why the teams had backed off, Guy had promptly set out to clear up a misconception which he'd been told the major league clubs had of him; that he might not be able to hit top-notch pitching. At this point in his life, he believed he'd satisfactorily shown that his greatest baseball attribute was his strong bat, and that his body was sturdy enough to withstand the rigors of 50 plus games in ten weeks. Trudging along the sandy path, he looked out over the calm blue waters of Cape Cod Bay and fastened his eyes on the sky at the blue-gray horizon.

"Are ya there, God? I haven't talked to ya for awhile because I've been kinda busy. But now I'm back" He walked a few more yards and then stopped and listened to the sound of small waves breaking on the nearby beach.

"I proved I can hit," he said aloud. The sound of his voice, small against the brisk breeze blowing across the sand, was like an echo in the wind. "And I did it for not just one, but *two* seasons in this league. I faced good pitchin' every day and did damn well." Viciously, he kicked at a mound of sand, and the force of his leg spun him sideways. "So where the hell are the offers? Will ya tell me?"

Still carrying on an imaginary dialogue with a neglected God, he started to jog. "And what the hell am I supposed ta do next? Should I try ta get inta college again?" His words, pulled from his lips by a current of air, were quickly lost in the ether.

Lowering his head, he began running hard now, against the wind. "I'm not gettin' any younger, ya know," he said, and chuckled at his own levity.

Maybe I should go back ta Boston and confront Fred O'Brien—learn the truth about what, if anything, he's doing—then tell him I no longer want him ta represent me. The thought came to his mind so clearly that it seemed like someone had spoken it in his ear. He glanced over his shoulder but there was no one there.

After that I could approach a few professional teams on my own, he thought, *or maybe get a real agent ta help me.* Suddenly all the tension seemed to drain from his body and he felt relaxed.

Dusk was setting in. The sun had disappeared behind stunted pines to the west. To the north, dark clouds had begun to pile up, and he could smell rain in the air. He slowed to a jog, the wind in his face. "But where would I get the dough ta hire an agent?" he said out loud, silencing the comforting voice. "Wish I had somebody ta help me. Ma and Pa? They don't know shit about stuff. And Frankie's so busy tryin' ta' make a livin' he never has a free second ta pee, let alone help me out."

Jogging over the sandy path with no shoes on was becoming increasingly difficult; the sand here, unencumbered by dune grass, was loose and deep beneath his feet. But even though his breathing became faster, he didn't seem to notice yet. "And Albert's back from the Berkshires, but he's keepin' a low profile so the Mob doesn't find him." He shook his fist at the sky. "Why the hell did You allow that ta happen? Answer me that?"

Since leaving home at the beginning of the summer, Guy's prayer life had diminished to the point where it was almost nonexistent. Without the graces that flow from God through prayer, he'd been turning to Him less and less as the summer had progressed. He'd reached a point where the God of his youth, who had carried him through many tight spots, had been largely forgotten. It's no wonder, then, that with no one to bounce this stuff off of, he felt that he was on his own, and largely inadequate.

Another thought came; one that momentarily confused him and started him thinking along a fateful line: *possibly, a few years in college might be the way ta get out from under O'Brien; maybe give a major league club some time ta look me over and a chance ta tie me up. That way, there might still be a chance for me ta play in the Northern League.*

He had covered more than a mile. Across the dunes to his right, he saw the green roof of a private hunting or fishing cabin set back in the marsh. His legs were beginning to burn now, and so were his lungs. *But where'll I get the funds for tuition?* he asked himself. *I don't wanna play football at a major college and risk gettin' hurt.*

And then it came to him—a thought that seemed, in his confusion and fearfulness, so logical that it stopped him in his tracks. The night was without moon or stars, and the clean-cut lines of Guy's face were now revealed by an occasional flash of lightening from the heavy clouds swirling low over the bay. *What about an academic scholarship? I might be able ta get another shot at Colgate or some other college, like Holy Cross, with an academic scholarship—if I can improve my grades and show I can do college work.*

Turning around, he started trudging back. The wind was worse, but it was now blowing from behind him. The smell of rain that had been in the air had moved northward with the heavy clouds carrying that liquid. Multiple stars were now overhead. Thinking along this new line, he didn't notice that it was much easier to walk. His brain simply made a note of it, his mind accepted it. *How do I go about that?* he asked himself. When the answer came, it was deceptively simple. *Kents Hill. That's how I can do it. A year there will prove that I'm capable of doin' college work.*

Rested, he again began to jog back in the direction of Sandy Neck Road. A broken shard of moon in a now cloudless sky lit his way. A big, impish grin spread across his face. *And Pete Herman's just the guy ta help me get in.*

Pete Herman *did* have part of the answer to one of Guy's dreams. But what Guy did not understand that night was that changing direction at this point in time was going to delay, even longer, the day when he might accomplish his primary dream of playing professional baseball.

*   *   *   *

Sandwich, MA
Thursday, August 19, 1937.
Main Street Bar & Grill
9:45 p.m.

It was late on a hot, sultry Cape Cod evening. Holding onto a three game lead for the past week, with fifteen games to go, Pete Herman, Big George Colbert and Francis "Cowboy" Crawley, the older ballplayers on the team, were visiting a bar and grill just down the block from the old Daniel Webster Inn on Main Street in Sandwich, the same establishment where the entire team had celebrated Merrill's tenth victory of the season a week or so before, and in which these older players spent many summer evenings.

A storefront-type bar with a limited food menu, like you find in a lot of small towns in America, the place had neon signs in each plate glass window; one advertising Bud, the other Miller's. Inside, a long mahogany bar ran along the left wall and a row of dark wood booths ran along the right. The atmosphere was not much, but the prices were right, if you weren't raking in much money.

The older guys were relaxing in there, demolishing a couple dozen crabs, quaffing a few cold ones and doing what they loved to do; talking baseball.

"Ain't nobody gonna catch them damn Yankees," Colbert was saying. "Who could do it at this stage? Detroit? The Red Sox? I don't see it."

"Nope!" Herman said. "Detroit's already changed managers twice. Bringin' Cochrane back again was *not* the brightest move, I don't think."

"The Red Sox don't have the *horses* this year," Crawley chipped in. "The curse lives on. It's been the same every year since they traded the Babe. Bad shit happens to them."[38]

"If the Sox catch the Yanks, it'll be a sign the world is comin' to an end," Herman agreed, stabbing a finger in the air for emphasis. "But I wouldn't count the *Tigers* out yet. Charlie Gehringer's leadin' the league in hitting. If he stays hot ..." He left his thought unfinished and reached for another fat crab.

"It's pitchin' that counts," Colbert fired back. "With six weeks ta go, Gomez and Ruffing are on track ta win twenty each."

Herman nodded agreement. "It's their year," he said and drained his beer.

"Pete? Can I talk to ya fer a minute?"

Concentrating on the crabs and their beer, no one had seen Guy walk in and approach their booth. He was alone.

"Guy? Sure." Herman started to slide in to make room for his young, hard-hitting outfielder, but Guy held up a hand to stop him.

"I'd like ta talk to ya alone," he said self-consciously.

---

38   He was referring to what baseball fans call "the Curse of the Bambino." The Red Sox had traded Babe Ruth to the Yankees because Sox owner, Harry Frazee, had needed money to invest in a Broadway musical entitled *No, No, Nanette*. The deal went down for $125,000 cash and a $300,000 dollar loan to Frazee. Since 1918, the Red Sox had not won a pennant. This so-called "Curse" continued until 2004, when the Sox beat the Yankees in the AL playoffs and then swept the St. Louis Cardinals in the World Series, thus ending the "Curse of the Bambino."

One reason Pete Herman had such a good way with boys was because he'd learned to read them well enough to tell when they were troubled. The other thing was, he always tried to be accessible for them.

So Pete took one look at Guy's face, pried himself away from his group and steered Guy past the authentic old mahogany bar where a few locals sat on barstools nursing their favorite brews and shooting the bull, past the long mirror with subdued red lights over it, and the rows of liquor bottles with names like Johnny Walker Red, Jack Daniels Black Label, Drambuie, and Crème De Menthe, to another booth all the way in the back where the two could talk privately. They settled in under a cloud of thick cigarette smoke. Herman gestured for the bartender, who took a quick look at Guy and brought over a draft Budweiser, a Coke and two glasses.

Herman poured himself a glass. "What's on your mind, young man?"

"I've been thinkin' about what I'm gonna do in September," Guy announced, very seriously.

"After the season's over?"

"Yeah."

"What d'ya *wanna* do?" Herman lifted his beer, drank some, and put the glass back on the table.

"Well, I wanna go ta college."

"I thought you were gonna play pro baseball?"

Guy dropped his gaze. For a second, he looked confused. "Yeah. Mr. O'Brien is workin' on that for me. But I haven't heard anything yet. And it's been awhile, ya know?"

Herman studied Guy's face and saw the momentary confusion. He filed it away in his head. He knew how good a ballplayer Guy was. Believing, like everyone else, that Guy had both the ability *and* the desire, he thought it was only a matter of time, so he was a bit puzzled.

"Have you applied anywhere yet?"

"No. For one thing, I don't have the tuition money. For another, at East Boston High, I took the clerical course, not the one that prepared kids for college. So there are a few courses I need if I'm gonna get accepted inta some college."

When Herman heard that, he knew what was coming. "You thinking you might like to attend Kents Hill for a year?"

Guy fidgeted with his Coke. "Yes, sir," he said, his voice real low.

Now Pete Herman was no dummy. Kents Hill was a prep school for good students. It didn't normally attract great football or baseball players from New England high schools. He knew a proven athlete like Guy could be a real plus up there.

"I think maybe I can help."

"But what about the tuition?" Guy wanted to know.

Herman paused, sipped some more beer, and studied the foam as it settled in his glass. Augusta's newspaper, which was delivered to just about everybody in Readville, picked up articles from the Boston papers. So he had read about Guy's high school exploits on the gridiron *and* diamond. He thought about how a good punter can help a bad offense by kicking it out of trouble when it can't move the ball. That problem had been dogging Kents Hill football forever. They *never* had a good offense. He also knew that a good punter could force an opposing offense to start a drive from inside its own twenty-yard line, and a team that always had to start from there wasn't going to score as often as a team that puts the ball in play out around its own forty. He looked hard at Guy.

"I hear you were quite a punter, and not a half-bad quarterback in high school," he said. "Would you be willing to play football as well as baseball if you came up there?"

Well, Guy had already thought it out before he came looking for Pete. The way he saw it, playing football in prep school wasn't the same as playing the game in the fourth or fifth best college football program in the country, like at Colgate. For one thing, prep school players weren't that big. Less chance to get hurt. So he jumped at it.

"Yes, sir."

"Tuition, room and board? Between four hundred fifty and six hundred fifty dollars. Don't worry. If you're willing to play football, baseball, and maybe a little ice hockey in between to stay in shape, and possibly work a bit in the dining hall, the money can be found."

Guy leaned back and his face lit up. He had a nice smile. "I learned to skate when I was four years old," he said. "Played a lotta pick-up ice hockey with the neighborhood kids who were on the high school hockey teams. On Saturdays and Sundays durin' the winter. Didn't do too bad against them, either."

Now it was Herman's turn to smile, and he smiled big. *I know one kid won't make for a winning football or baseball team,* he thought. *But with someone like Guy out there, we won't lose quite as often or as bad. And if I recruit Guy, that'll make me look good. Maybe even help me hold onto my job.*

"You can start making your plans, Guy. I'll call the office tomorrow and get them to send the application papers down here so you can fill them out right away. Then I'll make a couple of other calls—about money—and get back to you in a day or two."

A few days later, on Tuesday, August 24th, the *Cape Cod Standard Times* printed photographs of Pete Herman, "Muggsey" Kelly and Guy Vitale. Captioned *WORKING TO KEEP BARNSTABLE FIRST,* here's what it said:

Shown above smacking the pill on the nose is Pete Herman, sturdy manager of the Barnstable team, stout batsman whose average is .408 and dependable first sacker. Sometimes he pitches. He is a teacher-coach at Kents Hill School, Maine, where he has been since his days at Boston College, where he was an outstanding athlete.

At left is John 'Muggsey' Kelly warming up. This is his fifth season with Barnstable. A good general utility man, he pitches, plays in the outfield, and at first. He is a senior at Boston College this fall and lives in Cambridge.

At the right is Guy Vitale of Barnstable, who has to his credit the largest number of base-hits of anyone in the Cape Cod League. He is shown coming in from the outfield after making several spectacular catches in a recent game against Bourne.

*   *   *   *

Barnstable, MA
Thursday, August 26, 1937
Harwich Field
3:45 p.m.

Fast forward to August 26th, 1937, exactly six days after I was born back in East Boston. Barnstable is at Harwich, game tied three all. An interesting thing happened. Let's let the *Times* describe it:

Barnstable came to bat first in the tenth, and Vitale, urged by lusty rooters, hit a single. A female voice in the stands said audibly, 'Lord, I wish Colbert would hit one over the railroad track!' The echo of her voice had not died away when the crack of Colbert's bat against the battered pill riveted attention to the flying sphere. It sailed up and out and over the railroad tracks, as per the previous order, but Ferdenzi, in left field, was after it like a shot and it was only good for three bases, the only multi-base hit of the game. Vitale thus scored one. Herman struck out for the second time; Giovannangeli, pinch hitter, hit to shortstop, was out at first. But Colbert had been watching events with a piercing glance, and was safe at home.

Well, we previously learned that George Colbert, who became a History teacher and coach at Franklin High School, was a big fan favorite. Just how much of a favorite and with whom, we weren't told. Until now.

CHAPTER 26

Cape Cod, MA
Saturday, August 30, 1937
Barnstable, MA
8:50 a.m.

On August 30th, with the season winding down, another list of leading batters was published. Bill Barrett of Harwich led all regular players with a .431 average. Normie Merrill of Barnstable was next, hitting .386. Palumbo, Orleans, was third hitting .382, and Dudley, Orleans and you guessed it, Guy Vitale followed closely, tied at .380.

Exclude the part-time players from the list and Guy was tied for the fourth spot in hitting at this point, with only a half-dozen or so games left in the summer season. This was what the *Times* said in its article that day:

> *The race for top batting honors in the Cape Cod League tightened last week as the averages dropped and the pitching on the whole improved. Barrett of Harwich continues to lead the circuit with 66 hits out of 153 times at bat and is pressed by Knowles of Orleans who played in only five games and collected nine hits out of 22 trips to the plate. The nearest regular player to Barrett is Norm Merrill of Barnstable with 66 hits out of 171 times at bat.*

The morning that article was printed Barnstable and Orleans, playing at Barnstable, recorded another ten-inning game. In this one, Guy again figured prominently. He seemed to thrive on pressure, excelling in these situations.

Orleans had been playing better ball recently. Barnstable, down by five runs in the sixth inning, sent three men to the plate with nothing to show for it. But in the seventh, the locals scored three times while Orleans came up with nothing. In the eighth, Barnstable plated two runs to knot the game at six all, and Barnstable's fans were beginning to hope.

Tenth inning; score tied. Orleans, up first, scored a run on singles by Leonard and Leahy, a pitcher who had come on for Orleans in relief. In Barnstable's half of the inning, Conway flied out to center and Kelley smashed a hard grounder to short but was thrown out at first base.

But Leahy's control was a bit shaky. The next batter, Crawley, was hit by a two-one pitch and went to first base. Herman, first ball swinging, hit a sharp smash to shortstop Lee, who fired wildly to first and Herman was safe. Crawley advanced to third on the play.

Guy, who'd been hot at the plate that day, was two for four. As he stepped into the batter's box, he was conscious of the boisterous Barnstable fans and also aware that the season was winding down. With Bourne breathing down their necks, they needed to win every game from here on out if they were to capture the championship.

Waiting for Leahy to toe the rubber, Guy's thoughts came fast and furious. *This guy's a pretty fair pitcher. Playin' for any other team, his record would be a lot better than it is. So what's he gonna do here?*

It was heat, at the knees, Guy's best pitch. He went down to get it, and drilled it between third and short into left field for a clean single. Crawley came in to score from third and the game was tied at seven, bringing Big George Colbert to the plate.

Colbert had also smacked two hits in four previous plate appearances that day. Showing no emotion, he stood upright in the box and waited for Leahy's delivery. When it came, he was ready. With a nice level swing, he met the ball squarely, driving it into center field for the hit that drove in his manager from third, winning the game for Barnstable.

Harwich beat Barnstable 4–3 on August 31st, in a close game where the outcome was never a safe wager until the final out was recorded. That same day Bourne, sensing a chance to overtake Barnstable, trampled a battered Orleans team, 15–3 at Orleans.

*   *   *   *

Cape Cod, MA
Tuesday, September 1, 1937
Barnstable, MA
1:00 p.m.

On September 1st with the hot, humid month of August in the books, the League standings read this way:

TEAM	WON	LOST
Barnstable	*26*	*16*
Bourne	*23*	*16*
Harwich	*24*	*18*
Falmouth	*21*	*19*
Orleans	*8*	*33*

You remember the days of pasteurized milk? Whether the bottles were delivered to your back door each morning, or you stopped at the grocery store to pick them up, the cream always rose to the top. It was something everybody noticed. Before long, an analogy was being tossed round. It was applied to people, organizations, and sports teams. Especially sports teams. Well, Barnstable was the cream that year.

In the week leading up to that eventful final day of the '37 season, excitement was building. Who would win the pennant? Barnstable? Bourne? Harwich? Which of these three would earn the right to fly that flag above its home diamond next year?

Although Barnstable had been playing some pretty good baseball, on September 2nd, the above report notwithstanding, Bourne had closed the gap and gone into first place, actually leading Barnstable by percentage points in the standings because of a brief end-of-August slump by Pete Herman's boys. But the club, sensing it could hang on and win the pennant again, rose to a new level; the ordinary players playing better, the good players playing exceptionally well. An example of what I mean came on September 3rd as Barnstable entertained Orleans at home. The *Times* again, the next morning:

> *King for a day was Bourne, as Barnstable climbed back onto the Cape Cod League throne yesterday by winning over Orleans 11–5 at Hyannis, while Falmouth at the home grounds took Bourne over the bumps for a 4–3 squeak, the margin of the win coming with one out in the last of the ninth.*
>
> *Diminutive but stout of heart, young Guy Vitale led the Barnstable offensive, getting four hits, one a double, out of five times at bat.*
>
> *[In the fifth] Crawley was Barnstable's opening batter. He promptly doubled to center field. Merrill followed with a double to right field, scoring Crawley and lessening the tension on the Barnstable bench considerably. Vitale hit a double down by third base, just inside the line, scoring Merrill—the first three men at bat in the game for Barnstable*

all hit doubles. Colbert hit the ball to Dennis and was out at first as Vitale went to third. Herman singled to third but Vitale couldn't move safely. Pilote hit to Sharkey who threw to Knowles to get Herman at second, and Knowles threw wildly, trying to get Pilote at first, allowing Vitale to score. O'Flaherty doubled to center field, scoring Pilote. At the end of the first inning, Barnstable led by four runs ...

Guy was not done at the plate. He singled in the fifth to drive in another run, as Barnstable went on to win that game, 11–5. Meanwhile, Falmouth playing at home upset Bourne in a close one, 4–3. Ruckstull and Plansky had great days with their bats, combining in the bottom of the ninth inning for the win. That, for Bourne, had to be heartbreaking.

Another example came the following day, September 4th, just two days before the final game of the season. Barnstable and Orleans squared off in Hyannis where many of the League games were played that summer. True, Orleans was the weakest team in the league, finishing last in the standings with a record of 11 wins, 38 losses. But it's an axiom in sports that a great team will play well against its good competition and will "beat up" on the lousy teams. That Saturday, true to form, Barnstable beat up on Orleans.

Rain was threatening as the game got underway. Barnstable's batting order looked like this:

Frank 'Cowboy' Crawley leading off and playing second base, Norman Merrill patrolling right field and hitting second, John 'Muggsy' Kelly was in left field, batting third, Guy Vitale playing in center field (and later, right field), batting fourth, George Colbert was again the catcher and he was in the fifth slot, Pete Herman was at first base, hitting in the sixth hole, A fellow named Pilote was at shortstop and hitting seventh, O'Flaherty playing third base, hitting eighth, and Giovannangeli was doing the pitching and hitting ninth.

Also seeing some action that day were John Spirada, an outfielder, pitcher Mike Maleski, William Conway, John Maloney, Roy Williams, Frank Zammarchi, Tominey and Marso.

The hurlers for both clubs, Giovannangeli and Leahy, pitched well for the first two innings, although Leahy's control of his curve ball was a bit shaky. Then things heated up. In the top of the third, two Orleans errors and a walk loaded the bases.

Guy, batting in the cleanup slot, came to the plate. This was a lineup change made several days before by manager Pete Herman, moving Guy back from third to fourth, because Colbert had hit a mild slump.

Patient at the plate, Guy worked the count to three and one. The next pitch was a hitter's pitch and he didn't miss it, lining a shot into left for the first of his two singles, driving in two runs.

Then in the fifth, Leahy completely lost the strike zone and gave up three singles, one to Guy, and two walks, as Barnstable plated four runs. Guy went two for five in the game, stole a base, scored a run himself, and played his usual reliable outfield as Barnstable won it 8–0.

Also on September 4th, the *Cape Cod Standard Times* announced its All-Star Cape Cod League baseball team:

> *Herman, Barnstable, Manager*
> *Colbert, Barnstable, catcher*
> *Donovan, Bourne, First base*
> *Crawley, Barnstable, Second base*
> *Gallagher, Bourne, Third base*
> *Berry, Bourne, Shortstop*
> *Plansky, Bourne, Left field*
> *Barrett, Harwich, Center field*
> *Vitale, Barnstable, Right field*
> *Boehner, Falmouth, Utility*
> *Merrill, Barnstable, Pitcher*
> *Sexton, Bourne, Pitcher*
> *Morris, Falmouth, Pitcher*
> *Kenney, Harwich, Pitcher*
> *Leahy, Orleans, Pitcher*

And here's what that same article said about Guy:

> *For the outfield, the selectors named Tony Plansky of Bourne at left, Bill Barrett of Harwich at center and Guy Vitale of Barnstable at right.*
> *Those weren't easy choices by a long shot. Here's the reasons why they were picked. Plansky, recalled by many fans as a mainstay at Bourne's pennant winning nine last year, is a heavy hitter and sure fielder. Barrett leads the loop in hitting and can snare them out of the. ozone if need be. Vitale, while not the leading hitter on percentage, has more safe bingles to his credit than any other man in the circuit*

and doesn't need a clothes basket to pull them in when someone else smacks them.

*   *   *   *

Cape Cod, MA
Monday, September 7, 1937
Barnstable, MA
1:00 p.m.

So the stage was set for a big finish. It could not have been scripted better or in a more exciting manner by a Hollywood screen writer. Barnstable, after losing three in a row the week before because of jitters, was now back to playing its best baseball of the summer. And, they were psyched!

On that windy Labor Day, Barnstable's ace starting pitcher, Normie Merrill was slotted to take the mound against Bourne, before a festive holiday crowd of fifteen hundred excited fans. Having beaten these guys three times already that summer, he was confident, as was the rest of the Barnstable squad. But it was the end of an exhausting season and Merrill was pretty tired, so anything could have happened.

Tension ran high among the players that morning, as Pete Herman announced his lineup. "Crawley—second base, Merrill—pitcher, Vitale—left, Colbert—catcher, I'll do first, Pilote—short, Giovannangeli—right field, Tominey—center field and O'Flaherty—third base." He paused and glanced down the third base line at a grandstand full of spectators, with many others, dressed in jeans, colorful shorts and an assortment of hats, standing along the foul line. Pulling his gaze away, he focused on his team.

"It's been a long season. You guys are a great bunch," he said, a bit emotionally. "Whatever happens today, it's been a real privilege for me to have managed ya this summer. Do I think we can win the pennant today? No! I *know* we can win the pennant today. So let's go do it!"

Well, it was a pitcher's duel for the first three innings. But in the fourth, Barnstable drew first blood. With one out, Herman singled to left. Pilote struck out, but Pete advanced to second when Giovannangeli drew a walk. Tominey, Barnstable's center fielder then hit a hard ground ball to Moran at third, who threw high to first. Herman scored and 'Gio' went to third. Tominy moved to second on the play. The next hitter was O'Flaherty. He sent a soft grounder to Berry at shortstop, who allowed the ball to go through his legs. Two more runs scored. So it was three-zip and Merrill had not given up a hit or a walk yet.

In the fifth, Barnstable padded its lead. Guy, who seemed to live for these pressure situations, stepped to the dish. Pumped by the large crowd of tourists mixed with locals, he stood deep in the box, in a straight stance. The first pitch was a fast ball, just off the corner, which he did not chase, for ball one. *It's gonna be another fast ball,* he reasoned. He guessed correctly, swung and lined a single to left field.

That brought up catcher George Colbert, who was again batting behind Guy. The burly local resident smashed a long double to left to drive him in.

Guy came to the plate again in the seventh. The stocky nineteen year-old, first ball swinging, chalked up the fifth and final Barnstable run when he reached first on an infield pop that dropped in safely (there was no infield fly rule back then), went to third on Herman's single through short, and scored on a bad throw to second by Bourne's catcher Spinney, who was trying to keep Herman from stealing second.

In this thrilling, storybook finish to the '37 season, Barnstable, blasted out five runs to capture the Cape Cod League pennant. For a jubilant Guy Vitale, it was a good day. He had two hits in four official trips, walked once, drove in a run and scored two runs himself. He also fielded his position in left flawlessly, with two putouts in his only chances, since Bourne wasn't hitting much out of the infield against Merrill that day.

Tony Plansky was in the lineup for Bourne that morning, but although he had four put outs in left field, perhaps tired at the end of a long summer season and unable to solve Merrill's assortment of pitches, he went nothing for three at the plate and did not figure in the game.

Later that afternoon, Bourne made up a rained-out game against Orleans, and drained by their morning contest with Barnstable, you guessed it, they lost four to one! That dropped them to third place with a record of twenty-six wins and nineteen losses, behind Harwich, who finished at twenty-seven wins, nineteen losses. Barnstable's record was twenty-nine wins, seventeen losses.

This was the way Christopher Price[39] described the rest of the game.

> *Despite an increasing wind, Merrill continued to work his magic. Keeping in mind that they only needed one win to take the crown, Merrill set down the Bourne team in order in the ninth inning to finish off his no-hitter. The Barnstable players were the league champions, and Norman Merrill had solidified his position as one of the best clutch performers in Cape League history.*

---

39 Christopher Price, *Baseball by the Beach: A History of America's National Pastime on Cape Cod,* Cape Cod Publications. 1998.

The *Cape Cod Standard Times* reported the game the next day, and commented:

> *Merrill, who has hit .385 in the League this year, and Vitale led the Barnstable batting forces and both the the Barnstable infield and outfield played 'heads-up baseball' to give their hurler champion support in the final game of the world series of Cape Cod.*

Just a couple of notes before we move on. That final game of the season? Barnstable's ace hurler Normie Merrill pitched the first no-hit, no-run game in Cape Cod League history. He did not walk a batter, either, and struck out four. Finishing the season with a thirteen and three record, Merrill's performance, which accounted for almost half of Barnstable's victories, was best in the league. He was named to the Cape All-Star nine a few days later, along with, guess who? Guy Vitale. Robert Leahy, the Orleans pitcher who lost to Barnstable on September 4th, was an Honorable Mention selection.

Christopher Price again, from his aforementioned book:

> *This win gave Barnstable its third title in four years, and would place them alongside Falmouth (which would close out the '30s having won five titles during the decade), as one of the teams of the decade. However, it would also mark the final Barnstable title, ending a dynasty. It is the ultimate tribute to Pete Herman and his players that they have been placed alongside of Orleans teams of the '50s and the Cotuit teams of the '60s and '70s in the pantheon of great teams of the Cape Cod Baseball League.*

Pretty high praise for a bunch of baseball players, huh? And Guy Vitale was one of them! Had the town of Barnstable fielded a team in '38, perhaps Guy and these same teammates would have played for them again. And perhaps Barnstable might have overtaken Falmouth in the number of titles won during the 1930s. We'll never know.

So! How did Guy do with the stick that summer? Not bad at all. According to "Uncle" Dudley Larkin, the Leagues' self-styled unofficial scout and guardian angel who achieved a measure of local fame by annually naming a Cape Cod League All-Cape nine for *The Boston Traveler*, Guy finished the season with a .401 batting average. I don't have any information as to where he got that figure, but that's what he wrote.

On September 8th, the *Cape Cod Standard Times* printed its final list of Cape Cod hitters:

> *BARRETT LEADS CAPE BATSMAN IN FINAL LIST*
>
> *Final compilation of the batting averages for the Cape Cod League season finds Bill Barrett of Harwich in possession of the lead with 77 hits out of 175 trips to the plate for an average of .440.*
>
> *More laurels must go to Normie Merrill, who pitched Barnstable into the pennant with a no-hit, no-run game, for exploding the old adage, Pitchers can't hit'. Merrill ranks second with 78 hits out of 198 times up for an average of .394.*
>
> *Another of the pennant winning aggregation, Vitale has 82 hits out of 211 times at bat for .389. These three have played the entire season. Plansky of Bourne has 57 out of 152, for .375 ...*

Here's the *Cape Cod Standard Times* list showing only the top five batters in the League in 1937:

Barrett, Harwich	*.440*
Merrill, Barnstable	*.394*
Vitale, Barnstable	*.389*
Plansky, Bourne	*.375*
Knowles, Orleans	*.373*

Examining the stats, we see that Guy, although not the leading hitter for average, had five more hits and thirty-six more trips to the plate than Bill Barrett, and four more hits and thirteen more at bats than Normie Merrill.

I know what you're thinking. But, 211 times at bat in forty-six games is a lot of plate appearances. That number clearly shows that Guy came to the dish to swing the bat, not to look for a free pass. By the way, in a year when the leading home-run hitter, George Colbert, muscled only seven dingers, Guy poled three.

And on September 10th, *The Enterprise, Falmouth, Mass*, in its column, *Sports in Vacation Falmouth*, reported the final team standings and said this:

> *As Falmouth dropped an 11-inning game to Harwich Monday afternoon and Norman Merrill of Barnstable pitched a no-hit, no-run game against Bourne the same morning the curtain dropped on the 1937 Cape Cod Baseball League. Barnstable's victory gave Pete*

Herman's team the league championship with room to spare. The
final standings:

TEAM	W	L	PCT.
Barnstable	29	17	.630
Harwich	27	19	.587
Bourne	26	18	.578
Falmouth	24	23	.511
Orleans	10	37	.213

A few days after the Cape Cod League season ended, "Uncle Dud" emerged from the cranberry bogs and sand dunes to name his "Cranberry Blossom Special" for 1937. Like the *Cape Cod Standard Times*, he picked Guy as one of three all-star outfielders, to complement Bill Barrett in center and Tony Plansky in left:

> *And to complete the outfield, is Guy Vitale, the East Boston boy*
> *who is heading for the West for the big show. One of the finest to show*
> *up in years, and the youngest to go on the team.*

Well, just who *were* those other two outfielders? I did some research to find out. Bill Barrett, from Cambridge, Massachusetts, had played nine years of major league ball, alternating between three American League teams; the Philadelphia Athletics, Chicago White Sox, and the Boston Red Sox. After retiring from professional ball in 1930, he continued to play amateur ball for fun. That was allowed back then. As mentioned earlier, league rules permitted each club to field two former professionals on its roster. 1937 found him playing center field for Harwich. No big surprise here—he led the league in hitting at .431, led the league in total bases, and tied for the lead in home runs.

We've already met Tony Plansky. The slick-fielding left fielder for Bourne hit .375 during the forty-six game season. He was the reason Guy did not get named to the All-Cape nine as the left fielder, his regular position that year, but had to settle for being named at another position.

At the end of the season, a photograph of this 1937 Barnstable team was printed in the *New Bedford Standard Times*. It's the same one printed on July 10th, 1937 in *the Cape Cod Standard Times*. Al Irish sent me a copy of it on March 31, 2004. The following players were shown:

Left to right, kneeling—Frank "Cowboy" Crawley, George Colbert, John Maloney, Guy Vitale, William Conway, and Roy Williams.

Left to right, standing—Manager Pete Herman, Norman Merrill, John Spirada, Mike Maleski, Frank Zammarchi, and John "Muggsy" Kelley. Missing from the picture were Norman Pilote, O'Flaherty, Tominey and Giovannangeli, because the picture was taken earlier in the season and these last few players joined the club later. Since the late arrivals contributed substantially to Barnstable's winning season, it makes one wonder how they felt about not appearing in the team photograph.

This same photo has been reprinted in Dan Crowley's book entitled, *Baseball on Cape Cod.*

And last but not least, an editorial appearing in the *Cape Cod Standard Times* on September 7th, 1937, summed up the good feelings prevailing in the area as an exciting baseball season came to a dramatic close:

BARNSTABLE, CHAMPION

As forecast some time ago, the finish of the Cape Cod League was a thriller. The fans who had been following the fortunes of Barnstable and Bourne particularly looked for a close race and they got it. Not until yesterday was that result made definite. The winner: Barnstable.

The rivalry between Barnstable and Bourne has been keen, and especially so in this year's race. Yet to the credit of both teams it can be said that in yesterday's championship deciding contest there was not one instance of bad conduct on the part of either players or fans. The game was clean, fairly close and interesting. The final score, 5 to 0, indicates a large margin for Barnstable, which was the case. But for some time the outcome was uncertain and throughout the Bourne players appeared a possible threat.

Whatever the financial standing of the teams, the Cape Cod League can look back on a successful season, as far as interest and attractions are concerned. Only a few games separated the winner from the fourth team in the standing. The late season games drew large crowds and developed a high pitch of enthusiasm. Some of the players were chosen for tryouts with higher leagues.

Of all the players probably none had greater satisfaction in yesterday's determining game than Merrill, the young man who capped a brilliant pitching season with his 13th victory, almost half of the contests won by Barnstable. He pitched a no-hit, no-run game. Merrill also performed well at bat, getting hits the first two times up. Behind him was flawless fielding support by Barnstable players determined to preserve the narrow lead they held.

Baseball as played in the Cape Cod League justifies its position as the national pastime. The game is invariably clean, it affords a common meeting place for sport lovers and a chance for friendly rivalry and bantering that promote the good feeling prevailing on the Cape. The season now closed should be an inspiration to the backers of the Cape cod League to plan for a renewal in an even bigger way next year.

CHAPTER 27

Pine Bluffs, WY
Thursday, October 28, 2004
703 Beech Street
9:05 a.m.

I didn't actually know my uncle had gone to a prep school until my Aunt Margaret sent me a copy of Guy's Army discharge papers, and there it was, under *Civilian Education,* on line 18—*Name and Address of Last School Attended: Kents Hill Academy, Kents Hill, Maine.* So I said, "What's this?" and decided to check it out.

First thing I did was to get on the Kents Hill web site at www.kentshill.org.

According to the information there, one Luther Sampson, a native of Duxbury, Massachusetts, founded Kents Hill School in 1824. Sampson, a Revolutionary War veteran and a religious man, had a great interest in kids, so he thought he'd use his resources to provide educational opportunities for young men and women. And he had a plan:

> *To offer an educational program calculated to inspire intellectual*
> *growth and develop character.*

That's what he wanted to do. So he picked up some land in the small town of Readfield, not too far from Maine's capital city of Augusta. When he first started the place he called it the Maine Wesleyan Seminary and College. According to the commencement day program for the Calls of '38 that was still its official name even when Guy went there, but nobody actually referred to it that way by then. Everyone called it Kents Hill Academy, the name to which it was later changed. Now, after another minor change, to Kents Hill School, it's still going strong, preparing young men and women to take their places in the world.

Next thing, I called the school and spoke to Matthew R. Crane, Director of Admissions and Financial Aid. Matt is an intelligent person, receptive and interested.

"If you can hold on, I'll look him up in the Alumni Yearbook," he offered.

I held the line for several minutes. Then, "There's no listing for him in this book," he said when he came back on. "But this isn't complete. It only lists people we've been keeping up with."

"Well, how can I find out if he actually went to school there in 1937?"

I could almost hear the wheels turning as he mulled over the problem. "We can help you," he said. I immediately liked his positive tone. "First, I can check to see if we have a file on him. His records will be in it. I can also check out the Yearbook for that year. Then, later today I'll make a few phone calls to some people who may have known him."

After we finished talking he turned me over to Cheryl W. Freye, who had a fancy title; Director of Institutional Research, Assistant to the Director of Development. She, too, was very helpful.

In answer to my question if Kents Hill was a separate town or part of another area, she told me more than I ever wanted to know.

"Kents Hill is a part of the town of Readfield, Maine," she laughed. "It has its own post office which I believe was started years ago because the school received such a large volume of mail—at least large for this rural area. The Post Office Building is actually owned by the school. The whole region around the school is referred to as Kents Hill, but legally it's in the town of Readfield."

I can't say enough good things about Cheryl. Over the next few months, she put me in touch with several people and provided a bunch of documents. The world's a better place with people like her in it.

A few evenings after my first contact with Matt and Cheryl, I got home late and found a cryptic message on my answering machine from a guy named Howard Doyle.

"Matt Crane spoke to me. Call this number as soon as possible and you'll learn a lot more about Guy."

Doyle was a member of the Kents Hill Class of '35 and he was the class agent. The phone number he gave me belonged to Chester Parasco, who had been in Guy's class at Kents Hill, went on to college and law school, and had a career as an insurance lawyer. He was now retired and living in Walpole, Massachusetts.

As we already know, in the 1930s the Athletic Director at Kents Hill was a big, nice looking young man named Edward Peter Herman. He also coached baseball, football and ice hockey at that school. Yep, he's the same fella who managed the Barnstable baseball team. He'd made a reputation for himself as a darn good baseball player a few years before. Played first base. Good hitter, fair glove man. Didn't have any interest in playing pro ball, though. Wanted to work with kids. So he parlayed his baseball reputation into the Athletic Director's slot and coaching job at Kents Hill, and in the summertime, he managed the Barnstable ball club to keep busy and earn some extra money. By the end of '37, he'd seen Guy play ball for two summers.

These things we already know. What we don't know with certainty was how Guy managed to show up at Kents Hill for the '37–'38 school year. But on that warm fateful evening in August 1937, a couple of weeks before the baseball season on Cape Cod came to an end, after their conversation in that Barnstable bar and grill, Pete Herman made some phone calls and put things in motion for Guy, who was practically penniless, to attend prep school and rub elbows with boys whose parents were people of wealth, power and influence, and who, themselves, might eventually become the same. The potential for a bright future was opening up for Guy.

*   *   *   *

Readfield, ME
Monday, September 13, 1937
Kents Hill School
8:45 a.m.

When Guy Vitale and his new friend, Chester Parasco, trudged across the quadrangle from Sampson Hall, their dormitory building, to Blethen House that opening day of school in 1937, on the way to their first class, the leaves on the tall oaks and maples growing on campus were already turning color and there was a hint in the air of the bitterly cold Maine winter to come.

Both boys were post-graduate (PG) students in the Academy Program, and football players. "But," Chester told me, "there was a difference. Guy was a born athlete. I was not."

"When I met Guy," Parasco continued, "he was five feet seven inches tall and weighed about a hundred sixty-five or seventy pounds. I found out right away that he'd been recruited by Pete Herman to play football, baseball and hockey. I didn't play baseball, but we both played football on that '37 team."

It didn't take long for Parasco and the other boys to size up Vitale. "He was the quarterback that year. A couple other kids competed for the job, but Guy beat them out. After all, he'd been a quarterback for his high school team and had made All-Scholastic in football twice. He was easily the best player on the team," Parasco reminisces. "On the other hand, I was the worst. I had speed and willingness but nothing else. Guy had everything."

Parasco chuckled as he told the story of his one claim to a dubious fame while at Kents Hill. It seems that the football team had another pretty good player, a fullback, who was counted on to help them win games in their league, which was made up of other prep schools and a couple of college freshman teams. One afternoon prior to the start of the season, during a scrimmage on the sparse fall grass, Guy called an off-tackle slant and handed off to this fullback who didn't find a hole where one was supposed to be. So he spun off a couple of tacklers and attempted to come around end. It was Chester's side of the field. He was playing defensive halfback. He moved up and made the tackle. After the whistle, Chet got to his feet. The fullback didn't. His leg was broken. He was lost to the team for the entire season.

"The guys didn't appreciate me very much after that," Chester said ruefully.

He laughs about it now, so many years later. But we all know how cruel kids that age can be to one another. Chester Parasco left unsaid the hurt of being ostracized by his pals on the team for part of the year, until things sort of worked out. I'll tell you about that in a minute.

As for Guy's intellectual prowess, Parasco recalled it this way. "We only had one class together, a course in U.S. History. Mr. Fifield was the teacher. In class Guy was a quiet sort; but it was obvious he was interested in American history. And he was bright."

*   *   *   *

Readfield, ME
Tuesday, September 14, 1937
Kents Hill School
9:00 a.m.

"Good morning class." The tall, gangly man closed the classroom door and strode to the front of the room. Dressed in a blue sport coat with leather elbow patches and tan slacks, he wore thick bifocals perched halfway down his nose, and his sandy hair was brushed straight back from his forehead. All of this gave him a scholarly air. "My name is Reginald Fifield and, like it or not, I've been assigned the task of teaching you U.S. History." Turning, he picked up a piece of chalk and with a flourish, scrawled his name on the blackboard.

The room became still. Guy Vitale sat in the second row next to the open windows, his new history book at his left elbow. Chester Parasco sat immediately to his right. Through the open windows, the crisp fall air entered, carrying the odor of burning leaves, and bringing with it a hint of the cold weather soon to come.

Fifield removed his bifocals and waived them at his class. "You will address me as 'Sir' or as 'Mr. Fifield,'" he announced. "Before we begin, I'm going to conduct a little poll." His Adam's apple bobbed up and down noticeably as he spoke. "Ready? Good. How many of you know the date upon which the Declaration of Independence was signed?"

No response. "No one? Humph." He strode to his desk. "What about this? Where were the thirteen original colonies located?"

Again no response from the students. Placing his glasses back on his nose, Fifield turned and took a step forward. "Just as I thought," he said contemptuously. "We've raised a generation who are, for the most part, historically illiterate." Glaring at the students as if he expected trouble from them already, he continued. "Well, I'll tell you what we're going to do," he said. "We're going to learn the importance of knowing History. You must realize that we have to know who we *were* if we're to understand who we *are* and know where we're *headed*. This is essential! You must learn to value what our forbears—and not just in the Eighteenth Century, but our own parents and grandparents—did for us, or you are not going to take knowledge of our history very seriously, and it can slip away."

Tossing the chalk back into the chalk tray, he again advanced on the class, his voice taking on an earnest quality. "If you've inherited a great work of art that's worth a fortune but you don't *know* that it's worth a fortune, you don't even know that it's a great work of art, and you're not interested in it, you are going to lose it."

Guy, a serious look on his face, nibbled on the end of his number two pencil. He'd never heard anything like this before. His young mind opened like a blossoming flower, and he smiled. *I think I'm gonna like this class*, he thought.

*   *   *   *

Readfield, ME
Saturday, October 2, 1937
Kents Hill School
3:00 p.m.

Kents Hill played seven football games that season, beginning with Maine Central Institute on October 2nd, at Pittsfield. The *Kennebec Journal* covered high school and prep school sports in the area like a blanket that year:

MCI ENTERTAINS KENTS HILL AT PITTSFIELD TODAY

MCI of Pittsfield will be hard pressed this afternoon as they play their second game of the season against a rugged eleven from Kents Hill at Pittsfield. Starting time is set for 2 o'clock.

Just how strong the Hilltoppers are no one really knows but the MCI preppers, classed by many in the state as having one of the best outfits in years will test them in what promises to be one of the best games of the year.

Maine Central Institute's backers had a lot to cheer about that day, as its team trounced the Hilltoppers twenty-one zip. But Guy got his feet wet as a prep school football player that afternoon, playing quarterback and doing some kicking.

*   *   *   *

Readfield, ME
Monday October 4, 1937
Kents Hill School
9:00 a.m.

It was cold in Readfield, and the wind, remnant of a nor'easter blowing itself out over on the coast, gusted against the gray stones of Blethen House, rattling the windows in their frames, making the students glad they were warm and dry inside.

Reginald Fifield had been teaching for several years. He was a sanely human person, intelligent and sensitive, especially where his students were concerned. His life experience had resulted in a humanness, a trustworthy ability to judge things, and an intensely stable personality, to which others—his wife, fellow teachers, and friends, for instance—reacted with unconcealed admiration.

Standing in front of his classroom, totally in control, he was conscious of the huge gap in learning between himself and his charges. The knowledge that he, and the other instructors at Kents Hill, must try to change that; must narrow that gap as much as possible in the limited time which they had available to them, weighed heavily on him for a brief moment.

Surveying this group of youngsters with a concern that he concealed, he feigned disgust, instead. His students had already grown used to this, had seen through it, and were already fond of him.

"You may have noticed," Fifield said, "that for the past three weeks, we've done lots of writing in this History class." He glanced around the room slowly, making eye contact with each student one at a time, not moving on to the next until sure he had the attention of each. "And I've not been grading you on your writing, but only on the historical substance of your work. Well, gentlemen and ladies," he paused and bowed slightly toward the two girls in the class, "as of this week, that will change. From now on, you will be graded on *writing* as well as *substance*. You will write as best you can. No, as of today, you will write better than you ever thought you could; carefully, thoughtfully, and often."

This announcement was met with loud groans from everyone and some foot-stamping.

"What?" Fifield continued, pretending to be surprised. "You don't want to write? You don't want to convey your jewels of knowledge to your most unworthy professor every week for the remainder of the year? You're reluctant to dazzle me with your lucid prose?"

"Sir!" one of the boys said. "We don't write so well. None of us do. We …"

Fifield cut him off. "Let me ask you a question, young man," he said. "What are your intentions after you leave these hallowed halls?"

"College, sir. And then into my father's business."

Turning to Chester Parasco, Fifield pointed. "What about you, Chester?"

"College and then law school, I hope," Parasco responded brightly.

It was Guy's turn. "And you, Guy?"

"I … hope to play pro baseball after I leave here, but if I don't get signed, then I'll go to college," Guy responded.

Fifield turned away, about to call on another student. Then he paused and turned back. "A professional baseball player, huh? I believe that's a first for my classes. I don't think I've ever had anyone whose ambition was to play professional baseball." He smiled thoughtfully. "But you still want to be a well-educated person, don't you, Guy?"

"Yes, sir."

"Good. My point is that the well-educated man … and woman … must write well. To accomplish this, you must read widely, grounding yourselves in the Classics and then going on from there. At college, you will probably take courses in writing and poetry. Those will be very valuable in your quest for mastery of the art of writing. But you will need to have a certain level of writing ability before then. I intend to help you reach that level."

More good-natured groans as Fifield paused. "And as you attain a certain writing skill, remember this. History! That's where the truly well-educated person must be fully versed. History of Western Culture! European History! Some dabbling into the History of Ancient Civilizations! History of Asian Cultures!" he paused again. "And, ahh, yes, don't forget the most important of all … the History of your own country—American History!"

"But, Mr. Fifield," One of the girls said. "Jack London and Ernest Hemingway became great writers, but London had no education, and Hemingway didn't know much about History."

"True, Elizabeth," Fifield said. "But Mr. London was a self-made man. He scratched out his education by *reading and writing* between work-shifts on boats, in logging camps and gold mines. And Mr. Hemingway, although he said 'the only way for a writer to learn to write is by going away and writing,' went away and studied under two of the greatest writers then living; Sherwood Anderson and Gertrude Stein."

Now at the back of the classroom, Fifield was conscious that every head was turned toward him. "There are exceptions to all general rules," he continued. "By implication, a general rule will have its exceptions. And those two were exceptions. But the rule is there, unchallenged. To be well-educated, one must read widely, know history, and learn to write well."

Guy Vitale, sitting next to the windows against which wind-driven rain was now beating, removed the pencil upon which he'd been chewing from his mouth and nodded in complete agreement.

And that was it for Guy—the moment in his academic life when he became a true student—something which few, even at the college level, ever do. This was the moment when he became interested in learning. Not just to pass a course or to get his diploma or a good job. Rather, his mind was opened to learning for learning's sake. As James W. Sire puts it in his jewel of a book, *Chris Chrisman Goes to College:*[40]

> … *to gain insight into the way the world really is or at least the way those who have thought about it and studied it think it is. They [the true students] are interested in integrating the way they think about one thing with the way they think about another and connecting the way they live with the way they think. True students make no distinction between formal academic study and personal study. They remain students throughout their lives.*

---

40   James W. Sire, *Chris Chrisman Goes to College; And Faces the Challenges of Relativism, Individualism and Pluralism,* InterVarsity Press, Downers Grove, IL. 1993.

And there's evidence that, throughout his later life, Guy *did*, in fact, maintain this quality.

*   *   *   *

Readfield, ME
Saturday, October 9, 1937
Kents Hill School
3:00 p.m.

The following week Herman's bunch of footballers traveled over to North Bridgeton to play long-time rival, Bridgeton Academy. In an article on the morning of October 7th hyping the game, the *Kennebec Journal* reported:

> *Bridgeton Academy will face its ancient rival in its annual football game to be played at North Bridgeton on this coming Saturday. For the past ten years these have been closely contested and usually are won by a narrow touchdown. This year all indications point to a great game and one of the largest crowds of the year are (sic)anticipated.*
>
> *Little is known of Kents Hill's strength this year except that last Saturday in their opening game they fell before a powerful MCI team 21–0. However, it has been reported that MCI has one of the best football teams to represent them for years and that they are capable of giving any one plenty of competition.*

Guy and his Hilltoppers lost 7–0. He called a good game, fired several passes that should have been caught but weren't, and as a result, had trouble moving the football. Kents Hill didn't score a single touchdown.

On Saturday, October 16th, the boys traveled all the way to Providence, Rhode Island for a game against the Brown University Freshman team. Maybe the bus trip was too long. They lost. Again, they didn't score.

Next, the Kents Hill eleven traveled to Orono, Maine, and squared off against a University of Maine freshman team making its second start of the season. It didn't come out well for Guy and his bunch. The *Kennebec Journal* saw it like this:

KENTS HILL AT MAINE TODAY

> *Orono, Oct. 21—The University of Maine freshman football team, which scored 32 points in its only game, meets Kents Hill School,*

which has not scored a point in three games, tomorrow afternoon at 2 o'clock.

"But despite the fact that Kents Hill has lost all of its contests, we expect a tough battle," asserted Phil Jones, coach of the freshman, who trounced Ricker, 32–0 last Saturday. "Kents Hill is always dangerous. It lost by one touchdown to Bridgeton which shows that it has considerable strength."

The weather was clear and cold on Friday, October 22nd as the teams took the field for the opening kickoff. The Maine freshmen won the toss and elected to receive. Guy was doing the place-kicking so, to avoid the possibility of a devastating runback which would put his team behind immediately, he kicked it into their end zone. Maine started on its own twenty and it took them just nine plays to score. But the extra point was blocked, so it was six to zip and that's the way it stayed until the beginning of the second quarter.

After the teams swapped ends of the field, the first Hilltoppers' possession stalled at their own forty-eight, and it was a punting situation. Guy, standing on his own thirty-four, got off a punt that rolled out of bounds on Maine's one-yard line.

Unnerved with their own goal line so close at their backs, Maine ran three plays that didn't go anywhere, and kicked it away.

Guy's team had the best of this exchange. Kents Hill's second series of downs started from their own forty-five, and Pete Herman was over on the sidelines thinking he had made a pretty good move bringing Guy to Kents Hill.

The Hilltoppers moved the ball down to the freshman's twenty-five yard line on several carries by Victor Lebednik, the new kid from Nashua, New Hampshire, who was taking the place of the fullback who had broken his leg earlier. It was second and seven.

Guy handed off to Lebednik again. Lebednik started around the left side, pulled up and tossed it downfield to Hebert, the left end. Hebert, who had a couple of steps on his defender, hauled it in for the score, and Kents Hill had its first touchdown of the season. Game tied six all, and Chester Parasco was breathing a little easier, thinking maybe people would start to forget that he broke the first string fullback's leg back in that pre-season scrimmage.

But a few minutes later, near the end of the half Maine scored again. They moved to Kents Hill's forty on a series a running plays and one pass play. Then their fullback, a guy named Reitz, tossed a fifteen yard pass to his end, Ray Harnish, who galloped down the sidelines to the ten-yard line. About to be tackled, he lateraled to Anderson who went in for the score. Reitz place kicked the extra point, and that's the way the game went down.

The late afternoon edition of the local newspaper reported it like this:

MAINE FRESHMEN TOP KENTS HILL, 13–6

Orono. Oct. 23—Kents Hill and the University of Maine freshmen took turns marching up and down the field during the first half today, but the freshmen added a forward and a lateral to edge out the preppers, 13–6.

FINE KICKER

In Vitale, Kents Hill has one of the best punters seen in Maine this year. Many of his boots traveled more than 40-yards from the line of scrimmage and on one occasion he cut loose with a 51 yard kick that rolled out on the Maine one-yard line …

So it was four games into the season, and Guy had already been noticed by the local press. I mean, we're talking fifty-five and sixty yard punts, and Pete Herman was walking around after the game saying "I told ya so," to anyone who'd listen.

Four days later, on October 26th, Kents Hill announced the names of its Honor Roll students for the first quarter. It was an exclusive list. Only fourteen students made it.

Guy was on the list. So was Chester Parasco.

Next up was Huntington School, in Boston, on October 29th. Kents Hill won, but I could not find an article about it, so I don't know either the score or how Guy did in that game.

On Saturday November 6th, Herman's boys were due to play Hebron Academy in the first of only two home games that year. Hebron was their traditional rival, and naturally, they wanted to win. Here's what the Kennebec paper said about the upcoming game;

KENTS HILL MEETING HEBRON; IS TRADITIONAL BATTLE

Kents Hill, Nov 4—The Kents Hill football team meets its traditional rival Hebron Academy at Kents Hill on Saturday at two o'clock.

Despite the fact that Kents Hill has won but one game, there is considerable interest being manifested in this meeting of these two teams

and the game should be interesting and as full of thrills as in past years
when respective records for the season meant little.

With his entire squad free of injuries, Coach 'Pete' Herman is able
to start the strongest lineup of the year with Hebert and Chamberlain,
ends; Fanning and Hurd, tackles; Tollman and Elliott, guards; and
Maguire at center. The backfield will consist of Douville, Greene,
Barolet, and Vitale.

I couldn't locate an article describing this game either, so I don't know who won.

On Thursday, November 11th, the Hilltoppers were pitted against Ricker Classical Institute in their season finale. There was a big turn-out of students and locals, since it was not only the last home game, but the final game of the season for Kents Hill.

This contest was a defensive struggle for the entire first quarter. Guy got to unlimber his leg several times. So did the other punter. The game was played mostly between the forty-yard stripes until mid-way in the second quarter, when Ricker's quarterback got hot and started completing passes to both his ends and a halfback coming out of the backfield. Ricker moved inside Kents Hill's twenty and it was first and ten from the eighteen. But Kents Hills' kids, fired up, put on the first of two goal line stands and Ricker didn't score. The game went into halftime nothing—nothing.

In the middle of the third quarter, Guy got his boys moving. Starting on their own twenty-five, with fullback sub Lebednik running off-tackle slants and power plays right over center, they moved all the way to Ricker's thirty-five. Then Guy called what had been a bread-and-butter play for them all season. Lebednik took the handoff, started around the left side, stopped and heaved a bullet to Hebert at the goal line and he took it in for the score. The unbelieving crowd screamed its approval.

What was it with this quarterback to fullback to left end play? The way Lebednik could pass, you wonder why he wasn't playing quarterback instead of Guy. Anyway, they got the six, and Guy place-kicked the extra point. Kents Hill seven, Ricker zip. Later, Kents Hill pulled another goal line stand in the fourth quarter to protect their fragile lead. They won it 7–0. That evening, the Kennebec paper called it this way:

KENTS HILL OVERCOMES RICKER CLASSICAL, 7–0

Kent's Hill, Nov. 11—The Hilltoppers only threatened once here
this afternoon, but it was enough to down a stubborn Ricker Classical

eleven, 7–0. A thirty-five yard pass from Lebednik, a substitute back, to Hebert on the end of a 75 yard march proved the final touch in the Kents Hill scoring.

Other than this, the locals failed to offer another threat while they had to stage two goal line stands to hold off a fighting Ricker team. Once in the second period and again in the final quarter, Ricker got its passing game into action and heaved its way into scoring territory. But each time the Hilltoppers were equal to the occasion and threw back both attempts …

So another year had passed, and Guy Vitale, showing amazing resourcefulness, had done what he needed to do; what he'd told his parents he *would* do. On the strength of his athletic skills, he'd been able to attend one of the most prestigious college prep schools in New England, and perhaps in the entire country. And, in addition to playing three sports, he had apparently done well academically. Just how well, we'll see later on.

CHAPTER 28

Pine Bluffs, WY
Saturday, October 30, 2004
703 Beech Street
9:00 a.m.

There were girls at Kents Hill, too. Lillian Beatrice MacDonald Washburn, who now lives in Jaffrey, New Hampshire, was president of the Class of '38. She was in the Junior College program, a two-year course of study for kids who wanted to go on to a full four-year college later.

"I knew Guy," she said. "He was a nice boy, well liked, quiet and serious. Struck me as the kind who was so nice he'd sleep with a smile on his face."

I wanted to know if Guy was a good student.

"Well, since he was with the Academy kids, we didn't have any classes together," Lillian said. "But my recollection is that he was. He was there to get the most out of life," she said. "He apparently wanted to get additional credits to go into a college of his choice. That's what the post-graduate program was for."

Did Lillian MacDonald know anything more about Guy?

"I knew he played football, because I used to watch the games on the weekends. I also know he worked in the dining hall some to help out with his tuition. During the week I didn't circulate much because I was so busy studying. I did the two-year Junior College program in one year by doubling up the courses. That kept me pretty busy."

"What about his social life? Did he date anybody while he was there?"

Lillian paused for a few seconds. "Ah, I don't really recall," she mumbled, a bit evasively. "You might want to talk with somebody else about that."

"Who'd be a good one to talk to?" I asked. "I noticed someone named Marie Theresa Greco listed on the graduation program; Italian and from Boston."

"Terry? Yes," she said. "She'd be a real good one to talk to. I think she lives in Florida now." With that she changed the subject, but my curiosity was aroused so I decided this was something to look into a bit more.

*   *   *   *

Pine Bluffs, WY
Saturday, October 30, 2004
703 Beech Street
2:30 p.m.

When I was a kid, there'd been a rumor floating around the family that Guy had had a bad experience with a member of the opposite sex while in his late teens or early twenties; really fell hard, but was greeted with either total and complete indifference or rejection. You'll recall that Guy, being devoted to his athletics, had not dated much if at all in high school. So his experience with girls had to have been meager by the time he arrived at Kents Hill.

Who was this femme fatale who had dared to reject my uncle? Details were scant. I didn't know whether this story was true or not, and if it were true, who the girl was, whether she had lived in Boston or somewhere else, or how or where they'd met.

They could have met at Kents Hill. Or on the Cape. Or it could have happened later. Or maybe not at all. I decided to track down Marie Greco. Not having anything but her maiden name, I made several abortive phone calls before realizing that it was going to be almost impossible without help. About to give up, I found the name "Janet Spalding Pratt," nee "Janet Elisabeth Spalding," in an issue of *Kents Hill Today,* the school's alumni magazine, sent to me by Cheryl Frye. Janet had been in the Junior College program with Lillian MacDonald. The magazine gave me a city and state; directory assistance did the rest.

"Yes," Janet said, "I knew Guy at Kents Hill, but not real well. Just to say 'hi' to." She chuckled. "I thought he was real cute. He had a turned-up nose and nice eyes."

"Did he have any close friends, either male or female while he was there?"

"Well, I know that Jack MacDougall was one of Guy's close friends. His real name was William John MacDougall, but we all called him Jack. He died back in the '40s. A brain tumor, I think. And Guy was also friendly with Vance Healy and Earle Smith, but they're both deceased, too."

"Did Guy date any of the girls at Kents Hill?" I asked.

"I'm not real sure, but I *do* know he didn't date anyone in the Junior College program. I seem to recall that he had a girl back in Boston."

"Anything else, Janet?"

"About Guy? He was real quiet. I knew he played football and hockey. He was a very good athlete. And I vaguely recall that he played baseball." She paused, thinking. Then, "I think he also worked as a waiter in the dining hall. He was there on a football scholarship, and most of those boys did that to help out with tuition."

I thanked Janet for her assistance and gave her my phone number. "If you think of anything else," I said, "please call me."

"One other thing, Mr. Sacco," Janet said. "You might want to talk with Terry Greco. She was from Boston, Italian and Catholic like Guy. They used to ride the bus over to Winthrop to church on Sundays."

"Have you got a number for her?" I held my breath.

"Sure. Terry's alive and well." She gave me a phone number in Florida.

*   *   *   *

Pine Bluffs, WY
Saturday, October 30, 2004
703 Beech Street
4:30 p.m.

Terry Greco Paquette, nee Marie Theresa Greco, had been from Arlington, Massachusetts. She'd married Hubert Leonard Paquette, and after his retirement, moved to Madeira Beach, Florida, to be near her brother, Edmond, who lived there. She didn't know that one of Guy's nephews, my cousin, Frank Vitale—Guy's brother Frank's oldest son—lived not fifty miles away, in Safety Harbor, and Guy's widow, my Aunt Margaret, lived north and east, in Sanford.

"I knew him well, Tony," Terry responded to my first question. "Thought he was a great kid. He was always friendly, and he had a good personality."

"Who were some of his friends?" I wanted to know.

"Guy was friendly with everybody," she said. "He was close with Vinnie Hebert but Vinnie's deceased now."

"Who did Guy date while he was at Kents Hill?"

Terry paused. "I'm not sure he dated anyone. He and I didn't date. I got to know him on our Sunday trips to Mass over to Winthrop. I was the only Catholic girl up there. All the Catholic boys rode the bus. I got to go with Mr. Herman, in his car. We went on Holy Days, too."

"Winthrop?"

"Yes. That's a small town not too far from Kents Hill. Oh, yeah. Guy was also friends with Bob Brown, but he was killed in a training accident while in the Service years ago."

"How did you get to know Guy well enough to see that he was always friendly and had a good personality?"

"Well, Kents Hill was such a small school back then, everybody knew everybody. I'd run into Guy at the games, mostly, or at the dances."

"Dances? Did he bring anybody to the dances?" Terry didn't know, she said.

Off the phone I searched my, by now, voluminous papers for the commencement program of the One Hundred and Fourteenth Graduation Exercises, for some of the names given me. There was no Vinnie Hebert listed. He may have been a member of the football squad mentioned earlier. But the name Vance Augustus Healy *did* show up. A second call to Terry Greco revealed that *she* had dated Vance Healy, that he had played baseball with Guy, but that he, too, was deceased. And she was certain that there'd been a kid named Vinnie Hebert at Kents Hill with them.

So, there we have it. With the exception of Janet Spalding Pratt's recollection that Guy may have had a girl in Boston, I drew a blank. Either he did not date anyone while at Kents Hill, or if he did, those girls were not willing to share the information.

*   *   *   *

Pine Bluffs, WY
Saturday, October 30, 2004
703 Beech Street
9:30 p.m.

Lillian MacDonald and Chet Parasco were *both* correct about one thing: Guy *was* a good student at Kents Hill School. In fact, he was one of just nine students—three girls and six boys in the Post-Graduate Program's Class of '38—who graduated Cum Laude.[41]

Where Guy found the time to do so much studying I don't know, because besides playing football, he also played ice hockey in the middle of the year, and baseball in the spring, lettering in all three sports. But he did it. At that stage in

---

41 The Kents Hill Chapter of the Cum Laude Society awarded him a certificate on May 16, 1938, although they spelled his name "Vitalie" instead of "Vitale." They weren't too familiar with Italian names up there back then.

his young life, he seemed to know what he wanted and how to go about getting it.

And the kid was good under pressure. Most of his efforts to this point had met with success. He was able to accomplish what he set his mind to do. College? The way now seemed open. A baseball future? Although doubts were there, it was not at all clear, yet, that O'Brien had let him down. Girls? We don't know much, but it seems that most of the young ladies found him … at least attractive at this point. And when they learned about his athletic prowess, to me it seemed impossible that he would face rejection at the hands of the female set.

*   *   *   *

Readfield, ME
Friday, May 27, 1938
Kents Hill School Dining Hall
4:30 p.m.

The school year had come to a close. Kents Hill's campus bustled with the sights and sounds of kids packing, saying their goodbyes, preparing to leave, knowing full well that for most of them, this would be the last time they'd ever see each other. Guy, whose bus to Boston would not leave until the next morning, was relaxing with Pete Herman in the dining hall. He was scrutinizing the list of the Cum Laude students, which he'd picked up at the Dean of Student's office earlier.

"Listen ta this!" he said and began reading the names in alphabetical order. "Emery Akeley, Pearl Berry, Robert Cunningham, Margaret Dow, Robert Hight, Barbara Smith, Stuart Smith, *Guy Vitale,* and John Wills." He looked up, a huge grin on his face.

"Congrats, Guy," his coach said. Herman was content, too; the Board had renewed his contract for another year with a substantial increase in salary, largely because of the kid sitting across the table from him. "When we talked about this last summer, I knew you felt college might be your doorway to that professional baseball career."

"Yeah," Guy responded, slapping the list on the table and reaching for his Coke. "But first," he said, "I needed to show I have what it takes ta do college work."

Herman tapped a finger on the list. "Well, you accomplished that, all right. Any college will be glad ta get ya. Decided on a school, yet?"

"Naw. But it's gonna be one with a darn good baseball program. I'm gonna talk with Mr. O'Brien about it."

Hearing that, Herman frowned slightly. "Once you get in, what're the chances a major league team will tie you up and help out with tuition and all?"

"Pretty good, I think."

"Well, ya did what ya had ta do." Herman sat back and beamed at Guy. "You can be justifiably proud a yerself. Cum Laude isn't Magna Cum Laude or Summa Cum Laude, but it's damn good in anybody's book." He paused, glanced at his hands and then at Guy. "I'm comin' down ta Boston next week," he said. "I'll stop by your place."

"That'd be great, Mr. Herman," Guy responded. "You can meet my ma and pa while yer there."

"Terrific," Herman said. "And maybe you can introduce me to Mr. O'Brien, too. I'd love to have a little chat with him."

*　　*　　*　　*

East Boston, MA
Friday, June 3, 1938
20 Breed Street
12:40 p.m.

True to his word, after school closed for the year, Peter Herman wrapped things up at Kents Hill and a week later, made the trip to Boston in his old Mercury sedan, arriving at Guy's home a bit after noon. Guy, who'd stayed out late drinking in one of the watering holes over on Bennington Street the night before, had only been out of bed for a few minutes. For him, the days of morning Mass and the Eucharist were a thing of the past and his prayer life had all but disappeared. He'd found that a few hours in a local bar, sopping up the accolades of people he did not know but who knew him or knew of his exploits on the gridiron and the diamond during his high school years, seemed to fill the hole in him left by the lack of parental love, affection and attention which he craved but had not received.

"Where are your parents?" Herman asked. "I'd like ta meet them."

"C'mon. I'll introduce ya to them," Guy responded.

Turning on the charm for which he was noted at Kents Hill and within his own family circle, Herman was pleased to see that he made a favorable impression on both Guy's mother and father. Afterwards, the two men walked over to Noyes Field, sat in the empty wooden grandstand and talked about baseball, the Cape Cod League, and the players with whom they'd hung out the previous summer. At the first lull in their conversation, Herman got down to business.

"Guy? How about you and me goin' ta see Fred O'Brien later this afternoon?"

"Today?"

"Yeah. Don't you think it's high time ya knew what he's been doing?"

Seeing doubt and concern mirrored on Guy's face, Pete trotted out all the reasons he could think of for setting up a meeting with Fred O'Brien that very day.

After listening for awhile, Guy saw the wisdom in Pete's idea. "Yer probably right," he said. "Let's go back ta the house. I'll call him and set it up." Reluctantly, he admitted to himself that he was both relieved that he would finally learn what, if anything, O'Brien had done, and grateful that his former manager and coach was interested enough to want to help him. *And God knows, I need the help,* he thought. *Something's wrong. I shoulda confronted Mr. O'Brien a long time ago.*

*   *   *   *

East Boston, MA
Friday, June 3, 1938
East Boston District Court Building
3:40 p.m.

"Guy tells me you're representing him with the major league scouts," Peter Herman said. Introductions over, he and Guy had taken seats in front of the desk in Fred O'Brien's second floor office in the building in which the Department of Parole and Probation was located.

O'Brien closed the door, shutting out the sounds of telephones and typewriters in the front office. Although the window was open, a smell of stale cigars hung in the air. Another year had taken a considerable toll on him. He had lost weight and his once-natty suit coat hung from his bony shoulders as if it belonged to someone else. His face had the florid look of the heavy drinker. His bloodshot eyes darted from Herman to Guy and back again, no doubt wondering why Guy had brought this man with him instead of his brother, Frank, and what tack he should take.

"Yes," he said, deciding quickly and shaking his head slowly from side to side as if recalling difficult times. "It's been hard work, too. Many meetings with scouts from the Yankees, Cleveland, Detroit—"

"Oh. So three teams are interested, huh?" Herman said genially.

"Well, n-n-not exactly," O'Brien stammered. "Ya see. These things take time."

He ran a hand through his thinning hair and began to speak fast, without making eye contact, his voice low, his words tumbling, somewhat garbled, from his lips.

Watching and listening, the tight smile Guy had worn as he entered O'Brien's office faded from his face. Herman's demeanor, too, changed noticeably. Crossing and uncrossing his legs, he was trying to understand, for Guy's benefit, what O'Brien was saying.

A dull anger began to gather at the back of Guy's mind. Studying the lined face of his old football and baseball coach, he took in the changes in the man; the signs of aging and stress, the ravages of alcohol consumption. *This has been goin' on for a long time,* Guy suddenly realized, as O'Brien's voice droned on.

"... and so I've had several talks with—" That's as far as he got. With a wave of his hand, Guy cut him off.

"Mr. O'Brien! It's been two years now. I wanna know what's *really* goin' on? How come nobody's signed me yet?"

The rest of the meeting had not gone well. Under Herman's not-too-gentle prodding, O'Brien revealed all. When the awful truth was finally exposed, it sat there naked, for all to see.

It was over. Silence reigned among the three. O'Brien, tears running down his aging cheeks, wrung his hands. Herman, his left foot resting on his right knee, looked away, concern written all over his face. Guy glanced from one to the other, understanding slowly dawning; the simple truth was that his high school coach had let him down. Greed, need and drink had intervened. The scouts had been repelled by O'Brien's demands, the major league teams had backed off, perhaps for good, and two whole years of Guy's life, years that should have been spent honing his skills under the watchful eyes of instructors in a major league team's farm system, had been wasted.

Finally, with a sound like a wounded animal, Guy rose from his chair, directed a withering glance at his old coach and burst from his office, throwing the door open so hard that it hit the wall with a loud bang like a gunshot, startling the secretaries at work in the outer office.

Guy, without a thought for Pete Herman, Fred O'Brien, anyone or anything else, ran down the stairs and out of the building, the horrible implications of what he'd heard searing through his fevered brain,. Anguished tears welled up in his eyes, obscuring his vision. Blindly, he ran into the busy street, narrowly escaped being hit by a yellow cab, made it across to the opposite sidewalk, and turned south.

He walked for a long time, perhaps covering two miles. Finally, feeling the need for some place to rest and think, he turned into a seedy, unfamiliar tavern.

"What'll ya have, kid?"

"Bourbon. On the rocks," Guy said. He'd heard his Barnstable teammates order that on the Cape.

"Yeah? You old enough ta drink?" the bartender asked. But he was already dropping ice cubes into a glass.

"Don't I look old enough ta drink?" Guy returned angrily.

"Don't get huffy wit' me, kiddo," the bartender said. "Jes bein' careful, is all. I don' need no law in here askin' questions 'bout me servin' any underage kids."

He poured three fingers of bourbon over the ice cubes and set the drink in front of Guy, who threw a dollar bill down on the bar, scooped up the glass and headed for a booth.

An hour later he left the saloon on shaky pins, having continued ordering and consuming drinks until he ran out of cash. It was dark by the time he, on automatic pilot, arrived home.

His brain was fuzzy. Not thinking clearly, he felt only that he needed to get away; from his ma and pa, from his home, from his few friends, from East Boston itself.

Opening his dresser drawer, he removed all the cash he had in there and stuffed it into his battered wallet. He tossed some clothing into the brown leather grip he always used, raced from the house without a word to his parents, and headed for the subway, his only thought to get to South Station and a train that would take him as far away as possible from the city of his birth, which, it seemed to him, had suddenly turned on him.

CHAPTER 29

South Boston, MA
Friday, June 3, 1938
South Station
10:00 p.m.

He didn't decide on New York City as the place he'd go until he reached the ticket window and the ticket clerk asked his destination.

"Where to, young man? New York?"

"Uh, yeah," he said rocking back and forth on his heels. "How much?"

Before boarding, he ducked into the all-night bar and package-goods store in the Station and bought a fifth of Kentucky Gentleman Bourbon. He asked the clerk to put it in a brown paper bag. Outside the store, he opened the bottle quickly and took a long swig. Some of the golden nectar dribbled from the corner of his mouth, ran down his chin and onto his neck. Replacing the bottle in its bag, he headed for the gate and the platform where the few passengers bound for New York City this late at night were already boarding.

Slipping into an all but empty Pullman car, he almost fell into a seat as the train lurched forward and moved slowly out of South Station. He was drunk now, but not falling down drunk, the way some people get. Just drunk enough to take the edge off the bitter thoughts threatening to engulf him. Only two other passengers occupied the car with him. *Good*, he thought. *I'll drink and sleep all the way down ta New York. Don't think. Drink 'n sleep, sleep 'n drink, all a way.*

*   *   *   *

New York City, NY
Saturday, June 4, 1938
Penn Station, Lower Manhattan
3:30 a.m.

He had made it. A feeling of relief overwhelmed him; a sense of escape, freedom.

From what, he didn't remember.

Most of his bourbon was gone now. "Sho thish ish ... New ... New ... New Yawk," he said aloud. There was no one around to hear him at that hour.

Now, two levels below the streets of Lower Manhattan, he paused and surveyed the empty platform. Black and white tiles, vacuous advertising bills, blue and red graffiti chalked on the walls, a few green trash containers; that was all there was. The trash containers reminded him of the one in the hall outside of O'Brien's Department of Probation office. The thoughts came flooding back. He was suddenly consumed by a sense of futility and defeat. A sharp pain kicked him in the pit of his stomach.

"Oh, Gawd!" he cried. "I'm so tired." Looking wildly around, he spotted an escalator and headed for it. *Shit*, he thinks. *Gotta go ... gotta go find ... what? what? Oh, yeah ... a place ta sleep.*

*   *   *   *

New York City, NY
Saturday, June 4, 1938
Lower Manhattan
5:30 a.m.

He had found a room in a four-story fleabag just down the street from Madison Square Garden, at the corner of 29th Street and 8th Avenue. *Lovely accommodations,* he thought. *Seventy-five cents a night's not a b-bad d-d-d-deal.* He paid for a whole week, pocketed the room key, went back out to an all-night liquor store he had passed on his way here, and purchased another fifth of Bourbon.

Returning to the hotel, he staggered into an ancient elevator and pressed the button for the fourth floor. He had not eaten anything since lunch the day before. His stomach did flip-flops as the elevator ascended.

In his room, he ignored a calendar displaying a naked woman engaged in an erotic pursuit and collapsed on the well-used bed, the springs complaining under his weight. Across the street, a rooftop neon sign cast a flickering red light through the room's only window. The ten by twelve foot room reeked of cigarettes, and from the tiny bathroom came the stench of urine, but he didn't notice. Soon he fell into a fitful slumber.

In his dream, he was being chased around the perimeter of a baseball field, just inside a high, chain-link fence, by a huge ballplayer with wildly-flowing hair and gappy teeth, resembling George Colbert without his catcher's mitt. The wire fence was crooked, angling this way and that like it had been erected by a crew of madmen. The man chasing him was hollering, "C'mere leetle fella," as he pursued Guy. Every time they passed first base, Fred O'Brien was there; drunk, cackling gleefully and shaking a finger at Guy. "Screwed ya, didn't I Gaetano?" he said. Guy woke, reached for the bottle next to his bed, drank deeply and returned to troubled sleep.

Another dream; he was standing in the batter's box waiting for a big pitcher with huge shoulders and arms to step onto the rubber. It was Colbert again. "Hit this one, leetle fellah," he said and threw a fast ball at Guy's head. Guy hit the dirt. "Strike three," the umpire yelled. It was O'Brien, a fifth of Jack Daniels in his left hand, his right hand above his head, the middle digit extended in Guy's direction. "You're outta heah!"

When he woke up again, his tee shirt was soaked with sweat. Sunlight streamed in through the windowpane. He'd forgotten to draw the shade. Because the window was closed, the room felt hot, and he could hear traffic noises from the busy street four stories below. Rolling onto his side, he got off the bed slowly. The exertion was almost too much. His head pounding like he was inside a kettle drum, he negotiated the short distance to the window and lowered the yellowed shade. Leaning over, he untied his shoelaces, removed his shoes and kicked them into a corner. He unfastened his belt, let his slacks drop to the floor, stepped out of them and kicked them into the same corner.

"Oh, shit!" he said, as the painful memories came flooding back. "God damn you, Fred O'Brien!" he said. Picking up the bottle from where he had dropped it a few hours earlier, he removed the cap, raised it to his lips, drank deeply, placed it on the floor again and rolled back onto the bed.

*   *   *   *

East Boston, MA
Wednesday, June 8, 1938
Ford and Breed Streets
4:30 p.m.

"So I checked the bus terminal and North Station," Frank Vitale said. He stood in the kitchen of his parents' apartment. Both his mother and father were there. "But nobody's seen him."

"Would they have recognized him, Frankie?" Nick Vitale asked, running a hand across an early stubble on his chin, a concerned look on his face.

"Yeah, Pa, they would've. His picture's been in the papers around here so much in the last couple years, nearly everybody knows Guy."

Rosaria turned from the sink where she was cleaning squid to put in spaghetti sauce for that evening's dinner. "What about South Station?" she wanted to know.

Nick whirled around and faced his wife. "Oh, so now all of a sudden, you care? In four years while he was in high school, you never expressed any interest in him—never once went to see him play baseball or football. Last summer and the summer before, you couldn't spare a *single* weekend to go down the Cape to see one of his games. No goddamn time. Now, you're concerned?"

Not used to long speeches from Nick, much less angry ones questioning her actions or motives, Rosaria's mouth dropped open. A retort began to form on her lips, but her husband cut her off. "You—don't—give—a goddam—about—your—son!" he said. With a contemptuous glance in his wife's direction, he turned to Frank. "Let's go," he said. "Maybe she's right and he caught a train from there."

*   *   *   *

South Boston, MA
Wednesday, June 8, 1938
South Station
5:15 p.m.

"Yeah, I seen him. Three, four nights ago." The ticket clerk said. A short, thin man with a hooked nose and close-set eyes, he wore a green eyeshade. "You his Pa?"

Ignoring the question, Nick gestured at the photo of Guy the man held in his thin fingers. "You sure?"

The clerk studied the photo again. "Yep," he said. "That there's Guy Vitale. He made All-Scholastic in football and baseball a couple years ago. Couldn't place him when he first come in the other night, but after he bought his ticket and left my window, I remembered where I'd seen him."

"He bought a ticket?" Frank Vitale asked. "Where to?" Reaching out, he took the photo of Guy from the man's hand and returned it to his jacket pocket.

"I wanna say New York City," the clerk responded thoughtfully. "Yeah, I'm sure of it. New York."

"Thanks for your help," Nick said, and started to turn away from the window.

"The kid in some kinda trouble, mister?" the clerk asked.

"No," Nick answered evasively. "Not at all. We just want to know where he went."

"I been wonderin' what became a Vitale since he played down the Cape last summer. All that talent? Really looked good down there. Guess it won't be long before he makes it ta the majors, right?"

*   *   *   *

New York City, NY
Thursday, June 9, 1938
Lower Manhattan
10:00 p.m.

When Guy finally came around, his head was splitting and his mouth was dry. A shower, a shave and something to eat at the nearby diner left him feeling only marginally better. As he walked back to his hotel the dreaded memory returned, and along with it *the thought*. It bombarded his consciousness until he wanted to cry out. He had never understood before how painful a thought could be; he'd always believed that thoughts were simply things inside his head. But now, his mind attacked unceasingly by *the thought, the clinging, putrid thought*—that he would never play big league baseball—he knew thoughts existed independently of himself and that they had hard rock surfaces that could smash you, leaving you in bits and pieces.

Outside his hotel, he noticed a small watering hole in the basement. He entered and climbed onto a stool at the bar. One corner of the dimly lit room was filled by a black piano. A short, fat, bald man sat on a stool playing bad jazz from the twenties and early thirties. A small stage was wedged into the other corner, but it was bare of combo or duo tonight. Cigarette smoke hung in the air like a thick, gossamer veil.

Ordering a drink, Guy sat there, trying to put his brain in neutral, numbly listening to the tinkling of the piano keys and gulping his bourbon on the rocks. He decided that he wanted to get drunk again quickly, before *the thought* returned. Finished with his first drink, he ordered another and worked it vigorously.

Later, working on his third drink, he was surprised to hear a voice at his elbow. "Ya want company, Mistah?" she asked.

He had not seen her come in. Glancing up he looked her over coldly, conscious that the two other men in the bar were doing the same. Dressed in a hot pink blouse, a tight black skirt way too short, and black boots, her intentions were painfully obvious. There was a stirring in his loins which he recognized as a feeling he'd had many times before but has always suppressed. This time, he knew he was not going to suppress anything. He was twenty-one years old and had never had sexual relations. *It might as well be her as anybody,* he thought.

"Yeah," he said and placed his arm casually around her waist, drawing her toward him until he could smell her cheap perfume and feel the warmth of her body. "Buy ya a drink?"

Knowing the drill, the bartender quickly moved to them. "What'll it be, Miss?"

"A Pink Lady," the girl said. That was code for pink lemonade with no alcohol, but Guy was so out of his element in this environment he wouldn't have known that, and if he'd heard, since he was already three-sheets-to-the wind, he wouldn't have known that, or even cared what she ordered.

The bartender brought her drink, along with another for him. "Down the hatch," Guy said.

She raised her glass to his. "A toast? To a real good lookin' guy and a great time tonight."

Laughing nervously, Guy touched his glass to hers and downed his drink. She sipped hers. He leaned over and kissed her on the mouth, noting that her thin lips were incredibly soft. He had not known what a kiss was like. Aside from his mother, he'd never kissed a woman on the lips before. The fury, the despair that had been sitting in his stomach since the meeting with O'Brien was suddenly submerged by other thoughts, other feelings. "I got thish room upstairs," he said huskily. "Wanna see it?"

Nodding, she drained her faux Pink Lady, rose and struck a theatrical pose. "Lead on, kind sir," she said, "If yer not too tight ta get offa the barstool."

*   *   *   *

New York City, NY
Friday, June 10, 1938
Lower Manhattan
7:30 a.m.

After leaving the train at Penn Station, Nick Vitale and his son rode an escalator to the surface—unaware that it was the same one Guy had used the week before—and walked out onto 8th Avenue at 30th Street. Tired after their train ride from South Boston, they paused, unsure what to do next, and not at all confident that they'd locate Guy.

Young Frank broke the silence. "Pa, I'm hungry. Before we do anything else, let's find someplace ta eat," he said in English.

A block further on, they spotted a diner at the corner of 29th and 8th, and, call it luck, fate or the hand of God working through the Holy Spirit, because Frank Vitale had a healthy appetite, they quickly got the break they needed.

Entering the almost empty diner, they slid into a booth and ordered breakfast. Over steaming coffee, they talked about what was ahead for them.

"This is a big town," Frank said glumly to his father as he chewed his eggs. "Maybe we shouldn't a come."

"Mm-hmm," Nick said, sipping his coffee and beginning to work on the first of two sausage patties. He was speaking his adopted language now, and proud of the fact that he'd mastered it so well. This, together with the success of his barber shop and the exploits of his youngest son, which seemed to be so important to his friends and acquaintances, had combined to give him a feeling that he actually belonged in America, and that he could succeed here. "Big enough that Guy might not have gone too far after he got off the train," he said perceptively. "But just *where* he'd have gone is a mystery."

"So, what do we do now?" Frank wanted to know.

Nick shook his head slowly. "I don't know," he said. But, his spirit boosted somewhat by the comforting food they'd consumed and the pleasant aromas of bacon, sausage, eggs and coffee that filled the place, he was more determined than ever to find Guy and bring him home. On a hunch, he whipped out Guy's photo and gestured to a waitress who was hovering nearby.

"Him?" she said, her nostrils flaring as if she smelled something bad. "Yeah he's been in here a couple a times. Drunk as a skunk both times. Somethin' sure is botherin' him."

Nick threw Frank a relieved glance and spoke again. "My dear, do you know where he's staying?"

"Nope," she answered. "But gimme that snapshot and I'll go ask my boss if *he* knows."

*   *   *   *

New York City, NY
Friday, June 10, 1938
Lower Manhattan
8:45 a.m.

And, with the help of a tip from the diner's owner, they *did* find Guy; in bed with a woman—a different woman from the one previously mentioned—and very drunk. Again. Or still. Suppressing his disappointment in his youngest son, Nick flashed a ten spot and dispatched the prostitute. Then they cleaned Guy up as best they could. A quick visit to the diner for food and several cups of strong coffee was all that was necessary to sober him up enough to make the return train trip to Boston.

I'd like to be able to tell you that Guy was no worse for wear; that the revelation from O'Brien and his experiences in New York had left him undamaged in any way. But t*hat* would not be true. In fact, he was very different after his father and brother had found and returned him to East Boston. At twenty, almost twenty-one, you'd think that the natural resilience of youth would have come into play, and he'd have bounced back quickly. But he didn't. And people noticed.

"After that, Guy was changed," Joe Rocciolo recalled.

"In what way was he changed?" I asked.

"He was even more of a loner than he'd been before. Everybody thought he'd had a breakdown, or something 'cause he was so different."

"Different?"

"Yeah. He began ta hang out in the saloons a lot. And he seemed angry the few times I saw him before he went back down the Cape, and very depressed," Joe said. "Ya couldn't talk ta him for long without him flyin' off the handle."

CHAPTER 30

East Boston, MA
Monday, June 13, 1938
Ford and Breed Streets
10:30 a.m.

"Why not, Guy?" Pete Herman, seated in one of two overstuffed chairs in the Vitale living room, asked. After Guy had burst from O'Brien's office and disappeared, Pete had driven back to Kents Hill and sadly waited for word from East Boston. When it came a week later, sensing that his young friend would need his counsel and some emotional support, he'd been prepared. That morning he had risen at the crack of dawn and made the trip from Readfield to Guy's home. "What'll ya do this summer if ya don't play ball again?"

Guy, pale and thinner than he'd been, deep circles from lack of sleep etched under his eyes, rubbed his temples with his thumbs. "The Cape again? Naw. I don't ..."

Expecting to hear something like this from Guy, Herman had his argument ready. Rising from his chair, he paced the length of the room and back. "Nothin's really changed, ya know. Ya still got the ability. And if yer gonna get ta the Bigs, ya still need ta showcase yerself."

"I don't think so, Pete," Guy said, his voice tired and flat.

"The world hasn't come to an end jest because a what O'Brien did—or didn't do."

Guy looked away. "I think I'll jest get a job at the shipyard and go ta work for awhile."

Dropping back into his chair across from Guy, Pete leveled a finger at his friend. "Shit, Guy. I figured you for a lotta things, but I never figured you for a quitter. That's what yer doin' isn't it? Quittin'?"

"What the hell's the difference?" Guy shot back hotly. "I've lost two goddam *years* because of O'Brien. Besides that," he raised a hand and began counting

269

on his fingers, "one, I haven't been able ta get inta college. Two, because a that I can't play in the Northern League. And *that's* where I really should be playin'. Three, I tore up the Cape Cod League the past two summers, but I'm no closer ta gettin' signed now than I was in '36. Possibly even less close."

Shaking his head, Herman pointed a finger at Guy. "Maybe so. But you put together one hell of a record. And on top a that, at Kents Hill you showed you're capable of doin' college work."

Guy yawned and stretched. His limbs felt heavy, like lead weights were attached to his arms and legs. "It's over, Pete. Don't ya understand? I jest don't care any more."

Herman scrutinized his young friend for a few minutes before rising from his chair. "I know you, Guy. I don't think that's true."

Silence. Seconds dragged into minutes. Neither spoke; Herman waiting expectantly, Guy too emotionally spent to respond.

Finally, Pete rose. "I gotta get back," he said. "Think about it for a few days. If ya change yer mind, I'll be at Kents Hill. Call me. Barnstable's not fieldin' a team this season, but I hear Falmouth is lookin' for a few good ballplayers. And they're payin' twenty a week plus room and board." He walked to the door and stopped. "A friend a mine's gonna manage Falmouth. If ya wanna play, I'll call him and arrange it."

*   *   *   *

Pine Bluffs, WY
Monday, November 1, 2004
703 Beech Street
10:30 a.m.

I know what you're thinking. Why did a kid like Guy, who obviously grew up with a certain amount of faith in God and at least a belief in and devotion to the Blessed Mother, take this bad break so hard? Why did he give up so easily? Why did it cause him to run off to New York, get blind drunk every day for a week, stay out all night and sleep most of each day, while, for the first time in his life, consorting with prostitutes and loose women?

The only answer I have is that Guy's boyhood faith may not have been very strong. He may not have had a close, personal relationship with Jesus, and because *that* was lacking, no deep relationship with God. What *was* there may have been built on a false or weak premise: that if he prayed and promised to be good, God would return the favor. I think the Roman Catholic Church calls this a 'bargaining relationship.' It's much like a person diagnosed with a fatal illness, who attempt to bargain with God to cure him: "If you restore my health, God, I'll go to church every Sunday."

During his high school years, he'd often prayed that God would give him athletic ability; success in baseball, football and even track. And he'd often asked God to help him play well in a particularly tough upcoming game or run hard in a race. He'd promised, in return, to go to daily Mass and receive the Eucharist. To Guy, it seemed that God heard his requests and granted them.

But we've seen that as he grew older, Guy's prayer life had gradually diminished. He stopped going to church during the week as he once did, and eventually even on Sundays; stopped receiving the Eucharist often; stopped saying the rosary daily, too. As these things happened, God's graces began to ebb until they were no longer flowing to him. It wasn't God that left *him*. God never leaves us, no matter what. But it was Guy who left God. Two summers on the Cape was all it took to, not necessarily lose his faith, but to put it on the back burner more or less permanently. Then, when adversity came, he found himself defenseless and without his friendship with Jesus to see him through.

Anyway, after his wild week in New York City, he *was* different. At home again, he withdrew from everyone; parents, brothers and sisters. Even his few friends saw less of him. He stayed to himself; brooding about what O'Brien had done, about the lack of any offers from the professional baseball teams, and about how unfair it all seemed.

A week after his return from New York, his anger had grown to a purple rage. He began to contemplate murdering his old coach, turning scenario after scenario over in his young mind about exactly how he'd do it. But every plan he made ended the same way; with him alone, behind bars in a small, damp jail cell. A few days more and he understood that he'd never commit murder—not cold-blooded murder, anyway—he just wasn't the type. So he put those thoughts aside, and instead, started spending even more time in the local watering holes in the Heights, drinking until the wee hours of the morning, after which, in a drunken stupor, he'd stagger home and fall into bed until late the next day.

Although he tried desperately to conceal it, deep down inside Guy felt the first stirrings of the idea that he might not be in control of his existence; that his life had taken on a life of its own. And that thought, without the comforting, supportive beliefs that God loved him unconditionally, and that he needed to place his entire trust in his Divine Father, sent paroxysms of panic surging through his mind, like alternating electric shock waves passing through his body.

He no longer even had that firm surface sense of self-confidence he once had, no longer seemed to believe that he could be successful at whatever he set his mind and heart on, no longer felt that everything would turn out all right, no matter what. In short, caught up in a deep sense of despair, and drowning in self-pity, he was experiencing that first crack in the often blind overconfidence of youth. Slipping into that abyss with him was the belief that there was no way out, that his quest for a college degree and a professional baseball contract would end in failure.

Sooner or later all of us experience it to a certain extent. I can remember when it happened to me. But for most of us, these feelings give way to a re-evaluation; sober thought about how to get what we want, and a determining on a course of action founded on hard work to develop our talents and accomplish our goals. Would twenty year old Guy Vitale do the same?

*   *   *   *

East Boston, MA
Thursday, June 23, 1938
20 Breed Street
10:30 a.m.

Of course Guy was going to play baseball that summer. Depressed? Angry? Awash in self-pity? A sense of futility and defeat? A loss of faith? Yes, he probably experienced all those things. But as Pete Herman had suggested, instead of making an immediate, irrevocable decision, Guy thought about it for a week.

Fortunately, the sport was in his blood by this time. I know baseball can do that to a person who plays the sport. It did to me, too. So what he prudently decided was this: no matter what, unless he lost both legs in a car accident or contracted some rare blood disease that sapped all his strength, he would play ball again that summer. *Who knows,* he reasoned, *maybe lightning will strike this year. Maybe some scout will decide ta recommend me and some major league team will decide ta gimme a shot.*

Going to the wall phone in the hallway, he dialed the operator and asked for help in placing a long-distance call to Readfield, Maine.

"Pete?"

"Yes."

"It's me. Guy."

"Guy! How are ya?"

"I'll live. Don't gloat. I wanna go down the Cape."

"I wasn't gonna gloat, Guy. But I'm sure glad ya made that decision. I don't think you'll ever regret it."

"Maybe yes, maybe no," Guy said wearily, and came right to the point. "Since Barnstable doesn't have a team this year, I guess it'll have ta be Falmouth."

"Stay near the phone for awhile. Bill Boehner is managing Falmouth this summer. I'll make the call and get right back to ya."

*   *   *   *

East Boston, MA
Sunday, June 26, 1938
20 Breed Street
10:30 a.m.

A few days after his conversation with Pete Herman, Guy packed his bag and, out of money because he'd spent just about every cent he had on what he was now, tongue-in-cheek, calling his "New York caper," and its aftermath, hitch-hiked to Falmouth on the Cape.

Where did Guy stay that summer? Connie Blackwell, of East Falmouth, attended many of the games and knew most of the players. I contacted her for two reasons. This was one.

"A lot of the players stayed in rooming houses," she said. "George Lilly put some of them up at his place. Also, Mrs. Mary Cobb ran a boarding house for them. He probably stayed at one of those places."

"Was that a good deal for them?"

"Yes, it was. Falmouth paid players between ten and twenty-five dollars a week. The manager usually got twenty-five. Most got ten to fifteen plus room and board."

So there he was, on the Cape for a third season. Somewhat out of shape because of all the drinking and carousing of the last month, he was not exactly eager to face the rigors of fifty-four baseball games in as many hot summer days. But he *was* determined to give it all he had—just one more time—and see what might happen.

*   *   *   *

Cape Cod, MA
Friday, July 1, 1938
Falmouth, MA
8:30 a.m.

According to an article printed in the *Cape Cod Standard Times* on Friday, July 1ˢᵗ, the team Guy would play for that summer was to be managed by Bill Boehner, a coach at La Salle Academy in Providence, Rhode Island, who was completing his fifth year in the Cape Cod League. Boehner would also play some at shortstop. The article continued:

> *A guarantee of extraction from any pitching holes in which the team may be thrown is given by Frank Cammaranno, playing first base for the Falmouth nine and completing his eighth year in the Cape League ...*
>
> *Rated as one of the most dangerous hitters in the League when a run or a hit is demanded in a pinch, Myron Ruckstull will be at second base for the Falmouth nine. Ruckstull is completing his 14ᵗʰ season in the League and was known as the grand old man of Cape baseball.*
>
> *John Spirada of Bridgewater will fill the hot corner position. Spirada was with the Barnstable nine last year, playing in the garden. He is a graduate of St. Anselm's College in New Hampshire and is known to Cape sports fans who followed his play with the Redskins football team last year.*
>
> *Selected as All-Cape catcher last year, George Colbert will be behind the plate for the Falmouth nine, an important cog in any Cape League machine.*
>
> *Playing both right field and pitcher will be Les Shatzer, while Guy Vitale, also taken from the ranks of the Barnstable nine, and one of the leading batters in the league, will be in center field.*
>
> *Wally Sullivan of Providence will be in the left field berth, also taking the hill when necessary.*
>
> *The twirling staff is large, including Frank Benyon of Providence, Al Nerbonne, Pawtucket hurler, Slug Mahoney of Taunton and Jerry Robbins of Falmouth, local pitcher.*

This piece, informative and even colorful, was not very accurate, as we will see. In fact, only Frank Cammaranno, Guy Vitale, and George Colbert actually played the positions in which the article placed them, while several of these players never suited up for a single game with Falmouth.

*   *   *   *

Cape Cod, MA
Tuesday, July 5, 1938
Falmouth Heights Field
1:30 p.m.

Apparently the powers that be in Barnstable were unimpressed by that wonderful editorial appearing in *The Enterprise, Falmouth, Mass,* at the end of the '37 baseball season. Despite urging to the contrary, they decided against fielding a team in '38. So only four teams competed in the Cape Cod League that summer. These were Bourne, Falmouth, Harwich and Orleans.

Was everyone reconciled that Barnstable did not have a League entry in '38? Decidedly not. *The Falmouth Enterprise* was so upset that the writer of its column, *Cape Circuit Chatter,* sub-captioned his column, *Baseball—Minus—Barnstable,* and referred to the situation regularly in his sports coverage throughout the season.

However, without a tough Barnstable outfit to contend with, Falmouth got off to a fast start over the Independence Day weekend with four quick victories. In fact, it was July 8th before they lost a game, and that was a 4–3 decision to Orleans. Here's what the *Cape Cod Standard Times* had to say about the first weekend of the season in its article on July 5th:

> *A declaration of leadership in the Cape Cod League was signed by nine members of the Falmouth team over Independence Day with a volley of four bangup victories and no losses.*
>
> *Falmouth laced Orleans on Saturday, 6–3 and downed Harwich in a 13 inning Sunday game 5–4. Falmouth came through in a clean sweep over Bourne in yesterday's battles with 17–0 and 9–0 wins.*

That 17–0 football score win over Bourne was reported this way:

> *Falmouth, July 5.—Collecting 20 hits for a total of 17 runs off the offerings of 16-year old Red Sliney and Al Sayce, who hurled in the relief role after pitching a full game Sunday, Falmouth walked all over Bourne for a 17–0 victory here yesterday afternoon.*

Falmouth's batting averages went skyrocketing as every player but Benyon, hurler, collected at least two hits, while John Spirada, former Barnstable player, led the slugging with two singles, two doubles and a triple in six trips to the plate …

Falmouth's lineup, which changed occasionally throughout the season, had Myron Ruckstull at second, leading off, Guy in center, batting second, John Spirada at third base, batting third, Frank Cammaranno at first, batting clean-up, George Colbert catching and hitting fifth, Lester Shatzer pitching in this game and hitting sixth, Wally Sullivan in right field hitting seventh, Bill Boehner at short hitting eighth, and Al Nerbonne in left hitting ninth.

Guy? He played the entire game in center field, got two base hits in five trips, was hit by a pitch, scored three runs and had three put-outs in the field.

On July 11th the first listing of batting averages was published. John Spirada, Falmouth's third baseman was leading the League's regular players with a .548 batting average, while two of Guy's other teammates, Ruckstull and Shatzer, were swatting at .455 and .441 respectively. Guy's average, despite his good intentions, was a mere .297.

On July 13th, when the first League standings were published, Falmouth was firmly ensconced in first place, with a record of six wins and three losses, while Harwich was in second place with four wins and four losses. But the season was still young.

*   *   *   *

Cape Cod, MA
Thursday, July 13, 1938
Falmouth Heights Field
1:30 p.m.

Because of poor conditioning during the previous month, and a short lapse into a lackadaisical attitude, Guy's start in the 1938 season was slow. In fact, Bill Boehner was so baffled by Guy's lack of effort that he dropped his center fielder down in the batting order to the seventh slot for a few days.

Perhaps since he'd never hit lower than fifth, that move jolted Guy out of his lethargy, because July 13th was the day he began changing things. In a losing effort against Orleans, he stroked two hits in five plate appearances, one of them the only triple of the game. His team lost 7–6, but it left eleven men on the base pads, as Orleans used three pitchers to subdue them.

On Friday, July 15th, however, it was a different story, as Falmouth turned the tables on Orleans 10–9. Guy, who had been elevated in the batting order to second because of his good showing on the 13th and 14th, picked up three hits in five trips, had three putouts in center field, and scored the winning run in the ninth inning. Here's how the *Cape Cod Standard Times* described it:

> *With two gone in the ninth, Ruckstull was given a base on balls, Vitale singled to center. Spirada smashed a high fly between home and first which was dropped by Harvey, Orleans catcher. Ruckstull came home with the tying run and Cammaranno hit a long double to score Vitale with the winning run.*

Three days later, in another losing effort, Guy was still batting second and went two for three. Patrolling center field again, he was busy out there, with eight putouts in the field but his team dropped the game to Harwich, 12–8.

On July 20th, an article in the *Cape Cod Standard Times* summarized events:

> *It's a long way from the cellar to the roof. But when the step of the ascendant is steady the path is one that is clearly marked.*
>
> *When the Cape cod League opened it appeared for a time that the bottom had fallen out of the League, that Falmouth would sweep the cranberry circuit with little trouble. But the wise baseball follower never leaves the field until the last ball has been pitched. A rising Harwich tide has been sweeping in slowly and has covered Falmouth, Orleans and Bourne under a cascade of hits.*
>
> *Falmouth began to lose steadily … since then it has been a battle of Falmouth and Harwich for the top position … From a 5–0 game lead Falmouth has fallen into second place …*

The next list of players' batting averages was printed on July 25th. Wally Sullivan of Falmouth was leading the League among regulars with a .459 average. Spirada, Ruckstull, Shatzer and Colbert were all ahead of Guy, but Guy had raised his average by 59 points, to .356. That was no small accomplishment in a league where every hurler was an above-average pitcher and had something going for him; either a good fastball, a wicked curve or a deceptive change-up, or all three.

*   *   *   *

Pine Bluffs, WY
Friday, November 2, 2004
703 Beech Street
12:30 p.m.

Wally Sullivan? Where had I heard that name before? I dove into my notes and soon came up with a letter from Al Irish dated September 26, 2002, to the effect that Wally Sullivan had played for Falmouth in '38, and was still alive and living in California. He even gave me Sullivan's telephone number. I wasted no time dialing it.

"Yes, I knew Guy Vitale in '38 on the Falmouth team," Sullivan recalled. "He was a nice person; quiet most of the time and a helluva good ball player. He could do everything; hit behind the runner, drive the ball in the alleys between outfielders, loft a deep fly ball to bring a runner in from third. He also had good speed and he stole a lot of bases."

"Did Guy ever tell you he wanted to play professional baseball?" I asked.

"Guy and me went into Falmouth for dinner together a few times. We had several good talks. We'd confide in each other. Yeah, he told me he wanted to play pro ball. I told *him* the same thing. But Guy was not out front like me, with a lot of noise. He was a likeable person. But self-contained."

"A loner?"

"Well, not in a bad way. People liked Guy. He liked people. But he had this … reserve about him."

"Can you recall who Guy hung around with that summer?"

"We all got along well. So we all palled around together. Guy was quiet, but he hung around with us. He had one friend he was close to—a fella who played first base. I can't remember his name."

"Was it Frank Cammaranno?"

"Yeah, that was it. He was a good ball player, too. Friendly with everybody, but he was close with Guy. Maybe because they were both Italian. They spent time together, even hung around the general store over on the hill, where we could get ice cream and soft drinks. There were not many places to go around there, unless you had a car. Most of us lived in houses close to the park. We could walk there and back."

"Did Guy date anybody down there on the Cape that summer?"

"No, I don't think so. He wasn't the type," Wally said.

"Can you remember anything specific about Guy?" I wanted to know.

Sullivan thought for a minute. "Well, in the evenings we'd cut across the field to go to dinner at the only restaurant in town. There was a cook there who drank a lot and was always drunk. We'd take turns bringing him home—whoever was free—walking him through the woods to his house. Guy did it more than anybody. Seemed as if he felt sorry for the man, ya know?"

"That's interesting," I said, recalling Guy's New York City spree.

"Yep. Guy was average size, very clean-cut, and liked to laugh a lot. I got along well with him. But he'd have these moods. He was well-built and tough, and one look at him would tell you that you wouldn't want to mess with him when he was in one of them."

"Where were you from, Wally?"

"I was from Edgewood, a suburb of Cranston, Rhode Island. I went to Northeastern University for my undergraduate degree and Boston University for a Masters. I tried out with the Red Sox while I was there, and played for Pawtucket for two seasons. They paid a hundred seventy-two dollars a week, which was nice money back then. We even played the Red Sox a couple of times. Eventually, Pawtucket became a Red Sox farm team."

Sullivan and I talked twice, for over an hour each time. He told me his wife had passed away five years before. It was clear that, although he had a daughter named Patricia and two sons, Philip and Shaun, he was lonely, and looked back on his baseball days fondly.

"For me, those were the happiest days of my life," he said. "They were a wonderful bunch of guys. You think back and say, 'God. They don't make 'em like that any more.'"[42]

A day or two later, I came across a photograph of Myron Ruckstull and Bill Boehner, printed in the *Cape Cod Standard Times* on Tuesday, July 26th, 1938. Its heading was *PILOTS OF FALMOUTH ENTRY*, and the caption under the photo said:

Holding the reins of one of the leaders in the Cranberry circuit are Captain Myron Ruckstull left, and Manager Bill Boehner of the Falmouth entry in the Cape Cod League. Both are familiar figures in baseball circles on the Cape.

---

42 Al Irish's letter to me dated September 26th, 2002 contained this: "Both Wally Sullivan (Northeastern's 1942 baseball [team] captain and [Oscar] Khederian are in Northeastern's Athletic Hall of Fame along with Neil Mahoney (most valuable Cape Cod League player in 1938) and Herb Gallagher. Herb was Northeastern's baseball coach when I was there and later became Athletic Director. He was Bourne's manager in 1939."

During my second telephone conversation with Wally Sullivan, I asked him about Ruckstull.

"Ruckstull! I remember him. An older guy. Been around forever. Was full of aches and pains. He was always hurting so much that it was actually comical how he'd carry on. But come game time, he'd be ready to play."

*   *   *   *

Cape Cod, MA
Wednesday, July 27, 1938
Falmouth Heights Field
1:30 p.m.

Two days after it published those batting averages, the *Cape Cod Standard Times* printed a photograph of Guy and three of his teammates, Frank Cammaranno, Lester Shatzer, and John Spirada. The baseball glove Guy was wearing in that photo was the one found in the trunk he left with my mother in early 1960 when he … Well, I'm getting ahead of myself. But just let me say here that I oiled that glove religiously, along with mine while he was away, keeping the leather soft and supple. I also tied a ball in it to shape the pocket, in case he ever wanted it back. But outfielder's gloves in that era were very small, not the long-fingered leather things they're using today. So that pocket-shaping idea didn't work very well.

On the 28th and 30th of July, Falmouth lost to Harwich, 8–7, and Guy went one for five at the dish, and to Bourne, 9–4, with Guy collecting one hit, a triple, which knocked in a run for his team in the sixth inning. In the Harwich game, Neil Mahoney made his appearance at catcher for them. Neil would be named Cape Cod Leagues' Most Valuable Player for 1938. The following year, he would be working for the Boston Red Sox, scouting for talent in the Northern and Twin States Leagues. Later, he'd go on to become Director of Player Development for the Sox.

CHAPTER 31

Cape Cod, MA
Friday, July 29, 1938
Falmouth Heights Field
1:30 p.m.

As July drew to a close, the Falmouth club appeared to break out of its slump, beating Bourne in a slugfest on Friday afternoon, July 29th 15–11. The game saw the two clubs pound out thirty-eight hits.

Guy prowled center field and had three putouts. At the plate, he went three for four and scored two runs, while collecting yet another triple—again the only one of the game—and showing off his speed on the base paths. Oh, and by the way; "Muggsy" Kelly, who pitched for Barnstable in '37, joined Falmouth's team and was once again one of Guy's teammates.

But three days later, on Sunday, August 1st, in a double-header against Orleans, Falmouth's woes resumed. Guy, playing in left field while his manager, Bill Boehner patrolled center, went three for five at the plate in a losing effort. He also hit a sacrifice fly and a double in this game. Later that day with Guy back in center field, Falmouth downed Orleans 7–3, and he turned in one hit in three plate appearances.

However, despite several good games with the stick, the list of batting averages printed on that day shows Guy's average down slightly from the week before, at .347.

On Tuesday, August 2nd, Falmouth beat Bourne 3–2. Guy figured prominently in this contest, which saw his teammates commit four errors and leave eight men on base, while beating Bourne's ace pitcher, Kendrick. Here's how the *Standard Times* described the game:

VITALE BRINGS HOME BACON

Falmouth, Aug. 3—A lone run in the sixth frame, the result of a stolen base, gave Falmouth a 3–2 victory over Bourne in a nip and tuck battle here yesterday afternoon.

Cammaranno opened the way in the second for Falmouth with a walk. Ziniti hit into a double play and Cammaranno scored on the play. Falmouth added another in the third when Surrette singled, Boehner flied out to center and Ruckstull doubled to bring in Surrette.

Bourne knotted the count in the fifth with Coyne singling and Kendrick going to first via the free pass route. Ferretti sacrificed and was safe on a muff by the third baseman. Mandeville cracked out a single to score Coyne and Sawyer hit into a double play with Kendrick scoring.

Vitale singled and pilfered second for Falmouth in the sixth. Shatzer walked and Ziniti grounded to first, Vitale going to third and coming home on Brochu's out …

So, in this one Guy collected two hits in four trips to the dish. His two hits amounted to a quarter of his team's eight that day, and he scored one of their three runs while ringing up three putouts in left field. With the season at the halfway mark, it seemed as if, despite a heavy heart, Guy had finally begun to focus on baseball.

But elsewhere, there were troubles in the Cape Cod League, as first Orleans and then Bourne raised the cry that they were short of funds and might be unable to carry on unless the fans contributed more at the games. To this point, Harwich was in first place, with Falmouth in second, chasing them.

On Thursday, August 4th, Falmouth lost a tough one to Harwich, 5–4, but Guy was again in the thick of things. Manager Boehner started it off in the fourth inning with a leadoff walk, but the old veteran, Myron Ruckstull, flied out to right field. Wally Sullivan then followed with a single and Cammaranno was out at first. That brought Guy to the plate and he smashed a hard ground ball between first and second that looked like it would go through for a base hit. Harwich's second baseman, McDonough, knocked it down but could not make the play, and the runners moved up. Ernest "Zip" Ziniti, Falmouth's new catcher, then blasted a single to score both runners. But Ziniti, not a great base runner, tried to score from first and was caught at the plate on a nice relay from Ferdenzi to Cash to Mahoney.

The following day, Guy collected three hits in four trips, but Falmouth lost to Orleans, 5–3, as Lester Shatzer took the loss on the mound. In this game, player-manager Bill Boehner gave everyone a scare when he was hit in the head by a pitched ball in the seventh inning and had to be revived on the field.

On Saturday, August 6th, Guy was two for five as Falmouth exploded for ten runs and demolished Orleans, 10–3. Then, in Sunday's game, Bill Boehner's bad luck continued as he fell over a fence while chasing down a ball in the outfield, was injured and had to be removed from the game.

*   *   *   *

Cape Cod, MA
Tuesday, August 9, 1938
Falmouth Heights Field
1:30 p.m.

On Tuesday, August 9th, Falmouth beat Bourne and Guy accomplished something most baseball players only dream about; a perfect day at the plate, going four for four. One of his hits was a double, and he scored three of his team's twelve runs. Falmouth's pitcher, Pinkham, yielded fourteen hits and six walks, but Falmouth only left three men on the base paths and that was the difference in the game.

The *Enterprise, Falmouth, Mass* newspaper column, *Cape Circuit Chatter*, had this to say about Guy's perfect day at the dish on Thursday, August 11th, as the writer, having fun with words, took some liberties with names:

RIGHT IN THE 'PINK' WITH PINKHAM
Vitale got four hits out of four trips to the plate on Tuesday and aided Pinkham in chalking up a victory over Bourne, 12–6. The club found itself right in the 'Pink' with Pinkham.

That day, the Cape Cod League Batting Averages were printed again. Connie Creedon, of Orleans led the League with a .429 mark. Wally Sullivan of Falmouth was in second, hitting .417, and Myron Ruckstull was in third, at .414. In the twelfth spot on that list with an average of .348, was Guy, while his friend, Frank Cammaranno, was three batters below him at .330. Tony Plansky, familiar to us from the 1937 season, was back again, playing left field for Bourne. His average at that stage? .318. And Bill Boehner, after the hard-luck week he had just experienced, saw his average plummet all the way to .260.

At this point in the Cranberry Circuit's season an exciting event occurred for young Connie Creedon, of Orleans. On the strength of his showing the previous summer and so far in '38, Creedon earned a tryout with the Chicago Cubs. The Orleans right fielder, who had a cannon for an arm, was asked to show up in Boston on Friday, August 5th, when the Cubs were scheduled to play the Braves, so Cubs skipper, Gabby Hartnett could take a look at him.[43]

Another interesting note: You'll recall that in the Cape Cod League of that era, teams were allowed to have no more than two former professional ballplayers on their rosters. Well, one of Falmouth's former pros was Rosy Ryan, who at one time pitched for the New York Giants. On August 8th, his curve ball working superbly, he tossed the Falmouth team to a 6–1 win over Harwich, giving up just one run, scattering seven hits and allowing only one free pass. At the plate in this one, Guy, back in center field, went two for two, one of them another triple, while scoring once and walking twice.

About Ryan's appearance in a Falmouth uniform, the Enterprise, *Falmouth, Mass* column, *Cape Circuit Chatter*, said this on Thursday, August 11th:

RYAN MAKES THINGS LOOK 'ROSY'

Falmouth lost to Harwich, Orleans and Bourne last week on Wednesday, Thursday, and Saturday. The crucial situation forced the management to seek additional pitching strength.

Sunday the club had Rosy Ryan on the mound and he made things look 'rosy' for Falmouth for the first time in days. The former New York Giant twirler limited Harwich to one run while his mates got 6 tallies.

Two years ago when Barnstable was in a nip and tuck struggle with Falmouth the up-Cape club sought Ryan's assistance. It has become an annual mid-season occurrence for Falmouth to S.O.S. Ryan.

Falmouth had better soft-pedal its praise of Ryan or else lose his phone number as the New York Giants may be wanting him back for their Pennant race.

---

43   Cornelius Stephen Creedon, five years later (the delay was probably because of the War), would make it to the Majors, but only briefly. Playing in just five games for the Boston Bees in the National League, he went one for four at the plate for an average of .250. Born in Danvers, MA July 21, 1915, he died in Santa Ana, CA on November 30, 1969.

*   *   *   *

Cape Cod, MA
Thursday, August 11, 1938
Falmouth Heights Field
1:30 p.m.

As the Cape Cod weather became hot and humid, play in the Cape Cod League continued hot and heavy for the next few days. Then, on Thursday, the 11th, Falmouth won over Bourne again, 6–4. Guy stole another base and had one hit in four plate appearances in that one, and *Cape Circuit Chatter* summed up the season to date, this way:

> PENNANT RACE TIGHTENS
> *Wednesday finds Harwich leading Falmouth by a full two game margin. Boehner's boys gained some ground the past week.… If the teams were to finish the season with their present line-ups, Harwich would appear to be in there. As it is there is no knowing who will be wearing Cape club uniforms between now and Labor Day.*

The following day, the *Cape Cod Standard Times* printed the League standings:

TEAM:	W	L	PCT.
Harwich	*21*	*10*	*.677*
Falmouth	*18*	*15*	*.545*
Orleans	*14*	*16*	*.467*
Bourne	*10*	*22*	*.313*

But all was *not* rosy for Falmouth, even when Rosy Ryan took the mound. The contest on August 12th was one example. In that outing, Harwich jumped all over Ryan for eighteen hits and eight runs, as they beat Falmouth 8–2, even though Ryan did not walk a single batter. Ryan had two problems in that game; a curve ball that was not working, and an umpire who would not give him the calls on the corners.

In fact, all was not rosy for Falmouth at *all*. Even though it had picked up three games on first-place Harwich in the win column, they were still five games behind in the loss column. And because of its streaky play, by the 15th of August, third place Orleans was breathing down Falmouth's neck, threatening to take over second place, as it defeated the Falmouth club 7–2 at Falmouth Heights Field. The *Cape Cod Standard Times* saw it like this:

> ### SCENE IS SET FOR LEAGUE SHAKEUP
> *Falmouth: Aug. 15—Three runs in the first frame formed the foundation for Orleans' 7–2 victory over Falmouth here yesterday afternoon and put the visiting club in striking distance of second place. Falmouth can only sit idly by today as Orleans seeks a victory over Bourne, which would put her in runner-up position.*

Well, the Falmouth boys were not about to relinquish second place without a struggle. On Tuesday, August 16th, in a hard-fought contest, they defeated Bourne 3–2 behind Rosy Ryan's excellent pitching, which earned him his second win of the season. Falmouth scored once in the third, on singles by Ryan, Brochu and Vitale. It scored twice in the sixth on Guy's second single, which drove in Lester Shatzer with what proved to be the winning run. Again, with the pressure on, Guy came through for his team.

Then, the following day at Bourne, Falmouth and Bourne played an error-filled game, which Falmouth won, 10–8. Guy, playing in left field, collected two hits in five plate appearances, and a newcomer, young Oscar Khedarian, joined the team at third base.

On the night of Thursday, August 18th, fans on the Cape were treated to the first appearance of the summer by the original Colored Giants of Philadelphia. The game, held at the Barnstable High School field, was the first game to be played under the floodlights on the Cape. The *Cape Cod Standard Times*, again:

> *Not only a good baseball game but a good 'show' is promised by Cape Cod officials for fans who attend a floodlight game between the Falmouth entry and the original colored Giants of Philadelphia tonight …*
> *… members of the squad have as much ability at clowning and amusing the spectators in a humorous way, as they have in playing ball, according to officials. It is expected the meet will be colorful.*

And *the Enterprise, Falmouth, Mass* column, *Cape Circuit Chatter,* said this about the upcoming game:

> *CAPE COD TO GET INITIATED TO NIGHT BALL*
>   *Tonight Falmouth is playing the colored Giants, under the lights at the Barnstable High School field.*
>   *Barnstable is going to have a Cape Cod League team on its field once this summer even if it is its ancient rival, Falmouth.*
>   *Local fans have much interest in the game, the colored Giants are always an attraction, and Falmouth is the choice of many Barnstable fans for this season and then the Barnstable Association may play a few night games next year when it is back in the Cape Cod League again.*

This was the first indication I'd seen that Barnstable might possibly be back in the League for the 1939 season.

Well, despite the fact that the Boehner-coached boys were playing their second game of the day, they apparently defeated the colored Giants handily. Their *first* game of the 18th had been against Orleans at Falmouth, an important one considering that, at this point, Orleans was threatening to dislodge them from their hold on second place. Falmouth rose to the challenge however, winning it 5–3. Guy patrolled center field and collected two hits in five plate appearances.

∗   ∗   ∗   ∗

Cape Cod, MA
Monday, August 22, 1938
Falmouth, MA
9:00 a.m.

In fact, Falmouth's team, sensing that it had a shot at winning the pennant, was looking mighty good. Over the previous weekend, it defeated Harwich convincingly on Saturday, 9–4 and on Sunday afternoon, 12–3. Feeling the pressure, Harwich dropped two games on Sunday, losing their morning tilt to Bourne, 7–6, so that by the close of the weekend, Falmouth had drawn even in the win column, and was only one game behind Harwich in the loss column. The standings, as reported by the *Cape Cod Standard Times* on Monday, August 22nd, read like this:

TEAM	W	L	PCT.
Harwich	*23*	*16*	*.590*
Falmouth	*23*	*17*	*.575*
Orleans	*19*	*19`*	*.500*
Bourne	*14*	*27*	*.341*

Also on Monday, August 22nd, the hitting stats were again published for the League. Eliminating Al Blanche, who had thirty hits in only sixty-six times up because he had not been playing regularly, Connie Creedon was still leading the loop with 65 hits in 153 trips to the plate. Wally Sullivan and Myron Ruckstull of Falmouth were next, with averages of .418 and .398, respectively. And, in the fifth spot—coming on like gang busters was—Guy Vitale, hitting .364. He had closed on the leader, going from twelfth the previous week to fifth—fourth if you only count the regulars—raising his average a whopping sixteen points in the bargain.

Was the stage set for a fantastic final two weeks of the 1938 Cape Cod League season? Would Falmouth continue its torrid wining pace and overtake Harwich, or would it wilt under the pressure? Are Cape Cod baseball fans about to witness a repeat of the thrilling 1937 season, when Barnstable and Falmouth battled down to the very last day, before the pennant was won?

CHAPTER 32

Cape Cod, MA
Tuesday, August 23, 1938
Orleans MA
1:30 p.m.

On the afternoon of Monday, August 22nd, Falmouth took advantage of five Orleans errors to pound out a 9–6 win, smashing fifteen hits in the process. And immediately after the game, WATCH FALMOUTH became the warning cry throughout the Cape Cod League, as fans noticed the torrid pace being set by that club.

Guy, encouraged by his progress over the past week, was on fire at the plate. He had three base hits in six trips to the dish, one of them a double. Playing in left field again, he turned in four putouts, while committing none of his team's three errors that afternoon.

Just two days later, on Thursday, August 24th, Falmouth took over first place from Harwich when it defeated Bourne, 9–3, while Harwich lost a close one to Orleans, 4–3. Here's how the *Cape Cod Standard Times* reported the game:

> FALMOUTH BATTERS OUT 15 HITS
> *Bourne, Aug. 25—Falmouth rode into the leadership of the Cape Cod League here yesterday afternoon on the wings of a wind which at times approached gale proportions and sent balls spinning to all parts of the diamond with Rosy Ryan scattering Bourne's hits throughout the contest while his teammates battered Drisko for 15 smashes ...*

And Guy Vitale continued his scorching pace at the plate, collecting two hits with the stick in four appearances. However, troubled by that wind in center field, he dropped a fly ball, one of his team's two errors in the game that day.

Also on the 25th, *the Enterprise, Falmouth, Mass* newspaper column, *Cape Circuit Chatter,* said this about the season, to date:

FALMOUTH RIGHT ON HARWICH'S HEALS

Cape League fans are following the games anxiously to see if Falmouth is going to knock Harwich out of number one position. What a difference one week makes! The speculation last week was whether or not Orleans would force Falmouth out of second place ...

The nip and tuck battle between Falmouth and Harwich reminds Barnstable fans of the League set up a year ago When Barnstable, Bourne, Harwich and Falmouth were in a thrilling pennant race which was not decided until Labor Day morning, when Normie Merrill pitched a no—hit, no-run game to clinch the flag.

Falmouth and Harwich squared off in two games on the 25th and 26th, and each earned a win and a loss. On August 25th, George Colbert returned to his catching post for the first time since July 25th, perhaps having, been out with an injury. Guy drove in one of Falmouth's four runs with a long fly ball that scored Lester Shatzer in the seventh inning as Falmouth won it, 3–2. However, next day Harwich turned the tables, 9–6. But Guy went three for five, scored two runs and committed no errors in left field. One of his hits, a single in the fourth, tied the game, and his double in the ninth, drove in a run.

On August 28th, the *Cape Cod Standard Times* printed the batting averages:

Connie Creedon, Orleans outfielder, continues to lead the parade of batsmen in the Cape Cod League among those who have played the bulk of the season's games. Creedon bats for .417, having collected 70 hits out of 168 trips to the plate.

Wally Sullivan comes second among the regulars with an average of .412 having hit safely 77 times in 187 times at bat. Two more of his teammates, Myron Ruckstull and Guy Vitale, are also well up among the leaders.

Ruckstull was in the third slot at .395, and Guy was now a solid fourth among the regulars, with a .364 average.

Falmouth squeaked by Orleans, 2–1 on August 29th, as Manager Bill Boehner, whose batting average had dropped to .247 because of nagging injuries, provided the offensive punch to keep his team out in front in the cranberry circuit by knocking in both runs with a triple and a double. In this game, Guy went one for four, with three putouts in left field.

And on the 30th, fifteen-year old Oscar Khederian's spectacular scoop of a ground ball at shortstop snuffed out a Harwich rally in the eighth inning and allowed Falmouth to earn a 10–7 win and move "under the shadow" of the 1938 Cape Cod League pennant. Khederian, a junior at Watertown High School, a suburb of Boston, also had a good day at the dish, collecting four hits in five plate appearances. Guy? Four hits in six trips, scored three runs and played a flawless left field the entire game.

*   *   *   *

Cape Cod, MA
Thursday, September 1, 1938
Falmouth, MA
8:00 a.m.

With the '38 Cape Cod League season rapidly coming to an end, interest was at a fever pitch. Local fans and tourists from Boston, Providence, towns up and down the Cape, and other cities and towns throughout New England, awaited the final outcome, and the announcement of those young men who would be recognized as *the best* in the League.

The choosing of all-star teams began on August 26th, with this piece in *The Enterprise, Falmouth, Mass*:

ALL CAPE LEAGUE TEAM

Myron Ruckstull	Second base	Falmouth
Thomas Palumbo	Third base	Bourne
Anthony Plansky	Left field	Bourne
Wallace Sullivan	Right field	Falmouth
Frank Cammaranno	First base	Falmouth
Guy Vitale	Center field	Falmouth
Irving Fay	Shortstop	Harwich
Neil Mahoney	Catcher	Harwich

THE ALL CAPE TEAM

As the Cape Cod League baseball season draws toward an exciting end, what with Falmouth wresting first place from Harwich, everyone starts selecting an All-Star aggregation. The Enterprise, as usual, announces its choice of players for the mythical nine. Here are the whys and wherefores for the above team: Center field: "Little Poison" is

*an appropriate nickname for Guy Vitale of Falmouth. The Guy can do
anything. He's fast on his feet, a clever ball hawk, and is slugging for
.364, fifth highest in the league. Who has a better right?*

And this article on Thursday, September 1st, in a newspaper I can't recall:

ALL-CAPE LEAGUE TEAMS ARE CHOSEN
*As the Cape Cod League goes down the home stretch, with Falmouth
leading, the choosing of all-star teams has begun. The League has but
four more days of play, winding up with the Labor Day double head-
ers. Harwich still has a chance to forge ahead and win the title, but the
odds are on Falmouth.*

The piece went on to name its selections. I found it interesting that it did not
pick Connie Creedon, who led the League in hitting in '38, on its first team, but
instead, selected Tony Plansky, who finished far down the batting list, as one
of its outfielders. Surely, sentiment played a role in their decision. Here are the
Enterprise's choices:

*Frank Cammaranno, Falmouth, 1st base
Myron Ruckstull, Falmouth, 2nd base
Thomas Palumbo, Bourne, 3rd base
Tony Plansky, Bourne, left field
Walter Sullivan, Falmouth, right field
Guy Vitale, Falmouth, center field
Irving Fay, Harwich, shortstop
Neil Mahoney, Harwich, catcher
Kittredge and Garfield Harris, Harwich, pitchers
Joseph Carpi, Orleans, pitcher
Charles 'Buzz' Kendrick, Bourne, pitcher
Rosy Ryan and 'Muggsy' Kelly, Falmouth, pitchers.*

And *The Harwich Independent* checked in with these players, which it considered the best of the Cape Cod League:

*Frank Cammaranno, Falmouth, 1st base
Myron Ruckstull, Falmouth, 2nd base
Thomas Palumbo, Bourne, 3rd base
Atilo "Tilly" Ferdonzi, Harwich, left field*

Guy Vitale, Falmouth, center field
Cornelius Creedon, Orleans, right field
Neil Mahoney, Harwich, catcher
Joseph Carpi, Orleans, pitcher
Garfield Harris, Harwich, pitcher
Rosy Ryan, Falmouth, pitcher
Charles Kendrick, Bourne, pitcher
Leonard "Pete" Dean, Harwich, utility man.

The Harwich Independent did not name a player at shortstop, but selected Pete Dean, as a utility infielder, who could no doubt fill that roll.

What about young Oscar Khederian, who joined the Falmouth club on August 17th? Perhaps because he'd missed approximately six weeks of the season, then played for awhile at third base before being moved to shortstop, the newspaper felt that he was not quite the best at either position.

Nice to see that Guy, finally, was selected as an All-star at the position he actually played most of the summer. That must have given him much satisfaction.

The *Cape Cod Standard Times* All-Cape selections were quite similar to the other newspapers. This is what that newspaper printed about Guy:

Guy Vitale—an All-Cape selection from Barnstable last year. He has been one of the big guns in the Falmouth offensive with an average of .364. Vitale, playing his third season on the Cape, won letters in football, baseball and hockey at Kents Hill School, from which he was graduated this [past] June. He makes his home in East Boston and hopes to enter Holy Cross.

So, it was almost over. Only a few games remained. The League standings as of September 1st looked like this:

TEAM	W	L	PCT.
Falmouth	30	19	.612
Harwich	27	21	.563
Orleans	23	25	.479
Bourne	17	32	.347

Although Harwich still had a mathematical chance to overtake Falmouth, most knowledgeable observers felt the race was over, the flag Falmouth's to take home. They were right. On Friday, September 2nd, Falmouth slipped by a stubborn Orleans team, 4–3, with Guy, Wally Sullivan and Frank Cammaranno all going two for four, while Harwich defeated Bourne, 3–2.

The following day, Falmouth dumped all over Orleans, 19–8, as many of Orleans' regulars deserted the team and left for home. Indeed, Orleans was forced to use the bat boy's brother and several players in civilian clothing, in order to field a team that day. Guy, apparently letting up a bit, went one for six at the plate.

*   *   *   *

Cape Cod, MA
Monday, September 5, 1938
Falmouth, MA
8:00 a.m.

The Labor Day games were all that remained. Attendance was light as many tourists closed out their vacations and headed for their homes in Boston, Providence, and other nearby cities. On Tuesday, September 6th, the *Cape Cod Standard Times* described the action this way:

> *After cinching the pennant on Sunday by defeating Harwich, its closest rival, 5–3, Falmouth, in a jovial mood, dropped both holiday games to Bourne yesterday as the curtain went down on the 1938 Cape Cod League season. Bourne beat Falmouth 12–10 in the morning game at Falmouth and topped the pennant winners 12–8 at Bourne in the afternoon contest.*
>
> *The league winded (sic) up its season on the lower Cape with two serious and well-played contests, Harwich winning both behind excellent pitching. Frank Hadley hurled Harwich to a 6–1 victory over Orleans in the morning at Orleans. The teams traveled to Harwich for the closing contest, which featured the four-hit 6–0 shutout, pitched by Harwich's Ed Ingalls.*

A day later, the *Cape Cod Standard Times* ran a very complimentary article on the Cape pitchers. Harwich's Ed Ingalls, a Harvard College graduate, mentioned above, was the pitcher with the best record that season, winning his first four starts in a row and later tossing a two-hit shutout in August, and a four-hit masterpiece on Labor Day. Lester Shatzer of Falmouth and Joe Carpi of Orleans, compiled records of eight wins and five losses, respectively, Shatzer for a winning team, Carpi for a losing club.

The final standings for the 1938 Cape Cod League:

TEAM	W	L	PCT.
Falmouth	32	22	.593
Harwich	31	23	.574
Orleans	24	30	.444
Bourne	21	33	.389

And the final listing of batting averages showed that Connie Creedon, of Orleans, the orchestra leader who graduated from Danvers High School in 1932, and St. John's Preparatory School a year later, and who'd had tryouts with the Boston Bees and the Chicago Cubs that year, had hung on to win the batting crown with an average of .420; 87 hits in 207 trips to the plate. Perhaps it was the war, but why it took this fellow five more years to reach the Majors, and why he only lasted there for such a short time, I do not know.

Wally Sullivan, from Edgewood, RI, making his debut in the cranberry circuit for Falmouth, finished in second place among the regulars and fifth place overall, at .402; he poled 88 hits in 219 attempts. His two seasons of play for Pawtucket, which eventually became a Red Sox farm team, had been extremely helpful to him in this league.

Veteran Myron Ruckstull came in third among the regulars at .396, thus proving that he could still hit the old "pill," even if it did look a bit more like a pill as it came to the plate.

And our boy, Guy, finished fourth among regular players and eighth overall, at .374, on the strength of a last-minute spurt of five hits in ten trips to the plate in the final two games on Labor Day, which raised his average ten points. Although Creedon, Sullivan and Ruckstull hit for higher averages, Guy ... well, I'll let the *Cape Cod Standard Times* tell the tale:

> *Guy Vitale, speedy Falmouth outfielder, collected the largest number of base hits during the season, batting out 93 for an average of .374 ...*

So there we have it. Despite his unnerving experience with Fred O'Brien and his utter despair at having "wasted two years," Guy's swan song in the Cape Cod League turned out extremely well. He collected more base hits than anyone in the League *again* that year, as he had done in '37, and finished high up on the list of batters. As I said earlier, baseball was in his blood. I know the feeling. It's hard to shake. Had he not decided, at Pete Herman's urging, to put aside his abject misery after the New York City debacle and play one last season on the

Cape, he would not have been part of this Falmouth championship team, and would not have met Oscar Khederian, who would play a role in Guy's life a bit later.

*   *   *   *

Pine Bluffs, WY
Monday, November 1, 2004
703 Beech Street
12:00 p.m.

Researching Guy's exploits in 1938, I was pleased. Day after day, newspaper stories chronicled his successes. But again I was surprised by something I'd uncovered. A minor mystery came to light, which cried out for an explanation.

Selected by the *Cape Cod Standard Times* as its All-Cape center fielder that summer, the article states that he hoped to enter Holy Cross in the fall of 1938.

Kents Hill, Colgate, and now Holy Cross. All were linked to him in newspaper articles or cartoon drawings appearing in newspapers. We've seen, explained and disposed of the first two. But Holy Cross? Where did that one come from? Well, here's my explanation in five words—Lenny Merullo and Frank Cammaranno.

In one of my telephone conversations with Lenny Merullo, he told me he had attended Holy Cross after graduating from Danvers Preparatory School. He told me he'd almost obtained a degree from there, but in his senior year, the school found out he'd been given financial help by a major league team, thus violating the rules, and invited him to leave. I guess that incident revoked his amateur status. He'd had to finish college elsewhere. But he acknowledged that Holy Cross's baseball program was a good one.

As we now know, Frank Cammaranno, who hailed from New Haven, Connecticut, was one of Guy's closest friends on the Falmouth club in 1938. A dentist in civilian life, Frank played a terrific first base, batted .358 that season, and was a unanimous All-Cape selection at that position. Further, Wally Sullivan told me that Guy hung out with Frank a lot that summer, and Connie Blackwell confirmed it. Well, in 1933, Frank Cammaranno graduated from Holy Cross, where he played baseball for four years and captained the team in his senior year.

Another interesting fact about Cammaranno—he took his dental degree from the University of Maryland Dental School at Baltimore, in June 1938—just before traveling north to Cape Cod to play baseball for Bill Boehner's Falmouth club.

At the end of the 1938 school year at Kents Hill, prior to their meeting with O'Brien, Guy told Pete Herman he was again looking into colleges and that he wanted to pick one with a "durn good baseball program." Because of what he knew about Lenny Merullo, he may have already been focusing on Holy Cross. And after a few weeks of friendship with Frank Cammaranno, he may have arrived at a decision to enroll there.

Did he make it? No. And I don't know why. My guess is that he started the process too late. Holy Cross, being a small Roman Catholic college with an excellent academic reputation, its classes probably filled quickly, thus making it important for anyone wanting to go to school there to apply perhaps as much as a year in advance.

One final note: Connie Blackwell's brother, George W. De Mello, was connected to the Falmouth team and may have played a few games for them in 1938. Somehow, he came into possession of two baseballs signed by all the players on the '37 and '38 Falmouth teams. Guy's signature is on the 1938 ball.

"My brother was *not* really on the team," Connie said. "He graduated from high school in 1938, and he may have played in a few games or practiced with the team. But he knew all the players and he even handled the team's money that year. George died in 1996 at age seventy-five after a career as a dentist. I got those two baseballs. They were of no value to me, but because of their historical interest, I donated them to the Cape Cod League's Baseball exhibit at Heritage Plantation in Sandwich."

Al Irish again: "George and Connie's father was John De Mello. He was vice-president of the Cape Cod League for most of the '30s. I can still picture him collecting donations from the fans seated on the bank along the third base line at the Falmouth Heights ball field. George De Mello [actually] played first base for Falmouth in the last game of the 1938 season. He did graduate from high school that year and later became a dentist with a practice in Falmouth."

Guy Vitale, East Boston high School, Class of 1936

He's shown here accommodating photographers of several Boston newspapers as he concludes his senior year on the East Boston baseball team, after hitting an amazing .621

Guy Vitale, as a young boy

Here, he's seven or eight years old. Photo was taken on the back porch of
his parents' home at 20 Breed Street

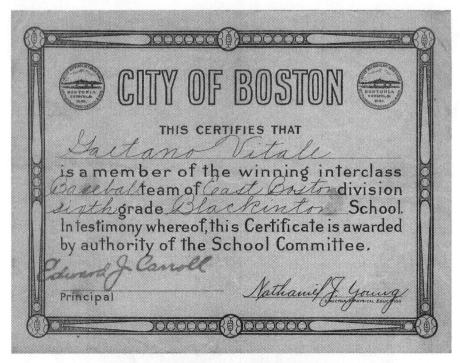

Blackinton Elementary School Certificate

Given to Guy Vitale for participating on the winning team in the East
Boston Division, 6th Grade team at Blackinton Elementary School

"You just swing this against the ball"

Said Babe Herman, big homerun hitter of the Brooklyn Robins, to Guy
Vitale and Ernest Siciliano, aided and abetted by Lefty Frank O'Doul, a
pretty fair country hitter himself, who seconded the motion. The boys
won places in the fungo hitting contest on the program sponsored by the
park department at Braves field yesterday.

East Boston High School Football Squad, 1935

As quarterback and Number one back, Guy is shown seated in front row, center, holding a football. To his right is Coach Fred O'Brien

THE NODDLER 21

SPORTS

Edited by ANTHONY AVOLIO, '36

East Boston vs. Brighton High

Our Blue and Gold football team, under the direction of Coach O'Brien, opened its schedule of the 1935 season by defeating Brighton High, 7 to 0. Although our boys were outweighed, they were by no means outplayed.

The first half proved to be a punting duel between our Guy Vitale, and Bill McSweeney of the Scanlon squad. Vitale booted a pair of sixty yarders that kept Brighton in home territory.

In the second half, things were different. After the kickoff, our boys started a march from their own forty-four yard line. Thrusts by Vitale and Geraci reached the Brighton twenty-five yard line, from which Tuck carried it to the thirteen. It was then, that a great cheer rose from the rooting section; Vitale had scored standing up to give our team its well earned victory over the Black and Orange. To top that, he also booted a perfect kick from placement to make the final score which read 7 to 0. As the game ended, our boys were again about to score.

Guy Vitale, no doubt, was the outstanding player. His kicking and rushing was exceptional.

Credit must also be given to the rest of the backfield consisting of Tuck, Geraci, and Cotrozza. These boys did much to keep the ball in Brighton territory.

The line did an excellent job in blocking and tackling the Brighton huskies, this being the chief reason that our boys came through with victory.

Our team received good support, which helped their fighting spirit a great deal. We have a good Captain, and a good team this year.

CAPTAIN GUY VITALE

FALL 1935

Page from East Boston High School's 1936 yearbook, The Noddler

This write-up of the Eastie—Brighton game glowingly describes Guy's role. Here, he's shown in his practice uniform

Boston Traveler's All-Scholastic Football Team, 1935

From that newspaper's November 30, 1935 issue, page 14. Guy was
selected as a fullback, even though he played quarterback that season.

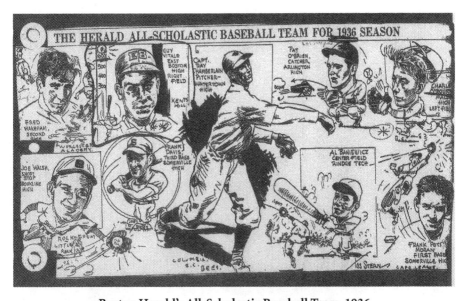

Boston Herald's All-Scholastic Baseball Team, 1936

Guy is in top row, second from left. Note the words "Kents Hill" next to his caricature.

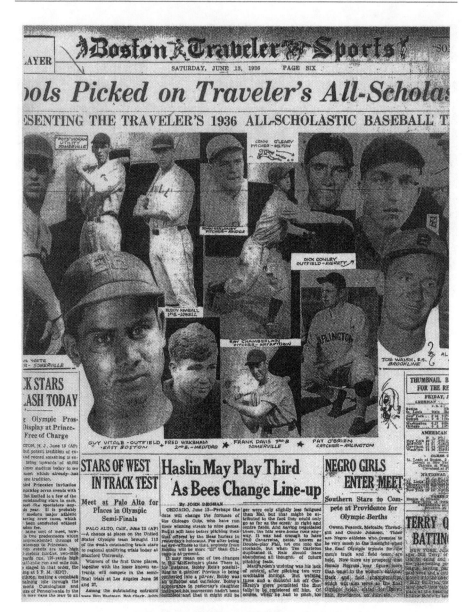

Boston Traveler's All-Scholastic Baseball Team, 1936

The Boston Traveler's Schoolboy Hall of Fame for 1936

At top and left of page, shows Guy Vitale winner of its award for 1936.
Other information shows results of a track meet

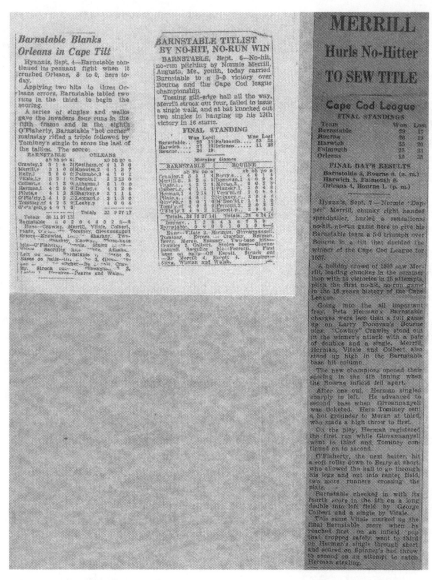

Above, left—Box score showing Barnstable's defeat of Orleans 8–0 Guy played left and right fields, in this tilt and had a good day with the stick.

Above, center and right—In a thrilling conclusion to the 1937 Cape cod League season, Barnstable shuts out Bourne, 5–0 to win the championship. Guy played left field in this game, collected two hits in four trips to the plate, and scored two of his teams five runs, as Normie Merrill tossed a no-hitter at Bourne, and shut them out in front of a festive holiday crowd of 1,500

Cape All-Star Nine

Player	Team	Position
Walter "Doc" Berry (Capt.)	Bourne	Short Stop
Jackie Oleks	Harwich	Third Base
William "Bill" Barrett	Harwich	Center Field
Anthony "Tony" Plansky	Bourne	Left Field
Guy Vitale	Barnstable	Right Field
Francis "Cowboy" Crawley	Barnstable	Second Base
Lawrence "Law" Donovan	Bourne	First Base
William "Mike" Ryan	Falmouth	Catcher
Normie Merrill	Barnstable	Pitcher
Walter Morris	Falmouth	Pitcher
Thomas Palumbo	Orleans	Utility Inf.

HONORABLE MENTION

Peter Herman, George Colbert, Peter O'Flaherty, Barnstable; Hal Spin... Charles Brycato, Milton Vergnani, Frank Escott, George Sexton, ... Kendrick, Bourne; Frank Cammarano, Robert Gendron William Boehner, Myron Ruckstull, Falmouth; Edward Britt, Charles Cahill, Johnny Laurek, Arthur Kenney, Harwich; James Dudley, Victor Dennis, Lou Athanas, Don Eastham, Robert Leahy, Orleans.

Top Photo: Cape Cod All-Star Team, 1937

Bottom Photo: Number 9, Guy Vitale, Barnstable, swinging for the fences.
Note spectators along the third base-left field line, watching the game.

Photo of the 1937 Barnstable Team

This 1937 Barnstable team won the Cape League championship on the
final day of the season with a 5–0 victory over Bourne. Norman Merrill
pitched a no-hitter for Barnstable to give his team a league-leading 29–17
record that year. (Courtesy Trayser Museum.)

1937

Photo of the Kents Hill Academy Football Team, 1937
Guy is shown in the second row, fifth from left. Pete Herman is the Coach

KENT'S HILL SCHOLL ICE HOCKEY TEAM, 1937–38.

Top Photo: Guy is in back row, fourth from right. Pete Herman is the Coach.

Bottom Photo: Guy is in first row, second from left.

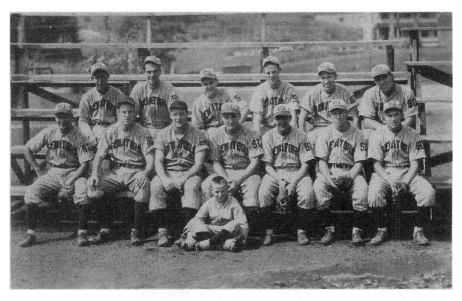

St. Johnsbury Senators, 1939

Guy is in the first row, left end.

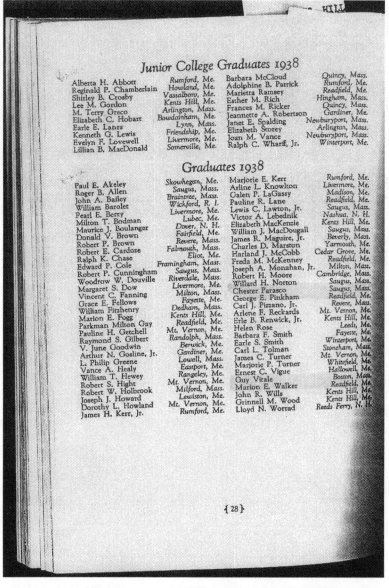

Junior College Graduates 1938

Alberta H. Abbott — Rumford, Me.
Reginald P. Chamberlain — Howland, Me.
Shirley B. Crosby — Vassalboro, Me.
Lee M. Gordon — Kents Hill, Me.
M. Terry Greco — Arlington, Mass.
Elizabeth C. Hobart — Bowdoinham, Me.
Earle E. Lanes — Lynn, Mass.
Kenneth G. Lewis — Friendship, Me.
Evelyn F. Lovewell — Livermore, Me.
Lillian B. MacDonald — Somerville, Me.

Barbara McCloud — Quincy, Mass.
Adolphine B. Patrick — Rumford, Me.
Marietta Ramsey — Readfield, Me.
Esther M. Rich — Hingham, Mass.
Frances M. Ricker — Quincy, Mass.
Jeannette A. Robertson — Gardiner, Me.
Janet E. Spalding — Newburyport, Mass.
Elizabeth Storey — Arlington, Mass.
Joan M. Vance — Newburyport, Mass.
Ralph C. Wharff, Jr. — Winterport, Me.

Graduates 1938

Paul E. Akeley — Skowhegan, Me.
Roger B. Allen — Saugus, Mass.
John A. Bailey — Braintree, Mass.
William Barolet — Wickford, R. I.
Pearl E. Berry — Livermore, Me.
Milton T. Bodman — Lubec, Me.
Maurice J. Boulanger — Dover, N. H.
Donald V. Brown — Fairfield, Me.
Robert P. Brown — Revere, Mass.
Robert E. Cardoze — Falmouth, Mass.
Ralph K. Chase — Eliot, Me.
Edward P. Cole — Framingham, Mass.
Robert P. Cunningham — Saugus, Mass.
Woodrow W. Douville — Riverdale, Mass.
Margaret S. Dow — Livermore, Me.
Vincent C. Fanning — Milton, Mass.
Grace E. Fellows — Fayette, Me.
William Fitzhenry — Dedham, Mass.
Marion E. Fogg — Kents Hill, Me.
Parkman Milton Gay — Readfield, Me.
Pauline H. Getchell — Mt. Vernon, Me.
Raymond S. Gilbert — Randolph, Mass.
V. June Goodwin — Berwick, Me.
Arthur N. Gosline, Jr. — Gardiner, Me.
L. Philip Greene — Lowell, Mass.
Vance A. Healy — Eastport, Me.
William T. Hewey — Rangeley, Me.
Robert S. Hight — Mt. Vernon, Me.
Robert W. Holbrook — Milford, Mass.
Joseph J. Howard — Lewiston, Me.
Dorothy L. Howland — Mt. Vernon, Me.
James H. Kerr, Jr. — Rumford, Me.

Marjorie E. Kerr — Rumford, Me.
Arline L. Knowlton — Livermore, Me.
Galen P. LaGassy — Madison, Me.
Pauline R. Lane — Readfield, Me.
Lewis C. Lawton, Jr. — Saugus, Mass.
Victor A. Lebednik — Nashua, N. H.
Elizabeth MacKenzie — Kents Hill, Me.
William J. MacDougall — Saugus, Mass.
James R. Maguire, Jr. — Beverly, Mass.
Charles D. Marston — Yarmouth, Me.
Harland J. McCobb — Cedar Grove, Me.
Freda M. McKenney — Readfield, Me.
Joseph A. Monahan, Jr. — Milton, Mass.
Robert H. Moore — Cambridge, Mass.
Willard H. Norton — Saugus, Mass.
Chester Parasco — Saugus, Mass.
George E. Pinkham — Readfield, Me.
Carl J. Pizzano, Jr. — Revere, Mass.
Arlene F. Reckards — Mt. Vernon, Me.
Erle B. Renwick, Jr. — Kents Hill, Me.
Helen Rose — Leeds, Me.
Barbara F. Smith — Fayette, Me.
Earle S. Smith — Winterport, Me.
Carl L. Tolman — Stoneham, Mass.
James C. Turner — Mt. Vernon, Me.
Marjorie P. Turner — Whitefield, Me.
Ernest C. Vigue — Hallowell, Me.
Guy Vitale — Boston, Mass.
Marion E. Walker — Readfield, Me.
John R. Wills — Kents Hill, Me.
Grinnell M. Wood — Kents Hill, Me.
Lloyd N. Worrad — Reeds Ferry, N. H.

{ 28 }

List of Graduates, Kents Hill Academy, Class of 1938

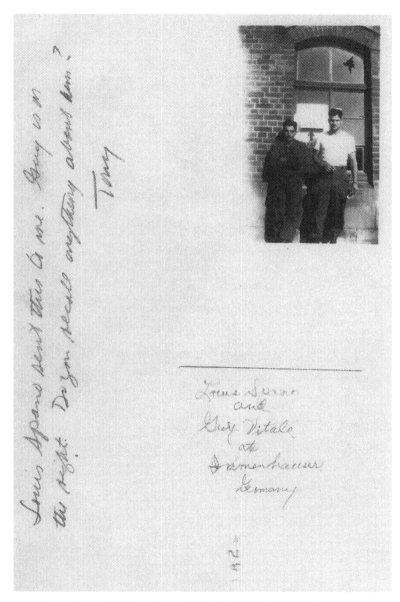

Photo of Guy and Louis Spano in Immenhausen, Germany

I sent copies of this photo to numerous members of the 311th Infantry
Regiment, asking if they knew Guy.

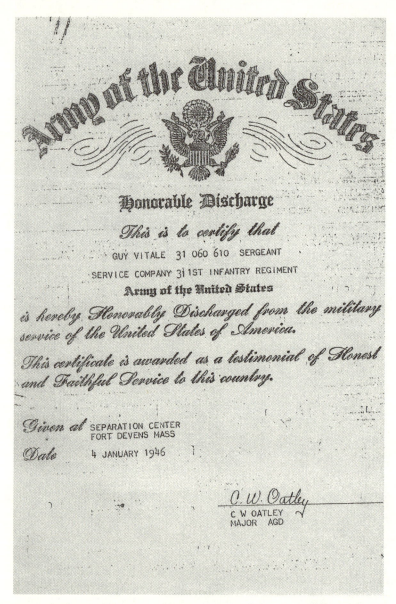

Copy of Guy Vitale's honorable discharge from the United States Army

PART FOUR

THE TWIN STATES
LEAGUE

CHAPTER 33

Pine Bluffs, WY
Wednesday, November 2, 2005
703 Beech Street
10:15 a.m.

In November 2000, after a trip to Baseball's Hall of Fame in Cooperstown, New York, my father-in-law, Paul Fenchak[44] brought me a half-page form—called a Contract Form—from their records. Significance? It showed that Guy Vitale played baseball in 1941 for the Salisbury Indians, in Maryland's Eastern Shore League. That was a surprise to me; one of many jolts I'd received since starting to research my uncle's life.

Two years later, I was ready to work on this topic. A few phone calls revealed that the Eastern Shore League was considered a professional league because the teams in it were loosely affiliated with major league ball clubs. Although there's some confusion here, the Salisbury Indians, the team for which Guy played, appears to have been connected with either the Washington Senators or Cleveland Indians organizations.

Up to this point, I'd understood that Guy played only unorganized ball; that he'd never signed a contract with any team in organized baseball. But here was conclusive proof otherwise; that he'd actually cracked organized baseball on the way to achieving his dream of playing in the Major Leagues.

I also learned that Baltimore's Enoch Pratt Library owned microfilm of *The Salisbury Times*, a daily newspaper published in those days, containing exten-

---

44 Paul Fenchak, born May 30, 1929 in Madera. PA. A pitcher, he rose to Double A ball, when an injury forced his retirement. He taught History and Social Studies for forty years in the school systems of New York, Pennsylvania and Maryland, until his retirement in 1990. A free-lance writer and scholar with a life-long love for learning, his work has appeared in Ukrainian American and other publications. Paul's home library consists of more than 3000 volumes.

sive sports coverage. Did that paper cover Salisbury Indians games in 1941? A trip to the library resulted in the proverbial pot of gold; articles covering the Indians for the 1941 season.

What does this have to do with the Twin States League? I know it's taking awhile, but I'm coming to it. One of the earliest articles I found, printed on April 30th, 1941, contained the first of many references to Guy and the Salisbury Indians. And the Twin States League:

> *INDIANS PLAY PARSONSBURG IN EXHIBIT*
> *SALISBURY CLUB WILL FACE HERCULES SATURDAY*
> Leo Venskus was scheduled to hurl for the Salisbury Indians today in their scheduled exhibition game with Parsonsburg at GordyPark. The tilt was set for 5:30 p.m.
> Another newcomer joined the ranks yesterday. He is Guy Vitale, a chunky looking outfielder from up Boston way. He may give Arnold and Sullivan a fight for one of the outfield posts.
> Signed to a contract earlier this week, he has had several years of semi-pro experience. During the past two seasons he played in the Twin States League and the Cape Cod circuit, a pair of unorganized loops.

Other articles revealed that the player-manager for the Salisbury club was Johnny Wedemeyer, who had pitched for the Bennington Generals the previous season. Also of major interest was a piece about the new Indians' owner; a man named Reubin Levin who hailed from—Bennington, Vermont.

Before reading the above-quoted article, I'd only known that Guy had played in the Cape Cod League, in '36 and '37. What he had done in the summers of 1938, 1939, and 1940, was still a mystery to me. Of course I wanted to fill that three-year gap. This article alerted me to the fact that Guy may have played on the Cape again—perhaps in 1938—and maybe even in 1939. However, no teams were mentioned.

Checking further, I found that my uncle *had* played a third year of ball on Cape Cod; for Falmouth, in 1938. I did the research and we know now that Falmouth won the league championship in '38, with Guy as a key member of that club. So one-third of this gap in his life had been filled.

But what about the Twin States League? Impressed by the record Paul Fenchak had uncovered at Cooperstown's Hall of Fame, established at the purported site of the 1839 invention of the game, I placed a long-distance call to the Reference Library located there. If I could pin down where this league had been located, I might be able to discover the team on which Guy had played during 1939 and, perhaps, 1940.

"Yes, there was a Twin States League," a researcher at Cooperstown's Library told me. "It was started in 1911 as a professional league and operated in New Hampshire and Vermont. But after about 1915 or so, it became a semi-pro league. Apparently it was still operating in the 1930s."

"What towns had entries in the League?" I asked.

"Well, when it first started in 1911, Springfield-Charleston Hyphens, Bellows Falls Sulphites, Brattleboro Islanders and Keene Champs were the entries," was his initial response. Later in the conversation, he recalled that Bennington and Charlestown may have also had teams in that early Twin States League.

Juggling continued research and writing with the ever-pressing necessity to earn a living, I put this section of the book aside while I developed the first few sections. Years later, on October 26, 2005, I began to seriously dig into what was left of this "gap" in my uncle's life.

Because of the Reubin Levin-Johnny Wedemeyer tie between Bennington and the Salisbury Indians, I decided to start with Bennington. A call to the Bennington Free Library was first. There, Lynne McCann turned me over to Wendy Sharkey, the Adult Reference Clerk in the Vermont History Room. Besides sporting a pleasant British accent, Wendy knows what she's doing. She found several helpful articles dealing with the early history of Bennington baseball and the Twin States League, one from *The Bennington Banner* dated March 21st, 1911:

TWIN STATES LEAGUE

SCHEDULE OPENS JULY 1 AND CLOSES ON LABOR DAY
The Twin States League will open the baseball season Saturday, July 1, and will play its last game on Labor Day, Monday, Sept. 4.
[As of this writing] Four clubs will battle for the pennant; Brattleboro, Bellows Falls, Springfield and Charlestown ...

That was corroboration of sorts, although not on all fours, with what the Cooperstown researcher had told me about the beginning of the Twin States League. So some progress was being made. But was the Twin States League of 1911–1915 the same Twin States League mentioned in the above-named article? And did Guy play for Bennington or one of the other teams in the Twin States League in 1939 and 1940? Or did he play somewhere else during those two years? I had no clue.

Back on October 30th, 2001, armed only with that *Salisbury Times* article, I had spoken to Lenny Merullo about this. It was from him that I first learned about the Northern League, the "connected" and "unconnected" thing, and the Twin States League.

"The kids who were connected or tied up by major league clubs played in the Northern League, which had at least four teams at that time," Lenny said. "A couple from around Saranac Lake in New York, and one each from Vermont and New Hampshire."

"Why did they play way out there instead of in the Cape Cod League?" I asked.

"During the middle and late 1930s the Northern League was the strongest amateur league in the country. There was little or no minor league baseball at the time, but the teams in that league were connected to major league teams. If a major league club was interested in a player, it'd recommend that he play for a certain team in the Northern League. I played in that League for the Burlington, Vermont club in [the summers of] '37 and '38. That team had players recommended by the Yankees organization. The Saranac Lake team was [made up of] players recommended by the Red Sox."

"Were there any other leagues around for the unconnected but better ballplayers?" I asked the question because of the *Salisbury Times* article.

"Yeah," Lenny said. "There was an amateur league called the Twin States League. It was an inferior league that ran at the same time as the Northern League, but it *did* have some good ballplayers. It operated in New Hampshire and Vermont, and had six or eight teams in it." Apparently Lenny was unaware of the first Twin States League in the early part of the 20th Century, but then why should he have been?

*   *   *   *

Pine Bluffs, WY
Thursday, November 3, 2005
703 Beech Street
11:45 a.m.

Continuing my efforts to unravel this mystery, I began placing long-distance phone calls, following leads that developed as I went along. With help from "Reg" Jones, a baseball aficionado living in Bennington, Joe Hall, of the Bennington Historical Society, and Bob Cummings, a local lawyer in Bennington, individuals who were very generous with their time, I learned much about Vermont baseball.

From Joe Hall, I got this: "My connection with the Bennington team started in the '40s. They were called the Bennington Generals, and during that period of time, they were in the Northern League."

"Were they connected to any major league team?" I asked.

"No. The earlier Generals were a semi-pro team from around 1930 until 1950. As far as I know, the Generals did not exist prior to 1930."

"Does the name Rubin Levin mean anything to you, Joe?"

"Yeah. Rubin Levin was a lawyer here in Bennington. He was interested in baseball and boxing. He died in the 1970s. His kids are still living, though."

"Did Levin ever own the Bennington team?" I wanted to know.

"No. The team was kind of a community thing. Didn't have one owner. But Jim Payotis, a restaurant operator here in town for years, was one of the prime movers." He paused. Then, "Another guy who might know something is Bob Cummings. He's a local lawyer here in town."

Hall gave me Cummings's telephone number and hung up.

*   *   *   *

Pine Bluffs, WY
Saturday, November 5, 2004
703 Beech Street
1:45 p.m.

Two days passed before Robert Cummings, Esquire, returned my call. He was friendly, interested and helpful.

"You're talking about the Northern League, Tony," he said. "Operated here in Bennington in 1940 and 1941. The teams played a seventy-game schedule. Back in the 1930s there *was* a Twin States League."

"Did you play ball for them?"

"No. I got involved with Bennington as a batboy around 1946."

"Was the Northern League connected to organized baseball during the time you're familiar with?" I asked.

"I don't think it was, but some pretty good ballplayers played in it. You remember Robin Roberts? Pitched for the Phillies in the National League. He played for the Montpelier-Barre Senators, and out of seventy of their games, he won eighteen."

"Robin Roberts? He was one of the best. Did you know Rubin Levin?"

"Oh, yeah. He was a lawyer and very well respected citizen here. Why?"

"Well, in 1941, he showed up as the new owner of the Salisbury Indians in Salisbury, Maryland. They were in the Eastern Shore League. My uncle played there during the '41 season. I understand Levin never owned the Bennington team. Is that right?"

"That's true." Bob thought for a minute. "Jimmy Payotis, who owned the Paradise Restaurant before he passed away, was involved with the team along with several others. It was a community effort."

*   *   *   *

Pine Bluffs, WY
Wednesday, November 9, 2005
703 Beech Street
9:45 a.m.

A few days later, Wendy Sharkey e-mailed me with the results of her preliminary research: *"It doesn't look like Bennington played in the Twin States League in 1939 or 1940. But they did play in the Northern League in 1940."*

The next day, Wendy reported this: *"In 1939, Bennington played in the Eastern New York State League. There was some debate about Bennington even fielding a team and whether it would get supporters. [To get money] team members had to hold fundraisers, etc.*

"In 1940, Bennington moved to the Northern League and played the following teams: Glens Falls Giants, Rutland Senators, Brattleboro, Saint Alban's, Montpelier Cards, Claremont Pilots, Burlington Maples … At least these were the games which were reported."

Well, at least this information confirmed what Lenny Merullo, Joe Hall and Bob Cummings had said about Bennington having had an entry in the Northern League in 1940.

Just when I thought I was getting somewhere, Wendy e-mailed me one last time: "I've checked the [Bennington] index and Guy Vitale does not appear at all for either 1939 or 1940," she told me "I've also been looking at batting averages for the Generals and there's no mention of Guy Vitale. I assume this means he did not play for them. There is no mention of the Generals until 1940. But," she said, "I'm sending you a photocopy of an article I found. It'll be interesting background for you."

*   *   *   *

Pine Bluffs, WY
Friday, November 11, 2005
703 Beech Street
9:45 a.m.

True to her word, two days later my snail mail brought the article she'd mentioned. What I read *did* seem to prove at least two connections between Guy Vitale and Bennington, Vermont—Rubin Levin *and* Johnny Wedemeyer. Here's that article from *The Bennington Banner* dated November 8, 1940. We'll deal with it in depth, later:

> ### ATTY LEVIN TO HEAD CLUB
> ### BECOMES PRESIDENT OF SALISBURY, MD., EASTERN SHORE LEAGUE BASEBALL OUTFIT; WEDEMEYER TO ACT AS MANAGER
> *Word has been received in Bennington and confirmed that Attorney Reubin Levin has become president of the Salisbury, Md., Eastern Shore League baseball team and that John 'Lefty' Wedemeyer, former star Bennington Generals pitcher will probably manage the team …*
>
> *Mr. Levin has long been interested in baseball in Bennington and vicinity and he was largely instrumental in bringing Northern League baseball to Bennington last summer.*
>
> *Salisbury is the largest town in the Eastern Shore League and it has won the pennant the last three years out of four. In 1937, it won considerable fame and was even called the "wonder team of the minors" in some quarters when two of its pitchers won over 40 games between them …*
>
> *Five Major League clubs have farms in the Eastern Shore League. Salisbury has long been a proving ground for the Washington American League team …*

After seeing this article, it now seemed more important than ever to find where Guy had played during 1939 and 1940. For the answer, I needed to look easterly over the rugged Green Mountains, and down along the banks of the Connecticut River.

CHAPTER 34

Pine Bluffs, WY
Saturday, November 12, 2005
703 Beech Street
10:00 a.m.

No mention of the Generals until 1940? How could *that* be? Enter Tony Marro, of the Bennington Historical Society, to whom I was referred by "Reg" Jones a few days later. "In the late 1930s, including 1939, the Bennington team was [called] the Paradise Diners and it played not other Vermont and New Hampshire teams but Eastern New York teams."

"Why did they do that, Tony?"

"Because although Brattleboro is only forty-five miles from Bennington, you have to go over the [Green] Mountains to get there. It was a much easier trip to Albany and Troy, and the teams in the Eastern New York State League were all located in that area, except for Kingston, which was further south.

"I spent the afternoon in the Bennington Library checking every box score for every game played by the Paradise Diners during the summer of 1939. There's no reference to Guy Vitale playing for them or any of the teams that came through Bennington that summer."

"Why was Bennington's team in '39 called the Paradise Diners?" I asked.

"Because their principle supporter, Jimmy Payotis, owned and operated the Paradise Diner in Bennington for many years. In fact, I think Payotis may have actually owned the team in '39. When the Generals were created as part of the Northern League in 1940, he also was very involved, but the club was actually owned by a group of more than a hundred people, most of them local businessmen."

Marro was able to further corroborate what Sharkey had told me: "The Paradise Diners that year [1939] played in the Eastern New York State League. I don't know what the Twin States League was. The only Twin States League that I know of in Vermont was in the very early part of the 20th Century—your 1911 date is correct and in fact may be the only year it existed—and that included teams from Bellows Falls, Springfield, Brattleboro and Keene, New Hampshire."

Marro promised to check a bit further. While waiting for him to get back to me, operating on the theory that Guy may have returned to the Cape Cod League to play in the '39 or '40 seasons, I again contacted Al Irish, who, along with Dudley Jensen, had emerged as my primary sources for information about the Cape Cod League.

"The 1939 season? I don't think so, because, if he had played that year I'd know about it," Al said. "And as to 1940, that would not have been possible because there was no Cape Cod League that year. It shut down after the '39 season, and didn't start up again until [after the war in] 1946. I'll check about 1939 and get back to you."

A few days later, Al called back to confirm that Guy had not played in the Cape Cod League for a fourth season.

On the same day, we … or I should say, Tony Marro, hit pay dirt, coming up with further information about the elusive Twin States League.

"The Twin States League was on the east side of the mountains and involved Vermont teams based in Connecticut River towns—Springfield, Bellows Falls and Brattleboro. I'm sorry to say I don't know how long it lasted, because when the Northern League expanded in 1940, both Bennington and Brattleboro had teams in it. That was the first year of the Bennington Generals. The Brattleboro team was the Maples, but I don't know if that was a new team just started that year or a long-standing team that just switched leagues."

The Connecticut River? My knowledge of New Hampshire and Vermont geography was extremely limited, so I dusted off my copy of Rand McNally's World Atlas. There, I learned that the Connecticut River is a long, meandering flow that forms the western boundary of New Hampshire and the eastern boundary of Vermont.

The Salisbury Times article I mentioned earlier said that Guy had played in the Twin States League—not the Northern League. So, if I was going to find anything more, I'd need to look for information in the towns that had entries in the Twin States League—Springfield, Bellows Falls, Brattleboro and perhaps a few others whose names I did not yet know.

*   *   *   *

Pine Bluffs, WY
Monday, November 14, 2005
703 Beech Street
10:00 a.m.

One of my sources in Bennington had told me that the *Brattleboro Reformer*, a local newspaper, had been in existence back in the early part of the 20th Century and its older issues were on microfilm at the Brooks Library in Brattleboro. I decided to contact that library and ask for help. I was referred to Dana Sprague, a writer who had written baseball articles for newspapers and was connected to the Society for American Baseball Research (SABRE). "There were actually two different Twin States Leagues," he said. "The first ran from 1911 to about 1915. It was a professional league. Later, there was another Twin States League which ran from 1938 to 1941. That was a semi-pro league."

As we talked, he recalled that a man named Bob Wood may have played in the Twin States League in 1939. "The only teams I know of in the Twin States League during that period were St. Johnsbury and, I think, Newport," he said. "But I'm not an authority on that league. My focus has been on the Northern League, from 1940 on."

"I've often wondered why my uncle didn't play in that league," I said. "One of his high school chums, Lenny Merullo, played there."

What Dana Sprague said next was just a tidbit of information dropped casually into the conversation. But it answered a question I'd asked myself over and over again while writing this book—why had he *not* played in the Northern League? And it confirmed what I'd earlier heard from several different sources.

"The players in that league were all college kids," he explained. "That was a firm rule. If your uncle was not in college at the time, he would not have been allowed to play in the Northern League."

*   *   *   *

Pine Bluffs, WY
Monday, November 14, 2005
703 Beech Street
10:00 a.m.

"Yeah," Bob Wood, from Keene, New Hampshire, said when I contacted him. "I played in the Twin States League. My brothers, Steve and Joe played there, too.

They hooked on with the Lancaster Pilots. I played for the Groveton Athletics. But it was only for about a month or so in 1939. Things weren't working out for us there, so we left and returned home."

"Does the name Guy Vitale mean anything to you?" I asked.

"No. I was only there for a short time, but I'm sure I'd remember that name if he'd been on the team."

"What cities had teams in the Twin States League back then?"

Bob thought for a minute before answering. "Groveton, St. Johnsbury and Newport are the only teams I remember. Might have been three more—maybe Berlin, Lancaster and Littleton." He chuckled. "I'm eighty-six years old and my memory isn't what it used to be."

"How did you happen to get involved in that league?" I wanted to know.

"Well, Neil Mahoney was scouting for the [Boston] Red Sox in '39. He later became Director of Player Development for them. Came up here and asked my two brothers and me to play ball. He'd sign guys and assign them to teams in the Northern League. Wanted us to play in the Northern League the next summer."

"Neil Mahoney? He played baseball in 1938 in the Cape Cod League. Same as my uncle," I told Bob.

"Look, I have a friend named George Hanna who played in the Northern League but knows a lot about the Twin States League. He was a lawyer here in Keene until he retired a few years ago." Bob gave me a number and hung up.

An hour or so later, I put in a call to George Hanna, who grew up in Keene but is now retired and living in Venice, Florida.

"Sure," he said. "Be glad to talk to you."

"Where did you play baseball, George?"

"I played my college ball at Dartmouth. Graduated in 1939. That summer, I played ball for the St. Albin's Giants in the Northern League. Vic Raschi pitched for us that season. The following summer, I went to Burlington. Played there in '40 and '41. Then after the war, I went back to Burlington and played there again."

"What can you tell me about the teams in the Twin States League back in '39, '40 and '41?" I asked.

"The teams in the Twin States League? Let's see; St. Johnsbury and Newport, Vermont, Groveton, Berlin, Lancaster and Littleton, New Hampshire." He paused.

"What about Keene and Brattleboro?"

"Nope. Not in the Twin States League. They had teams in the Northern League, though." Pausing, his mind replayed a pleasant memory. "I batted against Robin Roberts the year he played for the Montpelier-Barre team," he said proudly. "Got three hits off him, too."

Armed with what Wood and Hanna had told me, I went on the internet to search for the Twin States League and found this:

> The Twin States League began in 1911 as a Class D League. Its teams were the Bellows Falls Sulphites, Keene Champs, Brattleboro Islanders, and the Springfield-Charlestown Hyphens.
>
> The early Twin States League ran from late June to early September, a schedule suited for college players looking to play summer ball. Colleges no longer allowed players to be paid as they did in the 1890s, so players often used pseudonyms. during a close pennant race, much energy was expended unmasking 'illegal' players, and the situation grew so confused that umpires would go to the mound before a game and call out the names of banned players.
>
> The [later]Twin States League had not signed the National Agreement placing the league under the control of the major leagues, so the league was not considered 'official.' Yet, many major league clubs sent injured or slumping players to the Twin States League teams and recalled them at will.

So, thanks to much help from a lot of wonderful people, I now knew the cities that had entries in the Twin States League. But I still didn't have a clue as to which team Guy had played for, and the only thing I had that connected him to that League was a newspaper clipping from *The Salisbury Times,* a newspaper on the Eastern Shore of Maryland, five hundred miles to the south. I'd need to keep digging.

*   *   *   *

Pine Bluffs, WY
Wednesday, December 14, 2005
703 Beech Street
10:00 a.m.

When writing a book, things go a lot smoother if you know where to look for your information. That was part of my problem; I didn't always know where to look. Supplied now with the names of cities that fielded teams in the Twin States League in 1939, I began making phone calls.

My first call was to the public library in Littleton, New Hampshire. I explained my problem to head Librarian Barbara Mellor, and she promised to do some research for me. On Thursday, December 22nd, 2005, she e-mailed me:

> *Hi, Tony—we were able to find out the following re your recent inquiry: Littleton DID have a baseball team in the Twin States League in 1939/40. The Littleton Team's name was the Littleton Collegians. In 1939 someone just listed as 'Vitale' played right field for the St. Johnsbury (VT) Senators. In 1940, Vitale's name is not mentioned in the line-ups for either Littleton Collegians or St. Johnsbury Senators.*
>
> *All this information came from 1939 and 1940 issues of the Littleton Courier on microfilm.*

Well, when I read that e-mail, you can just imagine how elated I was. Here was what seemed to be the proof I'd been searching for. Guy Vitale *had* played ball in 1939! And he *had* played in the Twin States League, just as he'd told that Eastern Shore journalist in 1941.

*   *   *   *

Pine Bluffs, WY
Thursday, December 22, 2005
703 Beech Street
10:00 a.m.

So far so good. My next call went to the Weeks Memorial Library in Lancaster, New Hampshire. Barbara Robarts was the Director there.

"Yes, Mr. Sacco, we have the *Coos County Democrat* newspaper on microfilm. It's a weekly, and it covered Coos County, New Hampshire, and Essex County, Vermont."

"Can you run a check to see if my uncle's name appears anywhere?"

Robarts agreed, but ended the conversation by saying it might take some time and that she'd get back to me after Christmas. However, her interest must have been piqued, because a few days later, Robarts checked in with this e-mail:

> *I have just finished reviewing all of the 1939 season for the Twin States League. At no point did I find Mr. Vitale referred to by anything except his last name. I have copied several sample pages of the statistics of the games in which he played if you would like those. He was not on the all-star team. … I would suggest that the Caledonian Record in St.*

Johnsbury would be more likely to have in depth material on him since he was one of 'theirs' …

The week after Christmas, Robarts' material arrived by snail mail. She'd copied short articles and the box scores from seven games, describing the St. Johnsbury Senators playing other teams in the League and winning handily. And each box score listed a Vitale, playing left field and batting in the fifth slot.

But Barbara was right when she said the first name of *this* Vitale was not mentioned anywhere in the material. So was this my uncle or, by some strange coincidence, a different Vitale?

*   *   *   *

Pine Bluffs, WY
Thursday, December 22, 2005
703 Beech Street
10:30 a.m.

Hoping to find conclusive proof that we had the right Vitale, I went to the phone again, this time placing a call to the St. Johnsbury Public Library. Lisa von Kahn, the Director there, was very excited.

"We don't get too many interesting research inquiries like this," she said. "Yes, we'll do a search of the St. Johnsbury *Caledonian-Record.* A volunteer research assistant will actually do the work, and she'll keep track of her hours. A donation would be nice, after she finishes."

"How long do you think it'll take?" I asked.

"I really can't say. But the holidays are coming up, you know. We probably won't start on it until after January 1st."

Most people say that holidays like Christmas and New Years go by too quickly. You've probably heard the expression, "Time flies when you're having fun!" But I'm here to tell you that, for me, these holidays did *not* pass quickly. Waiting for word from Lisa was like … watching paint dry.

Finally, on Friday, January 13th, 2006, I opened an e-mail from her:

> *Dear Mr. Sacco,*
> *Our volunteer is busy at the microfilm machine going through the daily issues of the Caledonian-Record from the summer of 1939 and is she ever having success! She already has a huge folder of printed pieces from the paper with news of the team including a fair amount about Guy Vitale himself …*

So there it was—conclusive proof that Guy had played baseball in the Twin States League in the summer of 1939. Perseverance had paid off. But information on how he had done that season would have to await the results of efforts by Lisa von Kahn and her volunteer researcher, Alice Carpenter.

CHAPTER 35

East Boston, MA
Friday, April 14, 1939
20 Breed Street
6:30 p.m.

He wasn't living with his mother and father any more; had moved out the previous fall after returning from Falmouth and hiring on at the shipyard as a Shipfitter's Helper. No one thing prompted the move—it had just seemed the right thing to do. *At twenty-one,* almost twenty-two, he'd thought, *a man ought to have a place of his own.* Besides, his new lifestyle didn't seem to fit in with a young man living under his parent's roof.

But his rented room was small and cramped, and he couldn't afford a phone of his own yet. Then too, the place was empty when he left each morning and no one was there to whom he could eagerly return each evening. So he had taken to going back to 20 Breed Street for dinner several nights a week, spending time with his mother and father; relaxing in their living room, now heated and comfortably furnished in a 1930s style, which made visiting easier and more comfortable.

Guy and Nick were in the living room talking quietly, Guy sharing with his father a tale about an incident that had occurred at the shipyard the previous day. Nick, because he'd worked there for several years as a Shipfitter's Helper, could relate and empathize with what his young son was telling him.

The hall phone rang. Rosaria, who'd been finishing up in the kitchen, passed through, and with a wave of her hand for them to sit still, she answered it.

"It's for you, Guy," she announced.

In the hall, Guy picked up the dangling receiver. "Hello?"

"Guy? It's me. Oscah."

"Who?"

"Oscah Khederian. From Watahtown, remembah? Falmouth last summah."

"Oh. Oscah. Sure, I remember. The vacuum cleaner at shortstop." Guy chuckled at his own humor. "Howaya, Oscah?"

"I'm good, Guy. Say, listen. Ya know I'm playin' fa Watahtown High again this yeeah."

"Figured ya would." He didn't really mean that. What he meant was that if he'd thought about Oscar Khederian at all since the previous summer, he would have figured the kid would play for his high school team again as a senior.

"Well, Ahtie Johns came by the otha day ta watch practice. I spoke ta him afta."

"Who's Ahtie Johns?" Guy asked.

"He's a seenya at Hahvaad College. Plays vahsity baseball and he's gonna manage the Berlin Red Sox in the Twin States League this summah."

There was a pause. Guy's eyes were on the faded, flowered print of the blue and white wallpaper, but his mind was busy "Ya gonna play for them?"

"Yeah. Ahtie was lookin' fer a shortstop. Since I ain't in college yet, I'm too young fer the Northern League, so that's the next best thing. You playin' ball anywhere this summah?"

"Naw. I'm workin' over at the shipyard. It's hard but the pay's good."

"Guy? Ahtie tells me St. Johnsbury's manager is in town. Needs some position playahs and was askin' about you. Ya interested?"

"You sign a contract, yet, Oscah?"

"Yep. Fifteen dollas a week. All the teams are payin' the playas either ten or fifteen a week. The pitchahs get more."

Guy's interest picked up. "Who's St. Johnsbury's manager?"

"Tom Bilodeau. He's frum Dorchestah. Went ta college in Minnesota, but he's back now. Goin' ta Hahvaad Law."

"Bilodeau? Neva heard a him. Why was he askin' about me?"

"Dunno. Maybe somebody tole him about ya. Say, look. I'll call Mr. Johns tonight and give him yer numbah. Maybe Bilodeau'll call ya tomorrah night."

*   *   *   *

St. Johnsbury, VT
Tuesday, April 18 to Friday, April 21, 1939
Caledonian Record
5:00 p.m.

Not only did Guy play for the St. Johnsbury Senators in 1939, but he was one of the first players signed. Apparently, the dream to play professional baseball was still strong; strong enough to overcome the good pay at the shipyard about which he'd told Oscar Khederian.

At a meeting held in the local Elk's Home on April 18th of that year, Club President, Harry Witters and Financial Director, Arthur Hafner, told the group that St. Johnsbury had landed Tom Bilodeau as player-manager, and that Bilodeau, who played college ball at the University of Minnesota, had already gone to work. So far he'd signed Ben Meyers, Milton Bruhn, Guy Vitale and Henry Bushey to play for the Senators, and was hot on the trail of others to fill out the roster.

Spanning the Sports, local sportswriter Ralph H. "Deak" Morse's column in the *Caledonian-Record* of Friday, April 21, 1939, said this:

> *Bushey and Vitale are the two other players that Bilodeau has announced and both were all-scholastic choices as high school players around Boston. Vitale has two years' experience in the Cape Cod League where he was one of the five leading hitters during both campaigns. He started at Colgate, was forced to drop school for a while, but will return again this fall. Further information on Bushey is expected within a few days.*

Morse doesn't mention how Bilodeau became aware of and made contact with Guy. But since Bilodeau played at least one summer in the Boston Twilight League, and since Ralph Wheeler managed a team in that circuit while functioning as Commissioner of the Cape Cod League, perhaps he suggested Guy's name to Bilodeau.

Now let's take another look at "Deak" Morse's column, where he mentions Guy. You see what I mean? There's that Colgate thing again.

Why did these journalists keep dredging up Colgate in relation to Guy? With just a few exceptions such as young Oscar Khederian, a senior at Watertown High in the spring of 1939, but signed to play for the Berlin Red Sox that summer, virtually all the ballplayers in the Twin States League were either *attending* or had *graduated* from college. And if they were among those who had already *graduated* from college, most had played semi-pro ball somewhere.

I think that at this point, Guy was deliberately conveying this information about himself to reporters, to give the impression that he, too, was a collegian.

∗   ∗   ∗   ∗

St. Johnsbury, VT
Monday, April 24 to Saturday, April 29, 1939
Caledonian Record
5:00 p.m.

1939 was the 100th anniversary of baseball, and the Major League's baseball image was enhanced by season-long celebrations all across the nation, of the game's centennial birth date. That spring must have been an exciting time for baseball fans in northern Vermont and New Hampshire. Why? Because it was in honor of the event that this new semi-pro league was set up, and six towns had pledged to send entries.

The Twin States League would not lack for newspaper coverage in its first season since the early part of the 20th Century. Five newspapers served the people of that area; the *Lancaster Democrat, Littleton Courier* and *Berlin Reporter* were weeklies. The *Newport Express* and St. Johnsbury's newspaper, the *Caledonian-Record*, were dailies. All had sports sections to keep local baseball fans current on high school, college and professional sports. On Monday, April 24[th,] 1939, the *Caledonian-Record* reported this:

> *TWIN STATES LEAGUE BECOMES A REALITY*
> *The signatures of representatives of the St. Johnsbury Senators, Newport Frontiers, Littleton Collegians, Lancaster Pilots, Groveton Athletics and Berlin Red Sox were affixed to a document at Lancaster yesterday afternoon that bound these six north country teams to the Twin States Baseball League. the League is now a reality ...*

The League's fifty-four game schedule was announced in the *Caledonian-Record* on April 24th. St. Johnsbury would open against the Newport Frontiers at Hazen Field, the Senator's home field, in the morning of June 24th. This was fitting because it was St. Johnsbury which had been the prime mover in establishing the new League. Later that day, the same two teams would travel to Gaines Park in Newport, to assist the Newport Frontiers with their home opener. "Deak" Morse said this about it:

> *The most important item of business to be transacted yesterday was approval of the schedule. It was thought that it might be necessary to alter somewhat the list of games drawn up at a meeting held in St.*

Johnsbury two weeks ago but each of the six clubs represented expressed their approval of the schedule as it stood and it was adopted.

The goal of the directors [of the St. Johnsbury Baseball Association] this year will be a minimum of $1,500 with hopes of $2,000 … it will be necessary to purchase new uniforms and if the $2,000 goal can be reached, the much needed grandstand will become a reality.

Why a grandstand? The Association's board of directors thought that building a grandstand and fencing the playing field would substantially increase revenue because tickets could be sold and fans encouraged to come inside the enclosed area to sit in the stands, rather than watching games from the parking areas or grassy fields beyond the outfield. Indeed, fencing the playing fields, although not fully achieved, seems to have been a common goal of all six clubs for the same reasons. Ticket prices ranged from fifteen to thirty-five cents, proceeds to be used to meet the team's payroll, which was between $300 and $350 per week.

The Senators did not lack for donors. According to Morse;

> *Businessmen and merchants are the heaviest contributors but one way or another a pretty good portion of them get a fair return on their money. Some of them even make a profit. One thing is certain about the League this year; it will draw a larger percentage of out-of-town patrons than ever before and that's where the merchants stand to pick up some extra cash. If an analysis of each dollar spent by St. Johnsbury people for baseball could be made, it would be found that a sizeable portion of it stays right here in town. The ball players … every week turn a certain part of it back into such essentials as board, room, clothing, etc …*

Businessmen certainly *did* contribute to the athletic life of St. Johnsbury. On Saturday, April 29th, the *Caledonian-Record* said:

> *The Fairbanks-Morse & Company … assured [League] President Harry Witters of the St. Johnsbury Senators Baseball Association today that they would furnish lumber for the erection of a covered grandstand at Hazen Field which will be erected at an early date this spring. A year ago the scale concern donated $500 towards the new surface at Hazen Field.*

Present plans call for an oblong stand 26 feet wide by 80 feet in length, which will comfortably seat 400 spectators. The stands will be erected the legal distance of 60 feet directly in back of home plate … The field this year will take care of the spectators comfortably and also has the usual conveniences for the players as the field house will be open to both the Senators and visiting clubs.

*   *   *   *

Pine Bluffs, WY
Monday, March 6, 2006
703 Beech Street
5:00 p.m.

To give you an idea of what sort of company Guy would play in when the season opened on Saturday, June 24th, let's take a look at the backgrounds of these first-to-sign ballplayers who would be his teammates.

Tom Bilodeau: originally from Dorchester, Massachusetts, he hit well over .300 at the University of Minnesota, the sixth largest university in the country at that time, and then showed that rumors about the pitching of semi-pro twirlers being superior to that at the college level were not necessarily true, by macing the sphere for over .500 in Boston's Twilight League games. In addition to managing the Senators, he'd play shortstop, first base, and take a turn on the mound if necessary.

Milton Bruhn: had also attended Minnesota, where he'd played varsity football and baseball for three seasons, hit over .300 each year, and fielded his position of catcher flawlessly. He was named All Big Ten Conference catcher in his junior and senior years. Following graduation, Bruhn had a chance to sign with the St. Louis Cardinals but accepted a position as a member of the football and baseball coaching staffs at Amherst College, instead.

Reino "Dick" Grondhal: signed to play third base, this member of the Harvard nine was hitting over .350 and fielding .964 in eight games as of the date he signed. He was also the Crimson's team captain. I didn't know that Harvard had ever fielded a good baseball team, the academics there being what they are, but an article in the *Caledonian-Record* dated Thursday, April 27th, 1939 revealed this:

Grondahl … has been pacing the Harvard team with some terrific hitting this season which has established the Crimson as one of the East's most powerful offensive teams. The Cantabs have shown such an impressive early season attack that they are being selected by many to replace Dartmouth as Eastern Intercollegiate [League] champions this year.

Eddie Casey: signed as the Senator's third outfielder, Casey played three years of varsity baseball at Dartmouth College, where he was one of the top hitters in the Eastern Intercollegiate League as a sophomore, with an average of .471. After college, he played semi-pro baseball and that fall, found a job at St. Mary's High School, in Milford, Massachusetts. The following summer he played ball with Bilodeau and also served as an instructor with the Tris Speaker Baseball School. Here's what the *Caledonian-Record* wrote about him on Wednesday, May 3rd:

> *With the signing of Eddie Casey, former varsity outfielder for three years with Jeff Tesreau's Dartmouth Indians, the outfield patrol of the St. Johnsbury Senators for the summer season of 1939 was complete today with the announcement by manager Bilodeau that Casey has given his consent to play with the St. Johnsbury nine this year. Guy Vitale, slugging East Boston boy, and Henry Buchie of St. Joseph's College at Washington, D.C., are the other outfielders.*

Harry "Zeke" Cleverly: a first baseman, after three years at Green Mountain Junior College in Vermont, where he was twice captain of his baseball team and hit .385, .421 and .506, attended Boston University, from which he graduated in '37. He earned letters in three sports; football, baseball and ice hockey. A good bunter, adept at pulling the ball through the hole, he almost never hit into a double play. His batting averages had earned him a place in Boston University's Athletic Greats of All-Time.

Although not professional ball players, these boys had played their baseball at some of the best colleges in America. The University of Minnesota is a good example. A large school, competition for each position on any of its sports teams was fierce, and tended to weed out the worst, permitting only the top talented players to make a team. Guy would be rubbing elbows with a far better caliber of baseball player than he'd ever played with before.

What about the managers? We've already learned a bit about St. Johnsbury Senator's player-manager, Tom Bilodeau. But who would manage the other clubs during this first season for the new League?

The Lancaster Pilots had signed Linn Wells, who coached baseball at Bowdoin College, to manage that team. He was one of three college coaches in the League. Elbert "Ebb" Caraway, coach at Massachusetts State College, was to pilot the Littleton Collegians. Philip "Pinkey" Ryan, baseball coach at St. Michael's, would guide the Newport Frontiers. "Chick" Toomey, in his mid-twenties, started out at the helm of the Groveton Athletics. He'd managed St. Johnsbury's team the previous season. The youngest manager of the group, 22-year old Arthur L. "Artie" Johns, of Medford, Massachusetts, captain of the Harvard Crimson varsity the previous year, would skipper the Berlin Pilots.

*   *   *   *

St. Johnsbury, VT
Monday, May 8 to Friday, May 26, 1939
Caledonian Record
5:00 p.m.

For approximately a month, Tom Bilodeau had been working fast and furiously to get all his position players for the '39 season under contract. Now, with first baseman "Zeke" Cleverly in the fold, manager Bilodeau could breathe a bit easier. He had accomplished that fete.

Apparently "Deak" Morse was a sportswriter who didn't sit on his hands, but liked to get out there to press the flesh, meet and greet. In his column of Friday, May 5th, he reports hearing comments about several members of the Senators nine:

> *During the course of the afternoon [at Memorial Field, Hanover] I buttonholed Joe Urban and George Hanna who were up with Littleton last year as you will remember. Both think very highly of Bilodeau and believe that he will bring a strong team to St. Johnsbury that will show splendid results. Urban had a good word for Eddie Casey with whom he played at Dartmouth and Hanna remarked that St. Johnsbury was indeed fortunate in landing Guy Vitale. Hanna predicts that the Greater Boston boy will ride the ball hard and often for the Senators.*

Yes, this is the same George Hanna who played in the Northern League, was a close friend of Bob Wood, and is quoted in the previous chapter, giving me a list of cities which had teams in the Twin States League in 1939.

Although his pitchers had yet to be revealed, Bilodeau, under some adverse scrutiny by local fans because he'd taken the place of popular Chick Toomey who'd managed St. Johnsbury's semi-pro club the previous season, felt justified in announcing his batting order for the first game, still six weeks in the future.

It seems he, at least, and perhaps a few others, were expecting big things in the hitting department from young Guy Vitale. Here's the *Caledonian-Record's* article, penned on Monday, May 8th:

BILODEAU SIGNS CLEVERLY AND ANNOUNCES HIS BATTING ORDER FOR THE FIRST GAME
*Meyers will Be Leadoff Man With
Vitale Batting Cleanup—Bilodeau bats Fifth*

With the signing of a first baseman, Harry "Zeke" Cleverly, Tom Bilodeau, 1939 manager of the St. Johnsbury Senators, was able to announce the batting order of the team for its initial game on Saturday, June 24th, today.

Bilodeau' batting order will be as follows:

Meyers, 2b,
Cleverly, 1b,
Casey, cf,
Vitale, rf,
Bilodeau, ss,
Grondahl, 3b
Bushey, lf,
Bruhn, c.

In selecting Cleverly to play the initial sack this season, Bilodeau again chose a player with whom he has had a great deal of contact and playing experience ... Meyers will be selected to bat in the leadoff position because of his exceptional ability to wait out a pitcher. Cleverly's regular batting position is second due to the fact that he is an exceptional bunter ... Casey, considered a consistent hitter by Bilodeau, will bat in the number three position, and the powerful Vitale is to be placed in the clean-up slot ...

Although Bilodeau felt comfortable with his efforts in putting together his position players, he *was* having some trouble signing pitchers for the 1939 season. So were all the other managers. One problem? Whether or not college underclassmen could play semi-pro ball for teams that paid them, had been much in the news recently. Just the week before, an announcement had been made by various college Athletic Directors that if college ball players wanted to maintain their amateur status, they could not play for any team which paid its players.

The very day that announcement was made, Bilodeau lost the one pitcher he'd already signed, a nineteen-year old stand-out from New Jersey. The boy planned to enter college the following fall, but would be ineligible to play for his college team if he signed on with the Senators and accepted cash for summer play. Wanting to play college ball, he was forced to decline Bilodeau's offer. That must have been an upsetting development for the Senator's young manager.

"Deak" Morse again:

> *For years there has been a hue and cry of the way the colleges have commercialized their football teams. Tickets to a big game start at $3.30 to the general public and go up to $4.40 and $5.50 and you're often lucky to get them at that price. Recently a whole flock of high pedigreed Eastern colleges sold their broadcasting rights to an oil concern. It's strange that they can rake in several hundred thousands themselves by exploiting an oil company but put a taboo on a lad who has a chance to make himself perhaps $25 or $30 during the short summer season in an honorable occupation and still talk about ethics. Just another case of the old oil.*

Morse's estimate of the amount these boys could earn during their summer of ball playing was a bit low. For example, St. Johnsbury planned to pay $10 or $15 per week to its position players, and a bit more to its pitchers. Still, his point is well taken, and it seems that this rule was honored in the breach, as many boys, wanting to play ball but needing to earn some money during the summer months, played under pseudonyms in order to do it. Until exposed, that is, as they usually were.

"Deak" Morse's *Spanning the Sports* column, on Wednesday, May 24th, contained another interesting item:

> *As yet no team has completed its roster. Lancaster must find another pair of pitchers, possibly three more, and the Senators also are in need of some chuckers. The other four teams are lacking twice as many players or more. Berlin has augmented its list, so the Boston Herald discloses, with Joe DeCesare, Everett High School captain and first baseman. Previously announced was Oscar Khederian of Watertown High who will probably play third base for the Red Sox this summer. DeCesare played brilliantly for Orleans in the Cape Cod League last year, while Khederian played a prominent part in bringing the League*

Championship to Falmouth. He is giving the ball a fearful going over
for Watertown this spring.

Of course, we know that Joey DeCesare did not "play brilliantly" for Orleans in 1938. He held down the first sack for them, but his team finished a distant third to Falmouth, with a record of 24 wins and 30 losses, and his final batting average was a mere .246.

Oscar Khederian in '38? Arriving late to Falmouth, he had played both shortstop and third base, and hit only reasonably well with a season-ending average of .289. He failed to make the All-Star Team at either position.

On the other hand, Guy Vitale was Falmouth's leading hitter in '38, and he also collected the largest number of hits of any batter in the League for the second year in a row with 93, finished the summer with a .374 average, fifth best among regular players, and was named to the All-Star Team at the end of the season, as its center fielder. In fact, his role was far more important than Khederian's in "bringing the League Championship to Falmouth." But although mentioning that Vitale had played two seasons in the Cape Cod League, Morse, at this point, did not seem to have been aware that Guy played in that League again in 1938, much less how well he actually did.

On Friday, May 26th the *Caledonian-Record* reported that Tom Bilodeau signed his first pitcher—Eddie Ingalls. Here's a portion of the article:

EDDIE INGALLS IS FIRST PITCHER SIGNED BY
TOM BILODEAU, WAS E .I. C. LEADING PITCHER
'37–'38.

News that will assuage the feverish anxiety of St. Johnsbury base-ball fans in regard to the pitching problem of the Senators for the 1939 season was given today by Tom Bilodeau through President Harry Witters' office. Bilodeau has signed Eddie Ingalls, leading pitcher in the Eastern Intercollegiate campaign in 1937 and 1938, and is fairly certain of having his choice of two out of three other excellent candidates ...

Ingalls was one of the players whom Bilodeau spoke highly of when he first came here to discuss the managership of the Senators with the board of directors. It has taken a good deal of perseverance on the part of Bilodeau to land the former Harvard ace as he had pretty well made up his mind to cast his lot in the Cape Cod League this summer.

Ingalls, a hard throwing right-hander, went undefeated at Harvard during his senior season in the spring of 1938. That summer, as we've seen, he pitched for Harwich in the Cape Cod League, finishing with seven wins and two losses, best won-lost record of all pitchers in that league, and was instrumental in keeping Harwich in the thick of the pennant race right down to the wire, tossing a two-hit game in August and finishing by shutting out Orleans with only four hits on Labor Day. In landing him, Tom Bilodeau was living up to expectations that he'd bring some real strong talent to the Senators for its first season in the Twin States League.

In all the articles leading up to opening day, no mention was made that this was the second time around for the Twin States League; that there had been an earlier, professional version which had operated from 1911 to 1915. Either this fact was so well known as not to need retelling, or, by 1939, it had been forgotten by everyone in the area, its memory, perhaps, lost in the mists of time.

*　　*　　*　　*

St. Johnsbury, VT
Monday, May 29 to Thursday, June 15, 1939
Caledonian Record
4:00 p.m.

Monday, May 29th, 1939, was a big day for Tom Bilodeau. He announced the signing of two pitchers from the University of Michigan's baseball team, Jack Barry, of Katonah, New York, and Dean Dubois, of North Troy, making him the first manager in the Twin States League to complete his entire roster for the upcoming season.

With these signings, the Senators club looked like this:

> *Guy Vitale, outfield,*
> *Henry Bushey, outfield,*
> *Eddie Casey, outfield,*
> *Dick Grondahl, third base,*
> *Tom Bilodeau, shortstop,*
> *Ben Meyers, second base,*
> *Zeke Cleverly, first base,*
> *Milton Bruhn, catcher,*
> *Eddie Ingalls, right-handed pitcher,*
> *Jack Barry, right-handed pitcher,*
> *Dean Dubois, left-handed pitcher.*

On the same day, Guy and his manager were again mentioned in a small article printed in *The Caledonian-Record*:

TOM BILODEAU AND GUY VITALE
START PLAYING BASEBALL
   Manager Tom Bilodeau and Guy Vitale, shortstop and outfielder respectively for the St. Johnsbury Senators, will get their first licks of the season in tomorrow afternoon with the Plymouth Cordage nine. The Plymouth aggregation will employ Bilodeau and his classy outfielder until the Twin States League season starts.
   Plymouth, one of the leading semi-pro clubs in Massachusetts, opens against the Hoyt Pals of Cambridge tomorrow

Nothing is known about why Guy started playing ball early that summer, nor why he picked the Plymouth Cordage outfit for which to play. And I don't understand if, to do that, he would have had to give up his job at the shipyard. Perhaps, except for its season opener, these semi-pro teams played their games in the evenings, and he landed there for a couple of weeks at the urging of Tom Bilodeau, who apparently felt the need to get a jump on the season, and believed that both he and Guy would benefit from the work. Certainly, one factor was that Plymouth paid its ball players. And you know what I'm thinking? That Guy, after a fall and winter of frequenting East Boston's bars and saloons, realized that if he were going to do well in St. Johnsbury, he needed to get into shape quickly. Here was a chance to accomplish that while earning a bit of extra cash as well.

Although no box scores were available for the Cordage games, a brief article in *The Caledonian-Record* on Thursday, June 1st, said the team won its opener by scoring seventeen runs on eighteen hits, and *"it is assumed that Tom and Guy got their share."*

On Saturday, June 10th, *The Caledonian-Record* printed another story about Guy, Tom, and the Plymouth Cordage nine:

BILODEAU AND VITALE STAR
ST. J. MANAGER HITTING FOR .556 IN TWO CONTESTS
HAS HIT TWO HOMERS AND VITALE HAS ONE FOR
PLYMOUTH NINE
   Confirmation the Manager Tom Bilodeau and Guy Vitale are getting in shape for their summer's campaign with the St. Johnsbury

> *Senators came to the Caledonian recently from Plymouth Mass, where*
> *that pair are playing for the Plymouth Cordage semi-pro nine.*
> *Bilodeau and Vitale both are hitting the ball hard and Bilodeau*
> *in particular is setting a terrific pace. In the two games which the*
> *Cordage nine has played to date—and won—Bilodeau has been at*
> *bat nine times, garnered five hits, five runs and has accepted thirteen*
> *chances without error. He has slammed a home run in each of the two*
> *games and has a batting average of .556.*
> *Vitale has likewise been at bat nine times and has thumped out*
> *three hits for a .333 average. He made two in the first game which the*
> *Cordage team played in and one was good for the circuit. Vitale has*
> *scored the same number of runs as Bilodeau, five …*

Albert J. Cavicchi, Chairman of Athletics and coach of the Plymouth Cordage Club, was quoted as saying: "Bilodeau played with my club last season and I think he is the greatest player I have ever seen outside of the Big Leagues. I can't understand why a player of his caliber hasn't been picked up by some scout. I do understand that he was made an offer by the Boston Red Sox, which he did not accept because it interfered with his education program at Harvard Law School."

About Guy, Cavicchi said: "Vitale has played with us for only two games but I can see that he is a very fine player. He is short and sturdy with plenty of power in his swing. He made a tremendous home run here during our first game and his fielding was sensational. I shall be very sorry to lose those two boys."

But with the Twin States League's season bearing down on them, he would shortly have to give up both of them. Tom and Guy played their last game for Plymouth, on Saturday, June 10th, which Plymouth won in the late innings, although only collecting four hits. Guy got one of the four. Tom walked twice, and his average dropped to .455, while Guy stayed right at .333, going four for twelve, while fielding a perfect .1000.

Although this short stretch of three games at Plymouth may have been good for Tom Bilodeau, it seems as if it was not for Guy, whose batting average of .333 was well below that of his manager's and not in accord with the stats he'd compiled the previous season at Falmouth. Was the pitching in semi-pro ball that much better than Guy had faced the season before? Was this a harbinger of things to come? If so, it was not that evident to observers during the last days leading up to the Senator's opening game.

Having finally been made aware of Guy's accomplishments the previous summer in the Cape Cod League, "Deak" Morse, in his column on Thursday,

June 15th, drew the attention of the St. Johnsbury fans to Guy's record, when he wrote:

> One of the directors of the St. Johnsbury club, interested in the work
> of the boys who will play for the Senators this year, and who played in
> the Cape Cod League last season, got some information from Sawyer
> Smith, League statistician. Vitale hit for .374 ... played in the League
> in 1937 and hit for .389. He was a member of the All-League team
> both years ...

The Senators team was scheduled to assemble in St. Johnsbury on the following Thursday, and would participate in its first practice on that morning. Those fans who were not early Bilodeau supporters raised questions as to whether or not the boys would have sufficient time before the opening game to gel as a unit. But when Morse reported that the players were "... all in good shape and the only practice needed was a bit of 'feeling out' by the infielders of one another ..." complaints fell off and fans decided to take a wait and see attitude.

CHAPTER 36

St. Johnsbury, VT
Friday, June 23, 1939
The Purple Onion Bar and Grille
8:45 p.m.

It was his first night in town. Guy, alone, sat at a table in the rear of this out-of-the-way roadhouse, which had been recommended to him by a member of the Board of Directors of the Senator's baseball club for its good food and live music. "And they have a blue grass outfit comes in on Friday nights," he'd said, "if ya like ta dance." So after checking into the room reserved for him at one of the player's boarding houses, he had decided to try it. *Besides,* he thought, *this place stays open 'till 2 a.m. It'll be a great place to come afta the games.*

He had just finished his dinner; a steak, a baked potato covered with sour cream and butter and a salad on which he slathered blue cheese dressing. Young men his age, even if they'd ever heard of it back then, didn't worry too much about cholesterol. He was dressed in a white tennis shirt, khaki slacks, over-the-calf blue socks, and brown penny loafers.

Satisfied with his food, he ordered his first bourbon and water, and glanced around the room. His gaze fell on two women, a red-head and a blonde, occupying stools at the bar across the room.

Guy assessed the situation as he stirred his drink carefully with a swizzle stick. His eyes roamed freely over the two women. *Not bad, not bad,* he thought. *Both built nice.* He sipped from his drink, and as he did, the red-head rose from her stool and headed for the ladies room. To get there, she had to pass close to his table. He watched her approach and sighed. Five feet two inches tall and nicely-dressed, her red mane fell below her shoulders. She had large breasts and a slim waist, and her compact figure revealed curves in all the right places. *She's stunning,* he though. *Like … a ripe piece of fruit.* But it was her buttocks, asserting itself under a tight skirt, which quickly demanded his attention. Opposite his table, she paused to search for something in her purse, looked up and smiled at him, and Guy thought he'd never seen such a gorgeous smile. He smiled back. *What have I got here,* he wondered, as she disappeared into the ladies room.

Moments later, that blue grass band he'd been told about entered and noisily began setting up its equipment for that evening's gig.

She's a bit older than me, Guy thought. He waited. It wasn't long. When she came out, she moved directly to his table. "You alone?" she asked.

"Yeah. Wanna join me?"

"Sure," she said. He rose gallantly as she pulled out the chair opposite him and slid gracefully into it. A young waitress came over and took their drink orders. When she'd gone, the woman examined him candidly. "You're not from around here," she said, as if making an important announcement.

"Go ta the head a the class," Guy responded. "I'm not."

"Where, then?"

"Boston. I'm here for the summah ta play baseball."

Her eyes widened. "You playin' for the Senators?"

"Umm—hmm."

Removing a pack of cigarettes from her purse, she tapped one out and offered the pack. He shook his head. Diving into the purse again, she came out with a lighter and handed it to him. Leaning forward, he lit her smoke for her, catching a whiff of her perfume as he did.

"Opening day is tomorrow," she said. She had a way of making everything she said sound like an earth-shattering observation.

"Right again." He lifted his glass. "You're two fer two. That calls for a toast."

"It's been in the newspaper all week," she said, lifting her glass to his. Their fingers made contact, causing an electric shock to pass from one to the other.

"Wow!" Guy said, grinning.

"Wow!" she echoed, and laughed a throaty laugh that he found pleasant to hear.

The band began its first tune. They were loud, about the best that could be said for them. A woman vocalist with straight, dirty blonde, shoulder-length hair stepped out front and began singing in a nasally-sounding voice.

Again Guy leaned forward, as much to get a bit closer to her as to make himself heard. "Your friend? Won't she be missing you along about now?"

She leaned toward him until their heads were only inches apart. Looking into her intense green eyes, Guy thought he could easily fall into them and drown. "No," she said. "She knows … she's used ta me. What's your name?"

"Guy."

She stuck out a tiny hand. "Prudence." An additional announcement.

They finished their drinks. "Want another?" Guy asked.

"Yes," she said, but as Guy twisted around to summon a waitress, she put a hand on his arm. "But not here. I don't care much for blue grass, but I'd like ta continue this evening in more … comfortable surroundings. I live alone a few miles outside a town. Let's go ta my place."

Guy nodded. "This could be the beginning of a beautiful friendship," he remarked.

She laughed loudly and began stuffing things back in her purse. "I know you don't have a car," she said. "I'm gonna go out and get inta mine. It's the blue Ford right out front. Don't keep me waiting."

*   *   *   *

St. Johnsbury, VT
Saturday, June 24 to Friday, July 7, 1939
Hazen Field
2:45 p.m.

Excitement was high in St. Johnsbury as opening day of the Twin States League's 1939 season dawned. The lineups for the first game had been announced the day before. Tom Bilodeau, aware of how well Guy had smacked the pill in the Cape Cod League, named Guy to start the season in the number four slot as his cleanup hitter, thereby showing early confidence in his twenty-one year old outfielder:

NEWPORT	ST. JOHNSBURY
Foley, rf	*Meyers, 2b*
Ryan, cf	*Cleverly, 1b*
Sheeran, 2b	*Casey, cf*
Benson, c	*Vitale, rf*
Clark, lf	*Bilodeau, ss*
Smith, 3b	*Bouchie, lf*[45]
Rosenbaum, 1b	*Bruhn, c*
Laramie, ss	*Grondahl, 3b*
Passabet or Anderson, p	*Barry, p*

---

45 I've seen this man's name spelled differently by several people: this way, and as Bushie and also Bushey.

Festivities were kicked off with a parade led by the St. Johnsbury band, from the Summer Street Common down Main Street and Eastern Avenue, to the Elks Home on Railroad Street, the Senators players riding in open cars.

Later, at Hazen Field, a flag-raising ceremony preceded remarks by Vermont's governor, George D. Aiken, who threw out the first ball, and the St. Johnsbury Senators and the Newport Frontiers took the field promptly at 3:00 p.m. for the first game. 1,119 paid fans saw the Newport nine defeat the home team 4–1.

On Sunday, June 5th, eight hundred Newport rooters turned out for the opening game in that town, and their team did not disappoint, beating St. Johnsbury 8–7. The Tom Bilodeau naysayers began squawking.

Guy, although listed as the starting right fielder for these opening games, played left field in both contests, as he and Bouchie switched their announced positions. And Guy was off to a slow start. Up to bat seven times, he banged out only one hit, scored no runs and made no errors in the field.

St. Johnsbury fans credited the poor Senator showing to the fact that they had been unable to practice together prior to opening day, because Tom Bilodeau and four other players, Guy among them, had not been able to leave Boston until the morning of Friday, June 23rd. Although a few players had practiced in St. Johnsbury on Thursday, the scheduled session on Friday had been rained out.

"Deak" Morse's column on Tuesday, June 27th contained this tidbit:

> Leading hitter in the Twin States League at the moment is Wally Benson of the Frontiers who has cuffed four out of eight for safeties … Guy Vitale hit one of those believe it or not shots at Newport when he rifled one through the box that was just a white blur but it struck second base, bounced straight up into the air and was taken for a putout.

As we previously learned, the Northern League was also functioning at this time. Its 1939 season began around June 16th with eight towns, Burlington, Malone, Montpelier, Plattsburg, Rutland, Saranac Lake, St. Albans, and Tupper Lake all being represented. By this time, that League had already played eleven games, and Saranac Lake sat atop the League standings with a 6–3 record with two rainouts to be made up later, followed by Burlington, at 7–4.

It's a good thing Guy received so much favorable press coverage coming into and at the season's outset, because, by July 3rd, after five games, his team was in second place with a record of 3 wins and 2 losses, but the chunky outfielder had two games where he was 0-fer and only one game in which he notched two hits. In stark contrast, Guy's fellow outfielder, center fielder Eddie Casey, was pounding the pill, with seven hits in fifteen official trips to the plate.

On July 6th, the *Caledonian-Record* printed batting statistics for the first time, up to and including games on Sunday, July 2nd, and Casey was leading the League in hitting. Guy was shown well down the list, hitting only .188, with five hits in sixteen trips. Obviously, something was ... well, maybe not wrong, but certainly different for him. Henry Bouchie, whose father passed away, left the team after only six games to attend the funeral. He did not return.

The *Caledonian-Record* of Friday, July 7th, printed new League standings. Some teams had played eight games, while others, because of bad weather, had played only four:

TEAM	W	L	PCT.
Newport	5	2	.714
St. Johnsbury	5	3	.625
Berlin	3	5	.375
Littleton	2	3	.400
Groveton	2	3	.400
Lancaster	1	3	.250

Now, here's some more interesting stuff. In "Deak" Morse's column in the same issue, we had this:

> Once again Northern Vermont and New Hampshire teams are seeing an improved brand of baseball. Each year the class of ball is better than the previous season. This year, it's plenty fast enough for what the towns can afford and if it stays at its present peak it is good enough.
>
> In his July 4th column, Ralph Wheeler of the Boston Herald says that Vermont must be recognized as the semi-pro baseball capital of New England, as it has four teams in the Northern League and two in the Twin States League. A point that Mr. Wheeler was not familiar with was that at the conclusion of the games on Independence Day three of the four Vermont entries in the Northern League were running 1–2–3 and the fourth team was at the head of its second division. In the Twin States League the two Green Mountain entries were at the top of the list ...

Is this the explanation for Guy's slow start at the plate? A brand of baseball better than he'd previously experienced? That may be part of it. Here's "Deak" Morse again:

> Ralph Wheeler rates the Northern League as the fastest semi-pro circuit in the East with the Twin States League next, followed by the Cape Cod loop ...

But there may also have been another explanation for the difference in Guy's performance—the loose, red-headed Prudence, who was anything but, with whom Guy connected on his first night in town. That woman's dark, smoldering sexuality was new to him. Although in the past women had not exactly flocked to Guy like bees to honey, he was a very attractive young man. Looking to spice up an otherwise humdrum existence in this small Vermont city, Prudence wasted no time inserting herself into our boy's life.

*   *   *   *

St. Johnsbury, VT
Monday, July 10 through Friday, July 21, 1939
Hazen Field
8:00 p.m.

"Vitale, Horne, Grondahl and Bruhn" Tom Bilodeau yelled, as his team came off the field to start the eighth inning of a game against the Lancaster Pilots. "Let's get a couple more runs."

"Dammit, you guys, it's the eighth and we're only up by two," Guy said as he tossed his glove on the grass beside the player's bench and picked up two bats. "We need some insurance runs this inning!"

"Huh," Bruhn said. "You should talk. You ain't had a hit yet today."

Guy shrugged off the remark and leveled a heavy look at his catcher "I'll get one now," he said with a nod toward Ted Anderson, the other team's pitcher who was on the mound taking his warm-up tosses. "He ain't so tough."

As Guy walked to the plate, guilt pricked him like numerous tiny needles. *I should nevah have stayed at Prudence's place last night,* he thought. "*I'm sure tired.*

Shut up! Shut up and just do it, he thought, the pressure building in his head as he addressed the plate and waited for the first pitch.

He swung and missed as a fastball came in over the outside corner. Fatigue and the alcohol he'd consumed the night before pulled at him. His arms felt like lead as he waived the bat back and forth through the strike zone. Surely this was not his bat. It was so heavy. *This'll be his curve. If he does what he's been doin' the last coupla innings.*

It was. Guy, ready for the pitch, swung and lined it over the shortstop's head into left-center field. The play was in front of him as he legged it around first and headed for second. He could see that the ball had skidded between the fielders and the Pilot's left fielder was running it down. Lowering his head, Guy extended his stride, thinking triple all the way.

The play was close at third. It wouldn't have been if Guy had slept in his own bed, *alone*, the night before. He beat the throw by a fraction of a second with a nifty fall away slide to the home plate side of the bag. Breathing hard, he dusted himself off and looked over at Bruhn, who gave him a thumbs-up from the edge of the dugout.

But that's all the Senators could muster, as Horne, who had taken Henry Bushie's place (yes, it's Bushie, not Bushey) so Bushie could attend his father's funeral, struck out on three pitches, and Grondahl and Bruhn did no better, to end the Senator's eighth inning, leaving Guy stranded at third base.

In the ninth, with one down and Guy playing left field, Haldane hit a bouncer to Bilodeau at short. Tom hurried his throw to first base, and Cleverly could not dig it out of the dirt. The next Pilot batter worked Jack Brady for a walk, bringing up the dangerous Elrod with the tying runs on base. Brady was tiring. He missed with two close pitches and came back with heat over the plate on the 2–0 pitch. Elrod got the fat of the bat on it and sent a screaming liner in fair territory down the left field line.

Oh, shit! That ball's hit hard and it's slicin' away from me, Guy thought. His energy at a low ebb, he did not get a good jump on it. At the last split second, just as players and fans alike thought the ball was past him, Guy extended his gloved hand, stabbed at the white sphere and caught it in his glove's meager webbing. Wheeling, he fired the pill into his cut-off man, but he'd made the catch so deep in the outfield that the runners moved up. Two outs, men on second and third.

However, at this point Brady bore down and struck out Lawrence to end the game. As Guy came off the field, Brady was waiting for him. "Hell of a catch, Guy," he said, slapping his left fielder on the back.

"Just thought I'd make it exciting," Guy responded, grinning broadly.

So the Senators won that game 4–2, which was nice. But they lost the next two games over the weekend. Berlin roughed them up 4–1 on Saturday, behind Al Hatch, of Tufts College, who scattered ten hits and gave up only one run, and the Groveton Athletics beat them 3-zip on Sunday afternoon, as Walter Jusczyk of Brown University, was even more impressive, tossing a four-hit shutout.

Guy patrolled left field in both contests, but, although he had a walk to his credit, he collected only one hit in eight official trips to the plate. The pair of weekend losses dropped St. Johnsbury into third place behind Newport and Littleton, with a 6–5 record. Guy, who'd turn twenty-two that October, was having his problems with the bat, although his fielding did not seem to be suffering from his evening sojourns at the home of the curvy Prudence, who was turning out to be anything but what her name suggested. So far, these two would meet each evening at *The Purple Onion,* and after dinner and a few drinks, would retire to her colonial-style farm house, to … get to know each other better. But that was about to change.

On Wednesday, July 12th, the Senators played Berlin on the Red Sox's home field, with young Jack Brady again taking the mound for St. Johnsbury. Scoring three runs in the top of the first, they hung on to win 3–2. In the ninth, they threatened to add an additional run, as Tom Bilodeau singled and Guy, who went one for two in the game, sacrifice-bunted him along to second. But here, Oscar Khederian showed how much he had matured in a year. Grondahl smashed a hard grounder to him at third. Khederian fumbled the ball momentarily but picked it up in time to trap Bilodeau between second and third, then caught Grondahl off first for a double play.

Apparently the playing surface in Berlin was not the best, but Guy and the Senators fared well on it. An article in the *Caledonian-Record* dated July 12th said this:

> *The Senators were the second team to go through a game on Berlin's difficult surface without an error. Vitale had six putouts in the outfield and fielded sensationally.*

And "Deak" Morse had also noticed how well the outfielders played despite trying conditions at Berlin and generally:

> *The fielding of the team is of exceptionally high order, and the outfield trio, whether it has been Vitale and Casey with either Bouchie or Horne, has been the greatest ball hawk outfit in the circuit.*

With League play about one-fifth complete, Newport was still ahead in the standings, but not by much, and the fans were being treated to some pretty good baseball. Sixteen round trippers had been poled so far, there had been only one or two one-sided games, and two triple plays and two shutouts had occurred.

But from the League's viewpoint, there was a problem. "Deak" Morse:

> *Some of the towns have not drawn as well as was expected but this is primarily due the fact that most of the parks are not enclosed. None of the clubs are in tough financial condition but the teams are not making the money they should. As stated before much of that trouble is due to the fact that those who want to crash the gate can do so or can see the game from outside the park. The first year of the League is certainly one of the most important ones and every effort should be made to collect from every person who witnesses a game.*

I don't think the gate was of any concern to Guy on Thursday, July 13th as his team scored a bunch of runs to beat Littleton 13–6. Both teams did lots of hitting. In the past in games like this, Guy expected to have a multi-hit game. This time, he did not. One hit in five trips with one run scored was all he could manage, and he did no better the next day, as his team hammered out eleven hits against Groveton in a game that ended in a 4–4 tie, called by the umpire after eleven innings because of rain. Guy was one for six in this one, although he was robbed of a hit by Tabaldi, Groveton's second baseman, in the seventh, on a grounder between first and second, and in the eleventh, a great shoe-string catch was made by Groveton's center fielder, Murphy, on a ball he hit right on the nose.

At this stage, Guy, who had moved in with Prudence (what people of that era referred to as "shacking up"), was starting to worry a bit on the inside about his performance. But he concealed it well. Although his hitting had been light so far, he had been able to keep the fans, the sportswriters, his manager, and his teammates happy with his excellent fielding. Here's what the *Caledonian-Record* said about that on Tuesday, July 18th:

> *Vitale keeps moving along at about the same pace, unable to move into the upper brackets but doing very satisfactorily and if he were given credit for the hits that he has taken away from the opposition in the outfield, he would be well over the .300 mark.*

Nice thought. But batting averages are figured on the number of hits made at the dish, not on anything done in the field. On Thursday, July 20th, a month into the season, the *Caledonian-Record* printed a new list of batting stats. Among regular players, Rube Dyer of Berlin was leading the league with a .422 average. In sixteen games, he'd been up to bat sixty-four times, collected twenty-seven hits and drove in sixteen runs. Eddie Casey of the Senators was in third place with a .383 average; sixty at bats, twenty-three hits and eighteen ribbies; Guy was well down the list with 15 hits in 60 at bats and only four runs batted in; an unremarkable .250.

The next day, Guy continued his "torrid" .250 pace by getting one hit in four plate appearances as the Senators latched onto first place by beating the Newport Frontiers 5–1 behind the six-hit pitching of Harry Eich. Guy's hit, a double into center field, drove in Ben Meyers. A batter later, Guy was forced at third by Eddie Ingalls, the Senator's light-hitting pitcher who'd been playing right field that day.

*   *   *   *

Pine Bluffs, WY
Tuesday, March 7, 2006
703 Beech Street
5:00 p.m.

I know what you're thinking. You're probably right. No athlete can perform at peak levels for very long while staying up late every night, drinking heavily and leaving his energy on the sheets in some woman's bedroom. In 1938, although Guy Vitale had engaged in this type of behavior for a full month or more, he had called a halt to it prior to the start of the baseball season. Cape Cod and the small town of Falmouth, where everyone knew everyone else and the bars were few and far between back in '38, helped him, after a slow start, to concentrate on his baseball, and that produced excellent results.

But St. Johnsbury, VT was a larger place and a different story. Opportunities to misbehave abounded in this bustling city, and Guy was not unwilling, from the start, to seek them out. Having fallen head-over-heals for his red-headed female friend, he was trying to live up to her level of sophistication. Also, competition in the Twin States League was decidedly better than he'd experienced in the Cape Cod League. For these two reasons, his hitting was suffering. All this created a type of pressure for which he was unprepared. It's not surprising, then, that his performance was not up to his level of the previous three seasons. I'm not going to belabor the obvious.

Now here's a good thing. Despite his only average performance at the plate so far, apparently he was well-liked by his manager, fellow players and fans. And once again he found himself on the team to beat for the League title. In the stretch drive, although his fielding faltered just a bit, his hitting *did* pick up some.

*   *   *   *

St. Johnsbury, VT
Saturday, July 22 through Monday, July 31, 1939
Hazen Field
5:30 p.m.

For the first several weeks of the season, the Newport Frontiers had been in first place, although not by much, with St. Johnsbury trying to catch them. Toward the end of the second week of July, that happened, and by July 22nd, Tom Bilodeau's boys, now knick-named "Bilodeau's Butchers" by sportswriters and fans, were playing some pretty good baseball, having won six of their last seven games. That included a 5–1 win over the Frontiers at Gains Park in Newport the day before, behind Harry Eich, who tossed a six-hitter. Guy went one for four, a double into center field, but was forced at third on a grounder to Clark Laramie at short, who tossed to Smith.

On the 22nd, the Lancaster Pilots halted the Senator's win streak, 3–2, as they could do little to solve the offerings of Norval Hunthausen of Notre Dame, who limited them to only four hits. However, St. Johnsbury was without the services of its star centerfielder, Eddie Casey, who'd been injured the week before. At the time, he'd been whaling the ball at a .383 clip. For Guy, however, it was a good day. He picked up two of this team's four hits and drove in both runs, the first time this season he'd accomplished that fete. But the same day, Newport's victory over Groveton cut the Senators lead to half a game.

Over that hot and humid weekend, the Senators lost two more at Hazen Field; a three-game losing streak, as the Berlin Red Sox manhandled them 7–0 on Saturday and Littleton defeated them 5–1 on Sunday, the first time the Senators had lost more than two games in a row. Guy? 0 for 4 with the bat and he had an embarrassing day in left. In the seventh inning of the Littleton game, with the bases loaded, DeCesare doubled over his head, clearing the bases. It wasn't much better for Guy at the plate. With two on and only one out in the fourth, Hatch, the Berlin pitcher, gave a masterful exhibition as he bore down and fanned Guy and Grondahl to end the inning. The following day, however, Guy collected one hit in three plate appearances, driving in two of his team's three runs. He got some good press. The *Caledonian-Record* on July 24th:

Jack Barry appeared to be in perfect form for the Senators and set the first 19 men to face him down in order. St. Johnsbury picked up hope in the fourth when Jawarski won a pass, was sacrificed to by Meyers and went to third on Bilodeau's stab to the mound. One run looked pretty imposing at the moment and little Guy Vitale was equal to the occasion for he poked a fast drive through second that none of the Collegians were able to lay a hand on.

Team standings in the Twin States League on Tuesday, July 25th, a month into the season, read like this:

TEAM	W	L	PCT.	GAMES BEHIND
Newport	14	8	.636	—
St. Johnsbury	12	8	.600	1
Berlin	13	9	.591	1
Littleton	8	11	.591	4–1/2
Lancaster	7	12	.368	5–1/2
Groveton	5	11	.313	6

That day, in his column, *Spanning the Sports*, "Deak" Morse reported that with the deadline for altering rosters only a few days away, Lancaster "has taken on Joe and Steve Wood" to play for them. We know from Bob Wood that his brothers, Joe and Steve, played for Lancaster, and he played briefly for Groveton, after coming from the Northern League where they had held down slots for the Plattsburgh entry. In fact, the only figures I could find for the Wood brothers show that Steve played in four games and collected four hits in eleven times to the plate. Joe played in three games, getting three hits in nine plate appearances, and Bob participated in four games for Groveton, played first base, and batted .143, with two hits in fourteen trips.

"Things weren't working out for us," Bob said, when I spoke to him by telephone at his Keene, New Hampshire home, "so we left and went back to New Haven before the season ended."

And on Friday, July 28th, Morse had this to say:

The half-way mark is just around the corner in the Twin States League and the various managers, if they plan any changes, must make them at once. Tom Bilodeau has intimated that he intends to stand pat on his lineup. That happens to be a pretty good tribute to a team of which it was said in a nearby town that neither the manager nor half of the players would be in St. Johnsbury after the first couple of weeks. Bilodeau has made less changes in his personnel than any other club. Joe Horne was here for a time to replace Bouchie and Chet Jaworski came in as a replacement for Horne. Harry Eich was taken on in place of Dean Dubois, but otherwise the team has remained intact, the same as the day it arrived here.

But the following day, Saturday, July 29th, Bilodeau made one change, bringing in Walter Murphy, a coach at Amherst College who had been captain of its baseball team in 1934, and had been playing semi-pro ball, to take Eddie Casey's place until the injured Senator's leading hitter could return to action.

During this same weekend, the Senators picked up a half game over second place Newport by beating both the Lancaster Pilots, 3–0, and the Berlin Red Sox, 10–7. Against the Pilots, Guy went 0 for 4 at the plate, but the Senators played great defensive ball, with Vitale, Cleverly and Bilodeau making fine plays. The Berlin game was perhaps Guys' best game of the summer, as he went three for three at the plate, getting singles in the fifth, seventh and eighth, and driving in three runs.

That weekend, the *Boston Sunday Post* ran a very favorable article on the Twin States League:

TWIN STATE LEAGUE HAS GREAT YEAR
Reorganized Loop Has Many College and School Stars

Berlin, N. H., July 29—For the first time in a score of years, followers of the national pastime in this particular neck of the woods are enjoying a high brand of baseball in the form of the Twin State League this year.

With Raymond E. Farwell, Wells River Vt., sportsman, business headliner as its president, the recently-organized Twin State diamond circuit composed of St. Johnsbury and Newport, Vt., and Berlin, Groteton, Lancaster and Littleton, N. H. passed the halfway mark of its 50-game schedule today.

SCHOOL COLLEGE STARS
The various aggregations in the loop are made up of outstanding schoolboy pastimers and college stars representing over 30 different institutions of higher learning. Arthur L. Johns of Medford, who captained the Harvard Crimson on the diamond during the past

season and who was awarded the Princeton A. A. trophy for his brilliant playing, is piloting the Berlin Red Sox. Tom Bilodeau, former Harvard baseball and football luminary has complete charge of the St. Johnsbury Senators.

Philip Ryan of St. Michael's College is handling the managerial reins of the Newport Frontiers, with Ebb Caraway, athletic director of Massachusetts State College, leading the Littleton Collegians. The Lancaster Pilots are managed by Linn Wells, Bowdoin College baseball mentor. John Murphy of St. Johns Prep is the leader of the Groveton Athletics.

Although the Twin State League's campaign is only half over, many top notch achievements have already been recorded in the books.

Ted Harwich, ex-Andover Prep ace slabster and Yale freshman strikeout king, hurled the League's first no-hit, no-run contest against the Lancaster Pilots a few days ago. Harrison is playing for the Groveton Athletics.

Al Hatch of Bennettsville, S C., and captain-elect of the Tufts College baseball nine, pitched a grand total of 34 consecutive scoreless innings for the Berlin Red Sockers against league competition. Al has allowed but seven earned runs in over 76 innings of pellet flinging.

Big Rube Dyer, former Boston Park League slugger, is leading the circuit in hitting with the lofty mark of .482. Dyer is regular backstop for the Berlin outfit. On the same team are Oscar Khederian And Georgie Yankowski of Watertown, Mass and Joey DeCesare of Everett, Mass, who won berths on the Boston Post All-Scholastic array of stars this past spring.

Also, on Monday, July 31st, Billy Murphy, who'd signed on at Groveton to take Chick Toomey's place, resigned as manager and was replaced by Stanley Slayton.

*   *   *   *

St. Johnsbury, VT
Tuesday, August 1 to Monday, August 14, 1939
Hazen Field
5:30 p.m.

"It isn't as good as it was because the college crop this year was under par," remarked Paul Kritchell, a scout for the New York Yankees, as he sat in the stands at Gains Field on Tuesday afternoon, August 1st, answering questions about the Northern League. The well-known Yankee scout had arrived in Newport on

Monday, fresh from a tour of Northern League towns where, in his opinion, baseball was being played "not so well as last year."

His fame having preceded him, Kritchell had come to Newport, where he was scheduled to watch the Frontiers and Littleton that Tuesday, and then trek to each of the other parks in the League until he'd seen every team play. In search of prospects, he had let it be known that he was interested in watching catcher Walter Benson, pitchers Carrol Rurak and Howard Anderson, and pitcher-outfielder Passabet of the Frontiers, pitcher Al Hatch and third baseman Oscar "Skee" Khederian of the Berlin Red Sox, and pitcher Ted Harrison of Groveton. Guy? Not mentioned. Nor was Rube Dyer of the Red Sox, or Eddie Casey of the Senators, at that time leading the League in hitting, with averages of .384 and .377 respectively. Makes you wonder.

Kritchell's presence in the area was noted by "Deak" Morse on Wednesday, August 2nd:

> *The fact that Paul Kritchell, famous scout of the New York Yankees is to stay in this sector long enough to see each of the teams in the circuit play, is a good testimonial to the circuit's strength. The following colleges are represented in the League: Harvard, Yale, Dartmouth, Michigan, Minnesota, Purdue, Wesleyan, Mass State, Villanova, William & Mary, Springfield, New Hampshire, Brown, Boston College, Boston University, Rhode Island State, Amherst, Bowdoin, Maine, Notre Dame, Colgate, Tufts, Clarkson, St. Michael's, St, John's of Brooklyn, and Fordham*

As previously mentioned, although there was no rule that all the players in the Twin States League must either be in college or have been college graduates, virtually all of them fit that bill. Except Guy, who was neither in college nor, although now old enough, a college graduate.

In a game against Ebb Caraway's Littleton Collegians on Wednesday, August 2nd, Guy collected two hits in four trips in a losing effort. Littleton, celebrating their manager's eighth wedding anniversary, showed off for Mrs. Caraway, who was in the stands, beating the Senators 12–4. Guy, continuing to show signs of wear, had his troubles in the outfield. Here's how the *Caledonian-Record* described it on August 3rd:

> *Eich [pitching for St. Johnsbury] got two straight strikes on Tirelis, wasted one, but sent the next one down through the slot and Tirelis fouled it off. The next one came over waist high and the Littleton*

catcher pickled it in a line over Vitale's head. It rolled toward the bank in left and slowly disappeared. Vitale found it but too late to make any close play at the plate …

In the ninth, Reil got on when Balme [a new shortstop for the Senators] pulled Bilodeau off the bag and Reil and Dadderio followed with successive singles. Caraway's grounder trickled through Balme and Wentzel got a hit to score the fourth run of the inning. Rice poked one to left that gave Vitale a chase but Guy failed to turn with the ball and was watching it all the way losing whatever chance he might have had to get it. He just tipped it as it was and Rice pulled up at third.

On the morning of August 3rd, stats were published up to and including the game on Sunday, July 30th. After twenty-four games, Guy had twenty-three hits in eighty-nine trips. His average at this point was .258. He'd driven in only nine runs on the season. Berlin Red Sox catcher, Rube Dyer, was leading the League at .381, while Senator's center fielder, Eddie Casey, now fully recovered from his injury, was in second place at .379, and Fran Reil of Littleton moved into third at .376.

With a month to go, Littleton led the League in team batting, at .302, Berlin was second with a .280 team batting average, Newport was third at .274 and St. Johnsbury was fourth at .252.

During the week of August 7th, the schedule called for the Senators to play eight games in seven days. Two of these were to be exhibition games at home, against Gorham. Even though it was a bit risky to play so many games in such a short stretch, it was done because Hazen Field was the best home field in terms of fan attendance, and there had only been one home game scheduled for that week; a lean week for the Club at the gate. And, Gorham had been making noises about joining the League in the '40 season.

The games were played on August 8th and 9th. A sizeable crowd saw Gorham defeat the home team, 4–1 in the first game. Guy managed one hit in four plate appearances. But only a small crowd of two hundred fifty fans witnessed the second on August 10th, surely a disappointment for the directors of the St. Johnsbury Baseball Association, who had hoped to pick up a few extra dollars from ticket sales. Guy was nothing for three in that one, another Senator loss, 4–3.

Despite all of Groveton's managerial problems, the town apparently was serious about its baseball. On Thursday, August 11th, a new ball park was dedicated by New Hampshire Governor, Francis E, Murphy, who afterwards, watched Groveton pitcher, Ted Harrison, pitch one-hit ball against the Senators for seven innings. But in the eighth, Bilodeau's bombers unloaded on Harrison with a vicious rally that chalked up six runs to get the win, 6–3. Guy played left and went one for three, a single to center, and scored a run, as the Senators were putting together another win streak and strengthening their grip on first place.

Friday, August 11ᵗʰ was a repeat of the previous day. Bilodeau's boys downed the Berlin Red Sox in Berlin, 6–3, knocking off their sixth straight win and extending their lead over Newport and Littleton by another game. At the close of the day, they were four games ahead of the Frontiers and six ahead of the Collegians. Guy, nothing for four at the plate, had five putouts in left field, and the *Caledonian-Record* took note, in its article Saturday, August 12ᵗʰ:

> *Grondahl, Bilodeau and Khederian worked nicely in the infield, while Vitale romped in the outfield for five putouts.*

But the weekend was coming up, with a single game scheduled on Saturday and a double header set for Sunday. Bilodeau's boys seemed to be having trouble winning on weekends lately.

Lynn Wells' Lancaster Pilots, firmly ensconced in fifth place, rose up and blasted the first place Senators on Saturday, 4–1 at Hazen Field, and on Sunday, before close to a thousand fans at Lancaster, the Pilots came from behind and nipped St. Johnsbury, 9–7.

In the first of Sunday's games, with the Senators behind in the bottom of the ninth, the first two men up drew walks. Jaworski then lined out to Linden in right field, who made a great catch to keep at least one and possibly two runs from scoring. That brought Guy to the dish.

This is it, Guy thought. *We don't score here, we don't win this game.* As he'd been taught, he was not going to help the opposing pitcher late in the game by being too anxious. He looked the first pitch over carefully as it missed the outside corner. Ball one.

He's gonna throw another fast ball, he guessed. It was heat alright, on the inside portion of the plate. Guy swung and missed. Concern lines visible on his brow, he stepped out of the batter's box and rubbed some dirt on his sweaty hands.

Guy stepped back in. *Curve? Or heat?* He wondered. *He hasn't thrown me his stuff, yet.* Thinking curve all the way, Guy was fooled by another fastball, which he didn't catch up to. The count was one and two.

Shit, he thought. *Looks like he's stickin' with his heat.* And this time Guy was right. Swinging a bit late, he sent a screaming liner down the right field line, which would have landed fair, but Linden again streaked over and made a fine catch to end the game, and Guy came off the field, perplexed that he could not buy a hit. It hadn't yet occurred to him that his reflexes were slowing a bit due to his nocturnal activity with Prudence.

The second game of the double header on Sunday could not be played because of rain. In these two Lancaster games, Guy was a combined one hit in eight official trips, while some miles away, "Skee" Khederian of the Berlin Red Sox, clubbed two home runs, one of them a grand slam, to lead his club to a 6–2 win over the Newport Frontiers.

Back on October 26, 2002, while researching Guy's time in the Cape Cod League, as described before, I came in contact with Al Irish. He wrote me a follow-up letter about several matters, one of which was Oscar Khederian:

> *Dear Tony ...*
>
> *I mentioned that I was involved with Northeastern baseball teams when in college. Wally Sullivan and Oscar Khederian were members of Falmouth's 1938 team and future stars at Northeastern. Khederian, from Watertown, must have been the youngest player ever in the Cape Cod League. You will note he was only 15 at the time. He was in the class of 1944 at Northeastern. Both Wally Sullivan (Northeastern's 1942 Baseball captain) and Khederian are in Northeastern's Athletic Hall of Fame ...*

CHAPTER 37

St. Johnsbury, VT
Tuesday, August 15 to Monday, August 28, 1939
Hazen Field
5:15 p.m.

With just three weeks left in the '39 season, Guy once again found himself in the thick of things. Not only were the St. Johnsbury Senators contending for the first League championship of the new Twin States League, but they were on top of the heap on August 15th, and even though they had lost their last two games to Lancaster over the previous weekend, the consensus was that they were the team to beat.

Pitching and defense wins games. That's the standard line in baseball circles. The Senators had not been hitting well, getting by with few base knocks. But they had developed a flare for coming through in the clutch; getting that base hit with runners in scoring position to drive across just enough runs to win. And the pitching? Bearing up well as a whole.

But it was on defense that these Senators excelled. Here's "Deak" Morse in his column on Tuesday, August 15th:

> *... in the field, the team is something terrific. They've taken many*
> *a sure fire hit away from the opposition with sensational defensive*
> *plays ...*

As we've already seen, he was talking about Guy's fielding as well as that of his teammates.

Now, the St. Johnsbury fans were beginning to speculate about just which ball club would win it all. These people weren't just average fans. They were baseball fanatics. Morse again, on the same day:

*With the race nearing the stretch some of the fans are starting to fig-
ure what kind of a break the Senators need to stay out in front. Some
say that .500 ball would turn the trick. If that were the case, the locals
would finish up with a record of 30 games won and 20 lost. In order to
duplicate that record, the Newport Frontiers would have to annex ten
victories in their remaining 14 games and Littleton would be forced to
win 14 out of 18. That's quite a strenuous task for either team, but it
would be more comfortable in St. Johnsbury if the Senators could win
two games to every one they lose.*

And nearing the stretch it was. The Senator's schedule called for eighteen
games over the last twenty days, with a crucial series to begin on Wednesday,
August 16th at Hazen Field and ending the following day at Littleton, against
a torrid Littleton club which had clawed its way into the third slot, and was
threatening to overtake Newport.

Well, despite the best of intentions, that next game, which the *Caledonian-
Record* described as a celebration of the Anniversary of the Battle of Bennington,
viciously fought 162 years ago on Vermont soil, resulted in another loss for the
Senators; this one in eleven innings. Ebb Caraway's club, behind the pitching
of Caraway and Fran Riel, gave up a lot of hits—seventeen in all—but only
nine runs, while collecting eleven hits and eleven runs off Harry Eich. Caraway
himself went two for six, one of them a grand slam with two down in the tenth
inning. For the Senators, that made it three losses in a row, and all three at the
hands of the Collegians.

Another thing about this game: Bilodeau's boys, who had been rather
impotent with the bats lately and spectacular in the field, reversed things and
pounded out seventeen hits, but committed four errors in the game. Guy, who
had one hit in five trips, drove in one of his team's nine runs, and had four putouts in left field, but he was now showing the effects of a strenuous season ...
and other things. The *Caledonian-Record*, again:

*Vitale made a fine play on Fred Riel's double earlier in the inning
but lost a possible putout in the next frame when he failed to see
Caraway's double as it came off the bat and slipped as he started for
it.*

Was Guy still seeing the pretty Prudence at this point? Yes, and I'm speculat-
ing that their relationship had reached torrid proportions, even if Guy's hitting
had not. Having moved to her farm earlier, his mornings were spent helping

her with chores around the farm, after which he'd report to the Senator's small-ish clubhouse, where he'd spend a few hours playing cards with his teammates before suiting up for practice or the game. He was even using her car to drive back and forth to town, sometimes with "Pru" in tow. Despite the age difference of eight years, and the press of her farm work, pretty Prudence had become a full fledged baseball groupie.

On Thursday, August 17th, the Senators ended their brief losing streak with a 4–2 win over Littleton at Remick Park in Littleton. This win was especially grat-ifying for them because the day before in their loss to the same team, pitcher Arthur Kenney had made some unwelcome remarks about them. Here's how the *Caledonian-Record* described this game, in which Guy collected two hits in four trips, scored a run and had two put outs in the field:

> *The Senators bench was riding Kenney viciously and their jeers reached a climax in the second when Vitale started the frame with a single and advanced as Bruhn rolled out to Kenney. Cleverly, the only left-hander on the team, reached the Littleton southpaw for a hit and Vitale came home on the play that would have been close if Tirelis had controlled the peg to the plate. Barry then fanned for the second out but Jaworski smashed out a hit in the right field sector which sent Cleverly home.*
>
> *Jaworski, Meyers, Casey, Cleverly and Fred Riel came out of the game with two safeties apiece. Guy Vitale, who was perturbed because the official averages for the season to date showed him as being at bat 143 times for a .203 average, should have read 125 times for a .232 [average], also came through with two base knocks.*

Well, this incident showed that Guy was paying attention, and that he was concerned enough about his poor showing at the plate to be upset over a mis-taken average printed in the newspaper the previous week. But over the next week, although Guy had several good games with the toothpick, going one for three once and two for four twice, his batting average picked up only a few points, and it was clear that he was tiring in the field.

On top of that, the Littleton Collegians refused to quit and were making things hot for the Senators. On Wednesday, August 23rd, Littleton defeated our boys 4–3 to reduce their lead to three and a half games, as Guy committed a pair of miscues that cost them the game. The *Caledonian-Record* again:

Caraway put the Collegians off to a fast start in the first inning when, with two down, he cuffed a hard liner over Bilodeau's head which rocketed right through Vitale and went deep into the pines for Eben's seventh round tripper of the season.

Littleton's third run came in the [seventh] inning as Tirelis dropped a fly into left. A combination "high sky" and a long run caused Vitale to drop the ball and Dodario laid down the conventional sacrifice. An error by Bilodeau on Skaza's bounder put Tiralis over.

But the following day against the Berlin Red Sox, St. Johnsbury's infield reeled off five double plays to bring their total for the year to fifty-one twin killings in forty games, as they defeated the Sox 6–0. Guy had another of those two hit games and raised his average to .248 for the season. "Skee" Khederian of the Berliners took over the League lead in runs batted in, with thirty-eight.

That Friday, August 25th, the Senators closed out their week with a double header against Groveton. They split it, losing the opener 8–1, but winning the nightcap 6–5. Guy was oh-fer in the first game. In the second game, he went two for five, scored one of his team's six runs, and had three putouts in the field. But he was charged with an error in each game. By the way, Bob Wood was no longer with the Groveton team at this point, and that club, under new Manager Slayton, had become a team to reckon with.

On Monday, August 28th, St. Johnsbury was hanging onto first place, with a record of 26 wins and 17 losses, a .605 won-lost percentage, and their nearest rival, Littleton, was three and a half games behind them. What about that other league? Here's how things stood in the Northern League on that date:

TEAM	W	L	PCT.	GAMES BEHIND
Burlington	39	24	.619	
St. Albans	38	24	.613	½
Rutland	38	24	.613	½
Saranac Lake	36	26	.581	2–1/2
Malone	29	33	.468	9–1/2
Plattsburg	26	350	.426	12
Montpelier	21	41	.339	17–1/2
Tupper Lake	21	42	.333	18

On Monday, August 28th, Morse reported that the Senator's twenty-four year old manager, Tom Bilodeau, became the first pilot in the League to get a vote of confidence from his directors. The previous day, club President Harry Witters, before the home half of the seventh inning, had announced that the Board of Directors had asked, and Tom had agreed, to handle the Senators again in 1940. Guy, on that morning, made an announcement of his own in the small farmhouse northwest of the city.

*   *   *   *

St. Johnsbury, VT
Monday, August 28, 1939
Prudence's Farm
9:15 a.m.

"… so I think it'd be best if I go back ta my room for the rest a the season." Having slept late like a married couple, the two were in the kitchen of Prudence's farm home, finishing a breakfast of thick bacon, scrambled eggs, toast, and coffee. The delicious aroma of freshly brewed coffee hung in the air, and sunlight streamed through the double windows above the sink. An opened box of breakfast cereal, a dish with one uneaten slice of buttered toast on it, and a pitcher of farm-fresh pasteurized milk straight from one of Prudence's cows, littered the table in front of them.

"What?" Prudence was surprised. "But … I thought you liked it here, Guy. I thought you liked *me*."

"I do," Guy responded. "I've nevah felt this way about anyone before. I think I love you."

Tossing a lock of red hair back from her face, Prudence rose from the table and stood, her back to the sink, dishes from last night's supper clearly visible behind her. "Well this is a fine way ta show it. Moving out, I mean."

"The problem is, I like you so much that I've let you become a distraction. I gotta do better this last week or …"

"Humph. Baseball! That's all you ever think about," Prudence said, her eyes flashing the anger she felt.

"That's what I'm here for, Pru. Don't be upset. It's only for a week."

But Prudence *was* upset. "If you leave now, you needn't bother ta come back," she said.

"But, Pru …" Guy began. His face anguished, he glanced uncertainly from the woman to his leather bag and back. "I gotta go," he said. "It's what I have ta do." Getting up from the table, he picked up his bag and walked to the door. "I'll come back afta it's ovah. Then we can talk." With that, he opened the door and walked out. The screen door slammed loudly behind him.

*   *   *   *

St. Johnsbury, VT
Tuesday, August 29 to Thursday, August 31, 1939
Hazen Field
5:15 p.m.

Only a week of the season remained. "Deak" Morse, on Tuesday, August 29th, said this about the pennant race:

> The six teams in the Twin States League are headed down the pike now with the season due to be concluded next Monday evening. It has developed into a two-team race with Lancaster already counted out and Newport and Berlin are through the minute the Senators win one game or the other two clubs lose one. Three Senator wins will still put Groveton out of the running.

Perhaps thrilled that their manager had been asked to come back, or possibly because they were so close to winning the League title, the Senators, behind very effective pitching by Barry, Eich and Brady, swept both ends of a twin bill against the Lancaster Pilots at Lancaster on Tuesday, August 29th. The Littleton Collegians, their closest rival, defeated the Groveton Athletics 9–2, to keep their mathematical chances alive, but St. Johnsbury's two wins all but crushed the hopes of the four other teams. They needed only two more wins to clinch the pennant.

In that double header, Guy went two for four in the first game, one of them a triple, scored a run and committed no errors. But in the second contest, Bilodeau's 11th inning home run with a man on was the deciding factor. Guy? Oh for four. And he committed one miscue, However, his sacrifice fly in the sixth brought home Meyers from third base with a vital run.

Before the games played on Wednesday, August 30th, St. Johnsbury's record was twenty-eight wins and seventeen losses. The closest competition was Littleton, three and a half games behind at twenty-five wins and twenty-one losses. To lose it at this point seemed impossible.

On the 30th, Groveton and the Senators squared off at Hazen Field, in another of their wild contests, and despite the home field advantage, Groveton won it 6–5. Because of the absence of a regular League umpire, an alternate arbiter was brought in to call balls and strikes. Apparently, a few of his calls were controversial. In the Groveton fourth for example, he missed a "perfect strike" to Groveton's pitcher, Johnny Bemben, which would have retired the side. Given new life, Bemben, on the next pitch, drove a fastball from Eddie Ingalls over the right field fence; a three-run homer. But in that game, Guy was two for four, stole a base and drove in two of his team's five runs, and it was clear that he was making a concerted effort, with only a week left in the season, to raise that batting average as much as possible. Meanwhile, Littleton was manhandling the Lancaster Pilots, 7–1 to keep its hopes alive. That weekend, Littleton and St. Johnsbury were scheduled to play two games. These might decide the League championship.

On Thursday, August 31st, hitting stats showed that Guy had indeed raised his average—from somewhere in the low .230s just two weeks before, to .256. That was a nice jump, but over all, not very impressive for a player trying to showcase himself in hopes of being noticed by a professional scout.

Well, you'd think that St. Johnsbury might be able to count on a little help from its friends when the chips were down; but the Berlin Red Sox failed to beat Littleton on Thursday, August 31st, and Newport's Frontiers walloped the Groveton bunch 9–3. The result would keep the League pennant race in doubt until at least Saturday afternoon.

Anyway, the final week of the new Twin States League's first season had arrived. Would St. Johnsbury hang on to win the pennant? Or would Littleton overtake them and snatch the flag from their grasp?

*   *   *   *

St. Johnsbury, VT
Friday, September 1 to Wednesday, September 6, 1939
Hazen Field
5:15 p.m.

On Friday, September 1st, "Bilodeau's butchers" and the Berlin Red Sox played to a 3–3 tie, as the game had to be called after ten innings because of rain. Meanwhile, the Newport Frontiers defeated the Lancaster Pilots 6–3 behind the six hit pitching of a kid who actually *was* from Colgate, Passabet.

Enjoying the excitement, nine hundred fans turned out for the game between the Senators and the Collegians on Saturday at Hazen Field, but the locals were disappointed. The streaking Littleton club chalked up its fifth straight win, 3–2 in ten innings, and Guy, disconcerted by the absence of Prudence from the stands, and possibly experiencing … withdrawal symptoms, was oh fer at the plate.

Sunday, September 3rd, was an eventful day for the Senators and fourteen hundred fans, as they lost the second of two crucial games to a Littleton club seeking to keep them from clinching the pennant over the weekend. The score of that one was 6–3, and it gave the Littleton team the series between these two clubs, six games to four. Littleton, smelling at least a tie for the pennant, was on a roll, which, on Monday morning, after the Berlin team beat the Senators, moved it into first place and dropped Bilodeau's boys into second for the first time since July 26th.

The Senators were scheduled to play two games that Monday. In the morning tilt, they lost, yes, that's right, *lost* to Artie Johns Berlin Red Sox, 7–2. It seemed that the tension of the Littleton series had been too much and, except for Guy, they could not muster much of anything. Harry Eich didn't have any stuff, and had to be replaced early by Jack Barry. Meanwhile, Al Hatch was at his best for the Sox. Here's what the *Caledonian-Record* had to say:

> *Guy Vitale was the only Senator to have any luck with Al Hatch. "Pizan" checked in with three hits in as many official trips, two of them being doubles and two of his hits playing a part in the scoring. Vitale doubled to right in the fourth with two out and Meyers on second to drive the first run in and he scored the only other run himself as he doubled to left in the seventh and came all the way around as Hatch threw the ball away on a play to first base.*

So, apparently free of his redheaded "distraction," Guy's attempt to concentrate on baseball showed, as he had a terrific game even though his team could not get a win that morning.

But his stamina completely deserted him in the afternoon game, and he came up hitless. A couple of bingles would have lifted that batting average to a respectable level. But it was not to be, as the Senators barely manage to eke out a 3–1 win over Groveton and Wally Jusczyk, who allowed only six hits and three runs.

And that's how it ended. The Senators and Collegians finished the season in a dead heat. Each team had won twenty-nine and lost twenty-one. Here are the final Twin States League standings:

TEAM	W	L	PCT.	GAMES BEHIND
St. Johnsbury	29	21	.580	TIE
Littleton	29	21	.580	TIE
Newport	26	24	.520	3
Berlin	24	26	.480	5
Groveton	23	27	.460	6
Lancaster	19	31	.380	10

The League's All Star team selections were announced on Wednesday, September 6th. It must have been disappointing for Guy to realize, as surely he did some time before this list was published, that for the first time in four seasons, his name would not appear among those designated as the best:

PLAYER	POSITION	TEAM		AVERAGE
John Dyer	*C*	*Berlin*		*.363*
Tom Bilodeau	*1B*	*St. Johnsbury*		*.362*
Rod Smith	*2B*	*Newport*		*.313*
Oscar Khederian	*SS*	*Berlin*		*.299*
Ebb Caraway	*3B*	*Littleton*		*.285*
Lloyd Rice	*LF*	*Littleton*		*.315*
Edward Casey	*CF*	*St. Johnsbury*		*.365*
Honey Beaton	*RF*	*Groveton*		*.311*
PITCHERS	*TEAM*	*W*	*L*	*PCT.*
Norman Hubbard	*Littleton*	*8*	*3*	*.727*
Edward Ingalls	*St. Johnsbury*	*8*	*4*	*.667*
Francis Riel	*Littleton*	*10*	*6*	*.625*
John Barry	*St. Johnsbury*	*9*	*6*	*.600*

On that same Wednesday morning, the *Caledonian-Record* printed a column letting the Senator fans know what each of their ballplayers would be doing after the season. Tom Bilodeau planned to play for the Plymouth Cordage team before returning to Harvard for his final year of law school. Here's what it said about Guy:

> *Guy Vitale: Plans to enter Colgate where he will go out for football.*
> *Home address: 20 Breed Street, East Boston, Mass.*

Yep, there's the Colgate thing again. More about that in a minute. A few days later, on September 9th, the final Twin States League stats were printed. Eddie Casey of the Senators took home batting honors with a .365 average, followed by Dyer of the Red Sox at .363, and Tom Bilodeau at .362. Oscar Khederian finished the season at .299. Guy? He was well down the list. In 53 games, he was at bat 205 times, scored 25 runs, made 52 hits which included 3 doubles, 4 triples, 0 home runs, and he drove in 26. His final average was .254. His fielding average was .943.

CHAPTER 38

Pine Bluffs, WY
Friday, March 31, 2006
703 Beech Street
10:39 a.m.

So the mystery had been solved. That gap in my knowledge of Guy's life labeled "1939" had been filled. When I started the research, I didn't know that the finished chapters of this section would read like a history of the first year of the modern Twin States League. Nor did I know how many wonderful people in New Hampshire and Vermont would help me in my quest.

And I'm not sorry I undertook the search, despite the fact that I discovered two disconcerting things; that against a higher caliber of ball player, my uncle's baseball talents seemed to lag, and that he'd lived with a woman eight years his senior, and had apparently fallen hard for her. Perhaps that rumor which had lingered in the family for so long, about a rejection in the love area, was now resolved, too.

But I *will* tell you one thing; the people who were involved in setting up the Twin States League were the cream of the crop. As a result of their efforts, a league was created that ran extremely well during its first year of existence, and came through the summer in fine shape, ready to continue on into a second season.

The first directors who met on April 24th, 1939 in Lancaster, and affixed their signatures to the document pledging their town entries to the new league deserve a lot of credit.[46] While researching this section of the book, I had seen some indication that the impetus for the new league began at St. Johnsbury, which, prior to 1939, had been a hotbed of semi-pro baseball, beginning with the Purina Mills team, filled with local talent, followed by the Sunset League,

---

46   These were Lee Gray of St. Johnsbury, Austin McAuley of Littleton, Irving Hinkley of Lancaster, Vaughn Chase of Groveton, Dr. Charles Schurman of Newport, and Dr. William Johnson of Berlin.

and two years of excellent semi-pro ball in the Green Mountain League. The St. Johnsbury Baseball Association, headed by its president, Harry Witters, and its Finance Committee chairman, Arthur Hafner, did a wonderful job guiding the fledgling Senators during that first season.

Managers Tom Bilodeau of the St. Johnsbury Senators, Linn Wells of the Lancaster Pilots, Elbert "Ebb" Caraway of the Littleton Collegians, Philip "Pinkey" Ryan of the Newport Frontiers, Arthur "Artie" Johns of the Berlin Red Sox, and Chick Toomey, Walter Jusczyk, and Steve Slayton of the Groveton Athletics, all had many start-up problems to overcome, and most proved themselves wise managers, capable of doing so.

And of course, the new League's president, Raymond Farwell, who on September 13th, 1939, at the St. Johnsbury Country Club, expressed himself as "greatly pleased over the outcome of the initial effort to organize [the League's baseball teams]." He also spoke of the whole-hearted cooperation he had received from the men who had worked with him as members of the Board. At the conclusion of President Farwell's remarks, as a token of appreciation, he was presented with a beautiful briefcase, inside of which was a second case. A motion that he be elected president again for the 1940 season met with unanimous approval, but was deferred until the organizational meeting to be held the following February.

The last word? That goes to "Deak" Morse, whose prose followed almost every game played that season by the teams in this fledgling League:

> *The official closing of the Twin States League will come this evening when a banquet will be held at St. Johnsbury Country Club to transact the final items of business. The League may well be very proud of its first year. Without a doubt there is not a single town that regretted signing a franchise last May. St. Johnsbury came through the year with a distinct profit, the best year in the history of the National Pastime.*

As for Guy Vitale? Well, please read on.

*   *   *   *

East Boston, MA
Tuesday, September 12, 1939
20 Breed Street
10:00 p.m.

The baseball season over, Guy hitched a ride back to Boston with "Skee" Khederian, in his beat-up 1939 Oldsmobile coupe. The car displayed a weathered, flat black paint job and an accumulation of dents, which gave it the appearance of having just come out of someone's barn, but it sported a flathead 6-cylinder engine and radiator, and was, in reality, a cool vehicle.

"My folks bought it fer me," Khederian explained proudly as Guy tossed his bag into the narrow space behind the front seat. "Jest so I could come out heah this summah." He turned the key in the ignition and revved the engine.

"Looks like ... you've given it a lotta use," Guy said diplomatically as he warily climbed into the leather-scarred, trash-filled passenger seat. "Listen, the record fer a trip from heah ta Boston is 6 hours and ten minutes. Lets' see what this wreck can do."

Khederian bared his teeth in what was a cross between a grin and a leer. "Must a been a little old lady drivin' a Packard," he said, and floored it.

Having seen the season-ending statistics, I wonder how Guy must have felt, sitting next to this kid from Watertown with the hot wheels, who played so well and finished the season with far better stats than he had. That was a complete reversal of the '38 season at Falmouth, and was probably an indication that Khederian was improving and would continue to do so, while Guy may have reached his peak; both in terms of his physical ability and his desire to play.

Anyway, the roads being what they were, they did not chop any time off the record Guy had mentioned, but he and his friend eventually wound up back in East Boston, where Khederian dropped him off at the corner of Ford and Breed Streets. Since he'd given up the room he'd leased prior to leaving for St. Johnsbury in June, a lonely billet in his mother's house awaited him.

That night, his first back at home, he lay on his bed, the same one in which he'd slept as a kid; the same twin bed from which he'd turned out every morning of his high school years, especially that mystical senior year, when he could not wait to get up each dawn, attend early morning Mass at St. Lazarus, and go off to receive the accolades of friends and others, over some new football or baseball fete.

There in the dark, awake, shoes off, staring up at the ceiling, for a brief moment, a montage of faces flashed through his mind's eye; his brother, Frank, his friend and manager, Pete Herman, the angry Prudence, who scorned his affections at the end and would not let him return to her, and Fred O'Brien— always Fred O'Brien's boozy face as he tried to talk his way out of trouble during that fateful meeting in his office a year ago.

It never failed to astonish him, the sudden sharpness of that painful memory as it stabbed through the veil of time. A part of him wished fervently that the pain would dull and eventually fade. But so far it had not, and he could summon it at a moment's notice during a period of solitude like now. The surface of the old wound had, of course, healed over as he tried to move on with his life, which was as much as he could hope for.

But how easily the gash re-opened. How humbling the reality that despite all his talent, all his best efforts in high school and three blazing summers on Cape Cod, he had not been offered a contract by any major league club. And despite all his hopes that some scout would spot him in St. Johnsbury, *that* had not happened either. At Kents Hill, he'd studied the famous 14th century poet, Chaucer. A line from one of his poems came to Guy's mind:

> *Thou shalt make castles, then in Spain,*
> *And dream of joy all but in vain.*

Why? Why? he asked himself in the blackness of his bedroom. He had no ready answer, was not prepared yet to admit, consciously, at least, that his staying out late, his drinking and his escapades in that quaint Vermont town with a somewhat desperate woman seeking temporary solace from a bleak existence who had welcomed him with warm, open arms, were the causes of his poor showing with the bat and his late season fielding lapses in the Twin States League.

Subconsciously, however, he knew, and the pain he experienced as he lay there, hands clasped under his head, staring at the ceiling, was as if someone had hit him with a clenched fist squarely in the solar plexus. Gritting his teeth, he tried to wish it away, but he could not. Guilt and disappointment washed over him in alternating waves. Finally, unable to cope, he searched wildly for his shoes and slipped them on.

I'll be alright, he told himself. *Tomorrow I'll be better. But just now, I think one a the local bars is where I should be.*

*   *   *   *

East Boston, MA
Tuesday, September 12, 1939
20 Breed Street
10:30 p.m.

Stepping outside into the humid September night, he debated which watering hole to grace with his presence. Santarpio's was closer than Calderone's, but he knew the place would be crawling with Fred O'Brien's friends; possibly O'Brien himself might be there. Every time his thoughts turned to his old coach, the anger welled up within, and he knew he didn't want to get anywhere near the man, for fear of what he might do.

It was late by the time Guy, his hair nicely combed, and smelling of after-shave, walked through the door of Calderone's. As he approached the door, his was a melancholy mood. His mind replayed a line from John Dryden's *Cymon and Iphigenia:*

> *Then hasten to be drunk,*
> *the business of the day.*

Ah, well … business of the night, he thought. *It's my business tonight.* Stepping inside, he paused, listening to the clinking of glasses and sounds of laughter, while his eyes adjusted to the dimly-lit interior. When they did, the first person he saw sitting at the bar was Joseph E. "Jimmy" Rosetti. Four years younger than Guy, he was only eighteen but, because he looked older, and was possessed of a fat bankroll and an affable, back-slapping manner, he'd been able to convince most of the barkeeps in East Boston that he was of legal drinking age. Not in the mood for company, Guy turned to leave, but he was too late. Rosetti had spotted him.

"Hey, Guy! Bambino! Good ta see ya," Rosetti said. Turning back to the bartender, he picked up his drink. "My friend and I'll take that table over there." He slid off the barstool, grabbed Guy by the elbow and steered him to a corner table.

Settled, Rosetti leaned forward. "So! I hear ya played ball in the Twin States League this past summah," he said.

"Yeah," Guy responded without enthusiasm.

A waiter arrived, placed two cardboard coasters on the table, glanced at both men and addressed Guy. "Let's see some ID, pal," he said in a guilty-until-proven-innocent tone. He didn't ask Rosetti for any. Just Guy. Seething, Guy reached for his wallet and flashed his ID. Satisfied, the waiter left to fill their drink orders.

"What team?" Rosetti wanted to know.

Guy, who had become used to regular sexual relations with Prudence, had been checking the place for single women. Seeing none, he turned his attention to his companion. "St. Johnsbury," he said. "We tied for the title."

"The bee's knees!" Rosetti responded. "How'd *you* do? Did ya git signed?"

Guy debated which of the two questions to answer first, but shrugged and did not respond to either. The waiter returned and placed their drinks on the table, along with their tab. Rosetti, who would later become a campaign worker for John F. Kennedy during his run for the House of Representatives in 1946, examined his drink. He'd heard that Guy had not done well. "You gonna play again next season?"

"I don't think so. I'm through with baseball."

Rosetti shook his head sympathetically. "Timing is everything," he said. "It's not enough ta do well in games if there ain't no scouts in the stands."

Trying not to be rude, Guy made the effort to engage. "True," he replied. "I was pretty sure I'd be signed when I graduated from East Boston. It didn't happen. Guess I've turned inta a cynic. A cynic is just a disappointed idealist, ya know."

Rosetti grinned. "Is *that* what you are?"

"I think so," Guy said. "I used ta always see life as ideal. Now, I don't."

"But," Rosetti said, raising his glass, "that didn't save ya from disappointment. You *are* disappointed ain't ya? Disappointed that yer not in the Bigs yet?"

Frowning, Guy didn't answer directly. "The only thing that can save somebody from disappointment is hopelessness." Raising his glass, he sipped the golden nectar. "But if ya don't have hope, then there's no point in livin'."

Rosetti leveled an evaluating glance at his older friend. "Oh? Well, if ya still have hope, then why don't ya play again next summah?"

Guy shrugged. "Maybe I'm jest tired of it. I'll probably go out and get a job."

"Where? At the shipyard?"

Guy raised his eyebrows at Rosetti's derisive tone. "Why not? I worked there last year for awhile."

Rosetti studied Guy's face for a few moments more before shaking his head and reaching for a menu. He didn't think Guy would be happy doing that for long. "You hungry? I ain't had nothin' since lunch an' I don't wanna go home drunk. All this heavy talk is okay, but principles don't mean nothin' unless yer well-fed."

Laughing despite himself, Guy picked up his own menu. He didn't tell Jimmy that going home drunk was *exactly* why he'd come here. "Yeah, I could eat somethin'. Some soup, maybe. They say 'soup can cure any illness, whether physical or mental'. So maybe it'll help cure what ails me."

Well, Did Guy play baseball in 1940 or did he give up the game that he'd loved so much and played since he was still wet behind the ears? Did he go to work, as he told Jimmy Rosetti he would?

*   *   *   *

Pine Bluffs, WY
Wednesday, April 5, 2006
703 Beech Street
1:00 p.m.

Remember Guy's oldest brother, Albert? Yes, that's right. The one thought to have been involved with the numbers racket in East Boston. Well, he died in 1940. His death is one of the few items of information I have about Guy and his family during that year. Here's what the *Boston Globe* printed about his accident on Tuesday, October 29th, 1940:

FALLS 55 FEET TO HIS DEATH

Somerville Man Killed at Everett Fuel Plant

Losing his grip on a steel beam 55 feet above the ground because the new gloves he was wearing were slippery, Albert Vitale, 29, of 16 Fountain Avenue, Somerville, plunged to his death from a building in the plant of the Eastern Gas & Fuel Associates, Rover Street, Everett, yesterday. Three other men were killed when a staging collapsed on the same project six weeks ago.

At the time of the accident, he was holding a rope to guide the upward progress of a 600-pound plate being hoisted up to his level where it was to be used for flooring. He was pronounced dead by Dr. Harris Bass, who said he had suffered multiple fractures of the head and body.

He was employed by the Bartlett-Hayward division of the Koppers Construction Company and leaves his wife, Mrs. Elizabeth Vitale and one child.

That one child was a cousin, Jeanne Vitale. Born September 9, 1935, she was only five years old when her father was killed. What this piece does not mention was that Albert's wife, Emma Hughes Vitale, erroneously referred to in this article as "Mrs. Elizabeth Vitale"—it won't come as a shock to anybody who reads newspapers that reporters sometimes get their facts wrong—was pregnant with their second child; my cousin Ronald Albert Vitale, was born shortly after his father died.

"My mother and father were married in 1934 at St. Mary's Church in East Boston," my cousin Jeanne told me. "They lived in an apartment at 20 Breed Street for awhile. But my father got mixed up with the gangs—the Mafia—he stepped on some toes. After they took shots at him and things got too hot, we moved out to Western Massachusetts, and lived in Huntington, in the Berkshires."

"Did you have any first-hand knowledge of this Mafia thing?" I asked.

"Well, no. But when my father died we went to live with my grandmother, Catherine Hughes, at 724 Saratoga Street. I heard these stories from members of the Hughes family."

Apparently Albert and his family had lived quietly in Huntington from 1935 until early 1940, when for some unexplained reason they moved back to the Boston area and took up residence in Somerville.

Al then went to work for the Koppers Construction Company, something which Jeanne did not know. She'd either always been told, or simply understood, that her father was working for New England Coke Company at the time of his death.

Now here's the interesting part. Jeanne has always maintained that her father was done in by the Mafia. Somewhere, somehow, she had heard that "… his safety belt let go. But people said his belt had been cut." Who? She didn't recall.

The *Boston Globe* article describing the incident makes no mention of a cut safety belt or any suspicious circumstances connected with or surrounding Albert's death. I find it difficult to believe that, had his safety belt been cut—and this would have been one of the first things checked by those on the scene, especially the police—they wouldn't have discovered that fact immediately, and begun an investigation. And investigations of that nature are almost impossible to conceal from the press.

Then, there's this. A leather safety belt is several inches thick. To cause it to "let go," a cut would have had to have been a substantial one. If it had been cut, when was the cutting done? If before Albert put it on and ascended to the level from which he fell, why wouldn't he have noticed it as he slipped it around his waist? And why wouldn't one of his co-workers have noticed that his belt was cut or torn as they worked together?

I also find it hard to understand why, if Albert Vitale feared for his life, he'd have returned to Boston with his wife and five-year-old daughter, thereby exposing himself to the continued wrath of his former gang members, if indeed they were former gang members whose wrath was continuing.

And what about the Mafia itself? Was this an instance of Mafia street justice? To be effective as an example to others, the act of "justice" must follow swiftly upon the heels of the perceived transgression. Had the Mafia bosses waited all this time to make an example of Albert Vitale? Surely, if they'd wanted to kill Albert for some reason, they'd have located him in Huntington and wasted him out there. Why would they have waited five years before doing it?

Jeanne Vitale, herself, reveals that once as a little girl in Huntington, she was approached at the corner store by some men who she thought may have been Mafia hit men from Boston. If she was correct, and they were the bad guys, that means the Mafia knew where Albert was. So why didn't they dispose of him at that time? No, there are several explanations as to who those men might have been, and none of them have anything to do with Mafia hit men from Boston.

But there is one story I find difficult to dismiss. Jeanne again: "In 1938 or 1939, my father and mother were visiting my mother's sister, my Aunt Mary Gormley, in East Boston," she related. "A car pulled up in front and my uncle saw some men in it. He told my father to run, and we left by the back door. Those guys sat out there for six hours before leaving."

Who were those men? Did they have any connection to anybody in Albert's past? Apparently, during the "six hours" they stayed there, they made no attempt to enter the apartment and gun Albert down. And if they were bent on killing Albert Vitale, they must have been stupid, indeed, not to have covered the back door, through which my cousin Jeanne claims her father, her mother and she, escaped.

And finally, what was the effect of Albert Vitale's death on his youngest brother, Guy? Several of his siblings had passed away prior to Albert's death, but those deaths had all occurred before Guy was born; Tony, Salvatore, and Bedelia. For Guy, thinking about his brother's death as he returned home from the gravesite on that dismal November morning, I think it had to have been the moment when, for the first time in his life, he understood mortality and death as something close and personal; not just something that happened to someone else's family.

PART FIVE

THE EASTERN
SHORE LEAGUE OF
MARYLAND

CHAPTER 39

Pine Bluffs, WY
Tuesday, April 18, 2006
703 Beech Street
9:45 a.m.

As I mentioned at the beginning of the section dealing with the Twin States League, in November 2000, after a trip to Baseball's Hall of Fame in Cooperstown, New York, my father-in-law, Paul Fenchak brought me a half-page form from their records, showing that Guy had played baseball in 1941 for the Salisbury Indians. Here was conclusive proof that my uncle had actually played professional baseball, although with a minor league team.

Even though I'd lived in Maryland since the age of fifteen, I knew nothing about the Eastern Shore League. But a few phone calls revealed that it was considered a professional league—a Class D league—because its teams were loosely affiliated with major league ball clubs.

Although there's some confusion about it, the Salisbury Indians Baseball Club appears *not* to have been connected to either the Washington Senators or the Cleveland Indians in 1941, even though its former owner, Poppa "Joe" Cambria had been the Senators' chief scout for several years.

With the name "Indians," I thought that perhaps the team had been sponsored by the Cleveland Indians organization. Not so. In fact, that season, the Salisbury Indians were the *only* team in the Eastern Shore League *not* sponsored by any major league team.

When Reubin Levin, Bennington, VT's baseball aficionado, bought the Salisbury team, it was big news in several places. For example, as mentioned in Chapter 36, in Bennington, *The Bennington Banner* ran this story, dated November 8th, 1940:

ATTY LEVIN TO HEAD CLUB
BECOMES PRESIDENT OF SALISBURY, MD, EASTERN SHORE LEAGUE BASEBALL OUTFIT; WEDEMEYER TO ACT AS MANAGER

Word has been received in Bennington and confirmed that Attorney Reubin Levin has become president of the Salisbury, MD, Eastern Shore League baseball team and that John 'Lefty' Wedemeyer, former star Bennington Generals pitcher will probably manage the team. Frank J. Kervan, Mr. Levin says, is to be assistant business manager.

Mr. Levin has long been interested in baseball in Bennington and vicinity and he was largely instrumental in bringing Northern League baseball to Bennington last summer.

Salisbury is the largest town in the Eastern Shore League And it has won the pennant the last three years out of four. In 1937, it won considerable fame and was even called the 'wonder team of the minors' in some quarters when two of its pitchers won over 40 games between them ...

Five Major League clubs have farms in the Eastern Shore League. Salisbury has long been a proving ground for the Washington American League team and has been operated by Joseph C. Cambria, chief scout of the Senators. Mickey Cochrane and Jimmy Fox are perhaps two of the greatest graduates of the league.

Mr. Levin has said that his position as president of Salisbury will not necessitate absence from his office in Bennington except for a few weeks during the summer season.

In this week's Sporting News, the Bennington attorney Stated that, 'I will operate the club along the lines of the Bennington team. About half of my players will come from semi-pro and the other half will be college boys. I have found that these boys get along well together, having a fine spirit of cooperation and make a fine team.'

The Salisbury park has a seating capacity of 3,500. Mr. Levin says, and is equipped with lights for night baseball. Salisbury itself is an attractive, progressive town, he adds, and somewhat larger than Bennington.

Levin, you'll recall, had been a prime mover in Bennington's baseball life, as a contributor and booster of the Bennington Generals. He played a significant role in transferring Bennington from the Eastern New York State League into the Northern League in 1940; a shift that was hugely popular with Bennington area fans.[47]

Maryland's Eastern Shore was predominantly a rural area, separated from the rest of the state by the Chesapeake Bay. Back in those days, sun worshippers reached its pristine beaches by traveling north or south on U.S. Route 40 to Glasgow, Delaware, and then turning southeast on either Highways 13 or 113. For years that was the only route to Ocean City, Maryland and the Federal government's secluded camping facilities at Assateague Island, until the early '50s when construction of the Chesapeake Bay Bridge was completed.

Eastern Shore people were solid, hard-working and unpretentious. Farmers and factory workers, tradesmen and fishermen, they enjoyed their sports; especially baseball. Their rural setting was pretty much a closed system. Periodically, there was talk of seceding from the rest of the state, which they perceived as liberal, out-of-control, and dangerous to their way of life.

Mr. Levin seemed to know how to get things rolling. He spoke early and often with members of the local press in the weeks leading up to opening day of the 1941 baseball season in Salisbury, and when The Eastern Shore League held its organizational meeting in Cambridge, MD on Monday, March 10th, with six cities represented, he was there representing Salisbury. Joe Barnes of Easton, Fred Lucas of Cambridge, John W. Perry of Centreville, Frank R. Grier of Milford, DE, and W. K. Knotts of Federalsburg also attended on behalf of their respective cities.

At this meeting, a rule was adopted allowing players to be signed, released, suspended and reinstated between games of a double header, if necessary.

Before returning to Vermont, Levin set about organizing a Boosters Club in Salisbury, to work in cooperation with the management on the operation of the ball club. About this, he was quoted in *The Salisbury Times,* saying:

"I want to give baseball around here back to the fans. So I urge anyone interested to attend the first Boosters Club meeting tomorrow night."

Since the Indians had won pennants the past three seasons during Cambria's ownership, and while managed by D'Arcey "Jake" Flowers in '38 and '39, and Gus Brittain in '40, when they got off to a 14–0 start, I wondered what he was referring to here. Were these comments, which sounded slightly demeaning, appropriate?

But his words must have had the desired effect, at least early on, because the following night, Tuesday, March 11th, twenty-five baseball fans turned out to meet him and his pilot, Johnny Wedemeyer, at the local Elks Club—a great

---

47   The press in Bennington spelled his name "Rubin." The press on Maryland's Eastern Shore spelled it "Reubin." I don't know which is correct.

turnout on such short notice—and heard the new owner set out his plans for the coming season and pledge his fullest cooperation with the Boosters.

"We want you to feel that this is your club," he said. "We want you to organize into a group that will work with us in seeing that Salisbury is again made one of the best baseball towns in the country." Again, that slightly demeaning tone; dismissive of all past efforts by locals to foster a great baseball atmosphere, which, had Mr. Levin been a bit more perceptive, he would have recognized. Three previous pennants had not been enough to alert him to this truth.

When it was Wedemeyer's turn, he outlined his plans and discussed a few of the ball players who would be coming to Salisbury that spring.

"I think Salisbury will have a young, aggressive ball club rather than a bunch of seasoned veterans whose peak in baseball had been reached in this league," he said.

Johnny also announced plans for a baseball school in Salisbury in April, and he asked those present to send any and all local ball players for a tryout with the Tribe.

"We're anxious to give any local boy a chance to make good in baseball," he added.

After a few remarks from C. Ray Hare, who acted as emcee for the evening, and Judge E. Sheldon Jones, a prominent baseball fan who regularly showed up at Gordy Park, the meeting was adjourned with an agreement to meet again the following week.

Several days later, Levin left town and returned to Bennington. But before leaving, he gave a final interview to *The Salisbury Times*, which was printed on Friday, March 14th, 1941:

LEVIN MAILS CONTRACTS TO
TEN INDIANS
SPRING TRAINING TO GET UNDERWAY APRIL 25

Reubin Levin returned to his home in Bennington, VT today but before leaving, he unloosed a list of 10 players to whom he has mailed contracts.

Coupled with those already signed, Levin said the list might well comprise the Indians' starting lineup next May 8, opening day.

'Of course, we'll have to get a look at them when they report for practice April 24 and 25,' he added.

Three pitchers are on the list, two of whom unmentioned as yet. They are Ace Healy and Frank Jackowitz, both of whom played semi-

pro ball around Boston last year. The third flinger is Leo Venskus, of Mexico, Maine, who has previously been reported as signed. Infielders to get documents are Charles Clariri, Frank Mulkern, Eddie Roubien and Phil Donovan …

And Monday evening, March 24th, *The Salisbury Times* reported the signing of the latter two infielders, Roubien, a second baseman who hailed from Brighton, and Donovan, a shortstop from Roslindale, both in Massachusetts.

Both were sought by manager Johnny Wedemeyer, in his plan to give Salisbury a young, aggressive ball club.
Roubien tried out with the Bennington Generals of the Northern League last year but didn't make the grade.

That's interesting. First, it confirms some of my earlier research, especially what Tony Marro had told me; that in 1939, the Bennington club had played in the Eastern New York State League, but in 1940, when the Northern League expanded, Bennington's team moved into that League and became the Bennington Generals.

Second, that Roubien had tried out with Bennington, in the Northern League, a fast semi-pro league to be sure, but still only semi-pro baseball, and did not make it. Here he is a season later, being signed to a contract by a professional Class D league in Maryland. What's the explanation for this? Reubin Levin in *The Times:*

He didn't get much of a trial, and Johnny seems to think he'll make a ball player.

And Donovan? What was his background? Well, he was nineteen years old and hit .360 for a three-year average in semi-pro ball around Boston. And he could play anywhere in the infield.

On Wednesday, March 26th, *The Times* reported that Reubin Levin had signed Warren J. Healy, a right-handed pitcher, and Henry Ciak, a receiver. Healy, an All-Scholastic selection while in high school in the Boston area, later played with Barnstable on the Cape, Owensboro in the Kitty League, and Woonsocket in the Rhode Island League. In 1940, he pitched for Roslindale in the Boston Parks League, a semi-pro circuit, where he started thirty-nine games and won twenty-three while only losing seven. Ciak came well-recommended, having played in the Northern League in the '40 season where he was the all-star catcher in the loop's annual "dream game."

And here's where another name from Guy Vitale's past surfaces. According to *The Times*, Mr. Levin:

> *... said he hoped to bring the popular Bobby Maier back again this summer. The two have failed to agree on salary, but Rube says they are closer together now than at any time during the negotiations.*

Remember Bobby Maier? He and Guy played together for Barnstable in the Cape Cod League back in 1936. After that, Maier disappeared from Guy's life, but resurfaced on Maryland's Eastern Shore in the summer of '38, when he played for the Salisbury club. He played for the Indians again in '39 and '40. In 1941, here he was apparently playing hard to get in the matter of signing a contract, because as of Wednesday, April 2nd, according to Levin, he was still unsigned but "negotiations were ongoing."[48]

Levin and his young skipper, Johnny Wedemeyer, were at least *trying* to develop a good rapport with Maryland fans on the Eastern Shore. One of the ideas they came up with was to hold a baseball school for local boys, the thinking being, according to Wedemeyer, that "it might be possible to find one or two from this section who could make the grade in organized ball." The camp was to be held prior to April 24th, which was the date set for the start of spring training for the Indians.

And area people, especially members of the Eastern Shore Sports Writers Association, seemed to be responding well to Levin's and Wedemeyer's message, holding a baseball banquet at St. Peter's Episcopal Church Parish House on Friday evening, April 4th, 1941. Seventy-five area dignitaries, including Harry S. Russell, League president, and Ed Nichols, president of the Writer's Association, turned out to listen. With Russell acting as toastmaster, the guests heard William S. Gordy, Jr., Salisbury National Bank president, talk about Eastern Shore Baseball in years past. Of course, Levin and Wedemeyer were also present.

---

48 In 1945, Bobby Maier played for the Detroit Tigers. Under manager Steve O'Neill, he appeared in 129 games, almost all of them at third base. Not a power hitter, in 486 plate appearances for the Tigers, he hit only one home run and drove in thirty-four, for an average of .263. At the end of that season, he went to the World Series with Detroit and hit 1.000, collecting one hit in one plate appearance.

$*$ $*$ $*$ $*$

Salisbury, MD
Monday, April 7 to Sunday, April 20, 1941
Gorsy Field
9:45 a.m.

Excitement was rapidly building. On Monday, April 7th, 1941, *The Salisbury Times* printed this story:

INDIANS [TO] OPEN CAMPAIGN AT HOME MAY 8
ALL-STAR GAME WILL BE PLAYED AT CAMBRIDGE

The Eastern Shore League formally adopted a 110-game schedule here yesterday and at the time began preliminary arrangements for an all-star game.

League president Harry S. Russell said the full schedule will be released on Friday.

Salisbury will open the season Thursday night, May 8th, with Cambridge, returning there the following date for the curtain raiser in that city …

Two other newsworthy developments occurred at the same time, one good, one possibly not so good. Here's what *The Times* said:

LEVIN WONDERS ABOUT PILOT'S
DRAFT STATUS
GETS REPORT WEDEMEYER CALLED BY ARMY

Reubin Levin was wondering today whether or not he has a manager for the coming season and also if there is any truth to the report that Bobby Maier, 1940 utility man, has finally come to terms.

A wire from a Boston friend of Levin's advised that Johnny Wedemeyer had been drafted, but the Indians owner refuses to believe the report until he hears from Wedemeyer.

The big lefthander had an order number which would have made him available at this time, but he telephoned Levin Saturday that he had previously enlisted in the Naval Air Corps reserves and was given a deferment of from three to six months.

> *Mrs. Margaret Mahadey said Saturday that she had received a let-ter from Maier in which he said he had signed his 1941 contract. When Levin arrived here Saturday night to remain until next Thursday, he said he had not yet heard from Maier.*
>
> *"Maybe his contract is in the mail, now," he said.*
>
> *Boston newspapers last week reported that Wedemeyer was in that city looking for baseball talent. The stories also mentioned the fact that Wedemeyer, along with 10 other members of last fall's Boston University football team, had signed up with the air corps reserve.*
>
> *Wedemeyer left Salisbury more than a week ago, telling friends that he expected to return in time to start his baseball school here April 10. During the past month he had received a questionnaire from his local draft board in Chicago.*
>
> *He had made known his air corps affiliation to friends here dur-ing the last few weeks, and Levin today said he was "almost certain" Johnny would be available to manage the Indians.*

Baseball fans are the same everywhere: whether it's St. Johnsbury, Vermont, or Salisbury, Maryland, they like a festive season opener. So a few days later, on April 9th, Reubin Levin announced plans for a "big opening day" at Gordy Field on May 8th. A parade preceding the first game, a band at the field to play during it, and dignitaries from both Salisbury and Vermont were to be in attendance. Nothing small about the man's thinking.

And on Monday, April 14th, *The Times* printed a short article noting that Johnny Wedemeyer, his draft status confirmed, would in fact be available to manage the Indians during 1941. For at least awhile.

Thursday, April 17th brought the news, in an article written by Harry Grayson in *The Times*, that Commissioner of Baseball, Judge Kenesaw Mountain Landis, who had given Boston Bees owner, Charles Francis Adams one year to sever his connections with baseball, was applying pressure on Adams to move along. This, because although Adams owned and operated a chain of grocery stores, he also headed up the Suffolk Downs Racetrack, which in Landis's eyes, made him persona non grata in baseball.

But Adams, whose grace period had now expired, had been attempting to sell the Bees franchise, which, along with the National League's Phillies, and the American League's Athletics, Browns and Senators, was one of the most unprofitable teams during the decade of the '30s. He was asking $400,000, a good price in ordinary times. But with a war on, he'd found no takers, although names like Casey Stengel and Bing Crosby were being bandied about as possible purchasers. Stengel had successfully searched the West Texas oil fields for investment funds, and had come up with $50,000 to invest. Crosby, at first interested, dropped out because of Adams's horse racing connection.

A discordant note was sounded for the Salisbury Indians in a shorter article on that day, letting Eastern Shore fans know that the Indians' baseball camp was off.

BASEBALL SCHOOL OFF BUT INDIANS WANT LOCAL TALENT

Because of his recent business trip to Boston, Johnny Wedemeyer will be unable to hold his baseball school at Gordy Park before the Eastern Shore League race gets under way.

The Salisbury Indians' manager, however, extended an invitation to all local ball-players to turn out for the Tribe's spring training period beginning next week.

Wedemeyer had planned to run the school from April 10 through April 24, at which time most of the Indians are expected here for training.

"I had business in Boston, was unable to get back here in time, and now there's nothing else to do but call it off" he said "I still want all ball players in Salisbury and the surrounding area to come out during our spring practice," he added. "If they've got anything, they'll get a chance to play with the Indians this summer."

Wedemeyer spent some time in Boston looking for more talent for the Tribe. He has 12 signed, but needs a few more to round out the team. Besides those signing contracts several are expected to come here at their own expense to try for the team.

Because he had spent four years at the University of Boston, Wedemeyer, originally from Chicago, had developed ties to the Boston area. Now, with opening day fast approaching and players in short supply, it was only natural for him to turn to Boston baseball talent to fill out his roster. And the team's owner was apparently allowing his young manager free rein in hiring players, limiting himself to sending out contracts to those recommended by Wedemeyer. In fact, Johnny made several trips to Boston prior to the start of spring training, contacting prospective ballplayers.

Meanwhile, Guy Vitale, who had set aside, although perhaps not completely given up, his dream to play professional baseball, was holding down a

Shipfitter's helper's position at the Bethlehem Steel Shipyard in East Boston, with, as far as I know, no plans to play ball in 1941. His lifestyle? His relationship with the Lord at a low ebb, he spent much of his free time in local watering holes around Boston, drinking and carousing until the wee hours of the morning several evenings each week, including Friday and Saturday nights. And on those weekend nights, he did not always go home alone.

*   *   *   *

Salisbury, MD
Monday, April 21 to Wednesday, April 30, 1941
Gordy Field
9:45 a.m.

Between thirty-five and forty players turned out on a sunny and humid day at Gordy Field, to go through their paces in front of Manager Johnny Wedemeyer. The date was Tuesday, April 22nd, 1941. Guy Vitale was not among them.

On hand that day were thirteen players under contract; eleven rookies and only two holdovers. Expenses for these guys would be paid by the club. Any others coming to camp would pay their own way.

Pitchers reporting this first day were Johnny Mikan, Leo Venskus and Warren (Ace) Healy, who, with Wedemeyer, would form the nucleus of the pitching staff. Healy was from East Boston.

Outfielders under contract were Peter Arnold, Joe Sullivan and Bobby Meier. Although he'd been a utility infielder the previous year, Maier was slated to play in the outfield that season.

Infielders included Bernie McLaughlin from Troy, New York at first base, Charles (Chuck) Caliri from Matapan, MA, Eddie Roubien, Phil Donovan and Joe Hood.

Catchers in camp were Hank Ciak and Joe Sandrin.

All these players had previously played semi-pro ball around Boston or other places in New England; except for Sandrin, who hailed from Chicago, and Ciak, who had played ball in the Northern League in 1940 for the Brattleboro, Vermont entry.

An article in *The Salisbury Times* on Monday, April 21st, reported this:

> Other players expected to report are those who have written
> Wedemeyer during the past few weeks asking for tryouts with the Tribe.
> Then he also has a few local fellows who expect to give it a whirl.

One of these is Jim Elliot, Wicomico High twirler who held Seaford hitless last week.

"He looks like a pretty good prospect," Wedemeyer said. He looked at the boy two weeks ago, and now that his arm is in shape, he's anxious to give him another examination.

Other local boys turned up for tryouts that morning; Clinton Hill and Dick Morris, infielders, Jack Mumford and Jim Nichols, both pitchers. All were from Salisbury.

The following day, April 22nd, eight more players arrived in camp, bringing the number to nineteen, and the newspaper reported that Reubin Levin had joined his team in the scheduled workout. After the drills, the few reporters on hand gathered around owner Levin.

"Mr. Levin? How did you like the workout?" one grinning reporter asked.

"Aw, hell," Levin said, clutching his back and camping it up for their benefit. "I'm not at all in shape. But these guys are." He gestured toward the ball players gathering up their equipment as they prepared to leave the field.

"That boy Hank Ciak stood out today," a reporter said. "He's big and rangy, and he seems to know how to handle pitchers."

Levin nodded. "You fellas know he played in the Northern League last year. For the Brattleboro, Vermont team." He smiled. "The fans in Brattleboro banned me from the town for stealing their star catcher."

Three exhibition games had been scheduled for the weekend; two against the London, Ontario Pirates, a farm team of the Pittsburgh Pirates training in Pocomoke City that spring, and the other against the Fitzberger All-Stars, a semi-pro club comprised of all-star players from Baltimore, which competed each summer in the Maryland Club League. At the close of practice on Friday, April 5th, Johnny Wedemeyer announced his roster—tentatively of course. Guy, at that point, was nowhere in the mix:

PITCHERS	AGE:	WGT:	BATS:	THROWS:	HOME TOWN
John Wedemeyer	24	200	L	L	Chicago, Ill.
John Mikan	21	195	L	L	Briar Hill, Pa.
Leo Venskus	22	185	R	R	Mexico, Maine.
Warren (Ace) Healy	22	185	R	R	Boston, Mass.
Frank Hiatt	19	175	R	R	Boston, Mass.
Ed Syren	18	170	L	L	Upper Darby, Pa.
George Lewis	23	165	R	R	Kingston, Pa.

INFIELDERS

Walter Mahoney	19	175	*L*	*L*	*Waltham, Mass.*
Bernie McLaughlin	22	180	*L*	*L*	*Troy, N.Y.*
Charles Caliri	19	180	*R*	*R*	*Boston, Mass*
Phil Donovan	20	170	*R*	*R*	*Boston, Mass.*
William Sullivan	20	185	*L*	*R*	*Boston, Mass.*
Al Gervan	21	180	*R*	*R*	*Boston, Mass.*
John Mulkern	22	175	*R*	*R*	*Boston, Mass.*
Clinton Hill	21	170	*R*	*R*	*Salisbury, Md.*

OUTFIELDERS

Robert Maier	22	185	*R*	*R*	*Dunellen, N.J.*
Peter Arnold	23	190	*L*	*R*	*Wilton, Maine.*
Joe Hood	20	185	*R*	*R*	*Boston, Mass.*
James Nichols	22	185	*L*	*R*	*Salisbury, Md.*

CATCHERS

Henry (Hank) Ciak	22	185	*R*	*R*	*Easthampton, Mass.*
Joseph Sandrin	20	180	*R*	*R*	*Chicago, Ill.*

So, here we had a roster of nineteen players. Ten hailed from Massachusetts; eight from Boston and two from elsewhere in that state. Two team members were from Maryland; both from Salisbury. Two boys came from Pennsylvania, two came from Chicago, two from Maine and one from New Jersey.

By the way, I could find no report of the Friday afternoon game against the London Pirates, but the Tribe split its other exhibition games that weekend. On Saturday, the Indians lost to the fast, semi-pro Fitzberger Club, 9–5 in a loosely-played game. Guy was not there. But they bounced back on Sunday afternoon to defeat the London Pirates, 7–6 in a ten-inning contest. Guy had still not made his appearance.

It's hard to believe that skipper Johnny Wedemeyer was pleased with the showing his boys made against these two semi-pro clubs. After all, Wedemeyer's guys were playing in a "connected" loop, on a club previously affiliated with the Washington Senators in the National League, and were expected to compete against other teams also affiliated with Major League clubs. Worried, he extended practice sessions to four hours daily, hoping to loosen up sore arms and melt off excess poundage, while working on the team's double play combination and drilling his outfielders to hit the cutoff man on relays to the infield. It's reasonable to assume that he was also continuing his shopping spree for ballplayers of a better caliber.

✷   ✷   ✷   ✷

Pine Bluffs, WY
Wednesday, April 19, 2006
703 Beech Street
9:45 a.m.

The question for me at this point became, how did Guy Vitale wind up on the Eastern Shore of Maryland in the summer of 1941? Newspaper articles *did* seem to prove at least two connections between Guy Vitale and Salisbury, Maryland—Reubin Levin *and* Johnny Wedemeyer. But we also had another possible connection between him and Salisbury; Bobby Meier. My attempts to contact Meier in New Jersey failed. But follow that one up with yet another possibility; that Johnny Wedemeyer, on one of his "business trips" to Boston, perhaps the one during which he recruited Healy, became aware of and made contact with Guy. Finally, that Healy or Dom Augliera, with whom Guy had played in the Twin States League, alerted Guy to the fact that the Salisbury Indians were looking for additional players. And what about the possibility that Guy, while working at the shipyard in '40, played semi-pro ball for one of the many Boston Parks League teams active at the time?

Exactly what the connection was between Guy, Reubin Levin and Johnny Wedemeyer may never be known. Was Guy acquainted with them prior to 1941? Had he met them, perhaps, while playing for the St. Johnsbury Senators? If so, where and how did they meet? In view of the so-so season he had turned in that summer, it's hard to believe that they'd have been impressed enough to seek him out two seasons later.

And what did Guy actually do in the summer of 1940? Did he play ball any-where? I can't answer those questions with any certainty, but I can and will speculate.

CHAPTER 40

Pine Bluffs, WY
Thursday, April 20, 2006
703 Beech Street
12:45 p.m.

In calling around, I learned that Baltimore's Enoch Pratt Library owned micro-film copies of *The Salisbury Times,* a daily newspaper published back in the 1940s, which, as we've already seen, contained extensive sports coverage. Did *The Times* cover the Salisbury Indians' games in 1941?

A trip downtown to the Pratt Library resulted in the proverbial pot of gold; *The Times* daily articles covering the Indians' entire '41 season. One, printed Wednesday evening, April 30th, 1941, contained the first of many references to Guy:

> *INDIANS PLAY PARSONSBURG IN EXHIBIT*
> *SALISBURY CLUB WILL FACE HERCULES SATURDAY*
> Leo Venskus was scheduled to hurl for the Salisbury Indians today in their scheduled exhibition game with Parsons—burg at GordyPark. The tilt was set for 5:30 p.m.
>
> Another newcomer joined the ranks yesterday. He is Guy Vitale, a chunky looking outfielder from up Boston way. He may give Arnold and Sullivan a fight for one of the outfield posts.
>
> Signed to a contract earlier this week, he [Vitale] has had several years of semi-pro experience. During the past two seasons he played in the Twin States League and the Cape Cod circuit, a pair of unorganized loops.

So Guy, having arrived on Tuesday, April 29th, was already making his presence felt. Was he actually signed on Monday, April 28th? If so, who signed him, Reubin Levin? Johnny Wedemeyer? Where? In Salisbury? Or was he signed in Boston, during Wedemeyer's earlier trip to that city, from which he returned on

April 17th, saying only that he "had business there," but from which *The Times* correctly deduced that he was "looking for some talent for the Tribe"?

And when the article referred to "the past two seasons," was it talking about the years 1939 and 1940? Although at first glance it would seem so, the piece could only have been referring to 1938 and 1939. Now, try to follow this logic.

In 1940, there was no Cape Cod League; it had folded after the '39 season, and according to Al Irish, did not start up again until after WWII. Al also checked and confirmed that Guy did not play in the Cape Cod circuit in 1939. Therefore, Guy must have been referring to 1938, when we know for a fact that he played at Falmouth.

And we also know Guy played ball in the Twin States League in the summer of 1939, for St. Johnsbury. From the wording of the article, we see that the Twin States League is mentioned first; probably because it was the league in which Guy had played most recently.

Well, you say, he could have played in the Twin States League again in 1940, couldn't he? Or maybe he finally was able to slip himself into the Northern League, where he'd always wanted to play? The answer to both questions is no. Here's why.

First, newspaper reports of the Twin States League's '40 season do not show a Vitale playing for any of the teams that year. That's conclusive proof that he was not back in the Twin States League in 1940.

Second, if Guy had played in the Northern League in 1940, surely he'd have mentioned it to the writer of this article, because he, like most others, knew *that* League was a superior league. But when talking to the reporter, he did not say anything about the Northern League.

But if Guy was referring to 1938 and 1939 when he spoke to *The Salisbury Times* reporter, why didn't he say anything about where he'd played in 1940? What happened to him in 1940? I think we can assume, and I've already made that assumption, that Guy did *not* play ball anywhere that year; that, discouraged, he set baseball aside and went to work in that East Boston shipyard, just as he'd told Jimmy Rosetti he might do.

*   *   *   *

Salisbury, MD
Thursday, May 1 to Saturday, May 10, 1941
Gordy Park
1:45 p.m.

On Thursday evening, May 1st, *The Times* reported the results of that exhibition game against Parsonsburg mentioned above, which our boys won big, 12–1, stating that more new players had arrived in camp and that almost all twenty-five ballplayers had participated in the contest:

> *Johnny Wedemeyer used the clash to give almost everyone on the club a chance to play, and a half dozen new players who arrived here yesterday also saw service for an inning or two.*
>
> *One of the newcomers is a likely-looking infielder from Somerville, Mass. His name is Dominic Augliera and he comes to the Tribe after one previous trial in organized ball. He played a few games with Erie, in the Mid-Atlantic League two years ago.*
>
> *Two outfielders were among the arrivals—Tom Sooy and Dick Haus. Then a new pitcher also came on for trial. He worked one frame and his name is Al DiBirino. Al hails from New York City where he has played several years of semi-pro.*

Time ran out for five players on Friday, May 2nd, as Johnny Wedemeyer rounded his club into final shape by trimming his squad to twenty-four men. Players let go were Al Gervan a second baseman, Bill Sullivan an outfielder, Joe Hood an infielder, and Ed Syren and George Lewis a pair of pitchers. Of this bunch, only Sullivan and Hood had been signed to contracts. The others had come in on their own, seeking to make the club.

The Salisbury Times, after reporting on the cuts, said this:

> *Two other newcomers in the ranks have impressed Wedemeyer. They are Guy Vitale and Dom Augliera. Vitale is an outfielder, while Dom is a shortstop and he seems to be giving Donovan a tough battle for the berth.*

Over the weekend of May 3rd and 4th, the Tribe had scheduled two exhibition contests; one against the Hercules Baseball Club, a pitching duel which they won 3–1, and the other, a Sunday afternoon game against Crisfield, in which Dom Augliera smashed a three-run home run to help defeat an outclassed Crisfield, Maryland team, 14–4, nailing down the shortstop's job for himself in the process.

Against Hercules, Guy played left field, collected two hits in four plate appearances and scored one of his team's three runs while committing no errors. *The Times* noticed:

> *Guy Vitale, one of the new outfielders, broke off a pair of hits in his debut in Tribal livery.*

I could not find the box score of the Crisfield game, but a reference to it in the above-quoted article said the Indians smashed fourteen hits and "a like number of runs," which I take to mean they were also victorious in that contest. But the Hercules game; was that game an indicator of good things to come for Guy?

Opening day had arrived, sunny, warm and humid, amid lots of fanfare—a parade, a band at Gordy Park, and many local dignitaries. The Indians were scheduled to open at home in the afternoon against the Cambridge Cardinals, and then travel to Cambridge that evening to help *that* team open; a day-night doubleheader, if you will. A hundred and ten games needed to be played between May 8th and Labor Day, so day-night ball games and doubleheaders would be numerous.

The Salisbury Indian's opening day lineup looked like this:

PLAYER	POSITION
Caliri,	*3rd Base*
Maloney	*1st Base*
Maier,	*CF*
Arnold	*RF*
Ciak	*C*
Vitale	*LF*
Augliera	*SS*
Kelly	*2nd Base*
Mikan	*Pitcher*

Yes, despite the fact that he'd only been there a week, and despite the fact that he may have taken the 1940 season off, while living a lifestyle incompatible with that of a top-notch, serious athlete, Guy Vitale had beaten out all his competition, impressing his skipper enough to win the starting left fielder's job. Keep in mind that a baseball team generally places its most reliable outfielder in that spot, since so many balls are hit to left field during the games.

The Salisbury Times, in its article on Thursday evening, May 8th, 1941, paid tribute to new Indian's manager, Johnny Wedemeyer:

SETS PRECEDENT IN ORGANIZED BASEBALL
STEPS FROM CAMPUS AND SEMI-PRO
TO MANAGERIAL JOB IN SHO' LOOP

———

It's a long jump from the campus and semi-pro ranks to a managerial berth in organized baseball, but Johnny Wedemeyer set that precedent when he signed last winter to pilot the new Salisbury Indians.

Wedemeyer's athletic career began in a Chicago high school and by the time he was ready for college, a scholarship awaited him at Boston University. His talents numbered baseball, football, basketball and swimming.

A lefthander and switch hitter, Johnny started as a first baseman, but for the past two seasons he has concentrated on pitching which led to recognition from major league scouts.

Wedemeyer met his boss, Reubin Levin, while hurling for the Bennington Generals last summer in the unorganized Northern League. Shortly after that, the latter acquired the Salisbury franchise and signed Johnny to skipper the Indians.

John is 24 years old, is six-foot two inches tall and weighs 200 pounds. A southpaw, he expects to take his regular turn on the mound this summer. His presence gives the Indians two lefthanders to throw against Sho' League opposition.

At Boston University, Wedemeyer took a commercial education [course] preparing himself for a career in business, teaching or coaching.

He turned down major league offers to come here with Rube and his reason is explained when he says, "I believe there is a definite place for a young fellow who understands the game from both the playing side and the business end."

Wedemeyer played varsity football at Boston U. With 11 other members of the team, he joined the Naval Air Corps Reserve and expects to take that up this fall.

The Boston U. angle to his story bears a good omen. Mickey Cochrane, who became one of baseball's greatest players, left that college to play ball in the Eastern Shore League with Dover in 1923.

A fine tribute to the team's young, inexperienced manager, and a vote of confidence, too, for the man who'd put together their city's team that season.

Friday evening's *Times,* on May 9th, reported the results of the first of the opening day games. It seems our gang lost their opener in front of approximately a thousand home fans, 12–10. Pitching was the problem. Johnny Mikan started the tilt, but the lefthander from Briar Hill, Pennsylvania, was removed from the game in the top of the seventh, leading 10–4. He'd given up four runs on five scattered hits, before a sore arm forced his departure.

Then the sky fell. Three other pitchers, including Wedemeyer, could not find the plate and walks loaded the bases several times, setting the stage for run-scoring singles. By game's end the Tribe had collected eleven hits but had given up twelve runs and blown a six-run lead, while Caliri, Ciak and Kelly each committed a miscue. Guy? Oh fer. Not an auspicious start. Chalk it up to opening day jitters. Still, the game probably left a sour taste in the mouths of Salisbury fans, who had watched a championship club perform in their town for the past several seasons.

The evening game at Cambridge was rained out, which allowed the boys to get some rest after the stress and excitement of those opening day activities.

On Friday, May 9th, the Indians were set to travel to Cambridge for that city's home opener. But that game, too, was called late Friday afternoon because of rain. The Indian's next game was at home Saturday night against the Federalsburg Athletics. I don't have the box score, but there's a reference in the article quoted below describing their win on May 10th, that Guy had a great day with the stick, going three for five.

The Salisbury Times issue of Saturday, May 10th, carried a photo of the Tribe's outfield. Captioned, *Indian's Picket Line,* it said:

> *Here's the starting outfield array Johnny Wedemeyer will throw at the Federalsburg A's at Gordy Park tonight. Those first two clubbers from left to right, Guy Vitale and Pete Arnold, are still unknown factors Bobby Maier, far right, is starting his fourth year with the Tribe as a .300 hitter.*

*   *   *   *

Salisbury, MD
Saturday, May 10 to Saturday, May 17, 1941
Gordy Park
6:00 p.m.

Well, after an opening loss and two rainouts, the Tribe had a successful weekend, scalping Federalsburg on Saturday evening, 9–7, and then doing it again on Sunday, 3–1. Guy faired well that weekend, too. Here's how the newspaper, on Monday, May 12th, described those games:

> HURLERS SHOW FORM. INDIANS WIN
> 'ACE' HEALY TURNS IN THREE-HIT, 10-INNING
> GAME AT FEDERALSBURG
>
> ---
>
> *A superb three-hit, ten-inning pitching job by Warren 'Ace' Healy, the steady chucking of Leo Venskus and some timely swatting by the*

batting cast enabled the Salisbury Indians to break into the win column over the weekend.

At Federalsburg yesterday, Healy ruined that city's opening day festivities by holding the home forces to three safeties, while his mates put together the markers in the 10th round for a 3–1 triumph.

Saturday night, before a chilled handful of the faithful at Gordy Park, Venskus hurled persistently to give the Tribe a 9–7 win over the little A's.

Thus the Indians, after losing their opener to Cambridge when their pitching fell apart, bounced back into the infant Eastern Shore League race.

The Tribe hitters were not to be outdone, however, in a weekend filled with first class hurling. Saturday night they collected 14 safeties off three A's chuckers. One of those was Bobby Maier's first home run of the season.

Yesterday they solved Reisburg for three tallies in the tenth inning to reward Healy for his pitching masterpiece.

Maier started the Sabbath rally with a single and stepped all the way home when Pete Arnold bashed a triple to distant places. As Meier reached the plate, the throw-in hit him in the neck and he collapsed to the dirt. Recovering in a half daze, he managed to fall across the dish for the Tribe's first run.

Hank Ciak kept the attack going with another safety that scored Arnold. Then, just to insure the victory, Guy Vitale, who had three for five Saturday night, banged a double off the fence to score Ciak.

A couple of free passes, a force out at second and a fly ball brought in the A's only run in their half of the overtime inning.

Besides handcuffing the little A's Healy fanned 10 and kept them under control throughout. Troubled by a sore arm during spring training, Healy is believed ready to take his turn on the hill.

Venskus hurled his second nine inning game Saturday night to win his first start in the Eastern Shore League. He limited the visitors to nine hits and displayed plenty of heart when he pitched out of a couple of tight spots. He struck out eight and walked but three.

Bobby Meier's homer hit the shirt factory roof in the fourth inning and scored Walt Mahoney ahead of him. The blow was one of three for the evening.

> *Everyone in the Tribe batting order had at least one hit with the exception of Dom Augliera, who managed to walk twice. Caliri and Arnold each had doubles …*

Meanwhile, in the Majors, the Cleveland Indians were leading the American League after four full weeks of play, while the New York Yankees were firmly ensconced in fourth place, as only two of their hitters, Bill Dickey (.371) and Joe DiMaggio (.320), were hitting over .300.

The local Indians didn't rest on their laurels after a good weekend. On Monday, May 12th, they stopped the Centerville Red Sox 4–1, behind the pitching of Jimmy Menz, a rookie from New Jersey, who looked good until he walked three Sox to load the bases in the ninth without recording an out. But Johnny Wedemeyer's relief effort was successful; he struck out the side to end Centreville's threat.

Guy again patrolled left field and collected one hit in four plate appearances. Bobby Meier, who had won the starting assignment in center field, extended his hitting streak to four, and, just like that, the Indians had a three-game winning streak going.

The following night, Tuesday, May 13th, Centreville suffered another defeat at the Indian's hands, but it took three Tribe hurlers, Menz, Hiatt and Wedemeyer, to subdue them, 9–6.

Bottom of the third, the bases loaded. Herb Kelly and Mahoney each had singled. Bobby Maier and Pete Arnold had struck out, but Mahoney moved to second on Ciak's grounder to Centreville's third baseman, Eddie Walls, whose high toss to first pulled Di Cesare's foot off the bag. Two down. The Salisbury fans were in the game, howling for a hit, as Guy stepped to the plate, worry lines creasing his brow.

When a hitter comes up to bat with the bases loaded, he's under pressure to put the ball in play and bring those runners home. With two outs, that batter's under even more pressure. Only a hit will do the trick. If he makes an out, the inning's over; the fans remember. The manager does, too. So Guy was concentrating hard on just one thing as he stepped into the batter's box; make good contact, get the fat part of the bat on the ball and drive it into the outfield.

The runners took their leads; Kelly in foul ground off third, Mahoney, a few feet off second, Ciak, from first, not being held. Guy didn't need to check his third base coach for the bunt sign; with two outs, it wasn't a bunting situation. He focused on Maire, trying to pick up the ball as it left the pitcher's hand, to see if it was going to be a fastball or curve, so he could adjust a split second sooner. Maire wound and threw. It was heat, inside, and Guy backed off.

Figures he'll work me inside, Guy thought. Maire toed the rubber again, wound and fired. Another fastball, inside again and Guy let it go by, but the umpire liked it on the corner for strike one. Guy again backed out, picked up some dirt, frowned at the ump and stepped back in. *Just meet the ball,* he thought. *Drive it up the middle.* One and one, the count.

Now, Maire was out there on the mound, trying to outguess the hitter. He was thinking that Guy had not seen a curve yet, so he would be expecting one on this pitch. So he tried to cross him up with another fastball, inside. But Guy, guessing heat on the inside corner again, had moved back in the box a bit. He was right on this one. Stride. Perfect swing, arms extended, wrists breaking at just the right time. The fat part of the bat met the ball and … drove it right back over the pitcher's mound and into center field. Base hit, and both Kelly and Mahoney scored as Guy pulled up at first with his only hit of the game, two RBI's, and a huge grin on his face. The Tribe added three more runs in the sixth, and then hung on to win it. Their win streak was now at four.

On Friday, May 16th, the Indians beat the Easton Yanks 14–10, in a slugfest that lasted two hours and thirty-five minutes, and saw Guy moved up in the batting order from fifth to third. He delivered a hit and scored two runs himself, apparently having reached base via walks. This game featured some sensational play in right field by Bernie McLaughlin, the Troy, New York railroad fireman, who had started in place of Pete Arnold. The win pulled the Indians into a tie for second place in the League standings.

On Saturday, May 17th, *The Times* published batting averages for Tribe players. Bobby Maier led the team with a .483 average. Mahoney was next at .454, followed by Donovan at .333, Augliera at .296, Arnold at .280, Kelly at .217. Guy, despite the good days with the bat in games mentioned, was hitting only .200.

That evening, Saturday, May 17th, the Tribe lost a tilt to Easton in a ten-inning struggle, 7–6, when the little Yankees shoved across a pair of runs in the tenth inning.

*   *   *   *

Salisbury, MD
Sunday, May 18 to Saturday, May 31, 1941
Gordy Park
6:00 p.m.

This two-week stretch saw the Salisbury club win four and lose four, and take a firm grip on third place in the League, behind the streaking Milford Giants, but closing on the Federalsburg Athletics.

But by Sunday, May 18th, the Indians were in second place. On that day, in a 15 inning epic, they rallied for six runs in the fifteenth, to defeat Federalsburg, 11–5. That extra inning game, the longest to date in the Eastern Shore League, enabled the Tribe to hold onto its recently acquired tie with the A's for second. Menz started the game for the Indians but gave way to Wedemeyer in the sixth, who went the rest of the way and got credit for the win, giving up only five base knocks, striking out ten and walking one. It was the second game this season in which he'd gone nine innings. It also saw Bernie McLaughlin, the acrobatic right fielder who'd wrested that position from Pete Arnold, crash into the fence so hard that he had to be removed from the field. Arnold took his place and rapped out three hits.

Bobby Maier hit safely both Saturday and Sunday that weekend, running his consecutive game hitting streak to ten in a row. Guy, who'd been moved up from fifth to fourth on the strength of a couple of good games with the bat, went only one for eight that day, a mini-slump that all hitters go through, but which can play hell with a fella's already-low batting average, and bring on additional pressure.

Also, three new players were added; Orest "Smokey" Intindola, a pitcher from Nutley, New Jersey, Hilliard Murray, another pitcher from Spring Hope, North Carolina, and Joe Castoro, a backstop from Hopewell, New Jersey.

On Monday evening, May 19th Intindola made his debut on the mound for the Tribe, and he did well, going nine innings and tossing a three-hit shutout at Federalsburg, as the Indians won it, 7–1, solidifying their hold on second place. Guy, playing left field again, collected three hits in five plate appearances while batting in the number three hole. Here's *The Salisbury Times*:

> *In the eighth, Augliera doubled to left and scored on two successive wild pitches. Guy Vitale, heavy hitting left fielder, had a big night both in the garden and at the plate. He drove out three straight singles to figure in the run-making. Then in the ninth, he saved Intindola possible embarrassment with a running, diving catch of Lewis's hard liner.*
>
> *Vitale raced near the fence, stretched out his arms and grabbed the ball. After that he fell, rolled over into the barrier, holding the ball so the umpire could see. The stands gave him a great hand.*

So you can see what this fella could do when he was keeping his nose clean; getting into bed early at night—alone—and cutting out the drinking.

However, a week later, our boys were back in third place behind the Easton Yanks and Cambridge, having lost several games and evening their record at eight wins and eight losses. Two of their losses were to the first-place Milford Giants, hottest team in the League at that time, 5–4 and 10–2. With those victories, the Giants equaled the Eastern Shore League record for consecutive wins by tying the record of fourteen, set twice before—by the Salisbury Indians.

In the 10–2 loss on Sunday, May 25th, Guy, hitting in the lead-off spot, laced two hits in four trips, but did not figure in the scoring, while teammate Bobby Maier hit a home run.

The following evening, Milford set a new consecutive win record at fifteen, with its victory over Centreville, while the Indians beat Easton, 2–1. Guy batted in the third slot in that game and picked up one hit in four appearances at the dish *The Salisbury Times,*

> *The Salisbury Indians made the most of their six scattered hits last night at Gordy Park to register a 2–1 triumph over the Easton Yanks as the Tribe snapped a two game losing streak.*
>
> *Both runs were driven in by Guy Vitale, who singled in the fifth to score Murray with the tying run. Then in the seventh, he came up with two on and batted in Herb Kelly.*

That night, the Indians won an eleven-inning, pressure-packed game against Easton, 7–5, to crawl within percentage points of second place, behind Milford and Cambridge. Leo Venskus hurled the full eleven innings, scattered ten hits, walked only three and fanned six. Guy, who went one for six, and Bobby Maier, who doubled in the eleventh, were the run makers who brought home the victory. After the game, Tom Sooy, Chuck Caliri and Pete Arnold were handed their walking papers by Reubin Levin.

The Milford Giants? Ran their consecutive win streak to sixteen in a row with a 9–3 win over the Centreville Red Sox.

On Friday, May 30th, the Indians split a doubleheader with the Cambridge Cardinals, losing in the afternoon, 4–3, and bouncing back in the nightcap, 1–0. In the loss, Guy had another good game with the wand, going three for five, driving in a run and scoring two of his team's three. But in the second game, he was oh-fer, finishing with three hits in nine plate appearances on the day.

In response to questioning by a reporter for *The Times* after the second game, Guy said: "Ya know, this is sure a wonderful game. We've been playin' it since we were kids. But the one thing baseball does is test you mentally at some point during each season. That's true whether you're hittin' .400 because you're always gonna go back down. And it's true if you're hittin' .100 because you're always gonna go back up. But at some point, it tests you, and right now it's testin' me. I can't seem ta put two good games back ta back with my bat."

On Saturday, May 31st, the League standings looked like this, as the Tribe was set to meet the league-leading Milford Giants at Gordy Park that evening:

TEAM	W	L	PCT.
Milford Giants	19	3	.864
Cambridge Cardinals	11	9	.550
Salisbury Indians	12	10	.545
Easton Yankees	8	13	.381
Federalsburg Athletics	8	15	.348
Centreville Red Sox	7	15	.318

The hitting stats were also printed on that date. Walt Mahoney was leading the Salisbury club with a .354 average. Bobby Maier was next at .325. Guy, who was keenly aware of his streakiness at the plate, did not make the list, although it showed hitters' averages all the way down to several players tied at .250.

*   *   *   *

Salisbury, MD
Sunday, June 1, 1941
Gordy Park
6:00 p.m.

From a baseball point of view, Guy's best game of the summer, and if not *the* high point, certainly *one* of only a few highpoints of his first season in professional baseball, came in a crucial game against first place Milford on Sunday, June 1st, 1941. Shame it was wasted in a losing team effort. Ironically, it would spawn the low point of Guy's season as well. Here's what *The Salisbury Times* said about the game:

VITALE HITS TWO HOMERS BUT INDIANS LOSE
GIANTS RALLY IN SEVENTH TO KEEP UP RUSH

MCKINNON'S HOME RUN WITH TWO
ABOARD CLIMAXES GAME

Despite two home runs from the bat of Guy Vitale, Salisbury's Indians lost to the Milford Giants yesterday, 8–4, as the league lead-

ers wiped out the Tribe's early lead with a six run rally in the seventh round.

The Redskins were enjoying a 3–2 edge going into the stretch frame and with Leo Venskus holding the Giants in check, the Tribe seemed on its way to its first victory over the pace-setter.

Mac McKinnon climaxed the big seventh with his eighth home run of the season with two mates aboard. Coming after three others had previously scored, the blow gave the Giants the ball game.

Venskus lost his second game of the season as the Delawarians pounded his offerings for 12 hits. He has won three …

Vitale's two home runs kept the Tribe in the ball game until McKinnon matched one of them in the seventh frame. Besides those two Ruthian swats, Guy had a pair of singles for a perfect day at the dish.

CHAPTER 41

Salisbury, MD
Monday, June 2 to Sunday, June 15, 1941
Gordy Park
6:00 p.m.

Monday, June 2nd was an off-night around the Eastern Shore League, but on Tuesday the Indians were shut out by the Centreville Red Sox at Centreville, 5–0. Guy? He was given his first night off since the opener. Johnny Wedemeyer patrolled left field, and a newcomer, Jim Campbell, a refugee from the Centreville club, played right field, as Guy was "on the sick list." Salisbury's record fell to twelve and twelve, while Milford won again, raising its record to twenty-one wins against only three losses.

Nothing was said about the nature of Guy's illness, but I'm going to speculate that after perhaps months on the wagon and obediently observing curfew, Guy celebrated his Sunday perfect day at the plate with a night on the town, from which he had not recovered sufficiently by game time the next day.

Did that sort of thing happen often in professional baseball? I think so. Probably less from celebrating good days, than from combating or dealing with the bad ones. In his book, *Beating the Bushes,*[49] Frank Dolson said this:

> *It's difficult getting accustomed to the pro baseball lifestyle: the long road trips, the three, four, even five days spent at a single place, the seemingly endless hours of sitting around, waiting to go to the ball park. Add that to the pressure of playing night after night, of sinking into one of those devastating slumps that even the good hitters go through, of making one bad pitch in the ninth inning and having it cost you a ball game or, even worse, of having somebody make a bad*

---

49   Frank Dolson, *Beating the Bushes,* Icarus Press, South Bend, IN. 1982.

play behind you or getting a bloop hit off you with the game on the line.

Is it any wonder that baseball and booze go together like ham 'n' eggs, like George Steinbrenner and turmoil, like scotch and soda?

To put it bluntly, there are a lot of men who develop drinking problems in pro baseball, and some out-and-out alcoholics. You'll find them in the dugouts, on the playing fields, in the front offices.

I think Guy was no different from countless other young men playing their first year in professional baseball. Drinking is a part of the game, so much so that it's a serious problem which often begins in the minors, where young ballplayers first find themselves with all that pressure to handle and lots of time to kill. Guy, the all-American boy who never drank, smoked or stayed out late while in high school, had been developing a susceptibility to alcohol abuse and an inclination toward pre-marital sex for at least three years, since his New York "caper" near the end of 1937. So, in Salisbury, a city of some two hundred thousand people and many hospitable bars, when, each night after the game, the older players would head for the nearest pub, Guy was not going to refuse to accompany them.

Meanwhile, funeral services for Lou Gehrig, who died on Monday, June 2nd, 1941, were held at a little vine-covered Episcopal Church around the corner from his home in the Bronx. Hundreds of prominent, somber baseball personages, including Gehrig's teammate, Babe Ruth, filed past his handsome mahogany coffin, and offered condolences to his widow. Afterwards, Ruth was reportedly seen in tears.

From Tuesday to Friday evening, there appears to have been a gap in the schedule. That was alluded to in the description of Friday's game as *Back on the Eastern Shore League warpath after almost a week of idleness ...* Perhaps it was bad weather. But the Indians came back to suffer a crushing defeat at the hands of Easton, 7–1, on Friday, June 6th. The loss left them a full game behind the second place Cardinals, whom they were scheduled to meet at their home field on Saturday. Guy went oh for four in that game, but on Saturday, June 7th, the latest stats were printed, and Guy's average was up to .256; he was definitely doing somewhat better at the dish.

But for the Indians as a team, things were not going well. *The Times* on Monday, June 9th, after noting that they'd won two out of three games over the weekend, announced the call-up of manager Johnny Wedemeyer to Uncle Sam's Naval Air Corps flight training program. Bobby Maier was named to succeed him in the managerial post:

> *Reubin Levin, owner of the Tribe, said that his 24-year-old south-paw pilot will bow out of the Eastern Shore League tomorrow evening at Gordy Park, taking the hill against the Federalsburg A's.*

Wedemeyer's swan song was a 6–2 triumph over Federalsburg on Tuesday, June 10[th.] Although he gave up fourteen hits overall, he bore down with men on base, striking out nine. Three double plays by his infield also helped. Guy went one for four with a stolen base. The win put the Indians into undisputed possession of second place, one game over .500; their record was fifteen wins and fourteen losses.

That Friday evening, June 13th, was scheduled to be Bobby Meier Night at Gordy Park. The plan was for Maier to sign his new contract as manager of the club during a ceremony at home plate, and receive a trophy for his service to the team during this and the previous three seasons. However, a drenching rain forced the game's postponement, although Maier took over the club that night.

And his first two games as manager of the Indians turned out well: a come-from-behind victory on Saturday, June 14th, against the Easton Yankees, 4–3, in ten innings, and a repeat of that fete Sunday afternoon, June 15th, winning 5–0, as Hilliard Murray tossed a four hit shutout at Easton. Guy was one for four, a double, and seemed to be in a not-so-hot groove of some sort, hitting at a .250 clip. That's not great for an outfielder.

But the Indian's fine showing over that weekend cut the Milford Giants lead to eight games, as Centreville helped a bit by whipping Milford twice. However, the Little Giants were still running away from the competition with a 25–7 record. Not a good thing for attendance around the League.

*   *   *   *

Salisbury, MD
Monday, June 16 to Friday, June 27, 1941
Gordy Park
6:00 p.m.

On Thursday evening June 19th, a smallish Ladies Night crowd of about five hundred fans watched the Indians slip past the Cambridge Cardinals, 4–3. Guy again went only one for four, but was given an ovation by the crowd for a great catch of Czaplicki's smoking liner in the eighth inning, to save at least one run.

A week later, on Friday, June 27th, Centerville, aided and abetted by new faces in their lineup, slipped into second place after handing Federalsburg a 9–7 licking, and the Senators took on the league-leading Milford Giants. Although Bobby Maier sent Leo Venskus to the hill, the Giants proved way too much for him and won the game 7–1, and Guy hurt his right leg and came up limping after attempting a diving catch of a line drive down the left field line in Milford's half of the seventh,.

Although he finished the game, Guy's injury proved more severe than anyone thought. But Guy knew it. And that's serious pressure. Here he was trying to make it in pro ball, and *this,* his first serious injury since he began playing baseball back at Blackinton Elementary School, had to happen. He was affected so badly that, after an unnerving session with the club's physician early that evening, he headed straight for a local watering hole, where he stayed until after 1:00 a.m., missing the surprise bed check pulled by his manager earlier that evening. His escapade was reluctantly reported to Reubin Levin the following morning.

*   *   *   *

Salisbury, MD
Saturday, June 28, 1941
Gordy Park
10:30 a.m.

"This isn't the first time Guy's missed bed check," Maier informed his boss. "After he hit them two home runs in that game a few weeks ago, he was out celebratin' several nights in a row."

Levin's brow furrowed. "Ya don't say."

"And that ain't all," Maier jerked a thumb in the direction of the door. There's a reporter from *The Times* outside. Says he's checkin' on a report that Guy was seen at a local bar early this morning."

"Aw, shit!" Levin said. "That's jest what we need."

"What should we do?"

Annoyed, wrestling with the team's financial problems, and under strain due to concern over his terminally ill mother, Levin made a snap decision. "I'll talk ta the reporter," he said. "You get Vitale in here, Bobby. I need ta talk ta *him,* too."

*   *   *   *

Salisbury, MD
Saturday, June 28, 1941
Gordy Park
12:00 p.m.

"Come in and sit down, Guy," Reubin Levin said an hour later as his young left fielder entered the small, windowless office under the grandstand at Gordy Park where the owner held forth. Levin, tie off, shirt collar open and sleeves rolled up in the sultry heat, gestured toward the vacant chair next to the one in which Bobby Maier was sitting.

"You sent for me?" Guy asked, shifting his weight off his injured leg. Feeling outnumbered, he nodded at Maier and sat, a worried look on his face.

"Yes, son, I did." Levin responded, adopting his fatherly tone. "You had a great game Sunday the first of June. Two homers in one day? Not too common around here."

"Thank you, sir."

"And you celebrated pretty hard that night, right?" Levin asked.

Guy looked startled. "Yes, sir."

"And for several nights after that, too," Bobby Maier added, tugging at his forelock.

"Celebrated so hard you weren't in any condition to play ball for a couple games," Levin rejoined, casting a baleful eye at his young left fielder. "So, Johnny had to give you some time off."

"Well, I …" Guy began. But Maier cut him off. "We don't have an official curfew rule around here, but we *do* conduct random bed checks," he said. "Johnny and I came by your room several nights that week. We know you weren't in bed by ten at least three nights in a row."

Guy, his face and neck crimson, lowered his eyes but said nothing.

Levin tapped some papers on his desk with a finger. "I got a report from the doc on your leg, this morning. Says you'll need at least a week." He sat back in his chair. "There was a *Times* reporter in here this morning, young fella," Levin continued. "He had a report that you'd been seen almost every night that week at a bar over on 8th Street, until the wee hours of the morning. Also last night. You wanna comment on that?"

"No, sir."

"It's true, then?"

"Yeah."

Levin turned to his new manager. "The other players know about this?"

"Some do. We're like most of the other clubs. At least two, maybe three heavy drinkers. For all I know, they may have been together last night."

The attorney-owner looked tired. He heaved a long sigh. "Guy, you know we can't tolerate this kind of thing," he said. "If all the players did it, the local press would be highly critical."

"And the fans." Maier added. "What would they think? We're already having trouble pulling them through the gates as it is."

Levin sighed again and leaned back in his chair. "I'm sorry, Guy, but I'm gonna have ta suspend ya for a few games," he said sternly. "We'll try ta keep it quiet, because the fans like you. They have a good impression of you. The other fellas will know, but we'll keep it inside the club, if we can."

"Should I leave town and go home?" Guy asked despondently.

"No. Rest the leg and keep a low profile 'til ya hear from me. It won't be long."

The three men stood. As Guy turned to leave, Reubin Levin said, "While you're off, Guy, I want ya ta stop and think. You've been given a chance to play professional baseball because you have some ability. In the field, you perform like a major leaguer. Your hitting needs work, but it's comin' along. Not many men can do what you can do. Don't mess up. If you really wanna play in the Bigs, show us when you come back."

That day, Saturday, June 28th, this item appeared in the *Salisbury Times:*

> *Injuries struck both Milford and the Indians in the recent series. Guy Vitale suffered a bruised leg and will be out for several days. Nick Solomon and Chick Price, Milford outfielders, are both out of the lineup with bone bruises.*

So that's how I see it. Because of his departure from the wagon, Guy was suspended. That suspension was papered over; covered up by the leg bruise he'd suffered, in order not to embarrass either him or the team. And Guy, knowing he'd deserved it, was not resentful. He simply did what he could to speed recovery from his injury while waiting out the suspension.

But to make matters worse for him, a newcomer, Larry Maranucci, from Albany, New York, arrived around the 28th of June, and was promptly inserted into left field in the series against Centreville. Maranucci marked his debut with two hits. Here's the way *The Times* described it on Monday, June 30th, 1941:

> *Larry Maranucci, the new left fielder, made an impression on the home fans Saturday night. He broke off two hits and walked twice,*

leading off the last inning of the second game with a double that started the winning three-run rally.

On Monday, *The Times* also reported that on Sunday, June 29th, New York Yankee slugger, Joe DiMaggio, in front of thirty-one thousand wildly-cheering fans, shattered former St. Louis Cardinal great George Sisler's nineteen-year-old record of hitting safely in 41 straight games His double in the first inning against the Senators tied Sisler's record, and his single in the seventh broke it.

In the same edition, the Eastern Shore League looked like this as of the last day of June:

TEAM	WON	LOST	PCT
Milford	34	11	.756
Salisbury	24	23	.511
Cambridge	24	23	.511
Centreville	24	24	.500
Easton	18	28	.391
Federalsburg	16	31	.340

At the same time, Reubin Levin, driven to the brink by poor attendance, was dipping into his own pocket to pay his ballplayers their full salaries. To attract more fans, he conceived a not very original plan; reduce ticket prices. *The Times* reported it this way:

INDIANS WILL SELL REDUCED PRICE TICKETS

ATTENDANCE DRIVE TO FILL EMPTY SEATS IS PLANNED

A campaign to fill empty seats at Gordy Park by selling 25,000 general admission tickets at a greatly reduced price will begin shortly, Reubin Levin, owner of the Salisbury Indians said today.

"We're going to try to make it as easy as possible for every fan in Salisbury and the surrounding area to support the Indians," Levin said as preparations were being made for the drive.

"I've already lost about $5,000 in this year's ball club," the little Vermont attorney admitted. "I'm anxious to keep baseball in Salisbury and I'm willing to take my present loss if the fans will just come out and keep the club going the rest of the season."

*   *   *   *

Salisbury, MD
Thursday, July 10 to Sunday, July 27, 1941
Gordy Park
7:00 p.m.

Although it's difficult to believe that *The Salisbury Times*, which followed the Indians so closely, would not have reported something more about Guy Vitale's absence, my search while at the public library in Baltimore found nothing else on this matter than what I've already described. Later, in June 2006, a search by Ginny Young and her assistant Nicole, at the Wicomico County Library in Salisbury, revealed only the information about the leg injury. I'm not even sure the fans *knew* he'd been suspended. They may have thought he had just been benched for awhile because of the injury or because of his spotty hitting.

In any event, on Thursday, July 10th, 1941, *The Times* reported on a dramatic, eleven-inning Indians win the night before over the first-place Milford Giants, 1–0, and Guy was still missing from the lineup. But in another article printed the same day, the paper reported this:

> Reuben Levin, owner of the Salisbury Indians, announced the sale last night of Dom Augliera to the Wilmington Blue Rocks of the Interstate League.
>
> Augliera, a fixture at shortstop since the season started, will report today to the Rocks, a member of the Philadelphia A's farm system.
>
> Poor attendance here this season made necessary the disposal of Augliera, Levin said.
>
> The reported sale price was $500, a figure far under that which Levin figured his promising recruit would be worth had he played out the season here.
>
> "I hated to do it," Levin said. "But with the poor crowds and general lack of baseball interest here, I had to let him go in order to keep the team operating here."
>
> Augliera was conceded as the shortstop prize of the year in the current Eastern Shore League season. He fielded well and with Jack Campbell, formed a double play combination which has already registered 37 twin killings. On top of that, he hit around .290.
>
> Manager Bobby Maier is expected to slip in at short to replace the departing Augliera and the club re-instated Guy Vitale to round out the outfield.

> *"It's a tough break for the faithful fans," Rube explained. "But something had to be done so that they could still have their baseball here."*
>
> *Attendance here as in other Eastern Shore League towns has been far below expectations. The strain was felt more here, however, because the club has no affiliation with the majors. Other outfits are partially financed by the big clubs.*
>
> *One crowd of 800 paid admissions watched the Indians opening night. Since then, top has been about 600 with a general average of about 300. Reduced prices, put in effect to lure the fans, have also cut the club's revenue, Levin said.*

So the Club actually went through with its reduced price ticket campaign, but apparently that did little or nothing to lure the fans back to Gordy Park. And amid gathering financial woes besetting his team, Guy Vitale was back on the Salisbury Indians team, re-instated on Wednesday, July 9th, to "round out the outfield." However, the time off may have been good for Guy. He marked his return to the lineup by going three for four and scoring three runs on Thursday evening, July 10th, in a 6–4 win over—the first-place Milford Giants again. *The Times* said this:

> *Putting on a revamped batting order, Maier went to short in place of Augliera, Guy Vitale resumed his duties in left field, and Henrickson went to center. Maranucci moved over to right.*
>
> *Manager Maier, who performed sensationally at short, drove in three of his club's six runs with his fourth home run of the year and a single.*
>
> *He and his mates clubbed Chris Hayden for 14 hits. Henrickson and Vitale had three blows apiece while Walt Mahoney came up with two as did Hank Ciak.*

This was only the second time the Indians had beaten Milford all season, but it cut the streaking Giant's lead to ten and a half games, while strengthening the Tribe's hold on second place. Cambridge and Centreville were tied for the third position, at this point.

Well, things changed quickly in the League that season. Between Thursday, July 10th, when they were in second place, and Tuesday, July 15th, when they handed the Cambridge Cardinals a 6–0 trouncing, the Indians had apparently been in a slump, because the report of this game has them moving up to a tie with the Cards for third place.

In the game on July 15ᵗʰ, Guy played left field again, rapped out two hits in four appearances at the dish, one of which was a double, drove in two runs, and scored two of his team's six runs. But sorry to say, by Thursday, July 17ᵗʰ, he was also slumping; an oh for four game at the plate, although to be fair, he *was* robbed of a sure single by Centreville's second baseman, Eddie Walls, who had a great game in the field and at the plate to help his club defeat the Indians in ten innings, 2–1.

Also on that date, the longest hitting streak in the Majors came to an end at fifty-six games, as Joe DiMaggio went hitless against the Cleveland Indians. 67,468 fans, the largest night crowd in baseball history, had jammed Cleveland's Municipal Stadium to see if DiMaggio could extend his consecutive game streak. Instead, they watched Ken Keltner make two sensational plays behind third base, and Lou Boudreau gather up DiMaggio's sharp grounder to short and turn it into a double play, to bring the streak to an end.

On Friday, July 25ᵗʰ, Guy had another two fer game, this one in an 8–4 loss to the Athletics; he rapped out a single and double, scoring both times. But the next day, the Eastern Shore League Averages recorded batting statistics for all players all the way down to .250, and Guy's name was not among them.

*   *   *   *

Salisbury, MD
Thursday, July 31 to Saturday, August 23, 1941
Gordy Park
8:00 p.m.

By the end of July, the weather was not the only thing that was hot on Maryland's Eastern Shore. The Milford Giants were making a shambles of the League's pennant race. Their record? Forty-nine wins and nineteen losses. Milford's closest competition was Cambridge, nine games behind in the win column, at forty wins, thirty-three losses. Next was Centreville, which at thirty-five and thirty-six, held onto third by mere percentage points over the Indians, who, at thirty-five and thirty-eight, had dropped below the .500 mark and into fourth place.

But on the night of Thursday, July 31ˢᵗ, in a 4–2 loss to Milford, Guy turned in another good game. *The Salisbury Times*:

> Gene D'Ambrosia hammered a home run in the fifth inning with two men aboard and the league leaders won 4–2.

D'Ambrosia's circuit swipe, his fourth of the year, wiped out a two-run lead built by the Tribe when Guy Vitale smashed a home run in the first inning with Denny Henrickson on base.

Guy's latest home run came against Milford's ace, lefty Bill Boland, from Brooklyn, New York, who chalked up his eighteenth win of the season that night, against no losses; his record of four shut outs was far better than any pitcher in the League. But Guy seemed to have solved him.

The following evening, it was the Cardinals. Guy and Hank Ciak were the Tribe's hitting stars, in a 7–0 loss that dropped them further behind Centreville. Guy and Ciak each had one hit, as Cards pitcher Jerry Curran threw a two-hit shutout at the Indians.

And the Tribe's troubles continued. The Easton Yanks defeated them twice in a double header on Sunday, August 3rd, 17–5 and 2–0. That made it three losses in a row, as the pitching seemed to have collapsed. In those two Sunday games, Guy collected three hits in eight plate appearances, but his efforts did not help.

Well, the Indians latest losing streak was finally snapped at five games, on Monday, August 4th, when they topped the Centreville Red Sox in the fastest game played in the Shore League that season, 3–0. Because Bobby Maier had no starting pitchers ready for service, he sent a new reliever, Pat Grazania, to the mound, and in his first start of the season he obliged his manager by throwing a seven-hit shutout, to keep his club mere percentage points ahead of the Easton Yankees. According to *The Times,* Grazania was aided by fielding gems from Maier, Mahoney, Vitale, Henrickson and Hynes. Guy went one for three in this game, and drove in one of his team's three runs.

But the next evening, Salisbury lost to the team breathing down their necks, the Easton Yankees, 6–5, and Easton took over fourth place from the Indians. Worse yet, their most dependable pitcher, Hilliard Murray, came down with a sore arm early in the game, and although he stayed on the mound for six innings before being relieved by Smokey Intindola, Easton cranked out thirteen hits against him. Guy went one for four and drove in a run for his team in the seventh, when they were playing catch-up ball.

That night, sitting alone at a table in a local diner, Guy pondered the situation over a no-frills supper of roast beef, mashed potatoes and brown gravy, which would set him back eighty-nine cents. It was the first time in his baseball career that he sensed the team he was playing for was not going to win or even come close to the League title.

We've got a terrific bunch a fella's, he thought. *And we care about each other, so we're tryin' hard ta play well as a group. But we're havin' a rough time. When we get the hittin' we don't seem ta get the pitchin' and vice versa.* He attacked his mashed potatoes for a few moments. *But there's almost a month of the season left. That's a lotta baseball. Plenty a time ta turn this thing around and maybe finish third or even second.*

On Thursday, August 7th, the Tribe eked out a 2–1 win over hapless Federalsburg to get back into the scramble for a playoff berth. Here's how *The Times* described it:

> *Frank Hiatt, the bespectacled youngster who hurled a few games for the Salisbury Indians the first two weeks of the season, returned here last night and pitched them to a 2–1 triumph over the Federalsburg Athletics.*
>
> *Hiatt, who was ineffective here earlier this year, had enough on the ball last night to hold the A's to five hits.*
>
> *His mates gave him great support. Vitale and Bobby Maier coming up with a pair of shoe-string catches on a pair of liners marked 'base hit.' Those two catches right there saved the ball game.*

So the stage was set for a crucial three game series with the league-leading Milford Giants, beginning the following evening at Milford. *The Times* again:

> *INDIANS STAGE SEVEN RUN RALLY, BEAT MILFORD*
> *VITALE SMASHES HOMER AS TRIBE COMES*
> *FROM BEHIND*
> *All season long the league-leading Milford Giants have been terrorizing the Eastern Shore League opposition with big one-inning explosions.*
>
> *Last night they fired a seven run salvo at the Salisbury Indians in the fifth frame … [but] the Indians scored seven runs themselves to take the ball game, 10–8.*
>
> *Bobby Maier led the batting attack against the Giants getting three for three. Guy Vitale smashed his fourth home run of the season over the Milford left field fence …*

But Guy's fourth long-distance clout of the summer was his only hit of the game in five plate appearances. It did nothing for his average. The batting stats were printed on Saturday, August 9th, and again, he was not hitting above .250, so his name did not appear on the list, the cut-off point of *this* list being at .253.

Tuesday evening, August 12th, saw the Indians defeat the Red Sox, 7–4, as Guy collected two hits in four trips to the dish, scored two runs and had five put-outs in left field. This win pulled the Indians within a game and a half of the fourth place Sox, who were three games ahead of them in the loss column.

On Friday, August 15th, with a patched-up batting order, the Indians lost a heartbreaker, 6–5, to the Easton Yankees, now securely in possession of third place. In this ten-inning ballgame, Guy got two hits, his second of the night coming in the tenth inning, in the midst of a rally. But with two on and two out, Maier stroked a fly ball to Ekdahl in center field to end the game.

After eighty-eight games, the Indians as a club were batting just .249. In hitting, they were in fourth place behind Milford, at .299, Cambridge, .258, and Easton at .252. It would seem that this was a pitcher's league.

On Wednesday, August 20th, 1941, I was four years old, and my uncle was playing ball for a hard luck Salisbury Indians baseball team on Maryland's Eastern Shore. That night, more than 1,100 rooters, the best crowd of the season at Gordy Park, watched their team drop a 3–1 decision to the Milford Giants, after playing them tough for nine innings. Intindola scattered seven hits, fanned five and only gave up two free passes, but still took the loss. Guy, in this one, stroked a double, which, had it happened in an inning with men on base, would have driven in enough runs to tie or win the game. And there was this in the *Salisbury Times* on Thursday, August 21st:

> *Vitale thrilled the crowd in the second frame with a running, one-handed circus grab of Yagiello's sure double or triple. He fell after the catch, rolled over several times and still held onto the ball. He got a great hand from the fans.*

However, on a sad note, that same article reported:

> *Word was received from Reubin Levin in Bennington, Vermont that his mother had died.*

At this point in the season, perhaps overwhelmed by the passing of his mother and the financial woes of his team, Reubin Levin decided to cut his losses and walk away from the Salisbury Indians, petitioning the Federal Court to place them in Chapter 11 receivership.

On Thursday, August 21st, the Tribe handed Milford another defeat, 6–2. They gathered nine hits off one of the League's best pitchers, Chris Hayden, who had been tough against every team, but who did not last beyond the fourth inning. Guy did his usual one for four at the plate, but his hit was a double, and he drove in a run, scored one and committed one error in the field. Although they won, the Indians failed to gain in the race for a playoff slot, because Centreville also won its game that night.

On Friday, August 22nd and Saturday, August 23^{rd,} games were scheduled against Centreville, offering the Indians a chance to gain ground. They were not up to it. On Friday, a ninth inning rally failed and they lost, 6–5. Hiatt, their starter, was relieved by Grazania in the second, and Salisbury thumped out ten hits against Red Sox pitchers, Ryan and Clifton. Phil Donovan was the big stick for the Indians, going two for four, while Guy nailed one hit, a double and collected another run batted in, but Tribe batters stranded nine men on the sacks, and that was the difference, as they fell three and a half games behind Centreville.

*　　*　　*　　*

Salisbury, MD
Sunday, August 24 to Saturday, September 6, 1941
Gordy Park
6:00 p.m.

With just fourteen games remaining on its schedule, the Salisbury club opened the last phase of the Eastern Shore League race on Sunday, August 24th by blanking Federalsburg, 4–0. Why not? Every team in the League was doing it to the A's by this point. Their record? 34 wins, 65 losses. Behind the four-hit pitching of Smokey Intindola, his mates scored some runs off Johnny Heenan. Jack Campbell's single, Henrickson's double, and Guy's single gave the Tribe the game in the first inning. Guy had eight putouts in left, and played errorless ball out there.

Meanwhile, second-place Cambridge slipped past Milford, 8–7, and cut the Giants lead to six games, not quite a pennant race yet, but making things a bit more interesting for the fans.

Only four teams would make the playoffs. To become one of them, the Indians needed to win five more games than Centreville's Red Sox over the last thirteen games—unlikely the way they'd been playing.

Although Guy's fielding was just short of sensational in left, his hitting had been decidedly below par all season. No doubt conscious of that fact, he attempted to bear down at the plate. Monday, August 25th was an example.

It was the bottom of the third, the home team up at bat, and the fans noisily suggesting what they wanted their club to do. Hiatt, Salisbury's pitcher, singled up the middle and Campbell walked. Henrickson was up. Guy, standing in the on-deck circle swinging a couple of bats, looked on. McLaughlin, the A's hurler got ahead of Henrickson quickly. With the count nothing and two, he swung and rolled a grounder to third, forcing Hiatt at that base. Guy's turn, with runners at first and second and only one out.

In prior years, this was a pressure situation in which Guy had excelled. Not so far this season. But he wanted to drive in at least one of those base runners. Standing deep in the box, he practice-swung the bat through the strike zone a few times, called time out as McLaughlin toed the rubber, stepped out and, with the fat part of the bat, knocked some dirt from his spikes.

Ready, he stepped back into the batter's box and took the first pitch for ball one. Again, Guy backed out; this time it was to get some dirt on his hands and wipe the sweat from his brow with a forearm. He was obviously playing head games with McLaughlin.

Back in, he took the next pitch for a called strike, stepped out again, and glared toward the mound. *He hasn't thrown his curve yet. This might be it,* he guessed as he leaned over and tapped the plate with the barrel end of the bat. It was, and Guy was on it. His picture-book swing had not deserted him and he drilled it over the shortstop's head into left field. His single scored Campbell from second base, for the Indian's second run of the game.

Guy was not done in this contest. Bottom of the sixth, score tied at two, here's how *The Times* described things:

VITALE'S HOMER GIVES TRIBE 3–2 WIN
VICTORY KEEPS CLUB IN RACE FOR PLAYOFFS

———

A rousing home run off the bat of Guy Vitale kept the Salisbury Indians in the battle for a playoff spot last night as the Tribe annexed a 3–2 decision from the Federalsburg A's out at Gordy Park.

Vitale's smash, his first of the year on the home lot, cleared the left field fence with plenty to spare. It was in the sixth inning, the score tied and Frank Hiatt, who went the route for the Redskins, was beginning to have his troubles.

> *The A's tied it up [in the sixth] ... but Vitale took care of things in the Tribe's half when he poled the pellet out of the park putting the Indians ahead again, 3–2.*

So, thanks to Guy's heroics—he went two for three and scored a run—the Tribe held on to win it and picked up half a game on the Centreville Red Sox, keeping them in the playoff scramble. The next morning, a nice photo of Guy appeared along with that story, captioned *Homer Beats A's.*

And he turned in more heroics the next evening, Tuesday, August 26th, as the Indians again beat the A's, 4–1, and gained a full game on Centreville. In the fifth, with Leahy on third and Campbell on second, Guy rifled a clean single to center field, scoring Leahy and Campbell. He then took third on a bad throw to the plate, and scored his team's fourth run moments later on Maier's sac fly. The Tribe was now just two games behind Centreville, with a couple of games coming up against that club.

But, on Thursday, August 28th, Centreville stopped the Indian's short winning streak, 7–1, even though Guy, hitting in the third slot, collected two hits in four plate appearances. His two bingles were among only five his teammates could muster that night, as they were almost shut out by Centreville's pitcher, Bechtol, who struck out nine.

On Tuesday, September 2nd, the *Times* printed an article which shed more light on the Indians financial straights:

RECEIVERS MAKE LAST APPEAL TO BASEBALL FANS

> *Ernest C. Clark and Charles E. Hearne, Jr., receivers for the Salisbury baseball club, issued a plea to the fans today for last minute all-out aid for the Indians.*
>
> *"When we took over the club two weeks ago," Clark said, "we hoped to make at least our operating expenses. But it's been a struggle to meet the light bill, feed the players and buy baseballs."*
>
> *"One big turnout tonight and another tomorrow night would go a long way toward paying the wages the boys have earned yet haven't received.*
>
> *"These fellows have been poorly paid all summer. To save Salisbury the embarrassment of dropping out of the Eastern Shore League two weeks ago, they agreed to finish the season, gambling that business might pick up.*

> *"Charlie Hearne and I told the boys we would try to save some-thing for them; at least part of their salaries.*
>
> *"True enough they've been unable to catch Centreville for that playoff spot, but in baseball, one team must be the loser.*
>
> *"In spirit and this business of sticking it out, these boys can't be beat. For those things alone, they deserve some help, win, lose or draw"*

Despite these kind words, try as they might, the Indians could not gain on Centreville. By Wednesday, September 3rd, with only two more games left, they were mathematically eliminated from all hopes of a playoff berth. That night, they played their last home game of the '41 season, dropping a 4–1 decision to the Easton Yankees. Guy, disappointed, went hitless, as his team left eleven men on base. But a walk gave him the honor of scoring his team's lone run of the evening. A base hit here and there could have changed this game's outcome, but it was not to be.

However, Clark was right about their spirit. As Salisbury was batting in the bottom of the ninth, Bobby Meier and Smokey Intindola huddled briefly next to the water cooler at one end of the dugout. Then, Meier disappeared down the runway into the locker room. Moments later, he emerged, carrying a pair of blue slacks, as the last out was made on the field and the game ended.

"Woooeee!" he said, raising the pants to his nose. "Fragrant."

This grabbed the attention of the others. "Hey," Guy yelled. "Those look like … what the hell are ya doin' with my pants?"

Intindola, trying to keep a straight face, stopped in front of Guy and gestured toward the flagpole in center field. "Well, we don't have a pennant ta fly out there this year, Guy," he said. "You won't mind if we fly these, will ya? Come on, everybody." Guy went along with the gag.

Here's how *The Times, on Thursday, September 4th,* described what happened:

TRIBE HAS NO FLAG, FLIES VITALE'S PANTS

> *It being the last home night of the year, the Salisbury Indians felt the need of some kind of ceremony to close the season. They decided a procession to the centerfield flag pole would be just right, so, out they marched and before the ceremony was over, the gang had raised Guy Vitale's blue slacks—the pair he has worn all summer—aloft on the flagpole. Guy admitted the garment hadn't been washed all summer.*

That same evening's paper contained the names of the Eastern Shore League All Star team for 1941. Although Guy was certainly popular with the fans and his teammates, he was not among the players named or even considered for the team.

From Salisbury, first baseman Walt Mahoney, who batted .265 for the season, was the only one to make it. Others considered but not chosen were shortstop and third baseman Phil Donovan, who hit .260, outfielder and manager Bobby Maier, who finished the season hitting .292, outfielder Denny Henrickson, at .260, and second baseman Jack Campbell, .257.

And of course, the next day, Thursday, September 4th—the final game of the season—the Indians lost to Easton, 6–1, collecting only three hits in the process. Guy, up only once, did not get a hit. In the article on Friday, September 5th, *The Times* said:

> Today, most of the boys departed for home, a share of them going to the New England states for a short, barnstorming tour with Reubin Levin, former owner of the club.

Batting averages for all players competing in the Eastern Shore League during the 1941 season can be found in the 1942 edition of the *Sporting News*, the official Baseball Record Book. Here are Guy's statistics, according to that publication:

PLAYER	G	AB	R	H	TB	2B	3B	HR	SH	SB	BB	HB	RBI	SO	PCT
Vitale, Guy, Salisbury	99	392	11	92	124	12	1	6	6	1	31	7	11	14	.235

Just one more word about this. It seems apparent that during 1941 this League was a pitcher's league. Bill Boland, Milford's ace, finished with a record of 20 wins and five losses, tops in the League. Only eleven position players finished the season with averages above .300. Remember Henry (Hank) Ciak, the all-star catcher from the Northern League's Bennington Generals in 1940? Well, he and Guy were among the very few players to stick with the Salisbury Indians for the entire summer. Ciak's batting average? .238; just three points better than Guy's.

The final standings for the 1941 Eastern Shore League were printed on Friday, September 5th, 1941. Of course, it had been obvious to Guy, as it had been to the others Salisbury players that Salisbury was not going to be in the thick of things at the end. This was contrary to Guy's experience during his three seasons on Cape Cod and contrary to his experience at St. Johnsbury in '39:

TEAM	WON	LOST	PCT
Milford	66	43	.606
Cambridge	61	46	.570
Centreville	57	52	.523
Easton	57	53	.518
Salisbury	51	59	.464
Federalsburg	35	74	.321

The next day, *The Times* reported the full extent of the Indians financial woes:

INDIAN'S DEBT MAY BE MORE THAN $3,000

MAY BE BAR TO FUTURE BASEBALL IN CITY, RUSSELL SAYS

League prexy Harry S. Russell came up with some heartening news yesterday for those fans who feared that the forthcoming play-offs, beginning tonight, might be the end of organized baseball on the peninsula.

"The Eastern Shore League situation has improved considerably over what it was a month ago," Russell said. "While it's true that all but two clubs suffered poor attendance, every effort will be made to keep the circuit going next year."

Salisbury experienced the worst season of all, the Loop head stated. "Outstanding debts amounting to Between $2,500 and $3,000 will have to be paid off at Salisbury before another club can operate."

The total indebtedness of the Indians is still unknown. Players' salaries in arrears amount to about $1,800, of which $600 was paid off by that amount on deposit with the league.

Other clubs in the wheel, though lacking sufficient attendance to pay the freight, are backed by major league outfits. Easton and Cambridge, now rivals for the pennant, have experienced an encouraging month as far as the turnstiles are concerned.

Russell added that he has been at work trying to interest other towns for next season with an eye toward making the circuit an eight club affair again.

The Hall of Fame at Cooperstown, New York, keeps records of every ball player who ever played organized baseball anywhere in the country, no matter for how long. As mentioned earlier, I'd obtained a copy of Guy's Contract Card from my father-in-law, Paul Fenchak, a truly educated man who, although retired, continued to learn and actively pursue research and writing projects.

Guy's card clearly shows that at the end of the 1941 season his contract was reserved by the Salisbury club with an eye to re-signing him for 1942. It also shows, however, that in January 1942, Guy applied for free agency.

Free agency? Did baseball in the '40s have this system, which tends to cater to big egos and create even bigger salaries while undermining the concept of loyalty to a team? I asked the Cooperstown researcher:

"Yes, free agency goes back to the 1890s, but back in the '40s it did not mean what it means today," he said. "Probably, it simply meant that if he intended to play ball again in '42, he did not intend to play for Salisbury."

That figures to be correct, especially if he were one of the ballplayers whose salary went unpaid when Reubin Levin jumped ship.

*   *   *   *

East Boston, MA
Monday, September 15, 1941
Bennington Street Apartments
9:30 p.m.

After the Eastern Shore League's season was wrapped up, Guy lost no time returning to Boston. But at his age—he was twenty-three and would turn twenty-four the following month—he didn't go back to his parent's home. Instead, he took a small efficiency in an aging, three-story apartment building on Bennington, a few blocks away.

The structure had fallen on hard times. Weeds had taken over the small lawn in front, which was brown from lack of care. The skimpy bushes along the walkway needed trimming, and the front door could have benefited from a coat of paint.

His apartment was small and sparsely furnished, with yellowing linoleum on the floor, no screens on the windows, and a kitchen that was so tiny he could barely turn around in it. But it was all he could afford because the pay had been skimpy in Salisbury and he had not saved very much of it. He needed to use what he *did* have sparingly, until a job at the Shipyard, where he'd applied immediately upon his return, came open. *I'm gonna be livin' on vapors until I can get work,* he thought ruefully.

Again, as at the end of the 1939 season when he'd returned from St. Johnsbury, he was bitterly disappointed in himself and his showing. Yes, he'd made it into professional baseball, but his first year of organized ball was not at all what he'd hoped it would be. Curiously, he did not feel the same level of regret and guilt that had weighed so heavily upon him at the close of the Twin States League's season. Still there had been that lost several weeks in the middle of the summer. *But that was only a short time,* he rationalized. Well if that had not been the reason for his poor showing, then why had he *not* done better? Had he peaked? Was this level of performance the best he could do? Was he now the best he'd ever be? Or was the quality of Eastern Shore League players simply so much better that he'd needed time to adjust after a year away from the game? *Maybe I shoulda at least played semi-pro ball in Boston last year,* he thought.

Moving to the refrigerator in the kitchen, he took a bottle of Miller's from it, rummaged through a drawer for a bottle opener, and popped the cap. Bringing it to his lips, he took several swallows before returning to a chair at the small table in what served as both living and dining rooms, and sitting heavily.

So should I play down there again next summah? he asked himself. *Or somewhere else. War's comin'. Everybody knows it.* Raising the bottle again, he drank deeply. His eyes, as dark as the night outside, intense, shining, stared out the kitchen window as if trying to see beyond the darkness, to glimpse, if he could, what life had in store for him. He shrugged. *I might not have any choice. With my draft status, Uncle Sam may be the one ta decide where I'm gonna be next summah.*

PART SIX

THE WAR YEARS

CHAPTER 42

Pine Bluffs, WY
Saturday, December 18, 2005
703 Beech Street
4:30 p.m.

On Sunday, December 7th, 1941 a Japanese military force of six aircraft carriers and four hundred twenty-three planes launched a surprise attack on Pearl Harbor. All remaining doubts on the part of the American people about whether we'd enter the war voluntarily or wait to be drawn into it, vanished literally overnight. Admiral Nagumo, the Japanese commander, selected a Sunday for the attack, hoping to catch the entire American fleet in port. Call it luck or call it an act of the Holy Spirit, but two aircraft carriers, the USS Enterprise and the USS Saratoga, and a battleship, the USS Colorado, were otherwise occupied at sea that day.

The enemy struck in two waves: the first, at 6:00 a.m., one hundred eighty-three fighters and torpedo bombers hit the fleet in Pearl Harbor and the air fields at Hickham, Kaneohe, and Ewa. The second wave, an hour and fifteen minutes later, struck the same targets.

The following day, President Roosevelt delivered a speech to a joint session of Congress. Behind him were Vice-President Henry Wallace and Speaker of the House, Sam Rayburn. To the President's right was his son, James, in uniform.

> *Yesterday, December 7th, 1941—a date which will live in infamy—*
> *the United States of America was suddenly and deliberately attacked*
> *by naval and air forces of the Empire of Japan ...*

In the short speech, President Roosevelt alluded to in-process negotiations between America and Japan at the time of this treachery:

437

The United States was at peace with that nation and, at the solicitation of Japan, was still in conversation with its government and its Emperor looking toward the maintenance of peace in the Pacific. Indeed one hour after the Japanese air squadrons had commenced bombing in Oahu, the Japanese Ambassador to the United States and his colleague delivered to the Secretary of State a formal reply to a recent American message. While this reply stated that it seemed useless to continue the existing diplomatic negotiations, it contained no threat or hint of war or armed attack.

It will be recorded that the distance to Hawaii from Japan makes it obvious that the attack was deliberately planned many days or even weeks ago. During the intervening time the Japanese Government has deliberately sought to deceive the United States by false statements and expressions of hope for continued peace.

The tone of this discourse mirrored surprise, disappointment, and even dismay by America's leaders at this shocking turn of events; the bombing of Oahu followed by the immediate torpedoing of U.S. ships on the ocean between San Francisco and Hawaii. Indeed, even much of the media appears to have been surprised. On the morning of December 7th, the *New York Herald-Tribune* carried a large photo on its front page of the Japanese Ambassador and his entourage making a good will call on President Roosevelt "in peaceful pursuit of a Pacific trade agreement."

Although the Japanese assault was a tactical surprise, America was not completely unprepared. The Selective Service Administration had been up and running for several years, and, as we saw in the case of Johnny Wedemeyer and his eleven Boston University football buddies, young men had been assigned draft numbers in anticipation of a call-up, and were actually being drafted for training. Still there was hope that they'd not be needed; a hope that was dashed for Guy and millions of men like him by the events of December 7th, 1941.

Of course, as they watched the situation unfold in Europe and Southeast Asia in 1940, Guy and many other young men must have understood that their lives might soon be altered by war. But until that "infamous day" they could not have been certain.

Prodded by the attack on Pearl Harbor, an outraged, still morally-sound America quickly embarked upon a mobilization program of unprecedented magnitude. Financial, human and physical forces were marshaled. To learn more, I again turned to historian Paul Johnson:[50]

> *Within a single year, the number of tanks built in America had been raised to over 24,000 and planes to over 48,000. By the end of America's first year in the war, it had raised its arms production to the total of all three enemy powers put together, and by 1944, had doubled it again, while at the same time creating an army which passed the 7 million mark in 1943. During the conflict, the United States in total enrolled 11,260,000 soldiers, 4,186,466 sailors, 669,100 marines and 241,093 Coastguardsmen.*

       *   *   *   *

East Boston, MA
Saturday, February 7, 1942
Fort Devens, MA
6:00 a.m.

Three weeks after returning from Maryland's Eastern Shore the previous September, Guy had been able to sign on at the Bethlehem Ship Building Company in East Boston, in his old position as a Ship Fitter's Helper. His duties included assisting in scraping, chipping, spraying and painting steel plates which were later used to make the hulls of ships, such as the Victory troopships, C-1 and C-2 freighters; cargo carriers turned out quickly and in assembly-line fashion to transport troops, tanks, trucks and other equipment to any war zone overseas where they might be needed. It was hard, dirty work and Guy hated it, but somebody had to do it, and it provided him with the money he needed to support himself until Uncle Sam crooked a long, bony finger in his direction.

And he knew *that* would be soon. Having turned twenty-four the previous October, Guy was the not-so-proud possessor of a draft number which guaranteed an early call-up if and when war broke out. Not having any other goals in life except to play professional baseball and go to college, and with war looming, he was satisfied, for the time being, to drift into a loose pattern of existence; rise early, go to work, eat dinner out, visit a local watering hole where he'd drink with friends, acquaintances or strangers—hangers-on eager to be seen in the company of a local celebrity like Guy—get pleasantly mellow, and

---

50   Paul Johnson, *A History of the American People*, HarperCollins Publishers, Inc. New York NY. 1997.

return to his empty room, usually alone except on weekends, to sleep until it was time to repeat the pattern the next day.

Back then, not much consideration was given to health problems which might be caused by inhaling lead paint or the various chemicals used in this type of work over a long period of time. But I've often wondered if there was any link between this early occupation and Guy's later health issues.

With the entry of the United States into the war in December 1941, a young, healthy and vigorous Guy Vitale was not surprised to receive in his mail in early February 1942, a notice from his local draft board to report for induction. To his chagrin, Guy was among the first men to be called up.

On the bleak morning of Saturday, February 7, 1942, exactly two months after Japanese forces struck Pearl Harbor, a yellow, unheated school bus loaded with thirty army draftees, Guy among them, drove through the main gate at Fort Devens Military Induction Center, and stopped in front of a small group of uniformed men, one of whom stepped aboard and addressed the chilled civilian inductees.

"Good morning," he said, grinning broadly. "My name is Sergeant Avery McCoy. You will address me as 'sir' or as 'Sergeant McCoy.' In a minute, you will leave this vehicle and form two parallel lines beside it, directly in front of those men out there, who've been given the almost impossible task of turning you civilians into soldiers." He gestured out the grime-streaked bus window, and thirty pairs of uncomprehending eyes glanced in the direction he'd indicated.

Moving to the back of the bus, Sgt. McCoy continued. "If you take more than two minutes to accomplish that task, you'll earn the undying enmity of me and the men out there. And that," he added, "will not be a good thing. FALL OUT!"

These young men were all from East and South Boston. They'd reported to their local army recruiting office at 5:30 a.m. that morning, carrying nothing but a small bag crammed with shaving gear, clean underwear and socks. Those who smoked also brought several packs of their favorite cigarettes, not knowing if or when they'd be allowed to purchase more. From here, later that day they were shipped to Fort McClellan, Anniston, Alabama for six weeks of basic training, followed by six more of advanced infantry training. At the close of his basic training, Guy's rank was Private. At the end of his advanced infantry training cycle, he was promoted to Private First Class.

In May 1942, he left Fort McClellan and joined the 311th Infantry Regiment of the 78th Infantry Division at Camp Butner, North Carolina, apparently as advanced cadre, to help establish the division in its new headquarters and role.

By July 1943, he had been promoted to the rank of Staff Sergeant, which is the third of four sergeant non-commissioned officer ranks.

For the next three years and eleven months, Guy Vitale, Serial Number 31060610, would live under a discipline and order that he'd never before experienced. His life would have a purpose not of his own making, although not entirely distasteful to him—defending the United States of America against foreign enemies.

*   *   *   *

Pine Bluffs, WY
Monday, June 12, 2006
703 Beech Street
8:45 a.m.

Before we get too far into Guy's army service, I think it would be good for readers who may never have been in the Armed Forces to understand how army divisions are numbered.

Phillip Carter, in his article, *How Are Army Divisions Numbered?* (2/28/2003) said the first thing to know is that the Army's divisions were numbered in the order in which they were created. The 1st Division was actually the first division. Then came the 2nd, 3rd, etc."

He went on to say that there are, of course, gaps in the sequence. Today's army [in 2003] has eight infantry divisions: the 1st, 2nd, 3rd, and 4th, along with the 101st. What happened to the rest of them? Well, the military has cyclically expanded in wartime, creating lots of new units—during WWII for example, the Army had infantry divisions running all the way up to the 106th. But during peacetime, most of the war units are deactivated, which accounts for the holes.

Carter asks another rhetorical question. How does the army pick which divisions to keep? Each unit has its own customs and history, and the Army basically preserves the ones with the most glorious lineage. Take the 101st Airborne Division, which has been part of the Army since 1942. During World War II, the "Screaming Eagles" parachuted into Normandy and fought their way across Europe, making a heroic stand at Bastogne during the Battle of the Bulge. The Army has kept the division on active duty ever since. During the same war, the Army's 100th and 102nd Divisions served no less bravely but somewhat less famously. Both were shuttered for good after the war.

So what was a Division comprised of during WWII? 10,000 to 15,000 soldiers, divided into three to five combat regiments and a number of support units. Regiments had 3,000 to 5,000 men and included several combat and support battalions. Each battalion had three to five line companies, and those companies broke down into three to five platoons of 20 to 40 people. Each platoon was made up of three squads of 8 to 12.

The 78th Infantry Division was established by the War Department on 5 August 1917, and was first activated on 23 August 1917—just two months before Guy's birth—at Camp Dix, New Jersey.[51] It consisted of four infantry regiments; the 309th, 310th, 311th, 312th, and three artillery regiments; the 307th, 308th, and 309th. Twenty thousand soldiers, draftees from Delaware, New Jersey and New York made up the original division.

The new division acquitted itself well in WWI, in France when deployment orders came. Movement overseas commenced on 18 May and was completed by 12 June 1918. During the summer and fall of 1918, it was the "point of the wedge" of the final offensive which knocked out Germany.

The 78th, known as the Lightning Division, was in three major campaigns during Word War I; Meuse-Argonne, St. Mihiel and Lorraine, earning three battle streamers and suffering heavy casualties—1,530 men killed in action and 5,614 wounded. The Division was demobilized in June 1919. Its insignia mirrors its nickname—a red semi-circle with a lightning bolt streaking through it.

In WWII, the 78th Division was, as I said, reactivated at Camp Butner, North Carolina on August 15th, 1942 as a Training Division, just in time for Guy, who was finishing his six months of basic and advanced infantry training, to be transferred to it. The initial 311th Regimental commander was Colonel Merritt E. Olmstead.

In October 1942, after being fleshed out to its full complement of men, the 311th was assigned the task of training replacements for shipment to other units. By the fall of 1943, the Timberwolf Regiment, along with the 78th Division, had earned the distinction of having trained more fighting men—between 50,000 and 60,000—than any other single unit.

By the fall of 1943, the 311th began a program of training its own personnel for combat. That had been accomplished by January 1944. As an ailing President Roosevelt, advised by his doctors not to leave the White house, gave his Annual Message to Congress in a fireside chat to the American people, the Regiment began leaving Camp Butner. The transfer to Camp Pickett, Virginia, was completed in March 1944. There it remained while absorbing some Air Corps personnel, until September, when it left Pickett and went to Camp Kilmer, N.J. to make final preparations for embarkation to the European Theatre and combat

---

51   According to military historians Jim McGovern and Col. Robert E. Wyllie.

in Belgium, France and Germany. The Siegfried Line, the Rohr and the Rhine Rivers, the Cologne Plain, the Remagen Bridgehead, and the Ruhr Pocket, were all campaigns that lay ahead along its road to Berlin, where, after six months of occupation duty, the 78th was officially deactivated in May 1946. By then, Guy, who'd been discharged on January 4, 1946, was a civilian again, in East Boston.

∗   ∗   ∗   ∗

Pine Bluffs, WY
Tuesday, June 13, 2006
703 Beech Street
8:45 a.m.

Back in June 2002 when I began researching the section of this book dealing with Guy's military service, I was faced with the perplexing problem of how I was going to find out what my uncle did in the service.

After mulling this over, I decided to send a letter to Elaine Howard, then President of the *Army Times* Publishing Company, headquartered in Springfield, Virginia.[52] If I could convince the paper to print a note asking anyone who'd served with or known Guy Vitale in the Army to contact me, maybe I could develop some information. I sent a letter on June 2nd, 2002. Nothing happened—for a while.

In September 2002, my wife and I were still living in Towson, Maryland. Upon returning from breakfast at a local Friendly's Restaurant on the morning of September 3rd, I was pleasantly surprised to hear a message on my answering machine from Joe Lemon, who informed me that he'd known Guy Vitale in the Army. He said to call him.

Born in 1918, and eighty-five years old when I spoke to him, former First Lieutenant Joseph F. Lemon was retired and living in Lewisburg, West Virginia.

"I saw your ad in the Army Times," he began.

"You knew my uncle?"

"Yeah. I was in Service Company, 311th Infantry Regiment. I commanded it for awhile at Camp Butner, North Carolina. We were nicknamed 'the Timberwolf Regiment' for reasons that I don't now recall. I knew Guy there, but since I was an officer and he was an enlisted man at the time, we didn't know each other well."

---

52 *The Army Times*, a high quality periodical popular with veterans was, I'd been informed, a weekly newspaper sent out to both active and retired army personnel.

Joe Lemon's memory proved very good. And clearly he enjoyed talking about those long-ago Army days. "I was commissioned a Second Lieutenant in April 1942, at Fort Benning, Georgia. In June '42, I arrived at Butner. The 78th Division was being re-activated, and arrangements needed to be made to receive all personnel. Guy was already there. I knew him casually because I was in the Supply Section of the 311th and Guy was in the Ammunition Section."

"How long did you people act as a training outfit?"

"Until September 1944, when we got orders to [begin training our own people to] ship overseas," Joe said.

"That's about a year."

"Yeah. We honed our skills, ya might say."

"Did the Regiment have a baseball or softball team?"

"Yes, it did," Joe responded. "Baseball. We also had a football team made up of former college players. I know Vitale played on the baseball team, but I don't know if he played football. I didn't play baseball, but I watched most of the games that summer. That was 1943."

"What can you tell me about that?"

"Well, I recall the team was well-organized and it played against other regimental teams. I think your uncle played as a catcher. Anyway, I recall him as energetic and highly-skilled; more advanced than the other guys."

"That figures," I said. "Guy was a really good high-school baseball player, who played lots of semi-pro ball, and one year, he even played professionally."

"I remember one time when a team of baseball players [from an all-star Navy Pre-Flight squadron] from Chapel Hill, North Carolina, came in to play our regimental team. They brought eight big league ballplayers with them. Ted Williams was one of them. They beat us pretty bad."

We chatted for a few minutes, and Joe, who ended up his army career as a Major, promised to send me the names of some men who served with Guy in Service Company, and a couple of photos he had hung on to since those days in the Army. It would be almost two years before he made good on this promise, and then only after I'd called him again to remind him. However, it was Joe Lemon who, during that time, signed me up as an Associate Member of the 78th Infantry Division. I still proudly carry the membership card in my wallet, and pull it out to show to others occasionally.

*   *   *   *

Pine Bluffs, WY
Tuesday, June 13, 2006
703 Beech Street
12:45 p.m.

Shortly after my reminder call, I received Joe's letter:

> *Here are some ex Sv. Co. 311ᵗʰ Inf members who might know Vitale stories.*

Enclosed were the names of Col. (Ret) George E. Hudson, Capt (Retired) Richard J. Jacobs, who was C.O. of Service Company, Master Sergeant Nick Manojlovich, and Col. (Retired) Joseph Lewandoski, who was at one time the Regimental Athletic Officer. Joe finished his brief note with this:

> *I'm almost certain that these four are still alive. Hudson and Lewandoski both stayed in the service so had 20–30 years in. Nick and I got out in '45 or '46, right after the war. We are all in late 70s or 80s. Think both Hudson and I are same age. 86 or 87 and the others are younger.*

Relieved and pleased that I'd now be able to develop some information about my uncle's military days, and anxious to begin, I started contacting these men.

Nick Manojlovich, born on November 30, 1921, retired and living in Monaca, PA., was eighty-four years old when I spoke to him. Eager to talk, he was very helpful.

"Service Company was made up of three sections; motor pool, supply, and ammunition," he said. "Guy was a buck sergeant when I knew him. He drove a truck for the ammunition section. He'd pick up ammunition and deliver it where it was needed."

"What else can you tell me about him?" I asked.

"Well, I remember in the summer of ['42 or] '43 at Camp Butner, Guy played baseball for the Regimental Team. I watched a few of the games; one when they played a team from Chapel Hill connected with the University of North Carolina, and another when they played some major league ballplayers who were in flight school. Ted Williams was one. I don't recall much about the games; just that Guy played and he was one of the better players."

Wanting to find out more about this, I contacted Joe Lewandoski, who, according to Joe Lemon, had been the Regimental Athletic Officer as a young Lieutenant.

"Sure," the eighty-eight year old former Special Services officer said when I'd found his number and called him. "I did that job for a short while. My initial assignment was as Special Services Officer. I was responsible for setting up physical fitness programs; Athletic teams, the band, orchestra, Glee Club, etc."

"Do you recall a baseball game where Ted Williams played against the 311th team?"

"Yeah. It was at Butner before we went overseas. He came with a group of professional ballplayers. The game was stopped after the third inning because they were too good for us."

"Did Guy Vitale play in that game?"

"Vitale? Yes. He was the catcher that day, and I remember him as one helluva good ballplayer."

"Really?" I was pleased to hear this.

"Yeah. Your uncle and I were not close, but I recall hearing about Guy when the coach of the team told me, 'we have a hard-hitting catcher from New England and he is going to help us.' But after setting up the entire program, I was re-assigned to a rifle company. I left the 311th in November 1943, joined the 3rd Division and served with them in Italy. I landed with them on the Anzio Beachhead. Say, listen. I'll write everything I remember about the game and send it to you. I've also got a clipping about it, which I'll copy and include with my letter."

And he did. A few days later, his letter arrived:

> The first 311th baseball team was a pick-up team made up of people from the original 311th cadre of about five hundred people. I helped organize it but don't recall who was the coach or manager. It included people who played in high school or college, or sandlot ball, and some minor league players but no major league talent. As fillers came in our Regiment attained its full strength of 4500. Enough minor league people came in to form two teams. The 311th Blues and the 311th Reds. When a major opponent was scheduled, like with the North Carolina pre-flighters, players were hand-picked and played as the 311th Timberwolf Varsity team.
>
> Some North Carolina Pre-flighters were Johnny Pesky, Mel Allen, Harry Croft, Buddy Hassett, Pete Appleton, Harry Craft, Joe Kohlman, Johnny Sain, Al Sago, Al Moriarty, and Ted Williams. I don't know how

> *many innings were played but we did not play nine because we wanted*
> *the major league players to mix with the 311th soldier audience.*
>
> *After the 311th baseball team started to fill up with minor league*
> *players I left the baseball team and started to pitch softball for the*
> *officer's team.*

In this letter, Lewandoski also mentioned that Colonel Merritt E. Olmstead, Regimental Commander from August 15, 1942 to June 27, 1944, attended many of the games that summer, and *Guy was one of his favorite players.*

Besides baseball and softball, Camp Butner apparently had a lot going for it. Three movie houses were in the Lightning Division area, each showing the latest films. And five chapels, all with electric organs made it possible for soldiers of every denomination to keep up their religious activity, if so inclined. There was also a Service Club for enlisted men, which had just about everything, including a social hall, dance floor, balcony, cafeteria, soda fountain and library with over 8000 volumes in it. On Friday nights a dance was held, and girls from Durham and other nearby towns were imported under the supervision of the U.S.O. Committee.

✳   ✳   ✳   ✳

Pine Bluffs, WY
Wednesday, June 14, 2006
703 Beech Street
8:45 a.m.

In April 2005, I called Nick Manojlovich again. He'd already told me that he had not worked with Guy while they were in combat; he'd been assigned to Regimental Headquarters with the job of calling Supply Company to request the amount and type of ammunition needed by different units that day, and Guy and Chief Warrant Officer Jack Carlton would see to it. But I wanted to try to jog his memory some more about Guy and the time the 311th was performing its training mission at Camp Butner.

"Glad you called," he said. "I remembered a couple more things. Guy and Carlton took a Ranger course together. Don't know how that turned out, though. Another thing. A fella named John Talley knew Guy and worked with him. If he's still alive he'll be able to fill you in about your uncle."

Immediately after this conversation, using my investigative skills, I searched for John Talley, who had originally been from Cedar Rapids, Iowa, but who, according to *Flash* Membership Secretary Herman (Red) Gonzalez, had gone inactive while in North Canton, Ohio. A search of two directories on the Internet turned up several persons with the name John L. Talley, but none of them was the man I was looking for. A Social Security Death Index search revealed that someone with that name, born in 1914, had passed away in 1991. That was probably my man. A dead end; no pun intended.

During my research, another name had surfaced: Russell F. Jouppi, of Manistee, Michigan, had served with Guy and had probably known him personally. I attempted to locate him, without success. A month later, while devouring the July 2006 issue of *The Flash*, I came across his obituary, written by his son-in-law, David Hendricks, who sent it to Nick Manojlovich, who forwarded it to *The Flash*. Jouppi passed away in April 2006. Had I known of him sooner, I might have learned more about my uncle's military service.

What had Nick said about a Ranger course? Why would Guy take a Ranger course? I wondered. *Wasn't advanced infantry training difficult enough for him?*

Other than the fact that they were an elite group of fighting men, I didn't know much about the Rangers. So I booted up, went onto the internet and pulled some information from Wikipedia, the free encyclopedia.

It seems that the 75th Ranger Regiment is a special operations force of the United States Army Special Operations Command (USASOC), headquartered at Fort Benning, Georgia. The Regiment is a flexible, highly-trained and rapidly deployable light infantry force with specialized skills which enable it to be used against a vast array of conventional and special operations targets.

The force specializes in airborne, air assault, light infantry and direct action operations, conducting raids, infiltration and exfiltration by air, land or sea, airfield seizure, recovery of personnel and special equipment, and support of general purpose forces. Each Ranger battalion can deploy anywhere in the world with eighteen hours notice.

In May 1942, during WWII, the 1st Ranger Battalion was set up and trained in Scotland under British Commandos. The 1st, 3rd and 4th Ranger Battalions served in North Africa and Italy under William O. Darby until, at the Battle of Cisterna in January 1944, most of the 1st and 3rd were captured.

On June 6, 1944, the 2nd Ranger Battalion scaled the 150-foot cliff at Pointe du Hoc to destroy a German battery of 155mm artillery. Under constant fire during the climb, when they reached the top they found only a small contingent of enemy soldiers; the artillery had been withdrawn. The guns were later discovered and destroyed, and the Rangers cut and held the main roads for two days before being relieved. Meanwhile, the 5th Ranger Battalion was landing on Dog White Sector of Omaha Beach, and the 6th was fighting in the Pacific theatre, leading the invasion of the Philippines.

An illustrious history, I thought. *So what did Guy and his friend, Chief Warrant Officer John S. (Jack) Carlton have to do to become Rangers?* I didn't have a clue. Then I remembered that in Joe Lewandoski's letter of April 9th, 2005, he'd mentioned something about Guy and Ranger training. I dug it out:

> *About Ranger Training. In 1943 a group of us were assigned to take a two-week Ranger Training course at Camp Cook in Tennessee. After completion of our training we came back to our units and trained them in basic Ranger tactics. I'm sure this is what your uncle did in connection with Ranger Training.*

Back on the Internet, I searched for U.S. Army Rangers and their training. I learned that a prospective Ranger begins with the nine week Basic Combat Training course. Upon completion, he moves on to Advanced Individual Training to obtain a Military Occupational Specialty (MOS). Next, the soldier must complete Airborne School. After that, if he's still alive and healthy, he must complete the Ranger Indoctrination Program for grades E-4 and below, or the Ranger Orientation Program for grades E-5 and above. Upon successful completion of all this, the soldier has earned his Ranger Tab and returns to his unit, a fully-qualified and operationally deployable Ranger.

Guy, Carlton, Lewandoski and the others did not actually do all that. Theirs was only a fourteen day assignment. Still, it had to be a tough couple of weeks. I found nothing in Guy's records to indicate that he'd completed this rigorous training assignment. But several members of his outfit, apparently impressed, told me that he'd done it.

Reviewing my notes, I chewed on the fact that John Carlton had been a Chief Warrant Officer. Yet he and Guy seemed to have been close. What of the rules against officers 'fraternizing' with enlisted men? To learn more, I contacted Joe Lemon again:

"Well ya gotta remember that Sergeants are considered non-commissioned officers, Tony," he reminded me. "Guy was in the Regiment's Supply Company. He worked for Chief Warrant Officer Carlton. It wouldn't have been unusual for them to become close friends."

"Know anything more about this Carlton?"

"Just that during his service time he was a single fella, like Guy. Hailed from Punxutawney, PA, where that ground hog thing takes place every spring. Carlton went back there after he got outta the Army, and died there shortly after the war."

What was Guy's reputation? What did others think of him as a soldier? To find out I contacted former 1ˢᵗ Lieutenant Henry L. (Hank) Miller, who'd been Supply Company's Chief Executive Officer for the months leading up to shipping overseas. Eighty-five years old in November 2005, when I spoke to him, he was living in Chico, California, about two hundred miles north of San Francisco.

"Yeah," he said. "I was Supply Company's CEO for nine months just before we went overseas. Guy was my Sergeant."

"Did you know him well?"

"He was my driver; drove my jeep for me. I didn't know him socially. Whenever we'd go into Raleigh on leave, we'd go our separate ways. Guy had his own friends and I had mine."

"Were you the unit's CEO overseas, too?" I asked.

Miller chuckled. "Nope. When we got on the damn boat, I found out I'd been relieved. [Although Major George Hudson was still in overall command of Service Company], I was no longer CEO and Dick Jacobs was put in my slot."

"That must have been a shocker."

"Yeah. I shipped over with Service Company, but was then assigned to Third Battalion."

"What was your opinion of Vitale as a soldier during the time you knew him?" I wanted to know.

"Of Guy? Competent. One of our jobs was to help prepare convoys of six to eight trucks, going to Nashville. Guy would 'wind them up'—set them out at one hundred yard intervals—he was a beautiful driver and a good soldier. Did his job well and was no trouble to anybody. Damn professional."

CHAPTER 43

Pine Bluffs, WY
Thursday, June 15, 2006
703 Beech Street
8:00 a.m.

In September 1943, after a year as a training outfit, the inevitable happened. The 78th Infantry Division, under the command of Major General Edwin P. Parker, Jr., was given orders that would eventually take it to the European Theater and into the thick of the worst fighting of WWII. I needed to learn more about this frightening, uncertain time in Guy's life, so I turned once more to Nick Manojlovich and Joe Lemon. I was able to reach Nick first:

"When you got final orders to ship out," I asked Nick, "did you and Guy go with the advance party?"

"No," he said. "That was in the summer of 1944. Neither of us went with the advance cadre. We were supposed to, but we were away on a three-day pass when the orders came out. But our [Regimental] Supply Officer, Major George E. Hudson, went over with them. Guy and I shipped over later with the entire main force, on the Carnavan Castle."

*   *   *   *

Pine Bluffs, WY
Friday, June 16, 2006
703 Beech Street
8:00 a.m.

According to its regimental history, the 311th Infantry Regiment shipped out from New York on October 13th, 1944 and the crossing took twelve days:

On Friday, October 13, 1944, members of the 311th Infantry stag-gered up the gang-plank of a troop transport so so loaded with equip-ment that a dramatic leave-taking of the last bit of American soil we were to touch for some time was quite out of the question. Contrary to the general forebodings, not a leg was broken during the perilous ascent and all the Timberwolves were conveniently stowed between decks of the Carnavan Castle in a matter of a couple of hours. The next morning the 20,251 ton ship, which was to be our home for twelve days, swung out into the Hudson to join her convoy and move out across the Atlantic, destination unknown.

What were Guy's thoughts as this chapter in his life came to an end, and another began? Did he reveal his feelings to anyone? We have a brief letter from him to his father, written from Camp Pickett, Virginia, as his unit prepared to leave for Camp Kilmer, New Jersey, and then to its embarkation point in New York:

Sep. 30, 1944
Sgt. Guy Vitale 31060610
Service Co. 311th Inf.
A.P.O. 78
Camp Pickett, VA.

Dear Pa:
Received your cigarettes, thanks a lot. Now, to give you a short resume of things at the present. You may not be pleased, no one is, but it had to happen sooner or later. We are leaving soon in a day or so; by the time you get this letter I may be gone from Camp Pickett. I don't know where I'm going, or how it will end up. Don't worry. I told you not to. I'll make out all right. Keep things running and someday I may be back. Don't write anymore until you hear from me. I'll try to write the first opportunity I get. Remember now don't worry. I'll write you as soon as possible.

Your son,
Guy

*   *   *   *

Pine Bluffs, WY
Friday, June 16, 2006
703 Beech Street
11:00 a.m.

This is truly a fantastic country! So rich in talented people. One night during World War II, an obscure Kansas City physician's receptionist named Frances Angermeyer, penned a 26-line prayer entitled "Conversion," which found its way into the pockets of an estimated six million soldiers. Some say it even made it into the hands of many on the other side

As the sun set at the close of the first day of the Allied invasion of France on June 6th, 1944, and darkness enveloped the blood-soaked beaches along the Normandy cost where thousands of American, Australian and British soldiers lost their lives that day, copies of the poem littered the sand. And as the war dragged on, copies were found in lifeless hands from the European Theater to the Pacific Theater.

A 1943 article in the Omaha World-Herald detailed the spread of "Conversion" among American soldiers. When Angermeyer heard about it, she was flattered that her work had reached millions, and she felt good knowing it had comforted the lonely and the dying.

One soldier later wrote to Angermeyer:

> *I came across your poem today. By tonight it had Found its way to every man in the company, and left its mark. Men have died near me. Men will die in the future, perhaps myself. But I know this: the thought you have left with us will last beyond whatever will come in the future.*

Here's the prayer:

CONVERSION
Look, God I have never spoken to You—
But now—I want to say "How do you do,"
You see, God, they told me You didn't exist—
And like a fool, I believed all this.
Last night from a shell hole I saw Your sky—
I figured right then they had told me a lie.
Had I taken time to see the things You had made,

I'd have known they weren't calling a spade a spade.
I wonder, God, if You'd shake my hand,
Somehow, I feel that you will understand.
Funny—I had to come to this hellish place,
Before I had time to see Your face.
Well, I guess there isn't much more to say,
But I'm sure glad, God, I met You today.
I guess the "zero hour" will soon be here,
But I'm not afraid since I know You're near.
The signal! Well, God, I'll have to go.
I like You lots—this I want You to know—
Look, now. This will be a horrible fight.
Who knows—I may come to your house tonight—
Though I wasn't friendly with You before,
I wonder, God, if you'd wait at Your door.
Look—I'm crying! Me! Shedding tears!—
I wish I'd known You these many years—
Well, I have to go, God, for now good-bye.
Strange—since I met You, I'm not afraid to die.

Shortly after reading this prayer, I learned that when my uncle's outfit had shipped out, it was heading for the European Theatre and what turned out to be some of the bloodiest fighting of the war, as Germans, their backs to the wall, tried desperately to stem the tide of a relentless Allied advance.

Upon being told the name of his troop ship, my thoughts went back to him at that time. In my mind's eye, I saw him standing at the rail in the stern, watching the tugs which had towed them out into the Hudson River cast off their lines, feeling the ship's huge engine start up and the vessel rumbling and shaking beneath his feet as he watched the coastline of the country he loved fade in the distance.

Had he, perhaps, smoked a last cigarette before going below to a restless sleep in a sling hammock, separated by only a few inches from the man above? Had this prayer ever found its way into the hands of this young man who, as a kid, had had a devotion—big time—to the mother of Jesus, but who no longer believed in much of anything? If it had, what thoughts, I wondered, had run through his youthful mind.

*   *   *   *

Pine Bluffs, WY
Friday, June 16, 2006
703 Beech Street
12:00 p.m.

So, for the men of the 311th, what was the crossing like? What was life like for these fighting men crammed together for two weeks on this British passenger liner converted to troop ship, as it knifed its way through the icy Atlantic?

Former Captain Richard J. "Dick" Jacobs, who now lives in Bradenton, Florida, had arrived at Camp Butner in August 1942, straight from Officer Candidate School (OCS), when the Division was being activated, "... was involved with Service Company from approximately the middle of 1943 through 1945." He remembers it this way:

"The Carnavan Castle was a troop carrier, [but had] lousy accommodations for troops. It had been converted, [had an] English crew [and was on the ship's] first outing as a troop carrier. The men had lousy quarters but the officers were treated like royalty. [We had an] officer's mess, with waiters in tuxedos, and a menu to order from. Wonderful food."

Jacobs, you'll recall, was placed in charge of Service Company when the unit boarded ship for the trip overseas, taking over from 1st Lieutenant Henry L "Hank" Miller.

This is how the regimental history describes the ship:

> *During peacetime, the ship had carried 659 passengers in first, second and tourist class accommodations, but there had been some changes made, for there were 3200 odd Timberwolves, to say nothing of the 1600 supplementary troops, consisting of the 78th Division Artillery, Signal and Quartermaster companies on the ship, and almost all of them in tourist class ...*

And Joe Lemon? What did he think? After talking about his health for a few minutes, which he described as "deteriorating," he reminisced:

"We shipped out in early October 1944. I remember because the Regiment had gone to Camp Pickett, Virginia. I was TDY at Benning while they were there. I rejoined the outfit at Fort Dix, New Jersey."

"What can you tell me about the trip over?"

"We went over on the H.M.S. Carnavan Castle, a British cruise ship re-fitted to carry troops. It was crowded!"

What was there for the men, jam-packed together as they were, to do during their almost two weeks aboard the Carnavan Castle? The Regimental Handbook again:

> A *few of the men amused themselves continually hanging over the rail, doubtless keeping a sharp look-out for stray whales. Most ... spent a good deal of their waking hours sauntering about the ship, sweating out the interminable PX lines, and reading pocket editions on the sunny forward deck.*
>
> *... Special Services operated aboard ship, and there were several planned activities to occupy our time. The Information and Education Section scheduled daily programs over the PA system, dealing with the customs and speech of France and England, as well as the daily news ...*

So glad they attempted to put a good face on it. But author Jack Sacco, (no relation) in his book, *Where the Birds Never Sing*,[53] a tribute to his father who'd fought in WWII, writes his dad's description of *his* Atlantic crossing aboard the U.S.S. Anne Arundel in December 1943, ten months prior to the Timberwolves embarkation:

> *It was deep into the night when I awoke to hear a strange creaking and moaning of the ship, as if she were struggling to stay afloat. I wasn't a sailor so I really didn't know what was going on. What I did know was that the whole boat was rocking this way and that, up and down, back and forth. We were in these little bunks that swung out from the wall and were stacked about four high, with just barely enough room to turn over without hitting the one above you. Even so, I was hoping I wouldn't get flipped out onto the floor. Life's tough enough without the damn room moving all over the place.*
>
> *I could hear a few of the guys making these seasick noises, but despite the constant motion of the ship, I really didn't feel queasy or anything. In fact, in a strange way all the gyrations were surprisingly fun. It was as if we were on a big ride at the fairgrounds. What concerned me*

---

53   Jack Sacco, *Where the Birds Never Sing*, Regan Books, a Division of HarperCollins Publishers, Inc. New York, NY. 2003.

was the idea that we might sink. That was the main reason I hadn't joined the Navy in the first place—sailors spend a great deal of their time on the ocean. And the ocean consists of a lot of really deep water. This happened to be the middle of the winter and we were somewhere in the middle of the North Atlantic, which meant that this particular water had to be quite frigid. In addition, there were Germans prowling around in submarines looking to blow us up before we could even get into the war. I thought about all that for a while. Then I figured what the hell and went back to sleep.

Curious as to how Guy may have felt when he first realized those German subs were out there prowling the deep, circling his convoy of battleships, cruisers, transport and troop ships like flies buzzing around a corpse as it sailed through 'Torpedo Alley' in a tight formation for protection, I called Joe Lemon again.

"Anything eventful happen on the way to England?" I asked.

"Naw. We *did* have some motor trouble for several days and fell behind the convoy. With German subs in the area, we had to do a lot of maneuvering to avoid a straight path. I think we arrived at South Hampton, England on October 25th, 1944."

Humph. Nothing eventful!

*   *   *   *

Pine Bluffs, WY
Saturday, June 17, 2006
703 Beech Street
4:30 p.m.

The Regimental Handbook[54] picked up when the H.M.S. Carnavan Castle arrived in England and deposited its cargo of Timberwolves on British soil:

> *Throughout the voyage there was much futile speculation as to our destination, but the answer to this troublesome question was resolved on the morning of October 25th when the green shores of England rose out of the morning mist and a representative of the British Army officially welcomed the men of the 311th to England. All day the decks were*

---

54   Available in a very well-done CD for $15.00 when I obtained it, by sending a check to John C. Swengel, 508 Orange Drive, A-12, Altamonte Springs, FL 32701.

458 Echoes in the Wind

lined with men ogling through field glasses, as the ship steamed along the coast and into the harbor of Southampton. As night closed in the last Timberwolf stepped onto the dock to be greeted with doughnuts and coffee by the Red Cross. The last stage of our journey was made in strange little compartment coaches which brought us to Bournemouth Station, England.

Former Captain Dick Jacobs again: "The ship landed on the west coast of England, on the south end. A fine string of hotels was there, and no distinctions [were made as to rank, etc]. All of us lived well."

This was corroborated by the regimental history:

> *The town of Bournemouth is in the county of Hampshire, about 100 miles from London. In peacetime, it was England's Miami, a sea-side resort in the middle of the Channel Coast, just north of the Isle of Wight. With the outbreak of war, however, bathers and umbrellas were replaced by invasion-repelling barbed wire and pillboxes ...*
>
> *Fall came early to Bournemouth that year, but snugly situated in our hotels and private homes, we could ignore the bitterness of the damp cold and regard the world with smug satisfaction.*

How did the troops occupy their time during the six or seven weeks they were billeted in Bournemouth? Here's the way the Regimental Handbook described it:

> *During a day of training on the beach, we were able to look forward to the pleasant evening of writing letters around our own firesides, or of wandering through the town on pass to one of the many Red Cross centers, pubs, theaters, or to the Pavilion dance hall. The latter was a very popular and elaborate rendezvous, with bar, restaurants, and a concert hall. After a snack at Marsham Court, a show and perhaps a glass of bitters, we would stroll back up the cliff-bordered boardwalk to the hotel and bed. Everything seemed quite wonderful then, and few complaints were heard about overseas service.*

A snack at Marsham Court? A concert? Drinks at a bar? On twenty-one dollars a week? Perhaps some of the officers, who were paid better, may have been able to live like that, but I doubt many of the enlisted men experienced this idealistic lifestyle during their brief stay in the land of the Union Jack.

And it *was* brief. On November 17th, 1944, orders were received to move out. Motorized elements, including Guy's Supply Company, returned by truck to Southampton, while the various infantry companies traveled there by train. Once assembled, their heavy equipment—trucks and tanks—was loaded aboard two LSTs, while the men embarked aboard an LCI for Le Havre, France. On this second, much shorter voyage, the men were supplied hammocks in which they slept, their only night aboard.

A different agenda was followed by the LSTs carrying the regimental vehicles. Due to inclement weather in the Channel, the fully-loaded LSTs were required to lay over in Southampton for two days. Guy would have been with this group. Underway again on the morning of November 20th, one of the LSTs—I don't know if it was the one to which Guy was assigned—collided with a hospital ship and had to return to Le Havre. Later, on November 25th outside of Rouen, the men and equipment aboard that vessel re-joined the main force. So if Guy had been with that group, he was back with his Regiment by that date.

*   *   *   *

Le Havre, France
Tuesday, November 28, 1944
Duclair, Normandy Province
3:00 p.m.

For the men of the 311th, their first contact with the Continent of Europe took place on a gray day in the third week of November 1944, when their LCI carried them across the last few feet of dark channel water and onto a wide, pebble-strewn beach. Burdened by backpacks and other equipment, many found it difficult to accomplish the one hundred yard walk to a ruined roadway, where the chaos clearly visible around them was an unspoken shock. There, a truck convoy waited to transport them to their next destination—the small French town of Duclair. The Regimental Handbook again:

> *Past shattered homes, wreath-bedecked fragments of shattered monuments ... we joined the eastward throng of evacuees, on bicycle or foot, laden with the sparse salvage of their homes. The verdant garden plots of the suburbs, each with its improvised dwelling, showed us the grim determination of the French to accept this challenge of fate realistically and practically ...*

Later that day, shadows growing long on a grassy plain outside of Duclair, the outfit de-trucked and completed the regimental bivouac, where they'd remain for the week leading up to Thanksgiving, living amid a sea of mud, checking and re-checking their equipment, hiking over the picturesque countryside wearing their newly-issued overshoes, and attending lectures and displays of German weapons and uniforms.

Next, the men boarded a truck convoy which took them to Yvetot and an endless line of railroad box cars slated to transport them to Tongers [or Tongeren] Belgium, at which they arrived on the morning of November 26th. A three-mile jaunt brought them to Piringen, a small Flemish town just forty miles from the front. They would enter the fray as Ninth Army reserves.

Since no one knew how long they'd be in Piringen, an extensive training program was begun. Special attention was given to small unit tactics, map reading, aircraft identification, mines, and booby traps. All vehicles were serviced for pending combat operations, a task which probably kept personnel from the Motor Pool Section of Service Company hopping. On December 9th, 2004, with Generals Parker, Rice and Camm in charge, they boarded trucks and headed to the front for one hundred and thirty days of combat in some of the fiercest battles of WWII; the Hertgen Forest, the Ardennes, the Race to the Rhine, Remagen, and Central Germany.

At this juncture, I learned from 85 year-old former Motor Pool Sergeant Ted Bardsley, who had been transportation sergeant, dispatcher, and repair man in the Supply Section, of another soldier who had known Guy Vitale well: Staff Sergeant Emil J. Krukar of Milwaukee, Wisconsin. A brief investigation to locate him followed, and turned up his wife, who informed me that "Emil died eighteen years ago. He had a heart attack," she said. "High blood pressure for a long time."

CHAPTER 44

The Hurtgen Forest
Saturday, December 9, 1944 to Tuesday, January 9, 1945
Headquarters, Jagerhaus Hunting Lodge
11:30 a.m.

The 311th Infantry Regiment was thrown into the line on December 9th, 1944, taking over seven thousand yards of front from the 13th and 28th Infantry Regiments in the Hurtgen Forest. The Timberwolf Regimental Handbook describes it like this:

> ... *establishing its CP [command post] in the Jagerhaus (Hunting Lodge). This relief was accomplished in a driving snow storm that put a white blanket over mother earth that was not to be removed for the next sixty days ... The Jagerhaus was the only building for miles around and it was blacked out: why this building was not blown off the face of the earth is a mystery to us; possibly the enemy gave us credit for having enough sense not to use it.*

I'm not going to describe every battle in which the 311th took part. I want to concentrate on my uncle and the men with whom he served as much as possible. Those who'd like to read about unit battles can find detailed accounts in the CD version of the now hard-to-come by Regimental Handbook mentioned above, and in an account of the Remagen Bridge written by Lt. General Frank A. Camm and printed in the July 2006 issue of The Flash.

But here's just a brief mention of the Regiment's first taste of combat, when it was part of a Division offensive in the Lammersdorf area. Four days after the offensive began on December 13th, the 311th was ordered to eject some enemy soldiers who had penetrated a unit on their left. In the brief skirmish, seventy Germans were killed and a "score" of prisoners taken.

Snow-lined foxholes and bough-covered holes were homes away from home during the Timberwolves' days in the Hurtgen. From December 9th, 1944 through January 9th, 1945, the 311th Infantry Regiment found itself in the thick of things. And even though at first they didn't know it, these guys were good. All that time and effort spent training others had not been wasted, as they covered a lot of ground and quickly captured territory and killed German troops.

Did Guy and his Ammunition Section of Supply Company do their job well? To answer that question, I turned to several people. The first was former Sergeant T-4 Laverne J. Lander, whom I contacted in August 2005. Retired, he was living in Saint Paul, Minnesota. On August 20th, a few days after our lengthy phone conversation, he wrote me a very helpful three-page letter:

> *Yes … I remember Guy, but he was not a close friend of mine. Our company numbered about 100 men. Our job consisted of supplying our regiment with everything needed to fight a war. This included mail, water, ammunition, gas and food.… Each of the persons was close to the people he worked with each day. I was in charge of the Regimental mail room, and worked with three others in handling incoming and outgoing mail.*
>
> *All I can say about Guy was he impressed me as a first class soldier who knew his job and did it well; a quiet person who was always in command of any situation.*

Enclosed with his letter was a photo he'd taken of Guy and another soldier, in Immenhausen. Lander concluded his note with a list of three names and addresses: Joe Lemon, Nick Manojlovich—both of whom I'd already contacted—and Louis J. Spano, the other person in the photo. I couldn't wait to contact Spano.

*   *   *   *

Pine Bluffs, WY
Monday, June 19, 2006
703 Beech Street
4:00 p. m.

Former Tech Sergeant Louis J. Spano, of Keyser, West Virginia, retired from Du Pont's Savannah River plant in 1982 at the age of sixty-two, was residing in Aiken, South Carolina when I caught up with him in August 2005.

"I sure do remember Guy Vitale," he told me.

After chatting for a few minutes, I asked him to send me a note of everything he recalled about my uncle. His letter arrived on August 28th, but I'm only now getting the time to write it up:

> I *was drafted in February 1943, so Guy was already at Camp Butner in North Carolina before I got there. Guy was our drill Sergeant in the Service Company and also taught us how to break down the M-1 rifle.... Everyone in our company really respected him. He was tough on us but always treated us great. I don't remember him going to town very much and there were some nice towns to go to. We left Camp Butner and went to Camp Pickett, Va., and then went to Camp Kilmer, N.J. for overseas.... Most of my memories [of Guy] are during combat training while we were in Camp Butner. I remember he went on many 5 mile marches with us and also on some 12 mile rat races. He took very good care of us. I've often thought about him and wondered if he was still living....*

Expecting to see something in his letter about their experiences in Belgium and Germany, naturally I was a bit disappointed. I filed Lou's letter, not knowing that his name would surface again later.

Next, I contacted former Private First Class W. James Price, who'd been a rifleman with "A" Company. Retired from the Baltimore investment banking firm of Alex Brown & Sons, Jim was living in Baltimore with his wife. I caught up with him on Monday, July 17[th,] 2006, while he and his wife were vacationing in New London, New Hampshire. He told me he'd joined the 311th at Camp Butner in the spring of '44. Just a few short months later, he was in Europe with them:

"No, I didn't have any contact with the truck drivers from the Ammo Section," Jim told me. "We didn't want those trucks or tanks anywhere near us."

"Why."

"Well, every time the Germans heard a motor, they'd zero in on that location with mortars. One time, a tank came into our position, which was just north of the Bulge. When the Germans heard the sound, they dropped mortar rounds on us."

"So how would you get your supplies?" I asked.

"We'd get notice when the supplies were coming. The trucks would park about a mile away and the ammo, food, medical supplies, and mail would be hauled in to us. There was lots of snow on the ground, and I recall that sometimes the supply people used dog sleds to bring it from the trucks to our position."

"Did your company ever run short of ammunition?"

"Nope. My recollection was that *we* never ran short. But I can't speak for other companies. Whether or not we ran short depended upon two things: one was how active we were at any given time. Sometimes, there was a lot going on. Other times, not much, which was fine with us. The second thing was whether they could reach us or not. That depended on what we'd been doing the past couple of days."

What about holidays such as Christmas 1944? Although I have nothing from Guy or anyone in Service Company, 311th about this holiday, I came across a letter in the July 2006 issue of *The Flash* written by John Swengel, "L" Company, 309th Infantry Regiment, who wrote from Altamonte Springs, Florida. The 309th moved into the line only four days after the 311th. I think his experience was quite typical; the needs of the men of the 309th similar to other regiments. Reading between the lines, it certainly shows the diligent workings of a supply company in keeping the men fed, clothed, and in contact with family and friends back home:

> *We had our introduction to combat on December 13, 1944; our objective was to take a small town in Germany. We were successful in taking our objective …*
>
> *Germany was very cold that winter, and there was a lot of snow. On December 16, the day the Battle of the Bulge began, we were moving into another town, and the Germans did not want us there. We were into the town, when we got word not to advance any further, but to hold what we had taken.*
>
> *We went into foxholes, not getting much sleep because of the cold and because we had to be on the alert for a counter attack. Our food for the next eight days consisted of K rations; three boxes the size of cracker jacks per day. Each night after dark we received a new supply of K rations.*
>
> *It seemed that time was endless. We didn't get enough sleep, were always cold, and quite concerned about what the Germans might do. Living in a foxhole was not the greatest.*
>
> *Christmas Eve came and after dark, we were told to get out of the holes, and move out. We then walked several miles and were directed into a building. We were given sleeping bags, and were able to take our boots off for the first time in several weeks, and then into sleeping bags.*

We slept on the floor, but it was quite comfortable. We were finally able to be out of the cold and lay down.

Christmas Day came and with it we had a hot breakfast, a Church service, and then a turkey dinner. We also received mail from home, and we were able to write letters home. We had a very enjoyable Christmas Day.

Really? Can you imagine? I will never, ever, complain about *anything* around a Christmas holiday, again.

*　　*　　*　　*

Pine Bluffs, WY
Tuesday, July 24, 2006
703 Beech Street
8:00 a.m.

Dissatisfied that I could not locate someone who'd actually worked alongside Guy Vitale during the months his Regiment was in combat, I contacted "Red" Gonzalez, Membership Secretary of *The Flash* once more, and asked him to go over his membership roster again.

"You might try John L. Talley," he said. "He was in Service Company, too, but his record here went inactive as of November 2001. He might be deceased. Last address we had for him was North Canton, Ohio."

Thanking him, I hung up and immediately began an investigation to locate Mr. Talley. This would have been Tec 5 John L. Talley, listed on the Service Company's roster as hailing from Cedar Rapids, Iowa, back in 1944. Turned out "Red's" hunch was correct. The Social Security Death Index listed Talley's date of death as November 19, 1991. Another dead end; no pun intended.

The 311th Infantry Regiment spent almost five months in combat. Arriving at the front in the Hertgen Forest on December 9th, 1944, it was not withdrawn until April 20[th,] 1945. That's a long time for men to be under such pressure. Outside in the cold German winter, living in foxholes dug into snow, ice, and mud, with rain and sleet as constant companions, a man could go to pieces emotionally just from the conditions spawned by his environment. Throw in the stress of enemy artillery, mortar, and sniper fire, with the possibility of sudden death or serious injury, and, of course, the duty to do what they were there to do—attack the enemy, take ground from him, and hold it against his counter attacks—and you can see that what these men had to endure was, well … unimaginable.

The Regimental history:

> *During the 311ᵗʰ Timberwolves' one hundred and thirty days of continuous combat, there are certain high-lights: the Hurtgen Forest, the Siegfried Line, Schmidt and the Schwammenauel Dam, Nideggen and the Roer bridgehead, the Cologne plain or the Race to the Rhine, Remagen, and the Ruhr Pocket. To tell the story of each of these would require volumes, for the story of each is full of life and death, bravery and fear, joy and sorrow, humor and pathos, and suffering and misery and pain …*

*   *   *   *

Pine Bluffs, WY
Wednesday, July 25, 2006
703 Beech Street
8:00 a.m.

Back in 2004, while researching for this section of the book, someone—I think it was Joe Lemon, but it could have been "Red" Gonzalez or Nick Manojlovich—had given me the name of Fred Purnell as a person who'd been an officer in Service Company. That was a reference to Captain Frederick Purnell, from Amherst, Massachusetts. Whoever it was also sent me a copy of an article and an obituary which appeared in *The Flash* in January 2003, sent in by his widow, Elizabeth M. Purnell:

> *Dear Red:*
> *This is very hard for me to write even though my beloved husband passed away almost a year ago, on December 25, 2001.*
> *You may remember me and Frederick Purnell from the 78ᵗʰ Infantry Division Battlefield Tour in October 1991, when we told you our unique love story.*

Elizabeth went on to say that she'd met Fred in Weiden, Bavaria while working as his secretary at the U.S. Military post there; he was a U.S. Military Government Officer from June 1945 to June 7, 1946. When Purnell returned to Boston, he married and had children.

According to Elizabeth, twenty-five years later, after the death of his first wife, Bernice E. Smith in 1970, Fred searched for her, caught up with her in

Wales, learned that she was still single, and invited her to visit him in Boston. Elizabeth Purnell again:

> *During that visit [May 1970] Fred proposed to me. We got married in Cardiff, Wales in August of 1971, followed by a beautiful church wedding at Lindau, on the island in Lake Constantine, Germany, on September 3, 1971.*
>
> *We lived first in Norwood, Mass until 1981, and then lived in South Deerfield end enjoyed 30 very happy years together. Fred's two sons and children have become my family. I am very fond and proud of them. Fred often said: finding me was the best thing for him to come out of WWII.*

A graduate of Amherst High School in 1934, Fred Purnell was two years older than Guy, but they served together in Germany for a time. Purnell had graduated from The University of Massachusetts with a BA degree, and was class valedictorian. While working toward a Masters, he enlisted in the Massachusetts Army National Guard, and when hostilities broke out, he was assigned to OCS at Fort Benning, Georgia.

A telephone call to Mrs. Purnell elicited the name and phone number of her step-son, Frederick Purnell, Jr., and, on April 20th, 2005, a follow-up letter from her which contained a faded, black and white photograph of an old building standing next to a grove of cherry trees in full bloom. The following cryptic message, in Fred's handwriting, appears on the back:

> *Cherry blossoms. Our home at Lippe (where Sgt. Vitale captured the P.W. and the volkstormer).*

Wish I could tell you that I'd been able to unearth someone in the outfit who could enlighten us about this incident, but other than finding that Volkstormer is a company in Germany which had once manufactured vehicles but now manufactures Viagra (It's true! I'm not making this up), I could not learn anything more.

Following up, I contacted Frederick Purnell, Jr., who was a Philosophy teacher at Queen's College (City University of New York) in Flushing, N.Y. listed in the *Princeton Review's* 2005 edition of *America's Best Value Colleges,* as ranking # 8 among the nation's "best value" colleges. Junior informed me that his father had been "a student at U. Mass and graduated in 1939. While working toward a Masters, he had enlisted in the Guard, went to OCS at Benning and finished there as a 2nd Lieutenant."

"Know anything about his wartime service?" I asked.

"Yes. He took part in several campaigns. The Bulge, Hertgen Forest, and Remagen Bridge operations. [As I understand it} the Germans had tried to blow up all the bridges across the Rhine. Demolitions [charges] were placed but all of them went off except this one." He chuckled. "The day the bridge collapsed into the Rhine—March 17, 1945—was the day I was born."

After the war in Europe ended, Fred Purnell, who'd attained the rank of Major by then, served as the U.S. Government's Military Officer at Weiden, until June 1946, when he returned to the States. He, like others in the Regiment, received the Bronze Star for valor.

✻   ✻   ✻   ✻

Remagen, Germany
Wednesday, March 7, 1945
Ludendorf Bridge
0600 hours

On March 7th, 1945, the 9th Armored Division's Combat Command B, led by Brigadier General William H. Hoge, and to which the 309th, 310th, and 311th Infantry Regiments had been attached, completed an eight-day, thirty-five mile advance, capturing forty-seven towns and some fifteen hundred prisoners, and entered Remagen, a 2000-year old city of leather tanners and wine makers on the banks of the Rhine, approximately twenty-five miles south of the German city of Bonn. What happened during the next days would earn the 311th a Unit Citation.

Those lines from Shakespeare's King Henry V came to mind:

> *He which hath no stomach to this fight,*
> *   Let him depart ...*
> *But we in it shall be remembered;*
> *   We few, we happy few,*
> *We band of brothers;*
> *   For he today who sheds his blood with me*
> *Shall be my brother ...*

For a written description of the activities of Service Company, see *Activities of Service Company 311th Infantry From 08–20 March 1945 Which contributed to the earning of the unit citation for the 311th Infantry,* compiled and written by Joseph F. Lemon, 1st Lieutenant, Infantry. Also of interest are the memoirs of previously-mentioned Lieutenant General Frank A. Camm, one of the 78th Division's commanding officers, printed in various issues of *The Flash* during 2005 and 2006. I've relied heavily upon both for what follows.

General Camm wrote:

> *Crossing the Rhine at Remagen was the Ludendorf Bridge. Built in 1918 by Allied prisoners during World War I, it carried two railway lines and a pedestrian walkway, and it was considered one of the finest steel truss spans over the Rhine. The Krauts planked it over during World War II to carry truck traffic as well as rail. This was one of forty-seven bridges spanning the Rhine that the Germans systematically prepared for destruction to take advantage of the last formidable natural barrier facing the Western allies before reaching the industrial heartland of Germany.*

Upon arriving, elements of the 9th Armored Division expected to see only the remains of the Ludendorf Bridge, since German forces, retreating before the Allied advance, had blown the bridges spanning the Rhine at Bonn, Cologne and Coblenz.

And as Fred Purnell, Jr. had said, German engineers had prepared the bridge for demolition. This was done in three stages. Camm again:

> *The first stage was blowing a thirty-foot crater at the bridge entrance blocking armored vehicles from dashing across the bridge. The second was emplacing explosives to detonate on order, collapsing the bridge into the Rhine. The third was preparing backup charges in case of failure of stage two. The Krauts blew the crater at 1520 when the 9th Armored Division approached the bridge. [But] 9th Armored Division shells or bullets apparently cut the electric circuit to the second stage explosives, since they did not explode when the Kraut engineers tried to set them off. When the Germans detonated their backup charge, it damaged the upstream truss, but failed to drop the bridge.*

So the bridge survived for a few more days, enabling it to play its historic role in this epic battle.

Meanwhile, Service Company was being kept busy. Using all its available vehicles, it transported the Regiment to Remagen, its trucks under artillery and small arms fire from a German army determined to keep the Yanks out, allowing its engineers to have yet another chance to destroy the bridge. When intelligence learned of a new attempt by the Krauts to do just that, General Hoge ordered his 27th Armored Infantry Battalion to seize it. Avoiding machine gun and small arms fire from the upstream east bank, A Company, commanded by German-born Lieutenant Karl Heinz Timmerman, reached the towers and railroad tunnel on the far side in fifteen minutes, while 9th Armored Engineers raced onto the bridge and cut all wires on the west and center spans to prevent electricity from setting off the caps of forty pound charges planted on the crossbeams under the decking. Then they dashed to the far side to cut the main cable controlling the entire demolition set up, dismantling a 500-pound TNT charge with time fuses planted on the bridge, which had failed to detonate. With the bridge secured, Armored infantrymen, engineers, tank destroyers and anti-aircraft crews rolled over it, transformed for the moment into the most important military objective on the Western Front. Here's what General Camm said:

> Some 8000 men made it across the bridge in less than a day. Of these, half were our 78th Lightning Division soldiers. For hours at a time, reinforcements could not cross when German artillery blasted holes in the bridge. Combat engineers, under heavy shelling, worked constantly to repair the damage so other troops could cross.

Apparently, the 311th Infantry was the first complete infantry regiment to make it across the Ludendorf Bridge, where it proceeded to enlarge the bridge-head by driving north along the east bank of the Rhine. Here, wooded hills, not high but steep, made life difficult for them.

Indeed, during the next ten days the Regiment captured Unkel, Scheuren, Rhembreitbach, Honnef, Rhondorf, the Dollendorf-Neider and Ober, Ober-Kassel, Konigswinter, and Beuel. However, accompanied at first only by a mobile kitchen, hot meals were at a premium until later, since the infantry kitchens were still with the train on the other side of the Rhine. The following day, the 78th Division became the first infantry division to get all its soldiers across the Rhine, and as Camm noted:

> It seems fitting that our 78th Division, that by its capture of Schwammenauel Dam, had made possible the great drive to the Rhine, was the first to cross the last great natural obstacle. Incidentally, this was the first assault crossing of the Rhine since 55 BC, when Julius Caesar forced a crossing of the Rhine twelve miles South of Remagen.

Meanwhile, after the 311th crossed over, it was separated from the rest of the Division, and supply became a problem. All they had was a portable water point operated by one of the Engineer battalions, and that would have to suffice for several days. Here's Joe Lemon:

> *The service train which was located at Palmershein moved on 9 March to the Appolinaris Bottling Plant, about 1 ½ miles east of Bad Neuenhahr. This move took approximately 8 hours due to the crowded conditions of the roads and the fact that in some places [only] one way traffic was allowed.*
>
> *While at this location the train was under artillery fire and it was there that the A T Company kitchen was hit and a 1 ton trailer was completely destroyed.*

But the following day, Regimental Supply Officer, Major George E. Hudson, set up class I and class III supply points on the east side of the river at Unkel. Although under constant artillery and mortar fire, their proximity to front line soldiers aided the Regiment's advance north along the east bank of the Rhine. Lieutenant Lemon again:

> *… The entire period of 08–20 March 1945 was one of great activity for Service Company and the Service train. The supply trucks had to make long hauls from the division quartermaster to the advance sections set up on the east side of the river. This necessitated crossing the bridges and long stretches of road which were almost always under enemy artillery fire. A 2 ½ ton truck loaded with* mortar *and small arms ammunition was hit at Remagen and destroyed …*

It was during this period that Staff Sergeant Guy Vitale had, perhaps, his closest brush with death.

*   *   *   *

Remagen, Germany
Thursday, March 15, 1945
Ludendorf Bridge
1100 hours.

The olive green, 2-½ ton trucks, loaded with 60 and 81 mm mortar shells, 30, 45 and 50 caliber small arms ammunition, hand grenades, and much needed gasoline for tanks, trucks, and jeeps, were traveling in an eight-vehicle con-voy, along the narrow, two-lane road over Appolinaris Mountain. It was broad daylight. The convoy was moving briskly, each driver nervously scanning the too-clear morning sky for any sign of the hated German Messerschmitt Bf 109's, some of which still prowled the skies despite almost complete American air superiority. As they reached the summit and started down the other side, engines screaming as the drivers downshifted into lower gears, the river and the bridge across it lay below them.

Guy was in the cab of the last truck, but he was not driving. Sleep had been hard to come by the past few nights due to almost constant shelling from German artillery and the need to keep the infantrymen supplied twenty-four hours a day, so he had pulled rank a bit, and ordered Private First Class Clarence T. Moneyhon, of Pasadena, Texas to get behind the wheel.

Before leaving the division quartermasters' location, they'd all been briefed on the condition of the bridge's surface and instructed on how to cross the river when fully loaded with munitions. They were to proceed one at a time, moving as fast as possible once on the bridge, until all were safely across.

Guy wound them up, spacing the trucks at one hundred yard intervals, and climbed into the passenger seat of his own vehicle.

"Okay, Moneyhon," he said, "Let's move out smartly."

Even though it was the middle of March it was still cold. The cabs of these trucks were unheated. Their breath was visible on the mid-morning air as they traded banter. A thermos of hot coffee rested on the console between them.

"How about pourin' me a cup a that java?" Moneyhon asked. "Or are ya savin' it all fer yerself?"

Guy unscrewed the top, poured a cup and handed it to his driver. "I'll let ya have some," he replied. Then he poured himself one, drank it quickly—it was not that hot—leaned back and closed his eyes. Within minutes, he was asleep.

As Guy slept fitfully, his heavily loaded truck, Moneyhon at the wheel, approached the west end of the bridge. Moneyhon had geared into low, slowing almost to a crawl, waiting for number seven, piloted by Tec 5 Worrell C. "Daddy" Jones, of Waverly, Illinois, immediately in front of them, to begin its crossing.

Near the west entrance to the bridge, a disabled tank sat, abandoned, next to a huge hole in the ground. A few feet closer to the bridge, the burned out hulk of a halftrack loomed, its machine gun barrel aiming crazily at the sky.

Suddenly the sky was full of German Messerschmitts diving at the bridge, strafing as they passed. Guy awoke from a sleep of peace to a world anything but peaceful. It took mere seconds for his brain to adjust; to see, hear and feel what was happening, and even as his vehicle rolled to a point perhaps thirty yards behind Jones' truck, that vehicle took a direct hit. Fire! Exploding shells, burning gasoline, thick, acrid smoke.

"God!" Guy yelled. "Pull this fuckin' truck over, Moneyhon! We gotta bail out."

But Moneyon needed no urging. Steering the vehicle off onto the narrow shoulder, he slammed on the brakes and turned the engine off. "Jones is still in the truck," he cried, as he and Guy left the cab by their respective doors.

Another Messerschmitt approached, its machine guns spewing death and destruction. Guy threw himself into a ditch, adjusted his helmet, poked his head up, and looked around. Jones' truck was burning fiercely. Mortar rounds were cooking off, sending metal shards in all directions, and black smoke poured from the cargo area.

It must be true, what they say about Texans being a courageous bunch. Moneyhon did not take cover in the ditch with Guy.

"Moneyhon! Get yer ass back here!" Guy yelled. But Moneyhon did not hear. Oblivious to the danger to himself, he raced to the burning truck, instantly appraised the situation, threw the driver's door open, pushed the wounded and unconscious "Daddy" Jones aside, and jumped in. Starting the vehicle, he slipped it into gear and moved onto the bridge as fast as he could reasonably go given the conditions. With smoke billowing out behind the truck and a bleeding Jones slumped in the passenger seat next to him, Pfc. Moneyhon drove that burning truck, ammunition exploding to the four points of the compass, across the Ludendorf Bridge, to safety.

Moments later it was over. The strafing aircraft had disappeared eastward. Rising from the ditch, Guy stared vacantly after the receding truck. "Waddaya know about that!" he breathed.

For his act of bravery, Pfc. Clarence Moneyhon was awarded the bronze star. "Daddy" Jones, his wounds superficial, was patched up and rejoined Service Company at Herborn, in May 1945. Captain Fred Purnell's photo of him on his first day back with his unit appeared in the June 1992 issue of *The Flash* along with many other photos taken by Purnell and forwarded to *The Flash* after his death, by his widow, Elizabeth.

*   *   *   *

Pine Bluffs, WY
Thursday, June 22, 2006
703 Beech Street
8:00 a.m.

By the time "Daddy" Jones returned to Service Company, the 311th was off the line and enjoying some well needed R and R, probably in Herborn. Here's a copy of Guy's letter to his father, written on April 22, 1945, just ten days after President Franklin Roosevelt's death on April 12th, only eight days before Adolf Hitler would commit suicide in an underground bunker in Berlin, and nine weeks prior to Nicola's own death on June 30th:

Mr. Nicola Vitale
20 Breed Street   *Sgt. Guy Vitale 31 060 610*
East Boston, Mass   *Ser. Co., 311th Inf. APO 78*
Germany   *c/o PM NY, NY*

4/22/45

Dear Pa
A few lines to let you know about things in general. We are off the line now. We have been up there since December 9. The place I'm in now is a nice peaceful town somewhere in Germany. I'm not allowed to say too much about it. We are resting and for once enjoying ourselves. The meals are good and sleep plentiful. I have no idea how long we will be here. The mail has been coming through very regularly. All the folks write. Have been receiving the packages and newspapers. That's about all I can write for now. Will write more later. Regards to all.

Son,
Guy

And a few months later, as a new German winter was setting in and Guy's service days were drawing to a close, he wrote this letter to his sister Mary, late in the war:

Germany,
Nov. 16, 1945

Dear Mary:
Here it is; the news you've been waiting for. I'm on my way home. I leave tomorrow. That is, I leave the Division. From here, a trip to France and then I sail. I don't know how long all this will take. According to past reports, it shouldn't take too long. I should be home about Dec. 10th.
Please don't write anymore. I will write from time to time, and when I get to the States I'll send a wire. I hope everything at home is

back to normal. I'm back in Immenhausen. Called back from Berlin. It's a good thing. Berlin is pretty rough on a man. I'm keeping my fingers crossed. I may be able to take $500 with me, I hope so. I can use it. That's about all. Regards to all at home; see you soon.

Brother,
Guy

And he did. I recall his arrival a few days before Christmas that year. My family was still living in Somerville, a suburb of Boston, at the time. True to his word, he sent my mother a telegram announcing his train's arrival. On that evening we all piled into the car and drove to South Station to meet the train from New York City and pick him up. On the way home, he convinced my father to stop at a liquor store in Ball Square for a case of beer, which he brought to our house.

Remember, he'd been in Berlin prior to returning Stateside, as part of the American Army of Occupation. Depositing himself in an overstuffed chair in our living room, using the case of beer as a hassock for his feet, he popped the cap on a bottle, drank long and deep, pointed a finger at my father, and announced, "The Russians are next!"

My mother? Knitting her hands together and pulling them apart in a kneading, rolling motion as she rushed from kitchen to living room checking on the meal she was preparing, and announcing to anyone who'd listen, "What a wonderful Christmas gift. Praise God!"

From all reports, during his unit's participation in the European Theater, Guy was a model soldier; he obeyed orders from his superiors, kept his nose clean, and performed his duties in an exemplary manner. He was well-liked by his peers; enlisted men and officers.

For his efforts, when discharged in January 1946, he had earned a Good Conduct Medal, Bronze Star (which is given for valor), the American Campaign Medal, the European-African-Middle Eastern Campaign Medal with three Bronze Service Stars, and a WWII Victory Medal. He also was authorized to wear the WWII Honorable Service Lapel Button, and the Combat Infantryman's Badge.

What prompted Guy's assertion that we'd soon be at war with the Russians? Nothing is known of his personal experiences during the summer of '45, while his outfit filled the roll of occupier in Berlin. What we *do* know is that the political situation in Europe during 1945 was complex. Commander of Allied

Forces, General Dwight D. Eisenhower, wanting only to focus on ending the war, refused to consider the future composition and makeup of the Continent after Hitler's fall from power. As a result, according to Historian Paul Johnson, these aspects did not enter into his thinking:[55]

> *Hence he [Eisenhower] refused to countenance the proposal of his chief British subordinate, General Bernard Montgomery, to throw the entire Allied might into a single direct thrust at Berlin, which might have ended the war in 1944, but embodied corresponding risks, and instead favored his own 'broad front' policy, of advancing over a wide axis which was much safer, but also much slower. As a result the Russians got to Berlin first, in the process occupying most of eastern Europe and half of Germany itself ...*

To paraphrase Paul Johnson, of course, in retrospect, this played right into Stalin's strategy of rolling back German troops in furtherance of his goal to control the maximum amount of territory and resources in the postwar period. Sticking to his military mandate of destroying Nazi forces and compelling Germany's unconditional surrender, Eisenhower resisted the temptation to jockey for postwar advantage. He halted when he felt his job was finished; that was upon reaching Berlin.

Monty may have been right. Because Eisenhower's approach was followed, the occupation of Germany was a joint affair among the then allies; the United States, Britain, France, and the Soviet Union. Forty-five years later, the mess *that* created was finally cleaned up, after the world had suffered through the annexation of several countries by the Soviet Union, the Berlin blockade and the Berlin wall. In the process, America spent the equivalent of $200 billion annually in today's dollars—it was called the Marshall Plan—to put Europe back on its feet.

But getting back to 1946, imagine the arrogance of Soviet troops, whose country now possessed much of Europe, when meeting American and British forces in the streets of Berlin. Perhaps in dealing with Russian soldiers on a daily basis, Guy was able to see or at least suspect what many intellectuals and pseudo-intellectuals of that period did not: that the Soviet Union was anything but a peace-loving People's Democracy with an earnest desire to better the conditions of the working peoples of the world.

---

55   Paul Johnson, *A History of the American People*, HarperCollins Publishers, Inc. New York NY. 1997.

At the 78th Division's Reunion in Chicago, in 1998, Rabbi Victor Weisberg dedicated his speech to those killed in action in WWI and WWII. Here's an excerpt. I can think of no more fitting way to close this section of the book than to quote him:

> ... *My uncle, may he rest in peace, served in the first world war and I lost two cousins in the second, but I believe that it was a righteous war and that when we fought we fought for God's sake and humanity's sake, and those who have taken their leave can rest in peace for the battle well fought and the war beautifully won ...*
>
> *And so we remember the snows may fall, and the winds may rage, the seasons change, ourselves grow a day or two older, raising new generations, wondering if they would respond to the call to the colors.*
>
> *We don't want to think that they wouldn't. We believe that national service made us better for responding. And we believe that those who have taken their leave have a memory and a repository that we must cherish and carry on, not in battle, necessarily, but carry on to the highest and best of our ability that they shall not have died in vain.*
>
> *May we remember them with blessing in our heart and gratitude in our soul ...*
>
> *May we remember them for all that they did then and they continue to do to make this country safe and prosperous ...*
>
> *May we remember them as we rise and pray for them.*

PART SEVEN

A PERFECT SPY[56]

---

56   The name of this section is taken from the best-selling novel of that title by John le Carre, Bantam Books, an imprint of Alfred A. Knopf, Inc. New York, NY. 1986.

CHAPTER 45

East Boston, MA
Saturday, February 9, 1946
Bennington Street Apartments
7:30 p.m.

Guy Vitale's date of separation from the United States Army was January 4th,
1946, but he actually arrived home in mid-December 1945, sufficiently recovered from the almost constant fear, deadening fatigue and accumulated sleep
loss of his months in combat, and well on his way to putting aside many of the
unpleasant memories that he'd accumulated along the way.

Unlike his summers playing baseball in Saint Johnsbury and Salisbury, in
the Army he'd learned to save some of his money, and he'd brought a sizeable
chunk of it home with him. Not wanting to burden my parents or his brother,
Frank, who was now living in suburban Melrose with his family, Guy took a
room in East Boston, in the same shabby apartment building on Bennington
Street in which he'd lived briefly before entering the army almost four years
before.

But he didn't attempt to find a job. Content for a time to tread water, relax,
and check out East Boston once more while he thought about his future, he
settled into a pattern of rising late, buying breakfast at a local coffee shop {there
were no McDonalds, Burger Kings or Wendy's back then], reading the morning
newspaper, and dropping in here and there on old acquaintances, whenever he
found one available. Feeling a pull in the direction of keeping his body fit, he
spent several afternoons each week at the East Boston High School's athletic
field, jogging and doing calisthenics. In the evenings, he amused himself at a
local bar, rehashing his high school football and baseball exploits and talking
about his war experiences with whomever would listen.

Well, after almost two months, vaguely uncomfortable with this lifestyle, and intelligent enough to know that he could not continue in this vein much longer, he knew he'd soon need to find a job.

"There's always the shipyard," an acquaintance he ran into at a local bar told him one night, when the subject came up.

Guy slammed his bourbon and ginger ale down on the dark tabletop so hard his friend jumped. "No," he said sharply.

"Why not?" The man asked, sipping his Budweiser.

Thinking about it for a few seconds, Guy glanced toward the mahogany bar, at the backs of several rum-sodden men he knew to be shipyard workers, and had no ready answer except that he wanted something different … something more. He shrugged. "The shipyard's out," he said.

So, what then? Day after day, he thought about it. Finally, he was forced to admit a scary truth. He didn't know what he wanted to do with his life. *It would help,* he thought, *if I could figure out some direction. But nothin' seems ta interest me.*

On the afternoon of the day he finally admitted that to himself, shaken, he stopped into the local church and slipped into a pew in the back. A quick glance around assured him that no one else was in the place. Kneeling, he quickly, almost furtively, asked the God he'd not prayed to in years, to show him what he was to do.

That evening, a cool, bleak Saturday in mid-February, showered and shaved in case he ran into a local broad who was looking for more than a drink or two, he was standing in front of the bathroom mirror, applying aftershave lotion liberally to his smooth, olive skin, when the telephone rang.

"Guy? It's Ann. How are you?" His sister and her husband, Al Tosi, had moved to Washington, D.C. several years before, where Al had taken a job with the Bureau of Engraving at a much better salary than he'd ever made as a junior draftsman in Boston. Childless, they had already purchased a two-story home at 714 E. 31st Street, N.E., with several bedrooms and a large, screened-in front porch on which they spent their evenings playing Gin and Royal Rummy.

"Ann? Oh, I'm okay. Getting ready ta go out."

"Glad I caught ya. Al and I were talkin' about you at supper."

"Why?"

"We were wonderin' if ya'd gotten a job yet?"

Guy bristled. "No, not yet. But I'm lookin'," he lied.

"Al heard that the Library of Congress is hiring some people. Good pay and benefits. And they give preference ta veterans."

His eyebrows went up. The bottle of aftershave went down. "I don't know, Ann. I hear it's expensive ta live in D.C."

"Well, if ya came down here, you could stay with us. We've got plenty a room. Another thing. George Washington University's nearby. Ya might be able ta go there at night under the GI Bill."

Guy thought for a moment. He was to say, later, that he did not know what moved him to this quick decision, which changed his life forever. Perhaps it was boredom. Or possibly, just not knowing what he wanted to do with his life. Or perhaps it was his prayer earlier that day. Anyway, he'd been slowly coming to the conclusion that Boston had little to offer or interest him. Always a loner, his few friends had either moved away or were busy with their own families. His mother had died in October 1943, and his father on June 30th, 1945, two months after Hitler committed suicide on April 30th, and seven weeks after Germany surrendered on May 8th. His brother, Frank, working nights at the *Boston Globe,* had little free time. Ann had moved, and although he was fond of his oldest sister, Mary, he had little in common with her, since she was ten years his senior and had marital problems of her own to deal with.

"You sure I could stay with you?"

"Yeah. Al says it's fine with him."

Guy sucked in his breath. "Who do I contact about that job?"

*   *   *   *

Washington, D.C.
Monday, February 25, 1946
714 31ˢᵗ Street, N.E.
7:30 a.m.

Even though it was still early in the morning, the District of Columbia's traffic was extremely heavy, as it was every day. Al Tosi turned his dark blue 1946 Plymouth Sedan off of Benning Road onto Minnesota Avenue and headed south in a line of traffic, toward the John Philip Sousa Bridge across the Anacostia River. Just before crossing the river, he'd turn onto Pennsylvania Avenue, which would take them into the heart of the Capital, where the Library of Congress and the Bureau of Engraving were located. It was Guy's first day on his new job.

"You nervous?" Al asked.

"No," Guy said, staring out the window on the passenger side. "Well, a little."

"I was nervous as hell on my first day at the Bureau," Al said, conversationally. "But after a couple of hours, everything was fine."

"Humph," Guy responded, indicating his disinterest in the subject. He was about to say more, but he did not want to pursue the matter with his brother-in-law and perhaps make him angry. He'd need to ride back and forth to work with Al for God only knew how long; at least until he was able to afford a car of his own, and had obtained a D.C. driver's license.

As they turned onto the congested bridge, Guy thought about how easily he'd obtained the job. He'd had to take a test, but it was so simple that a high school kid could have passed it. Then his name had been placed on a short list containing other names, but with many assistant librarian positions open, he'd had to wait less than two weeks before hearing that he'd been accepted. His month-to-month lease had been paid through the end of February. After informing his landlord that he was leaving, he packed his belongings into a bag, boarded a train at South Station, and left Boston and the Bay State behind.

Removing a pack of Camels from his short-sleeved shirt pocket, he tapped one out, lit up, took a deep drag, and exhaled it in the direction of the open car window. "What time will you pick me up?"

"At ten after five, right on the corner at 2nd Street," Al said. "Don't be late. Traffic's always bad around there at that time."

They proceeded northeast, with Guy resuming his examination of the buildings along Pennsylvania Avenue. He was not that interested in the job he'd been hired to do, one of several Assistant Librarians, each in charge of the numerous new collections which the Library of Congress was rapidly acquiring. What he wanted the job for was so he could, as soon as possible, enroll at nearby George Washington University's night school and resume the pursuit of that elusive college degree, which Uncle Sam would now pay for. He had no idea at the time how events would unfold.

*   *   *   *

Pine Bluffs, WY
Tuesday, July 25, 2006
70 3 Beech Street.
9:30 a.m.

After the cessation of hostilities in WWI, the United States, eager to return to a peacetime footing, rushed to demobilize. As a result, the country was unprepared for the Juggernaut that was Hitler's opening move of Word War II. Although American mobilization was swift and had begun even before Pearl Harbor, still, valuable time was spent in returning to a war mode, and *that* resulted in the loss of lives. Having learned its lesson, the United States did not fall into the same trap *after* WWII regarding either military preparedness or intelligence gathering.

As far back as 1944, prominent New York City lawyer, William J. (Wild Bill) Donovan, who had gained the President's confidence, first in his capacity as Coordinator of Information, as Roosevelt's unofficial liaison to Sir William Stevenson, chief of British Security Coordination (BSC), and later as wartime Director of the Office of Strategic Services (OSS), had proposed to Roosevelt the idea of creating a new intelligence agency directly supervised by the President, "... which will procure intelligence both by overt and covert methods and will at the same time provide intelligence guidance, determine national objectives, and coordinate the intelligence material collected by all government agencies." And Sir William thought of such an agency as:

> *... a worldwide intelligence service to maintain the security of the democracies in the critical years ahead with safeguards against abuse of power. The safeguards were to have taken the form of a central authority made up of responsible citizens working within the framework of democratic government. Those safeguards were the most important feature, of the proposals, anticipating the problems and moral dilemmas that would finally explode in the 1970s.*[57]

But Roosevelt died from a massive cerebral hemorrhage on April 12, 1944, before implementing Donovan's suggestion.

Moreover, although eventually accomplished, getting it done was not easy. At first, seeing no further need for a coordinating intelligence apparatus which combined strategic warning and clandestine activity into one agency, and assured by the military services, the State Department, and the FBI, that to continue the OSS would be a duplication of function, Harry S. Truman, elevated to the vacant presidency after Roosevelt's death, abolished the OSS on September 20, 1945.[58]

However, by January 20, 1946, only four months after the OSS had been dissolved, either as part of a plan, or because Truman had changed his mind, the Central Intelligence Group (CIG) was formed, despite strong opposition from the aforementioned agencies. The following year, Congress, reacting to the rising hostility of the Soviet Union and the condition called "The Cold War," passed the National Security Act of 1947, which set up an information gathering agency. On September 18, 1947, the CIA came into being, as did the

---

57   William Stevenson, *A Man Called Intrepid*, Ballantine Books, New York, NY, 1976.
58   Ibid.

National Security Council. Both would grow rapidly into the gigantic operations with their unaccountable budgets that we know today. Rear Admiral Roscoe H. Hillenkoetter was appointed the CIA's first director (DCIA), and he served in that capacity until early in the Eisenhower Administration.

Later, Allen Dulles took over that post. Dulles was the younger brother of John Foster Dulles, foreign affairs advisor to the Republican presidential candidate Thomas E. Dewey in 1948—yes, recall that now famous, or rather infamous, Chicago Daily Tribune headline—"Dewey defeats Truman"—and Secretary of State in the Eisenhower years.[59] Under Allen Dulles's tutelage, the CIA rapidly expanded and developed a sense of independence from Congressional oversight, which led to later problems beyond the scope of this book.

But in June of 1949, thirty-one year old Guy Vitale, his days occupied as an Assistant Librarian at the Library of Congress while he worked toward that much-coveted college degree at George Washington University, would become one of the CIA's first recruits.

*   *   *   *

Washington, D.C.
Friday, June 3, 1949
Library of Congress
3:55 p.m.

On June 3rd, 1949, the New York prosecution of Alger Hiss was occupying the headlines as national media reported the epic opening statements of the prosecutor, U.S. District Attorney Thomas Murphy, Hiss's defense counsel, Lloyd Paul Stryker. Guy Vitale, engrossed in a review of his notes for Professor Warren Reed West's course on *The Constitution of the United States,* for a Political Science exam at George Washington University that evening, was unaware of the man's presence until he heard someone clear his throat.

"Mr. Vitale?"

Frowning, he looked up. "Yes. What do you need?"

In front of his desk stood a well-dressed, crew-cut, very physically-fit man, wearing a three-piece suit and a quirky grin. He flashed a thin, wallet-type identification card, too fast for Guy to actually see it well.

"Henry Barnes, Central Intelligence Agency." He tucked the ID in his back pocket. "May I talk with you?"

---

59   Anthony J. Sacco, *Little Sister Lost,* Writers Club Press, an imprint of iUniverse, Inc. Lincoln, NE. 2004.

Closing the book, Guy placed it flat on his desk and glanced at his wrist-watch. "I only have a couple minutes" he said. "Gotta grab some supper before I go ta class tonight." He gestured to the single chair in front of the desk. "Sit."

Barnes let his eyes wander around the room for a moment, before pulling out the chair and sitting. "You're a bachelor living with your sister and her husband," the man said. "You've made very few friends since coming to D.C. after getting out of the Army. You're attending George Washington University and have been for three semesters. Your final exams are this week."

Guy's eyes narrowed. "How do ya know all that?"

"We've … I've been watching you some," Barnes said.

"What d'ya want with me?"

"Mr. Vitale, I'll come straight to the point. A minute ago, I said I work for the Central Intelligence Agency. We're looking for new people to join us. We think you might want to be one of them."

Reaching into his shirt-pocket, Guy extracted a pack of Camels, pulled one out, and searched his desktop for matches. Barnes, ready with a lighter, extended it toward him and flicked it. Guy leaned forward until the tip of his cigarette made contact with the flame, inhaled and sat back. He had already decided that he was not going to stay on at the Library after he finished college; that he'd be looking for something else. But he was uncomfortable and a bit uneasy that this stranger seemed to know these things about him.

"Yeah? What makes ya think I'd wanna do *that?*"

"Oh, call it an informed guess." He handed Guy a business card. "If you're interested, be at this address tomorrow morning at 9:30. I'll meet you there and introduce you to someone who can tell you more."

"Tomorrow's Saturday," Guy said matter-of-factly.

The man smiled. "It's okay. Some of us work on Saturdays, too."

*   *   *   *

Washington, D.C.
Saturday, June 4, 1949
2436 E Street, NW
9:15 a.m.

The address on the card Barnes had given him was the headquarters building of the old Central Intelligence Group, the CIA's predecessor organization. Guy was fifteen minutes early. Despite trying to convince himself that he was not terribly interested in working for some governmental bureaucracy, he'd decided after turning in the evening before to go to the address and listen to their pitch.

What harm will it do? he reasoned. *I can still get back in plenty a time ta study for Monday night's International Law exam.* Which meant he needed to do a complete review of Professor John Withrow Brewer's course; *A Development of Legal Institutions.* A serious student, Guy had prepared for each of his classes, doing the reading assignment as he went along, so he was not terribly worried.

Awakening early, he showered, shaved carefully, and dressed in the new suit he'd purchased with his second paycheck the year before, but had had scant opportunity to wear. Leaving the house at 714 31st Street to catch a bus, he admitted to a certain excitement, and as he approached the building on foot a half hour later, a quickening of his pulse rate.

Dropping his unfinished cigarette to the sidewalk, Guy crushed it under his foot, and, with a spring in his step, mounted the brick stairs to the imposing front door. Before he could press the bell, the portal opened and Agent Henry Barnes, wearing the same three-piece suit he'd worn the afternoon before, stood there, his hand extended in greeting.

"Guy!" he said. "May I call you Guy? I'm glad you came. You won't regret it."

Shaking the man's hand, Guy noted the strength of his grip and that they were about the same age. He accompanied Barnes into the house, down a hall, the walls of which were lined with beautifully-framed prints of past presidents, and into a room at the far end. Here, standing at a heavily-curtained window overlooking the street, was Lieutenant General Hoyt S. Vandenberg. Appointed in June 1946 to replace Rear Admiral Sidney Souers as CIG's first Director, he served as its second Director until its merger with the CIA. Vandenberg was act-ing for the CIA in an unofficial capacity at this point, doing recruiting. Another man, dark, thin mustache, blue blazer and regimental tie, sat quietly on a sofa to the right of the General's desk, resting a thin file on his knees.

From his days in the Army, Guy immediately identified the rank, although not the identity of the man with whom he was meeting. *Impressive*, he thought. Vandenberg introduced himself, extended his hand for Guy to shake, and intro-duced the fourth man in the room.

"And this gentleman is Mr. Copeland." Mike Copeland was one of many CIA case officers who had cut their teeth in the OSS. He shook Guy's hand and retired to his couch, from which he observed everything but said nothing dur-ing the entire interview.

"I'm sure Agent Barnes told you a bit about why you've been invited here, Guy," Vandenberg began. "Our organization was first known as the Central Intelligence Group. We were set up by the President to absorb the old OSS. That process was accomplished quickly. I came aboard in June a year ago. By

July, I was able to tell the National Intelligence Authority that we'd begun to take over all clandestine foreign intelligence activities."

"Is that what you do?" Guy asked, and was conscious that his question might sound unintelligent to this man; that in fact he might sound like a young child trying to impress its elders. *What is it about these guys?* he wondered. *They seem so much more mature than me. Even Barnes.*

But Vandenberg understood how to put underlings at ease. He made a non-descript hand-gesture and smiled. "Well, yes. For almost two years now, we—first CIG and now CIA—have tried to comply with Mr. Truman's requirements: to create a structure that can collate the best intelligence gathered by several departments, and to make that structure operate."

Guy's head was spinning. "I thought the State Department handled that stuff. And the Army has an intelligence branch, too, right?"

"Correct. But the President wanted to centralize these different agencies. Otherwise, the friction and waste of resources would continue. Wild Bill Donovan, Chief of the former OSS, was of the same opinion. He saw the need for one centralized agency to gather information that will, as he put it, 'aid in solving the problems of peace.'"

Guy was silent as he digested what he was hearing and tried to imagine what part he might play in all this. Vandenberg broke the quiet.

"Our funding will vastly improve with this session of Congress. It's been limited 'till now. We'll be hiring many new agents. Men like you, Guy. We've already begun interviewing."

"How did you decide to approach me?" Guy wanted to know.

At this point, Agent Barnes entered the conversation. "We know what we're looking for in our new agents. There's a certain … profile. We think you fit that profile."

Guy was tempted to ask what that profile was, but instead, looking a bit confused, he glanced at his shoes. Seeing this, General Vandenberg picked up. "We're offering a good salary, lots of benefits, including full medical and dental coverage, and retirement pay, which you'd be eligible for after twenty years of service."

"It sounds awfully good," Guy said tentatively.

"And," Vandenberg continued, here's the best part. Your years in the military will help. Although you'll need to serve a full twenty years, you'll start off at a higher pay level than if you'd had no military service."

Hearing that, Guy became fully engaged. "One thing." He glanced over at Barnes. "I want to finish college. Get my degree. Will I be able to do that?"

"Probably," Vandenberg hedged. "If you sign on, you'll have to put school off for awhile in order to undergo training. After that? It's up to you."

"Do I need to decide right this minute?"

"No," Barnes said. "Take a few days to think it over. I'll come by to see you next week."

*   *   *   *

Washington, D.C.
Saturday, June 4, 1949
2436 E Street, NW
10:20 a.m.

Guy had left. Vandenberg, with a glance at Copeland, collapsed into an executive chair behind the oak desk and loosened his uniform tie, waiting for Barnes to return from seeing Guy out.

"Will he commit, do you think?" he asked as Barnes returned and tossed himself into an overstuffed chair across from the desk.

"I think so. He's the type the Company likes," Barnes said.

"What do *you* think, Mike?" Vandenberg asked.

Copeland opened the file he was carrying, but did not look at it. He leaned forward. "He's young, but he's been around the block a time or two. He doesn't rattle. I like that."

Vandenberg extracted a pack of Old Golds from his uniform's jacket pocket, pulled one out, tapped it on the desk and lit up. "Makes a good appearance," he said. "Wears his hair short back and sides, speaks reasonably good English, was a top student in a not-too-great high school, but Cum Laude at a damn good prep school, and is now trying to get a degree. Shows he's intelligent and inquisitive, though not the overly intellectual type."

Copeland nodded as the General took a deep drag on his cigarette. "He's a decent linguist, too." He tapped the open file on his lap. "Speaks Italian well, and has some French."

"While he was in the Service, did he have any trouble with authority?"

"None." Copeland said. "Seems to understand discipline."

The General stood and addressed Barnes. "Give him 'till the middle of the week," he said. "Then go see him. Bring along an invitation to the Company party at Langley next weekend. If he's on the fence, rubbing elbows with some of the boys and girls should do the trick."

*   *   *   *

Pine Bluffs, WY
Monday, June 26, 2006
70 3 Beech Street.
9:30 a.m.

I don't think anybody who hasn't lived it can adequately describe the life of a spy: the forced distance and for the most part unwelcome sense of alienation from loved ones and friends; the need to live a cover story as a nice guy who'd temporarily lost his way, and the more or less constant fear of discovery. An unsettling lifestyle if there ever was one.

But at this point, Guy, ruggedly handsome in a boyish sort of way, was in his prime. At a loss for what to do with his life, yet full of zeal and urgency to get on with it, the idea of working for the CIA appealed to his senses of adventure and patriotism. *I'll be doing it for America,* he reflected. *Protecting my country and the free world from its enemies.* And then there was this other thing; a quality which the men he'd met possessed, of self-assurance. *Barnes, too,* he thought. *He's near my age, but he's much more self-confident and sophisticated than me. What do they know that I don't?*

So it wasn't surprising that when Henry Barnes came to see him the following week, his decision was a resounding "yes." The next day, he gave the Library his week's notice. At the end of that week, having cleared out his desk, he embarked on his new career as a field agent in training for the Central Intelligence Agency, the most powerful intelligence gathering agency for the strongest government then on the world scene.[60]

Yes, of course he told his sisters, his brother and brothers-in-law that he'd changed jobs. But he never told any of his family what he did for the CIA. When asked, he said he was a clerk, but was always vague about his actual duties. His cover story? A man drowning his sorrows about what might have been—that elusive baseball career—in heavy drinking while trying to make something of his life in the Nation's Capitol.

---

60   His official file, opened upon his employment in 1949, was #39049.

*   *   *   *

Williamsburg, VA
Sunday, July 6, 1947
Camp Peary, Virginia
8:30 a.m.

Established during WWII as a Navy Seebees training base, Camp Peary, a 9,275 acre base on the banks of the York River southeast of Richmond, Virginia, was officially transferred to the Central Intelligence Agency sometime in 1951, for use as a place to train its agents.

According to a 1998 article by John Pike, FAS, the CIA's Special Training Center was used by the CIA's Directorate of Operations "for training [of its people in everything] ranging from the Basic Operations Course to advanced weapons and explosives training, driving techniques, field surveillance, infiltration and exfiltration, and paramilitary skills."

That was during and after 1951. But where did the fledgling CIA train its agents prior to that? The previously mentioned book, *A Man Called Intrepid*, which describes the clandestine activities of the office of British Security Coordination (BSC) prior to and during WWII, provided a possible answer with its references to a mysterious Camp X in the Canadian wilderness:

> *[Bases in] Bletchley and Bermuda were important to BSC for detection. Camp X gave BSC its punch. These closely guarded acres of Canadian farmland were separated from the United States by a stretch of some of the blackest, coldest water in the world, a dramatic contrast with Bermuda, thrust far forward into a sea surrounded by war action but lapped by warm waters.*
>
> *Here, agents trained, guerilla devices were tested, and Hollywood-style dummy buildings were constructed in imitation of important Nazi hideouts.*

Camp X, located near the Toronto-Kingston highway along the north Shore of Lake Ontario, was approximately 300 miles northwest of Manhattan, where it could easily be reached during WWII by BSC, OSS and FBI personnel. Recruits could cross the border undetected, but unauthorized visitors would find it difficult to reach because its southern approaches were guarded by forty miles of lake water, and its northern boundary protected by dense woods. Perimeters on east and west were patrolled by British commandos:[61]

> *These veterans of raids along the enemy coasts in Europe, now the protectors of Camp X, were skilled in the use of the hatpin, the thin copper wire, and other homely, silent, lethal weapons that would not needlessly alarm the local inhabitants or draw the unwelcome attention of the local constabulary.*

It was here that Ian Fleming, of later James Bond fame, trained. And it was probably here that the CIA sent its agents in the early days. And it was here, I believe, that Guy received his initial instruction.

Later, when Camp Peary, known as "The Farm," became the CIA's official training site, Guy probably traveled there to practice surveillance and counter-surveillance techniques, clandestine communication methods, brush passes, servicing dead drops, physical conditioning, driving courses, advanced firearms and explosives training, a three-day seminar on silent killing, night landings in rubber boats on sandy shores, falling out of airplanes at low altitudes, dipping into secret inks, and learning Morse Code. It's not known how long this training would have lasted back in those days, but obviously, Guy successfully completed it. His army Ranger training, his familiarity with weapons, his experience driving many types of army vehicles, and his perceived need after leaving the Army, to keep his body in some sort of physical shape despite his drinking, probably helped him get through.

And for Guy, there was this other change. Very much in the public eye during high school and later while playing baseball on Cape Cod and in the Twin-States League, and on Maryland's Eastern Shore, he quickly learned that he was, from that time forward, obliged to seek anonymity. "The less anyone knows about the personal life of an agent, the better," became an unwritten law. All records about him after 1949 were erased from their respective resting places, whether at the Library of Congress, in the files of the Civil Service, or at George Washington University.

As a corollary to that, the fledgling spy apparently learned and put into practice early, the lesson that in the dangerous intelligence game, everybody talks, so be careful in whom you confide.

---

61   William Stevenson, *A Man Called Intrepid*, Ballantine Books, New York, NY, 1976.

*   *   *   *

Pine Bluffs, WY
Wednesday, November 15, 2006
703 Beech Street
8:15 a.m.

Not much is known about what Guy did during his early years with the CIA. Since intelligence analysis is an important part of national security decision-making, I suspect that he was first trained as an analyst. In that job, he'd have come face to face with the problems inherent in the production process of that specialty, such as the uncertainty factor. When an analyst taps into the various data streams, he soon learns that he can rarely get a complete picture of what is happening in a foreign country, even regarding a single issue. Thus, he must pull together bits and pieces of information to form a picture. Since there will always be gaps, any report he issues rests on a foundation of assumptions, inferences and educated guesses; not unlike the process a lawyer goes through in building a case. Both inductive and deductive reasoning ability is essential, and the analyst must try to convey to anyone who will read his report, a sense of his uncertainty. A good analyst does this by employing caveats, so as not to convey a greater degree of certainty than he actually possessed about the subject. That's why former CIA Director George Tenet was quoted as saying in 2004: "In the intelligence business, you are almost never completely wrong or completely right."

It *is* known that Guy served, early on, in at least one real cold war hotbed: Athens, Greece. His future wife, Margaret Esther Spencer, at one point, worked as an Administrative Assistant for the American Ambassador to Greece. Exactly when that was, I don't know. But it *is* known that Guy and Margaret met in Athens while she was so employed, and he was assigned there.

Anyway, in exchange for whatever he did, whatever risks he took, and the dangers he overcame, he was paid a "competitive" salary every two weeks, and in certain circumstances, overtime compensation, holiday pay, night differential, Sunday premium pay, bonuses and allowances. Whether or not all of these applied to field agents is unknown. How his salary reached him while stationed in Athens is also unknown; perhaps some was paid in drachmas, the Greek currency, and the rest deposited directly to a bank account stateside, upon which only he could draw.

According to my Aunt Margaret, during a visit in the summer of 2003, Guy was not a desk jockey in the CIA's Athens section. He was a *field agent*. But was he part of the regular military intelligence detail attached to most U.S. Embassies?

Again, according to Margaret, Guy had a "military cover." I understood her to mean that he wore the uniform of one of the U.S. armed services, and lived on military bases instead of at the U.S. Embassy near the Byzantine Museum while performing his duties. Regardless of where he hung his hat, unlike civilian spies, uniformed spies were not protected by any form of diplomatic immunity. If exposed in a foreign country unfriendly to the United States, a uniformed spy could be taken before a firing squad and shot. Now *that's* pressure.

On December 20, 1956, Guy was issued a pseudonym: Hugh C. Jeston. However, he was never issued an alias. That pseudonym, which appears to have been a northern European or British name, does not seem to fit a man who was so obviously a Mediterranean type. I have no indication that he was ever called upon to use it, so perhaps it didn't matter.

1957 found him again in the Athens sector of the Greek capital, a city of several million inhabitants nestled in a bowl surrounded by mountains, and because of atmospheric inversion, frequently immersed in smog that irritated the eyes and lungs. The Greeks have a word for it: *nefos.*

What he did there is unknown. Perhaps it was part of a continuing assignment, or a totally new one after a short tour of duty stateside. Was his job to meet with and facilitate the transfer of an occasional East European defector through Athens and onto a waiting freighter, bypassing all legal channels? Did he pause in his dangerous work at midday, to eat his lunch in one of the burgeoning symbols of globalization: McDonald's, Burger King, or Wendy's? Or did he seek out one of the kiosks or small restaurants off Syntagma Square to sample the local food and drink?

In the spring of that year he sent a postcard to my mother. It showed a foreboding, black and white outcropping of rock called the Acropolis, crowned by Athena's sacred temple, the Parthenon. His note, scrawled on the back, like someone who is busy and can think of little to say, or ... someone who wants to say very little, is undated and unsigned:

> It stands on top of the Acropolis. Quite impressive, I see it every day.

A magnifying glass is needed to make out the postmark's date, almost obliterated now by the passage of time: *April 29, 1957.* I believe the card was another example of his having learned the lessons of secrecy: the less said to anyone about where he was living and working or what he was doing, the better.

A few years later, in mid-January 1960, while I was still living at 619 Chestnut Avenue, in Towson, Baltimore County, Maryland, he sent my mother a trunk full of his stuff and a brief note. One of the things in that trunk was his old baseball glove; the one he used in high school and when he played baseball down the Cape. There are newspaper photographs in existence showing him wearing it. Whether he also used it later, in the Twin States League and in the Eastern Shore League, I don't know.

Another was a pistol, which he said he'd taken off a dead German officer during the war. I think it was a Lugar, but that might just be the romanticized memory of a kid dangling on the edge of hero worshipping. Later, he reclaimed the pistol. Why not? It was cold, like the street weapons some cops carry as backup guns, completely untraceable if it ever needs to be used. The day he came for it, he said, "Watch," and broke it down quickly, told me the names of each piece, and showed me how to load and unload it. There was no holster with it. He simply put it in his jacket pocket and left.

But I still have that glove. I rubbed it with linseed oil two or three times a year to soften the leather and keep it in good shape in case he ever wanted it back.

He never did. Years later, on another of his infrequent visits, we sat in the living room of my parents' home on tree-shaded Chestnut Avenue, with its brick fireplace, gumwood paneled walls, ivory wall-to-wall carpeting, and spacious screened-in side porch, on which I sometimes slept on very hot summer evenings. I reminded him I still had the glove, pulled it from my closet, and showed it to him.

"Do you want to take it with you?"

A small smile. Grasping it in his hands, he turned it over, examining it like someone remembering events long past, but not altogether happy. A curious look spread across his face. Handing it back to me, he dropped his gaze and looked away. "You keep it," was all he said.

CHAPTER 46

Pine Bluffs, WY
Thursday, November 16, 2006
703 Beech Street
8:15 a.m.

According to John Newman, an Assistant Professor at the University of Maryland and a former military intelligence officer,[62] the Eisenhower Administration had not paid close enough attention to Cuba during the events in 1959 leading up to Fidel Castro's triumphant entry into Havana in early January 1960.

> *Preoccupied with Krushchev's secret speech [delivered by Krushchev to the Soviet Union's 20ᵗʰ Congress of the Communist Party in 1956], the missile gap, and crises in Hungary, Suez, Syria, Lebanon, Indonesia, China, and Berlin in the years 1956 to 1958, the United States was caught off guard when the insurgency in Cuba, having quietly grown beyond the capability of President Batista to control it, exploded with Castro's sudden seizure of power in January 1959.*
> *While U.S.—Cuban relations deteriorated and the CIA began to consider 'eliminating' Castro, Soviet—Cuban relations improved dramatically …*

Taken in context, this opinion seems to unduly focus on only developments in Cuba during 1959, displaying little understanding that the world, even back then, was a complex sphere, with lots of events taking place simultaneously. Europe, for example, was a hotbed of activity during that year, which marked the twentieth anniversary of the outbreak of WWII. Dwight D. Eisenhower,

---

62   John Newman, *Oswald and the CIA*, Carroll & Graff Publishers, Inc. New York, NY. 1996.

the man who had commanded the victorious allied armies, and who had orchestrated European recovery through the Marshall Plan, now President of the United States, spent at least two weeks in September 1959 touring the Continent, taking part in ceremonies commemorating that event. The central foreign relations theme of his Administration was his quest for relaxation of tension with the Soviet Union. "People want peace so much," Eisenhower said on British TV, "that governments ought to get out of their way and let them have it." But the Communists met Eisenhower's efforts to relax tensions by proclaiming that "peaceful coexistence" meant that the West must abandon partitioned West Berlin and accept the conquest of the captive nations of Eastern Europe.[63]

However, the Cuban thing *was* truly bothersome to Eisenhower because it showed that, Monroe Doctrine or not, the Soviet Union had successfully pulled into its orbit a small island nation just ninety miles from the shores of the United States. By the end of 1959, the Cuban problem had reached crisis proportions in Washington. The Eisenhower Administration had grasped that the situation required action of some sort, and the National Security Council (NSC) was grappling with the problem. Here's Newman again:

> *On December 10, 1959, during the discussion on Cuba at the 428th Meeting of the National Security Council (NSC) Vice President Nixon asked, "What was the Communist line toward Cuba? He gathered that the Russians did not object to a tough line on the part of Cuba." Richard Bissell, the CIA's Deputy Director of Plans, replied that "the Soviets encouraged a tough anti-U.S. line in Cuba under the guise of nationalism." In other words, the Cuban problem was, from its inception, fundamentally linked to the larger U.S.-Soviet power struggle in the minds of U.S. decisionmakers. At the following 429th meeting of the NSC on December 16, Nixon told those present he "did not believe that Cuba should be handled in a routine fashion through normal diplomatic channels.[64]*

Also, according to Newman, it was one day after this NSC meeting that Allen Dulles approved a recommendation "that thorough consideration be given to the elimination of Fidel Castro:"

---

63 See Nikita Khrushchev's 7000 word article in *Foreign Affairs Magazine*, September 1959.

64 John Newman, *Oswald and the CIA*, Carroll & Graff Publishers, Inc. New York, NY. 1996.

*Over the years we have learned much about the Castro assassina-
tion planning that Dulles approved on that December day, including
this detail from the 1975 final report of the Select Committee to Study
Governmental Operations With Respect to Intelligence Activities,
United States Senate (SSCIA) known as the "Church Committee."
On December 11, 1959, J.C. King, head of CIA's Western Hemisphere
Division, wrote a memorandum to Dulles observing that a "far left"
dictatorship now existed in Cuba which, "if permitted to stand,
will encourage similar actions against U.S. holdings in other Latin
American countries." One of King's four recommendations was: thor-
ough consideration be given to the elimination of Fidel Castro.*[65]

Whether or not this information was communicated to the NSC is
unknown. But at its 429th meeting just a few days later on December 16th, with
both President Eisenhower and Vice-President Nixon present, the topic under
discussion was covert ways to overthrow Castro, even to "eliminate" him.

In any event, it was clear by the end of '59 that the U.S. government was
expending a lot of time and energy at its highest levels on the Cuban problem.
But one should not assume from this that it was totally occupied with Cuba
while ignoring developments in Europe: especially Eastern Europe.

One more interesting item: At the end of 1959, an obscure American expa-
triate named Lee Harvey Oswald, wrote to his brother, Robert, from a hotel in
Minsk, where he'd taken up temporary residence:

*I have chosen to remove all ties with my past, and so I will not write
again, nor do I wish you to try to contact me, I'm sure you understand that I would not like to receive correspondence from people in
the country which I have fled. I am starting a new life ...* [66]

Now let's get back to Guy. We know that in mid-January 1960, he sent that
trunk full of his personal belongings to my mother. His cryptic note to her
accompanying the trunk said:

*I'll be gone for a while. If I don't make it back, everything in the
trunk is yours.*

---

65 Ibid.

66 Ibid.

This indicated that he'd be going somewhere to do something which might prove dangerous. What that was, is not known. Because the Cuban thing had dominated the news during that time period, my family always assumed that his mission was one outside the country and that it had something to do with Cuba. Imagine my surprise, then, all these years later when I began researching, and found otherwise. Here's what I discovered among the CIA's previously classified records, de-classified and made public later.

On February 25, 1960, a "Confidential" form entitled *Investigative File Memorandum* was filled out by then Deputy Chief of the CIA's Clearance Branch. The man's name is redacted everywhere on the memo, an [03] appearing where his signature should have been. But the memo references Guy:

> *Subject recently returned from an overseas assignment and the security file has been reviewed. It was recommended to the Chief, Interrogation Research Branch that the routine polygraph interview usually scheduled after an individual returns from an overseas tour of duty be waived.*
>
> *The Interrogation Research Branch file will be reviewed and a final determination made whether or not a repolygraph will be necessary.*
>
> [03]
> *Deputy Chief, Clearance Branch.*

This is proof that Guy was, in fact, sent overseas. But if not Cuba, then where? Having returned from his overseas assignment, and apparently having acquitted himself well while gone—I guess just coming back alive from some overseas assignments says something about an agent's competence—his satisfied bosses at the CIA wasted no time in preparing Guy for another task. What that was I don't know, but on May 2, 1960, a form entitled *Request for Domestic Cover List Entry Change* was filled out:

Subject:	*Guy Vitale*
Entry:	*Inclusion of subject on the Domestic Cover List is requested for the reason noted below. When notified that cover has been established, subject will be specifically authorized and instructed to conceal his Agency affiliation.*
Change:	*Subject is currently included ... (unreadable)*
Reason:	*Subject is a recent EE Returnee from [15–16]. Since a short tour in Headquarters and reassignment to the*

> *Field is planned for subject, please establish necessary backstopping in order to facilitate this plan.*
>
> Cover: *No cover in use—Type Suggested: (specify whether official or nonofficial)—DAC*
>
> *Approved by Central Cover division. CSJ.*
>
> *Requesting Official—[03]*
>
>   *Title—EE Personnel Officer*

Now, without help from a CIA official who actually knows what these in-house abbreviations and redactions mean, one could spend a lifetime trying to figure them out. But unable to get help, I was left to my own devices. I *was,* however, able to determine that EE meant Eastern Europe. So the entry, "… EE Returnee …" meant that he'd been sent somewhere in Eastern Europe on his overseas assignment. The thing is that Eastern Europe was, at the time, behind the Iron Curtain.

To which Soviet bloc nation was Guy sent? I don't know. What had his mission been? Don't know. This form makes no reference to it. Is [15, 16] a redacted reference to the country or countries to which he was sent? Probably.

From the above-referenced documentation, I now believe that, with things as they were in February 1960, he was sent to Eastern Europe on a mission of some importance, and some personal danger; a mission from which he was not completely confident that he'd return.

*   *   *   *

Pine Bluffs, WY
Friday, November 17, 2006
703 Beech Street
8:15 a. m

What the second form referenced above *does* clearly show is that by May 1960 Guy was being prepared for a stateside assignment requiring some sort of cover arrangements. The letters DAC mean Domestic Assignment Cover. What does [03] mean? Don't know. But on May 11, 1960, just a few days later, in a Memorandum to the Chief, EE, attention: Mr. [   ] we see this:

> *Subject: [   ]*
>
>   *Establishment of [   ] Cover Backstop. Reference: Request for Domestic Cover 2 May 1960 File No. K-4849*

All information concerning this cover is available in the Official
Cover and Liaison Section, CCD (Central Cover Division)

/S/Paul P/Stewart,
for Joseph M. Adams, Chief,
Official Cover and Liaison, CCD.

Guy was issued Unit ID Card No. 1205, *For Domestic Use Only.* Also on May 11, 1960, referencing the same file number—K-4849—another memo:

To: Chief, Records and Service Division, Office of Personnel
From: Paul P. Stewart, for Harry W. Little, Jr., Chief, Central Cover Division.
   1) *Cover arrangements are in progress and have been completed*
      for the above-named subject.
   2) *Effective 1 April 1960 it is requested that your records be prop-*
      erly blocked to deny subject's current Agency employment to an
      external inquirer.

Then, on September 30, 1960, someone whose signature is indecipherable issued a memo regarding Guy:

Today I informed [   ] of WH that subject is okay for assignment
to [   ] as an SI courier.

SI means Special Intelligence. On December 22, 1960, a memorandum for Chief, Personnel Security Division, OS:

Subject: Vitale, Guy—DDP
The above individual is under consideration for clearance for
Special Intelligence. Your recommendation is requested concerning
the granting of such clearance, together with any information or com-
ments which may be pertinent.

/S/unreadable

Chief, Special Intelligence Security Branch, OCI

So it seems that by the end of 1960, Guy had been assigned to the Special Intelligence Division as a Special Intelligence Courier.

*   *   *   *

Pine Bluffs, WY
Saturday, November 18, 2006
703 Beech Street
8:00 a. m

In November 1967, Guy filed an Outside Activity Approval Request[67] form, stating that he would visit *Munich, West Germany for three weeks. Will make social contact with Miss Margaret Spencer.* The visit was to take place from December 23, 1967 to January 19, 1968, apparently for the Christmas holiday. *In the Description of Outside Activity For Which Approval is Requested* section it says: *In engaging in the requested activity I will make no reference to, or discuss any CIA assignments or duties nor will I make reference to or discuss my CIA employment except as authorized by Headquarters Regulation 10–7.*

On December 11th, a note was added in the section titled *For completion by Employee Activity Branch and Return of Original to Employee. 12/11/1967: Experienced traveler under DAC cover. Other than [03], (unreadable) is an Agency employee, [24] will not be controlled.*

A year later, on October 28, 1968, he filed an identical *Outside Activity Approval Request.* One block contained this statement: *visit to Munich, West Germany, December 24, 1968 to January 13, 1969. Will be in contact with Miss Margaret Spencer, and socially with M.O.B. Personnel.* On this form his name and grade appear as Guy Vitale, GS-8, and the letters *DDP/WH/COG* appear in the block labeled *Component.* On November 1, 1968, the same memo was added as in the *Request Form* of the previous year: *1 November 1968: Experienced traveler under DAC cover. [24,] will not be visited.*

At that time, Margaret Esther Spencer still had a couple of years left before she could call it quits and collect her pension. The reason for these annual requests was so Guy could travel back and forth to Munich to visit her during her Christmas vacations from her State Department job.

Was Margaret Spencer simply an Ambassador's Administrative Assistant? Despite my aunt's protestations that she was not a spy, there's some evidence to the contrary. More about that later.

---

67   This and all the other CIA documents mentioned in these later chapters were culled from the records of the National Archives in Silver Spring, MD. They had been de-classified, made public, filed at the National Archives, and released in 1998 as part of the CIA's Historical Review Program.

CHAPTER 47

Pine Bluffs, WY
Monday, November 20, 2006
703 Beech Street
9:15 a.m.

On November 22, 1963, President John F. Kennedy was shot and killed in Dealey Plaza, Dallas, Texas. Lee Harvey Oswald was arrested and charged with the murder. It was alleged that Oswald, using a Mannlicher-Carcano 6.5-millimeter Italian rifle he'd purchased from a mail order house, had fired the fatal shots from a sixth floor window of the Texas School Book Depository on Elm Street.

On the evening of November 29, 1963, seven days after Kennedy was killed, Vice-President Lyndon Baynes Johnson, elevated to the office of President, signed an executive order creating the *President's Commission on the Assassination of President Kennedy,* which became known as *the Warren Commission.* A year later, on September 24, 1964, *the Warren Commission* released its report concluding that there was no "persuasive evidence" that Lee Harvey Oswald was involved in a conspiracy to assassinate President Kennedy.

The Commission's conclusions were attacked by critics almost immediately, including President Kennedy's brother, Attorney General Robert Kennedy. In a meeting with White House aide, Arthur Schlesinger on December 9, 1964, this dialogue purportedly took place:[68]

"What about Oswald?" Schlesinger asked.

"There could be no serious doubt that Oswald was guilty," Kennedy replied, "but there was still argument if he had done it himself or as part of a larger plot, whether organized by Castro or by gangsters." Kennedy said that Hoover

---

68   G. Robert Blakey and Richard N. Billings, *Fatal Hour; the Assassination of President Kennedy by Organized Crime,* Berkley Books, New York, NY. 1992. Times Books Edition, 1981.

thought Oswald had done it by himself, but CIA Director Mc Cone thought two people had been involved."

Was there one shooter or two? A conspiracy? Several conspiracies? Many think *the Warren Commission's* investigation was not thorough enough. Conspiracy theories began to appear, and to this day they still abound. Here's a list:

1) The CIA and Anti-Castro groups, acting together, had killed the President because of the Bay of Pigs debacle and/or because he was preparing to pull American troops from Vietnam.
2) Vice-President Lyndon B. Johnson, at the time of Kennedy's death the subject of four major criminal investigations involving govern-ment contract violations, misappropriation of funds, money laundering, and bribery, had done it with help from Malcolm Wallace, a convicted mur-derer with whom Johnson had been linked.
3) J. Edgar Hoover and the Mafia, had done it, because Bobby Kennedy was vigorously prosecuting mob bosses after his brother, Jack, became President; Hoover, because he'd rarely acknowledge mob existence, must have had extensive ties to the Mafia.
4) increasing pressure brought upon them by Bobby Kennedy. The Mafia had been working closely with the CIA, attempting to assassinate Fidel Castro.
5) The Soviet Union, aided by the KGB had done it, along with killing or attempting to kill the leaders of twelve nations.
6) Roscoe White, a Dallas police officer, acting as part of a three-man assas-sination team, had done it. I bet you haven't heard that one before.
7) The Cubans had done it, retaliating for the many CIA attempts on the lives of the Castro brothers.

Conspiracy theories 1 and 4 above, at first glance appear far-fetched; too absurd to be believed by any responsible persons, much less anyone in the U.S. Government, right? Not so.

In the early 1970s, when Democrats had large majorities in both Houses of Congress, the Church Committee—named for its Chairman, Democrat sena-tor Frank Church—attacked the CIA as if it were Adolf Hitler's Nazi Party. As a result, the Agency was gutted, hampered and hamstrung with endless bureau-cratic regulations, including one that prohibited it from sharing intelligence with the FBI. We'd pay for *that* one later, on September 11, 2001.

In 1980, Congressman Ron Dellums (D-CA), a Fidel Castro sympathizer, vowed "to totally dismantle every intelligence agency in this country, piece by piece, nail by nail, brick by brick." In 1993, the Democrat caucus elected Dellums chairman of the House Armed Services Committee by a vote of 198–10. The liberal *New York Times* observed the event by showering Dellums with praise.

That's not all. Throughout the '90s, Senator John Kerry (D-MA) repeatedly voted to cut billions from intelligence services budgets, so money could be spent on something more important, like reducing class size.

*   *   *   *

Pine Bluffs, WY
Monday, November 20, 2006
703 Beech Street
9:25 a.m.

Because these theories were believed by many, when the Church Committee's budget had been exhausted and it was dissolved, the House Select Committee on Assassinations was established in September 1976, by the U.S. House of Representatives, to conduct a full and complete investigation of the circumstances surrounding the deaths of John F. Kennedy, Robert Kennedy, and Martin Luther King, Jr. It operated for the four remaining months of the 94th Congress, expired at the end of that time, but was reconstituted on January 4, 1977 by a unanimous consent request dealing with House Resolution 9 of the 95th Congress. To make a long story short, because there was opposition to the appointment of yet another Committee to study President Kennedy's death, after some machinations to handle that, House Resolution 433 was passed setting up the Committee until January 3, 1979, the duration of the 95th Congress.

In 1977, after the resignation of its first Chief Counsel, the Committee hired Professor G. Robert Blakey, to fill that slot. Blakey, who served on the law school faculty at the University of Notre Dame for many years, had been selected to participate in the Attorney General's Honors Program at the Department of Justice in 1960, and worked as a Special Attorney General in that office, in the Organized Crime & Racketeering Section from 1960 to 1964. Naturally, with his extensive background in matters dealing with organized crime, the Committee soon became pointed in the direction of investigating mob influence in the murder of President Kennedy.

As part of the Select Committee's investigation of the Kennedy assassination in 1978, it was conducting inquiries into whether or not the CIA had withheld certain facts and information from the Warren Commission. These items included ties by Lee Harvey Oswald and Jack Ruby to Carlos Marcello, boss of the oldest Mafia family in America, and Sam Giancana, the Mafia family boss in Chicago, with whom Kennedy, it was alleged, had shared a mistress, Judith Campbell Exner.

Scott Breckenridge was the Principle coordinator for the House Select Committee. On August 23, 1978, he received this memo from Norbert A Shepanek, the CIA's Chief of Policy and Coordination Staff, Liaison and Oversight Control, apparently in response to a request from Blakey to the CIA a short time before, asking for "all files, index references and documents" pertaining to Greg (sic) Vitale and Calvin Hicks:

	23 August 1978
MEMORANDUM FOR:	*Mr. Scott Breckenridge*
	Principal Coordinator, House Select
	Committee on Assassinations
FROM:	*Norbert A. Shepanek*
	Policy and Coordination Staff,
	Liaison and Oversight control
SUBJECT:	*Response to Reference*
REFERENCE:	*OLC 78–2590/1 17 August 1978.*

1. *There is no Mr. Greg Vitale but we assume the reference is to Mr. Guy Vitale. Both Mr. Guy Vitale and Mr. Calvin Hicks have retired. The following information is provided so that the HSCA may make arrangements for interviews directly if they wish to do so:*

    A) *Guy Vitale*
       107 N. Virginia Avenue
       Sanford, Florida 32771
       Tele: 323–5369
    B) *Calvin Hicks*
       1608 Imperial Ridge
       Lascruses, New Mexico 88001
       Tele: 522–7905

2. *The pseudonyms and aliases assigned to Messrs. Vitale and Hicks are contained in the separate cover attachment keyed to this memorandum with date of issue indicated.*

3   *Files will be made available when they are received from Archives.*
                                                            Norbert A. Shepanek
    SEPARATE COVER ATTACHMENT TO MEMORANDUM
1) *The pseudonym of subject in paragraph 1A was Hugh C. Jeston,*
    issued on 20 December 1956. No aliases.
2) *The pseudonym of subject in paragraph 1B was Wallace K.*
    Ledbetter, issued in October 1950. The alias Calvin Wilson Carl is
    recorded in September 1963. No other aliases are listed.

I obtained this memorandum from the National Archives' CIA Historical Review Program's records released in 1996, through Martin McGann on April 3, 2003, and Martha Wagner Murphy on July 14, 2003. Both were Archivists on the Special Access and Freedom of Information Act (FOIA) Staff. I'd contacted them by telephone on April 3rd and July 11th respectively, and requested the information. From it, I confirmed an earlier discovery; that the HSCA had wanted to interview my uncle about something as part of its investigation, and had sought his address from the CIA. An interview was a preliminary step to issuance of a subpoena for a witness to testify before the Committee.

What was the Committee's interest in Guy? What was the avenue of inquiry upon which they thought he and Calvin Hicks might be able to shed light? In February 2005, I spoke by telephone with Blakey and followed that conversation up with an e-mail of four questions. But Blakey was uncooperative, citing the length of time that had expired since these events took place, and his busy schedule.[69]

On March 28, 2003, I spoke with the aforementioned John Newman, an adjunct professor in the University of Maryland's Honors program, by telephone, at his Lost River home near the George Washington National Forest in West Virginia. I asked him if, in his research regarding Lee Harvey Oswald, he'd ever come across the name Guy Vitale?

"Yes," he said. "Many references to him. He was Mafia, wasn't he?"

That was a bit of a shock. "Not that I know of," I said, recovering quickly. "My uncle was a CIA employee for twenty years."

"Well, I spent years researching records at the National Archives in College Park. The Adelphi Drive location is a nice place to work. Plenty of parking and all. I was working on my book, *Oswald and the CIA* during that time."

"What did you find out about my uncle?" I asked.

---

69 Notes of conversation and follow-up e-mail dated February 3. 2005, between the author and Professor G. Robert Blakey regarding HSCA's interest in retired CIA agents Guy Vitale and Calvin Hicks.

"It seems to me that I found references to him in the box dealing with Mob records. I didn't open a file on him, though."

"Why not?"

"I can't recall. Perhaps what was there was not closely enough connected to my subject."

In this conversation, Newman, a former intelligence analyst in the U.S. Army's Military Intelligence Branch for twenty-one years, was friendly and seemed willing to help. He suggested that I go to the Archives, pull the records to which I'd already found references, and then the following Tuesday, we could meet there.

"I can review what you found and interpret for you and direct you to the most important records," he said.

However, after visiting the Archives, my attempts to contact him by telephone to set up a meeting were unsuccessful. He never returned my calls.

Also, after seeing the name Calvin Hicks connected to Guy's name on the above-mentioned memo, I attempted to contact him. Although the phone number was still a working number, neither he nor any of his relatives ever returned my calls.

So I was unable to determine what the House Select Committee on Assassinations wanted with Guy. But here's what I *do* know. Beginning in late 1960, Guy was being prepared for overt activity of some kind within continental United States. As part of that preparation, his CIA affiliation and some other records were blacked out by the CIA, so that any inquiries regarding Guy's possible employment there would be deflected. Mafia Don Carlos Marcello operated extensively in and around New Orleans, and had ties to Lee Harvey Oswald. After Kennedy was assassinated, the CIA attempted to backtrack on Oswald, fill in his activities in the New Orleans area, and find out more about his time in Mexico City while he visited the Russian Embassy there. In files at the National Archives, Guy Vitale's name was found in boxes of records dealing with the Mob, contained in the JFK materials stored there. In the mind of John Newman, at least, Guy was somehow linked to the Mafia.

Was Guy involved in attempts by the CIA to infiltrate Marcello's operation? Or was he given the task of backtracking on Oswald in either New Orleans or Mexico City? We'll probably never know.

PART EIGHT

GUY'S RETIREMENT YEARS

CHAPTER 48

Washington, D.C.
Friday, February 28, 1969
Central Intelligence Agency
9:00 a.m.

On February 28, 1969, Guy retired from the CIA. He was fifty-one years old, a nice age to retire and, for many who do it at that age, early enough to begin another career, or travel, write a book, and renew old family relationships and friendships. But Guy did none of these.

Instead, within a few weeks thereafter, he left the United States and took up residence in Munich, West Germany, to be near Margaret while she completed her final State Department assignment. Having suspended almost all ties with his remaining blood relatives years ago, and having only a few friends within the CIA itself, this decision was probably not a difficult one.

Retiring from an intelligence agency like the CIA is not an easy process: it does not just happen. There are numerous exit interviews, some decorous, some tedious and uncomfortable. First, there's an application to be filled out. Guy's *Application for Retirement* gives his retirement address as No. 1 Thiemastrasse, Apartment 31, Munich, Germany. His correspondence address was listed as the same. That's also the address to which they'd be sending his retirement checks, at least for awhile.

In April 1969, a letter was written to Guy by Richard Helms, then Director of the CIA, acknowledging his retirement. It's a little-known fact that Helms had started his spy career in the 1940s as a member of the OSS, and had gradually risen through the ranks until he held the top position in its predecessor organization. This letter, probably a form letter written to all CIA employees when they retired, shows that the Agency had another address on file for Guy, in Washington D.C. Released under the CIA's Historical Review program in 1998, the letter said:

1 April 1969
Mr. Guy Vitale
1730 H Street, N. W.
Washington, D.C.

Dear Mr. Vitale:

As you bring to a close more than twenty-six years of service to your country, I want to join your friends and co-workers in wishing you well and hoping that you find the years ahead filled with enjoyment and satisfaction.

It takes the conscientious efforts of many people to do the important work of this Agency. You leave with the knowledge that you have personally contributed to our success in carrying out our mis-sion. Your faithful and loyal support has measured up to the high ideals and traditions of the Federal service.

May I express to you my appreciation and extend my best wishes for the years ahead.

Sincerely,
Richard Helms
Director

A cryptic handwritten note at the bottom of this letter states: *Do not send retirement letter to Germany. Subject will probably request upon return to the U.S.*

When he actually rented that room at 1730 H Street, N.W., how long he lived there, or even if he ever lived there at all, is unknown. Did he have it while living with Ann and Al Tosi during those early years in Washington? Was it his sanctuary? Had he leased it as an escape from somewhere or something? His safe house away from all other safe houses? The one and only place he could go to be totally free? Or, had he taken the room to protect his sister and brother-in-law from the dangers inherent to his occupation; to have an address at another location in case his cover was penetrated and someone sought to exact revenge upon him by going after his family? Had he, at any time, imposed anything of himself on that room, or was he simply a transient guest there?

Perhaps I'm attaching too much importance to this bit of information. Maybe it was simply a room which he leased later, for those times when he returned to the United States from overseas assignments or returned to Washington after assignments elsewhere in the U.S. Nothing more.

Anyway, along with this letter from Helms was one from Louis J. Mazza, Chief of the CIA's Employment Services Branch, announcing that Guy would received a Bronze Retirement Medallion for fifteen or more years of CIA service.

Guy's retirement application listed his office assignment at the time as WH/COG and his date of final separation was *28 February 1969,* after twenty-two years of civilian service with Uncle Sam. Twenty-two years? This apparently included his two years with the Library of Congress—civil service employment—and his twenty years with the Agency, but does not include his four years of military service.

Next, Guy had to undergo an interview. The *Interview Form* appears in his records.

Name of Subject: Vitale, Guy
Reason for Interview: Retirement—28 February 1969
Permanent Address: Thiemestrasse, Munich, Germany. Apt 31
Present Title, Grade and Division: WH—GS8—COG
Details of Contemplated Travel: Germany
Badges, Passes, Keys and credentials: EJ 998
Clearances:
Cover: Covert

1. *ALL PHASES OF SECURITY WITH RESPECT TO SUBJECT'S RESPON-SIBILITIES TO THE ORGANIZATION WERE FULLY AND COM-PLETELY DISCUSSED.*

2. *SUBJECT WAS ADVISED THAT ALL INFORMATION RECEIVED AND COMPILED BY THE AGENCY IS OFFICIAL DATA, AND IS THE PROP-ERTY OF THE U.S. GOVERNMENT AND THAT NO OFFICER OR EMPLOYEE HAS ANY PROPERTY RIGHT IN SUCH INFORMATION.*

3. *SUBJECT WAS INFORMED THAT THE SECURITY REGULATIONS AND THE SECRECY AGREEMENT APPLY, NOT ONLY TO INTELLI-GENCE INFORMATION: BUT ALSO TO ANY STATISTICAL, ORGA-NIZATIONAL AND ADMINISTRATIVE INFORMATION OF WHICH HE IS COGNIZANT.*

4. *SUBJECT WAS INSTRUCTED THAT INFORMATION PERTAIN-ING TO INTELLIGENCE OPERATIONS, SOURCES AND METHODS PECULIAR TO THE AGENCY MAY NOT BE DIVULGED TO PERSONS IN OTHER GOVERNMENT AGENCIES, EVEN THOUGH SUCH PERSONS ARE FULLY SECURITY CLEARED WITHIN THEIR OWN DEPARTMENTS.*

5. *SUBJECT WAS INFORMED THAT SHOULD ANY QUESTION ARISE ON SECURITY MATTERS HE MAY COMMUNICATE WITH THE AGENCY FOR ADVICE AND GUIDANCE.*
6. *GENERAL: (COMMENTS, CRITICISMS OR SUGGESTIONS AND KNOWLEDGE OF ANY INCIDENTS OR ACTIVITIES OF PERSONS WHICH SEEMED TO HAVE A SECURITY SIGNIFICANCE.)*

Curiously, Guy did not have to sign this form, it is undated, and the signature of the interviewer is illegible.

Next came a document called a COMMUNICATIONS INTELLIGENCE DEBRIEFING OATH:

> *It has been determined that I no longer require Communications Intelligence in the performance of my official duties. Therefore, I am aware that my right to see this material and have access to information pertinent to it has ceased. Pursuant to the obligation which I incurred, under oath, at the time of my indoctrination for Communications Intelligence, I reaffirm that I will never divulge any information which I have acquired as an authorized recipient or producer of Communications Intelligence, nor will I discuss with any person any of the inferences concerning Communications Intelligence which I may have formed through knowledge acquired by me by virtue of my cleared status.*
>
> *I have today re-read the statute dealing with the subject of Communications Intelligence (18 U.S. Code 798), and I understand its provisions, penalties and implications.*

This document was signed by Guy, witnessed by someone named D.P. Whitehill, and dated 26 February '69.

Margaret and Guy were married on April 8, 1969, not quite two months after he retired. The ceremony took place at the home of her sister, Ella Katherine Spencer Fletcher, in Maitland, Orange County, Florida. Katherine's husband, Dean Roger Fletcher and daughters, Ruth Anne and Jennifer Fletcher, were also present. Why was the wedding not held in a house of worship?

"I was raised in the Methodist Church," Margaret[70] told me during one of our telephone conversations in November 2000. "After returning to Sanford, I began going back to church there. Since Guy was Catholic, there was a problem

---

70   Margaret Esther Spencer was born July 13, 1923, into one of Sanford's pioneer families. She died Saturday, August 6, 2005, in Sanford, FL at the age of 82.

of where to get married. We resolved it by getting married at the home of my sister, in their front room, before a Justice of the Peace named George or Gary Adams." This was an interesting bit of information. I'd understood for years that my uncle was what we call a "lapsed Catholic" i.e. one who never attended church. Actually, the Church has always claimed many individuals as Catholics who have not recently set foot inside a Catholic Church.[71] But I'd often wondered how Guy saw himself. Did he continue to self-identify as a Catholic long after he'd stopped attending Mass? Apparently he did.

Later, I learned that Margaret had been a member of the First United Methodist Church in Sanford. Her pastor was the Reverend James Bradshaw.

The bride and groom were both older. Guy was fifty-one when he tied the knot; would turn fifty-two that October. It was his first marriage. I won't say how old Margaret was, but it was her first marriage, too.

A few months after their wedding, an interesting note turned up in Guy's CIA personnel file:

> *21 October 1969*
> *MEMORANDUM FOR THE RECORD*
> *Subject: [06] #189638 NEE [08] Subject was married on 8 April 1969*
> *to Guy Vitale #39049. Subject's spouse is a former Agency employee*
> *who retired in February 1969.*
>
> *[03]*
> *Employee Actions Section*

As I said earlier, there is some evidence that Margaret was also a spy. It's flimsy, but this is it. She had been assigned a file at the CIA—number 189638; six months after their marriage, she is the subject of this Memorandum. Why? Presumably the Agency had no further need to keep tabs on Guy, who'd retired months before. Was this simply a file opened as part of a background check on her? Were they being diligent in checking out Margaret to see if she might be or had ever been an agent of a foreign power? Did they suspect her of some ulterior motive in marrying Guy, their own former agent? Or was it her personnel file at the Agency. Yes, I know. As proof that she may have actually worked for the CIA, it's kind of thin. But when you combine it with the common knowledge that State Department personnel working out of our Embassies overseas often worked for the Agency? Well ... you decide for yourself.

---

71   Roger Hunter-Hall and Steven Wagner, *The State of the Catholic Church in America, Diocese by Diocese,* Crisis Magazine, February/March 2007.

*   *   *   *

Munich, Germany
Thursday, May 1, 1969
No. 1 Thiemastrasse, Apartment 31
7:00 a.m.

When his alarm clock began making noises, Guy Vitale rolled over and punched the button to stop its incessant clamor. It was 7 a.m. He'd gone to bed at 10 the night before, after watching some TV and enjoying a glass or two of a German Riesling, which he found to his liking, and had slept straight through. He lay on his back staring up at the ceiling. He was content; or at least the next thing to content that he'd ever been.

After they'd returned to Munich from Sanford, he and Margaret had had a week to settle into their routine as a married couple, in the apartment they'd had since at least November 1967; to get used to living together as husband and wife, before she'd had to return to her office at the Embassy in Athens.

Laying there, images of his new bride moving about in her small apartment in the Mets neighborhood of the Greek capital flooded his mind; Margaret, in a white, terrycloth bathrobe, laying out her clothing for a day at the office: a black linen skirt, a white silk blouse, and black pumps. Margaret, later in the morning at her desk, proofreading State Department reports for her boss, the Ambassador, before sending them in for his signature. *I miss her already,* he thought, as he threw back the covers and headed for the bathroom to shower and shave, before getting his breakfast and heading to the library for a few hours of reading newspapers from countries around the world, in their own languages. *Can't wait 'till she finishes up and we can be together every day.*

*   *   *   *

Sanford, FL
Thursday, January 8, 1970
107 N. Virginia Avenue
10:00 a.m.

After Margaret retired in 1970, the couple gave up their Munich apartment, returned to the U.S. and settled in Sanford, where her family was from, and where she'd grown up. Margaret's mother, Ruth Roberts Spencer, was still alive and living there at the time

Sanford is a charming Florida city, surrounding Lake Monroe, at the head of the navigable portion of the St. Johns River. The place is named after Henry Shelton Sanford, who purchased the land west of what was then known as Mellonville in 1870, and planned the new town as the transportation hub for all of southern Florida.

Sometime later—possibly while Margaret's mother was still living, but certainly after she died—the couple moved into a ranch-style home at 107 North Virginia Avenue, which is in a pleasant, middle class neighborhood on the south shore of Lake Monroe. Their street, lying between N. Scott Avenue to the west, and Shirley Avenue to the east, runs vertically to the Lake, and the house is only a few doors from the shore at the end of their street.

Of some interest is the fact that All Souls Catholic Church is only one and a half miles from this location, and Fort Mellon Park only three quarters of a mile away, right on the water. Both are within walking distance of the house, if one wanted to visit either spot.

So what did Guy do to fill his time in Sanford, Florida? "Guy enjoyed taking long walks," Margaret told me in one of our telephone conversations. "He also had a relationship with two local dogs."

"Really?"

"Yes. He gave them names. One he called Rommel, after the German Army General in the North African Campaign. The other he named Montgomery, which was the name of the British General during the same period."

I could just picture my uncle, walking down North Virginia Avenue, stopping to greet these two neighborhood dogs; perhaps stooping to pick up a stick or a rock to fling in their direction and watching them run to retrieve it and return it to him.

"Did Guy ever become involved in local sports there?" I asked.

"Well, even after all those years, Guy still enjoyed football and baseball, so he did some football coaching in the local recreation council league for a while. Volunteer stuff. Not baseball though." Why not? It was still too painful, I think.

His continued interest in football was confirmed for me by Ruth Anne Fletcher,[72] Margaret's niece and a cousin of mine by marriage, when I spoke with her on the telephone in February 2007:

"We were close to him, my sister Jennifer and I. Guy liked to go to high school football games, and he'd often take us with him. I recall that he also liked to watch football games on TV. Whenever we visited, he was always watching a ball game of one kind or another."

---

72   Now Ruth Anne Fletcher Franke, she is married to Doug Franke and resides in Thief River Falls, MN where the couple moved in 2001.

"What else did Guy do to fill up his time?"

"I saw him on weekends a lot during the school year," Ruth Anne said. "He did lots of gardening around there, along with Maggie; he built a patio for her in the back. And when they closed in the carport and turned it into a bedroom, he worked with the contractor on that."

"The house already had three bedrooms," I said. "Why did they do that?"

"It was for my grandmother. She lived in the same house and died in that room."

"Do you recall anything else about Guy?" I asked.

"Well, I liked him. He was an easy-going softie, very laid-back, and always had a smile on his face. He never 'shushed' us, and I never saw him angry or upset."

"Did he ever take you and Jennifer anywhere?"

"Well, I remember some bamboo fishing poles that we used, to go fishing down the end of the street, in the Lake," Ruth Anne said. "We enjoyed going there. One year Maggie cooked a Thanksgiving dinner for us, but most of the time, my sister and I would play in the back yard, climbing the trees and running around. My favorite thing was when Uncle Guy would take us to the local A&W for hamburgers and root beer floats, or stuff like that."

This was good information, but a bit hard to hear. My uncle, twenty years old when I was born and away a lot playing ball, was not around to develop a bond for himself with the children of his oldest sister and brother. Later, the war took him away again. After that, it was off to Washington, D.C. for him, and his career with the CIA. So he was not a part of our lives as we grew up. We didn't know him very well. Had things been different, perhaps there would have been that bond, that relationship for him with his blood nieces and nephews. We'd have liked that.

However, for my part at least, I was happy for Guy that he'd actually *had* that kind of family relationship, even if it was with his wife's sister's kids, instead of with *his* sister's and brother's children. I believe they filled a gap in his life, one which needed filling; and they did it well. And I'm thankful to them.

Some time during his retirement years, Guy developed coronary artery disease, perhaps from an accumulation of cholesterol in his arteries. That can, and sometimes does, produce acute kidney failure, which is what happened in his case. When did this occur? When I spoke to her in February 2007, Ruth Anne could not recall:

"Guy died only eight months to a year after my grandmother, so I don't remember [when he actually began having problems]. But it must have been during the last year or two of his life."

In some cases, kidneys, those two bean-shaped organs, each about the size of a fist, located at the back of the upper abdomen on either side of the spine, will recover normal function after a few weeks of treatment. But Guy's did not, and he eventually progressed to the next stage; chronic kidney failure. That resulted in end-stage renal disease, requiring that he be placed on dialysis, a mechanical filtration system for removing toxins and waste from his body.

Also possible as one method of treating this type of medical condition is a kidney transplant, in order to survive. Perhaps it was considered for Guy, but for some reason, he did not follow up with it. The end was near.

*   *   *   *

Pine Bluffs, WY
Tuesday, February 6, 2007
703 Beech Street
1:00 p.m.

Guy Vitale's struggles in this life came to an end on Friday, April 24, 1987. He was sixty-nine years old. He'd been a patient in Central Florida Regional Hospital in Sanford for several days, suffering from severe cardiomyopathy. The immediate cause of his death was ventricular flutter fibrillation, as a result of chronic renal failure. As noted above, he'd also had coronary artery disease for some time.

On Sunday, April 26th, the *Orlando Sentinel* printed a brief obituary:

> *GUY VITALE, 69, 107 N. Virginia Ave., Sanford, died Friday. Born in Boston, he moved to Sanford from Munich, West Germany, in 1970. He was retired from the CIA. He was a member of the CIA Retirement Association and an Army veteran of World War II. Survivors: wife, Margaret Spencer, Sanford; brother, Frank, Melrose, Mass. Brisson Guardian Funeral Home, Sanford.*

A memorial service was held a few days later, on Wednesday, April 27th, at Brisson Guardian Funeral Home, also in Sanford.

I obtained a copy of his death certificate from the *Sentinel* in late February 1997. As far as it goes it is accurate. Short, but accurate.

Apparently, Margaret or someone in her family also sent information to the *Boston Globe.* On May 2nd, 1987, that newspaper printed another notice of his death:

GUY VITALE, 69
RETIRED CIA EMPLOYEE

A memorial service was held Wednesday, April 27, at Brisson Guardian Funeral Home in Sanford Fla., for Guy Vitale, a retired CIA employee, formerly of Boston.

Mr. Vitale died April 24, in Central Florida Regional Hospital, Sanford. He was 69.

Born in East Boston, Mr. Vitale graduated from East Boston High School and George Washington University, where he majored in Political Science and law.

Mr. Vitale moved to Sanford in 1970 from Munich. He was a member of the CIA Retirement Association, and was a World War II veteran.

He leaves his wife, Margaret (Spencer) Vitale of Sanford, and a brother, Frank Vitale, of Melrose.

Burial was in Evergreen Cemetery in Sanford.

This one is not accurate, however. As we've already seen, although he did major in Political Science at GW, he only spent three semesters there before entering the CIA. Records obtained from George Washington, and checked at Credentials, Inc., a group specializing in checking attendance and degrees earned for employers and licensed private investigators such as myself, confirmed this. Further, he did not major in law; no one does until they attend law school. I suppose what the person providing this information had intended to say was that Guy was in the pre-law course at GW. Did he ever intend on going on to law school? Probably not. But his consummate interest in history apparently was what pointed him into that course of study.

Since both obituaries mentioned membership in the CIA Retirement Association, I contacted Norm Glover, then working for that organization, to see if he had any information about Guy.

"No, Mr. Sacco," he said. "We never published an In Memoriam for him because we were never notified that he had died. His dues were paid through 1987. In 1988, we dropped him from the rolls."

"Without investigating?"

"That's correct. We have no staff to inquire as to why any membership lapses, and we simply assumed that he'd either voluntarily dropped it for some reason, or had passed away."

*   *   *   *

Pine Bluffs, WY
Wednesday, February 7, 2007
703 Beech Street
1:00 p.m.

On August 6, 2005, my aunt Margaret passed away at the age of eighty-two at her home in Sanford. She'd had cervical cancer for several years. Unable to attend her funeral, I spoke to Ruth Anne, who called me a few days later.

"Aunt Margaret died at home," she said. "My mother, Jennifer, and her minister, Jim Bradshaw, were with her."

"That's comforting to know," I said. The next day, I ordered her obituary from the *Orlando Sentinel.*

Before putting the final touches on this book, I wanted to touch base with the Reverend Bradshaw.

"I came to First United Methodist Church in June 2000, so I didn't know your uncle," he told me. "And I didn't know Margaret very well."

"Was she active in Church affairs?" I asked.

"No, she wasn't. And she never came to church services, either," Reverend Bradshaw said. "But she had been in the local hospital three or four times since I came to Sanford, and each time she was hospitalized, I'd visit her there. So I *did* know her."

"Would you say she was a religious person?"

"Religious in the sense that she believed in God, yes. But she never mentioned Jesus. People in that generation seldom talked about their relationship with Jesus Christ, because they thought it sounded like they were bragging." He paused. "But she was not opposed to receiving prayer."

"Did she ever mention her husband, Guy?"

"Once when I visited her at home [shortly before her death]. A car port attached to the house had been converted into a bedroom. It was much lighter and cooler than the other bedrooms, so she'd been moved in there, at her request, by Hospice [personnel]. She told me it had been converted by her husband."

My thoughts went back to our visit in the summer of 2004. We'd spent a delightful four or five hours together, leaving only when she tired. Margaret walked us to our rented car. As my wife and I were getting into the vehicle, Margaret pointed to the car port-bedroom and explained that Guy had worked on it. "When it's time, I'll move in there to die," she said.

EPILOGUE

Alone, I stand on the shore of a sea of memories, some in vivid color, warm and friendly; others in black and white, cold and bleak. I cannot swim in the comfort of any of them just now.

My job is done. When I started writing, I did not know what I'd find; what my research would uncover, where it would lead, or even if I could complete the entire task.

The effort was a labor of love; love for a man I did not know well at all, but for whom I developed feelings as strong—no, stronger—than if he'd been my father or brother, and with whom I empathized almost completely.

As I said when we started out, Guy Vitale had at least two dreams. One was to get a college degree. The other was to play major league baseball. Both were goals he strived for, flirted with and came close to achieving. But in the end, because of some really lousy things that happened, certain events and circumstances, you could say, and even a couple of bad decisions on his part, like an echo in the wind, his dreams slipped away and were lost.

Who is to say what Guy's life would have been like had Fred O'Brien's greed not intervened. If the Red Sox, Yankees, or Tigers had signed him to a contract right out of high school, would he have made it to the Big Leagues? Everyone I interviewed, and some I did not, who saw him play baseball believed without a doubt that he would have, after the obligatory year or two of seasoning in the minors. And if that had happened, life, for him, would certainly have been different.

But don't get me wrong. I do not believe my uncle was a failure. It's just that I think his life was not what he had hoped it would be when he started out. Who could have imagined, though, what would happen? Remember that old adage, "truth is stranger than fiction"? Well, I believe that Guy Vitale's life proves its truth.

So what am I saying? I think, even though his life hummed right along, that later on he was disappointed and possibly even bitter about some things;

I believe the baseball episode really got to him. And the college bit? Well, there were signs that, although he tried hard to get his degree, not getting it may have held him back at several points in his life, especially during his CIA career.

After he went into the Central Intelligence Agency, he lived a life of heroism, sacrifice and patriotism. If, as Oliver North recently wrote,[73] "Heroes are people who place themselves at risk for the benefit of others ..." then Guy Vitale certainly was one of those heroes. His was not the heroism of the professional athlete on the gridiron or the baseball diamond, as perhaps he had once contemplated. Instead, he achieved another, more lasting heroism. But it was earned at substantial cost; a lonely existence, sometimes lived in faraway places and under circumstances that often exposed him to grave personal danger; a price few of us are willing to pay.

You remember Moe Berg? He was a catcher for Chicago and Boston. Played fifteen years in the Bigs and got his life story written up in a book[74] because he had done some cloak and dagger work for the United States before, during and after World War II.

But Berg's service pales by comparison to Guy's. After his four-year stint in the Army, Guy went back into the service of his country again. But this time it was for a *career*, not just a couple of years, like Berg.

As I've said, my mother and the rest of the family thought Guy had been sent into Cuba after Eisenhower approved that CIA plan to do away with the two Castro boys and Che. We've seen that that was incorrect, although I never learned why Guy was sent behind the Iron Curtain in Eastern Europe during that time frame. Perhaps it was precisely because so much of the CIA's resources were being expended on the Cuban crisis, so many of the top agents occupied with it, that his bosses turned to Guy. That assignment was what initially earned him the respect and admiration of his CIA peers.

What I also know is that he served in Greece for a long time; that he was involved, somehow, in the CIA background investigation of Lee Harvey Oswald, the fruitcake who shot former President Kennedy, that he may have been sent to Mexico City to back check on Oswald's comings and goings down there, and that he may also have had something to do with infiltrating the Mob, attempting to discover what, if any, connection it had to Mr. Kennedy's death.

As my research and writing progressed, I was at first pleased, then puzzled and finally awed to find that this quiet loner and I shared, from a distance, the

---

73   Oliver North, *Diddling While Americans Die*, GOPUSA, 2/19/2007.
74   Louis Kaufman, Barbara Fitzgerald, and Tom Sewell, *Moe Berg; Athlete, Scholar... Spy*, Little Brown & Co. First Edition 1975.

same dreams; that we each held, as we grew up, the same hopes—to get a college education, to play big league baseball, and to live a life of service to others.

Unlike Guy Vitale, I *was* able to attain that college education, and even a law degree, and these led to a good life as a lawyer, farmer/horse breeder, investigator and writer; an interesting and rewarding existence for any man, by any standard, although not without a few bumps along the way. But I certainly understood—and shared—Guy's strivings, his failings and his successes, although at different times and in different places.

From my brief, three-year "career" as a football player, I came to realize that we shared the same skills and feel for the game that had made Guy a high school star, and me, someone who might have been. For me, the spirit was willing but the flesh was weak—and would not withstand the stern rigors of the game, without damage. That was what caused me to switch to soccer, to stay in shape for the sport I, like Guy, loved most—baseball.

And like Guy, who achieved his goal of a life of service—service to his country—I was able to spend twenty-three years serving others as a practicing lawyer, a career both intellectually stimulating and personally rewarding.

But also like Guy, one of our shared dreams—to play professional baseball in the major leagues—was not attained, although he, because he possessed skills superior to mine, came closer to that elusive goal than I, with one year of organized ball under his belt before WWII forced an end to his participation. As it was for him, the possibility was there for me, but only for a fleeting moment. And just as with him, for many and varied reasons, it proved unattainable. For both of us, it will remain forever an echo in the wind.

SOURCES

BOOKS:

Blakey, G. Robert, and Billings, Richard N. *Fatal Hour; the Assassination of President Kennedy by Organized Crime.* New York, NY: Berkley Books, 1992. Times Books Edition, 1981.

Burkert, Nancy Ekholm and Langton, Jane Langton. *Acts of Light, Emily Dickinson,* Boston, MA: New York Graphic Society, Little, Brown and Company, 1980

Dolson, Frank. *Beating the Bushes.* South Bend, IN: Icarus Press, 1982.

Hunter-Hall, Roger, and Wagner, Steven. *The State of the Catholic Church in America, Diocese by Diocese.* Crisis Magazine: February/March 2007.

Johnson, Paul. *A History of the American People.* New York, NY: HarperCollins Publishers, Inc., 1997.

Kaufman, Louis, Fitzgerald, Barbara, and Sewell, Tom. *Moe Berg; Athlete, Scholar ... Spy,* New York, NY: Little Brown & Co. First Edition 1975.

le Carre, John. *A Perfect Spy.* New York, NY: Bantam Books, an imprint of Alfred A. Knopf, Inc., 1986.

Newman, John. *Oswald and the CIA.* New York, NY: Carroll & Graff Publishers, Inc., 1996.

Noble, William. *Writing Dramatic Non-Fiction.* Forestdale, VT: Paul S. Erikson, Publisher, 2000.

Price, Christopher. *Baseball by the Beach: A History of America's National Pastime on Cape Cod.* Cape Cod Publications. 1998.

Pyle, Howard. *The Merry Adventures of Robin Hood,* New York, NY: Grosset & Dunlap, Publishers, 1952.

Rawlings, Marjorie Kinnan. *South Moon Under.* New York, NY: Charles Scribner's Sons, 1933.

Sacco, Anthony J. *The China Connection.* Lincoln, NE: iUniverse, Inc., 2003.

Sacco, Anthony J. *Little Sister Lost.* Lincoln, NE: iUniverse, Inc., 2004.

Sacco, Jack. *Where the Birds Never Sing.* New York, NY: Regan Books, a Division of HarperCollins Publishers, Inc., 2003.

Sire, James W. *Chris Chrisman Goes to College; And Faces the Challenges of Relativism, Individualism and Pluralism.* Downers Grove, IL: InterVarsity Press, 1993.

Stevenson, William. *A Man Called Intrepid.* New York, NY: Ballantine Books, 1976.

Wolff, Rick, Ed. *The Baseball Encyclopedia. The Complete and Official Record of Major League Baseball,* 8th Ed. New York, NY: Macmillon Publishing Company, 1969.

ARTICLES:

Earle, Ed. "Vitale's Booting Key to Game." *The Boston Herald,* November 2, 1935.

Earle, Ed. "Sensational Pass Clutches by King Set Stage for South Boston to Crack East Boston's Unbeaten Record, 13–7." *The Boston Herald,* November 27, 1935.

Dalton, Ernest. "East Boston Takes Brighton by 7–0 Score." *The Boston Globe,* October 18, 1935.

Dalton, Ernest. "The Globe's 1936 All-Scholastic Diamond Nine." *The Boston Globe,* June 22, 1936.

Mooney, J.W. "Hyde Park Thrashes South Boston 27–0. East Boston defeats Charlestown 13–0 in Nightcap." *The Boston Post,* November 1, 1932.

Mooney, J.W. "Eastie-Southie Battle to Scoreless Tie." *The Boston Post,* November 23, 1932.

Mooney, J.W. "Boston Schoolboy Season Kicks off Today." *The Boston Post,* October 3, 1933.

Mooney, J.W. "East Boston and Southie in Tie." *The Boston Post,* November 28, 1933.

Mooney, J.W. "East Boston Tips Over Southie. Vitale Goes Over For Score of Noddle Islanders." *The Boston Post,* November 28, 1934.

Mooney, J.W. "Hub Schoolboys Play Suburbans All—Star Teams From High Schools in First of Series Tonight at Town Field at Dorchester." *The Boston Post,* June 17, 1935.

Mooney, J.W. "Latin Smothers Memorial, 19–0; Takes advantage of Breaks to Win. East Boston Cops Other Half of Twin Bill." *The Boston Post,* October 18, 1935.

Mooney, J.W. "First Defeat For East Boston High. Southie Team Smashes its Perfect Record By 13 To 7 Decision As Capt. King Stars." *The Boston Post,* November 27, 1935.

Mooney, J.W. "Post All Teams For 1936 Named." *The Boston Post,* June 15, 1936.

North, Oliver. "Diddling While Americans Die." *GOPUSA,* February 2, 2007.

Morse, Ralph H. "Deak." *Spanning the Sports, Caledonian-Record,* April 21, 1939.

Morse, Ralph H. "Deak." *Spanning the Sports, Caledonian-Record,* April 24, 1939.

Morse, Ralph H. "Deak." *Spanning the Sports, Caledonian-Record,* May 24, 1939.

Morse, Ralph H. "Deak." *Spanning the Sports, Caledonian-Record,* June 15, 1939.

Morse, Ralph H. "Deak." *Spanning the Sports, Caledonian-Record,* June 27, 1939.

Morse, Ralph H. "Deak." *Spanning the Sports, Caledonian-Record,* July 7, 1939.

Morse, Ralph H. "Deak." *Spanning the Sports, Caledonian-Record,* July 12, 1939.

Morse, Ralph H. "Deak." *Spanning the Sports, Caledonian-Record,* July 28, 1939.

Morse, Ralph H. "Deak." *Spanning the Sports, Caledonian-Record,* August 2, 1939.

Morse, Ralph H. "Deak." *Spanning the Sports, Caledonian-Record,* August 15, 1939.

Morse, Ralph H. "Deak." *Spanning the Sports, Caledonian-Record,* August 29, 1939.

Stout, Vic. "East Boston Winner on Hyde Park Forfeitures." *Boston Traveler,* December 11, 1934.

Stout, Vic. "Spotlighting the Schools." *Boston Traveler,* November 6, 1935:

Stout, Vic. "Tie for Individual Scoring Honors." *Boston Traveler,* November 19, 1935.

Stout, Vic. "Spotlighting the Schools." *Boston Traveler,* November 22, 1935.

Stout, Vic. "Rugged Clash at Fenway Tomorrow As East Boston Meets Southie Rival." *Boston Traveler,* November 25, 1935.

Stout, Vic. Traveler Names All-Scholastic Baseball Team for 1936." *Boston Traveler,* June 13, 1936.

UN-ATTRIBUTED ARTICLES:

"No Deal for Herman." *The Boston Post,* October 18, 1932.

"East Boston Winner 11–10." *The Boston Post,* May 10, 1935.

"Noddle Islanders Buried By Jamaica" *The Boston Post, May 15 1935.*

"East Boston Whips Charlestown Nine." *The Boston Post,* May 18, 1935.

"O'Brien To Field Good E. B. Team. Noddle Islanders May Have Another Fine Campaign." *The Boston Post,* October 9, 1935.

"South, East Boston Vie." *The Boston Post,* November 26, 1935.

"East Boston Cops Fifth Win, 20–0 over Jamaica Plain." *The Boston Globe,* May 15, 1936.

"Trade Team Buried By East Boston, 16 To 7." *The Boston Post,* June 1, 1936.

"Cape Cod Baseball Begins." *Barnstable Patriot,* July 1, 1937.

"Johnny Maloney Sure To Make Kents Hill Team." *The Boston Post,* July 2, 1936.

"Cape Cod Baseball Begins." *Barnstable Patriot,* July 1, 1937.

"Three-Fifths of Cape League Thrown Into Tie for First Place." *Cape Cod Standard Times,* July 18, 1937.

"Working To Keep Barnstable First." *Cape Cod Standard Times,* August 24, 1937.

"Cape Cod Standard Times Announces its All-Star Nine." *Cape Cod Standard Times,* September 4, 1937.

"Barrett Leads Cape Batsman In Final List." *Cape Cod Standard Times,* September 8, 1937.

"Sports in Vacation Falmouth." *The Enterprise, Falmouth, Mass,* September 10, 1937.

"Barnstable Champion." *Cape Cod Standard Times,* September 7, 1937.

"Bill Boehner's Falmouth Nine Boasts Top Talent." *Cape Cod Standard* Times, July 1, 1938.

"Falmouth off to Fast Start." *Cape Cod Standard Times,* July 5, 1938.

"Vitale Brings Home Bacon." *Cape Cod Standard Times,* August 3, 1938.

"Right in the 'Pink' With Pinkham." The *Enterprise, Falmouth MA. Cape Circuit Chatter,* August 11, 1938.

"Pennant Race Tightens." *The Enterprise, Falmouth, Cape Circuit Chatter,* August 12, 1938.

"Falmouth Batters Out 15 Hits." *Cape Cod Standard Times,* August 24, 1938.

"All Cape League Team." *The Enterprise, Falmouth, Mass, August 26, 1938.*

"Indians Play Parsonsburg In Exhibit. Salisbury Club Will Face Hercules Saturday." *The Salisbury Times,* April 30th, 1941.

"Twin States League Schedule Opens July 1 and Closes on Labor Day." *The Bennington Banner,* March 21st, 1911.

"Twin States League Becomes A Reality." *Caledonian-Record,* April 24[th,] 1939, "Bilodeau Signs Cleverly And Announces His Batting Order For The First Game." *Caledonian-Record,* May 8, 1939.

"Eddie Ingalls Is First Pitcher Signed By Tom Bilodeau. Was E.I.C. Leading Pitcher in '37–'38." *Caledonian-Record,* May 26, 1939.

"Tom Bilodeau And Guy Vitale Start Playing Baseball." *Caledonian-Record,* May 29, 1939.

"Bilodeau And Vitale Star. St. J. Manager hitting for .556 in two contests. Has Hit Two Homers And Vitale Has One For Plymouth Nine." *Caledonian-Record* June 10, 1939.

"Twin States League Has Great Year." *Boston Sunday Post,* July 30, 1939.

"Atty Levin To Head Club. Becomes President of Salisbury, Md., Eastern Shore League Baseball Outfit; Wedemeyer To Act as Manager." *The Bennington Banner,* November 8, 1940.

"Falls 55 Feet To His Death. Somerville Man Killed at Everett Fuel Plant." *Boston Globe,* October 29, 1940.

"Levin Mails Contracts To Ten Indians. Spring Training To Get Underway April 25." *The Salisbury Times,* March 14th, 1941.

"Indians [To] Open Campaign At Home May 8; All-Star Game Will Be Played At Cambridge." *The Salisbury Times,* April 7, 1941.

"Baseball School Off But Indians Want Local Talent." *The Salisbury Times,* April 17, 1941.

"Indian's Picket Line," *The Salisbury Times,* May 10, 1941.

"Hurlers Show Form. Indians Win. 'Ace' Healy Turns in Three-Hit, 10-inning Game at Federalsburg." *The Salisbury Times,* May 12, 1941.

"Indians Top Federalsburg 7–1; Augliera, Vitale Figure." *The Salisbury Times,* May 19, 1941.

"Indians Down Easton, 2–1; Vitale Drives in Both Runs." *The Salisbury Times,* May 26, 1941.

"Vitale Hits Two Homers But Indians Lose. Giants Rally in Seventh to Keep up Rush." *The Salisbury Times,* June 1, 1941.

"Johnny Wedemeyer called Up. Tribe Names Bobby Meier to Manage." *The Salisbury Times,* June 9, 1941.

"Milford Too Much for Tribe, 7–1. Injuries Strike Both Teams." *The Salisbury Times,* June 28, 1941.

"Indians Will Sell Reduced Price Tickets. Attendance Drive To Fill Empty Seats Is Planned." *The Salisbury Times,* June 30, 1941.

"Indians Defeat Giants in Eleven; Augliera Sold to Wilmington Blue Rocks, Vitale Re-instated." *The Salisbury Times,* July 10, 1941.

"Indians Have Giants Number; Henrickson, Vitale Have Big Night." *The Salisbury Times,* July 11, 1941.

"Indians Lose, 4–2. Vitale Clouts homer in Losing Effort." *The Salisbury Times,* July 31, 1941.

"Tribe Slips Past Federalsburg, 2–1. Maier, Vitale Star Defensively." *The Salisbury Times,* August 8, 1941.

"Indians Top Giants in Slugfest, 10–8. Vitale Smashes 4th Homer As Tribe Comes From Behind To Win." *The Salisbury Times,* August 9, 1941.

"Giants Defeat Indians in Thriller, 3–1. Vitale Stars in Outfield. Reubin Levin's Mother Dies." *The Salisbury Times,* August 21, 1941.

"Vitale's Homer Gives Tribe 3–2 Win. Victory Keeps Club In Race For Playoffs." *The Salisbury Times,* August 25, 1941.

"Receivers Make Last Appeal To Baseball Fans." *The Salisbury Times,* September 2, 1941.

"Tribe Has No Flag, Flies Vitale's Pants." *The Salisbury Times, September 4, 1941.*

"Batteries for Barnstable." *Cape Cod Standard Times,* July 9, 1936.

"Batteries for Barnstable." *Cape Cod Standard Times,* August 20, 1936.

"Batteries for Barnstable." *Cape Cod Standard Times,* August 27, 1936.

"Batteries for Barnstable." *Cape Cod Standard Times,* September 3, 1936.

"Batteries for Barnstable." *Cape Cod Standard Times,* September 10, 1936.

TELEPHONE INTERVIEWS:

Blakey, Robert G., Professor, House Select Committee on Assassinations, and follow-up e-mail February 5, 2005.

Bradshaw, Rev. James, Pastor, First United Methodist Church, Sanford, FL, February 18, 2007.

Crane, Matthew R. Director of Admissions and Financial Aid, Kents Hill School, October 28, 2004.

Cummings, Bob, Esquire, Bennington, VT, November 5, 2005.

Franke, Ruth Anne Fletcher, Thief River Falls, MN, February 14, 2007.

Freye, Cheryl W., Director of Institutional Research, Assistant to the Director of Development, Kents Hill School, October 28, 2004.

Gonzalez, Herman (Red), Pittsburgh, PA, *Flash* Membership Secretary, April 12, 2005, + July 16, 2006.

Hack, Bruce, Historian, Cape Cod Baseball League, October 14, 2004.

Hall, Joe, Bennington Historical Society, Bennington, VT, November 3, 2005.

Hanna, George, Venice FL, November 14, 2005.

Hudson, George E., Apopka, FL.

Irish, Alfred G., Member, Old Timers Advisory Committee, Cape Cod League, January 9, 2002, October 26, 2002, November 12, 2005, November 15, 2005.

Jacobs, Richard J. "Dick," Bradenton, June 16, 2006.

Jensen, Dudley, Member, Old timers Advisory Committee, January 10, 2002, October 14, 2004.

Jones, "Reg," a baseball aficionado, Bennington, VT, November 3, 2005.

Lander, Laverne J., Saint Paul, MN, August 15, 2005, and follow-up letter from him dated August 20, 2005.

Lemon, Joseph F., Lewisburg, WV, September 3, 2002, August 8, 2004, June 16, 2006.

Lewandoski, Joseph, San Antonio, TX, April 5, 2005, and follow-up letter from him dated June 13, 2006.

Lollman, Jeanette, Records Department, Colgate University, October 24, 2004.

Manojlovich, Nick, Monaca, PA, August 10, 2004, April 2, 2005.

Marro, Tony, Bennington Historical Society, Bennington, VT, November 12, 2005.

McCann, Lynne, Director, Bennington Free Library, Bennington, VT, October 26, 2005.

Mellor, Barbara, head Librarian, Littleton Public Library, Littleton, New Hampshire, December 14, 2005, follow-up e-mail from her, December 22, 2005.

Merullo, Lennie, September 25, 2001, October 10, 2001, October 30, 2001, and November 5, 2001.

Miller, Henry L. (Hank), Chico, CA, November 3, 2005.

Newman, John, Ph.D., Lost River, WV, March 28, 2003.

Parasco, Chester, Esquire, November 4, 2004.

Paquette, Terry Greco, nee Marie Theresa Greco, Madeira Beach, Florida, October 30, 2004.

Peterson, Carl, Archivist, Colgate University, October 21, 2004

Price, W. James, Baltimore, MD, July 17[th,] 2006.

Purnell, Elizabeth M., Amherst, MA. July 25, 2006.

Purnell, Frederick Jr., Flushing, NY, July 26, 2006.

Robarts, Barbara, Director, Weeks Memorial Library, Lancaster, NH, December 22, 2005.

Rocciolo, Joseph, October 1, 2001, September 15, 2004, October 16, 2004, October 20, 2004, October 22, 2004, and numerous others.

Sarro, Joseph, Historian, Boston Public Library, October 2, 2001.

Scarafel, Judy, President, Cape Cod League. September 19, 2001.

Sharkey, Wendy, Adult Reference Clerk Vermont History Room, Bennington Free Library, Bennington, VT, October 26, 2005.

Sprague, Dana, Society for American Baseball Research (SABRE), Brattleboro, VT, November 14, 2005.

Spano, Louis J. Aiken, SC, August 23, 2005.

Stone, Vicki, Assistant, Alumni Office, Colgate University, October 23, 2004.

Sullivan, Walter "Wally," September 26, 2002.

Summers, Robin, Associate Director of Alumni Affairs, Colgate University, October 20, 2004.

Vitale, Frank, November 10, 1995.

Vitale, Ronald Albert, Charlestown, MA, April 6, 2006.

von Kahn, Lisa, Director, St. Johnsbury Public Library, St. Johnsbury, VT, December 22, 2005.

Washburn, Lillian Beatrice MacDonald, Jaffrey, New Hampshire, former President of the Kents Hill School Class of '38, Junior College program, October 30, 2004.

Winter, Jeanne Vitale, Winthrop, MA, April 6, 2006.

Wood, Bob, Keene, NH, November 14, 2005.

OTHER:

Angermeyer, Frances, Kansas City, Kansas, Poem entitled: *"Conversion."*

Baccigalupo, George "Red," retired Fire Chief, Winthrop, MA. Personal interview, August 11, 2002.

Combat Journal: The Story of the Timberwolf Regiment of the 78th Lightning Division in World War II. 1944–1945. This handbook of the 311th Infantry Regiment is available in a very well-done CD for $15.00 when I obtained it, by sending a check to John C. Swengel, 508 Orange Drive, A-12, Altamonte Springs, FL 32701.

Howard, Elaine, President, *The Army Times.* Army Times Publishing Company, Springfield, VA, letter to her dated June 2, 2002.

Rocciolo, Joseph, East Boston Sports Historian, Boston, MA. Personal interviews, August 10, 11, 12, 13, 2002.

978-0-595-45522-5
0-595-45522-0

www.ingramcontent.com/pod-product-compliance
Lightning Source LLC
Chambersburg PA
CBHW051219050326
40689CB00007B/736